450

Russian Intellectual History: *an Anthology*

Russian Intellectual History

an Anthology

MARC RAEFF
Columbia University

With an Introduction by Isaiah Berlin

SPONSORED BY THE RUSSIAN INSTITUTE

OF COLUMBIA UNIVERSITY

NEW JERSEY: HUMANITIES PRESS
SUSSEX: HARVESTER PRESS

Reprinted in 1978 in the United States of America
by Humanities Press and in England by Harvester
Press by arrangement with the author.

(U.S.A.)   ISBN 0-391-00904-4 (cloth)
                   0-391-00905-2 (paper)
(ENGLAND) ISBN 0-85527-834 X (cloth)
                   0-85527-844- 7 (paper)

MANUFACTURED IN THE UNITED STATES OF AMERICA

Preface

The purpose of this anthology is to acquaint those unable to read Russian with the writings and ideas that have helped to shape the social and political consciousness of modern Russia. Most of these documents of the eighteenth and nineteenth-century intelligentsia have never before appeared in English translation. To be sure, the outlines of the ideas agitating the Russian intelligentsia have been presented in textbooks, translations of Russian prose and poetry, and recent scholarly studies. But the literary masterpieces only partially reflect prevailing attitudes and ideas, and they do not convey the process of reasoning that underlay the creation and acceptance of these ideas. As for scholarly research, no study—however detailed and brilliant—can do justice to all facets of an individual's (or group's) intellectual concerns. We feel that there is no substitute for the reader's own intellectual curiosity and perception in uncovering the treasure of ideas in what he reads.

An anthology is by definition never complete, and any effort at catholicity is self-defeating. Several considerations have determined our selection of material:

First, we have chosen relatively short articles and essays in order to include full texts (with two minor exceptions). By presenting complete pieces, we hope to convey to the reader the process of thinking and the writing style of the Russian intelligentsia. In keeping with this policy, the translators have tried to strike a balance between preservation of the style and flavor of the original on one hand and readability on the other.

Second, we have chosen pieces that reflect what seem to have been the principal preoccupations of the Russian intelligentsia: their self-image and Russia's cultural relationship to the Western world. These concerns dominated discussions in salons, literary circles, and lecture groups, and they took permanent form in essays, pamphlets, and tracts. Many of the selections we have included also focus on the nature of modern industrial civilization. Because the technological revolution burst upon the Russians as an external force rather than as a gradual organic development, it was easier for them to perceive its basic characteristics, problems, and implications. These writings may thus be of interest to those concerned with understanding the major technological and social trends of contemporary Western civilization, as well as to the student of Russian history and literature.

Third, no writings by major revolutionary figures have been included, for several reasons. Despite its enormous impact on the destinies of Russia, Marxism remained an imported ideology; whatever changes the Russians introduced were the practical results of accidental circumstances rather than the product of conscious intellectual effort. Moreover, the major pamphlets of the most influential Marxist leaders—Plekhanov, Lenin, and Trotsky— are now readily available in English. As for the non-Marxist revolutionary movements, their literary heritage is limited to party programs and propaganda leaflets, which are mediocre in intellectual content and which contributed nothing to the discussion of the fundamental issues that concerned the Russian intelligentsia.

Fourth, we decided not to include selections by influential men such as Aleksandr Radishchev, Aleksandr Herzen, or Nikolai Chernyshevskii, whose seminal works are too long to be presented in full and have already been published in easily accessible translations.

Fifth, we have omitted the writings of several religious thinkers, such as Konstantin Leont'ev, Nikolai Fedorov, Vladimir Solov'ev, and Nikolai Berdiaev, because they had little impact on Russian political and social thought at the time. (Many of the significant social and political essays of Solov'ev and Berdiaev are already available in translation.)

This volume includes an Introduction by Sir Isaiah Berlin characterizing the Russian intelligentsia, headnotes discussing each author and the significance of his writings, and a bibliography of books that provides historical and biographical information about these authors. Footnotes explain those allusions central to an understanding of the writer's argument. In general, however, editorial apparatus has been kept to a minimum. We hope that the essays, unencumbered by ready-made interpretations and glosses, may suggest new insights to the open-minded and curious reader.

Our translations have been made from the best published Russian texts available. All authors' notes have been preserved. Dates follow the Julian Calendar, in force in Russia until 1918. Russian words and names have been transliterated according to the Library of Congress system, slightly simplified to modernize spelling.

We wish to acknowledge our debt to the Director and staff of the Russian Institute of Columbia University, who encouraged this enterprise and generously financed the translations and technical assistance. Throughout all stages but the last, the critical eye of the Institute's editorial assistant helped to catch many a slip of the pen and infelicity of expression in the translations.

MARC RAEFF

Columbia University

Contents

vii

Russian Intellectual History: *an Anthology*

Introduction

ISAIAH BERLIN

This volume is intended to shed light on Russian intellectual history. What, the potential reader may well ask, is intellectual history? It is not a clear and self-explanatory concept. Such terms as "political history," "economic history," and "social history," however vague their frontiers, however much they may overlap with one another, are not in this sense obscure. They denote accounts of what certain more or less definable groups of human beings have done and suffered, of the interaction between their members, of the deeds and destinies of those individuals who have been influential in altering the lives of their fellows in certain specific ways, of the interplay between them and external nature or other groups of human beings, of the development of their institutions—legislative, judicial, administrative, religious, economic, artistic—and so on. Similarly, the idea of a history of the arts and sciences, however many difficulties it presents in practice, is easily grasped in principle: the concept of a work of art or of a scientific discovery or invention, and of the circumstances in which it is achieved, is relatively clear. But what is intellectual history? A history of ideas? What ideas and conceived by whom? Not ideas in any one well-demarcated province; accounts of mathematical, philosophical, scientific, esthetic, technological, and economic ideas all belong to histories of their respective "technical" disciplines. Yet it is clear that the mere juxtaposition or combination of these histories does not itself make a general history of ideas.

Leaving this problem undiscussed, let us, for the sake of argument, concede that it is possible to ask what ideas and perhaps, more vaguely, what attitudes were prevalent in a given society at a given time; moreover, that it is possible and indeed tempting to speculate about the influence of this or that body of ideas on a particular turn in the history of the society in question; in addition, that it may reasonably be argued that a particular school of thought exaggerates, or underestimates, the part that is played by particular ideas, or of ideas in general—that Idealists or Marxists or Positivists were right or mistaken when they supposed that a revolution or a war would not have occurred, or taken the form that it took, had it not been for certain beliefs or ways of thought in the mind of this or that individual, this or that group. Historians, philosophers, and sociologists quarrel about whether such ideas or attitudes are themselves by-products of some non-mental process—geographical or economic or biological—or, on the contrary, are independent forces, not to be fully explained in terms of anything other than themselves. What is the subject of such speculations and disagreements? If not the specific ideas that belong to specific disciplines, then what? General ideas, we shall be told. What are these? This is much more difficult to answer. In the end, no more than an approximation can be attempted here: by general ideas we refer in effect to beliefs, attitudes, and mental and emotional habits, some of which are vague and undefined, others of which have become crystallized into religious, legal, or political systems, moral doctrines, social outlooks, psychological dispositions, and so forth. One of the qualities common to such systems and their constituent elements is that, unlike a good many scientific and common-sense propositions, it does not seem possible to test their validity or truth by means of precisely definable, agreed criteria, or even to show them to be acceptable or unacceptable by means of widely accepted methods. The most that can be said of them is that they are to be found in that intermediate realm in which we expect to find opinions, general intellectual and moral principles, scales of value and value judgments, mental dispositions, and individual and social attitudes—everything that is loosely collected under such descriptions as "intellectual background," "climate of opinion," "social mores," and "general outlook"; that which is often referred to in ordinary language (this is part of our Marxist inheritance) as ideology. It is this ill-defined but rich realm and its vicissitudes that histories of ideas or "intellectual histories" supposedly describe, analyze, and explain.

The existence of such histories is itself a symptom and a product of that growth of human self-consciousness which has generated distinctions between, on the one hand, this realm—home of ideologies, outlooks, attitudes, myths, rationalizations, and the like—and, on the other, the better-ordered kingdoms populated by the concepts and propositions of the more developed exact sciences and disciplines. The history of ideas, as a branch of knowledge, was born in Italy and grew in Germany (and to a lesser extent in France and England) in the eighteenth century. In due course interest in it spread both east and west. In no country was there a greater degree of historical self-awareness or was greater or more intense attention paid to ideological issues than in Russia in the nineteenth and twentieth centuries.

It is in Russian writings that such titles as the "history of social thought" (obshchestvennaia mysl') or the "history of the intelligentsia" are most often found. Other countries have produced historians of culture or of civilization; Russia is the home of the history of general opinions, of the beliefs and general intellectual outlook of educated persons affected by the progress of the arts and sciences and by political, economic, and social phenomena, but not necessarily involved in professional concern with them—of the outlook of amateurs, not experts. There are many historical causes of this: the isolation of educated persons in tsarist Russia at the beginning of the nineteenth century; the conflict of the Western character of humane studies with Russian reality; the coincidence of the emergence of Russia as a world power with the rise of romantic ideas, particularly in Germany; the decay of religion among the educated and the search for a moral and spiritual substitute; the repression by the government of free political and social activity and, as a result, the forcible canalization of the quest for self-expression and individuality—especially in its acute, rebellious forms—into the realm of thought, which, for this reason, became the opium of the civilized, their only substitute, pale as it was, for action. This is not the place for the discussion of this large subject. Whatever the reasons, there is no doubt that ideas were taken more seriously, and played a greater and more peculiar role, in Russian history than anywhere else. Hence an anthology of Russian ideas can explain more about Russian behavior than a similar compilation applied to other peoples. And yet there is a paradox here, for few of these ideas were born on Russian soil.

At this stage it is relevant to repeat the second question raised above: Whose thoughts are the proper subject of intellectual history? It is perhaps an idle inquiry, and one that rests on a vulgar misconception of both thought and action, to seek to identify the exact origin or authorship of a belief or an ideal that has played a part in human history. Who invented the idea of democracy? Or the rights of man? Or duty or honor or individual responsibility—or, for that matter, mathematically perfect figures, or objectivity, or progress, or any of the other concepts and categories that have dominated the Western world? Nevertheless, some attributions can be made. The fundamental concepts of Western political theory evolved in Greece, not in India or Judea; so did those of mathematics and the natural sciences: the Stoics first discussed causality in the modern sense, and they and the Epicureans first argued about the solution to the problem of the freedom of the will. A clear distinction between individual and collective responsibility may be found in Jeremiah before we encounter it elsewhere; the contrast between love and justice as governing relations between human beings is not (despite the *Antigone*) of Greek origin, whereas that of impersonal natural law is; and so on. New beginnings—ideas that transform thought and action—do occur. Radical innovations are rightly attributed to Plato and Aristotle, Epicurus and Euclid, the authors of the Book of Isaiah and the Gospels, of the Roman Digest and the Code Napoléon, to Descartes, Kant, Marx, Darwin, and Freud. No doubt these men had forerunners, and the seeds of their doctrines may be found elsewhere, but it is their formulations, however arrived at, that have made the critical difference and have affected thought, feeling, and practice in a decisive fashion. Such identifications are still more certain within specific provinces of thought, even outside the natural sciences: Spinoza is the true father of higher criticism, Montesquieu of the comparative method in history, Saint-Simon of technocracy, and so on.

What part has been played in this advance by the Russians? They have contributed their full share of genius in mathematics and the natural sciences. Their poetical achievement is of unique magnificence; their novelists of the nineteenth century tower above all others; musical talent continues to flower to this day on Russian soil—since the beginning of the nineteenth century Russia has in no sense been a cultural backwater. But in the realm of general ideas her most striking characteristic is not inventiveness but a unique degree of responsiveness to the ideas of others. This Russian trait has proved to be a major factor in the modern world. That objective truth exists, that it can be discovered, and that life, individual and social, can be lived in its light—this belief is more characteristic of the Russians than of anyone else in the modern world. To take ideas with complete seriousness itself transforms them; this is a crucial corollary of the central insight of both Marx and Freud into the unity of thought and practice. No matter where an idea may have been born, writers, artists, critics, the educated minority in the capitals, and, at their hands, a growing number of sincere and idealistic semi-educated Russians elsewhere sought to discover the truth in its light and to shape their lives accordingly. A capacity for rigorous reasoning from premises believed to be true even if they led to unpalatable conclusions, intellectual enthusiasm, integrity, courage, and the rational conviction that only if a man understands the truth and lives by it can he rise to his full stature and be happy, creative, wise, and virtuous—these convictions, inherited from the Age of Reason, were never abandoned by the vanguard of Russian society. It is this faith that, for good or ill, has enabled it to move mountains. Others have invented ideas or come upon them, delighted in them, paid serious attention to them or played with them, conceived them as expressions of their own creative, self-assertive personalities or regarded them with scientific detachment as part of their professional task, while their private and inner lives were, at times, lived in a different province and at another level. But the Russian intelligentsia, or at least those of its members who set their stamp on Russian mental development in the nineteenth century (and on the Russian Revolution in the twentieth), went much further: it surrendered itself to what it believed to be true with a lifelong singleness of purpose seldom known outside of religious life in the West. The intelligentsia did not embrace the whole of educated Russian society—far from it—but it constituted its most active element. Nor did it always fully live up to its professions (no educated Russian needs reminding that two of the most passionate and effective enemies of serfdom—Nekrassov and Turgenev—did not, in fact, liberate their own serfs). But its words inspired others to acts of heroism and martyrdom.

Above all, it preached and practiced the notion of the unbreakable unity of men's nature. The idea of professionalism—the division of what one does as an expert from one's activity as a human being, the separation of public métier from private life, the notion of man as an actor who plays now this role, now that—has always been weaker in Russia than in the West. Differentiation of functions, specialization, a tidy social system in which every man has his place and his calling, has never been a central Russian idea in theory or practice. Even in the early eighteenth century,

Feofan Prokopovich (the first writer presented in this volume) was not merely a bishop, a clerical administrator, and a theologian but also a social and political reformer and an educator. As for Lomonosov, what realm of Russian spiritual development did he regard as alien to him? Poet, physicist, grammarian, educator, composer, administrator and universal sage, the "Russian Leonardo" stands worthily at the head of that extraordinary procession of many-sided personalities who are characteristic of Russian civilization. No doubt in a country without a true tradition of scholastic learning, where—despite occasional heresies and the penetration of Western ideas among the immediate neighbors of Roman Catholic Poland—there occurred no Renaissance and no Reformation, a small élite of educated persons was obliged to do everything for their benighted brothers. Novikov was not a man of great intellectual power, but he became all that he could be; he left none of his intellectual, artistic, or social gifts—such as they were—undeveloped. In what other country did eminent professors of chemistry or serious experts in ballistics become renowned composers? Where else did (and do) artists see themselves not as purveyors of objects, no matter how beautiful, but as heralds and prophets, solely because they take it upon themselves to speak in public? In Russia (and where else to a comparable degree?) this act alone has been conceived of as imposing on the élite the task—indeed, the sacred duty—to say only what is true, or only what they truly believe and are prepared to express and defend with their lives, so that any effort to escape this, any deception or self-indulgence, is viewed as being not merely esthetically false, but morally treasonable.

Every one of the figures included in this volume has this characteristic in some degree. While Shcherbatov was no more earnest and admonitory than contemporary European, and in particular German, historians, Novikov was a martyr to the public interest. Fonvizin was a traveler, an essayist, and above all a writer of satirical comedies whose primary purpose was, if anything, even more patriotic and didactic than that of his peers in the West. The famous historian Karamzin was consumed with concern for the future of his country, to which the past, which he recorded with such love, labor, and literary talent, was but the noble opening. He set the tone for Russian conservatism much as Burke did for its English prototype. While the central notions of both these founders may have had their obvious origins in France and Germany and the ancient world (with tributaries in the case of Karamzin from Byzantium and the Orthodox Church), the emphasis in each case was not on a true account of the facts for their own sake, but on the application of such truths to the present or the immediate future. It was this moral and social concern that gave their ideas dominant influence over their own generation and the entire nineteenth century. Pnin is an even better example of this universalizing tendency. He was a far smaller figure than, say, Humboldt, but his aims were no less wide: his entire life was dedicated to translating the ideas of the Enlightenment for use at home; they emerged, as one would expect, drastically transformed.

As for Chaadaev, Professor Raeff gives us the notorious "Philosophical Letter," the originality of which, characteristically enough, consisted not in the presentation of new ideas but in the denunciation of his country for its cultural inferiority to the West, for lacking anything authentic or original of its own. Chaadaev's attack, with its deification of Western traditions, ideas, and civilization, was the key to later Russian "social thought." Its importance was enormous. It set the tone, it struck the dominant notes which were echoed by every major Russian writer up to and beyond the Revolution. Everything is there: the proclamation that the Russian past is blank or filled with chaos, that the only true culture is in the Roman West, and that the Great Schism robbed Russia of her birthright and left her barbarous, an abortion of the creative process, a caution to other peoples, a Caliban among nations. Here, too, is the extraordinary tendency toward self-preoccupation which characterizes Russian writing even more than that of the Germans, from whom this tendency mainly stems. Other writers, in England, France, even Germany, write about life, love, nature, and human relations at large; Russian writing, even when it is most deeply in debt to Goethe or Schiller or Dickens or Stendhal, is about Russia, the Russian past, the Russian present, Russian prospects, the Russian character, Russian vices, and Russian virtues. All the "accursed questions" (as Heine was perhaps the first to call them) turn in Russian into the notorious *proklyatye voprosy*—questions about the destinies (*sud'by*) of Russia: Where do we come from? Whither are we bound? Why are we as we are? Should we teach the West or learn from it? Is our "broad" Slav nature higher in the spiritual scale than that of the "Europeans"—a source of salvation for all mankind—or merely a form of infantilism and barbarism destined to be superseded or destroyed? The problem of "the superfluous man" is here already; it is not an accident that Chaadaev was an intimate friend of the creator of *Eugene Onegin*. No less characteristic of this mental condition is Chaadaev's contrary speculation (not quoted in this volume) that was also destined to have a career in subsequent writing, in which he wonders whether the Russians, who have arrived so late at the feast of the nations and are still young, barbarous, and untried, do not thereby derive advantages, perhaps overwhelming ones, over older or more civilized societies. Fresh and strong, the Russians might profit by the inventions and discoveries of the others without having to go through the torments that have attended their mentors' struggles for life and civilization. Might there not be a vast positive gain in being late in the field? Herzen, Chernyshevskii, Marxists and anti-Marxists, were to repeat this with mounting optimism. But the most central and far-reaching question was still that posed by Chaadaev. He asked: Who are we and what should be our path? Have we unique treasures (as the Slavophiles maintained) preserved for us by our Church—the only truly Christian one—which Catholics and Protestants have each in their own way lost or destroyed? Is that which the West despises as coarse and primitive in fact a source of life—the only pure source in the decaying post-Christian world? Or, on the contrary, is the West at least partially right: if we are ever to say our own word and play our part and show the world what kind of people we are, must we not learn from the

Westerners, acquire their skills, study in their schools, emulate their arts and sciences and perhaps the darker sides of their lives also? The lines of battle in the century that followed remained where Chaadaev drew them: the weapons were ideas which, whatever their origins, in Russia became matters of the deepest concern—often of life and death—as they never were in England or France or, to such a degree, in Romantic Germany. Kireevskii, Khomiakov, and Aksakov (to cite only those included in this volume) gave one answer, Belinskii and Dobroliubov another, Kavelin yet a third.

Ideas traveled from the West and, transmuted by Russian logic and Russian passion, acquired an influence which would have astonished some of their authors. The Russian intelligentsia was bred on Western doctrines, movements, and events: French eighteenth-century skepticism, scientific materialism, and positivism; German historicism, romanticism, and idealism; the principles and dogmas of the French Revolution and of its aftermath; the new rational organization created by Napoleon; European revolutions in the early years of the nineteenth century, for which centralized France acted as a model; the Utopias of Saint-Simon, Fourier, Owen, Cabet, Leroux; the counterattacks of Maistre, Bonald, Schelling; the destruction of metaphysics by Comte, Feuerbach, Strauss; the social doctrines of Sismondi, Mill, Spencer, and the Darwinians. All had their fervent disciples in Russia. Dostoevsky was exiled for reading the celebrated philippic by Belinskii (included in this volume), which, in its turn, was an expression of the democratic radicalism that, everywhere in the civilized world, called for revolt in the name of reason, justice, and human freedom. This was the creed in the name of which, not many weeks after Belinskii's death, revolutions broke out in all the great capitals of the European continent. The intellectual preoccupations of Western thinkers—the relations of mind to body, of scientific to moral truth, of the individual to society, the patterns of history, the goals toward which humanity should (or is compelled to) march, the issue of freedom and determinism, of culture and the masses, of the primacy of economic versus political factors—these issues were matters of deep concern to the best minds of Europe. Yet even though they were not without influence on practice, they remained for the majority matters of theory. But for the Russian radicals and their conservative opponents they were questions of desperate urgency, causes for which men were prepared to risk their prospects and their lives, as they later fought (and died) for or against Populism or Marxism, or in the name of one of the variants of these creeds against another. The reader of Turgenev's *Fathers and Sons*— and to some extent *On the Eve* and *Virgin Soil* too—finds himself in the world which Chernyshevskii and Dobroliubov, Kavelin and Annenkov described and, by and large, condemned. Nothing like it existed in the West; the total and unquestioning, at times fanatical, intellectual and moral dedication of the intelligentsia, its purity of character and unswerving pursuit of the truth, and the horror with which any lapse from integrity—collaboration with the enemy, whether state or Church or other obscurantist powers—was regarded by it, are probably unique in human history. Unless this is grasped, the later history of Russia, not merely intellectual but social, economic, and political, cannot be adequately understood.

The history of the development of these psychological characteristics is another story. Suffice it to say that the seeds of Marxism here fell on the most fertile soil imaginable; and their growth was fostered by a mood of stern renunciation of the world and passionate social faith not known in Europe since the Jacobins, perhaps since the Puritans.

Yet to identify this attitude with educated Russian opinion in general would be a serious distortion of the facts. For this attitude was not characteristic of any Russian born before the nineteenth century—Russian art and thought in the early decades of the nineteenth century had far more in common with contemporary movements in the West than is often supposed. When Mérimée translated Pushkin's prose, or when Pozzo di Borgo described Chaadaev as being *"un Russe parfaitement comme il faut,"* these discoveries may have been a source of surprise in the West, but they should not have been so. For society in Petersburg and Moscow (the world described in *War and Peace*) was highly civilized by any Western standard, and Russian literature and art of the early part of the century were for the most part its direct expression. On the contrary, Bazarov in Turgenev's *Fathers and Sons* is, if not a caricature, a stylized and exaggerated portrait of the "men of the sixties," and Pisarev, who proudly acknowledged his kinship with Bazarov, preached a crude and violent form of positivism that became less characteristic toward the end of the century. Chernyshevskii, Pisarev, Tkachev, and Nechaev represented peaks of passionate and narrow dogmatism which, together with Dostoevsky's obsessed and equally uncharacteristic vision, and Chekhov's studies in futility, contributed to the notorious synthetic image of the "Slav soul" that has in the West so often been mistaken for reality.

During the two reigns that preceded the Revolution the leaders of the Russian intelligentsia, both radical and moderate, Marxist and anti-Marxist, and the writers and artists who belonged to their world, lacked neither breadth of knowledge nor balanced imagination nor critical judgment nor—although they have often been accused of it—sober common sense. Anyone who doubts this proposition should tear himself away from Chernyshevskii's *What Is to Be Done?* or Pisarev's *Destruction of Esthetics* and turn to the arts and letters, and still more the social and political literature, of the years preceding and immediately succeeding the abortive Revolution of 1905. This "Silver Age" of Russian culture—in the realms of science (including the social sciences) and the humanities as well as that of pure art—is part and parcel of a great European advance and not the peculiar achievement of a remote, barbarous, exotic, or unbalanced civilization.

The last essays reprinted in this volume are products of a later and more skeptical generation. Two of these are classical expositions of a generation's own view of itself on the part of the disillusioned Russian intelligentsia, and in particular of the notorious chasm that divided the educated from the uneducated, deprived the educated of "organic" connection with the society which they criticized and sought to guide, and rendered them incapable of influencing events. The last piece, the swan song of the old intelligentsia, takes the form of a correspondence between a famous and aging critic and his friend and contemporary, a greatly gifted, civilized, and influential symbolist poet, about the crumbling of the world in which both were brought up. The critic, Mikhail Gershenzon, a Jew, confesses to being crushed by the enormous burden of the unforgotten, unburied past—the weight of tradition too heavy to be borne by those who are, for good or ill, steeped in Hebraic as well as Western culture with its obsessive historical sense. The poet, Viacheslav Ivanov, who speaks as a "Hellene" and an heir of Byzantium, seeks a synthesis of pagan classicism and Christianity, of Dionysus and Christ, through which the individual, if not the masses, can be transformed and saved. This is the final, fascinating, and tragic document of a declining civilization, overwhelmed by a cataclysm partly of its own making, consciously averting its eyes from the "new shores" toward which the postrevolutionary society was to drive full steam ahead. It is the social and political outlook of this civilization, and the impact on it of the West in the two centuries that preceded the epoch-making (for once this term preserves its literal meaning) collision in our own day of two worlds, that this volume calls up from the half-forgotten past.

1.

Feofan Prokopovich

1681-1736

Russia's dramatic turn to the West, the modernization of many of its institutions, and the Europeanization of its upper classes were largely the work of Peter the Great. But of course the energetic tsar-transformer (*tsar' preobrazovatel'*) did not find the ground completely unprepared, for a slow and timid Westernization had already begun in the seventeenth century. Nor was Peter alone, for he found ambitious and capable men to help him in his task. Muscovy's Westernization had been much furthered by the Ukraine's earlier contacts with Poland and particularly by the establishment of schools patterned on Western Jesuit educational institutions. The best known of these schools was the Academy at Kiev; among its outstanding pupils and teachers was Feofan Prokopovich. Peter the Great discovered Feofan on his visit to Kiev after the battle of Poltava, and brought him to St. Petersburg.

Feofan became Peter's most loyal and energetic assistant in church and educational affairs, and one of Peter's main propagandists. His sermons and tracts extolled the Russian ruler and promoted his policy of Westernization. Most important and best known in this connec-

tion were "Dukhovnyi reglament" (Spiritual Regulation), 1721, which established the principles of Russia's official church life until the end of the Empire, and "Pravda voli monarchei" (Justice Is the Monarch's Will), 1722, a theoretical justification of the autocratic power of the Russian monarch. In both works Prokopovich relied heavily on Western European literature and historical experience.

After Peter's death, Prokopovich, as archbishop of Novgorod and Pskov, continued to work actively for the Westernization of Russian intellectual life. The school he founded in Novgorod and his close connections with the leading figures of the budding modern Russian literature and scholarship—Kantemir and Tatishchev, respectively—made him a pivotal figure in Russian society. In 1730 Feofan played a decisive role in preserving intact the power of the autocrat when he helped Empress Anne reject the limiting conditions the Supreme Privy Council was trying to impose on her.

The present sermon gives in brief all the theses that Prokopovich later developed at length, with a wealth of supporting citations, in "Pravda voli-

13

monarshei." Delivered at a time when Peter's relations with his son Alexis were strained to the utmost, these tracts were meant to justify the Tsar's disinheritance of his first-born and to warn of the dire consequences—a new Time of Troubles—that would inevitably follow if the Tsar's will were to be opposed.

Feofan Prokopovich's legacy in the domain of political theory and practice was as ambiguous as the sources of his thought were varied. On the basis of the scriptural injunction of obedience to the just ruler he justified blind submission to the modern functions and forms of political authority with which Peter the Great had endowed the Russian state. At the same time he bolstered his position with rational arguments based on the doctrine of natural law and the writings of contemporary Western political theorists. Thus on the one hand he helped to create the Russian ruler's image of himself as an autocrat, requiring absolute obedience from his subjects, and on the other he gave the educated elite some of the most useful intellectual weapons with which to challenge the autocrat's demand for unquestioning submission.

Sermon on Royal Authority and Honor

How It Is Established in the World by God Himself,
and How Men Are Obliged to Honor Kings and Obey Them,
and Who the People Are Who Oppose Them and
How Great Is the Sin They Have

In the Year of Our Lord 1718,
on the Sixth Day of April
in Reigning St. Petersburg, on Palm Sunday

Christ's triumphal entry into Jerusalem gives us cause to speak on exactly what the present time, in season and out of season, has been commanding us to preach. We see how great is the joy among the people, how agreeable the meeting; at the very rumor of the coming of the Messiah the whole city

Translated by Horace G. Lunt from Feofan Prokopovich, "Slovo o vlasti i chesti tsarskoi . . . ," in *Sochineniia Feofana Prokopovicha*, ed. I. P. Eremin (Moscow, 1961), pp. 76–93. The sermon was first published on August 18, 1718, in St. Petersburg in pamphlet form.

arises, many strew their garments along the way, many cut and bring palm branches, the emblems of the conqueror; everyone cries out the triumphant "Hosannah"—even the little children do. The archpriests and the scribes are vexed at this, but they avail not; the "holy" Pharisees, bursting with envy, are hastening to cut off the celebration, but they cannot.

Do we not see here what honor is done to the King? Does this not call us all not to be silent about the duty of all subjects to esteem the supreme authority and about the great resistance to this duty that has been exposed in our land at the present time! Let no one think that our intention is to compare an earthly king to the heavenly one.[1] May we never be so foolish, for the Jews welcoming Jesus did not know Him to be the King of Heaven. Now, from the Holy Scriptures and the Old Testament it was possible to know that the coming Messiah was God; yet at the time of Christ the theology of the Jews was already blind, filled with many foolish fables, so it knew not the Messiah either by His person or by His deeds. The Kingdom of the Messiah seemed to them to be an earthly one and His salvation only a liberation of the Jewish race from the rule of the Gentiles. Even the disciples of Christ were in the same ignorance. For that was what Peter thought when, as the Lord was foretelling His own passion and death, he said, "Let it not be for Thee, Lord," and he received the answer: "Get thee behind me, Satan! For thou thinkest not the things that be of God, but those that be of men" (Matt. 16:22–23).[2] That was what the same Peter thought when, having feasted his eyes on the spectacle of the Transfiguration, he cried, "It is good for us to be here" (Matt. 17:4). That was what the sons of Zebedee thought when they wished to be first in Christ's glory, nor was the understanding of the rest any better; for St. Luke witnesses that when Christ was prophesying about His death and resurrection, "they understood none of these things: and this saying was hid from them, neither knew they the things which were spoken" (Luke 18:34). And if the Apostles, who were walking near the Light, were so in blindness, what shall we say of the others, put into darkness by the teachings of the rabbis? Now because the Jews, even with such a low opinion of Christ's kingdom, hastened to give Him so much honor that they dared to make an unusual holiday for His coming— for this palm-bearing ceremony took place right on the great Feast of the Tabernacles—have we not then just cause to speak of honor due a king?

But whatever the Jews thought of the Messiah (that they may have thought He was God I do not dispute, but I do not believe it), our subject still has a place here. For we have models in God's Word for taking God's honor and love to be a reason for man's love and honor, not in equality, but as an example. The Apostle John says, "If a man say, I love God, and hateth his brother, he is a liar; for he that loveth not his brother whom he hath

[1] The word *tsar'* in Church Slavonic refers to the kings of the Old Testament as well as to the Roman caesars and emperors of later times. Prokopovich intentionally exploits this meaning and the word's identity with the Russian word meaning "supreme ruler," i.e., emperor (in general), tsar (of Russia)—a being higher than kings and princes. The English reader should, therefore, keep in mind that "king," "caesar," "emperor," and "tsar" in this text are all renditions of the single word *tsar'*.—Translator.

[2] All biblical quotations are translated from the Russian version of the Bible.—Editor.

seen, how can he love God whom he hath not seen?" (I John 4:20). Paul says, "The husband is the head of the wife, even as Christ is the head of the church: and he is the saviour of the body. Therefore as the church is subject unto Christ, so let the wives be to their own husbands in everything. Husbands, love your wives, even as Christ also loved the church" (Eph. 5:23–25). And Paul says again, "And no man taketh this honour unto himself, but he that is called of God, as was Aaron. So also Christ" (Heb. 5:4–5). And many sayings of the same sort can be collected.

It is meet and fitting therefore that, taking the occasion of today's solemn honor offered up to the King of Israel, we serve our need by simple and clear speech because of the sin which has come to be in Russia in these times. That we serve our need, I say, for we see that not a small part of the people abides in such ignorance that they do not know the Christian doctrine concerning lay authorities. Nay more—they know not that the highest power is established and armed with the sword by God and that to oppose it is a sin against God Himself, a sin to be punished by death, not temporary but eternal. But many think this originates in mere human provisions or overriding force, and that it is fitting to fear the powers for their anger, so powerful and terrible, and not to fear them for conscience' sake.

We will then today with the help of God throw down and destroy this mad opinion by bringing forth the invincible words of God and the witness of men which is established on them. Let us hope in the grace of the Lord that every man who is simple in heart and obedient to the truth will spit on this opinion about the powers. Yet if anyone purposely wants to be blind, let us send him off with the brief word of the Apostle, "If any man be ignorant, let him be ignorant" (I Cor. 14:38), or of the Apocalypse, "He which is filthy, let him be filthy still" (Rev. 22:11).

What shall we say first? The real doctrine has today (and had in the old days) opponents who do not consider themselves ignoramuses, yet who spin theology out of the Scriptures. They do so as grasshoppers fly—winged animals, to be sure, but like great worms, with wings not up to the body; if they take it into their head to fly off, they fall at once to the ground. And so do these present bookmen try, as though winged, to be theologians; however, because of the crudity of their brains, they appear as babblers, understanding neither the Scriptures nor the power of God. Let us give them first place, let us hear them first, that the truth may then come forth like the sun after the clouds have been driven away.

The ancient monarchomachs, or fighters against kings, appeared even during apostolic times, for St. Peter thunders against them in his second epistle, in the second chapter: "The Lord knoweth how to deliver the godly out of temptations, and to reserve the unjust unto the day of judgment to be punished: but chiefly them that walk after the flesh in the lust of uncleanness, and despise government. Presumptuous are they, selfwilled, they are not afraid to speak evil of dignities" (II Pet. 2:9–10). And the Apostle Jude speaks of the same ones in similar but very cruel words, for he compares them to devils and Sodomites, saying: "Likewise also these dreamers defile the flesh, despise dominion, and tremble not to speak evil of dignities"

(Jude 1:8). And Paul seems to be pointing his finger at these same men, teaching them in his epistles to submit to the authorities, as we shall see later.

But what is it that these presumptuous men of old based their opinion on? On Christian freedom. For hearing that Christ achieved freedom for us (the Lord speaks of it to us Himself, and we read of it in many places in the epistles of the Apostles), they interpreted this to mean that we are free from obedience to the powers and from the law of the Lord. For thus Jude speaks of them, "For there are certain men crept in unawares, who were before of old ordained to this condemnation, ungodly men, turning the grace of our God into lasciviousness" (Jude 1:4). Similarly St. Peter too speaks of them in the place I already mentioned: "While they promise their disciples liberty, they themselves are the servants of corruption" (II Pet. 2:19).

The wretches did not know or even want to know where Christian freedom lies. Christ freed us by His cross from sin, death, and the devil, that is, from eternal damnation, if we believe in Him in true repentence. This is the same as our being redeemed from the oath of the law; the same as our not being under the law, but under grace; the same as the law dying for us that we may be living gods; the same as our being saved from the power of him who had the power of death, that is, the devil, and any other comparisons at all that may be found in the Scriptures (Gal. 3:13, Rom. 6:15, Gal. 2:19, Heb. 2:14). Christ freed us too from the legislation of ritual and from human inventions, supposedly necessary for salvation but in fact arbitrary, as the Apostle instructs us more than once. However, this is not the time to expound on this in detail. But Christ did not give us freedom from obedience to the laws of God nor from due submission to the reigning powers; on the contrary, He affirmed this, as will be shown later.

So much for the presumptuous men of old. However, they have their followers even today: thus the Pope, excepting himself and his clergy from [obedience to] the state authorities, but deluding himself that he has the power to give and take away the scepters of kings; and thus the Anabaptists, forbidding a Christian to hold authority—fantasies which will be destroyed in my next section.

Let us recall just a little more about some of our wise men. There are some (and God grant that there be not many of them), either deceived by a secret demon or cast into darkness by melancholia, who have a monster in their thought that makes them consider sinful and abominable anything wondrous, merry, great, and glorious they see, even though it is just and correct and not displeasing to God. For example, they like a rainy day better than clear skies; they rejoice more in sad news than good; they love not happiness itself. And I do not know how they think of themselves, but they think of others this way: if they see anyone healthy and of good behavior, then of course [they think] he is not holy; they would like all men to be ugly, hunchbacked, gloomy, unfortunate—and only in such a condition would they love them. The ancient Greeks called such men misanthropes, that is, men-haters. And there is an old and wonderful story about one, Timon by name, an inhabitant of Athens. He was so ill of this passion and, hating good conduct among men, so thirstily wished misfortune to his fatherland that in the end he went mad. He was so blinded and deluded that he believed someone really had told him that all Athenians were going to hang themselves. And at once he rushed out glad and joyful among the people and proclaimed in this wise: "Men," he said, "Athenians! I have a great tree in my garden, and on it there are many strong branches. And I want to cut it down for a building I need on the spot; so come hang yourselves quickly, I beg you, for I cannot wait long." Are there not misanthropes like that today? Perhaps not in so great measure; yet there are spiteful and dejected men.

And they most of all do not tremble to dishonor dignities; they not only fail to hold all temporal powers to be God's work, nay they scorn them as abomination. For they know not what true humility and spiritual poverty are; but since they judge by outer appearance, they despise all that is great and glorious and put it down as sin. Thus they do not want to think of the supreme power as being just and made lawful by God.

However, they too are not without arms, they think they have a bit of theology from the Holy Scriptures; not that they might have turned away from a passage they have not understood (as happens with others), but for their ready evil they have brought out an uncomprehended passage. This is, they say, the word of Christ Himself: "For that which is highly esteemed among men is abomination in the sight of God" (Luke 16:15). From this they deduce that wisdom, power, glory, and every human authority are abominable in the sight of God. We are beholding the height of theology, O listeners! And who cannot see how powerful and effective it is for the simple and ignorant, especially when it is proclaimed with mellowed words and an emotional countenance, with sighings and noddings of the head? Thus the angel of darkness is transformed into the angel of light! Let us therefore expose his vileness and remove this seeming weapon from him! We ask you, O excellent theologians, what are we to understand when we hear the Psalmist praising Divine Providence precisely because it raises the poor man from the ground and lifts up the beggar from the dung heap to seat him with princes, with the princes of his own people? What are we to understand here? According to your wise way of thinking, one has to interpret thus: Providence raises the poor man from the ground and lifts up the beggar from the dung heap, that is, takes his holiness away from him, to seat him with the princes of his own people, that is, to throw him down into abomination. "That which is highly esteemed among men is abomination in the sight of God." See what abomination we sink into if we follow you! Stand then and behold the power of the word of the Lord! This word the Lord spoke to the Pharisees who were mocking His teaching: "Ye are they which justify yourselves before men; but God knoweth your hearts: for that which is highly esteemed among men is abomination in the sight of God." Behold here what sort of high esteem He called abomination: the justification of the Pharisees, which is to give themselves airs with the appearance of holiness, to catch the eyes of men by means of hypocrisy. For if all our righteousnesses are filthy rags before the eyes of God, as Isaiah says (Isa.

64:6), and if Paul so little admired his own gains that he counted them as vanity and dung when placed against the price of salvation (Phil. 3:8), how much more abominable in the sight of God are mere seeming virtues. This is the sort of high esteem which the just man had who spoke before God about himself: "I am not as other men are: I fast twice in the week," and so on (Luke 18:11–12). With this sort of esteem did the wretched Pelagius vaunt himself. And who else is great and high-placed because of it? You, blind ones (I was about to say hypocrites), you yourselves (with whom we are now talking) are thus high-placed! You arouse such admiration with your outward poverty, your gloomy faces, and your whole Pharisee hide (a lamentable business!), you arouse admiration in men and you deceive the hearts of the innocent! Yet this word of the Lord is not directed at the high esteem of government authorities, for the lowliness that God loves is found also in purple robes when a king confesses before God that he is sinful and places his hopes solely in God's mercy, as did David, Constantine, Theodosius, and the rest. On the contrary, the Pharisee's high esteem lives even in a beggar's dress. And here most of all, then, the quoted word of the Lord thunders against you, damned hypocrites—and you have not perceived it: "Ye are they which justify yourselves before men; but God knoweth your hearts: for that which is highly esteemed among men is abomination in the sight of God."

But now, having gotten rid of these men of filthy words like so much mud, let us go forth onto the clean and smooth road and examine what provision concerning human power is taught us by Nature herself and the word of God. Now, this speech is no longer only for a few gloomy, meek persons, but for everyone, every sex, age, and human condition, for poor and rich, sick and strong and famed, and simply for all who are not cattle, not beasts.

Let us first of all ask our very nature what it tells us about this matter. For besides Scripture there is in Nature herself a law laid down by God, for the Apostle says, "When the Gentiles, which have not the law, do by nature the things contained in the law, these, having not the law, are a law unto themselves: which shew the work of the law written in their hearts" (Rom. 2:14–15). Laws like these are in the heart of every man: to love and fear God, to protect one's own life, to wish for a never-declining posterity for the human race, not to do to others what one does not wish for oneself, and to honor one's father and mother. Our own conscience is both the teacher and the witness of these same laws. For what is this indefinite gnawing we feel in our thoughts in connection with an evil deed, even a secret one, known only to ourselves? Surely this power was sown in our nature by the Creator. Therefore also Paul, when expounding (in the passage mentioned above) the law written in men's hearts, points out the certainty of this and says: "They show the work of the law written in their hearts, their conscience also bearing witness, and their thoughts the meanwhile accusing or else excusing one another, in the day when God shall judge the secrets of men" (Rom. 2:15–16).

And behold, might there not be in the number of natural laws this one, too, that there are to be authorities holding power among nations? There is indeed! And this is the very chief of all laws. For because, on the one hand, Nature orders us to love ourselves and not to do to others what we do not like ourselves, while, on the other, the ill will of a depraved race of man does not hesitate to break this law, always and everywhere a guardian has been desirable, a defender and a strong fighter for the law, and this is the power of government. This thought does not occur to many men. Why not? Because living safely under such guardians, they do not reason about their good position, for they are used to it. Yet if anyone were to try to live with men outside such a system, he would at once become aware how bad it is without authority. We have the tale of Vejdevut, the first leader of the Prussians and Zhmuds.[3] His people, not being under any authority, when they had suffered many an ill from outsiders and from each other, were forced to ask him, as an intelligent man, for advice for their own improvement. Vejdevut addressed them thus: "If, men," he said, "you were not stupider than your own bees, it would be well with you." They asked in what way they were stupider than bees. "In that," he said, "the bees, these small and speechless insects, have a king, while you, men, have none." They burst into applause at the advice and that very hour urged him to become their ruler. But there is no time to cite witnesses to this. To speak briefly, the whole world is witness, all nations are witnesses. And if we ever find some coarse vile nation without a chief (though not entirely so; for at least every household has its own manager), we ordinarily compare its men to cattle and describe them by the saw "neither king nor law." For we hold it certain that supreme authority receives its beginning and cause from Nature itself. If from Nature, then from God Himself, the Creator of Nature. For if the principle of primary authority comes from man's condition and agreement, yet because the natural law written on man's heart by God demands a powerful protector for itself, and conscience (which itself is also the seed of God) urges him to seek the same thing as well, therefore we cannot help but call God Himself the cause of the authority of governments. From this, then, it is likewise evident that Nature teaches us too of the obedience due to authorities. Look within yourself and consider this: Governmental authority is necessary to natural law. Will your conscience not tell you at once: Therefore not to obey authority is to sin against natural law? Consider this: The powers act so that we live in safety. Will your conscience not tell you at once: Therefore not to wish authorities is to wish the destruction of man? Consider further: I see that authority has been made lawful by God for us through our own sane understanding. Will your conscience not lead you on: Therefore to resist the powers is to resist God Himself? And that is the same thing even the atheists (though they are not following their consciences) advise: that God should be preached among the people. Why? Otherwise, it is said, the people will become discontented with the powers. It is evident therefore that man's conscience sees that authority is from God and urges man to fear the powers for the sake of God.

---

[3] Prokopovich has taken this reference from a sixteenth-century Polish chronicle account (M. Stryjkowski, "O Wejdewucie, królu pierwszym Pruskim, z Litalanów wybranym, i o Litwonie i Samocie, synach jego," 1582).—Note in Russian edition.

Now then let us hear the written word of God, which is already very well known, and, apart from the fact that God shows us sovereignty through our own consciences, we will see that by His own Providence He makes up a part of sovereignty, and He seals the establishing of governments (by whatever just means it may take place) with His blessing and gives orders that they be obeyed. What light appears here? What harvest of mighty reasons? The books are full of them, both the books of the law and the historical ones, the books of the Psalms and the Prophets; and the Gospels and the writings of the Apostles agree with them. Who could number them in detail and fit in every word! It is enough to recall a few. Listen, therefore, every rank and age! Listen to the sublime word: "By me kings reign and the mighty decree justice" (Prov. 8:15). Who is speaking? The Wisdom which existed before all ages and is consubstantial with the Father—is not this alone enough? Divine Wisdom expounds Its own great glories and exults in this deed: "By me," It says, "kings reign." Who is not frightened by this alone? What spirits are not cowed? Can we count the words of God, which are "pure words: as silver tried in a furnace of earth, purified seven times" (Ps. 12:6), can we, I say, dare to count the words of God as foolish fables, O Christians? Let us hear more of the same Spirit's agents in agreement. Daniel speaks to the ear of this world: "Let the living know that the most High ruleth through the kingdom of men, and giveth it to whomsoever he will" (Dan. 4:17). He also calls out: "Blessed be the name of God for ever and ever, for wisdom and understanding and might are His, and He changeth the times and the seasons, He setteth up kings and He removeth kings" (Dan. 2:20–21). The speaker of Proverbs preaches: "The king's heart is in the hand of the Lord, as the rivers of water: he turneth it whithersoever he will" (Prov. 21:1–2). The Apostle Peter exhorts: "Submit yourselves to every ordinance of man for the Lord's sake: whether it be to the king, as supreme; or unto governors, as unto them that are sent by him for the punishment of evil-doers, and for the praise of them that do well. For so is the will of God, that with well doing ye may put to silence the ignorance of foolish men" (I Pet. 2:13–15). The teacher of the nations cries out: "Let every soul be subject unto the higher powers. For there is no power but of God: the powers that be are ordained of God" (Rom. 13:1). And let no one think, "We do not have to submit ourselves!" The powers are strong and terrible, they will bend one willy-nilly to mind them. The Apostle anticipates and overturns this thought; he teaches clearly that we must be obedient not because of fear but also for conscience' sake (Rom. 13:5), and that he who is not submissive to the authorities is resisting God. For when he has said that the powers are ordained of God, he adds at once: "Whosoever therefore resisteth the power, resisteth the ordinance of God: and they that resist shall receive to themselves damnation" [Rom. 13:2]. And again: "For he is the minister of God to thee for good. But if thou do that which is evil, be afraid; for he beareth not the sword in vain, for he is the minister of God, a revenger to execute wrath upon him that doeth evil. Wherefore ye must needs be subject, not only for wrath but also for conscience sake. For, for this cause pay ye tribute also: for they are God's ministers, attending continually upon this very thing" [Rom. 13:4–6]. A wondrous thing indeed! You might say that Paul had been sent by the king himself for such a sermon; he exhorts as zealously and persuasively as though pounding with a hammer, he keeps repeating the same thing again and again: there is no power except from God, the powers are ordained by God, the minister of God, the minister of God, they are God's ministers. This is not idle repetition; he is teaching from the wisdom given him. This is not flattery. It it not one desirous of pleasing men who speaks, but Christ's chosen vessel. He drums away so actively in order to make sensitive and vigilant Christians and not to allow anyone to doze even for a short time. And I beg you all to think carefully—what more could the truest minister of the king say?

Now let us add to this doctrine as its crown the names and titles fitting for high powers; they are not vain, for they were given by God Himself, and they adorn kings better than purple robes and diadems, than all their magnificent outer trappings and dignity, and together they show that such great power is from God Himself.

But what titles? What names? They are called gods and christs [the anointed ones]. The saying of the Psalms is renowned: "I have said, Ye are gods; and all of you are children of the most High" (Ps. 82:6). This statement refers to the authorities. Paul the Apostle is in agreement with this too: "There be gods many, and lords many" (I Cor. 8:5). But even before these two, Moses also had named the powers: "Thou shalt not revile the gods, nor curse the ruler of thy people" (Exod. 22:28). Now what is the cause of so exalted a name? The Lord Himself explains in John his evangelist that they are called gods because "unto them the word of God came" [John 10:35]. And what other word can we cite? Unless perhaps the instruction given to them by God to defend the administration of justice, as we read in the Psalm mentioned just now. For their power, therefore, given them by God, they are called gods, that is, the representatives of God on earth. Theodoretus speaks of this elegantly: "Because God is truly a judge, the court has been entrusted also to men; for this reason they are called gods, as imitators of God in this" [Theodoretus of Cyrrhus, on Ps. 81:1].[4]

The second name, christ, which is to say the anointed, is so frequent in Scripture that it would take a long time to enumerate the places. And who needs an explanation of why kings are called so? For this name "anointed" itself is clear; it means "he who is established and justified by God to reign." And he is said to be anointed from the ancient ceremony when those chosen for kingship were anointed with oil as a sign of God's grace, which gave blessing for this.

And these quotations, for all their brevity, suffice as perfect proof that the powers of government are the work of God Himself.

It is time to show what honor we owe the authorities, what love and faithfulness, what fear and obedience. But this seems to be superfluous talk:

---

[4] Theodoretus' commentary on the Psalms was translated into Slavonic in the Golden Age of Bulgarian literature. There is an eleventh-century copy of it, and numerous references show its popularity in Slavic lands throughout the Middle Ages.—Translator.

for who, knowing perfectly that power is from God, can doubt or ask about doing honor to authority? Unless he is doubtful even of honoring God Himself.

Now in my foregoing words you have heard the preaching of the Apostles that he who resists the powers is resisting God and that one must obey not only out of fear of wrath but also out of conscience. You have heard Peter's teaching about the same thing; you have heard how Peter and Jude revile those insane lovers of freedom who tremble not to speak evil of dignities; you have heard God's preaching through Moses, "Thou shalt not revile the gods, nor curse the ruler of thy people."

Let us add to this the following admonitions of Paul: "Servants, be obedient to them that are your masters according to the flesh, with fear and trembling, in singleness of your heart, as unto Christ; not with eyeservice, as menpleasers; but as the servants of Christ, doing the will of God from the heart; with good will doing service, as to the Lord, and not to men" (Eph. 6:5–7). And he repeats the same thing to the Colossians, in the third chapter: "Servants, obey in all things your masters according to the flesh; not with eyeservice, as menpleasers; but in singleness of heart, fearing God: And whatsoever ye do, do it heartily, as to the Lord, and not unto men; knowing that of the Lord ye shall receive the reward of the inheritance: for ye serve the Lord Christ. But he that doeth wrong shall receive for the wrong which he hath done; and there is no respect of persons" (Col. 3:22–25). And to Timothy: "Let as many servants as are under the yoke count their own masters worthy of all honour, that the name of God and his doctrine be not blasphemed" (I Tim. 6:1). And he commands Titus to exhort "servants to be obedient unto their own masters, and to please them well in all things, not answering back, not purloining, but showing all good fidelity, that they may adorn the doctrine of God our Saviour in all things" (Titus 2:9–10). If there is such a strong apostolic doctrine about both every master and every servant (for it is stated in general terms), then how much stronger and firmer it is concerning the authority of government and concerning men subject to it as to the Lord's anointed, the representative of God.

But we cannot pass by what amazes us mightily and fortifies this truth as with adamantine armor. And that is the fact that the Scriptures order obedience not only to the good powers, but also to the perverse and the faithless ones. For everyone knows that holy saying of Peter: "Fear God. Honour the king. Servants, be subject to your masters with all fear; not only to the good and gentle, but also to the froward" (I Pet. 2:17–18).

Yet someone might think that this is advice, not a command, and that this befits a Christian as a matter of humility and gentleness, and not by truth itself and duty. But this is a deceitful thought and a vain doubting. For we see how other scriptures agree with this, how this was concluded in word and deed by our forefathers in the Old Testament, and by the true Christians under grace.

Who was King Saul, who does not know him? And how did David think of him in his kingship (David, I say, not just any man), David, who knew that Saul had been rejected by God, while he himself had already been anointed to reign (I Sam. 24)? What did David do? When his friends counseled him to kill Saul, his enemy, he became afraid at the very words and cried out: "The Lord forbid that I should do this thing unto my master, the Lord's anointed, to stretch forth mine hand against him, seeing he is the anointed of the Lord" (I Sam. 24:7). He said the same thing at another time to similar counselors, and, after the murder of Saul, he ordered his murderer to be put to death (II Sam. 1), always offering the same reason, that he was the anointed of the Lord.

You will say, whatever sort Saul may have been, still he was the one anointed to kingship by the public command of God and therefore was made worthy of that kind of honor. Good, then tell me—who was Cyrus, King of the Persians? Yet God calls him His anointed in the book of the Prophet Isaiah (Isa. 45). Who was Nebuchadnezzar of Babylon? Yet God commands Israel to serve him, in the book of Jeremiah the Prophet (Jer. 27). Who was Nero of Rome? Yet Peter teaches, Paul teaches zealously to honor him for conscience' sake. And how strong this doctrine was has been attested over many centuries and in various places among Christians who knew God's law well: the Christians obeyed the powers in Persia and Parthia; they obeyed in Africa under the Vandals and in Italy under the Langobards. And what will we say about the Christians in all the enormous extent of the Roman state of the time! From the beginning of the preaching of the Apostles right up to Constantine the Great, through three hundred years, there were ten of the most ferocious persecutions, which brought to light so great an army of martyrs, and though sometimes a rumor of some small Christian revolt might start, it never did happen.

It is not that I do not know what a stubborn heart thinks here: "The Christians did not have such strength." Nay, here an ignorance of ancient historians is speaking. About two hundred years after the birth of Christ there was such a multitude of Christians that, according to the testimony of Cyprian the martyr in his epistle to Demetrianus, they had sufficient force to defend themselves from the rapine and torment of the torturers. And be so good as to listen to what Tertullian had testified about this even before Cyprian. For he speaks thus in his Apology to the faithless Romans [37:4]:

If we had wished to be your enemies openly, not just your secret avengers, would the force of our numbers and troops have been too poor? The Moors, the Marcomanni, and the Parthians themselves, and any other peoples of whatsoever size, but of one place within their own confines, surpass in numbers, I suppose, one race that belongs to the whole world? We are but of yesterday, yet we have filled everything that is yours: cities, islands, fortresses, meeting places, councils, campaigns, the camps themselves, the palace, the senate, the market place—we have left you only your temples. [. . .] If we should tear away such a multitude of people from you and go to a far country, the loss of so many inhabitants of whatever sort would shame your rule, nay punish you by its very act of desertion. You would be horror-struck at your solitude, at the silence and stupor, as of a dead city. You would have to seek someone to govern.

Thus far Tertullian.[5] And after this he tells how the law of the Christians forbids them to revolt and keeps them in such humility. If therefore it is so, if Christians have to be subject even to perverse and faithless rulers, then how much more must they be utterly obligated to true-believing and true-judging lords! For the former are masters, but the latter are also fathers. And what do I say! This autocrat [Peter], all autocrats, every one is a father. Now in what other command will you find place for this duty of ours to honor the powers from the soul and for conscience' sake if not in this one: "Honor thy father!" All the teachers, wise in God, affirm this, thus Moses the Lawgiver himself instructs. And what more? The powers are the most primary and very highest fatherland, for on them depend not some single man, not one house, but the life, the integrity, the welfare of a whole great people.

It is indeed already time to finish. But one doubt remains that can be like a thorn in the conscience; let us pull it out quickly and finish the sermon.

Someone might think (and many do think) that not quite all men are bound by this obligation, but some are excepted, namely, the clergy and the monks. This thorn—or better say sting, for this is the sting of the serpent—this is the papal spirit, but I do not know how it touches or applies to us: for the clergy is a different work, a different rank among the people, and not a different state.

And as there is one job for the army, another for the citizens, another for doctors, another for various artisans, yet all with their work are subordinate to the supreme powers; so also the pastors and teachers and simply all those concerned with spiritual affairs have their own work, to be God's servants and the performers of His mysteries, yet they are subject also to the command of the governmental powers that they remain in the performance of their calling—and to punishment if they do not so remain; and how much more subject if they do not fulfill the obligation they have in common with the rest of the nation. Perhaps someone might think that we have already spoken entirely too long; but I beg you, listen patiently first to see whether we have powerful reasons for this, and then judge as you will.

Even before the written law, when God was preparing Moses to make him the leader of Israel, when He was sending him to Pharaoh and giving him as a helper Aaron, who was intended for the priesthood, He gave the command to Moses that he was to be instead of God to Aaron (Exod. 4[:16]).

Now if we look at the church of the Old Testament, there is no place for doubt (I Chron. 23), for it is well known that there all the priests and Levites were subordinate to the king of Israel in all things. Let us give some examples of this. David divides the priests into twenty-four groups, and defines the service to be performed by each of their ranks. He also, when sending the priest Zadok and with him the Prophet Nathan to anoint his son to the kingship, calls himself their lord. That is David. What about Solomon? He puts down from his office Abiathar the high priest, who had caused Solomon's brother Adonijah to seize the king's throne against his father's will, and condemns him to death, but for Abiathar's previous serv-

---

[5] Prokopovich quotes Tertullian with omissions and not always accurately.—Translator.

ice to his father, Solomon makes him the gift of his life. And there is a multitude of examples like this. Christ Himself orders that the things that are Caesar's are to be rendered unto Caesar; He gives this order to the high priests and the scribes and the elders, as St. Mark (Mark 12) writes in detail, and Luke (Luke 20). For if it is so in the Old, why not also in the New Testament! For this law about the powers is a moral, not a ritual, law having its roots in the Decalogue itself, and for that reason it is not changeable, but eternal, abiding as long as this world remains.

But let us question the New Testament separately. And here we see the truth even more clearly. For besides the fact that the Lord Himself gave the powers tribute in His own name (Mark 12) and that Paul appeals to the court of Caesar (Acts 25) and that Peter writes his first epistle, in which he teaches that one must honor the king, not only to the laity but also to the clergy (as is clear from the fifth chapter)—apart from these statements and others like them, there is Paul's invincible word: "Let every soul be subject unto the higher powers" (Rom. 13:1). Now why does he say "every soul" unless it be to subject everyone, without selection, without exception, to the powers? And would it have been difficult to add "every soul, except presbyters or pastors"?

But when he embraces everything all around—"every soul"!—how can one except the clergy from that? Unless that is the way our passions rationalize. Yet why am I using my own words in this struggle? Let us hear the teacher of the whole world, Chrysostom: "Showing," he says, "that these regulations are for all, even for priests, and monks, and not for men of secular occupations only, he has made this plain from the outset by saying as follows: *Let every soul be subject unto the higher powers,* if you be an apostle even, or an evangelist, or a prophet, or anything else at all" (Chrysostom, Homily on Rom. 13:1). What more do we want, then? It is fitting to urge only what Paul so zealously fights for before the powers (Acts 9 and 23), and he himself had the knowledge that it was proper for him to suffer. Chrysostom interprets Paul's words so precisely that you would say he was hired to do it; and yet he certainly showed by his own acts what sort of a manpleaser *he* was.

One ought to bring in still more evidence: the regulations of the Christian councils, teachers, and kings. For their words too are founded on God's Word. But for brevity, in passing as it were, let us only touch on a few. The ecumenical councils were convoked at the command of emperors; at these same councils judges instated by the emperors were in charge. They watched to see that the business went on decently, they tamed the turbulence and noise of the bishops, as was the case in Chalcedon (Acts of the Council of Chalcedon, 1), it was they the bishops asked for directions if someone wanted to read a message or take the floor. The acts of the council show this clearly. And if it is not so, then call me the world's greatest liar. At the time of the first council, at Nicaea, complaints against the bishops were given to Constantine. Though Constantine did not deign to investigate these slanders and burned the complaints, nevertheless he did it while expressing displeasure at the internal quarrels among the clergy as being matters not in keeping with the dignity of their rank, and not on the grounds that he had no power to judge them. The same monarch at the same council directed the bishops to seek out the truth only from Holy Scripture, not by any other proofs. At the fifth council it was Emperor Justinian's order that the chairman be Mina, the patriarch of Constantinople. The same emperor harshly punished Vigilius, the Pope of Rome, for his stubbornness and troublemaking, as Nicephorus writes in Book 26, Chapter 17; we will not cite unjust works. At the sixth council the chairman was Constantine Pogonatus himself.

What then will we say about the laws of the emperors, where for bishops and presbyters and the whole body of churchmen there are laid down various regulations, orders, and punishments for cause! We see much of the same kind of thing in the composition of the ancient laws which were collected at the order of Justinian in the book called the Code, much, too, in the laws promulgated by Justinian himself, and much in the Novels of the most recent emperors.

But if one were to enumerate all this in detail, it would be a book and not an ordinary sermon. For the lovers of truth even these suffice; for the stubborn and stiff-necked, however, nothing could be enough.

When, therefore, we see statements and arguments of such force and in such quantity, even though it be not all of them, that attest to the inviolable, hardly even touchable greatness of the powers of government, as if we really were all listening to our own consciences, then it would be better for kings to remain safe and carefree because of the shield of this truth than because of the military force surrounding them—then who would not spit upon a frivolous view of the powers! Who will not become indignant at the haughty disdain that fails to do great honor to the glorious state, of surpassing gigantic strength!

Nature has witnessed for us, the unlying word of God has witnessed for us that the high powers are from God; the Scriptures have taught us sufficiently how much obedience we all owe to the powers, the perverse as well as the good ones, not only from fear of their anger but also for the sake of our consciences; both divine and human testimony have shown clearly how every soul without exception is subject to this obligation. Where now are those ancient freedom-lovers, the presumptuous ones that were not afraid to speak evil of dignities? Where is the head of headless Rome, deluding himself that the scepter and kingly sword are his own instruments? Where are the humble-sly hypocrites who have despised as abomination this great work of God, given to the world as its strength? O damnable affair! O the troubles of our times! What adequate indignation can we arouse? What tears shall we not weep? How can we have enough heart to be sufficiently concerned? How contrary to the hard truth is the affair our present age has shown us! Some have thought not only of reducing the powers of government, the honor due the God-given tsar (enough right there to warrant eternal condemnation), but of begrudging both his scepter and his life! But whose desire is this? The mules and lions were not enough; the grasshoppers came too, and the vile caterpillar also.

It has come to the point that the most useless people have mixed into the affair! And an abominable and impudent one it is too! And even the dregs of the nation, cheap souls, men good for nothing else, born only to eat up other men's labors; these too are against their sovereign, they too are against the Lord's anointed! Why, you ought to marvel when you eat bread, and say, "From where has this come to me?" In truth the story of David, against whom the blind and the lame raised a revolt, has been renewed for us (II Sam. 5). People will think, "Now what's he blathering about?" One should not look at one's poverty but at one's conscience! A fine conscience! We'll set up a mirror for it!

Two men went into a church—to steal, not to pray. One was in fine dress, the other in rags and tatters. Now the agreement between them was not to steal for their common profit, but what each grabbed was to be his. The ragged man was more experienced and at once rushed to the altar and the throne and rapaciously plundered everything there. Envy seized the other. And as though out of true zeal he said, "Don't you fear God? How could you dare to approach the holy throne in rags!" And he replied: "Don't shout, brother, God doesn't look at your clothes, He looks at your conscience." This is the mirror for your conscience, O ye without sin! To place your conscience on your tongue and then boast of your conscience, when you ought to weep and groan. And what is more, you have to have evil-portending dreams for people! Sleep on, wizards! Oh, you unfeeling man! Who cannot catch a whiff of the atheist spirit in you.

But let my words be directed to you, honorable and noble men, glorious in rank and deed, even you who can be called by the name of the whole nation: O Russia! I doubt that the poverty of the preacher will greatly lessen the importance of the sermon, and I confess that I am unworthy of such listeners. But I beg you, when you hear the Gospel read by any man whatsoever, do you not believe? So here, too: look not at the face of the speaker but at the Word of God, and converse not with me, but let each man converse with his own understanding.

Since God has so commanded us with regard to the supremacy of the state, what reasons will excuse us, if someone dares not to be obedient to the state! And if one is actually resisting God Himself when he resists powers that are perverse and do not know God, then what word can we call it, not merely resisting, but even more, daring against the true-believing monarch, even him who has so benefited Russia, so that from the beginning of the All-Russian state, however many may be found by historians, they cannot point out one equal to him. All state obligations depend on these two things, on the civil, I say, and the military. Who in our land has ever managed these two as well as this man? Renewed Russia in everything, or rather given her a new birth? What then, is this to be his reward from us? For it was by his providence and his own labors that everyone received glory and freedom from care, while he himself has a shameful name and a life full of misery? What a scandal this is! What a shameful blemish! Terrible to his enemies, this man is forced to fear his subjects! Glorious among foreigners, dishonored among his own! And when by his many cares and efforts he is bringing untimely old age upon himself, when for the integrity of his fatherland, disregarding his own health, he is hurrying toward death as though at a gallop, why, some think he is living too long! If the law of God did not hold us back, the very shame of such ingratitude would be strong enough to hold us back. All nations refuse to suffer this one accusation against themselves, that they are unfaithful to their rulers, for on the contrary, they all consider it great glory to die for their sovereign! Are you alone, O Russia, going to lag behind all nations in this? The foreign writers of yore, even though they made fun of our nation for many things badly done, yet have praised us for faithfulness to our sovereigns so much that they have presented us as a model for others. And exactly when Peter had already wiped out all former mockery by such great glory, then the former glory of faithfulness began to fade! Is such the fortune of Russia, not to have full glory? Our most furious enemies are amazed at this, and although this news about us is pleasant for them (for it pleases their jealousy), still they curse such madness and spit upon it. And let us watch that this saying does not grow up about us: the monarch is worthy of so great a country, but the country is not worthy of such a monarch.

But this sin is not rewarded by shame alone. It brings after it a storm, a gale, and a terrible cloud of innumerable woes. Kings do not descend from the throne easily when they descend involuntarily. At once there is tumult and quaking in the country, bloody private quarrels among the great, but among the small men of good conscience wailing, weeping, affliction, while evil men, like fierce beasts loosed from their bonds, attack in waves everywhere, plundering and murdering. Where and when has the scepter been transferred by force without a great deal of blood, the sacrifice of the best men, the destruction of great houses? And just as it is difficult to keep a house whole when the foundation is undermined, so it is here too: when the higher powers are overthrown, all society shakes on the verge of collapse. And it is rare that this disease in states is not unto death, as can be seen from the historians of the world. But what historians do we need? Is not Russia herself witness enough? For I think that she will not soon forget what she suffered after the misdeeds of Godunov and how close she was to final destruction. Oh, even if (again I say) we did not know God's law, would not just this one most trying vision of the things that followed be enough? But it is an evil that is hard to doctor, when demented men neither look on the past nor deliberate about the future, while, delighting in some alluring illusion, they rush blindly to their ruin.

Therefore, finally, let us put it to every man that in all our doings and makings, first, last, and always, we must realize that this present doctrine is needed, like a special seal: this is the unerasable and inescapable judgment of God. Let us not deceive ourselves, orthodox men! The doctrine presented here that one should honor the government powers is a true one; for also Holy Scripture is the true Word of God Himself, witnessed by its internal explanations and powerfully effective strength and the fact that its great prophecies have come to pass.

Let us not doubt, therefore, that the judgment of God is coming also to those who resist His word. And when will this be? Grieve not, the Lord will come and He will not delay. Say not, "The Lord is late." For lo! the judge is standing at the door; only watch what word you give Him in this. For if He judges deserving of fiery hell those who blame their brethren for foolishness, what judgment will He give those who are displeased with their sovereigns and tremble not to speak evil of dignities? If He condemns those who have not been merciful to one of the little ones as though they had not been merciful to Him Himself, how then will He condemn those who scheme against His own representative, who partakes of the divine name, the anointed of the Lord? Oh, what utter callousness, if anyone is not frightened by this! For here it is not only those who oppose the powers who must tremble but also those who are obedient out of fear of wrath, and not for the sake of conscience.

Now such men will escape the sword of the king, for they have been obedient for fear of his wrath; yet they will not escape the judgment of God, for they have not been obedient for conscience' sake. Where then will you be, you who have despised both the wrath of the king and your own conscience and are daring to stand against the scepter and the health of the powers? Are you terrified or not? We are all terrified that this might hasten the wrath of God with his vengeance in this world against our fatherland.

But provide the best for us, the best, O God! Guard us by Thy mercy! To our great ingratitude we have added this, too, that we have not recognized many of Thy good deeds, shown forth to us in Peter; we confess therefore that we are unworthy and have been ungrateful. Yet our sins and Thy mercy are not in this world alone. Do not deal with us according to our lawlessness, but reward us for our sins. Lord, save Thine anointed and hear him from Thy holy heaven. Lord, save the Tsar and hear us! Make him glad in Thy salvation! Guard him by Thy gracious blessing! May Thy hand be on all his enemies, may Thy right hand find out all them that hate him. Be thou exalted, Lord, in Thine own strength; so will we sing and praise Thy power. Amen.

2.

Mikhail Vasil'evich Lomonosov

1711-1765

The versatile genius Mikhail Vasil'evich Lomonosov has frequently been described as the Peter the Great of modern Russian culture. His role as innovator and reformer in the realms of literature, grammar, and scholarship was very much like Peter's in the political domain. Little wonder that Lomonosov was an ardent admirer of the first Emperor. The panegyric below reflects his sincere feelings and is more than the fulsome official praise expected on the occasion of a public ceremony. Behind the traditional formulas of the encomium we can sense Lomonosov's pride in and genuine gratitude for Peter the Great's accomplishments in transforming Russia. The Emperor is hailed as the energy-giving principle of modern Russia, the creator of the new status and power enjoyed by the Russian nation. Although Lomonosov recognized that Peter's work had antecedents in seventeenth-century Muscovy, he contended that only the personal qualities of the Emperor made the country's transformation possible.

Lomonosov's oration, of course, cannot be read as an objective description of Peter's work. But it marks an important step in the process of mythologizing Peter's reign. While Prokopovich was thinking (and speaking) still in a traditional religious framework, Lomonosov was arguing in terms of a secular conception of state power and national interest. Historically, the myth that Peter the Great was the source of everything that is modern in Russia proved to be more important for Russian thought and feeling than his actual deeds. By singling out for praise the personal elements, Lomonosov contributed to the formation of a political tradition that assigned absolute value to voluntaristic (i.e., goal-directed) and rational (in Max Weber's sense—i.e., as opposed to traditional) leadership in social and cultural change. Implicitly, all the basic questions asked by the Russian intelligentsia involved taking a stand toward this tradition of political behavior. Little wonder that Peter's innovations became a focal point in all nineteenth-century political and philosophic discussions.

Panegyric to the Sovereign Emperor Peter the Great

Of Blessed and Everlastingly Honored Memory

At the Solemn Celebration of the Coronation
of Her Imperial Majesty, the Supremely August,
Most Autocratic, Great Sovereign Empress
Elizaveta Petrovna, Autocrat of All Russia

My listeners, as we commemorate the most holy anointing of our most gracious Autocrat and Her coronation as Sovereign of the All-Russian state, we behold God's favor to Her and to our common fatherland, favor like unto that at which we marvel in Her birth and in Her coming into possession of Her patrimony. Her birth was made wonderful by omens of empire; Her ascension to the throne is made glorious by courage protected from on high; Her acceptance from the Lord's hand of Her Father's crown and splendid victories is infused with reverential joy. It may be that there are still those who are in doubt whether Rulers are set up on earth by God or whether they obtain their realms through chance; yet in itself the birth of our Great Sovereign compels conviction here, inasmuch as even at that time She had been elected to rule over us. Not the dubious divinations of astrology, based on the position of the planets, nor yet other manifestations or changes in the course of nature, but clear signs of God's Providence shall serve as proof of this. PETER's most glorious victory over His foes at Poltava took place in the same year as the birth of this Great Daughter of His, and the Conqueror riding in triumph into Moscow was met by the coming into the world of ELIZABETH. Is this not the finger of Providence? Do we not hear a prophetic voice in the mind's ear? Behold, behold the fruition of that bliss promised to us in auguries. PETER triumphed in victory over external enemies and in the extirpation of traitors; ELIZABETH was born for similar triumphs. PETER, having returned the crown to the lawful Sovereign, made His entry into His Father's city; ELIZABETH entered the human community in order that Her father's crown should afterward revert to Her. PETER, having protected

Translated by Ronald Hingley from Mikhail Vasil'evich Lomonosov, *Sochineniia,* Vol. IV (St. Petersburg, 1898), pp. 361–91. The speech was delivered on April 26, 1755, to commemorate the coronation of Elizabeth; it was first published in St. Petersburg in 1755.

Russia from pillage, brought joy, secure and serene, in place of gloomy fear; ELIZABETH saw the light of day that She might pour the sunshine of happiness over us and free us from the gloom of sorrows. PETER led in His train numerous captives, conquered no less by His magnanimity than by His courage; ELIZABETH was delivered from the womb that She might thereafter captivate the hearts of Her subjects with philanthropy, gentleness, and generosity. What wondrous destinies ordained by God do we behold, O ye who hearken to me! Victory together with birth, the delivery of the fatherland with the delivery of the child from the Mother, the extraordinary triumphal procession and the ordinary rites of birth, swaddling clothes together with triumphal laurels, a baby's first cry mingled with joyous applause and acclamation! Were not all these things an earnest of Her Father's virtues and of Her Father's realm to the child ELIZABETH who was then born?

How much Almighty Providence did lend aid to Her own heroism on the path to the throne is a matter whereof joyous memories shall not grow silent throughout the ages. For it was moved by the power and spirit of Providence that our Heroine brought salvation and renewal to the All-Russian state, to its observed glory, to the great deeds and designs of Peter, to the inner satisfaction of our hearts, and to the general happiness of a large part of the world. To rescue a single man is a great deed; but how immeasurably greater is the salvation of an entire people! In thee, our dear fatherland, in thee do we behold abundant examples of this. Angered by the internecine feuds, perfidies, pillaging, and fratricides of our forefathers, God once bound thee in slavery to a foreign people, and on thy body, stricken with deep wounds, He laid heavy fetters. Then, moved by thy groans and lamentations, He sent thee valorous Sovereigns, liberators from slavery and suffering, who, joining together thy shattered limbs, did restore and increase thy former power, majesty, and glory. From no lesser downfall has the Russian people been rescued by the Great ELIZABETH, whom God has brought to Her Father's throne; but in a fashion even more deserving of astonishment. Internal diseases are more calamitous than external; likewise a danger nurtured in the bosom of a state is more harmful than attacks from without. External sores heal more easily than internal injuries. But when we compare the healing of Russia from defeat inflicted externally by the weapons of barbarians with the astonishing cure of a hidden internal ailment accomplished by ELIZABETH's hand, we find the reverse. Then, in order to heal external wounds, fields and rivers were empurpled no less with Russian than with Tartar blood. In our blessed days great-hearted ELIZABETH swiftly, without any suffering on our part, destroyed the disease which had taken root inside Russia, and it was as if She did heal the ailing fatherland with a single word filled with divine power, saying: *Arise and walk, arise and walk, Russia. Shake off thy doubts and fears; and filled with joy and hope, stand forth, exult, and rise to eminence.*

Such are the images evoked in our thoughts, O Listeners, by memory of the joy then aroused! But they are magnified when we consider that we were then freed not only from oppression but also from contempt. How did the nations judge us before our delivery? Do not their words still echo in our memory? The Russians, the Russians have forgotten PETER the Great! They do not repay His labors and services with due gratitude; they do not install His Daughter on Her Father's throne; She is abandoned and they do not help Her; She is rejected and they do not restore Her; She is scorned and they do not avenge Her. Oh, how great is the shame and derision! But the incomparable Heroine has by Her ascension to the throne removed disgrace from the sons of Russia and shown to the whole world the truth— that it was not that our ardor was lacking, but that Her magnanimity was all-enduring; that it was not that our zeal failed, but that She did not wish the spilling of blood; that it was not to our faintheartedness that these things must be ascribed but to God's Providence, which deigned thereby to show His power and Her courage and to redouble our joy. Such benefactions did the Almighty ordain for us by the ascension of Great ELIZABETH to Her Father's throne! Then what is our present celebration? The summit and crown of the things heretofore mentioned. The Lord has crowned Her wondrous birth, has crowned Her glorious ascension, has crowned Her incomparable virtues. He has crowned Her with grace, heartened Her with hopeful joy, and blessed Her with resounding victories, victories which resemble Her ascension. For just as internal enemies have been conquered without bloodshed, so also have external enemies been overcome with little loss.

Our Monarch is robed in purple, is anointed for imperial rule, is crowned and receives the Scepter and the Orb. Russians rejoice, filling the air with applause and acclamation. Enemies quail and blench. They slip away, turning their back on the Russian army, hide beyond rivers, mountains, swamps; but everywhere the strong hand of crowned ELIZABETH hems them in; from Her magnanimity alone do they receive relief. How clear are the auguries of Her blessed rule, which we see in all that has been said above, and how we joyously marvel at their longed-for realization! Following the example of Her great progenitor, she gives crowns to Sovereigns, calms Europe with peaceful arms, consolidates the Russian inheritance. Gold and silver flow out of the bowels of the earth, giving pleasure to Her and to the community; subjects are relieved of their burdens; neither within the realm nor beyond its bounds is the soil stained with Russian blood; the people multiply and revenues increase; magnificent buildings arise; the courts are reformed; the seeds of learning are planted in the state, while everywhere there reign dearly loved peace and quiet and an age which resembles our Monarch Herself.

And so, since our incomparable Sovereign has raised up Her Father's realm as presaged by birth, gained by courage, confirmed by Her triumphant coronation, and adorned by glorious deeds, She is in justice the true Heiress of all His deeds and praise. Therefore in praising PETER we shall praise ELIZABETH.

Long ere this the arts and sciences should have represented His glory in clear portrayals; long have they wished to laud the incomparable deeds of their Founder at a special grand assembly, but, knowing how great an art is required to frame a speech worthy of the subject, they have remained silent until this day. For of this Hero must be said what has never yet been heard of others. There is none equal to Him in deeds, nor is there any precedent in rhetoric which the thought might follow to plumb without mishap the depths of the vast number and grandeur of His deeds. But it was finally decided that it was better to show a deficiency of eloquence than of gratitude, that it was better to compose a discourse graced by sincerity and couple it with words of converse spoken in studied simplicity than to remain silent amid so much acclamation on this festive occasion. And this is especially so since the Almighty Lord has enhanced the beauty of all our celebrations by sending in the person of the young Sovereign, the Grand Duke PAVEL PETROVICH [the future Paul I], a universally longed-for pledge of His divine favor to us, which we see in the continuation of PETER's line. And so, abandoning timorous doubt and yielding to zealous daring, we must use, or rather exhaust, whatever spirit and voice we have in praise of our Hero. As I embark on this undertaking, with what shall I begin my discourse? With His bodily endowments? With the greatness of His strength? But it is manifest in His mastery of burdensome labors, labors without number, and in the overcoming of terrible obstacles. Shall I begin with His heroic appearance and stature combined with majestic beauty? But apart from the many who vividly call to mind an image of Him engraved in their memory, there is the witness of those in various states and cities who, drawn by His fame, flocked out to admire a figure appropriate to His deeds and befitting a great Monarch. Should I commence with His buoyancy of spirit? But that is proved by the tireless vigilance without which it would have been impossible to carry out deeds so numerous and great. Wherefore I do immediately proceed to present these deeds, knowing that it is easier to make a beginning than to reach the end and that this Great Man cannot be better praised than by him who shall enumerate His labors in faithful detail, were it but possible to enumerate them.

And so, to the extent that strength and the brevity of limited time will permit, we shall mention only His most important deeds, then the mighty obstacles therein overcome, and finally the virtues which aided Him in such enterprises.

As a part of His grand designs the all-wise Monarch provided as a matter of absolute necessity for the dissemination of all kinds of knowledge in the homeland, and also for an increase in the numbers of persons skilled in the higher branches of learning, together with artists and craftsmen; though I have given His paternal solicitude in this matter the most prominent place, my whole speech would not be long enough to describe it in detail. For, having repeatedly made the rounds of the European states like some swift-soaring eagle, He did induce (partly by command and partly by His own weighty example) a great multitude of His subjects to leave their country for a time and to convince themselves by experience how great an advantage a person and an entire state can derive from a journey of inquiry in foreign regions. Then were the wide gates of great Russia opened up; then over the frontiers and through the harbors, like the tides in the spacious ocean, there did flow in constant motion, in the one direction, the sons of

Russia, journeying forth to acquire knowledge in the various sciences and arts, and, in the other direction, foreigners arriving with various skills, books, and instruments. Then to the study of Mathematics and Physics, previously thought of as forms of sorcery and witchcraft, but now arrayed in purple, crowned with laurels, and placed on the Monarch's throne, reverential respect was accorded in the sanctified Person of PETER. What benefit was brought to us by all the different sciences and arts, bathed in such a glow of grandeur, is proved by the superabundant richness of our most varied pleasures, of which our forefathers, before the days of Russia's Great Enlightener, were not only deprived but in many cases had not even any conception. How many essential things which previously came to Russia from distant lands with difficulty and at great cost are now produced inside the state, and not only provide for our needs but also with their surplus supply other lands. There was a time when the neighbors on our borders boasted that Russia, a great and powerful state, was unable properly to carry out military operations or trade without their assistance, since its mineral resources included neither precious metals for the stamping of coins nor even iron, so needful for the making of weapons with which to stand against an enemy. This reproach disappeared through the enlightenment brought by PETER; the bowels of the mountains have been opened up by His mighty and industrious hand. Metals pour out of them, and are not only freely distributed within the homeland but are also given back to foreign peoples as if in repayment of loans. The brave Russian army turns against the enemy weapons produced from Russian mines by Russian hands.

In the establishment of the sizable army needed for the defense of the homeland, the security of His subjects, and the unhindered carrying out of important enterprises within the country, how great was the solicitude of the Great Monarch, how impetuous His zeal, how assiduous His search of ways and means! Since all these things exceed our capacity for admiration, shall we be able to describe them in words? The sire of our all-wise Hero, the Great Sovereign Tsar ALEKSEI MIKHAILOVICH of blessed memory, among other glorious deeds, laid the foundation of a regular army, with which He had great success in war, as witnessed by His victorious campaigns in Poland and by the provinces restored to Russia. But all His attentiveness to military matters was cut short by His death. The old disorders returned, and the Russian army was better able to show its strength in numbers than in skill. How much this strength later decreased is clear from the unavailing military undertakings of the time against the Turks and Tatars and, most of all, from the unbridled and ruinous mutinies of the strel'tsy,[1] which were the result of lack of proper discipline and organization. In such circumstances who could dream that a twelve-year-old youth, kept away from the conduct of state affairs and shielded from evil only by the sagacious protec-

---

[1] Literally, "musketeers," a corps of professional soldiers established in the sixteenth century. By the end of the seventeenth century, however, their military value had declined, and many of them were engaged in trade and crafts in peacetime. Their mutinies contributed to the political instability during the minority of Peter the Great. In 1698 Peter liquidated them.—Editor.

tion of His affectionate Mother, amid ceaseless terrors, and amid spears and lances drawn against His relatives and well-wishers and against Himself, could have begun to establish a new regular army, whose might the enemies were to feel very soon afterward. They felt it and trembled, and now the entire universe is justly amazed by it. Who could imagine that from what seemed to be a child's game so great an enterprise could arise? Some people, seeing a few young men in company with their young Sovereign handling light weapons in various ways, were of the opinion that this was nothing more than an amusement to Him, wherefore these new recruits were called Toy Soldiers. Others, being more perceptive and noticing the bloom of heroic high spirits on the Youth's face, the intelligence shining from his eyes, and the quick authority of His movements, reflected that Russia could then already expect a valiant Hero, a Great Monarch. But to recruit many great regiments of infantry and cavalry, to provide all with clothing, pay, weapons, and other military stores, to teach them [His] new Articles of War, to establish properly constituted field and siege artillery (for which no little knowledge of Geometry, Mechanics, and Chemistry is needed), and above all to have skilled commanders everywhere—all this might justly have seemed an impossibility; for a notable lack of all these means and loss of Sovereign power had removed the least hope and remotest probability of such a thing. Yet what was it that ensued? Contrary to general popular expectation, contrary to the disbelief of those who had abandoned hope, and in the teeth of the hostile intrigues and venomous murmurings of Envy itself, suddenly PETER's new regiments thundered forth, arousing joyous hope in loyal Russians, fear in their opponents, and amazement on both sides. The impossible was made possible by extraordinary zeal, and above all by an unheard-of example. In former times the Roman Senate, beholding the Emperor Trajan standing before the Consul to receive from him the dignity of Consul, exclaimed: "Through this thou art the greater, the more majestic!" What exclamations, what applause were due to PETER the Great for His unparalleled self-abasement? Our fathers beheld their crowned Sovereign not among the candidates for a Roman consulship but in the ranks of common soldiers, not demanding power over Rome, but obedient to the bidding of His subjects. O you beautiful regions, fortunate regions which beheld a spectacle so wondrous! Oh, how you marveled at the friendly contest of the regiments of a single Sovereign, both commander and subordinate, giving orders and obeying them! Oh, how you admired the siege, defense, and capture of new Russian fortresses, not for immediate mercenary gain but for the sake of future glory, not for putting down enemies but to encourage fellow countrymen. Looking back at those past years, we can now imagine the great love for the Sovereign and the ardent devotion with which the newly instituted army was fired, seeing Him in their company at the same table, eating the same food, seeing His face covered with dust and sweat, seeing that He was no different from them, except that in training and in diligence He was superior to all. By such an extraordinary example the most wise Sovereign, rising in rank alongside His subjects, proved that Monarchs can in no other way increase their majesty, glory, and eminence so well as by such gracious condescension. The Russian army was toughened by such encouragement, and during the twenty years' war with the Swedish Crown, and later in other campaigns, filled the ends of the universe with the thunder of its weapons and with the noise of its triumphs. It is true that the first battle of Narva was not success-ful; but the superiority of our foes and the retreat of the Russian army have, through envy and pride, been exaggerated to their glorification and our humiliation, out of all proportion to the actual event. For although most of the Russian army had seen only two years' service and faced a veteran army accustomed to battle, although disagreement arouse between our command-ers, and a malicious turncoat revealed to the enemy the entire position in our camp, and Charles XII [of Sweden] by a sudden attack did not give the Russians time to form ranks—yet even in their retreat they destroyed the enemy's willingness to fight on to final victory. Thus the only reason the Russian Life Guard, which had remained intact, together with another sizable part of the army, did not dare to attack the enemy thereafter was the absence of its main leaders, who had been summoned by Charles for peace talks and detained as prisoners. For this reason the Guards and the rest of the army returned to Russia with their arms and war chest, drums beating and banners flying. That this failure occurred more through the unhappy circumstances described than through any lack of skill in the Russian troops and that PETER's new army could, even in its infancy, defeat the seasoned regiments of the enemies, was proved in the next year and subsequently by many glorious victories won over them.

It is to you, our now peaceful neighbors, that I address my words: When you hear these praises of our Hero's deeds of war and my eulogies of the Russian army's victories over you, consider yourselves honored rather than disgraced. For to stand long against the mighty Russian people, to stand against PETER the Great, against the Man sent by God to astound the uni-verse, and in the end to be conquered by Him is more glorious than to conquer weak armies under poor leadership. Justly consider the boldness of your hero Charles to be your true glory; and assert, with the whole world's agreement, that there was scarcely any man who could hold out in the face of his wrath, had not God's wondrous Providence set up PETER the Great against him in our fatherland. PETER's bold regiments, organized on the basis of a regular army, proved by a quick succession of victories what ardent zeal and what great skill in the art of war they had acquired from wise instruction and example. Leaving aside the many victories, which the Russian army had learned to count by the number of its battles, not mentioning the great number of captured towns and stout fortresses, we have sufficient witness in the two main victories at Lesnaya and Poltava. Where else did the Lord manifest greater favor to us? Where else was clearer revelation given of [how great were] the successes achieved by PETER's blessed initiative and zealous ardor in instituting the new army? What more miraculous or im-probable event could have ensued? An army with a long-standing regular tradition, which had been brought from enemy lands renowned for their battle prowess under the leadership of commanders who had spent all their time in the practice of war, an army lavishly equipped with all kinds of weapons, shunned battle with the new Russian regiments, greatly inferior in numbers. But the latter, giving their opponents no rest, by swift movement overtook them, fought, and were victorious; and the enemy's chief commander barely escaped captivity with a few remnants to take the dolorous news to his Sovereign. Although the latter was greatly disturbed, yet in the confidence of his bold and impetuous spirit he still spurred himself on against Russia. He still could not be convinced that PETER's young army could stand against his matured forces advancing under his own leadership and, putting his trust in the audacious encouragement of a conscienceless traitor to Russia, did not hesitate to enter the border regions of our homeland. He tried to win over Russia with arrogant arguments and already considered that the whole North was beneath his heel. But God, in reward for unceasing labors, granted PETER a complete victory over this contemner of His efforts, who, contrary to his expectations, became eyewitness of our Hero's unbelievable successes in warfare and could not even in flight escape from the haunting thoughts of Russia's steady courage.

Having covered Himself and His army with glory throughout the world by such famous victories, the Great Monarch finally proved that he had been at pains to establish His army mainly in the interests of our safety! For He decreed that it should never be dispersed, even in times of untroubled peace (as had happened under previous Sovereigns, frequently to no little loss of the country's might and glory), and also that it should always be kept in proper readiness. Oh, truly paternal solicitude! Many times did He remind the loyal subjects close to Him, sometimes tearfully embracing and begging them, that the renewal of Russia—undertaken at such great pains and with such marvelous success—and most particularly the art of war, should not be neglected after Him. And at the very time of general rejoicing, when God had blessed Russia with a glorious and advantageous peace with the Swedish Crown, when ardent felicitations and the deserved titles of Emperor, "the Great," and "Father of His country" were being offered, He did not lose the opportunity to impress publicly on the Governing Senate that, though one may hope for peace, one must not grow slack in military matters. Did He not hereby give a clear sign that these high titles were not pleasing to Him if not accompanied by the preservation and maintenance of a regular army forever in the future?

Having cast a quick glance over PETER's land forces, which came to maturity in their infancy and combined their training with victories, let us extend our gaze across the waters, my Listeners; let us observe what the Lord has done there, His marvels on the deep, as made manifest by PETER to the astonishment of the world.

The far-flung Russian state, like a whole world, is surrounded by great seas on almost every side and sets them as its boundaries. On all of them we see Russian flags flying. Here the mouths of great rivers and new harbors scarcely provide space for the multitude of craft; elsewhere the waves groan beneath the weight of the Russian fleet, and the sounds of its gunfire echo in the chasms of the deep. Here gilded ships, blooming like spring, are mirrored on the quiet surface of the waters and take on double beauty; elsewhere the mariner, having reached a calm haven, unloads the riches of faraway countries to give us pleasure. Here new Columbuses hasten to unknown shores to add to the might and glory of Russia; there a second Tethys dares to sail between the battling mountains; she struggles with snow, with frost, with everlasting ice, desirous to unite East and West. How did the power and glory of the Russian fleets come to be spread over so many seas in a short time? Whence came the materials, whence the skill? Whence the machines and implements needed in so difficult and varied an enterprise? Did not the ancient giants tear great oaks from dense forests and lofty mountains and throw them down for building on the shores? Did not Amphion with sweet music on the lyre move the various parts for the construction of those wondrous fortresses which fly over the waves? To such fancies would PETER's wondrous swiftness in building a fleet truly have been ascribed if an exploit so improbable and seemingly beyond human strength had been performed in far-off ancient times, and if it had not been fixed in the memory of many eyewitnesses and in unexceptionably reliable written records. In the latter we read with amazement, while from the former in friendly conversation we hear—and not without emotion—that it cannot be determined whether PETER the Great gave more pains to the founding of His army or His navy. However, there is no doubt that He was tireless in both and exemplary in both. For, seeking knowledge of everything which might happen in land battles, He not only went through all the ranks Himself, but also tried out for Himself all the crafts and kinds of work, that He might not overlook a neglect of duty on the part of anyone nor require of anyone efforts beyond his powers. In the navy, too, there was nothing left untouched, untried by His keen mind and industrious hands. From that very time when the contriving of a boat (which, though small in dimensions, was great in influence and fame) aroused in PETER's unsleeping spirit the salutary urge to found a fleet and to show forth the might of Russia on the deep, He applied the forces of His great mind to every part of this important enterprise. As He investigated these parts, He became convinced that in a matter so difficult there was no possibility of success unless He Himself acquired adequate knowledge of it. But where was that to be obtained? What should the Great Sovereign undertake? It had formerly been a sight to behold when an immense throng of people poured out to see the entrancing spectacle on the fields of Moscow, as our Hero, still little more than a child—in the presence of the entire imperial household, of illustrious dignitaries of the Russian state, and of an illustrious gathering of the nobility, now joyful, now fearful of harm to His health—labored at laying out a regular fortress like a craftsman, digging moats and piling up earth for embankments behind the ramparts like a common soldier, giving orders to all as a Sovereign, setting an example to all, like an all-wise Teacher and Enlightener. But greater still was the amazement that He aroused, greater the spectacle that He presented to the eyes of the whole world when, becoming convinced of the untold benefits of navigation—first on the small bodies of water in the Moscow area, then on the great breadth of Lake Rostov and Lake Kubensk, and finally on the expanse of the White Sea—He absented himself for a time from His dominions and, concealing the Majesty of His Person among humble workmen in a foreign land, did not disdain to learn the shipwright's craft. Those who chanced to be His fellow-apprentices at first marveled at the amazing fact that a Russian had not only mastered simple carpentering work so quickly, had not only brought Himself to the point where He could make with His own hands every single part needed in the building and equipping of ships, but had also acquired such skill in marine architecture that Holland could no longer satisfy His deep understanding. Then how great was the amazement that was aroused in all when they learned that this was no simple Russian, but the Ruler of that great state Himself who had taken up heavy labors in hands born and anointed to bear the Scepter and the Orb. But was it merely out of sheer curiosity or, at the most, for purposes of instruction and command, that He did in Holland and Britain attain perfection in the theory and practice of equipping a fleet and in navigational science? Everywhere the Great Sovereign aroused His subjects to labor, not only by command and reward, but also by His own example! I call you to witness, O great Russian rivers; I address myself to you, O happy shores, sanctified by PETER's footsteps and watered by His sweat. How many times you resounded with high-spirited and eager cries as the heavy timbers, ready for launching of the ship, were being slowly moved by the workmen, and then, at the touch of His hand, made a sudden spurt toward the swift current, inspiring the multitude, encouraged by His example, to finish off the huge hulks with incredible speed. To what a marvelous and rousing spectacle were the assembled people treated as these great structures moved nearer to launching! When their indefatigable Founder and Builder, now moving topside, now below, now circling round, tested the soundness of each part, the power of the machinery, and the precision of all the preparations and, by command, encouragement, ingenuity, and the quick skill of His tireless hands, rectified the defects which He had detected. In this unflagging zeal, this invincible persistence in labor, the legendary prowess of the ancients was shown in PETER's day to have been not fiction but the very truth!

What pleasure was afforded the Great Sovereign by the successes in maritime affairs achieved through His zeal, to the indescribable benefit and glory of the state, may easily be seen from the fact that He not only bestowed awards on those who had labored with Him but also gave the unfeeling timber a glorious token of His gratitude. The Neva's waters are covered with vessels and flags; its banks cannot hold the great multitude of the assembled spectators; the air vibrates and groans with the people's exclamations, with the noise of oars, the voice of trumpets, and the sound of fire-breathing engines [guns].[2] What happiness, what joy does heaven send us! Whom does our Monarch come out to greet in such magnificence? A

[2] Lomonosov is alluding here to the public ceremony organized by Peter the Great to salute the first ship he had had built for the Russian fleet. The ship, constructed in the 1690's on one of the lakes near Moscow, was brought to St. Petersburg, and the new fleet massed on the Neva rendered it honors.—Editor.

decrepit little boat! But one that occupies pride of place in the new and mighty Fleet. Contemplating the majesty, beauty, might, and glorious deeds of the one and at the same time the smallness and feebleness of the other, we see that no one in the world could have achieved such things without PETER's titanic daring in enterprise and tireless vigor of execution.

Exemplary on land, peerless on the waters in His might and military glory was our Great Defender!

From this brief account, which contains but a small part of His labors, I already feel fatigue, O my Listeners; yet I see the great and far-reaching field of His merits before me! And so that my strength and limited time may suffice to complete the drift of my discourse, I shall make all possible haste.

For the foundation and bringing into action of so great a naval and land force, and also for the construction of new towns, fortresses, and harbors, for the joining of rivers with great canals, for the strengthening of frontiers with ramparts, for long-lasting war, for frequent and distant campaigns, for the construction of public and private buildings in a new architectural style, for the finding of experienced persons and all other means for the dissemination of science and the arts, for the maintenance of new court and state officials—how vast a treasury was needed for these things anyone can easily imagine, and conclude that the revenues of PETER's Forefathers could not suffice for this. Wherefore the sagacious Sovereign did strive most earnestly to increase internal and external state revenues without ruining the people. And He had the native wit to perceive that by means of a single institution not only would great gains accrue to the treasury, but the general tranquillity and safety of His subjects would also be assured. For at a time when the total number of the Russian people and the place of residence of each person were not yet known, there was no curb on arbitrary conduct, and no one was forbidden to change his place of residence or to wander about as the whim took him. The streets were filled with shameless, loafing beggars; the roads and great rivers were often blocked by the thieves and by whole regiments of murderous brigands who brought ruin to towns and villages alike. The wise Hero converted harm into benefit, laziness into industriousness, pillagers into defenders; when He had counted the multitude of His subjects, He bound each one to his dwelling and imposed a light, but fixed, tax; in this way the internal revenues of the treasury were increased, and a definite amount of such revenue was assured—and, likewise, the number of persons on recruiting lists. Industriousness and strict military training were also increased. Many who, under previous conditions, would have been dangerous robbers He compelled to be ready to die for their country.

I say nothing of the assistance afforded in this matter by other wise institutions, but will mention the increase of external revenues. Divine Providence aided the good designs and efforts of PETER, through His hand opening new ports on the Varangian [Baltic] Sea at towns conquered by His valor and erected by His own labors. Great rivers were joined for the more convenient passage of Russian merchants, duty regulations were established, and commercial treaties with various peoples were concluded. What

benefit proceeded from the growth of this abundance within and without
has been clear from the very foundation of these institutions, for while
continuing to fight a burdensome war for twenty years Russia was free from
debts.

What, then, have all PETER's great deeds already been depicted in my
feeble sketch? Oh, how much labor still remains for my thoughts, voice, and
tongue! I ask you, my Listeners, out of your knowledge to consider how
much assiduous effort was required for the foundation and establishment of
a judiciary, and for the institution of the Governing Senate, the Most Holy
Synod, the state colleges,[3] the chancelleries, and the other governmental
offices with their laws, regulations, and statutes; for the establishment of the
table of ranks and the introduction of decorations as outward tokens of
merit and favor; and, finally, for foreign policy, missions, and alliances with
foreign powers. You may contemplate all these things yourselves with minds
enlightened by PETER. It remains to me only to offer a brief sketch of it all.
Let us suppose that before the beginning of PETER's enterprises someone
had happened to leave his native Russia for distant lands where His name
had not thundered forth—if such a land there be on this earth. Returning
later to Russia, he would see new knowledge and arts among the people,
new dress and customs, new architecture and household furnishings, newly
built fortresses, a new fleet, and a new army; he would see not only the
different aspect of all these things but also a change in the courses of
rivers and in the boundaries of the seas. What would he then think? He
could come to no other conclusion than that he had been on his travels
for many centuries, or that all this had been achieved in so short a time by
the common efforts of the whole human race or by the creative hand of the
Almighty, or, finally, that it was all a vision seen in a dream.

From these words of mine, which reveal scarcely more than the mere
shadow of PETER's glorious deeds, it may be seen how great they are! But
what is one to say of the terrible and dangerous obstacles encountered on
the path of His mighty course? They have exalted His honor the more! The
human condition is subject to such changes that undesirable consequences
arise from favorable origins, and desirable consequences from unfavorable
origins. What could have been more unpropitious to our prosperity than
that, while He was engaged in reforming Russia, PETER and the country
were threatened by attacks from without, by afflictions from within, and by
dangers on all sides, and dire consequences were brewing? The war hampered domestic affairs, and domestic affairs hampered the war, which worked
injury even before it had started. The Great Sovereign set out from His native land with a great embassy to see the states of Europe and to acquire
knowledge of their advantages, so that on His return He might use them for
the benefit of His subjects. Hardly had He crossed the frontiers of His domin-

---

[3] I.e., the government departments established by Peter the Great on the Swedish model,
including the College for Foreign Affairs, the State Chamber (for taxation), the College
of Justice, the College of Comptrollers, the War College, the Admiralty, the College of
Commerce, the Treasury (for state expenditures), and the College of Mining and Manu-
factures. See *Polnoe sobranie zakonov*, 1st series, No. 3255 (December 12, 1718).—Editor.

ion than He everywhere encountered great obstacles which had been set up secretly. However, I do not mention them now, since they are known to all the world. It seems to me that even inanimate objects sensed the oncoming danger to Russia's hopes. The waters of the Dvina sensed it and opened a path for their future Master amid the thick ice to save Him from the cunning snares that had been laid. Pouring forth, they proclaimed to the shores of the Baltic the dangers which He had overcome. Having escaped from danger, He hurried on his joyous path, finding pleasure for His eyes and heart and enriching His mind. But alas! He unwillingly cut short His glorious course. What conflict He suffered within Himself! On the one hand was the pull of curiosity and of knowledge needful to the homeland; on the other hand there was the homeland itself, which had fallen on evil days and which, holding forth its hands to Him as to its only hope, exclaimed: "Return, return quickly; I am rent within by traitors! Thou art traveling in the interests of my happiness; I recognize this with gratitude, but do Thou first tame those who are raging. Thou hast parted from Thy household and with Thy dear ones to increase my glory; I acknowledge it eagerly, but do Thou allay the dangerous disorder. Thou hast left behind the crown and scepter given to Thee by God and hidest the rays of Thy Majesty behind a humble appearance for the sake of my enlightenment; with joyous hope do I desire it, but do Thou ward off the dark storm of turbulence from the domestic horizon." Affected by such feelings, He returned to calm the terrible tempest.[4] Such hindrances impeded our Hero in His glorious exploits! How many enemies surrounded Him on all sides! From abroad war was made by Sweden, Poland, the Crimea, Persia, many eastern nations, and the Ottoman Porte; at home there were the *strel'tsy*, the dissenters, the Cossacks, and the brigands. In His own household villainies, hatred, and acts of treachery against His most precious life were fomented by His own blood. To describe all in detail would be difficult, and it would be painful to hear! Let us return to the joy of a joyous era. The Almighty helped PETER to overcome all grievous obstacles and to exalt Russia, fostering His piety, sagacity, magnanimity, courage, sense of justice, forbearance, and industriousness. His zeal and faith in God in all His enterprises are well known. His first joy was the Lord's house. He was not just a worshiper attending divine service, but Himself the chief officiant. He heightened the attention and devotion of the worshipers with His monarchic voice; and He would stand somewhere away from the sovereign's place, by the side of ordinary choristers, before God. We have many examples of His piety, but one shall now suffice. Going out to meet the body of the holy and brave Prince Alexander,[5] He moved the whole city and moved the waters of the Neva with an act full of devotion. Wondrous spectacle! At the oars were the Bearers of various Orders, while in the stern the Monarch Himself was steering and, before all the people, lifting His anointed hands to the labor

---

[4] Allusion to the rebellion of the *strel'tsy* in 1698, which interrupted Peter the Great's first voyage to Western Europe.—Editor.

[5] Reference to the transfer of the body of St. Aleksandr Nevskii, Prince of Novgorod who defeated the Teutonic Order in 1240, for burial in newly founded St. Petersburg.—Editor.

of simple men in the name of His faith. Made strong by His faith, He escaped the frequent assault of bloodthirsty traitors. On the day of the battle of Poltava the Lord shielded His head with power from on high and did not permit the death-dealing metal to touch it! As the Lord had once crumbled the wall of Jericho, He crumbled before PETER the wall of Narva —not while blows were being struck from fire-breathing engines, but during divine service.

Sanctified and protected by piety, He was endowed by God with peerless wisdom. What seriousness in counsel, unfeigned brevity of speech, precision of images, dignity of utterance, thirst for learning, diligent attention to prudent and useful discourses, and what unwavering intelligence [showed] in the eyes and entire countenance! Through these gifts of PETER, Russia took on a new appearance, foundation was laid for the arts and sciences, missions and alliances were instituted, the cunning designs of certain powers against our country were thwarted, while among Sovereigns some had their kingdoms and autocratic rights preserved, and to others the crown wrested from them by their foes was restored. Complementing the wisdom lavished on Him from on high and clearly manifested in everything which has been said above was His heroic courage; with the former He astounded the universe, with the latter He struck fear into His enemies. In His most tender childhood He showed fearlessness in military exercises. When all the observers of a new enterprise—the throwing of grenades on to a designated place—were exceedingly fearful of injury, the young Sovereign strove with all His might to watch from nearby, and was scarcely restrained by the tears of His Mother, the pleas of His Brother, and the supplications of dignitaries. On His travels in foreign states in pursuit of learning, how many dangers He scorned for the sake of Russia's renewal! Sailing over the inconstant depths of the sea served him for entertainment. How many times the waves of the sea, raising their proud crests, were witnesses of unblenching daring as, cleft by the swift-running fleet, they struck the ships and combined with raging flame and metal roaring through the air into a single danger, but failed to terrify Him! Who can without terror picture PETER flying over the fields of Poltava amidst His army, drawn up for battle, a hail of enemy bullets whistling around His head, His voice raised aloft through the tumult urging His regiments to fight bravely. Nor couldst thou, sultry Persia, halt our Hero's onset with thy swift rivers, miry swamps, high mountain precipices, poisonous springs, burning sands, or sudden raids of turbulent peoples, as thou couldst not stop His triumphal entry into cities filled with hidden weapons and guile.

For the sake of brevity I offer no more examples of His heroic spirit, O my Hearers, and I make no mention of the many battles and victories that occurred in His presence and under His leadership; but I do speak of His generosity, the generosity characteristic of great Heroes, which adorns victories and moves the human heart more than bold deeds. In victories the courage of the soldiers, the help of allies, and the opportuneness of place and time have a share, and chance appropriates the greatest share, as if taking what belongs to it. But everything belongs to the conqueror's generosity alone. He wins the most glorious victory who can conquer himself. In [this victory] neither soldiers, nor allies, nor time, nor place, nor yet that chance itself which rules over human affairs have even the slightest portion. True, reason admires the victor, but it is the heart which loves the man of generous spirit. Such was our Great Defender. He would lay down His wrath together with His weapons, and not only were none of His enemies deprived of their lives merely because they had borne arms against Him, but they were even shown honor beyond compare. Tell me, you Swedish generals who were captured at Poltava, what did you think when, expecting to be bound, you were girt with your own swords which you had raised against us; when, expecting to be put into dungeons, you were put to sit at the Victor's table; when, expecting mockery, you were hailed as our teachers. What a generous Conqueror you had!

Justice is akin to generosity and is often linked with it. The first duty of rulers set over nations by God is to govern the realm in righteousness and truth, to reward merit and punish crime. Although military matters and other great concerns and, in particular, His premature death much hindered the Great Sovereign in establishing immutable and clear laws for everything, yet how much labor He expended in this matter is testified beyond doubt by the many decrees, statutes, and regulations, the drafting of which deprived Him of many days of relaxation and many nights of sleep. God has willed that a Daughter like unto so great a Sire should complete these things and bring them to perfection during Her untroubled and blessed rule.

But though justice was not established to perfection in clear and systematic laws, yet was justice inscribed in His heart. Though not everything was written in books, it was carried out in fact. At the same time mercy was favored in the courtroom in those very instances when villainies which had hindered many of His deeds seemed to compel severity. Of many examples, one will serve. Having forgiven many distinguished persons their grievous crimes, He proclaimed His heartfelt joy by taking them to His table and by firing cannon. [However,] He is not made despondent by the execution of the *strel'tsy*. Imagine to yourselves and reflect on what zeal for justice, pity for His subjects, and His own danger were saying in His heart. Innocent blood has been shed in the houses and streets of Moscow, widows are weeping, orphans are sobbing, violated women and girls are moaning, my relatives were put to death in my house before my eyes, and a sharp weapon was held against my heart. I was preserved by God, I endured these things, eluded danger, and took my way outside the city. Now they have cut short my beneficial journey, openly taking up arms against the homeland. If I do not take revenge for all this, averting eventual doom by means of execution, I foresee town squares filled with corpses, plundered houses, wrecked churches, Moscow beset by flames on all sides, and my beloved country plunged into smoke and ashes. For all these disasters, tears, and bloodshed God will hold me answerable. Mindful of this ultimate judgment, He was compelled to resort to severity.

Nothing can serve me so well to demonstrate the kindness and gentleness of His heart as His incomparable graciousness toward His subjects. Superbly endowed as He was, elevated in His Majesty, and exalted by most glorious deeds, He did but the more increase and adorn these things by His incomparable graciousness. Often He moved amongst His subjects simply, countenancing neither the pomp that proclaims the monarch's presence nor servility. Often anyone afoot was free to meet Him, to follow Him, to walk along with Him, to start a conversation if so inclined. In former times many Sovereigns were carried on the shoulders and heads of their slaves; graciousness exalted Him above these very Sovereigns. At the very time of festivity and relaxation important business would be brought to Him; but the importance did not decrease gaiety, nor did simplicity lessen the importance. How He awaited, received, and greeted His loyal subjects! What gaiety there was at His table! He asked questions, listened, answered, discussed as with friends; and whatever time was saved at table by the small number of dishes was spent in gracious conversation. Amid so many cares of state He lived at ease as among friends. Into how many tiny huts of craftsmen did He bring His Majesty, and heartened with His presence His most lowly, but skilled and loyal, servants. How often He joined them in the exercise of their crafts and in various labors. For He attracted more by example than He compelled by force. And if there was anything which then seemed to be compulsion, it now stands revealed as a benefaction. His idea of relaxation was to change His labors. Not only day or morning but even the sun at its rising shone upon Him in many places as He was engaged in various labors. The business of the governmental, administrative, and judicial offices instituted by Him was carried on in His presence. The various crafts made speedy progress not only through His supervision but also through the assistance of His hands; public buildings, ships, harbors, fortresses ever beheld Him, having Him as guide in their foundation, supporter in their labor, and rewarder on completion. What of His travels or, rather, swift-soaring flights? Hardly had the White Sea heard the voice of His command before it was already felt by the Baltic; scarcely had His ships' wake disappeared on the waters of the Sea of Azov before the thundering Caspian waves were making way for Him. And you great rivers, the Southern Dvina and the Northern Dvina, Dnieper, Don, Volga, Bug, Vistula, Oder, Elbe, Danube, Seine, Thames, Rhine, and others, tell me, how often were you granted the honor of reflecting the image of PETER the Great in your waters? Will you tell me? I cannot count them! Now we can only contemplate with joyous amazement the roads along which He went, the tree under which He rested, the spring that quenched His thirst, the places where He labored with humble persons as a humble workman, where He wrote laws, where He made plans of boats, harbors, and fortresses, and where at the same time He conversed with His subjects as a friend. In His care and labors for us He was in constant motion, like the stars of the sky in their course, like the ebb and flow of the tide.

In the midst of fire in the battlefield, amid weighty government deliberations, amid the diverse machinery of various crafts, amid a numberless multitude of peoples engaged in the building of towns, harbors, and canals, amid the roaring breakers of the White, Black, Baltic, and Caspian seas and of the very Ocean itself—wherever I turn in spirit, everywhere do I behold PETER the Great in sweat, in dust, in smoke, in flame; and I cannot convince myself that it is not many PETERS everywhere, but a single one, not a thousand years, but one short life. With whom shall I compare the Great Sovereign? In both ancient and modern times I behold Rulers termed great. And in truth they are great when compared with others; but compared with PETER they are little. One has conquered many states but has left his own country untended. Another has vanquished a foe who was already called great, but has spilled the blood of his citizens on all sides solely to gratify his own ambition and instead of a triumphal return has heard the weeping and lamentation of his country. Some were adorned with many virtues but, instead of lifting up their country, were unable to keep it from sinking. Some have been warriors on land but have feared the sea. Some have ruled the waves but feared to put in to shore. Some have loved learning but feared the drawn sword. Some have feared neither steel nor water nor fire, but have lacked understanding of man's estate and heritage. I shall quote no examples except that of Rome. But even Rome falls short. What was achieved in the two hundred and fifty years from the First Punic War to Augustus by Nepos, Scipio, Marcellus, Regulus, Metellus, Cato, and Sulla —as much was achieved by PETER in the short period of His life. Then to whom shall I liken our Hero? I have often pondered the nature of Him whose all-powerful hand rules sky, land, and sea. Let His breath blow and the waters shall pour forth; let Him touch the mountains and they shall be lifted up. But a limit has been set to human thoughts! They cannot grasp the Deity! He is usually pictured in human form. And so, if a man must be found who, in our conception, resembles God, I find none excepting PETER the Great.

For His great services to the country He has been called Father of the Country. But the title is too small for Him. Say, what name shall we give Him in return for begetting His Daughter, our most gracious Sovereign, who has ascended Her Father's throne in courage, vanquished proud enemies, pacified Europe, and lavished Her benefactions on Her subjects?

Hear us, O God, and reward us, O Lord! For PETER's great labors, for the solicitude of CATHERINE, for the tears and sighs that the two Sisters, PETER's two Daughters, poured forth when taking Their farewell, for all Their incomparable benefactions to Russia, reward us with length of days and with Posterity.

And Thou, Great Soul, shining in eternity and casting Heroes into obscurity with Thy brilliance, do Thou exult. Thy Daughter reigns; Thy Grandson is heir; a Great-grandson has been born in accordance with our desire; we have been exalted, strengthened, enlightened, and adorned by Thee; by Her we have been delivered, enheartened, defended, enriched, glorified. Accept as a sign of gratitude this unworthy offering. Thy merits are greater than all our efforts.

3.

Mikhail M. Shcherbatov

1733-1790

Throughout his life Prince Mikhail M. Shcherbatov—administrator, historian, publicist—was an energetic advocate of the special status and privileges of the old established nobility. As a deputy to the Legislative Commission of 1767 he argued with passion and asperity against perpetuating open access to the nobility on the basis of service and merit. At the same time he advocated special economic privileges, including certain monopoly rights, for the nobility. In "O povrezhdenii nravov v Rossii" (On the Deterioration of Russian Morals), a tract which he wrote toward the end of his life, he berated his contemporaries for having forsaken the virtues and traditions of their Muscovite ancestors and accepting the domination of parvenus and favorites. The source of these evils of Russian life, he believed, was to be found in the reign of Peter the Great.

And yet Shcherbatov did not fail to see also that the new Russia, respected as a world power and graced with numerous cultural achievements, was the direct creation of Peter the Great. Shcherbatov was particularly well placed to know what Peter had tried to do—and actually succeeded in doing—because Catherine II had entrusted him with the responsibility of preparing Peter's public and private papers for publication.

The two selections below illustrate the ambivalence with which a member of Russia's educated elite in the second half of the eighteenth century approached the heritage of Peter and his country's remote past. The struggle between the principles that Max Weber called "tradition" and "rationality," so clearly evidenced in Shcherbatov, was to become a basic element in the social and political thought of the Russian elite throughout the nineteenth century.

Petition of the City of Moscow on Being Relegated to Oblivion

MOST GRACIOUS PRINCESS!

A very ancient city, formerly of the tsardom and now of the Empire of Russia, throws itself at the feet of its Monarchs, pleading that it may be released from its eighty-four years of oblivion, that it may be restored to its Monarchs' favor, and that it may raise its hoary head in rejoicing to know its past services remembered!

Seeing the oblivion to which I have so long been relegated, I have been meditating on my former estate, and I venture to place before my Sovereign a brief account of my services and fealty, as also of my labors, so that my diligent endeavors, for many a century, to please the rulers of Russia will not be lost to memory; and if this does not save me from oblivion and abandonment, let it at least bear testimony that I cried out in grief and anguish, but that stern Fate triumphed over labors and justice, services and mercy.

I shall say nothing of my origins, veiled in the darkness of time . . .[1] the city which 429 (459?) years ago, after the ruin of Vladimir, was chosen by the Grand Duke Ioann Danilovich to be his princely Seat. Was I not the first to raise my head against the ravagers and conquerors of Russia, which is to say the Tatars? Was it not from my very bosom that the Grand Duke Dimitrii Donskoi went forth with his armies to destroy Mamai's host? Did I not suffer grievous devastation under that same Grand Duke at the hands of the evil Tokhtamysh, and were not the corpses piled high within my walls, my burnt buildings, and the soil red with the blood of my citizens—were there not so many signs of my diligent zeal? Was it not from within my walls that issued forth the victorious armies which added Odoev, Kozel'sk, Mozhaisk, Viaz'ma, Belev, Vorotynsk, and Smolensk to the Russian state? Was it not from within my walls that emerged the armies which, during the civil strife instigated by Prince Andrei Vasil'evich, brought down his overweening pride and put the child Tsar Ioann Vasil'evich [Ivan IV] on the throne?

[1] Some words are obviously missing here.—Note in Russian edition.

Translated by Valentine Snow from Mikhail M. Shcherbatov, "Proshenie Moskvy o zabvenii eia," in *Sochineniia*, Vol. II (St. Petersburg, 1898), pp. 53–64. The article originally appeared in *Chteniia Moskovskogo obshchestva istorii i drevnostei rossiiskikh*, I (1860). It was probably written in 1787 (eighty-four years after 1703).

Later, it was again from within my walls that the armies marched forth which conquered Kazan, Astrakhan, and Viatka; while Novgorod and Pskov, which had enjoyed liberty, were also forced to surrender to me; and the bells that had announced their town meetings, brought to my walls and hung in my embrasures, are signs of my loyalty. The invading forces of Devlet-Girei surrounded my walls and burned my suburbs; eminent sons of mine died on this occasion, but my loyalty was not shaken, and soon thereafter I had the pleasure, almost, to see from my embrasures the defeat of that selfsame Devlet-Girei at Molodi, where one of my beloved sons, Prince Vorotynskii, won his fame. Later still, other armies marched forth from within my walls to conquer Polotsk, part of Lithuania, and Livland; and although by a turn of fortune Russia lost these conquests, my loyalty to my Tsars held the balance between misfortune and victory. The Tatars who came in the days of the young Tsar Feodor Ivanovich [Ioannovich] beleaguered my walls in vain; they were driven forth and scattered, leaving behind only relics of my sons' victory, and the Donskoi Monastery is an eternal and faithful monument to that event.

Torrents of tears flowed from my eyes when the death of the Tsar Feodor Ioannovich ended the line of my Tsars, the line of the rulers who had occupied the Moscow throne—Riurik, St. Vladimir, and Vladimir Monomakh. In my anguish, I did not know where to seek surcease. Giving preference to a marital union over ancient happenings, I chose her who had shared his bridal bed to rule over me, and upon her abdication and at her command, I raised her brother Boris to my throne. His villainy was then concealed from me; I knew not that his hands were stained with the innocent blood of my former Sovereigns. But what was a mystery to me, was plain in the sight of God; during his reign Boris was beset by anxiety, while his son was struck down by ferocious foes. On that occasion I was led astray—led astray, but not disloyal. When the Pretender came, I thought him to be the last scion of my Sovereigns, and I took him to my bosom with joy, crowned him with the Tsar's crown, and gave myself into his power. My actual deed was culpable, but my heart was innocent. The Pretender's imposture was soon revealed, and my beloved sons took up their arms, defended their faith and their country, took the brigand prisoner and, having proved his guilt, had him put to a cruel death. Deprived of the solace and hope of being reigned over by a direct descendant of my ancient Sovereigns, I then turned my eyes to my deliverer, to the blood of Riurik and Vladimir, to the close kinsman of my Tsars, and gave the crown to [Shuiskii]. His reign was a time of troubles; pretenders multiplied, Russian blood flowed everywhere, and Russia, divided against itself, was on the brink of destruction. Tearing at my entrails, unable to offer resistance, I chose to let the Tsar—who was no descendant of Tsars—perish that Russia might be saved, and handed him over to the Lithuanians, so that Russia might find peace under Sigismund's son. But this mistake of mine called forth fresh misfortunes: the Poles, having taken possession of part of Moscow, would neither send us Władysław nor keep their promises, and my last day was drawing nigh when my own beloved sons, Trubetskoi and Pozharskii and other Russians, driven into exile by internecine strife, delivered me from the enemy's yoke and, after all my sufferings, left me free to demonstrate my perfect allegiance to my Sovereigns. According to all natural and national laws, when a royal line dies out the people recovers its original right to choose a new Sovereign or to change its laws. Did I take advantage of this? I did not. I chose Mikhail Feodorovich Iur'ev Romanov, a kinsman on the distaff side—a grandson of the brother of the Tsaritsa Anastasiia Romanovna—who was then a minor and in exile, and raised him to the Russian throne. Straining all my strength to help the youthful Tsar, I freed Russia from internal strife, as also from the Swedes and the Poles; I brought his father, Filaret Nikitich, back from captivity; and I made his rule respected. I maintained the same loyalty to his son and to his grandson, the Tsar Feodor Alekseevich, but he was mowed down by death in the flower of his youth and I was once again to be ruled by children. I first put on the throne his young brother, the sharp-witted Peter, and then, after the *strel'tsy* [2] uprising, his brother Ivan [V]. Resisting all the *strel'tsy* mutinies, in the midst of perils I protected him [Peter] with my shield and with the bodies of my beloved sons; I was the first witness of his childish, but heroic, pastimes; and in his absence I remained faithful to him. Alas! he left me. Whether out of necessity, to build a fleet, to institute commerce, and to direct in person the war then taking place, or out of disdain for my ancient customs, he transferred his capital to the newly built city bearing his name.

Streams of tears flowed from my eyes, as though I were a widow; gay voices were heard no longer within my walls and the dulcimers hung silent from dead boughs. Oft though resounding victories and useful enactments rejoiced my heart, yet my soul was pierced by the rare and brief glimpses of my Monarch vouchsafed me. My best citizens left my walls to found their homes in a strange land, and crowds of peasants were sent to cultivate a marshy and infertile soil; my buildings, which no order was given to restore, fell to ruins, and it was forbidden to erect new ones. At last death claimed this Sovereign, who had lived long if we count his labors, but not long enough for the weal of Russia. His successor, Catherine, passed away shortly thereafter; and Petr Alekseevich [Peter II], grandson of Peter the Great, ascended the throne of Russia while yet a child.

My eyes rejoiced in the sight of the young Sovereign, and hope was reborn in my heart when I saw his love for the city of his ancestors. But even as a shadow passes, so passed my happiness; and this youthful Monarch, like a lily in bloom, was cut down by the scythe of death.

There remained, as heirs to the throne, two young sisters and two aunts; and the great nobles, met in conclave, chose Anne, daughter of the Tsar Ioann Alekseevich; but in so choosing they set limitations to her power and sovereignty. Having always been treated by my Sovereigns with magnanimity, I could not tolerate any restrictions of their power, and shortly thereafter, annulling all conditions, I threw myself unreservedly on her mercy.

Alas! She, too, repaid me by removing herself from within my walls, and I never set eyes on her face again during her entire reign.

[2] "Musketeers"—body of regular soldiers (see note on p. 36).—Editor.

From that day on I have been deprived of the joy of seeing my Monarchs dwell within my walls. Elizabeth and Catherine, who is Empress now, have honored me but briefly by their presence. Alas, their presence only showed my Sovereigns' displeasure with me; no sooner do they arrive in the city which is the ancient capital of their forefathers than they hasten to leave it, in order to return merrily to the shores of the Neva. Neither the assemblage of nobles, descendants of men who shed their blood in the service of their country, nor the multitudes of common folk whose joyful shouts testify to their loyalty and allegiance to their Sovereigns, nor the holy places famous for many miracles, where the saints beloved of God are buried, nor the tombs of their ancestors, nor the ancient buildings where my former Sovereigns, who laid the groundwork for Russia's might, used to dwell, nor my beautiful surroundings are able to attract and hold their hearts.

In my sorrow, I seek to justify this most grievous action of my Sovereigns by casting a glance at the beauty of the newly created city, the majesty of the river that flows through it, and the flourishing trade that goes on in it. But most gracious Princess, look at my condition! My ancient ruins still can please and are still useful—they please because they represent my very antiquity and that of Your Empire, and they are useful in that they are a reminder of many a service performed for the country. In me You will find an ancient palace—neither vast nor beautiful—surrounded by a golden fence; it is here that Tsar Ioann Vasil'evich lived; and here, too, is to be seen the window through which the Unfrocked Monk [Grigorii Otrep'ev, the first Pretender] tried to escape from the punishment that threatened him, but, having incurred the wrath of God, broke his leg, was carried into the royal palace, and suffered just retribution for his crimes. Here, too, still stands the Great Portal where the traitor Basmanov was punished at Shuiskii's hands and from which Naryshkin, a martyr for his Tsar, was hurled down on the spears of the *strel'tsy*. The places are still known where Iazykov was murdered by the *strel'tsy* for his loyalty and where the two Dolgorukiis, father and son, were killed. The sacred buildings, erected by Your ancestors and bearing witness to their piety, are all memorials to their virtues and reminders that it was here that You took the Imperial crown; it was here that You were anointed with the sacred oil; it was here that You were made a Monarch by a solemn rite, in order the more fully to command the love and fealty of the people. But why do I list these famous spots? Could I enumerate them all in the space suitable for a petition? There are temples within my walls which are monuments celebrating victories and conquests, such as the Cathedral of the Intercession of the Holy Virgin (*Pokrovskii Sobor*). Others have been erected to commemorate some great defeat of the enemy, such as the Church of the Intercession of the Holy Virgin at Kudrino, which commemorates the defeat of the second Pretender, known as the Thief of Tushino. Others still mark some catastrophe; thus, Ilya Obydennyi was erected in memory of a plague. The Monastery of Purification (*Sretenskii Monastyr'*) commemorates two events: the bringing of the ikon of the Holy Virgin of Vladimir to Moscow and the freeing of Russia from Temir-Aksak. The very streets and landmarks remind us of famous happenings. The ruins in Trubnaia Square recall the well-known defeat of the Poles; Zamoskvorechie was the scene of the valiant resistance against Devlet-Girei, where many of my sons perished; the Arbat shows that the Tatars held some parts of the city and that their baggage trains used to stop there; Bolvanovka recalls where they lived; and so forth. Thus a Russian citizen of some education cannot take a step without remembering the loyal labors of his forefathers for their country and Sovereign and being inspired thereby.

The rushing waters of my river have neither the breadth nor the purity of the Neva's waters, and, being today without care, daily lose of their purity; yet the succulent fish that live therein show that they could be clean, and they certainly do not inflict such diseases on the residents as are caused by the waters of the Neva.

If Your Majesty's merciful eye were to gaze upon me, if Your frequent presence were to restore my youth, vast buildings would most successfully be erected within my walls, and the art of the new architects, set in the midst of the edifices of antiquity, would lend me a double beauty. Kolomenskoe, Vorontsovo, and other villages that surround me could, with their more salubrious air, take the place of Peterhof and Tsarskoe Selo; and their fertile fields would not be marshland but would yield abundant harvests, illustrative of the abundance of the Monarch's mercy—or, to put it another way, they would serve as a reminder of the beneficent hand which feeds the universe. The Sovereign's heart would rejoice, and I would rejoice in my Sovereign.

My central situation within the Empire would be convenient in that all news could reach the government more speedily, and the Monarch's power, spreading evenly in all directions, would nowhere be less strong; the great nobles not only would see on every side monuments to the labors and loyalty of their forebears, but would become better acquainted with the heart of the country and more familiar with the people's needs; into the bargain, being closer to their villages, by their own management thereof they would encourage others to better management, and the conjunction of these private benefits would benefit the entire country.

Lastly, can my Monarchs be deterred by the trade which flourishes in Peter's city? For, extensive as it is and profitable as it is, yet the bulk of it comes not from the region of St. Petersburg but from the plenitude of other parts of Russia, which lie closer to my own city; my rejuvenation will also greatly increase state revenue, as the nobles, being far from the port, will find it less convenient to obtain foreign merchandise, their love of luxury and ostentation will diminish, and their example, influencing others, will remedy this evil which has crept into Russia.

Deign to glance, most gracious Sovereign, at the petition which a city grown old in loyalty to its Monarchs humbly presents to You; deign to see my services, my fidelity and that of my children, and my former and present usefulness to Russia, so that I may not, like a rejected slave, be deprived of the sight of my Monarchs, and that my children, who serve You, may not be forgotten in Your sight! They bear no less ardent a love to You and to their country than those who have the good fortune to surround You, the only difference being that the latter live in the hope of Your favor, while the former cherish the same sentiments without such hope. Gladden my old age, and their zeal; let Your presence give them the resolution and greatness of soul by which their fathers were inspired; and be Thou my reviver in my old age, as the reviver also of the moral virtues and the happiness of Russia!

[The Pace of Russia's Modernization]

Approximate Evaluation of the Length of Time
Russia Would Have Required, in the Most Favorable
Circumstances, to Attain by Her Own Efforts, without the
Autocratic Rule of Peter the Great, Her Present State of
Enlightenment and Glory

CONDITIONS IN RUSSIA BEFORE PETER THE GREAT

The Russian people used to be devout to the point of fanaticism, regarding Christians of all other confessions as infidels; for example, it was held to be a sin and a dishonor to have visited Germans in their *sloboda*.[1] They [the Russians] were superstitious, as witness the fact that Prince Vasilii Vasil'evich Golitsyn, the most enlightened man of his time in Russia, used to summon fortunetellers and observe the moon, seeking to divine his future. They were falling under the rule of the clergy, in proof whereof it may be cited that Patriarch Nikon was deemed to be a saint for having offered resistance to the Tsar Aleksei Mikhailovich.

They had no education, and many of the greatest nobles did not even know their letters.

The boyars were haughty and arrogant beyond measure, and the rank-and-file nobility (*dvoriane*) lived in their houses as hangers-on and servants.

The nobility served from their estates, but even so not all of them came to the place of service when summoned; and since they served without pay, they could neither perform their duties outside the country for long nor,

---

[1] A *sloboda* was a section of town settled primarily by members of one social group or profession. The reference here is to the section near the walls of Moscow where all foreigners were required to live in the seventeenth century.—Editor.

Translated by Valentine Snow from Mikhail M. Shcherbatov, "Primernoe vremiaischislitel'noe polozhenie, vo skol'ko by let, pri blagopoluchneishikh obstoiatel'stvakh, mogla 'Rossiia sama soboiu, bez samovlastiia Petra Velikago, doiti do togo sostoianiia, v kakom ona nyne est' v rassuzhdenii prosveshcheniia i slavy," in *Sochineniia*, Vol. II (St. Petersburg, 1898), pp. 13–22. The article originally appeared in *Chteniia Moskovskogo imperatorskogo obshchestva istorii i drevnostei rossiiskikh*, I (1890).

within the country itself, be long away from their homes; to take which into account, terms of service were prescribed for them.

The *mestnichestvo* [2] system was abolished in 1682, but no new order was instituted, and as before men were elevated to the rank of boyar because they came of a great family rather than because of merit. As may be seen from various family trees, many a *stol'nik* [3] became a boyar directly, and young men often held high office; thus Prince Ivan Iur'evich Trubetskoi was a boyar before he was twenty. And it is to such men that the most important matters of state were entrusted.

There was hardly any trade, either foreign or domestic; such as there was was so scanty as to be unworthy of the name; for handicrafts were unknown, the consumption of goods was very low, and there were neither men versed in foreign commerce, nor ports. The only port was the city of Archangel, which, in addition to the difficulties raised by its situation in the northern-most part of Russia, the problems of navigation on the Dvina, and the length of the journey around Norway, was almost wholly in the hands of the English, who controlled this trade.

The lack of trade and consumption of goods led to a shortage of money and its inadequate circulation.

Neither manufactories nor handicrafts existed, and the simplest articles had to be obtained from foreigners.

There were judiciously planned government agencies, such as the Treasury, the Office of the [Army] Rolls, the Office for Local Administration, the Criminal Prosecution Office, the Office for Serf Affairs, and the Offices for the Administration of Vladimir and Moscow,[4] but they had neither rules nor regulations, nor yet proper court procedures. Everything was done according to custom. Although laws existed—both through the Code of Laws [5] and through new enactments—there was no order in their application.

A standing army was not maintained; the backbone of the state was the gentry, who served from their estates and were summoned when needed by the Office of the Rolls; but never did all of them come to the appointed place, nor yet all in good time; those that did arrive were neither properly armed nor in any way organized, and as they served at their own expense they would depart too soon. The *strel'tsy* [6] were instituted, but they numbered barely ten thousand men. They were undisciplined troops, disobedient to their officers; they spent their time in trade or engaged in a craft and cared nothing for their duty. Training in the arts of war was to them a

---

[2] A complicated system (originating in the sixteenth century) of calculating an individual's seniority in service on the basis of birthright, relative standing of the family, and the service merits of members of the family.—Editor.

[3] A court rank whose bearers were not members of the boyar duma (*boiarskaia duma*). Ranks giving right to membership in the duma (*dumnye chiny*) were those of *boiarin* (several categories), *okol'nichii* (literally, "one close to" the person of the sovereign), *dumnyi dvorianin* (duma nobleman), and *dumnyi d'iak* (duma clerk).—Editor.

[4] *Palata Zolotaia, Razriadnaia Palata, Zemskii Prikaz, Razboinyi Prikaz, Kholopii Prikaz, Vladimirskii Sudnoi Prikaz,* and *Moskovskii Sudnoi Prikaz.*—Editor.

[5] The so-called *Ulozhenie* of Tsar Alexis, dating from 1649.—Editor.

[6] "Musketeers"—body of regular soldiers (see note on p. 36).—Editor.

burden, a march unbearable, the enemy a thing to fear; because of their readiness to mutiny they were only a danger to the throne and to their commanders.

There was no fleet. The Tsar Aleksei Mikhailovich, desirous of seeing the Russian flag on the Caspian Sea, had vessels built on the Volga; but the frigate *Orel,* constructed by foreign shipbuilders, suffered a wreck, and this intention was abandoned. This is a clear proof of how much the Russians detested every innovation.

There were no fortresses, nor knowledge of how to build them; tall towers and walls were the only fortifications the cities had, and these could be breached by a few cannon balls. Our people neither knew nor dreamed of the uses of breastworks and crossfire.

Cannon there were, but such cannon as befitted an ignorant people—that is to say, not cast to specifications, too long, too thick, and with mouths too large—and the gun carriages were worse still, being convenient neither for transportation nor for rapid firing.

Abounding as she did in various ores, Russia had no gold, silver, copper, or iron of her own; aye, even iron had to be brought from Sweden, for there were none who recognized the ores and none who knew how to mine, treat, and refine them.

CALCULATION

Such, in part, were conditions in Russia prior to their correction by Peter the Great.

In 1682 an Academy was founded at the Ikonospas Monastery, where Latin and Greek were taught, and Aristotelian philosophy.

Let us suppose that this school had been in every way successful; even then, at least two generations would have been needed before Russians became convinced of the usefulness of learning and grew to detest ignorance. Hence, for education to spread even so far as to result in some two hundred Latin scholars acquainted with ancient philosophy would have required not less than sixty years; for while the first generation, clinging to its former convictions, was among the living this [change in attitude] was not to be expected, and the second generation too would have been of like mind—and I agree with all the calculators in allowing thirty years for each generation.

But what would the scholars have learned in this Academy? They would have studied the Greek and Latin tongues, Aristotle's philosophy and his categories, the subtle and often incomprehensible reasoning of Plato, and theology; they would have read the best writers of Athens and flourishing Rome, and the Fathers of the Church. But would they have known of the new discoveries made by the new men? Would they have studied the new system of light and the inventions of physics, chemistry, and mathematics? No, for they would have made it a rule to hold no commerce with those of other faiths, being the more hardened in their hatred since the dominant

Church forbade all communication with heretics and schismatics. Thus our land, being as it were separated from all other parts of the world, would have had either to discover everything for itself or to overcome its hatred of foreigners and enter into communication with them. The first would have required thousands of years, and even then could not have been accomplished without travel. How much time, then, would have been needed to overcome hatred of foreigners? I put it at three generations at least, or ninety years, and am the more confirmed in this conviction as we have seen that although Tsar Ioann Vasil'evich, desiring to introduce some degree of education, invited foreigners to Russia, and although Godunov made still greater efforts to that end and even sent young Russians to study abroad, neither the sciences nor the arts were fostered thereby and hatred of foreigners did not abate a whit.

Once some degree of learning and knowledge had been acquired and some habit formed of maintaining relations with foreign peoples, it would have been necessary to grasp the newly invented sciences and study the art of war, the casting of cannon, and military and civil architecture. But here fresh obstacles would have been encountered. First of all, the pride of the Russian nobility, not tamed by despotism to this day, would not have allowed them to accept unknown, and often lowborn, foreigners as masters in their own country. And how could they have learned through travel? Their attachment to their families and their homes, the low revenue from their villages, and their luxurious style of living would have made it impossible for the Russian nobles to travel abroad; and so a new habit would have had to be formed, for which at least another thirty years must be allowed. Yet even then what would they have learned? They would have studied the organization of foreign armies, without comparing their characteristics with the characteristics of the Russian; returning to their own country, they would have begun to do everything in the foreign way, without making adjustments, not fearing censure as foreigners would, and so would have done everything wrong. Even today we see many instances in which men unfamiliar with Russian conditions attempt to introduce foreign customs, and what they do is badly done. Let me give one example. The Russian army will not be handicapped by shortages; if it is out of bread, the soldiers themselves will reap the wheat and thresh the grain, mill the flour, and bake the bread. The [German] Emperor's army, on the contrary, must have everything made ready for it, and if it should happen to lose its bakers, it will starve in the middle of a rich countryside. And yet there was an intention to introduce this system in the Russian army and, disdaining its capacities, to incur unnecessary inconvenience. Hence I conclude that it is far better for any innovations to be introduced not by natives who have studied abroad but by imported foreigners; for although the latter are not familiar with our domestic conditions, yet, being directed by those who are, and having neither family influence nor protection, but being rather surrounded by envy, they will be the more cautious in their actions.

But since it would have been desired that all improvements and innovations be introduced by Russians themselves, once they had acquired learning, such introduction, with all the shilly-shallying, would have taken at least thirty years. And even so it is unthinkable without autocracy, in the case of the army, because of the need to levy taxes and recruit soldiers.

Still, let us suppose that all this could have been achieved; it would then have been necessary to wage war in order to gain ports. Let us again assume that the war would have been in every way successful. The war itself, the conclusion of the peace treaty, the sending of men to study navigation, and the construction of a fleet would have required another thirty years.

I shall pass over in silence manufactories and handicrafts, trade (of which we still have none), and the art of mining (which is at a very low level in Russia), and I shall forgo the calculation of the number of years that would have been required to bring all these to their present condition. Not counting these, according to the foregoing calculation 210 years would have had to elapse from the founding of the Ikonospas Academy; in other words, Russia would begin to reach her present state—without, by the way, having won any glory for herself—in about the year 1892, and that only on the assumption that during this long period of time there had been no disturbance, either from within or from without.

And who can guarantee that during all this time there would have been no sovereign in Russia who destroyed by thoughtless action the improvements introduced by two or three of his forebears and thus prolonged still more the period required for Russia's enlightenment? Who can affirm that other sovereigns who reigned during this time, such as Charles XII of Sweden and Frederick II of Prussia, would not have conquered large parts of Russia's territory? In that event, when would she have attained enlightenment, and what would have become of her present glory?

Having studied these lines with diligence, do not judge the time Russia would have required, by the unaided efforts of her people, to reach a satisfactory condition, in the light of what she is today; but judge it bearing in mind her former state and her prejudices, and examine by degrees how long it would have taken her to cure any one of her ailments. Or judge rather by yourselves; since you too are moved by prejudice, you who have been enlightened by Peter the Great, consider how difficult it is to extirpate it among the people. And, laying aside these vain conceits of mine, render praise and gratitude unto Peter the Great, for although much of his work has been undone since his death, yet the foundations he laid resist weakness and envy, vanity and corruption; and this Monarch, imprisoned in his tomb, yet continues to defeat his enemies and to bring glory to Russia.

4.
Nikolai Ivanovich Novikov

1744-1818

The Russian who did the most to popularize enlightened attitudes and notions among his countrymen in the second half of the eighteenth century was without any doubt Nikolai Ivanovich Novikov. His public activities were numerous and varied; they made him a leading force in Russian journalism, publishing, public education, and philanthropy. He helped to spread culture and learning into the remotest corners of European Russia and to instruct an entire generation of the Russian nobility. Novikov was a leading Freemason and suffered arrest and banishment when Catherine II closed the Masonic lodges and persecuted their members in the belief that they were spreading subversive and revolutionary ideas. As a dedicated Mason Novikov saw in the individual's moral development the principal foundation of his social and material happiness and progress. Novikov's activities, therefore, centered on the spiritual improvement of the individual. Under Russian conditions of the time this was no easy task, and one must marvel at the results Novikov achieved. The high value he put on man as a moral individual capable of spiritual progress explains his great concern for education. If future generations of Russia's elite were to be better than their parents, they had to be exposed to higher values and given an upbringing consonant with their calling in life. Quite naturally, freedom of expression (that is, freedom of the press) ranked high on his list of "political" demands. But, like most progressive noblemen and Freemasons of his time, while critical of administrative practices, he was not unalterably opposed to the principles of the Russian state. His task, he felt, was moral improvement and reform of manners, not the transformation of Russia's political and economic system.

[On Man's High Estate]

GENTLE READER!

The publishers of this review, in embarking on their undertaking, are so moved by fear and hope that they are still in no condition to disclose their intention forthwith.

Our group consists of only ten; and our ages, added together, do not exceed thirty years. Such extreme youth barely brings us to the "Morning Light" of our lives; hence, as with all young persons, although we set great hopes in our industry and diligence, yet we dare not presume that many will deign to read us.[1]

For over nine days now we have been meditating on how to attract a large number of readers. Our gathering resembled the Athenian Areopagus. It had so important and dignified an air that awe-inspiring Minerva herself would have been pleased with it; yet withal, we were unable to come to any decision. Whatever was suggested appeared to us either extremely young or very old, either unduly devious or too straightforward, either very short or unconscionably lengthy; in a word, at the end of our confabulations we realized that our desire to be publishers not only was not accompanied by sufficient boldness but was not even prompted by ambition, vanity, or pride.

At last there spoke up a well-beloved fellow-member of our circle, whose small, deeply sunken, penetrating eyes and long nose, accenting the sharp features of his dry face, always reveal what he is thinking, and whose custom it is not to speak save when Venus is in conjunction with the Sun.[2] This fellow-member, addressing us, asked: "Friends! Are you certain that our compatriots will be inclined to read what, in your opinion, constitutes the

---

[1] In the opinion of a Soviet student of Novikov, the reference here is to the total number of years for which the ten members of the editorial board had belonged to their Masonic lodge. *Utrennii svet* was the mouthpiece of the Masonic circles with which Novikov was connected. Cf. notes to *N. I. Novikov i ego sovremenniki*, pp. 496–97.—Editor.

[2] An ironic self-portrait of Novikov. *Ibid.*, p. 497, note 4.—Editor.

Translated by Valentine Snow from Nikolai Ivanovich Novikov, "[O vysokom chelovecheskom dostoianii]," in *Izbrannye sochineniia* (Moscow, 1951), pp. 381–87. The essay served as the introductory editorial to the first issue of *Utrennii svet* (Morning Light), published by Novikov and a group of his Masonic friends from September 1777 to August 1780. First published in St. Petersburg, the review was moved to Moscow in 1779. In all, thirty-six issues appeared (in four parts). The essay is unsigned, but internal evidence and Novikov's usual editorial practices indicate that it came from his pen. Cf. L. B. Svetlov, ed., *N. I. Novikov i ego sovremenniki: izbrannye sochineniia* (Moscow, 1961), p. 496.

best of the new writings? Are your quills sharpened in the newest French fashion? Have England and the land of Germany supplied the subject matter of your compositions?" So saying, he sat down with great dignity, mopping his flushed brow.

Even as somber clouds are dispelled by a loud roll of thunder and allow free passage to the sun's ray, so were our souls suddenly filled with light on hearing this question. Whereas our learned disputes concerning the choice of material had been lively and noisy, a profound silence now reigned among us. For a long time we stared at each other, not knowing what we should think, say, or do; and so we begged him to extricate us from this new difficulty by giving us wise counsel. "This you must do," we said, "because you have rudely awakened us from a most pleasant slumber." We had to plead with this moralist, a resolute foe of weakness, imperfection, and vice, for a long time. At last his patriotic attachment to his beloved country overcame his obstinacy, his burning desire to do something for the good of his compatriots opened his humanitarian heart, and this is what he said:

"Friends! The matter regarding which I questioned you is without doubt of such importance that you could not even have broached it in your earlier consultations. All your efforts and your artistic undertakings, all the learned pieces you might carefully edit would be vain and useless if they did not please our readers. I am far from doubting our compatriots' love of reading, but we are in no position now to decide a matter which time must settle. Let us assume, however, for argument's sake merely, that love of reading has not yet spread through all Russian cities. Will we be released from our obligation to our countrymen, merely because some of them forget their duty toward themselves? Rather, should not our zeal for their welfare be intensified? Should we not then direct our efforts with greater foresight and intelligence toward giving pleasure to those of our compatriots who read and attracting the notice of those who do not read to something that will be useful to them? Those readers who have fallen under the spell of the works of certain foreign writers, with their tinsel glitter, will soon recover if they see their dream beauties, like the snowflakes which sparkle in our air in winter, melting away at the rising of the sun of truth. Thus my question should not cause you to doubt your intention, but merely make you cautious in carrying it out; for it brings before you the whole orientation of this review of ours and gives you this unspoken advice: *Be useful to men of good sense.*

"I might end my speech here and leave the rest to your commendable zeal, were it not that I see in your eyes an impatient desire to hear my detailed conclusions. Hence, contrary to my inclination, I shall now speak at somewhat greater length than is my wont. We cannot, it seems to me, choose a better field for our labors than the *hearts* and *souls* of our beloved compatriots. These compatriots of ours are rational beings, consisting of *body, soul, and mind.* Let us leave it to the hairdressers, tailors, and inventors of new fashions for females to improve their appearance; let us leave it to skillful physicians to heal their bodily ailments; and let their *souls* and *minds* be our exclusive concern. Let us offer healing and strengthening substances for those. Consequently we must fill the pages we publish with truths which have their basis in human nature, truths which derive from all of creation and are by it explained. Do you wish me to advance supporting evidence? Very well—bear with me a few minutes longer.

"If we systematically investigate the heavens, the earth, water, air, and fire—in a word, all of creation—we shall essentially be studying man, because of whom all Nature's works are worthy of discussion. The majestic sun and all the magnificent host of stars would not merit our attention, did not their beneficent influence prove to us how much they do for our welfare. The three realms of Nature would be of little worth, did not experience show that man was created master of them all. The whole vast field of learning and the arts would become an empty, arid mirage not worth mentioning, did not the arts and sciences work to improve the human heart, to increase human well-being, and to broaden the soul and its powers. Everything proves to us that among the tangible objects with which we have become familiar over many long years, there is nothing finer, nobler, or more majestic than man and his qualities, which flow from the source of all good. Hence it follows that we are not mistaken—and who will blame us for the great and noble self-love that we show in holding man to be the focal point of this created earth and of all things! Nothing can be more useful, more agreeable, and more worthy of our labors than that which is closely bound up with man and the object of which is his virtue, well-being, and happiness.

"We all seek ourselves in everything; the causes which move us would be weak and ineffective if, in undertaking any task, we forgot ourselves or our hopes of pleasure, joy, or well-being. Indeed, nothing pleases and delights us more than our own selves. It is surprising that we are fond of conversations of which we are the subjects and constantly seek to learn what others are saying about us? Do we not note a generous response even in callow youth when we deign to praise its endeavors? The most misguided man will not long resist if the error of his ways is pointed out to him in a gentle manner. Hence if it were possible to teach men in general to regard themselves as examples of goodness and virtue, as being the crown of all things, then each man in particular would be brought to consider himself an important and worthy part of this crowning whole. My friends, how can you doubt that you will find many readers for a publication which will speak of the readers themselves—provided only that by a skillful selection of material you seek to foster the inborn human desire to acquire knowledge?

"The fact that many people are ignorant of matters which concern themselves will be a great aid to you. Most men, allowing their thoughts to roam over the limitless expanse of the world, wish to know of all possible things that exist, and yet remain ignorant of, and alien to, their own small world. Many do not regard the *science of self-knowledge* as necessary and demanding great diligence but, rather, deem it not particularly useful, a homely craft, and easiest of all to learn. Others appear to think that they should study this, the highest, science after they have learned everything else. Still others—and how numerous they are!—prey to inconstancy, flit, like greedy bees, from one flower of knowledge to another; the vastness of the field and the great number of fair flowers in it cause them to lose their way in these meadows of delight and never to return to the fragrant amaranth of their own selves. Finally, yet others, more numerous than all the rest, neglect useful matters in favor of useless ones; they stray from the straight path, taking some trifle for a thing of importance, and hence never attain to the study of themselves. Is it surprising then that *self-knowledge* is a branch of learning which is as yet little known among men?

"We cannot deny that there are some people who spend their entire lives doing nothing but looking at themselves, but they examine only the surface of man. Their *self-knowledge* is not the kind from which the ancient Egyptian and Greek sages promised us such great benefit.

"Such knowledge, my friends, cannot thwart your undertaking; and it will help you all the more if, with all gentleness, you hold before some persons who are as inconstant as butterflies! the *mirror of truth* and show them the way from the surface of their bodies to the inside of their hearts.

"The whole vast field of higher, middle, and general ethics lies open to us in our self-appointed labors. Let us apply ourselves to some parts of it that are bare and uncultivated. Let us not fear those mocking and denigrating wits who pronounce *moralistic writings* dated and superfluous. To raise *virtue,* much looked down upon in the world, to its majestic throne, and to show vice in all its nakedness as base and contrary to human nature, is a praiseworthy labor, even if it does not go beyond intention, even if there is not sufficient strength of character to pursue it. The more our hearts solemnly assure us that no other intention will guide our pen, the more calmly and indifferently shall we bear all mockery and invective addressed to our *Morning Light,* until at last the *great sun* of the enlightening *spirit* rises over our land; and we shall then gladly vanish in its rays.

"Man, as I have already said, is a high and exalted being. Divine revelation teaches us, in addition, that he was made before all other creatures, in the image of the All-Highest, and that the Almighty breathed life into him. This circumstance is in itself so weighty and significant that it can readily inspire in us the greatest respect for a creature which was so honored by its own Creator; consequently we must produce writings commensurate with the importance of our task and treat man's qualities with due solemnity. We will permit ourselves to deal otherwise only with people who themselves trample underfoot their high estate and abase a condition worthy of respect, who resist the noble tendencies inherent in them, who willfully deny pure human feelings. Such people deserve that we should regard them as savage beasts in human guise and, for the honor of mankind, should treat them more severely than our inclination to gentleness would have us. Let universal satire be the scourge with which we chastise the vices of such nonhumans. And let it be our inviolable law to inflict such punishment on the vices alone, and not on persons, inasmuch as they are human beings. In our pages the vice and the man, two separate objects, shall be as two parallel lines, which can never meet. Let us, my friends, endeavor above all to love man, in order that, being all-tolerant and refraining from personal criticism, we may the better with our writings promote *virtue;* and if, as we do so, love of all mankind serves us as our Pole Star, we shall easily pass among the rocks that surround us and launch a strong attack against vice, wickedness, and inhumanity.

"The ancients have left us many beautiful writings, of great literary merit, on such important matters. Time and circumstance have buried most of these under ruins. Let us rescue them, my friends, let us give them to our compatriots in their own tongue. In this way we will restore the honor of antiquity for the good of our country and, in addition, we will often have occasion to lead our readers to the doors of good taste and rational knowledge. The modern age owes thanks to a few individuals endowed with great intelligence who have discovered the ways of gaining knowledge of man and his nature. Many great minds have dared to penetrate to the very depths of the human heart, and have made public their observations. Let us not disdain anything that furthers our purpose, even though there is prejudice against it.

"Let us regard as invaluable whatever can serve our aim, that is to say, can promote the welfare of our fellow-countrymen. I know, my friends, how remote we are from malice and pride, and how ardently we desire that all our beloved compatriots should join us in our labors to attain our common goal. Hence you must allow all those who have acquired new knowledge of themselves and of man in general to fill some of our pages with their writings. Welcome them and encourage them in this socially useful task; assure them that they will greatly oblige us by submitting their work to us. They can address their letters to the bookdealer who will sell our review, and we shall see to the rest with the greatest pleasure. What a delightful hope dawns in my heart! We shall thus have an opportunity to meet many great minds, true patriots, and honest men. In ancient times, Diogenes looked for them with a lantern, but even today, my friends, one does not come across them on every street!

"Finally, in order to avert any suspicion of cupidity, you should not conceal from your fellow-citizens the use you intend to make of the profits from this review. Why not let the world know that you have decided that all the money received from the sales of the review will go to maintain schools for poor children? [3]

"True, the left hand need not always know what good deeds the right hand does; and when good deeds are made public knowledge they lose their inner worth, so that the doers become no better than Pharisees. But the situation here is quite different; the founding of such schools cannot be kept a secret. They require considerable and constant support. Your good example may move other well-disposed people to do likewise. Their love for their poor, uneducated compatriots will be strengthened thereby; they will be glad to share the burden which others have readily agreed to place on their shoulders—a light, agreeable burden which can hurt no one and which can do great honor to the country and to humanity. Hence, where a good deed

[3] The reference is to the educational institutions supported by the Freemasons in St. Petersburg, *Ibid.,* p. 497, note 8.—Editor.

should serve as a public example, the modesty that would conceal it would be deserving of censure. Audacity and fearlessness are always attractive, and people are often moved by them as by an irresistible force. When Plutarch in his work on chance wrote that it is possible to speak of one's own good actions without a qualm, may he not have been thinking of such a case?[4] I believe that we not only may make such an announcement without any fear of being thought vainglorious, but that it is our duty to do so. If we thereby open a new door to our dear compatriots and show them a new path to the weal of mankind, we shall prevent them from saying that they were not afforded an opportunity to show their love for men, for their fellow-citizens, and for their beloved fatherland."

This was the conclusion of our good fellow-member's remarks. After a thorough examination, we decided that, except for his last proposal, he said nothing with which we were not in complete agreement. We decided that these views of his should be published instead of a foreword to our review, as there are always certain difficulties attendant upon the writing of a foreword to any new work. There are few writers who do not tremble when composing a preface for their books. Fortunately, our beloved fellow-member has spared us that labor; and we have now no need to appease criticism or to seek to attract attention. Our respected readers will, without such effort on our part, learn of our purpose and of what they can expect from our review in the future.

Following the example of Thucydides, we have not bequeathed our treasure to them for all time, and therefore are not obliged to inform them of its price. They already know both our intention and our fear—and time will show which was the better founded!

---

[4] The reference is to a translation of Plutarch's essay that appeared in the first issue of *Utrennii svet. Ibid.*, p. 498, note 9.—Editor.

On the Upbringing and Instruction of Children

With a View to the Dissemination of Useful Knowledge
and the Promotion of General Well-being

INTRODUCTION

Anyone who has given even a little thought to the influence of human actions on human well-being, and more especially to the influence of rearing on the rest of a person's life, will recognize that the upbringing of children is of great importance both for the state and for each individual family. With the best of laws, with religion itself, with the arts and learning flourishing at their highest, the state would have very poor members if the government should neglect this one subject, which in every country is the groundwork for all the rest. The most perfect system of justice does not make the functionaries upright or the judges incorruptible; religion itself cannot prevent its unworthy devotees from sometimes using it as a cloak for the vilest vices and abusing it to further their evil intentions; the best-conceived police regulations[1] can have little effect if honesty, sincerity, love of order, moderation, and true love of their country are virtues foreign to the citizens. Everything depends on each person being educated in the virtues appropriate to his calling and station in life. But when should such education take place, when can it take place, if not at the age at which the soul lies open to every impression and, as yet undecided between vice and virtue, may just as readily harbor noble sentiments, grow accustomed to equitable rules of conduct, and become rooted in virtue as it may give itself up to base carnal desires and the flames of passion, be misled by deceitful examples, and develop an unfortunate inclination toward folly and vice? Thus the prosperity of the state and the well-being of the people inevitably depend on public morality, and this in turn depends on upbringing. Al-

---

[1] The term "police regulations" (*zakony blagochiniia*) is used here in its eighteenth-century sense of administrative supervision and regulation of public and private behavior. —Editor.

Translated by Valentine Snow from Nikolai Ivanovich Novikov, "O vospitanii i nastavlenii detei," in *Izbrannye sochineniia* (Moscow, 1951), pp. 417–38. The article first appeared in *Pribavlenie k Moskovskim vedomostiam* (Moscow, 1783).

though law, religion, decorum, learning, and the arts may be used as auxiliary means for the fostering and protection of morals, yet once the morals
have been impaired, all these cease to be of benefit. The rushing stream of
corruption breaks down such defenses, makes impotent the law, disfigures
religion, arrests the advance of every useful branch of learning, and makes
the arts the slaves of stupidity and luxury. Upbringing alone is the true
engenderer of good morals; through it, an aptitude for virtue, a habit of
order, a sense of measure, a patriotic spirit, a noble national pride based on
truth and knowledge, a contempt for weakness and for anything trifling or
ostentatious, and a love of simplicity and nature, together with all other
humanitarian, public, and civic virtues, must be implanted in the hearts of
citizens; through it, men and women must be educated in accordance with
their sex, and each particular class of society so that it may fulfill its proper
function. When the rearing of children has reached the acme of perfection,
everything else will be made easy; the laws will be universally obeyed;
religion, simple in its majesty, will be what it always ought to be, which is to
say, the source of every virtue and the mainstay and consolation of the
spirit; learning will become an inexhaustible wellspring of genuine benefit
to the state; the arts will adorn existence, ennoble emotion, and become a
means of encouraging virtue; citizens of every class will be true to their
appointed station in life; and general industry, strengthened by moderation
and a good domestic economy, will afford the most populous nation security
from want and contentment with its condition.

This is how important the rearing of the young is for the state and for the
universal father of that great family, which is to say, the sovereign. Being
aware of this, our great monarch, from the outset of her glorious rule, has
shown a ceaseless concern with the spread of proper upbringing in her
Empire. Does not this wise maternal concern oblige each one of her subjects
who is the father of children to endeavor to foster her benevolent intentions
in the bosom of his own family, all the more so as each father is further
prompted to do so by his duty and by his own interest? For truly the
upbringing of children is of the utmost importance not only for the state
and the sovereign but for every private family, every father and mother.
Even should there be parents who are so blinded by their round of activities
that they can calmly bear the thought that they will give a scoundrel or a
fool to the world or, having badly brought up their daughter, will have her
make an unhappy marriage and thus give rise to whole generations of bad
and therefore unhappy persons—even such parents should at least dread the
thought that their neglected children will punish them for their lack of care
and, instead of being a joy and consolation in their old age, will destroy
their pleasure and peace of mind. Every friend of humanity would wish that
no family might recognize itself in that image, but every attentive observer
will find that—alas!—a good many parents are still in that condition.
Many to whom God has given everything that men call needful for felicity
are unhappy in their old age for the sole reason that their children have
brought them sorrow instead of joy, that the son's debauchery perturbs or
altogether shatters the family, or that the daughter's follies make her an

object of general contempt. How doubly bitter must such parents find this injury when in their hours of reflection (which even those who lead the most mundane and frivolous existence are bound to have) they discover that they themselves, by careless upbringing, laid the foundation for their children's vices or follies, that they themselves braided the whip which now punishes them for their unconcern.

Yet it may be that neither unconcern nor neglect is the reason why many of the young who enter society are bad persons and worthless citizens; it may be that the knowledge which is necessary for upbringing in the home is lacking; it may be that certain prejudices and harmful customs prevent the spread of such knowledge. For truly it cannot be said of our nation that parents are not concerned with the upbringing of their children. A family is hardly to be found which, having insufficient means for a private education [tutors], does not send its children to school; and there are many families which at great expense maintain tutors and governesses for their children, and teachers of languages, dancing, and drawing. Hence obviously there is something that works against these good and praiseworthy efforts of the parents and makes them at the very least useless to the main object of upbringing. It may be that even with much care and money spent on the children's rearing and with the most constant and varied instruction given to them, the true education of the heart and mind is neglected. Whether the guess we hazard is correct or not, we leave it to the gentle reader to decide. It is possible, while providing tutors and governesses for the children from their tenderest age, to bring them up badly; it is possible, while spending many thousands on their education, to do nothing for their true welfare: namely, when these endeavors are directed toward giving them such knowledge and accomplishments as will enable them to shine in society, while the first, great, all-important task of upbringing—the education of the heart—is neglected; when, instead of teaching them to think correctly and helping them to recognize truth and goodness, their heads are filled with wind and, instead of refining their wills and inclining them to love what is good, noble, and great, their sensibilities are bent toward trifles or even toward folly and vice. It will undoubtedly be difficult to prove to some parents that this can happen in families where the children have tutors and governesses; but this confidence in their own arrangements, this false security they have, imagining that they have done everything necessary for their children's upbringing by engaging tutors and governesses for them—that is the first thing they must discard; besides, their own circle of acquaintances may offer them living proof of what we have said. It is certainly true that the rearing of children is a difficult and complex matter, in which it is very easy to omit something, and yet in which every omission causes everlasting harm unless it is noticed and corrected in time. It is a special and subtle science, which presupposes great knowledge and which in the execution demands much observation, attention, and enlightened practical sense. No one is born knowing it, nor is it developed in the course of life, as in the life of a plant or a butterfly; it must be learned through well-chosen reading, through experience and reflection. Hence it is not surprising that this science (its name is pedagogy) is still little known; nor is it surprising that it should be known least of all by the very class of people who here are usually entrusted with the private education of a child, and who perhaps have to be chosen for lack of better available; but neither is it surprising that in many families children are badly reared.

These considerations and the sad experience which teaches us that books are still seldom read, that mistaken thriftiness, wasteful use of time, excessive love of entertainment, and Heaven knows what else prevent the cultivation of a taste for reading and useful information—these considerations and this experience have led us to make generally known, by publishing them in the *Vedomosti* [Record or Gazette],[2] those rules and principles of upbringing without grasping and following which all arrangements and expenditures will for the most part go for naught. In so doing, we shall take into account the best works of foreigners[3] and shall be happy if we succeed in fostering enlightenment in this matter and awakening a general firm desire to undertake this great and important task.

ON THE GENERAL AND ULTIMATE AIM
OF UPBRINGING AND
ON ITS COMPONENT PARTS

Every human enterprise which requires planning and time for its execution is carried out successfully only when we first clearly visualize its object and never lose sight of this throughout the process of execution. Only then are we able to discuss rationally every step taken in this enterprise, test every means that offers, understand and surmount every obstacle. Let us also follow this general rule of common sense in the important enterprise of child-rearing! We shall therefore begin by inquiring into the true, genuine, and ultimate aim of upbringing. This investigation will at the same time provide an answer to the question: What type of upbringing is really the best? It will also clear the way to an understanding of all the main component parts thereof. The reason why honest and conscientious parents so seldom attain their aim in rearing their children may also be revealed in the course of this investigation; possibly we shall discover that this occurs only because they are not aware of the principal aim of upbringing and, taking certain extraneous ends and means for the main purpose, devote all their attention to them.

We have seen in the foregoing section that the duty of parents to bring up their children as well as possible stems from their duties to the children, to

---

[2] There were several periodicals named *Vedomosti* in eighteenth- and nineteenth-century Russia. They usually included official notices of interest to readers in a particular city or province. The first regular journal established in Russia by Peter the Great in 1702 was also entitled *Vedomosti.*—Editor.

[3] One of the outstanding works on this subject, namely, the Englishman Locke's treatise on education, was translated into the Russian language long ago—but how many have read it? [John Locke's *Some Thoughts Concerning Education* (London, 1693) had been published in Moscow in 1759, in a translation by N. Popovskii.—Editor.]

the state, and to themselves. Hence it follows that the achievement of the true purpose of upbringing must also result in the discharge of those duties. And since, finally, the duty of the parents to their children is to promote their well-being as far as possible, and their duty to the state, in respect to their children, is to produce useful citizens, it is clear that the well-being of the children and their usefulness to the state constitute component parts of the aim of upbringing.

Having accepted these principles and examining, in the light thereof, the various special purposes which arise in the rearing of children, we shall see that these special purposes can in no way be the principal aim of upbringing and that, on the contrary, that aim is nothing other than to educate the children to be happy people and useful citizens. Let us suppose that one father should decide at all costs to make his son a man of learning, and another to bring up his son as a man of the world, and a third to teach his son to be a skillful artist or a merchant; all these fathers might labor greatly to carry out their intention, but they might not be fostering the true welfare of their children, for with all these accomplishments it is possible to be a bad and hence an unhappy person. They would, of course, give their children education of a kind, but they would by no means discharge their duty toward them and would even fail in their duty toward the state, for a bad man is always a bad citizen as well.

Thus these and similar special purposes, or education for a particular calling, in no way constitute the principal aim of upbringing. No father should boast of having fulfilled his duty in rearing his children if he has merely achieved one of these purposes, or even several. These are extraneous concerns which, as means to the main goal, may be good and praiseworthy, depending on the circumstances; [4] but the main object of upbringing, as we have already pointed out, is to raise children to be happy people and useful citizens. All other definitions, being imperfect, will fail to encompass the full scope of upbringing; only the one given above does so. Let us now proceed with our investigation.

We believe that by the inquiry so far and the definition of the true main object of upbringing we have indicated to parents a goal which should enable them to recognize the straight path they must follow. As mentioned above, they must never lose sight of this goal if they do not want to stray into various by-paths, and they must attain it if they want to acquire the great merit of having reared their children in the best possible way. But it is only by expounding this general and principal rule of upbringing that we

---

[4] We say "depending on the circumstances," for not always, not in all circumstances, are such special purposes good and praiseworthy. For example, not only would it not be good and praiseworthy, it would be very foolish for a father who had a naturally stupid son to try to make a learned man of him; or for another to try to make a painter or a virtuoso of a son whose birth and wealth destined him for political affairs and the great world; or for a third to educate his son for high society when this was incommensurate with his birth and means. Such special purposes are good and praiseworthy only when they are consonant with the circumstances of parents and children, for then they serve as both worthy and necessary means for the achievement of the principal aim of upbringing, as we shall shortly show.

can bring them closer to that rather distant goal and guide them along their dark road. At the same time, this exposition will confirm the justice of that general and principal rule, for it will be seen that all the component parts of upbringing may be deduced from it.

Our children must be brought up to be happy persons and useful citizens. In this connection, experience and our physical nature remind us that health and a strong constitution contribute greatly to our feelings of pleasure, and that in childhood the foundation is laid for the health and strength, and also for the weakness and ailments, of the body. We now see the first important component of upbringing: it is care of the body. The duty of parents is to see to it that their children have a strong and healthy constitution. Scientists call this component of upbringing physical education; and it is the first because the training of the body must begin before any other kind of education can take place.

No person can be contented and happy, or a good citizen, if his heart is agitated by immoderate desires which lead him either to vice or to folly: if his neighbor's prosperity moves him to envy, if cupidity drives him to seek another's property, if his body is weakened by lust, if ambition and hatred deprive him of peace of mind, without which no pleasure is possible, or if, finally, his heart holds so little religious feeling that the thought of death plunges him into dejection and hopelessness; yet all this depends on the education of the heart in youth. Hence follows the second main component of upbringing, the education of the heart; this is what men of learning call moral education.

Depending on the social class to which a person belongs, it is necessary for him, for the benefit of the state and for his own contentment, to have a greater or smaller amount of knowledge, a higher or lower degree of enlightenment; certain classes of society even require a definite level of scientific knowledge. The cultivation of the mind in general promotes a high degree of human welfare, and every person is the more useful to the state the more cultivated his mind. Hence follows the third main component of upbringing, the enlightenment or education of the mind.

Thus upbringing is divided into three main component parts: physical training, relating only to the body; moral training, for education of the heart; that is, the shaping and guiding of the children's natural feelings and wills; and intellectual training, relating to the enlightenment or education of the mind. We have deduced all three of these from the rule derived from the general and ultimate aim of upbringing, namely, "Bring up your children to be happy persons and useful citizens."

Each of these three components has its own rules, principles, and modes of action, without which it cannot be properly carried out, and which we will enunciate later in accordance with the division we have proposed.

Some of what we say may appear strange or even laughable to some of our readers, as, for example, the fact that we include training of the body in the science of education; for there are parents who imagine that the only thing necessary for physical training is to feed their children well. Other parents may be offended because, owing to the subject matter of this treatise, we speak frankly of what is good and praiseworthy in child-rearing, as also of what is bad and deserving of censure, and in so doing we may mention abuses of which they themselves are guilty. But it is not our purpose to while away the time of our readers or to lull them to unawareness of their harmful prejudices; rather is it our sincere and heartfelt desire to make known a necessary and generally useful truth. We cannot, therefore, take such considerations into account but must conscientiously strive to eschew anything that can encourage sinful slumber, which is so prejudicial to moral improvement.

Now that we have reached the end of our first section, let us briefly summarize what has gone before. We saw at the very outset that the upbringing of children is a matter of great importance both for the state and for each individual family; we saw that parents have a triple duty to bring up their children in the best way possible; and we have described both the beneficial results of a good education and the sad consequences of education neglected. Having thus proved the need for the best possible kind of upbringing, we first endeavored to discover what is the best kind. To this end, we attempted to ascertain the final or principal object of the parents in rearing their children, or, to put it another way, the general and ultimate object of upbringing. Our analysis showed us, first, that special ends, which are often mistaken for the principal task, are not the principal task or the main object of upbringing. It showed us that these are extraneous matters, which may in some circumstances be good and laudatory, but the fulfillment of which does not discharge the parents' duty toward their children; for they are not the main object and, being extraneous to it, can be truly good and praiseworthy only when they are properly used, in accord with the circumstances of the parents and children, and when they serve as a means to the principal end. Our analysis next revealed to us that the ultimate principal aim of education is "to bring up one's children to be happy persons and useful citizens." We took this maxim to be the main general object of upbringing and, if we treat upbringing as a science, to be also its first and general principle. We confirmed the validity of this maxim when, in analyzing it, we found that it encompasses the parents' entire duty as regards the upbringing of their children and contains all the main components of education. We discovered that these components are three in number (physical, moral, and intellectual education), and ascertained the principal content or object of each and its relation to the main object. We have thus become aware of the vast scope of upbringing; and we have also seen that these three main components of upbringing are all closely linked, inasmuch as they naturally derive from the main object, or the primary principle, which we have mentioned.

Thus, from all that we have already said about upbringing, we have learned no more than that! And indeed, it is not much; as against the whole subject, it is very little. Altogether, we have learned no more than the necessity, the main object, and the scope of upbringing, and we still know nothing of its actual practice, nor of what should be done at the same time, what separately, and what avoided. Undeniably, we are only on the doorstep. But, unless we are greatly mistaken, the general considerations we have set out in an orderly and coherent manner in order to clear our way should be very useful to most of our readers. They should, in our opinion, not only explain and rectify some ideas relating to this important subject but also clearly indicate the only path to the desired goal. They should show that those parents are wrong who either try to educate their children's minds alone, neglecting the so necessary education of the heart; or, in educating the mind, give no thought to their children's probable future station in life; or, through lack of care or bad practices, rear their children in poor health; or, lastly, are so inept at upbringing that they neglect everything that is essential and try, on the contrary, to inculcate only such knowledge and accomplishments in their children as will flatter their own vanity, being of the kind that catch the eye. These, while they may not actually harm the minds and hearts of the children, will certainly do nothing to educate them. Moreover, the general considerations we have set forth should eradicate the delusion that parents can bring up their children well without special knowledge, without reflection, and without great care. They should, on the contrary, make it clear that the task of upbringing, which is so comprehensive, requires so many different activities, and continues over so many years, demands not only a certain amount of knowledge, but also close attention, much reflection, and considerable caution if it is to be performed well. Lastly, the general considerations expressed herein, and especially the division of upbringing into its three main components, ought to serve as a guide enabling us to lay down more conveniently the particular rules thereof, and enabling the reader more readily to find them.

But we cannot yet proceed to the guide itself, for we see before us various other stumbling blocks, which hamper proper upbringing in general, in addition to the unawareness of the importance, object, and scope of good upbringing to which we have already referred. Hence it behooves us to try to clear away these obstacles in a special section, before we can begin to expound each of the different components of education.

SOME OF THE PRINCIPAL OBSTACLES IN THE WAY OF A GOOD UPBRINGING

There are certain circumstances which, without being part of upbringing and having to do only with the arrangements for it, yet have an immense influence on the upbringing of children, so that they may become either auxiliary means or obstacles to a good upbringing, depending on their good or bad utilization. Some of them are such that anyone is, or should be, able to see their effect on the education of children; while others, on the contrary, seem so far removed from the content of education that few see their link with it or their influence on upbringing; yet that influence is great and indisputable.

We deem it useful, for a number of reasons, to treat all these circumstances in a special section, and to begin by putting down what we have to say about them, in order to give some advance warning of certain principal obstacles in the way of upbringing, although we could have commented on them separately, in connection with each main component of upbringing.

Generally speaking, they include: (1) the parents' mode of life, (2) the domestic household arrangements, (3) the parents' treatment of tutors and governesses, and, lastly, (4) the selection of these persons.

And so in the present section we shall discuss these matters and their connection with upbringing. We should like to repeat our general preliminary observations, that all of them, severally or jointly, depending on their good or bad utilization, serve either as aids or as obstacles to upbringing.

Firstly: The parents' mode of life is an obstacle to upbringing if they are given to some coarse vice or lead such a flighty and frivolous existence that they have no time for useful and instructive association with their children. Nothing has a stronger influence on the young souls of children than the force of example, and, of all examples, none leaves a deeper and more lasting impression than the example set by their parents. We wish that our readers would enshrine this principle in their hearts, for it has been confirmed by experience in all ages. It is one of the great truths of upbringing that are extremely useful for the entire moral education of children and may never be lost sight of without great harm ensuing.

Children should hold their parents in greater respect than all other persons whom they have occasion to see; for the children's complete dependence on their parents, of which they are daily and naturally aware, is of itself conducive thereto, even if the parents use no special means, no instruction or admonition, to attain that end. This feeling can be extinguished in children only exceptionally if they constantly witness debauched behavior on the part of their parents, and their disrespect for the latter is a sure sign of very poor upbringing—so natural is this feeling in the young! Similarly, how natural it is that the parents' example should leave a mark on the young hearts of children, laid bare to every impression! Therefore it is easy to mold a child's heart if the example set by the parents is moral and instructive. Therefore experience teaches us that poor parents, who have little or nothing to spend on the upbringing of their children, often rear them to be better people than do many rich and noble families. Yet for the same reason it is extremely difficult, if not impossible, to inculcate virtuous inclinations and aptitudes in children if their parents' example shows them nothing save the coarsest or the most foolish vices. Where the father is a spendthrift or gambler, where the mother leads a dissolute life, or where both are mercenary, unjust, hard and cruel to their fellow-men, there moderation, thrift, chastity and marital fidelity, fairness, love of one's neighbor, and generosity are virtues of which the children know nothing, and their tutors and governesses will be unable to prevent them, even in childhood, from embracing this or that vice to which they may be susceptible at their age. We are, however, writing for enlightened persons, and so we prefer to assume that no admonition of ours is necessary in the case of blatant vice, especially as the danger of such examples must be obvious to everyone.

Yet even if we exclude the coarser vices, the life the parents lead may be an obstacle to proper upbringing if it is so frivolous and scatterbrained that they never do anything important and have no time for association with their children. It is not necessary for the parents to be constantly at work or to spend the major part of the day with their children; for they may certainly enjoy the pleasures to which their wealth and station in life entitle them without thereby harming the upbringing of their children. But it is absolutely necessary for all parents to set their children the example of useful endeavor and never serve as a model for sleeping one's life away or frittering it away on trifles, and to foster their children's education by engaging them in suitable conversation for at least an hour a day. Thus if the son knows that his father daily spends several hours in his study, engaged in serious reading or writing or some other occupation, if the daughter, likewise, sees her mother busy with household management, appropriate needlework, or the like, that in itself will suffice as a good example on the part of parents who maintain tutors and governesses. Furthermore, if the parents, as mentioned above, help the tutor for only an hour a day in properly directing the children's education, and if the tutor is skilled, he can readily make harmless the effect of any other diversions in which the parents are compelled or tempted to engage. On the other hand, where the morning is spent in sleep or on trifles, and the rest of the day at table and at cards, the children naturally develop a dislike for any serious occupation, come to regard eating, drinking, sleeping, dressing, paying visits, and playing cards as the lot of man, or at least as their own, and deem it ridiculous that their tutor should attempt to incline them to other and more difficult pursuits. Thus it happens that the unhappy disposition is developed which is most often to be found in young men of good family: a sybaritic softness which weakens a man, makes him incapable of any glorious endeavor, and renders him unduly sensitive to every misfortune and inconvenience; a laziness which leads him to regard slumber as the highest good and lowers the human condition to that of animals; a flightiness which shuns any important and useful endeavor, which is drawn only to the trifling and the unnatural, which always seeks pleasure yet is not conducive to real enjoyment and thus leads to folly and debauch, and particularly to the unfortunate predilection for card-playing which has ruined so many families. Did but such parents know how great and pure a joy it is to observe the young souls of children at all stages of their development, to test and direct their inclinations, to take part in their innocent pastimes, and, in some cases, to be able to say with justice: "This vigorous, industrious boy, that quiet, gentle, delightful young girl, are the product of my upbringing!" —then their own nature would move them to more frequent association with their children and they would thereby be distracted from their frivolous life. But as their hearts are wholly drawn to the artificial and noisy pleasures of high society, they do not know this and are in no position to feel these pure and natural pleasures. They must then, combating their inclination, listen to reason and to the voice of parental duty, and change their life at least in some measure; the example of childless persons of their own class can serve as no excuse for them, since it cannot be denied that parents have more reasons than others to organize their life with care.

Secondly: The domestic household arrangements are an obstacle to upbringing when they fail to set an example of certain civic and social virtues which should be inculcated in the children. Every household is a miniature government in which the children are offered the example of various relationships, various tasks, the manner in which they are discharged, and so on. These examples, as they are good or bad, make a good or bad impression on the children; and this impression is educational because the example is constant, continuous, and reinforced by the parents' respect. We refer above all to order and cleanliness. Order is the soul of all undertakings, the alleviator of all difficulties, the aid to various amenities and pleasurable enjoyment of life, and our preserver from manifold vexations. Cleanliness (in every respect) refines the senses generally, enhances physical beauty, promotes health, and makes a man attractive in society. Society shuns a slovenly person, particularly when that person is a woman, and such a person is always lacking in fine sensibilities.[5] Thus order and cleanliness are two qualities which must especially be instilled in children. These qualities also enter into the smallest details of everyday life, so that every household offers daily examples of them, or of their lack. It is impossible to describe every particular case in which the children can find in their household examples of disorder and uncleanliness, but we must cite a few, in order to make our point clear and to draw attention to certain disorderly ways which are generally regarded as unimportant. We refer particularly to disorderly ways of which for the most part the servants are guilty, while their masters, because of negligence, indulgence, or mistaken thrift, either overlook or actually cause them. They manifest themselves in various details of housekeeping, service, waiting on table, and so on. In a household where there is order and cleanliness in all these matters, where every command given by the masters is scrupulously complied with, where every need is taken care of at the proper time, where nothing is ever lacking, and so on, it is easy to accustom the children to order and cleanliness, for they see daily examples thereof. Where, on the other hand, the servant replies to every order, "At once, Sir," but carries it out two or three hours later or not at all, and is not punished; or where the major-domo neglects to buy firewood until the last logs have been used up, thus forcing the tutor and children to freeze for half a day; where the valet cleans his young master's boots or shoes by spitting on them and polishing them with his hand, because he would have to buy a brush with his own money; where uncouth rustics who would arouse repugnance in any properly brought-up person wait on table; where the children wear fine, expensive garments to go out but torn and stained clothes at home; where their beds are mean and dirty; where the floor or

[5] There is a book on disgusting customs in Poland, entitled *Orangutan.* If half of what it says about Polish ladies is true, no one will be tempted to marry a woman of Polish birth. For that reason the book may also serve other women as a serious admonition on personal fastidiousness.

oven bench is used to sleep on and coats make do for blankets; where, finally, these are not singular occurrences but the custom, approved by the parents—there it is hardly to be wondered that the children, if they are not altogether lacking in finer feelings, should at any rate deem order and cleanliness expendable and troublesome virtues. For low and trifling as the circumstances here mentioned may appear, it is well known that nothing is so low and so trifling that it cannot promote or hinder the attainment of great objects, and that in upbringing the greatest objects are attained through a multitude of small means. Hence it is an undoubted and highly useful truth that upbringing is like a complicated machine, consisting of many different springs and gears, each of which must bring another into motion if the proper operation is to be brought about.

Thirdly: The parents' treatment of tutors and governesses may serve either as an aid or as an obstacle to upbringing, depending on whether the parents encourage these persons in their service or subject them to annoyances, the children's respect for them being either fostered and strengthened or weakened and altogether destroyed thereby. Obstacles to good upbringing are found in particular in the following three cases:

1. When the parents fail to keep their promises to tutors and governesses when it is a question either of paying them the salary contracted for or of providing them with other small amenities.

2. When out of a mistaken and ignoble thriftiness they refuse to provide the tutors and governesses with the necessary tools for instruction and education.

3. When they treat these persons with contempt or allow their servants so to treat them.

Morally speaking, the first case is nothing less than flagrant injustice and actual dishonesty; it is what Holy Writ calls "muzzling the ox that treadeth out the corn." [6] Tutors and governesses, in devoting their time and efforts to a family, rely on its honor. However, it is not enough to say that such an action is unjust and shameful; since it relates to upbringing, it is also extremely unwise, for it causes displeasure and vexation to these persons and consequently harms the children and the parents themselves. There is perhaps no task that requires so much good will and such constant tranquillity of spirit as that of the teacher and educator. Failing these, a tutor cannot accomplish what he is there to do. Although he can discharge his duties without good will and a tranquil mind—since all duties can be discharged in many different ways—yet beyond doubt he will do everything badly. Not only will his instruction fail of its purpose, since its main requirement is to make learning easy and interesting for the children, something which cannot be accomplished without great care, forbearance, and good will on the teacher's part; but the education of the heart will also be endangered, for it requires even greater attention than instruction, and depends far more on the tutor's attitude toward the children than on his admonitions.

[6] I Tim. 5:18.—Editor.

But how can the tutor be expected to retain these qualities, so necessary for the children's well-being, and not to feel indignant and vexed, when the parents themselves show so little good will toward him and transgress, or allow transgression of, his incontestable rights? This occurs most often in respect to those small amenities the provision of which depends on the major-domo or the servants. In this connection, tutors in certain houses are subjected to incredible indignities and perfidious tricks: either they must apply themselves to win the friendship of these creatures, which they can only acquire by daily plying them with vodka to drink, or none of their needs will be seen to. We have known of contracts in which the most trifling details were mentioned and duly agreed upon, because the preceding tutor, who had failed to take this (frequently useless) precaution, had been deprived of them. Truly, one fails to understand how some parents can stoop to such actions, as ignoble as they are unjust. They cannot be excused even when the tutor is bad, for without good will a bad tutor will become even worse. And what will happen to the children if he should stoop to the base means which alone can protect him from the parents' miserliness or poor household management? If, on the other hand, he is an honest and high-minded man, such treatment of him is flagrant injustice, for he in no way deserves to be deprived of what he requires and to be delivered to the servants for dishonor and abuse. Parents should dismiss bad tutors as quickly as they can, and bear in secret their punishment for having made an unwise choice. But all tutors without exception, so long as they are in charge of the children, should be given what they are entitled to voluntarily, decently, without invective and without deceit.

The parents' treatment of the tutor is also an obstacle to proper upbringing if they refuse to supply the necessary books and other tools of instruction and education. We would have to write a whole book if we were to enumerate all the harmful consequences of ill-considered thriftiness in certain households; health, order and cleanliness, the upbringing of the children and peace in the family, all these are sacrificed to such thoughtless false economy. Let us therefore confine ourselves to the subject under discussion. The harm caused consists in the fact that the tutor is subjected to annoyance and that the good results which can and should be produced by the educational tools he asks for are frustrated. No artist or artisan can do anything without the tools he needs; there is a saying that a student without a book is like a soldier without a rifle. Nevertheless, in some households tutors lack even for books. Grammars and dictionaries are almost alone in being universally recognized as necessary. It should not be difficult to explain to some parents that books relating to the sciences are also needed, as well as various books for reading. Some parents even demand that the tutor should buy the books with his own money, or at the very least they are unable to understand why three children should need more than one grammar book and one dictionary. Where other tools, in addition to books, are required, such as prints, terrestrial and celestial globes, mathematical instruments, and the like, such parents always feel that these can be done without or that the tutor should pay for them out of his own pocket. Even

when the children require the most trifling furnishings, such as a blackboard or a desk, the parents either say no to the tutor, regarding these
things as unessential, or commission the major-domo to buy them; both are
equally frequent occurrences. He, being even more convinced than his
masters that these objects are not needed, either fails to carry out the order
or takes so long about it that by the time the blackboard and the desk are
bought the tutor has left the house. Yet a blackboard and a solid, comfortable desk are far more useful and necessary than twenty other objects in the
house which cost a hundred times as much; for with the use of the blackboard it is possible to explain many things to children which they would
otherwise find difficult or impossible to grasp, while it is bad for the children's health to write at a desk which is too high or too low or which
wobbles. Hence it is very wrong for parents to refuse the tutor such trifles,
which he obviously needs for the children's good, and to subject him to the
chicanery of a muzhik who should not be permitted to have any say in any
matter concerning the tutor. Parents should readily and agreeably furnish
the tutor on his first demand not only with such trifles but with anything
else he may ask for the children, and should in addition thank him for his
concern for the children's welfare. Otherwise, he will certainly abandon his
concern and will make do with what the parents provide, and the children
too will have to get along as best they can where their education is concerned.[7]

A far more common and serious obstacle to upbringing is created when
the parents treat the tutor with contempt and permit their servants to do
likewise, for both the instruction and the moral education of the children
are hampered. The education that the tutor is able to impart to the children is based on the trust they have in him, and that trust is in turn
founded on esteem, love, and respect. Lacking such trust, there is not much
a tutor can do with the children. Neither his admonitions nor his example
will make much impression on them, for they will not regard them as
important and will pay no attention; while if he scolds or punishes them,
they will not reform but will only be angry at him, for human beings, and
especially children, cannot without anger accept censure and punishment
from a man they do not respect or love, even when these are intended to
correct them. Thus respect, love, and the consequent trust the children
place in their tutor are the sole groundwork for all the good he can do
them. Parents wreck this groundwork and undermine the very foundations
of all instruction and education when they treat the tutor with contempt or
allow servants so to treat him. The person whom the child is to respect must
have the respect of the father and mother. This truth is as incontestable as
that all men must die. Such respect, however, consists not only in showing

[7] Such making do, when it is the general rule, is extremely unwise and causes untold
harm. For example, it is possible to build a house without using a saw. But if the ax is
used as a makeshift, a great deal of time will be wasted; and if the workman hacks with
an ax at timbers that have already been joined together, he will so weaken the joints that
the house will fall apart ten years sooner than if it had been built properly. Is that not
exemplary thrift?

him common courtesy, but in treating him as a highly valued friend of the family, in never speaking of him disdainfully in front of the children, in not demanding from him the sort of humble servility that is expected from the valet or the man who waits on table, and in not permitting those persons to show contempt for him by their actions (examples of which are too numerous to be listed here). A child readily distinguishes between the fashionable simulation of ordinary politeness and true respect; it will not listen to the tutor's exhortations and will remain indifferent to his scolding as soon as it notices that the parents disdain him or have less respect for him than for the *diad'ka* [8] or for the major-domo. Yet in some households these persons are the tutor's judges, and their verdict determines the masters' whole attitude toward him!

But what if the tutor is not the kind of person who can command respect and be treated as a friend of the family? Our answer is: dismiss him, and in choosing another heed well what we say below about the selection of tutors.

That a bad tutor is a great obstacle to a good upbringing is as obvious, in our opinion, as that a bad wife is an obstacle to domestic bliss. Yet everyone knows that even today there are a great many worthless persons wandering about our land who call themselves tutors. The need for the children to learn foreign languages and the insufficient number of good native [Russian] teachers have forced parents to pay tutors very high salaries; and this has attracted to our country a multitude of foreigners who had never in their lives before given a thought to the care and instruction of children— still less read the necessary books—who are themselves very badly educated, and who in their own country plied the lowliest trades; but here they are all engaged to bring up our young, and some of them receive staggering pay for it.[9]

Without doubt, many excellent people have also been attracted to our country; yet the bad still outnumber the good, and it is therefore very difficult to find a good tutor. Parents know all this; yet many of them act in such an irresponsible way in selecting a tutor for their children that they engage him even without a university examination, which would at least

---

[8] A male servant especially entrusted with the care of his master's son after the latter was taken from his nurse. Frequently the *diad'ka* retained charge of the boy until late adolescence (or even beyond, as did Savel'ich in Pushkin's *The Captain's Daughter*) and was entrusted with his physical care, while the tutor or teacher had the responsibility for his intellectual and moral development.—Editor.

[9] In order to show our readers that we are not alone in thinking so and that this evil is known in Germany as well, we should like to quote a passage which may be useful in another way too: "If you ask a French barber in St. Petersburg or Moscow what he intends to do with the young man to whom he has been engaged as tutor at 400 or 600 rubles, he will reply that he wants to *ouvrir l'esprit et former le coeur* [open the mind and form the heart] of his charge. This is the usual boastful reply which he stole somewhere, but he will not go into further detail. It is even difficult to make him understand that a more detailed approach is useful and necessary. One must first draw to his attention the concepts *perruque, friser, cheveux* [wig, to comb, hair] and then show him, by analogy, that making a wig or opening a mind, a number of special rules are required all of which must be known in order to be applied" (see *Versuch über den Kinderunterricht*, p. 229).

assure them that the man of their choice was not entirely unfitted for his important task. Two prejudices, in particular, lead parents astray in the selection of tutors. The first is that they insist on the tutor's speaking correct French without an accent; the second is that they imagine that every native Frenchman possesses this ability, which they deem to be the main characteristic of a good tutor. These are both prejudices, and very harmful ones, for they often cause children to be placed in the hands of the worst persons. Since knowledge of the French language is a necessity, parents cannot be blamed for demanding it in the tutor; if, however, the tutor has a solid and theoretical knowledge of the language, does not altogether mispronounce it, and in addition possesses some of the other accomplishments and qualities necessary to a good tutor, then perfect correctness and elegance of pronunciation are of very small importance and parents should not insist on them. For both the tutor and the children can correct their pronunciation in social intercourse; and, if all the other qualities of a good tutor are present, the lack of perfect French pronunciation is but a trifle, because of which an otherwise capable tutor should not be rejected. Least of all should those parents be concerned who either speak French correctly and without an accent themselves and can therefore teach their children to do likewise, or live in cities where especially good teachers of French are to be found.

It is altogether ludicrous for parents to imagine that it suffices to be born a Frenchman to speak and understand French perfectly. In France, as in other countries, the populace speaks its own language badly and understands it still less; for proper knowledge of any language is to be obtained only from books, and a correct pronunciation from frequenting good society, and neither of these pursuits is for the common people. Thus among the French, too, there are people who speak French as badly as our own populace speaks Russian. A language teacher whose pronunciation is perfect cannot for that reason alone be a good teacher, and still less a tutor, for to be the first requires a thorough and scholarly knowledge of the language, while to be the second demands still other qualities and qualifications which uneducated and uncultivated persons do not possess.

Parents who understand where their true interests lie in the choice of a tutor must try, as far as possible, to ascertain the following:

1. Whether the tutor reasons clearly and logically.

2. Whether his character is sufficiently flexible and adaptable to enable him to treat children in accordance with their age (without himself acting childishly).

3. Whether he is, generally speaking, a man of good morals.

4. Whether he has a clear and sound (rather than deep or extensive) knowledge of the languages and subjects which he is to teach.

5. Whether his pronunciation of those languages is at least passable, so as not to furnish a stumbling block and obstacle for the children.

6. Whether his manners are such as to serve as an example to the children.

These are the principal characteristics of a good tutor, and not his having been born a Frenchman or having a perfect and elegant pronunciation, for a man having those last two characteristics may be a bad tutor.

A combination of all these qualities, however, is far more rarely to be found in local tutors than a good French accent. The question thus arises: What are the parents to do? Should they engage a tutor abroad? Not every family has the means and the opportunity to do so; and when the tutor who has been engaged through correspondence arrives, it often turns out that a better one could have been found in our own country. There is also another great inconvenience, which is that the tutor does not understand a word of our language and is not familiar with our ways and customs. This is so great a drawback for the upbringing of children that we would advise every family in this position to maintain the tutor for a whole year outside the household, asking nothing of him but that he should learn the local language; for, if he does not know it, he will do more harm to the children in one year than he can undo in three.

In these circumstances, it is certainly difficult to find good tutors. But cannot this difficulty be surmounted? Is it not possible to educate worthy private teachers and tutors here in our own nation? Do we want to abandon the upbringing of our children to foreigners for evermore? Anyone who knows Russian realizes that the Russian language so shapes all the organs of speech that it is not difficult for any Russian to learn French and German perfectly if he so desires. This is borne out by experience, for all our compatriots who have had an opportunity to learn these languages by using them speak them very well. Hence the need to know the French and German languages should not prevent us from having our own excellent private teachers and tutors, especially as in our capital cities there is ample opportunity to learn both these languages thoroughly and to become accustomed to pronouncing them correctly through association with others. Why is it, then, that we still do not have good tutors of our own and must rely on foreigners?

In point of fact, this is caused by two minor circumstances, which we can alter whenever we wish; they are as follows:

Firstly, that young students have no opportunity to visit good homes and be thus trained for the tutor's calling.

Secondly, that the calling of tutor itself is, if not disdained, at any rate not as respected as it deserves and as it ought to be if we are to obtain worthy tutors from among our own nationals and render foreigners superfluous.

Our young people are able to study all the languages and subjects which a tutor has to know; there are excellent institutions for this purpose in both our capital cities. But in no school, seminary, or university can a young man learn the manners which a tutor needs even more than languages and sciences. These he can acquire only by having ample opportunity to see and to frequent the society of cultivated people; for only society and social intercourse in general educate a man, and they must be used especially to educate those who are called upon to educate others. But how are our young students to have such an opportunity, when the homes of the nobility are closed to them? Young men who can acquire polish in their own families through the company of cultivated people do not accept the post of tutor; and those who do accept such posts live either at home, in families which do not entertain such company, or in seminaries, in the monotony of academic life, which is suitable for the training of a scholar but not of a tutor. Thus if the class of persons who will take up the duties of private teachers and tutors is to be given an opportunity to acquire much-needed polish, patriotism must come to the aid of legislative power, and rich and prominent families must open their homes to young students, admit them to their board and their amusements, and thus afford them a chance of acquiring the kind of education which no public school can give.

But in order that the young men so educated should desire to take up the calling for which they will thus have been prepared, and not prefer some other occupation to it, we must overcome the contempt in which the calling of tutor is apparently still held and accord to it the measure of respect to which it is entitled. If the most illustrious of our nation would adapt our first proposal and open their homes to young students, they would strike the first blow at this foolish prejudice against people who are concerned with a task so important for the nation and for private families as the upbringing of children. But in order to eradicate this prejudice altogether or to allow it currency only among the rabble, the more prominent must make a special effort to make the tutor's calling respected; to this end, they must treat every skilled and honest tutor with courtesy and show contempt for anyone who does otherwise; they must refute and rebut any unfair views on the status and dignity of tutors and thereby disseminate among the people the great and necessary truth that an educated and honest man who brings up the children of a family well does a great deal for the common weal and, although he holds no rank or title, is greatly deserving of admiration and respect.

In this way, the unfortunate situation in which parents who need tutors now find themselves could be changed in a short space of time. Young students would have an opportunity to be trained for the calling of tutor through social intercourse and, having been thus educated, would not hesitate to embrace an occupation which would promise them an honorable estate and adequate emoluments. In this way our nation would in a brief time have excellent tutors of its own, who, if they did not displace all foreign tutors, would at least force out the bad ones and send them back to their true calling.

We shall end at this point our section on the main obstacles in the way of upbringing, and with it the general preliminary considerations on our subject. Unless we are mistaken, by setting out these necessary preliminary considerations we have made it possible for the reader to apply with understanding and assurance the specific rules of upbringing which we will now enunciate under the three main headings thereof. Too, if our compatriots' desire to give their children the best possible upbringing is commensurate with our eagerness to help them do so, we venture to hope that what we have said already and what we still have to say will not be a sermon delivered in the desert but a word of benediction at the appropriate time.[10]

---

[10] Following this introduction, Novikov gives a detailed discussion and summary of the contents of each of the three aspects of upbringing. These sections—quite long and wordy —have been omitted, as they are merely a restatement of the opinions commonly held on these matters in the eighteenth century.—Editor.

5.
Denis Ivanovich Fonvizin

1745-1792

In his two famous plays *The Hobble-dehoy* (*Nedorosl'*) and *Brigadier* (*Brigadir*) Denis Ivanovich Fonvizin castigated the manners and values of Russia's Westernizing nobility in the reign of Catherine II, and through his criticism he struck at the basic political and social shortcomings of his time.

Fonvizin was close to Count Nikita I. Panin (1718–83), who had unsuccessfully tried to reform the administrative structure of the Empire. They shared the opinion that, above all, Russia needed institutional safeguards against the arbitrary actions of its rulers and the deleterious influence of their favorites. The main task, they felt, was to protect the persons and property of the members of the educated classes of Russia; the Russian who had assimilated the cultural and moral values of Western Europe had the right to be treated with respect.

For Fonvizin, as for many enlightened thinkers of the West, the solution lay not so much in reforming institutions (which were only as good as the men who staffed them) as in developing virtuous attitudes in all men, particularly those entrusted with the government of others. Hence his sharing of the Enlightenment interest in Chinese moral philosophy and his reliance on the moral leadership of the monarch. Laws were the expression of this leadership and the guideposts for the citizen's moral progress.

Ta Hsüeh

Or That Great Learning Which Comprises
Higher Chinese Philosophy

A grandson of Confucius and a certain disciple of this famous Chinese philosopher wrote, in conformity with his teachings, two short works, one of which, the one introduced here, is called Ta Hsüeh [*The Great Learning*], *and the other* Chung Yung [*The True Mean*]. *China, under the influence either of prejudice or of the truth which shines in these exquisite writings, has applied itself to their study for more than twenty centuries now and has preserved this ancient heritage with great piety. The frequent changes which have ensued since the days of those illustrious men—changes in taste, in the people's sophistication, and in government itself—have still not destroyed the general high esteem in which they are held; neither have they taken away the excellence of their style nor obliterated the beauty of their beneficial teachings. And even if they have suffered a certain change, their value has only been increased thereby, inasmuch as philosophers and all citizens of good sense consider them the most magnificent monuments of ancient eloquence and love of wisdom. We hope later to contribute a translation of the* Chung Yung.

True wisdom consists in enlightening one's reason and purifying one's heart, in loving men and instilling love of virtue in them, in overcoming all obstacles which prevent one from achieving union with higher goodness, and in cleaving to that alone.

Blessed the man who knows the goal toward which he directs his course! The road which he must follow presents itself to his eyes in precisely delineated form; as soon as he treads upon it, hesitations and doubts fly away, peace and quiet cause flowers to grow beneath his footsteps, truth illumines him with its brilliant beams, all virtues enter his soul in unison, and with

Translated by Ronald Hingley from Denis Ivanovich Fonvizin, "Ta Gio, ili velikaia nauka, zakliuchaiushchaia v sebe vysokuiu kitaiskuiu filosofiiu," in *Sobranie sochinenii*, Vol. II (Moscow, 1959), pp. 231–42. Fonvizin's translation of the famous Chinese classic *Ta Hsüeh* was made, with minor omissions, from the French version of Abbé Pierre Marial Cibot (1727–80). It first appeared unsigned in the *Sankt-Peterburgskii Vestnik* for May 1779 and was obviously a vehicle for expressing Fonvizin's own ideas about rulership. His explanatory notes, which only elaborate points made in the text, have been omitted.

those virtues come joy and the pleasures of unalloyed bliss. But woe to him who takes the branches for the root and the foliage for the fruit, confusing the immaterial with the essential and not distinguishing ends from means. To understand the proper ordering of one's duties and to assess their importance is the beginning of wisdom.

O wisdom, divine wisdom! Such were thy teachings to remote antiquity. A monarch who wished innocence and truth to hold sway in his dominions made the proper administration of his provinces his first concern. He would begin by setting his own house to rights, his first care being to order his own conduct; so as to order his own conduct, he strove chiefly to correct his inclinations; he sought above all firmness in his undertakings, endeavoring principally to define his own thoughts; in order to define his thoughts, he extended his deliberations even to the first cause and final end of all creatures, and formed thereof a clear conception.

And in very truth, a clear conception of the beginning and the end of all creatures did give precision to his thoughts; precise thoughts confirmed his undertakings; the strengthening of his undertakings helped him to correct his inclinations; having ordered his own conduct, he found it easy to institute good order in his house; the order which held sway in his house assisted him in the good administration of his provinces. And finally, ruling serenely over his provinces, he became an example to the whole state and increased virtue therein.

In this respect there is no difference between a sovereign and the most humble of his subjects; virtue is the root of all good; its pursuit is the most vital and important task in the whole of life. If a man has no care for virtue, the corruption of his heart will soon communicate itself to his conduct, and he can then build nothing but ruins. To turn the essential into the immaterial and the immaterial into the essential is to unseat all reason.

1. Wen Wang, says *Shu Ching* [Classic of History],[1] "freed his spirit from errors and vices. Ching Tang [2] meditated day and night, and in all matters observed the enlightened law of Tien [Heaven]. Tao carried the pursuit of virtue to the highest point of perfection."

The example of these great sovereigns shows us in an instant how much we owe to dignity of spirit and whence we may draw the rays of its wisdom and glory.

2. On the bowl of Ching Tang could be read: "May thy main care be to purify thy virtue each day; become more perfect every day, and be each day a new man."

It is said in the book *Shu Ching:* "Try to correct and reform the manners of the people." We read in *Shih Ching* [Classic of Poetry]: [3] "Although the Chou were the most ancient sovereigns of this Empire, they owed the good will of Tien, which called them to the throne, solely to the zealous endeavors of Wen Wang to restore virtue in his provinces." Follow these great examples and constantly increase your endeavors to emulate them.

[1] A book of ten chapters excerpted by Confucius from historical chronicles.—Editor.

[2] Li Yüan (T'ai Tsu), founder and ruler (A.D. 618–26) of the Tang dynasty.—Editor.

[3] A collection of about three hundred poems collected and revised by Confucius.—Editor.

3. It is written in *Shih Ching:* "The provinces governed by the Emperor himself extend for a thousand li; each family inhabits and tills the land which has been allotted to it." And one may also read here: "Mien Man perches on the trees which stand on the hill." "Alas!" preached Confucius. "The little bird knows where it must make its nest. Then why does man not know this? Can it really be that the rays of that reason which enlighten him show him less than the bird learns from its natural instinct?"

We read in *Shih Ching:* "O Wen Wang, how pure and surpassingly beautiful was thy virtue! Oh, how wondrous and brilliant was it! It came close to holiness." This means that as a lord he strove to secure his people's well-being, as a subject to discharge his duties to his sovereign, as a son to honor his illustrious parents, as a father to show love for his children, and, finally, as an ally to carry out all his obligations faithfully.

We read in *Shih Ching:* "As a bamboo growing on the banks of the Ki, constantly crowned with new foliage, spreads its branches abroad and extends in all directions greenery which delights the eyes, just so does the benign sovereign Wen Wang present himself to our gaze. His soul is like gleaming ivory adorned with carvings, like a precious stone which has been fashioned and cut; his perfection is his own achievement. Oh, what loftiness in his thoughts! What nobility in his feelings! What charm of manner! What dignity in his entire person! His fame shall be deathless, as are his virtues." "Like gleaming ivory adorned with carvings"—these words of the bard signify the ardor of this great sovereign in correcting his ideas and purifying his thoughts; the words "like a precious stone which has been fashioned and cut" denote his striving to put right his deficiencies and perfect his virtues; the exclamations "Oh, what loftiness in his thoughts! What nobility in his feelings!" show us that the happy success of his endeavors and strivings was the consequence of his unceasing watchfulness over himself; the two following exclamations, "What charm of manner! What dignity in his entire person!" instruct us that the beauty of his soul revealed itself in his appearance and instilled love of virtue, proclaiming in his eyes its tender charms and majesty. The fine conclusion, "His fame shall be deathless, as are his virtues," tells us most expressively that, as long as men preserve the concepts of righteousness and truth, so long will they hold dear the memory of a sovereign who attained the summit of wisdom and virtue.

Shih Ching also says: "O Wen Wang! O Wu Wang! Your blessed reigns can only be reached by thought that goes back through many generations of men. But who does not know the marvels you performed, and who is not filled with memories of you?" In their wisdom the wisdom of their successors was strongly founded and by it is guided; their benefactions implanted great goodness in our sovereigns and constantly arouse noble feelings in them.

The people themselves enjoy the comforts and pleasures, the amenities and abundance produced by their farsightedness; wherefore also their memory, this memory so dear to all hearts, shall be carried on from age to age and never be expunged from the human heart.

4. "Without doubt," preached Confucius, "I can give litigants a hearing

and pronounce judgment, but I find little glory for myself in this. The true and worthy glory of a sage consists in drying up the source of litigation and in surrounding the throne of justice with virtues so great that it has no need either of the scales or of the sword." But how is one to fetter, or at least to restrain, those passions which fan into flames the ashes of chicanery? How is one to secure victory for that wisdom which would drive a bad conscience to despair, strike fear into self-interest, and put malice to flight? This is what I call exterminating the root.

5. Think little of yourselves. Abhor evil to the extent that it is hateful and ugly. Love good to the extent that it is lovable and fine, that is, with all your soul, and sweet calm will bring about a pleasurable condition of contentment with yourself. The wise man always has his eyes open to his conscience and everywhere obeys its voice. The foolish man degrades himself with evil deeds when there are not witnesses to them, and shamelessly gives himself up to the most disgraceful dissipations. If he beholds a wise man coming toward him, he is already filled with fear, and, hurrying to conceal his loathsomeness, clothes himself in the false guise of innocence. Vain cunning! Even the least penetrating of eyes pierce the ultimate secrets of a hypocritical heart. There is no secret in the soul which conduct does not reveal. For which reason the wise man seeks this alone—to take precautions against his own conscience. "Oh, how necessary it is," preaches Confucius, "to protect oneself against that which the blind see and the deaf hear!"

The rich man adorns and embellishes his dwelling; everything in it signifies abundance. So it is with virtue. The body it inhabits receives from it the imprint of majesty and serenity, proclaiming to the eyes that virtue opens the whole soul and feeds it on draughts of delight and tranquillity; so necessary is it for a wise man to dwell secure in his good undertakings.

6. By the righteousness of the heart alone are vices corrected and virtues acquired. But this righteousness, so precious and so essential, cannot stand against the powerful buffeting of passions. A stormy flash of wrath casts it down, the cold shiver of fear shatters it, the sudden trembling of timidity shakes it, and pale grief plunges it into tears as into waves. How can the heart save its righteousness from a storm in which it is not itself saved from shipwreck? Scarcely has the storm started when the heart begins to seem an exile from itself. Then a man looks and does not see, listens and does not understand. The sweetest food loses its flavor and pleasantness. Oh, the madness of passions! How fierce their grip! But the madness is advantageous and the grip beneficial, for they show that without righteousness of heart it is impossible to be assured even of outward show of virtue.

7. Vain is the hope of instituting good order in the home if one does not first endeavor to order one's own conduct. Is it possible indeed to require from others that which one cannot secure from oneself? How can one even ask this of them? Then does a man follow the slippery slope of his own weaknesses. Instead of mollifying men's hearts with tenderness, arousing self-respect in them, restraining them by fear, winning them over by kindness, and attracting them by marks of esteem, he forgets himself and brings shame on himself, becomes the object of contempt, and draws near to dan-

ger; he goes too far and then retreats, becomes blind and rash, is diminished and humiliated; nor can it be otherwise—the heart pulls in the direction toward which it is itself proceeding. Oh, how few men there are who see the weaknesses of those they love and the good qualities of those they hate! "A father," as the saying has it, "knows neither the faults of his son nor the good qualities of his fields." Therefore above all things let virtue be enthroned in your soul if you wish it to reign in your house.

8. O you emperors and monarchs, rulers of the world, who have been set above our heads by the Most High, what can the people expect from your wisdom if it does not open your eyes to your illustrious houses so that you may govern them with your solicitude. A great monarch serves as an example for his entire state from inside his own palaces. The virtues which he has restored to them, and which flourish around him, attract the eyes of all, proclaiming far and wide the presence of dutifulness and unsullied ways. And indeed he cannot but be loved and honored, his dignitaries cannot fail to receive respect and obedience, nor can the wretched fail to obtain help and relief, when filial respect, fraternal love, and charity impart more distinction to his illustrious house than the purple which adorns it. In the words of the song: "The mother presses her baby to her breast, she holds it in her embrace and kisses it many times; it still cannot speak, but she guesses its very wishes by the secret feeling of love." Before she was yet a mother, nature had already instilled this feeling in her heart. The birth of a baby only caused it to manifest itself.

Even more effectively does the example of the imperial family open the way for love of virtue and for that inclination toward goodness with which all men are born on this earth. If friendliness and kindness unite all hearts in the monarch's household, imitation will increase and multiply these qualities and spread them abroad forever in all families. But if injustice and wickedness enter therein, then all is lost; then will this spark cause a conflagration and bring about general ruin. The force of this reasoning is that a single word may destroy everything, but a single man may save everything. The beneficence of Yao and Shun passed from their hearts into the hearts of all their subjects; by contrast Chieh and Chou [4] imparted to their subjects their own ferocity and degraded them with their own vices. In vain does a sovereign forbid that which he permits himself, for then no one will obey him. It is proper that he should be entirely free from those vices which he is seeking to exterminate, and that the virtues which he is encouraging should be constantly a part of him; then let him expect everything from his subjects and set all his hopes in them. Never did a people set itself against the example of its emperor or become unworthy of it.

We read in *Shin Ching:* "In springtime the peach tree, crowned with blossom and foliage, delights all eyes with the pleasant glow of its beauty; such is a young bride as she enters the halls of her bridegroom; the meekness and pleasantness which accompany her steps enter all hearts." The virtues of a sovereign and of his illustrious household find the hearts of their subjects even better disposed; they fly to meet them and receive them.

[4] In a note Fonvizin likens Chieh and Chou to Nero and Caligula.—Editor.

In the words of the song: "Oh, how he honors his elders! How he loves those that are younger!" A sovereign who is a good brother eloquently teaches his subjects to be the same, and he will attain the very purpose of government if he is guided solely by the feelings of his heart and the tranquillity of his family.

9. If a sovereign honors and respects the advanced years of aged men and the virtue of the wise, if he grants distinction to the superior qualities of statesmen and to the excellence of gifted persons, if his heart aches for the tears of the wretched and for the deprivations of orphans, then will his delighted peoples of their own accord embrace all that is most tender and dear in filial respect, brotherly love, and fond sympathy. His heart will conquer their hearts, becoming their prime mover and lawgiver. If he wishes to travel even further along this path and never go wrong, let him put away from the sovereign that which he finds distressing in his subjects, and avert from his subjects that which they find repellent in their sovereign; let him avoid the fatal paths on which his predecessors lost their way, and let him not walk himself along those paths on which his successors may go astray. Let his right hand not strike those whom his left hand favors, and let his left hand not favor those whom his right hand strikes; let him not require acts which he himself would not agree to perform, and let him constantly put himself in the place of his subjects, that he may see his own place the more clearly.

In the words of the song: "O beloved and most dear sovereign! Father and mother of your people! Do you wish to be worthy of this praise? Cleave to your people and take to heart all their inclinations. Make them your own, and be like a father and mother, loving all which is favorable to their children, and hating all which is unfavorable to them."

In the words of the song: "O mountains of the south! Your proud summits present to the gaze nothing but massive stone cliffs, hanging horribly in the air. O Yin! Thou dost strike greater terror into the eyes of thy despondent people; trembling do they lift them up unto you." Emperors! Fear to resemble this hated overlord, or your throne will fall under the burden of arrogance and its ruins will be your grave.

In the words of the song: "When the Han dynasty ruled over all hearts they regarded Han Ti alone as more exalted than they and made themselves into his precious likeness. O you who have come after him, measure the height of his fall with your eyes, and let it teach you that the higher your calling, the more difficult it is to follow." Such is the unanimous voice of all the ages. The love of subjects gives scepters and crowns. Their hatred wrenches them away and shatters them. Wherefore a truly wise sovereign strives above all to be strong and to increase in virtue, for he knows that the more virtuous he is, the more favor he enjoys amongst his subjects; and the more favor he enjoys amongst his subjects, the more his provinces will grow, and together with these provinces possessions and riches in abundance. Virtue is the unshakable foundation of the throne and the inexhaustible source of power; riches and abundance are only its adornment. If a sovereign is deceived in this matter and takes the immaterial for the essential, then will his subjects, corrupted by his example, cast off the burden of the laws and pollute with plundering and robbery all those channels which his greed will tap to divert to himself the sources of wealth. The more gold and silver flow toward an avaricious sovereign, the more do hearts grow cold and distant; the more wisely a sovereign expends his treasures, the more do hearts go out to him and become filled by him. This is a law of all ages. Curses, which defile the lips as they issue from them, rend the ears into which they enter. When a sovereign's avariciousness corrupts the honesty of his subjects, then does their dishonesty disperse the treasures amassed by his injustice.

It is written, in *Shu Ching:* "The supreme governor of our fates does not arrive at the same decision forever." This means that with the same hand whereby he sets on the throne sovereigns able to preserve its glory by their virtue and justify its destiny—with that same hand he overthrows others who disgrace the throne with their vices and compel his justice to overthrow them. "You ask," a certain great minister said to some envoys, "what is the most precious and honorable thing in the state of Ch'u? Our customs answer you—it is virtue."

No less excellent is the answer of the wise Ch'ü Yüan. By law his nephew was to be called to the throne on the death of his father, the former ruler. The sovereign from whom this heir sought protection promised to clear the way to the throne for him. Everyone assured him that he might lose all by delaying. "Shed your tears," said Ch'ü Yüan to his nephew, "and lament the death of your father without giving thought to anything else. Though you are a wandering exile, the great duty of filial love should be more precious to you than the crown."

"Alas!" cried Wu King, grieved by the memory of a war which had been unadvisedly undertaken and was proceeding unsuccessfully. "I do not seek loftiness of intellect in a minister in whom I might put my trust, but I seek true reason, a righteous heart, and a great and noble spirit such as would cause him to honor and respect worth without feeling envy, to bring on and patronize talent without petty prejudices, to honor and encourage virtue with that tender kindness and zealous ardor which we manifest in everything which concerns us directly. With such a minister how tranquil I should be about the future fate of my house and of my peoples! But if my choice should fall on an arrogant man, one who would fear, remove, hide from me, or hem in all those whose ability, knowledge, zeal, obedience, and honor might vex his pride and prick his envy—then, however elevated his intellect and talents, what would become of my descendants and peoples? Will not my whole country be thrown into utter ruin?" Such ministers are born to destroy and ruin states. Only a wise sovereign is able to reject their services, banish them from his person, rid his country of their presence, and confine amongst barbarians those in whom barbarian vices dwell. In this sense Confucius preaches: "The beneficence of a sovereign shines forth as much in his severities as in the gentle manifestations of his kindness." If a monarch has not the confidence of spirit to summon merit from afar to receive honors, if he puts from him the path of merit and lets thorns grow on it, if he puts his trust in men whose malice is known to him or does not remove his entire confidence from them immediately, then it is himself whom he strikes down, opening the door to the greatest calamities. To make a favorite of a person whom all hate, or to despise a man honored by all, signifies an insolent betrayal of all those concepts of justice which nature has set in men's hearts; it is to provoke murmurings and to enter that cloud which conceals an arrow ready to strike. This is the message of all the ages, this is what all men's consciences repeat: Loyalty, righteousness, and honor are the true buttresses of the throne; it is cast down by pride, cunning, and malice.

Why stray along the winding, gloomy paths of false policy when wisdom reveals a way so clear, and one which leads so directly to the achievement of the desired end? Is it your desire that blessed prosperity should animate the entire body of the state, bringing the warmth of health and a feeling of gaiety into all its members? Then increase the number of useful citizens whose diligent enterprises may create and produce wealth; decrease the number of lazy inhabitants, whose dangerous parasitism swells expenditure and waste; let unceasing labors increase the state's benefits, and let the wisdom of merit spread them wide. A sovereign's true glory consists in making rich, not in being rich himself; he desires treasures only in order to distribute them. But the more beneficent he is, the more does he find in his subjects full generosity and tenderness of feeling. Their zeal conquers all obstacles to the execution of his designs, and they guard their own property less than a treasure which has been entrusted to them.

So we conclude our discourse. All sources of wealth flow for the state, but there are some on which the sovereign must never draw. Propriety itself forbids this to his dignitaries as well. One of the ancients said: "He who feeds horses for his chariots does not bring an offering of game. He who offers cold fare at a banquet does not feed the poultry himself; and he who bears command in war over a hundred chariots would be ashamed to grow rich by impudent levies, and would rather see himself robbed than commit base extortion." Justice is the richest and most inexhaustible treasure of a state. The sovereign must ceaselessly increase this priceless treasure; in it alone will he be rich. The magnificence of a state is a fruit of the sovereign's wisdom and virtue; anyone who presumes to think that it is the effect of his riches has a base soul and lacks cordial feelings. Unhappy the sovereign who hearkens to a minister conversing with him in this wise, and who gives his power into such a minister's hands. All the wise men of his state together will not be able to fill in the pit which he is digging beneath his feet, or to prevent his falling into it. The income obtained by saving does not belong to the state, which can be rich only in justice and virtue.

A Discourse on Permanent Laws of State

Supreme power is entrusted to a sovereign solely for the benefit of his subjects. Tyrants know this truth, but good sovereigns feel it. A monarch enlightened by the lucidity of this truth and endowed with great qualities of soul, being invested with unlimited power and striving (insofar as a mortal can) for perfection, will himself straightway feel that the power achieves real majesty only when it deprives itself of the capacity for doing evil. And indeed all the brilliance of the throne is but an empty gleam if virtue does not sit thereon at the sovereign's side; yet if one imagines him as a person of such superior intelligence and feeling that he would never separate himself from the common weal but would subordinate all his intentions and acts to this principle, who can suppose his unlimited power to be restricted by such subordination? Rather has it the same nature as the power of the All-Highest. The reason why God is almighty is that He cannot do anything except good; and that this inability might be an eternal token of His perfection, He instituted principles of everlasting truth, unalterable by Himself, whereby He governs the universe, and which He Himself cannot transgress without ceasing to be God. In the same way, a sovereign, like unto God and the recipient on earth of His almighty power, cannot signify his might and worth except by instituting in his state unalterable rules, based on the common weal, which he himself could not infringe without ceasing to be a worthy sovereign.

Without these rules, or, to put it more exactly, without permanent state laws, neither the condition of the state nor that of the sovereign is stable. There is no buttress to strengthen their common powers. No ordinances, however highly beneficial in intention, have any basis whatever. Who can defend their durability? Who can guarantee that a successor will not choose to destroy in a single hour everything which was established during all previous reigns? Who can guarantee that the lawgiver himself, persistently surrounded by persons who strive to conceal the truth from him, will not destroy today what he created yesterday? Where one man's whim is the supreme law, there no firm common bond can even exist; there is a state but no homeland, there are subjects but no citizens, there is no body politic with members united by the tie of mutual rights and duties. Partiality

Translated by Ronald Hingley from Denis Ivanovich Fonvizin, "Rassuzhdenie o nepremennykh gosudarstvennykh zakonakh," in *Sobranie sochinenii*, Vol. II (Moscow, 1959), pp. 254–67. The essay was written in the 1780's but was not published in Fonvizin's lifetime.

becomes the sole guiding principle of every enactment, for it is not the sovereign's temper which accommodates itself to the laws but the laws which accommodate themselves to his temper. And what confidence or respect can laws enjoy if they lack the essential feature—conformity with the common weal? Who can manage his affairs in a place where, without any just cause, an act permitted today qualifies as a crime tomorrow? There each man, being subject to the caprices and injustice of those more powerful than himself, considers himself under no obligation to observe, when dealing with others, standards which others do not observe in dealing with him.

Under these circumstances impudent ignorance requires proofs of natural laws, of palpable truths, and is unwilling to obey them unless ordered to do so, while, on the other hand, the senseless command of a powerful person is carried out unquestioningly with servile sycophancy. Then anyone who can do so issues commands, but no one governs anything, inasmuch as governing belongs to laws which suffer nothing above themselves. Then are subjects enslaved to the sovereign, while the sovereign is usually enslaved to an unworthy *favorite*. I have called him "unworthy" because the term "favorite" is never applied to a man of merit who has given true service to his country but usually to a person who has attained high degree by his success in the cunning art of pleasing the sovereign. In a condition so corrupt, the abuse of absolute power is carried to unbelievable lengths, and there is no longer any distinction between what is the state's and what the sovereign's, nor between what is the sovereign's and what his favorite's. Everything hangs on the latter's whim. Each man's property and safety are undermined. Spirits grow despondent, hearts are depraved, and the manner of thinking becomes base and contemptible. The favorite's vices not only gain currency but are almost the sole means of obtaining preference. If he loves drunkenness, all highly placed persons become infected with this filthy vice. If his spirit is a prey to violence and bad education has taught him a base mode of conduct, then during the period of his ascendancy noble conduct is quite sufficient to block the path to good fortune; but if Providence in violent anger with the human race permits the sovereign's soul to be captured by a monster who stakes all his ambition on making the state a helpless victim of his acts of violence and the sport of his caprices; if all his twisted impulses urge him to seek supremacy solely through wealth, titles, and the power to injure; if his glance, his bearing, and his speech betoken merely "Worship me, for I can destroy you"; if his unlimited power over the sovereign's soul is accompanied by numberless vices in his soul; if he is proud, insolent, cunning, greedy for wealth; if he is a voluptuary, shameless, and lazy—then the moral blight becomes general, all these vices spread abroad and infect the court, the city, and finally the country. All youth becomes haughty and adopts a tone of mutinous contempt for everything worthy of respect. All the bonds of the established order are broken, and—ultimate outrage—neither a life spent in serving the country nor a rank obtained by true service can protect a respected man from the impudence and insolence of worthless females who are little more than children and have been exalted by mere chance. Guile and cunning are accepted as the main principle of conduct. No one goes the way natural to him. No one thinks of being deserving, but all seek to gain advantage by serving. At a period so favorable to unworthy persons, what reward can true services expect, or, to put it more strongly, is there any way for a thinking citizen of noble ambition to remain in service? What rank, what mark of honor, what state position has not been sullied by the greedy touch of favoritism? When a man has devoted his life to military service, is it pleasant for him to earn command of a regiment when yesterday's corporal, a person completely unknown, for some unknown reason today becomes a regimental commander and even takes precedence over an officer who is seasoned in service and is covered with scars? Is it gratifying to be a judge when one is not permitted to be just? Now avid greed completes the general corruption. Men's thoughts are occupied solely by devising means of enrichment. He who can do so plunders, while he who cannot steals; and when a sovereign builds his edifices on sand without immutable laws of state, and, constantly issuing particular regulations, thinks to abolish tax-farming operations harmful to the state, then he does not know that in his state immunity from all punishments for crime has long ago been farmed out, and that in the minds of shameless plunderers it has become a pure matter of calculation to work out how much profit a crime will bring and how much a decree of pardon will cost. But when justice has been turned into a mart, when one may fear to lose one's own property unfairly and hope to take another's unjustly, then everyone hastens to enjoy unreservedly that which he has in his possession, pandering to his own corrupted passions. And what can hold back the onrush of vice when the idol of the sovereign himself has raised the banner of lawlessness and dishonor in the very imperial palaces before the eyes of the whole world; when, shamelessly indulging his lusts, he openly mocks the holy bonds of kinship, the principles of honor, and the duty of humanity, daring to trample on laws human and divine before the face of the lawgiver? I do not enter into the details of the disastrous condition of those affairs which he has grabbed and placed under his own special authority; but in general we see that the love of power which has infected him turns all heads, while the spirit of idleness, which has implanted in him all the hell of boredom and impatience, is spread far abroad, and the habit of sloth takes root all the more powerfully because zeal for labor and service has almost been proclaimed ludicrous idiocy.

After everything stated by me and confirmed by living example, do we not see clearly that the most absolute power does not rest with that sovereign who expects to consolidate his autocracy through a minimum of state laws? Enslaved to one or several of his own servants, wherein is he an autocrat? Surely not in being held in thrall by unworthy persons? Like a transparent body whose inner workings can be plainly seen, he vainly writes new laws, proclaims the prosperity of the people, and lauds the wisdom of his rule. His new laws will be nothing more than new rituals which confuse the old laws, the people will still be oppressed, the nobility humiliated, and, in spite of his own detestation of tyranny, his rule will be tyrannical. The nation suffers no less because the sovereign has not himself taken to tormenting it but has given it up to be plundered by monsters with whom he is infatuated. Such a position cannot even subsist for long. As hearts become extremely embittered, all private interests, fragmented by the nature of despotic rule, gradually unite to one end. Suddenly all strive to break the bonds of intolerable slavery. And what is the state then? A colossus that has been held up by chains. The chains burst, the colossus falls and automatically disintegrates. Despotism, which is usually born of anarchy, very rarely fails to return to anarchy.

To avert such ruin a sovereign must know fully and exactly all the rights of his majesty, so that he may, first, preserve the respect of his subjects for them and, second, not himself transgress the bounds set to his rights by the most autocratic of all powers on earth—the power of sound reason. A sovereign attains the first of these goals by righteousness, the second by meekness.

Righteousness and meekness are rays of divine light, proclaiming to men that the power which rules them has been established by God, and that it deserves their reverent obedience; consequently every power which is not marked by the divine qualities of righteousness and meekness, but which gives rise to injuries, acts of violence, and tyranny, is a power not from God but from men, whom the miseries of their times have caused to yield to force and lower their human dignity. If a nation in such a disastrous situation finds the means to break its fetters by the same right as that by which they were imposed, it acts very intelligently if it does break its fetters. The issue is clear. Either the nation is now within its rights in restoring its own freedom, or no one had the right to take away its freedom. Who does not know that all human societies are based on voluntary mutual obligations which are dissolved as soon as men cease to observe them? The obligations between a sovereign and his subjects are equally voluntary, for there has never yet been a nation on this earth which has compelled anyone to become its sovereign by force; and if the nation can exist without a ruler but the ruler cannot exist without a nation, it is obvious that the original power rested with the nation and that, when the ruler was established, the question was not what he would grant to the nation but with what power the nation was investing him. And is it possible that a nation should itself voluntarily enact a law permitting the ruler to dispense injustice without being called to account?

Is it not a hundred times better for a nation to have no laws at all than to have one which gives the sovereign the right to commit all kinds of outrage? This great truth should be ever present in his mind, for the very reason that he has been made ruler in the interests of the state and that his own welfare must be inseparable from the happiness of his subjects.

When one considers the relations between a ruler and his subjects, the first question which presents itself is: What is a ruler? He is the very soul of that society over which he rules. Weak is the soul which cannot control the capricious urges of the body. Unhappy is the body ruled by a soul devoid of reason, which gives either its full trust or no trust at all to the feelings which are its true ministers. Relying on them, it carelessly takes a molehill for a mountain, a planet for a mere speck. But if it despises the service of the feelings and becomes so obsessed with its own importance that it decides to see with its eyes closed and hear with its ears blocked, what true decision is then to be expected from it, and to what misfortunes does it not bring itself?

The ruler, who is the soul of the body politic, shares a similar fate. If he opens his ears to all kinds of suggestions, while averting them from all kinds of ideas, truth no longer enlightens him; but if he himself does not acknowledge truth's supreme authority over him, then all his relations with the state are corrupted at their source. Distinctions arise between his own welfare and that of the country; straightway hatred of him becomes implanted; soon he himself begins to fear those who hate him and to hate those whom he fears. In a word, all his power becomes illegitimate, for that power cannot be legitimate which sets itself above all laws of natural justice.

An enlightened intellect brings a ruler to this conclusion, free from all doubts and in all its clarity, but an enlightened ruler is nevertheless a man. He is born as a man, dies as a man, and during his life sins as a man, for which reason it is necessary to consider what the nature of human enlightenment is. Between man's primitive condition in natural savagery and true enlightenment the distance is as great as from an unplumbed abyss to the top of the highest mountain. A man requires a whole life's span to ascend this mountain, but if, having climbed it, he permits himself to overstep the line which divides the mountain from the abyss, then nothing can check his fall as he plunges back into his original ignorance. The enlightened ruler stands on the very brink of this terrible abyss. The guards who protect him from falling are righteousness and meekness. The moment he wrenches himself out of their arms, his ruin is accomplished, the light in the eyes of his soul grows dim, and, flying headlong into the abyss, he shrieks dementedly: "Everything is mine. I am all. All is nothing."

An enlightened monarch who cleaves to righteousness and meekness will never be weakened in his true majesty, for it is a quality of righteousness that it cannot be shaken either by prejudices, friendship, inclinations, or pity itself. Mighty and weak, great and small, rich and poor, all stand on the same level—the good ruler is good to all, and all his favors are related not to private advantages but to the common weal. Pity is aroused in his soul not by the plaintive countenance of a self-seeker who is trying to deceive him but by the real poverty of unfortunates whom now he does not see and whose complaints are often not allowed to reach him. Whenever he performs an act of grace toward some dignitary, he keeps his whole people in view. He knows that only service to the state is rewarded out of state resources, that the state is not obliged to pay for the gratification of his private passions, and that every tax not exacted in the interests of the state is robbery both in substance and in form. He knows that the nation, sacrificing part of its natural freedom, has entrusted its welfare to his care, justice, and worthiness, that he is responsible for the conduct of those to whom he entrusts the administration, and that, consequently, their crimes, if tolerated by him, become his crimes. In vain might a ruler think to justify himself by the fact that he himself is guiltless toward his country and that he is thereby fulfilling his entire duty to it. No, his innocence is the payment of a debt which he owes to himself, but he still remains the debtor of the state. He is obliged to answer to it not only for the evil which he has done but also for the good which he has left undone. Every act of connivance is his fault, every cruelty is his fault; for he must know that indulgence toward vice is the encouragement of villainy and that, on the other hand, the severest justice meted out to human weaknesses is the greatest wrong to humanity. Unhappily for his subjects, a ruler sometimes goes through a phase when he can think of nothing except the fact that he is a ruler, while at other times he can think of nothing except that he is a man. In the first case he usually resembles an evil man in his actions, while in the second case he is inevitably a bad ruler. In order to avoid these two extremes the ruler must not forget for a single instant either that he is a man or that he is a ruler. Then is he worthy of the name "all-wise." Then does he find a place for justice and mercy in all his deeds. Nothing transgresses its proper bounds. He who disturbs the general peace by his conduct is handed over to the full severity of the laws. He who dishonors himself by his conduct is punished by the ruler's scorn. He who does not show zeal for his office loses his post. In a word, a righteous ruler continually corrects vices, turning on them a stern brow, and strengthens virtue by calling it to high honors.

Righteousness makes a ruler respected, but meekness, this virtue so dear to humanity, makes him beloved. It reminds him unceasingly that he is a man and rules over men. It keeps out of his head the unhappy and foolish thought that God created millions of people for the sake of a hundred men. Between a meek and a proud ruler there is a palpable difference, in that the one obliges people to adore him in their hearts, while the other compels them to worship him outwardly. But he who compels men to worship him clearly feels in his inner heart that he is only a man. By contrast, the meek ruler is never exalted by the humiliation of humanity. His heart is pure, his soul righteous, his mind clear. All these superlative qualities present to him a vivid picture of all his duties. They repeat to him every hour that the ruler is the first servant of the state; that his privileges have been extended by the nation only so that he should be able to do more good than anyone else; that in virtue of the public power entrusted to him he can grant honors and privileges to private persons but nothing to the nation itself, since it is the nation which gave him everything he himself possesses; that in the interest of his own welfare he should shun the power to do evil; and that, consequently, to wish for despotic power implies a desire to be in a position to wield such pernicious power. Can the inability to do evil be a source of distress to a ruler? If it is, surely this can only be because it is always a source of distress to an evil man to be deprived of the opportunity to do evil. The right of the despot is the right of the strong—but this is the same right that a thug arrogates to himself. And who cannot see that the saying "Might makes right" (*Pravo sil'nogo*) is intended in irony? In sane reasoning this combination of words is never encountered. Might compels, but right obliges. What, then, is that right which is obeyed not from duty but from necessity, and which is lost to might at that very moment when greater might dislodges it from its position? Let us go into the nature of this alleged right in yet greater detail. If I am not strong enough to resist someone, does it follow that I am morally obliged to recognize his will as the principle of my conduct? True right is that which is recognized as good by reason and which consequently gives rise to a certain feeling within us that obliges us to submit voluntarily. Otherwise submission is not a matter of duty, but of compulsion. And where there is no duty there is no right. God Himself, in His capacity as an Almighty Being alone, does not have the slightest right to our obedience. Let us imagine an all-powerful being capable not only of compelling us to do anything but also of destroying us entirely, and let us imagine that this being should decide to make us unhappy, or at least not to show any concern whatever for our welfare. Would we feel in our hearts the duty of obedience to this higher will which tended toward our ruin or neglected us? We should perforce yield to its overwhelming might, and the relationship between God and us would be a purely physical one. God's right to our reverent obedience rests solely in His quality of supreme goodness. Reason, which recognizes the use of His supreme power as good, counsels us to come to terms with His will, inducing hearts and souls to obey Him. Can a supremely good being take pleasure in obedience extorted solely by fear? And is such odious obedience becoming to a creature endowed with reason? No, it is unworthy of a reasonable master and of reasonable servants. Might and right are completely different both in their nature and in their *modus operandi*. Right requires merits, talents, and virtues. Might needs prisons, fetters, and axes. It is quite superfluous to enter into discussions about different forms of government and to investigate where a ruler is more autocratic and where he is more restricted. A tyrant is a tyrant wherever he may be, and the right of a people to maintain its being is eternally and universally unshakable.

The true felicity of ruler and subjects reaches perfection when all enjoy that tranquillity of spirit which comes from an inner assurance of security. This is the real *political freedom* of a nation. Then everyone is free to do that which is permitted, and no one compels anyone to do that which is not to be done. So that a nation may possess this freedom, it behooves government to be so instituted that the citizen cannot fear abuse of power, that no one may become the sport of violence and caprice, that no one through the mere whim of power may suddenly be raised from the lowest degree to the highest nor cast down from the highest to the lowest, that an account should be given to all men whenever an individual is deprived of property, honor, or life, and that, consequently, everyone should be able to enjoy his property and the privileges of his status without hindrance.

Since, then, a free man is one who does not depend on any person's whim (and, by contract a despot's slave is he who has no other right to his possessions than that afforded by imperial grace and favor), this interpretation lays bare the indissoluble link between political freedom and the rights of *property*. The rights of property include the right to make use of property, but without freedom to use one's property, what does this right mean?

In the same way freedom cannot exist without rights, for in such a case it would have no point. Thus it is clear that it is quite impossible to infringe upon freedom without destroying the rights of property, just as it is impossible to destroy the rights of property without infringing upon freedom.

In investigating what constitutes the supreme welfare of states and peoples, and what forms the true aim of all legislative systems, we shall inevitably find two crucial points, to wit, those which have just been the subject of discourse: *freedom* and *property*. Both these privileges, and also the form in which public power is to be exercised, must be implemented in a manner consonant with the physical situation of the state and the moral temper of the nation. The sacred laws which govern their implementation are what we understand by the term "fundamental laws." Their clarity must be such that not even the slightest misunderstanding should ever occur and that monarch and subjects should in equal measure derive from them a knowledge of their duties and rights. It is precisely on these laws that their common safety depends, and the laws must consequently be permanent.

Let us now imagine a state which includes a greater expanse of territory than any state in the known world and which is the least populated in the world in proportion to its size; a state split into more than thirty large regions and consisting, one may say, of only two cities, in one of which people live mostly of necessity, and in the other of which they live mostly from inclination; a state fearsome through its large and bold army, so situated that at times it is liable to be entirely destroyed through the loss of a single battle; a state which attracts the attention of the entire world by its might and glory, and which a leaderless peasant, whose human appearance alone differentiates him from a beast of the field, can bring, so to speak, in a few hours, to the very brink of ultimate ruin and disaster;[1] a state which provides other lands with sovereigns, while its own throne depends on the opening of taverns for a bestial horde of ruffians engaged in safeguarding the monarch's person; a state where all political estates are found but where none of them has any privileges and one differs from another only in its empty appellation; a state governed by daily decrees, often of a mutually contradictory nature, but lacking any stable code of laws; a state where men are the property of other men, where a person in one walk of life has the right to be both plaintiff and judge with respect to a person from another walk of life, and where consequently each man may be forever a tyrant or a victim; a state where the most respected of all estates, which has the duty of defending the fatherland jointly with the sovereign and of corporately representing the nation, guided exclusively by considerations of honor—to wit, the nobility (*dvorianstvo*)—now exists in name alone and as a status which may be sold to any scoundrel who has robbed his native land; [a state] where illustrious rank—that single goal of the noble spirit, that worthy reward for services to the country performed by generation after generation—is eclipsed by patronage which has swallowed up all the

---

[1] The reference is to the peasant rebellion led by Emel'ian Pugachev that swept the Volga region in 1773–74. The entire paragraph is a critical description of the state of Russia under Catherine II.—Editor.

nourishment of true ambition; a state not despotic, for the nation has never surrendered itself to the arbitrary rule of the sovereign and has always had civil and criminal tribunals responsible for defending innocence and punishing crimes; a state not monarchic, since it lacks fundamental laws; [a state] not aristocratic, for its higher administration is a soulless machine controlled by the whim of the ruler; [a state not democratic, for how] can a land have any resemblance to a democracy when the common people, groveling in the darkness of deepest ignorance, silently bear the yoke of cruel slavery?

An enlightened and virtuous monarch, finding his empire and his own rights in a condition of such disharmony and disorganization, begins his great service by immediately safeguarding general security through unalterable laws. In this important matter he must not lose sight of two considerations. The first is that his country requires to be healed immediately of all the evils brought to it by the abuse of absolute rule. The second is that nothing can bring final ruin to the country so swiftly as the sudden and unprepared grant of those privileges which are enjoyed by the peoples of Europe, with their sound institutions. Attached herewith is a separate draft of what might be the first fundamental laws based on this consideration.

In conclusion, it is proper to recognize the truth that the chief science of government entails knowing how to make people capable of living under good government. In this matter no personal decrees of the ruler are of any avail. The ordinance "Be good" does not fall under any heading in the Statute on Public Order.[2] It would be futile to engrave it on signboards and set them up on desks in government institutions; for if it be not engraved on men's hearts, all administrative offices will be badly managed. The establishment of sound customs does not require splendid and solemn rites. It is a quality of true greatness to perform the greatest of deeds in the simplest possible manner. Common sense and the experience of all ages show that it is the ruler's good conduct alone which promotes good conduct in his people. It is he who holds the lever by which to turn men to virtue or vice. All men's eyes are on him, and the aura which surrounds the sovereign illumines him from head to foot before the whole people. His slightest movements are hidden from no one, and such is the happy or unhappy condition of the sovereign that he can conceal neither his virtues nor his vices. He judges the people, and the people judge his justice. And if he relies so much on the corruption of his nation that he thinks to deceive it with spurious virtue, then he is himself grievously mistaken. In order to appear a good ruler it is absolutely necessary to be one; for, however vicious men may be, their minds are never so depraved as their hearts, and we see that those very persons who are least attached to virtue are often the greatest connoisseurs of virtues. To be known is the inescapable destiny of rulers, and the worthy ruler is not afraid of it. His first title is the title of honest man, and to be known is the punishment of the hypocrite and the true reward of the honest man. He, having become known to his entire nation,

[2] PSZ 15 379, April 8, 1782. The General Police Regulations (*ustav blagochiniia*). See note on p. 68 for connotations of this term.—Editor.

at once becomes its exemplar. The respect which he pays to merit and to age is the most formidable possible barrier to all insolence and effrontery. As a good husband, a good father, and a good master of his house, without saying a word the sovereign establishes·internal tranquillity in all homes, arouses love of children, and in supremely autocratic fashion forbids every man to step outside the bounds of his condition of life. Who does not love that sovereign who is a wise man? And what cannot a beloved sovereign make of his people? Let us leave to one side all subtle analyses of political rights and ask ourselves sincerely who of all sovereigns on earth is most truly endowed with absolute power? The soul and heart cry aloud in unison: "He who is most loved."

6.
Nikolai Mikhailovich Karamzin

1766-1826

Few individuals proved to be more influential than Nikolai Mikhailovich
Karamzin in leading Russian feeling
and thought from eighteenth-century
rationalistic cosmopolitanism, by way of
didactic sentimentalism, to the romantic
nationalism of the nineteenth century.
In a sense, he helped Russia's educated
elite to discover the existence and moral
worth of the Russian common people
and to find new reasons for pride in
their country's past. If Lomonosov's
nationalism was manifested primarily
as pride in Peter the Great's leadership
and the new power of his re-created
Russia, Karamzin's was expressed as an
emotional affinity with the cultural and
moral traditions of the Russian nation
both before and after Peter the Great.
In insisting that Russians must become
cultivated individuals, Karamzin was
only doing what dramatists and satirists
had done throughout the eighteenth
century. But he was a pioneer in recognizing that true culture also implies an
upright heart, a genuine feeling for the
good in people. Karamzin's emphasis on
heart and feeling was still didactically
sentimental, but it ushered in the
sophisticated and complex romantic literature and thought of Russia. The same
spirit informed his approach to history.
High-flown descriptions of the moral
traits of the heroes in Russia's past served
to justify the role and glorify the accomplishments of the Russian state. His
greatest claim to remembrance (and his
most powerful impact on Russian intellectual history) remains the fact that
his *Istoriia gosudarstva rossiiskogo* (History of the Russian State), 1818–26,
popularized Russia's past among the
educated and provided the intellectual
foundation—as well as a constant source
of inspiration—for the new national
pride which had been nurtured in the
battles against Napoleon and was given
its literary expression by the writers of
Pushkin's generation.

Love of Country and National Pride

Love of country may be *physical, moral,* and *political.*

Men love the place where they were born and raised. This attachment is common to all people and all nations; it is the work of nature and should be called *physical* attachment. The native land is dear to one's heart not because of the beauty of its landscapes, its clear sky, or its pleasant climate, but on account of the enthralling memories that enfold, so to speak, the dawn and cradle of manhood. There is nothing dearer in the world than life; it is the first bliss—and the beginning of any auspicious event possesses a certain special charm for our imagination. Thus for tender lovers and friends the first day of their love and friendship remains brightly lighted in memory. The Laplander, born almost in the grave of nature, nonetheless loves the cold gloom of his land. Move him to happy Italy, and his eye and heart will turn to the north as does a magnet. The bright radiance of the sun will not arouse in his soul such sweet feelings as will a gloomy day, the howling of the storm, the falling of the snow—they remind him of his native land! The very arrangement of the nerves, formed in man according to climate, ties us to our native land. It is not without reason that physicians sometimes advise an air cure; not without reason that the inhabitant of Helvetia, when removed from his snowy mountains, fades and falls into melancholy, then revives when he goes back to wild Unterwalden or stern Glarus. Every plant thrives better in its own climate; the law of nature is immutable, even for man. I do not say that natural beauties and advantages have no effect whatever on the general love for one's native land—some lands richly endowed by nature can be so much the dearer to their inhabitants. I am saying only that these beauties and advantages are not the main foundation of men's physical attachment to their country, for otherwise this attachment would not be general.

We get used to those with whom we grow up and with whom we live. Their soul *conforms* to ours, becomes a kind of mirror of it; it serves as the means of our moral satisfaction and becomes the object of the heart's inclination. This love for fellow-citizens, or people with whom we grow up, receive our education, and live is the second, or *moral,* love of country. It is as common as the first, the local or physical love, but it is stronger at some

Translated by Jaroslaw Pelenski from Nikolai Mikhailovich Karamzin, "O liubvi k ote-chestvu i narodnoi gordosti," in *Izbrannye sochineniia,* Vol. II (Moscow, 1964), pp. 280–87. Originally published in *Vestnik Evropy,* No. 4 (Moscow, 1802).

ages, for time strengthens habit. One need only see two fellow-countrymen who discover each other in a foreign land—with what pleasure they embrace and hasten to pour out their souls in intimate conversation! They may be seeing each other for the first time, but already they are acquainted and on friendly terms, forging their personal bond through whatever ties them both to their native land. It seems to them that, even if they speak in a foreign tongue, they understand each other better than they understand others; for there is always a certain similarity in the character of fellow-countrymen, and the inhabitants of one state always form, so to speak, an electric circuit transmitting the same impression through the most remote coils or links. On the shores of the most beautiful lake in the world [Geneva], mirroring a bountiful nature, I happened to meet a Dutch patriot who, out of hate for the Stadholder and the adherents of the House of Orange, had left his country and settled in Switzerland between Nyon and Rolle. He had a wonderful little house, a physics laboratory, a library; seated at his window, he could view the most splendid panorama of nature. Walking past the little house, I envied the owner without knowing him; and when I got acquainted with him in Geneva, I told him about it. The response of the phlegmatic Dutchman astonished me by its animation: "No one can be happy outside his fatherland, where the heart has learned to understand the people and formed habits dear to it. The people of no other nation can replace one's fellow-citizens. I am not living with those with whom I lived for forty years, and I am not living the way I lived for forty years. It is difficult to adjust oneself to new habits, and I feel sad!"

But the physical and moral attachment to one's country, the effect of nature and of men's qualities, still do not constitute the great virtue for which the Greeks and Romans were renowned. Patriotism is love of one's fatherland's welfare and fame and the desire to further them in all respects. It requires the ability to reason—and that is why not everybody possesses it.

The best philosophy is that which bases man's duties on his happiness. Such a philosophy will tell us that we should love what is useful to our country because our own welfare is inseparable from it; it will tell us that the country's enlightenment provides us with many pleasures in life, that its tranquillity and virtues serve as a shield of family joys; that its glory is our glory; and that, if it is humiliating for a man to call himself the son of a contemptible father, it is no less humiliating for a citizen to call himself the son of a contemptible fatherland. In this way, love of our personal welfare gives rise in us to a love for the fatherland, and personal self-esteem develops the national pride on which patriotism rests. Thus the Greeks and the Romans regarded themselves as the first nations and all others as barbarians; thus the English, who in modern times are better known for patriotism than are others, think more of themselves than others do of themselves.

I dare not think that in our Russia there are not many patriots; but it seems to me that we are unnecessarily *humble* in thinking about our national dignity. Humility, however, is harmful in politics. Whoever does not respect himself will certainly not be respected by others.

I do not say that love of country should blind us and make us believe that we are better than all others in every respect, but the Russian should at least know his own worth. Let us agree that some nations are in general more enlightened than we are because their circumstances have been more favorable; yet we should also realize all the favors that fate has shown the Russian nation. Let us boldly take our stand alongside the others, and clearly speak our name, and repeat it with noble pride.

We do not need to resort to fables and fictions, like the Greeks and Romans, to extol our origins; fame was the cradle of the Russian nation, and victory the herald of its existence. The Roman Empire found out that there were Slavs, for they came and destroyed its legions. The Byzantine historians speak of our ancestors as a wonderful people whom nothing could resist and who differed from other Northern peoples not only in their valor but also in a certain knightly graciousness. In the ninth and tenth centuries our heroes amused themselves by terrorizing the then new capital of the world—they needed only to appear before the walls of Constantinople to obtain tribute from Greek emperors. In the eleventh century the Russians, always preeminent in valor, also stood second to no other European nation in enlightenment—thanks to close religious ties with Constantinople, which shared with us the fruits of its learning; in the time of Iaroslav many Greek books were translated into the Slavonic language. To the honor of the stalwart Russian character, Constantinople was never able to acquire political influence over our fatherland. Our princes loved the wisdom and the knowledge of the Greeks, but they were always ready to punish them by force of arms for the slightest sign of effrontery.

The splitting up of Russia into many principalities and the discord among its princes laid the ground for the triumph of the descendants of Genghis Khan and for our long-lasting calamities. Great men and great nations are exposed to the blows of fate, but even in the midst of disaster they show their greatness. Thus Russia, rent by a cruel enemy, was perishing in glory. Whole cities preferred certain annihilation to the shame of slavery. The inhabitants of Vladimir, Chernigov, and Kiev sacrificed themselves to national pride and in so doing saved the name of Russia from defamation. The historian, exhausted by these unhappy times as by a frightening, barren desert, takes rest on the graves and finds consolation in mourning the death of many worthy sons of the fatherland.

But what nation in Europe can boast of a better fate? Which one among them has not been in chains several times? In any case, our conquerors terrified both East and West. Tamerlane, sitting on the throne of Samarkand, fancied himself Emperor of the world.

And what nation broke its chains so gloriously and took such a glorious revenge on its ferocious enemies? There was only need for a firm and courageous prince to sit on the throne, and after a sleep, or drowse, the nation's power and courage announced their awakening with thunder and lightning.

The times of the false Pretenders present again a sorrowful picture of unrest; but soon love for the fatherland enkindles the heart—the citizens, the peasants demand a military leader, and Pozharskii, bearing the marks of his glorious wounds, arises from his sickbed. The virtuous Minin serves as an example; and anyone who cannot give his life for his country gives to it everything he possesses. Neither ancient nor modern history can show us anything more moving than this general, heroic patriotism. In the reign of Alexander it is permissible for the Russian heart to wish that some worthy monument erected in Nizhnii Novgorod (where the voice of love of their country first resounded) should revive in our memory a glorious period of Russian history. Such monuments elevate the spirit of the nation. The modest ruler might not forbid us to inscribe on this monument that it was built in his *happy* time.

Peter the Great, who *united* us with Europe and showed us the benefits of enlightenment, did not for long humiliate the national pride of the Russians. We looked at Europe, so to speak, and at one glance we assimilated the fruits of her long labors. No sooner had the great monarch told his soldiers how to use their new arms than they grasped them and rushed forth to fight the first army of Europe. Generals appeared on the scene, today still pupils, tomorrow examples for their teachers. Soon others could, and had to, borrow from us; we showed how to defeat the Swedes, the Turks—and finally the French. These famous republicans, who talk even better than they fight and who so often harp on their fearsome bayonets, in Italy fled at the first brandish of Russian bayonets. Knowing that we are braver than many, we do not know anyone who is braver than we. Courage is a great quality of the soul; a nation distinguished by it should be proud of itself.

In the art of warfare we have accomplished more than in other arts because we have engaged in it more, necessary as it has been for buttressing the existence of our state. However, it is not only of military laurels that we can boast. Our state institutions rival in wisdom the institutions of states that have been enlightened for several centuries. Our civility, the tone of our society, our taste astonish the foreigners who come to Russia with a false notion of a people who were considered barbarians at the beginning of the eighteenth century.

Those who envy the Russians say that we have only a very high degree of *imitativeness*. But is this not a sign of admirable development of the soul? It is said that the teachers of Leibnitz found in him, too, only *imitativeness*.

In the sciences we are still behind others because—and only because—we occupy ourselves with them less than do others and in our country the estate of scholar has not so wide a scope as, for instance, in Germany or England. If our young noblemen who study *were able really to complete their studies* and devote themselves to science, we would already have had our own Linnaeuses, Hallers, and Bonnets. The achievements of our literature (which requires less learning but, I venture to say, even more intelligence than the so-called sciences) prove the great talent of the Russians. How long is it since we have known what style is in poetry or in prose? And in some fields we can already compete with foreigners. The French had Montaigne philosophizing and writing as early as the sixteenth century. Is it any wonder that in general they write better than we do? Is the wonder not, rather, that some of our works can stand beside the best of theirs in vividness of thought and the fine shadings of style? Let us only be just, dear fellow-citizens, and we shall recognize the value of our own. We shall never be wise with foreign wisdom and never famous with foreign fame. French and English writers can do without our praise, but Russian writers need at the very least the attention of Russians. The disposition of my soul is—thank God! —quite the opposite of that of a satirical or quarrelsome spirit, but I make bold to reproach many of our lovers of reading who, being better acquainted with the works of French literature than the inhabitants of Paris, do not even want to look at a Russian book. Do they wish to have foreigners inform them about Russian talents? Let them read French and German critical journals, which do justice to our talents on the basis of some translations.[1] Who would not be ashamed to be like D'Alembert's nurse, who, while living with him, heard with great amazement from others that he was a clever man? Some excuse themselves on the ground of their poor knowledge of the Russian language; this excuse is worse than the guilt itself. Let us leave it to our dear society ladies to declare that the Russian language is crude and unpleasant, that *charmant* and *séduisant*, *expansion* and *vapeurs* cannot be expressed in it, and that, in a word, it is not worth the effort it would take to know it. Who dares to prove to the ladies that they are mistaken? But men do not possess such an amiable right to judge wrongly. Our language not only lends itself to lofty eloquence and sonorous, picturesque poetry, but it is also able to express tender simplicity and the voice of the heart and feelings. It is richer in harmony than French, more capable of expressing the effusions of the soul in its tones; it offers more *analogical* words, that is, words conforming to the action expressed; an advantage possessed only by root languages. Our misfortune is that we all want to speak French and do not think of taking the trouble to cultivate our own language. Is it strange, then, that in our conversation we are unable to express some subtle nuances? One foreign diplomat said in my presence that our language "must be very obscure," since, according to his observations, "when Russians speak it, they do not understand each other and immediately have to turn to French." Don't we ourselves give ground for such absurd conclusions? The language is important for the patriot; and I love the Englishmen because they prefer to *whistle* and *hiss* in English [when] conversing with their dearest loves rather than speak in a foreign language, which almost every one of them knows well.

There is a limit and a measure to all things. Like an individual, a nation always begins with imitation; in due time, however, it *ought to be itself,* so as to say: *I do exist morally!* Now we already have such knowledge and taste that we could live without asking: How do they live in Paris and in London? What do they wear there, what are their means of travel, and how do they furnish their houses? The patriot hurries to appropriate for his country what is beneficial and necessary, but he rejects slavish imitation in trifles, which is degrading to national pride. It is good and necessary to learn. But woe to the man or the nation that forever remains a pupil!

[1] For example, the worst French translation of Lomonosov's odes and various passages from Sumarokov received the attention and praise of foreign journalists.

Up to the present time, Russia has steadily risen in the political as well as [in] the moral sense. One may say that Europe respects us more from year to year—and we are still only in the middle of our glorious course! Everywhere the observer sees new *fields of knowledge* and discoveries; he sees many fruits, and even more blooms. Our symbol is an ardent youth—his heart is full of life, he loves activity, his motto is: *"Toil and hope!"*

Victories have cleared for us the road to prosperity; glory is the right to happiness.

The Book Trade
and the Love of Reading in Russia

Twenty-five years ago there were in Moscow two bookstores whose sales did not amount to even ten thousand rubles a year. Now there are twenty of them, and altogether they have approximately two hundred thousand rubles in annual receipts. And how many lovers of reading have been added in Russia? This is [a] pleasant [thought] to everyone who desires progress and knowledge and who knows that love of reading promotes them more than anything else.

Mr. Novikov was mainly responsible for the spread of the book trade in Moscow. He leased the university print shop, increased the number of mechanical devices [used] in book printing, ordered translations of books, opened bookstores in other cities, in every way tried to get the public interested in reading; he was successful in guessing the general taste, nor did he neglect individual taste. He traded in books as a rich Dutch or English merchant trades in the products of all lands—that is, with intelligence, insight, and farsighted consideration. Previously Moscow newspapers had had a circulation of no more than six hundred copies. Mr. Novikov made them much more interesting; to the political articles he added a variety of others; and, finally, as a free supplement to *Vedomosti* [Record or Gazette] [1] he put out the *Detskoe chtenie* [Children's Readings], which was liked by the public because of the novelty of its subject and the variety of its materials, despite the amateurish translation of many pieces. The number of subscribers multiplied annually, and in ten years it had reached four thousand. In 1797 newspapers became important for Russia because they began to print imperial orders and other state news, and at present the circulation of the Moscow newspapers has reached approximately six thousand. Undoubtedly this is still not enough considering the size of the Empire, but it is quite a lot in comparison with the previous circulation; and in hardly any other country has the number of those interested in reading grown so fast as in Russia. It is true that many noblemen, even those who

[1] See note on p. 71.—Editor.

Translated by Jaroslaw Pelenski from Nikolai Mikhailovich Karamzin, "O knizhnoi torgovle i liubvi k chteniiu v Rossii," in *Izbrannye sochineniia*, Vol. II (Moscow, 1964), pp. 176–80. Originally published in *Vestnik Evropy*, No. 9 (Moscow, 1802).

are well off, still do not take newspapers; but already the merchants and the townspeople like to read them. The poorest people subscribe to them, and even the most illiterate wish to know *what is reported from foreign countries!* One of my acquaintances happened to observe a group of pastry hawkers gathered around a man reading aloud; they were listening with great attention to a description of a battle between the Austrians and the French. He inquired and learned that five of them had pooled their resources and subscribed to the *Moskovskie vedomosti,* although four of them did not know how to read; however, the fifth managed to make out the letters while the others listened.

Our book trade cannot compare to the German, French, or English trade. But what can we not expect in time, judging by the progress of our book trade every year? There are bookstores now in almost every provincial capital. The riches of our literature are brought to every fair, along with other goods. For instance, the noble ladies from the countryside during the St. Macarius fair "stock up" not only on mobcaps but also on books. Formerly traders traveled through the villages with ribbons and rings; now they travel with *learned goods;* and while most are not able to read themselves, in order to tempt the amateurs they relate the contents of novels and comedies in their own very amusing way. I know of noblemen who have an annual income of no more than five hundred rubles but are collecting, in their own words, "little libraries," and rejoice in them. While we heedlessly throw around fine editions of Voltaire and Buffon, they do not let a speck of dust fall even on a copy of Miramond; [2] they read every book several times, and read it again with renewed pleasure.

The curious will probably want to know what kinds of books are sold most in our country. I asked this question of many bookdealers, and all, without even thinking, answered, "Novels!" No wonder, for this genre is undoubtedly captivating to the larger part of the public; it takes possession of the heart and the imagination, shows pictures of "Society" and of people like ourselves in interesting situations, represents the strongest and at the same time the most ordinary passion in its various effects. Not everybody can philosophize or put himself into the place of the heroes of history, but everybody loves, has loved, or has wished to love, and he discovers himself in the hero of the novel. It seems to the reader that the author speaks to him in the language of his own heart; in one reader the novel stimulates hope, in another pleasant reminiscences. As far as this type of literature is concerned, there are in our country many more translations than original works, and consequently the foreign authors' fame outshines that of the Russians. At present Kotzebue is immensely fashionable; and as once upon a time Parisian bookdealers wanted *Lettres persanes* from every author, so our bookdealers demand from translators, and even from authors, Kotzebue, the one and only Kotzebue! Novel, tale, good or bad—it makes no difference, if only the title page carries the name of the famous Kotzebue!

[2] F. Emin, *Nepostoiannaia fortuna, ili pokhozhdeniia Miramonda* (Fickle Fortune, or the Adventures of Miramond) (St. Petersburg, 1783; 2d ed., Moscow, 1781; 3d ed., St. Petersburg, 1792).—Editor.

I do not know about others, but I rejoice. If only people read! Even the most mediocre novels, even those written without any talent, foster enlightenment in some fashion. Anyone who is captivated by *Neschastnyi Nikanor* [Nikanor, the Unfortunate Nobleman] [3] stands below the author's level of intellectual cultivation, and he does well to read the novel, for undoubtedly he learns something from its ideas or the way they are expressed. As soon as there is a great distance between the author and the reader, the former cannot have a strong influence on the latter, no matter how intelligent he may be. For everyone something close is needed—for one, Jean-Jacques, for another Nikanor. As physical taste as a rule informs us whether food will satisfy our need, so a reader's moral taste reveals the true correspondence between the subject and his mind; however, this mind can lift itself up gradually, and he who begins with the *Neschastnyi Nikanor* often reaches Grandison.

All pleasant reading exercises an influence on the intellect, without which the heart cannot feel nor the imagination function. In the poorest novels there is a certain logic and rhetoric, and anyone who reads them will speak better and more coherently than the complete ignoramus who has never opened a book in his life. In addition, contemporary novels are rich in all sorts of knowledge. When an author takes it into his head to write three or four volumes, he uses every means to fill them, and even resorts to all the sciences. At one time he describes some American island, making exhaustive use of Büsching; at another he explains the nature of the island's vegetation, checking on himself with the help of Bomare. In this way the reader learns about geography and natural history, and I am convinced that in some German novel the planet Piazzi will soon be described more thoroughly than in the *Peterburgskie vedomosti*.[4]

People mistakenly think that novels can be harmful to the heart; but usually they glorify virtue or point a moral. It is true that some characters are both attractive and depraved. But in what respect, precisely, are they attractive? In certain good traits with which the author has relieved their blackness—consequently, the good triumphs in the evil itself. Our moral nature is such that the heart will never be satisfied by the portrayal of bad people; never will they become its favorites. What novels are liked best of all? Usually the sentimental ones. The tears shed by the reader always flow from a love for the good, and they nourish that love. No, no! Bad people do

---

[3] M. Kamarov, *Neschastnyi Nikanor, ili prikliucheniia rossiiskogo dvorianina G.* (The Unfortunate Nikanor, or the Adventures of the Russian Nobleman G.) (Moscow, 1775; 2d ed., 1787–89); a very popular novel patterned after the novels of Prévost.—Editor.

[4] Anton Friedrich Büsching (1724–93), German economist, was the author of *Neue Erdbeschreibung* (13 vols.; Hamburg, 1754–1807; trans. in part as *A New System of Geography*, 6 vols.; London, 1762). He was also the editor of a politico-statistical journal, *Magazin für die neue Historie und Geographie*, 1767–69.

Jacques Christophe Valmont de Bomare (1731–1807) was the author of a widely known *Dictionnaire Raisonné Universel d'Histoire Naturelle* (1st ed., Paris, 1764; 5th ed., Paris, 1800).

The small planet Ceres was discovered by the Italian astronomer Piazzi in January–February 1801.—Editor.

not even read novels. Their harsh souls are not susceptible to the gentle impressions of love and cannot be concerned with the fate of tenderness. The vile money-grubber, the egoist—will he find himself in the charming hero of the novel? And what interest does he take in others? We do not disagree that the novels make the heart and imagination . . . *romantic.* And what harm? In a way, the better for us inhabitants of the cold and iron North! It is certainly not the romantic hearts that are the cause of the evil in the world about which we hear complaints everywhere, but the rough and the cold-hearted; that is, just the opposite! The romantic heart causes itself more grief than it causes others, but it loves its grief and would not exchange it for the pleasures of the egoists.

In a word, it is good that our public reads even novels.

Foreword to History of the Russian State

In a certain sense history is the sacred book of a nation, the main, the indispensable book, the mirror of its existence and activity, the table of revelations and rules, the ancestors' bequest to posterity, the supplement and explanation of the present, and the example for the future.

Rulers and legislators act according to what history teaches, and consult its pages as does a navigator at his charts. Human wisdom needs experience, and life is short. It is necessary to know how from time immemorial riotous passions have disturbed civil society, and by what means the beneficial rule of reason has curbed their tempestuous drive, in order to establish order, to conciliate the interests of human beings, and to grant them such happiness as is possible on earth.

But the ordinary citizen, too, should read history. It reconciles him to the imperfections of the manifest order of things, as something usual in all ages. It consoles him when the state suffers calamities, by bearing witness that in bygone times similar events—and even more terrible ones—occurred and the state did not disintegrate. History feeds moral feelings and by its righteous verdict disposes the soul to a justice which assures our good and the harmony of society.

So much for its usefulness. But how many pleasures for the heart and the mind! Curiosity is natural to man, both the enlightened man and the untutored. At the famous Olympic games the noise ceased while the crowds listened in silence to Herodotus as he read the legends of bygone ages. Even before they know the use of letters, nations love history; the old man shows a lofty grave to the boy and relates the deeds of the hero resting in it.

Our ancestors devoted their first efforts in the art of writing to the religion and to historiography; deep in the shade of ignorance the nation listened avidly to the stories of the chroniclers. Inventions, too, are pleasing, but for full satisfaction one must deceive oneself into thinking they are the truth. History—in opening graves, resurrecting the dead, injecting life into their hearts and words into their mouths; in refashioning empires fallen into decay; and in presenting the imagination with the various passions, morals, and deeds of a procession of centuries—widens the boundaries of

Translated by Jaroslaw Pelenski from Nikolai Mikhailovich Karamzin, "Predislovie," in *Istoriia gosudarstva rossiiskogo*, Vol. I (5th ed.; St. Petersburg, 1842–43), pp. ix–xiv. The book was published in St. Petersburg over the years 1818–26; the Foreword is dated December 7, 1815.

our own existence; thanks to her creative power we live with people of all times, see and hear them, love and hate them. Not yet thinking about benefit, we enjoy contemplating the varied events and characters that capture our minds or feed our sensibility.

If any history, even when written without skill, can be pleasant, as Pliny contends, all the more so can the history of one's native land. The true cosmopolite is a metaphysical being or such an unusual figure that there is no need to speak about him, either to praise or to condemn him. We all are citizens, in Europe and in India, in Mexico and in Abyssinia; everyone's personality is closely bound to his fatherland—we love it because we love ourselves. Let the Greeks and Romans capture our imagination! They belong to the family of mankind, and they are no strangers to us in their virtues and weaknesses, their glory and disasters. However, a Russian name has for us a special charm; my heart beats even faster for Pozharskii than for Themistocles or Scipio. Universal history with its great memories adds beauty to the world for the intellect, but Russian history adds beauty to the native land where we live and feel. How attractive are the banks of the Volkhov, the Dnieper, and the Don when we know what happened on them in times long past! Not only Novgorod, Kiev, and Vladimir but also the huts of Elets, Kozel'sk, and Galich become interesting monuments, and mute objects become eloquent. Everywhere the shadows of bygone centuries create images before our eyes.

Besides the special value which Russia's chronicles have for us, her sons, they have also a general value. If we take a look at the expanse of this unique state, our minds are stunned—Rome in its greatness, ruling from the Tiber to the Caucasus, from the Elbe to the sands of Africa, never equaled this state. Is it not astonishing that lands separated by the eternal barriers of nature, immeasurable deserts and impenetrable forests, cold and hot climates—that [lands like] Astrakhan and Lapland, Siberia and Bessarabia, could make up one state with Muscovy? And is her population—a congeries of different races, different in appearance and far apart in level of civilization—any less astonishing? Like America, Russia has her savages; like other countries of Europe, she displays the fruits of age-long political life. One need not be a Russian, one need only be a thinking individual in order to read with interest tales from the history of a nation which by dint of its courage and fortitude won domination over one-ninth [1] of the world, opened up countries till then unknown to anyone, brought them into the universal system of geography and history, and enlightened them in the Divine Faith, merely by setting them a better example, without recourse to the violence and villainy to which other devotees of Christianity resorted in Europe and in America.

Let us agree that for any non-Russian the deeds described by Herodotus, Thucydides, and Livy are more entertaining in every respect, that they manifest greater spiritual power and a more lively play of passions, since Greece and Rome were popular states and more enlightened than Russia;

[1] "One-seventh" [correction by Karamzin on his personal copy of the *Istoriia gosudarstva rossiiskogo*].—Note in Russian edition.

yet we can confidently say that certain events, scenes, and characters of our own history are no less interesting than those of ancient times. Such are the heroic deeds of Sviatoslav, the terror of Batu, the uprising of the Russians in the time of [Dimitrii] Donskoi, the fall of Novgorod, the conquest of Kazan, the triumph of national virtues during the interregnum. Oleg and the son of Igor, giants of the twilight; the blind Vasil'ko, the simple-hearted hero; the benevolent Monomakh, friend and defender of the homeland; Mstislav, called Valiant, terrible in battle and examples of gentleness in time of peace; Mikhail of Tver, so renowned for his greathearted death; the ill-fated, truly courageous Aleksandr Nevskii; the hero youth who was victor over Mamai—these, even in sketchy outline, have a powerful effect on the imagination and the heart. The reign of Ivan III is in itself rare treasure for history; at least I do not know of any monarch more deserving to live and shine in her sanctuary. The rays of his glory fall on the cradle of Peter—and between these two autocrats [there are] the amazing Ivan IV; Godunov, who deserved his good fortune and his misfortune; the strange false Dimitrii; and, behind the throng of valorous patriots, boyars, and citizens, the regent of the throne, Patriarch Filaret with his sovereign son, bearer of light in the gloomy distress of our state; and Tsar Alexis, wise father of the emperor whom Europe called "the Great." Either all modern history should be silent, or Russian history has a right to attention.

I know that the battles fought in connection with the internecine strife of the appanage (*udel'nyi*) period, ceaselessly thundering in the time span of over five centuries, are of little value for the mind, that this topic is rich neither in ideas for the "pragmatic" historian [2] nor in beauties for the painter; but history is not a novel, and the world is not a garden, where everything should be pleasing—history portrays the real world. On earth we see majestic mountains and waterfalls, blooming meadows and valleys, but also how many barren sands and cheerless steppes! Yet travel, on the whole, is pleasant for a man with lively feeling and imagination; even in the deserts one may see delightful sights.

Let us not be superstitious in our high respect for the historical writings of antiquity. If from the immortal work of Thucydides one were to omit the invented speeches, what would be left? A bare narrative of the internecine struggles of Greek cities—crowds doing evil and slaughtering one another for the honor of Athens or Sparta, as in our country for the honor of Monomakh's or Oleg's dynasty. There is not much of a difference if we forget that these half-tigers expressed themselves in the language of Homer, that they possessed the tragedies of Sophocles and the statues of Phidias. Did the profound artist Tacitus always depict for us what was great and remark-able? With tender emotion we see Agrippina carrying the ashes of Germanicus; with a sense of pity we behold the bones and armor of Varus' legion scattered in the forest; in horror we watch the unrestrained Romans' bloody feast illuminated by the flames of the Capitol; with loathing we see monstrous tyranny devouring the remnants of republican virtue in the capi-

---

[2] In the eighteenth century the objective and exemplary writing of history (as contrasted to the teleological approach of Church writers) was called "pragmatic."—Editor.

tal of the world—but tedious litigation of cities concerning the right to have a priest in one temple or another and dry obituaries of Roman officials cover many pages in the work of Tacitus. He envied Livy because of the richness of his subjects; while Livy, who wrote smoothly and eloquently, sometimes filled entire books with information about skirmishes and robberies which were hardly more important than the Polovtsian raids. In a word, the reading of any history requires a certain patience, which is more or less rewarded by pleasure.

The historian of Russia could, of course, after a few words about the origin of her principal nationality and the composition of the state, present the important, memorable traits of the earliest period in a skillful picture and begin the detailed narrative from the time of Ivan, or from the fifteenth century, when there occurred one of the greatest political creations in the world; he could easily write two or three hundred eloquent, pleasant pages, instead of the many volumes that are laborious for the author and tiring for the reader. However, these surveys, these pictures are no substitute for chronicles, and whoever has read only Robertson's Introduction to the *History of [the Reign of] Charles V* does not have a thorough and true notion of Europe in the Middle Ages. It is not enough that an intelligent man who has glanced over the records of past ages should give us his comments; we must ourselves see the events and the participants—only then do we know history. Will the author's vaunting rhetoric and the reader's comfort condemn to oblivion the deeds and fate of our forebears? They suffered, and their disasters prepared our greatness. And should we not wish to hear about it, should we not know whom they loved and whom they blamed for their misfortunes? Foreigners can omit what is boring to them in our early history. But are good Russians not obliged to show more patience, following the precept of state morality, which makes respect for ancestors a virtue of the educated citizen? Thus I have thought and written about the Igors and the Vsevolods like their contemporary, looking at them in the dim mirror of the ancient chronicle with untiring attention, and with genuine respect; and if instead of living, whole images I have presented only fragmentary shadows, it is not my fault—I could not add to the chronicle!

There are three types of history: the *first* is contemporary history, like that of Thucydides, in which an eyewitness speaks about events; the *second*, like that of Tacitus, is based upon fresh oral accounts close to the time of the events; the *third* is drawn only from written sources—for instance, our history up to the eighteenth century.[3] In the *first* and *second* types, there is a lively play of intellect and imagination on the part of the historian, who selects what is most interesting, colors, adorns, and sometimes *creates* without fear of exposure. He can say, This is what I *saw*, this is what I *heard*—and, criticism being silenced, the reader is not prevented from enjoying the beautiful descriptions. The *third* type is the most limiting for talent. Not a single feature can be added to what is known; no question can

[3] Only from the time of Peter the Great do oral accounts begin for us; from our fathers and grandfathers we have heard much that is not in the books about him, Catherine I, Peter II, Anne, and Elizabeth.

be asked of the dead. We say what the contemporaries have passed on to us; we are silent if they were silent. Just criticism will close the mouth of the light-minded historian, for he must present only what has been preserved of the past in chronicles and archives. The ancients had the right to invent *speeches* in accordance with the character of the people and with the circumstances—an invaluable right for true talents, and Livy, in using it, enriched his books with the power of intellect, eloquence, and wise admonitions. We, however, contrary to the opinion of Abbé Mably, cannot wax oratorical in history. New achievements of reason have given us a clearer notion about history's characteristics and aims; sound taste has established fixed rules and has forever separated historical writing from poetic narrative, from flower gardens of eloquence. It has left to history the role of being a true mirror of the past, a true echo of the words in fact pronounced by the heroes of the ages. The most beautiful invented speech will disfigure history, which is dedicated not to the glory of the writer, the pleasure of the reader, or a didactic, moralizing purpose, but solely to truth, which in itself becomes a source of pleasure and utility. Like natural history, human history does not tolerate fictions; it presents only what is or was, but not what *might have been*. It is said that history is full of lies. We should rather say that in history, as in human affairs, there is an admixture of lies; however, the truthful character is always more or less retained—so that we can form a general idea about people and events. All the more exacting and strict should criticism be; all the more impermissible it is for the historian, in order to show off his gifts, to mislead honest readers, and to think and speak for heroes who have long lain silent in their graves. What is left to him who is, so to speak, chained to the dry documents of early times? Order, clarity, power [of expression], and picturesqueness. He creates from the substance given him; he will not produce gold out of copper, but he should refine even the copper. He should know the value and properties of everything. He should find what is great, wherever it is hidden, and uncover it, and not grant to the petty the rights of the great. There is hardly a subject so poor that in it art could not manifest itself in a form pleasing to the mind.

Until now the ancients have served us as models. Nobody has surpassed Livy in beauty of narrative nor Tacitus in power [of expression]—and this is the important thing! In the historian, nothing—not a knowledge of all the laws in the world, the learning of the Germans, Voltaire's wit, nor even the depth of Machiavelli's thought—can replace the talent to depict events. The Englishmen are proud of their Hume, the Germans of Johannes Müller, and justly so [4]—both are worthy competitors of the ancients, not imitators, for every age, every nation gives particular coloring to the skillful historian. "Do not imitate Tacitus, but write as he would have written in your place!" is the rule for the genius. Was Müller, by frequently inserting moral *maxims* into his narrative, trying to be like Tacitus? I do not know. However, is the

[4] I am speaking only of those who have written an entire history of nations. Ferreras, Daniel, Maskov, Dalin, and Mallet are not the equals of these two historians. However, while enthusiastically praising Müller (the historian of Switzerland), the experts do not praise his Introduction, which can be called a geological epic.

desire to show off one's intellect or to appear profound not against good taste? The historian offers opinion only in explanation at points where his ideas serve to supplement the description. We may observe that for serious minds these maxims are either half-truths or complete commonplaces, which have no great value in history, where we seek deeds and characters. Skillful narrative is the duty of the historian, but a good thought added of himself is a gift. The reader demands the first, and is grateful for the second once his demand has been met. Was this not the view of the wise Hume, who was sometimes extremely prolific in elucidating causes but who was restrained to the point of niggardliness in giving his own reflections? He was the historian whom we might have called the most perfect among modern historians, if he had not unnecessarily estranged himself from England, and if he had not unnecessarily prided himself on his impartiality and in so doing chilled his fine work! In Thucydides we always see a Greek from Athens, in Livy a Roman, and we are captivated by them, we believe them. The feeling of "we," "our" enlivens the narrative; and whereas crude partiality, the result of weak reason or a weak soul, is intolerable in a historian, love of country gives his brush-stroke ardor and power and appeal. Where there is no love, there is no soul.

Let me turn to my work. Not allowing myself any invention, I have sought for expressions in my own mind, but ideas only in the sources. I have sought spirit and life in crumbling parchments. I wished to unify what has been handed down to us by centuries into a system clear and coherent in the harmonious correlation of its parts. I have described not only the disasters and glory of war, but everything that belongs to men's civic existence: the achievements of the intellect, the arts, customs, laws, industry. I have not been afraid to speak with seriousness of the things that our ancestors respected—without being false to my own time, without pride or mockery, I wanted to describe the beginnings of our spiritual life, the centuries of credulity and legend; I wished to represent both the character of the period and the character of its chroniclers, since the one seemed necessary for the other. The less information I found, the more I valued and used what I did find, and the less selecting I did—for it is the rich, not the poor, who choose. It was necessary either to say nothing or to say everything about such-and-such a prince, so that he would live in our memory not only as a bare name, but with a certain moral physiognomy. Making an exhaustive study of the materials on the remotest history of Russia, I was cheered by the thought that there is some inexplicable fascination for our imagination in a narrative about distant times—there are the sources of poetry! Contemplating open space, does not our glance usually dart past everything that is near and clear, to the horizon's end, where the shadows grow thick and dark and the impenetrable begins?

The reader will notice that I do not describe events one at a time, by years and days, but combine them so that they may be more readily imprinted on the memory. The historian is not a chronicler. The latter considers only chronology, whereas the former is concerned with the nature of events and their interrelations; he may make mistakes in the allocation of space, but he should allocate its proper place to everything.

I am myself aghast at the number of my footnotes and excerpts. The ancients were lucky—they did not know this trifling work, in which half the time is lost, while the mind is bored and the imagination withers. The painful sacrifice offered to authentication is, however, unavoidable. If all our materials had been collected, published, and emended by criticism, then I would only have to give references; but when most of them are in manuscripts, and obscure, when hardly anything has been worked over, explained, and agreed upon, one must be armed with patience. The reader is free to look into this varicolored jumble which at times serves as evidence, at times as explanation or supplement. For the devotee everything is interesting—an old name, a word; the smallest detail of antiquity gives food for thought. From the fifteenth century on I make fewer excerpts, for the sources increase in number and become clearer.

The learned and famous Schlözer said that our history had five main periods: from the year 862 to Sviatopolk, Russia should be called "a'borning" (*nascens*), from Iaroslav to the Mongols "divided" (*divisa*), from Batu to Ivan III "oppressed" (*oppressa*), from Ivan to Peter the Great "victorious" (*victrix*), from Peter to Catherine II "flourishing." This idea seems to me clever rather than profound. (1) Even the period of St. Vladimir was a period of greatness and glory, not of *birth*. (2) The state was *divided* even before the year 1015. (3) If it is necessary to designate periods according to the internal conditions and external activities of Russia, can one lump together into one period the times of Grand Duke Dimitrii Aleksandrovich and of [Dimitrii] Donskoi, mute bondage and victory and glory? (4) The period of the false Pretenders was marked more by ill fortune than by victory. Our history can be divided much better, and with greater truth and modesty, into *earliest* history from Riurik to Ivan III, *middle* from Ivan to Peter, and *modern* from Peter to Alexander. The system of appanage principalities (*udel*) was the characteristic feature of the first period, the autocracy of the second, and a change in civil customs of the third. However, it is not necessary to set boundaries where geography provides the natural division.

Having willingly, even zealously, devoted twelve years—the best period of my life—to work on these eight or nine volumes, I may have the weakness of wishing for praise and being afraid of censure; but I make so bold as to say that for me this is not the most important thing. The desire for fame alone could not have given me the constant and prolonged persistence necessary in such an undertaking if I had not found true pleasure in the work itself and if I had not had the hope of being useful, that is, of making Russian history better known to many, including my severe judges.

With gratitude to all those, living and dead, whose intellect, knowledge, talents, and artistry have guided me, I throw myself upon the indulgence of my good fellow-citizens. There is only one thing we love and wish for: We love our native land; for it we wish well-being even more than glory; it is our wish that there may never be a change in the firm foundation of our greatness, that the precepts of a wise autocracy and of the Holy Faith may more and more strengthen the union of the parts. May Russia flourish . . . at least for a long, long time to come, if on earth there be nothing immortal except the human soul!

December 7, 1815

7.
Ivan Petrovich Pnin

1773-1805

Concern for the moral state of Russia and the "discovery" of the common people by some members of the elite in the last quarter of the eighteenth century found their best literary expression in *A Journey from St. Petersburg to Moscow,* published in 1792 by Alexander Radishchev, Director of the St. Petersburg Department of Customs.[1] Catherine II hastily banned the book, had the privately printed volumes burned, and exiled its author to Siberia. But Radishchev's passionate outcry against bureaucratic tyranny and the dehumanizing effects of serfdom did not go unnoticed. The most significant parts of his book circulated in manuscript among the progressive elite, and something of a circle of "Radishchevites," comprising young officials and litterateurs, was in

[1] A. N. Radishchev, *A Journey from St. Petersburg to Moscow,* ed. Roderick P. Thaler (Cambridge, Mass., Harvard University Press, 1958), is an easily available translation of this seminal document of Russian social thought. On Radishchev one may usefully consult D. M. Lang, *The First Russian Radical: Alexander Radishchev (1749-1802)* (London, 1959) for biographical data and Allen McConnell, *A Russian Philosophe: Alexander Radishchev (1749-1802)* (The Hague, 1964) for an insightful discussion of his ideas.

existence during the first years of Alexander I's reign. Ivan Petrovich Pnin was the oldest, best-educated, and most prominent member of this circle. Following in the footsteps of his master, he saw in serfdom the crux of all of Russia's ills and problems.

But Radishchev's book had in truth been only a cry of anguish and indignation meant to awaken the sense of moral responsibility in the Russian elite. Pnin, on the other hand, was not content with mere denunciation. Taking comfort and hope in the avowed desire of Alexander I to do something about Russia's needs, he sought a solution through changes in social and economic institutions. Like most of his contemporaries, Pnin had been shocked by the excesses of the French Revolution and the rise of Napoleon. He therefore rejected what he believed to have been their main cause: abstract rationalism and theoretical assumptions about the nature of man. Drawing his inspiration from Montesquieu and the example of England, he wished to see in Russia a harmonious, stable, and well-ordered society based on the rule of law. This could be easily achieved, he thought, if everyone had an economic stake, as well as a specific social role, in the nation's progress.

In spite of his gradualism and emphasis on education and enlightenment, Pnin continued to rely on the government for leadership. Like most of his contemporaries he did not see the paradox inherent in preparing society for a role of initiative and autonomous activity by means of state guidance and control. But even his moderate approach was rejected by the Russian autocracy, and his pamphlet was prohibited and destroyed by the police. The fate of Pnin's book made questionable even the possibility of a constructive relationship between the imperial government and the intelligentsia.

An Essay on Enlightenment with Reference to Russia

L'instruction doit être modifiée selon la nature du gouvernement qui régit le peuple.
—J. A. Chaptal

Fortunate are the rulers and the countries in which a citizen, free to think, can impart without fear the truths involving the common weal.[1]

WHAT SHOULD TRUE ENLIGHTENMENT CONSIST IN?

If the Creator of worlds, according to the great Euler, should decide to kindle a new star in the boundless spaces of heaven, several years would elapse before its rays reached us. In the same manner, the lamp of enlightenment lit by the benevolent hand of the wise legislator will not illuminate the moral sphere with its radiant glow until a long time has passed. Thus future centuries must be the mirror of what the legislator does today. His creative spirit must, without fail, project itself into that remote distance, into that mental world, and carefully investigate what effect his present undertakings may have on future generations.

Translated by Marc Raeff from Ivan Petrovich Pnin, "Opyt o prosveshchenii otnositel'no k Rossii," in *Sochineniia,* ed. I. K. Luppol, notes by V. Orlov (Moscow, 1934), pp. 121–61. The Russian text is reproduced from the only surviving copy of the 1804 edition (St. Petersburg, 147 pp.). Passages in angular brackets (⟨ ⟩) were inserted by hand on the 1804 copy. Apparently these passages from Pnin's manuscript had been cut by the censor in 1804.

[1] Paraphrase of text on p. 157.—V. Orlov.

Since Riurik's time, Russia has had many masters. Each has left on her some imprint of his power, and history pictures with fair accuracy all the shadings of this power, as well as the coarseness of those times. Russia has had many masters, but few rulers. At first glance, to "command" and to "govern" seem to designate the same thing, but they differ vastly in their true effects. One may hold command over a state without governing it; for autocratic power, flowing from a single will rarely directed to any particular goal, almost always depends on the disposition of the individual. To govern a people, on the other hand, means to be solicitous of them: to administer justice, uphold the law, encourage industry, reward virtue, spread education, support the Church, reconcile the promptings of honor with those of usefulness—in short, to bring about the common good and to open the way for everyone freely to seek this single goal of the citizen, through rules laid down toward that end, an established order, and wise activity. Thus Domitians and Caligulas only *commanded* Rome, but Lycurguses and Solons *governed* Sparta and Athens.

The history of these great legislators clearly shows to what extent laws adapted to the morals and spirit of a nation, consonant with the climate and local conditions, endure, resist change, and are strong enough to retain their power during several centuries. Peter the Great, that immortal monarch, the father of his country, among his many tireless efforts for the good of the people displayed a true spirit of legislation when he established the Senate and granted it the rights of the highest judiciary. It was in this period of such glory for her that Russia, given a regular form of government, joined the ranks of European monarchies. The genius of this wisest of sovereigns could brook no limitations, no gradualness in the organization of exceedingly complex fields of government. Wishing to organize all of Russia at once, wishing to see the country in a flourishing state in his own lifetime, he frequently took measures that did not have the desired success and, in some cases, even had the opposite result. Had Peter the Great had able assistants to match his own perspicacity and farsightedness, he would, without doubt, have advanced by at least fifty, if not a full hundred, years the attainment of those objectives on which he had set his sights. But as there was a great dearth of such men and as he had to train them himself, he could proceed toward his goal but slowly and with extraordinary effort. There is an idea that has become almost a commonplace and has unfortunately settled in the minds of great men—one that even took hold of the reformer of Russia: the idea that *an ignorant people must be ruled by fear and harsh laws.* Such a notion is as unjust as it is contrary to nature. For the ignorance of a people is but the sign of their infancy; that is, the people collectively are at the same age as each citizen, taken individually, who is cut off from experience, knowing neither the direct bonds that tie him directly to other citizens nor his real obligations toward the authority governing him, and who, as a result of his sad ignorance, is liable at every step to errors which in all justice require correction rather than punishment. An ignorant adult is like a strong infant who, following the unreasoned impulses of his desires, is as eager for the good as for the bad. When we see a man harming himself by preferring evil to good, we must conclude that he is deceiving himself, that his imagination is misleading him, that his passions are driving him to evil. When a man denies hmself the pleasures he could enjoy, he obviously does it with an eye to still greater and longer-lasting pleasures or a remote happiness which he hopes to attain by these deprivations or even short-term forbearance. Not for a moment of his life can man separate himself, so to speak, from himself; in everything he attempts or undertakes, in whatever he does, the object is always to secure some good or avoid misfortune. When we see him weep over the burial urn of anyone essential to his heart—his spouse, his child, or his friend—we see him weeping over himself. It is not the cold and unfeeling dust that wrings tears and pity from us, but the awareness of having lost our pleasure and happiness; there are times when this feeling of loss drives a sensitive person into his grave. Consequently, in all his thoughts, passions, and deeds man is hoping, according to his lights, to find happiness; for this reason, too, the art of the legislator who undertakes to draw up laws for a people in a state of ignorance should consist in directing the private passions to a single goal comprising the general good. And men can be led to this goal not by harsh punishments, which only harden their souls, but through *enlightenment*. Let us, therefore, consider what *enlightenment* is. Among all questions of politics none preoccupies philosophers more than this one. How many books have been published on popular education! Every philosopher in turn has not failed to make a system and to propose it to the world as the best, at least in his opinion. And in truth by its importance the subject deserves the greatest attention, especially on the part of a ruler whom circumstances favor in his desire to educate the peoples under his rule.

Enlightenment, in the present meaning, consists in every member of society, whatever his status, fully knowing and discharging his obligations; that is, in the authorities, for their part, piously fulfilling the obligations of the power entrusted to them, while the people of lower rank consistently carry out the duties of obedience incumbent upon them. When neither of these two estates exceeds its limits and they maintain the proper balance in their relationship, then enlightenment has attained its goal. There are men who judge a people's enlightenment by the number of its writers; that is, where there are more writers there is more enlightenment. According to these people, France should be considered the most enlightened country in the world because of its abundance of writers. But with all this brilliant learning, France is far from true civilization.[2] For wherever enlightenment reigns, peace and happiness are the portion of every citizen. But as long as the power entrusted to the authorities by society is used for ill, as long as subordinates constantly overstep the bounds and the equilibrium of civil relationships is lost, a country will hardly be happier than if it were plunged into dark ignorance, even though its population be composed exclusively of scholars and philosophers.

France has made a horrible revolution in her transformation; she is tear-

---

[2] Used in the eighteenth-century French sense denoting a cultured and well-ordered society.—Editor.

ing at her own vitals and thirsting for blood everywhere. Instead of restoring the necessary strength to the state, which, according to her, has long been debilitated, instead of strengthening the state and giving everything a firm foundation, France turned for help to her supposed wise men, who, in the guise of legislators—or, to speak more accurately, of destroyers—instantly demolished all the former government institutions and on the sad ruins laid the foundations of a constitution most horrible in practice and seductive in its principles. But experience has shown the weakness of these foundations, and how easy it was to subvert them, for the fate of the country is already in the hands of a foreigner.

The French Legislative Assembly completely departed from its true object when it drafted the constitution presented to the people on June 24, 1793.[3] Maybe some will tell me that it could not have been otherwise and that under such circumstances such consequences usually follow. As I understand it, they mean by this that the whole revolution was undertaken for the sake of Bonaparte, to elevate him to the throne of the Bourbons, to offer him the title of emperor, and to hand over to him far greater power than was previously enjoyed by the French kings. I agree that there is nothing France has not done for the glory of the First Consul, but I fail to see what she has done for her own glory.

But as the present condition of France is the result of her revolutionary constitution, which kindled the flames of discord in the very heart of France and has thrown its baneful sparks into other countries, it may not be useless to see how a class of men renowned for their learning and enlightenment could have given such a senseless foundation to the laws on which must rest the security and happiness of all.

This constitution of theirs contains more metaphysical disquisitions than simple intelligible truths. It is not surprising, therefore, that the people could not understand the constitution, as it exceeded their comprehension. It is doubtful that even the legislators themselves understood it well when they adopted as its basis, first, the *rights of man,* then *liberty,* then *equality,* and, finally, *property,* as if the latter derived from these rights. What a striking contradiction! What absurdity in the very foundation of the laws! Wishing to draw the laws from a natural source, these metaphysician-legislators drew them from their imagination.

Are the *rights of man* in any way in accord with the *rights of the citizen,* and what *rights* can *natural man* possess, a man we can conceive only in our minds? Primitive or natural man, living by himself, without any relations to others, is guided only by *natural impulses or needs* which he satisfies himself. As long as he remains in this state, nothing distinguishes him from other animals. Consequently, having only *needs,* natural man cannot have any *rights,* for the very word "rights" implies the existence of certain relationships, conditions, and sacrifices in return for which this general pledge of individual well-being is obtained. Man became acquainted with *rights until then unknown to him,* only at the moment when he left the womb of Nature for that of society; these rights differ as much from his primitive

[3] Reference to the Constitution of 1793 drafted by the *Convention Nationale.*—V. Orlov.

needs as natural man himself differs from a citizen. Any man can become a citizen, but a citizen can no longer become a natural man. Man's passage from a state of savagery to that of society is in accordance with the aims of Nature, but the passage of the citizen from society to savagery would be contrary to Nature. Every moment of his life primitive man is concerned with self-preservation, and this feeling never leaves him. In contrast, a true citizen is ever ready to sacrifice himself and cares less for his own preservation than for that of his fatherland.

From this it can be seen that the *imaginary rights of man* are opposed to the *rights of the citizen*. A system striving to spread these rights of man leads to ruin, plants the seeds of discord, kindles a universal conflagration, and, shaking the very foundations of kingdoms that were centuries in the building, ends by bringing about their fall.

From the seed of this first law of the rights of man must inevitably have sprung the *tree of liberty*. Its fruits are enchanting from the outside, but they contain a hidden poison capable of overpowering the reason, inflaming the imagination, and causing that madness and rage of which France alone could give examples—examples the world's annals will record in letters of blood.

Is this the light that legislators ought to have shed on those laws on which the happiness of both present and future generations depends? Thinking to outdo Nature herself, who seemed too simple to them, they insisted, against all reason, on trying to bring about their hypothetical happiness for the people through this visionary procedure. No, the way they chose is a horrible abyss that will forever engulf nations and lead to the portals of the temple in which truth reigns, repudiating such laws.

Is their idea of liberty not a completely metaphysical one? [4] Taking as the basis for their fundamental laws their own poorly understood notion concerning the nature of man, they do not hesitate to call themselves citizens in other respects, and on citizens they undoubtedly impose obligations far greater than their imagined rights of man and thus only provide ground for revolt and dissension.

Had they studied human nature with greater care, they would have seen that liberty, the idol they worshiped, was nothing but the phantom of their inflamed imagination; it had never been man's lot, whatever his condition. If we follow man into the depths of the primeval forest and bring him out from this horrible abode onto the stage of life in society, we shall find that in neither case can he possess the kind of liberty they have postulated. Indeed, in the first case man is completely dependent on his natural needs, and in the second on the laws of society.

When in the state of nature a man tormented by hunger attempts to take away food from another, he, of course, does it from necessity, driven by the instinct of self-preservation and the compulsion of his needs; in this instance force is nothing but the weapon Nature has given for the satisfaction of

4 See Article VI of the French Constitution.

these needs. If man had no needs at all, there would be no necessity for force. For as long as the senses are silent, this force remains inactive; it awakens only with the stirring of the senses. The state of nature is not, therefore, as many philosophers define it, the right of the strong, but the need of the strong; for, as I have noted earlier, right cannot be associated with the state of primitive man—such right would in no way differ from the rights of bears, wolves, and other animals ruled by the force of their natural impulses.

By the same token, when man enters society and receives the name of citizen, he is, so to speak, reborn and begins a new form of existence. As he sees himself amidst men who have the same desires, feelings, needs, and passions as himself, he becomes aware, at every step, of their influence and of his own reactions to them, comes to feel that his happiness is inseparable from theirs. This need for others which he has found in himself, and which has showed him that, for their own welfare, the others have an equal need for him, reveals to him the full extent of his duties. These duties have produced the laws, the laws have imposed bonds of dependence, and amidst his fellow-men, in society, man has become *less free* than he was in his primitive state.

But this is not all. To give their constitution the appearance of perfection, these legislators have included the notion of equality, a notion that has cost them so much blood and has been destructive of all *property* rights. Here indeed is the fitting fruit of the tree of liberty they have planted! The spirit of anarchy has thrown all civil relationships into confusion; it has given weapons to depraved idleness to be used against virtue, to laziness against industry, to caprice against order; it has violated the sacred rights of property; and, lastly, stifling the feelings of the heart, it has risen against God Himself, destroying the sacred altars and temples erected to His glory which provide the sole consolation of the wretched.

Wherefrom did they invoke this *equality*, this offspring of dissension?[5] I find it neither in the history of past centuries nor in Nature's womb. What happy, happy people, do they think, ever governed itself by anarchy? In what stage of the infancy of human society did Nature show examples of this quality that delights their souls? No, had they wanted to follow Nature, they surely would have learned that it is not their pernicious equality, but the *inequality* of men's forces which has united men and which still preserves them. This is why the weakest have united to protect themselves against the attacks of the strong and by concerting their individual forces have set up a common force or, what is the same, a law to maintain equilibrium and prevent abuse. Consequently, from the *inequality of men's forces* there arose societies, from societies arose laws, and civil welfare and stability came to depend on these laws.

These considerations ought to be sufficient to show the perniciousness of such a system, its unnaturalness, its remoteness from true enlightenment

[5] *Ibid.*, Article III.

and from the true goal, which should be the *greatest happiness of the greatest number of men.*[6] These considerations, I believe, are especially necessary since they touch on most important questions concerning both the legislators and the people. The former will see what deep reflection is required for [writing] all the new regulations to be introduced, how essential it is to conform to the spirit of the nation and to respect its prejudices. The people, for their part, will realize the disastrousness of governments of the type resulting from the revolutionary constitution of France; for, however magnificent the rights contained in this constitution, no one, as experience has showed, has enjoyed them in fact, and liberty and equality, the phantoms pursued by the French, vanished after luring them into an abyss of misfortunes. Lastly, the people will be convinced that all estates—from peasant to monarch—are essential, for each and every one of them is but a link in the chain that is the state. It is dangerous to break this bond of society; on the contrary, it should be preserved by all possible means. *Therefore it is the part of the legislator in his wisdom to instill in each estate the need for interdependence, to set for each the limits it would be too horrible to overstep, to define the rights of each estate, prescribe its duties, and devise the means for preventing abuses arising out of disloyalty and selfishness.* The question then arises: If inequality of estates is necessary for the preservation of society, is it requisite that *all estates should have the same degree of enlightenment?* This is the problem to be solved.

By the nature of its government Russia is a monarchy, and for this reason it has a particularly great need for inequality among estates, for this is its strongest support. If inequality of status, therefore, is of such importance to the state, it follows that every political institution must be composed of truly worthy, experienced, and loyal men who are well known to society as much for their benevolence as for their talents and zeal. Otherwise the civil *offices* will be wanting in the force necessary for their operation; they will be brought to a standstill at every turn, they will be seriously disrupted, and eventually the fate of the entire society will depend on chance. That is why the distribution of government posts must be carried out with the utmost care. Experience teaches us all too well that any partiality, though affording a few individual benefits, brings the greatest harm to all of society. The result is a lack of respect for civil institutions that ought to be esteemed; and while this disrespect is not shown openly but lurks deep in the heart, it does lead to contempt, which in turn frequently produces hatred. This is the fire smoldering beneath the ashes! This is the reason why *inequality of status* becomes unbearable and a heavy burden, why it enrages the mind, and often breaks the social bond.

However different political institutions may be, they all serve a single purpose, namely, the preservation of the property and personal security of the citizen. ⟨There is no man (however cruel and unjust he may be) who would not acknowledge, and deep down in his heart be convinced of it, that property is the foundation of justice, the source of all civil laws, and the

---

[6] This must necessarily be the goal of all laws, says Beccaria in *Dei delitti e delle pene* (Considerations on Crime and Punishment).

soul of society, and that its preservation depends on the personal security of the citizen. What is the use of putting effort and labor into the acquisition of property when everyone's life and death depend on chance, when the unrestrained will of some pasha may destroy the happiness of many honest citizens and deprive them of their possessions? In such a situation, when everything is uncertain, the best talents are destroyed, the beneficial spirit of industry and diligence is extinguished, and, in a debasement of human dignity itself, men are even kept as in a dark dungeon, where one can hear only the sound of pitiful sighs and the clanging of heavy chains. The rule of violence and ignorance allows of no rights; everyone is either a tyrant or a victim. Turkey is an obvious witness of this. Violence and ignorance, which inform its government and which hold nothing sacred, together ruin the citizens, indiscriminately victimizing without respect of persons. Frequently, therefore, the fate of the sultan and the fate of the lowliest beggar both depend on the madness of the former and the whim of the latter. Nations and rulers usually find themselves in this miserable condition when the night of ignorance lies on the lids of reason and the rays of enlightenment are unable to pierce through them, when genius dare not spread its wings to soar with its accustomed speed to the high abode of truth, when dissension, distrust, and fear separate men from one another, displacing the solidarity and mutual trust which fasten the bonds of life in society. The enlightened patriot will pity the fate of these nations and will say to himself that only those countries are truly well off where the power of government, based on sensible and humane principles consonant with the aims of civil society, accepts the following basic law: The greater a citizen's security in his person and property, the greater his zeal, activity, and happiness, and consequently, the greater his usefulness and loyalty as a citizen of his state.

Then it is that love of country becomes a diamond shield against which neither the thunderbolts of enemies, the perfidy of villains, nor the storms of rebellion can prevail; then it is that this love kindles the citizens' souls and spurs them on to those great and wonderful deeds that we read about in history with admiration and delight. There is no passion that could raise the spiritual powers any higher, that would be more abundant in virtues, sacrifices, and great examples. Through it, a state is feared abroad and prosperous at home; the arts, the crafts, and the sciences obtain their temples; in it laws find their surest safeguard, and monarchs their strongest support. Thus, if *love of country* is a passion so salutary for society, and if the wisdom of the laws safeguarding the citizen's property and personal security nourishes and strengthens it, then every enlightened government ought to foster it in the hearts of its citizens and work toward the welfare of all men without exception, and not only that of a few. It is not the splendor of its court, the magnificence of its courtiers, nor the unlimited power of the nobles that proclaims the prosperity of a state, but rather the good government and the condition of its people.) Property! Sacred right! Soul of society! Source of laws! Mother of plenty and of pleasure! Only where you are respected, where you are inviolable is the country blessed, is the citizen secure and happy. But the sound of chains puts you to flight; you shun slaves! In neither slavery nor anarchy can your rights exist, for you dwell only in the realm of laws. Property! There can be no justice where you are not.

In what incomprehensible way does the edifice of society last when it lacks proper foundation, when the rights of property are violated, when justice is known in name only and is obtained more through money or patronage than through observance of the law? Then everything is completely uncertain, everything rests solely on chance. One instant, and the social edifice is no more; one instant, and its ruins will proclaim the people's misfortunes.

O Russia! All my thoughts, all my desires are aspiring for you. Dearest homeland! Our hearts overflow with the sweetest feelings when they turn to you! What delightful thoughts are produced by your vast expanse when our imaginations contemplate you! Your scepter holds sway over half the globe, numerous peoples obey you, in your bowels are all the treasures of nature! Blessed Russia! Your glory resounds amid your trophies, your sword is terrible to your enemies! Captivated by your heroism, Catherine strove only to exalt you! She succeeded. You are surrounded by a forest of rustling laurels. But now the tempests of war have subsided, the angel of peace has inherited the scepter, and a sweet quiet, accompanied by joy and happiness, animates the hearts of your children. Beloved homeland! Alexander too is laying up glory for you, the true glory worthy of this virtuous monarch. He desires your enlightenment, he desires to extend the realm of your moral potential; it is his desire that the sciences and the arts thrive beneath a canopy of laurels and olive trees and that, fired by love of country, the citizen's first virtue, reason—this gift of heaven—delineate the people's bliss without fear and in all freedom. Taking the talented under his lofty protection, he encourages it with his attention, and by setting an example himself he summons all to virtue. Lastly, desiring to root manners and customs in *true enlightenment*—the foundation, the happiness, and the power of empires —he intends to give full luster to the glory acquired by the force of your arms.

Seeing such concern, such a striving for the good, and such love of the country on the part of his monarch, what Russian will not be touched to the bottom of his heart and fired with enthusiastic zeal for everything the monarch's genius shall ordain? The example of virtue shining from the throne creates an impression that is stronger than law itself; for the law comes into operation only when circumstances require it, while the ever-present example serves as a permanent object lesson and stirs us to emulation. Men always eagerly imitate those whom they deem essential for their happiness. But can anyone exercise greater influence on general well-being than the sovereign? And that is why the safest and surest way of guiding men to virtue is, without doubt, through the example set by the sovereign power.

Russia has four estates. The first is the *agricultural,* the second consists of the *burghers,* the third of the *nobility,* and the fourth of the *clergy.* Of these four estates, only one—the agricultural—suffers hardship in that it is liable for services over and above the obligations to the state to which its members are and ought to be subject, for everything that is required from the tiller of the soil for the good of the state is as justified as it is necessary. Any additional requirement is an evil, and the legislator should apply all his efforts to prevent it. How is it possible that the fate of this most useful of estates, on which the might and wealth of the country depend, should be in the hands of a few individuals, who at times treat its members even worse than their own cattle, forgetting that they are human beings like themselves, human beings who feed them and even cater to their whims. Horrible thought! How reconcile it with the goal of civil societies or with justice, which is their foundation? The great Catherine obviously felt the need of correcting this abuse when she demanded in her most wise and profoundly humane *Nakaz* [Instruction] that "all occasions that put man into bondage should be avoided (oh, divine words!), except in the case when extreme necessity compels it; but even then it should not be for the sake of *private benefit* but for the *good of the state.*" However, she says, "this would occur but very rarely." [7]

"Laws," she continues, "can make favorable provision for the personal property of slaves." [8]

Also "it *would be most necessary,*" she says, "to prescribe by law that [landowners] handle their levies with greater consideration," etc.[9]

Then she adds that "agriculture cannot prosper when no one has anything of his own." [10]

Here we have features worthy of the sensitive heart of the most wise legislatrix! Here we have the true foundation for the political edifice! *Without property,* of course, there cannot be that vivifying activity that is the soul of the body social. *Without property* all legislation exists only on paper. In the *absence of property,* public affairs barely move, and everything has an air of exhaustion, sadness, lifelessness, and, consequently, unhappiness. Lastly, where there is *no property,* where no one can safely enjoy the fruits of his labor, there the very *raison d'être* for human association is eliminated, the tie binding society is already broken, and, rising out of the existing conditions, the future is like a black cloud harboring a frightful storm.

Thus, the legislator's most important object is to make laws defining the property of the agricultural estate and protecting it against infringement —in a word, rendering it inviolable. Only when such laws come into existence will it be time to instill into this estate a sense of its rights and obligations. It is only then that the benefits of industry can be impressed upon it; only then will it be possible to tie the farmers securely to the land as the source of their happiness and prosperity. Only then will it be possible to undertake their education with confidence, to open the way to true enlight-

---

[7] Nakaz kommissii o sostavlenii proekta novogo ulozheniia [Instruction to the commission for the drafting of a new code] (Moscow, 1767), Ch. XI, § 253.

[8] *Ibid.,* Ch. XI, § 261.

[9] *Ibid.,* Ch. XII, § 270.

[10] *Ibid.,* Ch. XIII, § 295.

enment, an enlightenment shedding on them its healing and beneficial light, which will then be in accord, not in conflict, with the benefits expected from it.

"There are countries," says the great Catherine, "where in every parish there are books on agriculture published by the government, to which every peasant can turn for guidance in his perplexity." [11]

Happy lands! Why can I not say the same about my own country? No, Russia still is not in that position. For where the government takes care to furnish guidance to the husbandman in his pursuits, it has first taken care to *secure his property rights.* "This is based on the simple principle," says this most wise of monarchs, "that any man takes better care of what is his own than he does of what belongs to someone else, and that he exerts no efforts over something he fears another may take away from him." [12]

But nothing is impossible to the ruler who, burning with a desire to do good, ceaselessly labors to bring it about, to the sovereign who by his great intentions alone has already won immortality. No, for Alexander nothing is impossible. The heart that beats only for the country's welfare, whose virtuous qualities find illustration in the manifesto of March 5, 1803, allowing peasants to redeem themselves from their owners, such a heart will surely find a way to put an end to abuses of the landowners' power over their peasants and to secure and protect the latter's property.[13] ⟨To this end I consider it necessary to explain what I mean by *property* and the *peasants' rights to their property.*

Taking into account the present state of affairs, I shall be guided in this case by reason, experience, and our own laws and state acts.[14] Mr. Boltin writes:

> Before the conquest of the khanates of Kazan and Astrakhan all peasants in Russia were free and could move at will from place to place. Their taxes were paid not as head taxes or household taxes nor on the basis of possessions but on the basis of plow land (*pashnia*): He who [worked] more land paid more taxes and in turn earned more himself; the lazy man who worked less land paid less in taxes, had fewer benefits and less scope in satisfying his whims. The land belonged either to the crown or to the nobility (*dvorianstvo*); those settled on it paid the sovereign according to statute or the individual owner by agreement. From his peasants the landowner could not exact anything beyond what had been agreed upon or was established by law or custom, unless he wished to be left without peasants and without income. But to prevent the untimely peasant moves from one place to another that would produce arrears and confusion in state revenue or halt work performed for landowners, the law set aside one

[11] *Ibid.* Ch. XIII, § 302.

[12] *Ibid.*, § 296.

[13] Reference to the Law on the Free Agriculturists (February 20, 1803, PSZ 20 620).—Editor.

[14] From here to p. 140 Pnin is actually quoting from Ivan Boltin, *Primechaniia na istoriiu drevniia i nyneshniia Rossii g. Leklerka*, Vol. I (St. Petersburg, 1788), pp. 206–15 (N.–G. Le-Clerc, *Histoire physique, morale, civile et politique de la Russie ancienne et moderne*, 6 vols., Paris 1783–94).—V. Orlov.

period each year, in the fall, around St. George's Day, for the peasants' departure. There were fixed rules for this moving and the tenant's payments to the landowner for the homestead were regulated.

Kholopy [15] were also free men and served on the basis of *indenture papers (kabala)* and *limited indenture contracts (letnaia)*; only prisoners of war and their children were slaves. But as the latter were put under the same heading as the former, the first group was called *indentured (kabal'nye) kholopy*, that is, those serving under contract, while the second group consisted of the *old*, or full, *kholopy*, that is, hereditary [*kholopy*] or serfs. Freemen entered into the former status voluntarily, as did foreigners, burghers, lower service nobility (*deti boiarskie*), and others, except for peasants; and, having agreed on remuneration, they gave promissory letters, pledging to serve either until the death of the person to whom the pledge was given or for a certain number of years. In the first instance the instruments were called indenture papers and in the second time contracts. A full or hereditary *kholop* could be sold by the master or given away as a present or as part of his daughter's dowry. An indentured *kholop* was bound only to the person to whom he had voluntarily given himself in bondage, and upon the latter's death again became free.

In order to root out vagrants, parasites, and others who did not want to be useful members of the community, landowners were forbidden to accept into service free men who did not give a written pledge certified by a court; in the absence of such a document, an owner could not sue, even though the man robbed him and fled: *Do not hold without indenture papers.*

It was then understood that liberty had been given to man solely for the good and benefit of the country and the individual himself and that, in taking thought for his own welfare, the individual should not forget what he and everybody owed to the country. Whoever forgot his duty was reminded by the law; and necessity compelled him to obey the latter. A free man could not make a living without associating himself with one of the estates of the realm. And once within one of them, he had to accept all the obligations of the association of which he had taken the name and become a member. Every status category was liable for a particular duty, work, or service to the state and its own fellowship; the lazy and the parasitical were not tolerated in any status.

Dissatisfied with their power over indentured *kholopy*, as described earlier, the landowners started to treat them like full *kholopy*; the servants, however, not wanting to be enslaved, resisted the landowners' claims and, banding together, presented a petition to Tsar Vasilii Ivanovich Shuiskii complaining of the landowners' infringements of their freedom. Tsar Vasilii Ivanovich decreed that only prisoners of war could be slaves, while *kholopy* should serve, as previously, according to the terms of indenture papers, lifelong or temporary. In this condition the *kholopy* remained until the census [of Peter the Great], which put them into the same category as peasants, as will be mentioned below.

To return to my first point regarding the peasants. When they were forbid-

[15] Farm laborers or servants.—Editor.

den to move from one place to another, every man had to remain forever where he was settled, himself and his descendants as well. Those settled on the land belonging to [private] landowners became tied to the latter, not as individuals like the *kholopy*, but as part of the land, without freedom to leave it. The landowners took advantage of the prohibition to move and extended their power over the peasants; they forced the peasants to pay a high quitrent (*obrok*) and to perform excessive work. The peasants, bound as they were, did not dare to refuse either, lest it be interpreted as disobedience, opposition, or rebellion. For the law that had deprived them of their freedom of movement had not set the limits of their labor and obligations. Misunderstandings regarding the limits of the landowners' power and the peasants' obligation at first occasioned many disputes and complaints, rebellion; but as the landowners were cleverer and richer, they could interpret the law to their advantage and make the peasants appear to be the guilty ones. Not even at this time, however, had the landowners the power to sell their peasants and indentured servants like cattle, or to transplant them like trees, from one place to another. The law forbidding the turning of peasants into bondmen prohibited this as well. The only distinction between peasants and slaves was that the former were a cut above cattle and trees. This distinction existed for a long time, imposing some limitation on the landowners' power over the peasants and the latter's advantage over full *kholopy*. Peasants were sold, mortgaged, given as dowry, and left as legacies to children (in patrimonial holdings, of course), but only with the land; no one as yet dared to separate them from the land and to sell them individually. The landowner's power over estate peasants was smaller still; they could not be sold or mortgaged, for the estate (*pomest'e*) was granted, in lieu of emoluments, for life and not in hereditary ownership. The owners were given the first pretext for selling peasants individually by the system of recruiting soldiers from a number of households; this showed that the peasants could be separated individually from the land and their families. The decree equating granted estates and patrimonies (*votchina*) and soon afterward the census, which, without differentiating between the indentured and the full *kholopy*, lumped them both into one category with the peasants, lent support to the masters who were attempting to exercise the same ownership rights in the two cases. After this, *kholopy* were transformed into peasants and peasants into *kholopy*, they were separated from their families, and, finally, they were sold for resettlement in families or individually. The landowners' power over the property and life of their peasants and *kholopy* then became as complete as the power they had had, according to the old law, over prisoners of war only. There was no law making the peasants personal serfs of the landowners; introduced little by little, the practice of turning peasants into household servants, in direct violation of the law, and of selling them individually under that name was at first tolerated, then condoned, then falsely interpreted, and, as a result of long usage, finally transformed into law.

As there can be no peasant without a landowner, so there can be no free man without property. Property appertains to freedom in the same way as submission relates to power and authority. While our peasants in former times were free, they did, however, have landowners. In status (*sostoianie*) they were free, but they were peasants in official function (*chinosostoianie*), in their occupation. By virtue of their free status they could move from one place to another; but by virtue of the duties of their occupation they were liable for submission, services, and the payment of a certain sum in quitrent to the owner of the land on which they were settled. All the lands belonged, and still belong, either to the state or to individual owners; an estate owner (*pomeshchik*) settled on state land is a lord. There was no land on which those settled were exempt from payment of land taxes. By virtue of their freedom the peasants had the same kind of property as is now possessed by state peasants; it consisted in movables over which they had complete and independent power. After payment of all dues fixed by law, everything they acquired through their labor served to increase their own property. The land was the property of the landowners, but the fruits of labor and trade were the property of the peasants. The property of both was protected by law; the peasant could not leave before the set time nor without paying the amount legally fixed for rental and usufruct; the landowner, for his part, could not require anything in excess of this amount or retain the peasant against his will. What has been said suffices to show that in old Russia the peasants, being free men, had both owners and property without having land; landowners possessed peasants without the power to enslave them and received quitrent from them without having the right to despoil them.

. . .[16] At that time peasant and *kholop* were two status categories, distinct from each other in all respects; some of the differences have since been abolished, and others still exist today. In old times, the main difference between the *kholopy* and the peasants consisted in the fact that the former were slaves (I mean the full *kholopy*, of course) and paid no taxes. The differences existing today are that domestic serfs have no households, do not engage in agriculture or trade, live close to their masters all the time, perform all kinds of services, tasks, and duties for them, and are fed, clothed, and maintained by their masters.

. . . The term "enumerated people" designated peasants, not *kholopy*. The Tatars introduced the census. Their *basqaqs*,[17] after taking a census of those who lived in houses and had lands, trades, and incomes, imposed a tax; and because they had been counted and taxed, they were called "enumerated people." Those who, like the slaves, had no houses, trades, or property did not figure in the census, paid no taxes, and were of unknown number; consequently they could not be called "enumerated." *Kholopy* went to war with their masters, but only to guard and serve them. From among the enumerated, that is, the peasants, men were recruited for service on the basis of one man per hundred households, completely equipped, with the households furnishing his maintenance and pay. Because the peasants moved freely from place to place, a census had to be taken of them every year. The census records showed how many men had to serve from each district, and these men gathered at the mustering place on schedule, according to orders. All nobles without exception had

[16] Here and later, ellipses indicate Pnin's omission of quotations from LeClerc given by Boltin.—V. Orlov.
[17] Tax collectors for the Tatar Khan.—Editor.

to do service, and those who did not appear on time were listed as absent (*v netiakh*) and deprived of their granted estates. The law did not specify the number of *kholopy* each landowner was to have with him in service; everyone took as many as he could or wanted, depending on his wealth and on his will. *Kholopy* performed the same services for their masters during the campaign that the shield-bearing squires had performed for the knights of old. For the boyars these services were performed by their "familiars" (*znakomets*) and lower service nobility; the former were usually nobles, the latter, free men among whom could also be found landless nobles and princes.)

Does this not clearly show the excellence of the government institutions related to this matter in the days of our forebears? They valued the human being highly, protected property, and safeguarded the citizen's security; the *kholop*, the peasant, and the master were equal before the law, everyone's rights were respected, the law balanced the mutual obligations of the estates; and, lastly, order was well kept in all things. Most wonderful institutions! You have changed with the times, you have been superseded by others which do no honor to our enlightenment and even debase human beings. Could we in truth be blamed if we turned to the original source and drew from it the laws which were once the blessing of the Russian people and of which they are now deprived? The sovereign is the lawgiver in Russia; he can do whatever he wills. And what monarch has found obstacles to the doing of good? Removing the people's fetters, restoring men to mankind and citizens to the state—these are the good deeds that render emperors immortal and godlike and impose a tribute of gratitude on posterity, which raises altars to them in replacement of their thrones.

If we compare the present condition of the peasants with that of olden times, we notice a most striking contrast. The peasants of the past were free, but ours are slaves; formerly they had property, but our peasants have none, for the law does not protect it; in the past they had rights, but our peasants are deprived of them. I agree that the condition of some who belong to conscientious and just owners is not so bad, that in comparing themselves with others they are satisfied with their fate, forget their bondage, and bless their masters. But on the other hand, how numerous are those who find themselves in the most wretched condition and drag out their days in despair, cursing their lives and their masters. {*It lies within the government's power to correct this evil and give back his dignity to the tiller of the soil.* Owners, allow me to ask you this: Is it just to expose the peasant's labors, efforts, and fortune to horrible uncertainty, to the ever-present fear of losing what he has acquired? Tell me, is it not so that we may give one another help, security, peace, and happiness that we live in society? Look at yourselves! You will see that [the peasants] are men just like you. If you complain when injustice is done to you, if you are quick to avenge a trespass on your property, and if you consider the fruits of your labor your inalienable earnings, then, in truth, can you blame the peasants, endowed by nature with feelings similar to yours, if they complain of the cruelty of some inhuman masters and of the injustice that, in addition to [imposing] a heavy tax burden, deprives them of the fruits of their most arduous labor and effort?} [18] All this proves that property is as essential to the men who work the soil as the landowners deem it for themselves. Without it laws have no foundation, and it would be futile indeed to undertake to draft laws unless property is made secure. Finally, as soon as peasants' ownership of property is recognized, they can no longer be denied the rights entailed. Let us then consider what property and property rights should consist in.

The condition of privately owned serfs at the present is that they have nothing of their own [to show for] but the most arduous labor performed in acquiring things they cannot call their own, for, being themselves their masters' property, they have no feeling of security whatever. The terrible abuse of the power of the landowners over their peasants, {the excessive power of the owners over them, the slavery in which the peasants are held,} the inhuman trade in peasants which is carried on, all humiliate Russia in European eyes to a degree that cannot be expressed without the deepest sorrow. For a Russian who loves his native land it is grievous, very grievous indeed, to witness in it things which happen in the homeland of the negroes. Enlightened England, however, wishes to improve the latter's unhappy fate; despite the lucrative trade, England prefers to give up all its benefits rather than go against nature, against the rights of humanity for which it has so much respect and which constitute the foundation of all its institutions. In truth, by this action England will acquire immortal glory, and the deed will be recorded in the annals of mankind as an example of love of humanity. In the same manner our sensitive, always considerate monarch was pained to see men being advertised for sale together with animals. He immediately put an end to this vile custom, which was unworthy of his reign. Russia, how wonderful will be the high noon of this reign if its dawn is already so magnificent! [19]

The two kinds of property—movable and immovable—have caused political thinkers no little difficulty in discussing what kind of property should be given to peasants who have none.[20] For my part, taking into account present conditions, I would like to see the privately owned serfs possess *at least movable property* with the provision that, while paying to the landowner the dues imposed on them, they would have this property entirely at their own disposal, without fear, and would be assured that no one could take it away from them. Consequently, not only must this property be hereditary and inviolable, but the master must in no way restrict his

[18] Braces indicate passages censored in 1818, when an attempt was made to publish a second edition of Pnin's tract.—V. Orlov.

[19] Reference to the decree of May 28, 1801, to the President of the Academy of Sciences, forbidding the advertisement of the sale of serfs in the Academy's publications.—V. Orlov.

[20] To the question put in 1766 by the Free Economic Society: "What is more useful to society, that the peasant own land or only movable property; and what should be the extent of his rights to one or the other kind of property?" M. Beardé de l'Abaye, doctor of civil and canon law at Aachen, sent in an answer which was awarded a prize of 100 *chervontsy* and a gold medal by the Society and which indeed contains everything that deep knowledge, thorough reasoning, and love of humanity, expressed in pleasant style, can produce. See *Trudy vol'nogo ekonomicheskogo obshchestva* (1768), Part VIII.

peasants in their desire to make new acquisitions. To ensure this it is *absolutely* essential to give the peasants the *possibility* of saving property of their own.[21] This *possibility* lies in the peasant's *right to appeal to the law and demand its protection, not only when his lord violates his property but also in cases of illegal demands by landowners and of the inhuman acts which peasants must unjustly suffer from some masters.* Good and honest lords need not be vexed by this. It is not for good people that laws are established, for if all men were good and honest there would be no need at all for laws, which are necessary only to restrain the ill-intentioned and bad people. This is what I mean by *peasant property and the peasants' right to their property.* Great benefit will result from laying a foundation in this way, whatever its inadequacies and limitations. The first step will be followed by another. Wise rules and time will extend this beginning; the mere fact that a beginning has been made will drive away despondency from the farmers' houses, courage will revive the peasants' spirits, industry will awaken them to new activity, self-assurance will give them new strength, and joy, filling their hearts, will break out as gay smiles on their gloomy faces.

Without going into the possible ways of giving the peasants their rights to property and security (as I have described them) and of promulgating laws necessary toward this end, let us suppose that these laws are already in existence, that their beneficent influence has been extended to all.[22] Let us then turn to enlightenment and consider what it should consist in with respect to the agricultural and the other estates.

To achieve the desired end in the surest way, to make certain that success crown such a philanthropic undertaking, it is essential first to lay a firm foundation. I find no better procedure toward this end than to define for each of the nation's four estates its major virtues, *which will serve as focal points for their enlightenment and as the bounds of their spheres.* For if zeal and assiduity unfailingly attend the exercise of these virtues, society will reap in abundance their sweet fruits, and the potential benefits will appear in their full radiance.

And so I find *industry* and *temperance* to be the virtues most seemly for the agricultural estate; *punctiliousness* and *honesty* for the burghers,[23] *jus-*

---

[21] This property should include cattle, poultry, manufactured articles and handicraft work, various tools used by the peasants in their work, and other household articles; also included should be the dwellings, threshing floors, and other buildings and possessions the acquisition of which is provided for by the manifesto of March 5, 1803.

[22] How are we to proceed in drafting these laws and what steps are to be taken toward this end? All this is not my affair but the government's. For my part, I have only endeavored to show the need for peasant security and property and the numerous attendant benefits to the state; I have only tried to define what this property should consist in and how far the peasants' rights should go. All the unfeasibility of promulgating the necessary statutes and regulations will disappear once we take into account the status enjoyed by the peasants of old Russia (who in this respect had all necessary statutes and laws) and become acquainted with the excellent arrangements recently made for the peasants of Livland, safeguarding their property, rights, and welfare.

[23] By this term I mean all members of the third estate in Russia.

tice and *ever-present readiness to sacrifice oneself for the good of the country* for the nobility, and, lastly, *piety* and *exemplary conduct* for the clergy. These virtues I consider paramount for these estates. As to other moral qualities, they should be common to all, for the greater the sway of morality over all citizens, the more clearly does the welfare of the state proclaim the excellence of its government.

Thus the system of education which I propose shows that its sole aim is to make the citizens first *virtuous* and only then *enlightened*.[24] Its aim is to prepare Russians, not foreigners, for Russia, to prepare sons useful to their homeland and not individuals who scorn all that is native and despise their own tongue. No, such people are unworthy of being called Russians, unworthy of the glorious adornment which this name implies. A Russian's heart ought to be filled with noble pride. A Russian ought to feel his superiority over all citizens of foreign lands, for he belongs to a state which possesses half the globe and which has Alexander as its monarch. I am convinced that when Russia attains her proper civilization, that is, when her moral forces correspond to her physical strength, this power will assure the happiness of the whole world.

We ought to consider now the benefit that can be brought about by inculcating the virtues I have suggested. I shall treat them in the same order in which I indicated them earlier.

Without any doubt the geographic location of Russia requires that the greatest attention and encouragement be given to agriculture, upon whose improvement and success depends the flourishing condition of this state. But as the prosperity of agriculture is based entirely on *industriousness,* which gives life, strength, and power to the body politic, it it is necessary to instill this virtue in the men of the soil, to impress on them the fact that industry can bring them plenty, satisfaction, and prosperity. However, everyday experience teaches us that industry without temperance is like a body without a soul, that these two virtues support and safeguard each other, and that the one cannot exist at all without the other. It is also well known that nothing is more harmful to man than drunkenness. By weakening the body it brings about premature old age and exhaustion and shortens life. While affording certain short-lived pleasures, intemperance produces lasting misfortune. Those who surrender to an excess of wine become like savages, incapable of work; their powers of reasoning are impaired, they are diverted from the performance of their duties, they become negligent, useless, and despicable, and not infrequently they are led to [commit] the most horrible crimes. Consequently, while a love of industry must be implanted and encouraged in the farmer, he must be no less impressed with the benefits deriving from temperance and with an aversion to drunkenness, which, in addition to the misfortune it causes him himself, does harm to the whole

[24] In this I am in full agreement with the opinion of M. Virey, whose work *De l'éducation publique et privée des français* has revealed many useful truths about education that may enlighten all those concerned with this question. [Reference is to Jules Joseph Virey's book published in Paris in 1802. Virey was the author of a very popular *Histoire naturelle du genre humain.*—Editor.]

state. These reasons seem to me sufficient to convince anyone that industry and temperance, the two virtues essential to this estate of citizens, must be closely joined.

What Russian who loves his country can witness with indifference the sad spectacle before his eyes? How can he disguise the sadness that fills his heart? No, it is his sacred duty to express it to his benevolent monarch. He should hide no idea, no observation that concerns the state's advantage, for every single minute of the life of a Russian ought to be a contribution to the well-being of Russia, to the happiness of the country.

Look at the husbandman, surrounded by his family, hurrying to the temple to make his heartfelt offerings to the bountiful God who has sent him such an abundant harvest. Look at the joy shining on his face and reflected on his young children walking before him. See how he hastens his steps as he approaches the temple. But—what a sudden change! He diverts his eyes from the temple and fixes them on another object nearby! He notices many of his companions, some stretching out their hands to him with exclamations, others rushing forward to meet him. His thoughts are distracted, the reverence felt in his heart vanishes, the force of example triumphing over them. He follows his friends, and it is not the portal to the temple of the true God that opens to them, but the doors of Bacchus' noisy and pernicious den. There, drinking themselves into insensibility, before the idol of self-interest he pays tribute at the expense of his labor, his health, and morality itself, his most precious possession!

Certainly such a spectacle deserves attention on the part of the government. For, harboring physical and moral evil and contrary to the high goal of true enlightenment, the spectacle demands that the most effective remedial measures be taken. A famous writer of the preceding century says that "government has been established to support morality; as soon as it contravenes morality, it becomes useless and loses its power over [the people's] hearts."

Punctiliousness and honesty should be the particular virtues of the merchant estate. Experience confirms their necessity. The English and the Dutch, who serve as examples to all trading nations, consider punctiliousness the soul of commerce. Through it a dependable and steady flow of trade is secured; punctiliousness gives trade its character. Russia's trade is coming of age; alliance and friendship with her are sought by the foremost trading powers, thereby proving the wealth of her production as well as her influence on foreign nations. It is, therefore, essential for the Russian merchants to possess a true spirit of commerce, a spirit nourished and sustained only by business punctiliousness and disappearing when the latter ceases to operate. But punctiliousness without honesty, or honesty without punctiliousness, cannot exist properly. A merchant who is not honest will always find himself on the edge of an abyss. Honesty alone gives rise to the confidence that is so essential to trade. An honest merchant's word is accepted like cash. But, above all, honesty is desirable because it most effectively counteracts the vile ambitions prompted by foul cupidity and dishonesty. These are the reasons requiring that these virtues be inculcated in the burghers and that they be held sacred and considered an ornament of the estate.

Our merchants' major vice is that they lack a, so to speak, sense of solidarity and never endeavor to support one another in case of misfortune. On the contrary, seeing the failure and impending ruin of a poor merchant, the wealthy one will not only withhold a helping hand but will even make haste to harass him, so as to take advantage of his misfortune.

Merchants who have become more or less rich disdain being merchants. To them this estate seems too lowly. They want to be nobles. Strange wish! Yet nonetheless they do desire it, and they do so because they do not believe that it is impossible for them. And indeed they do reach their goal, obtain ranks (*chiny*), and become noblemen. But what is there to say about these new noblemen? What can they say about themselves? Instead of an answer they will show letters patent and display a charter of nobility and the hundred or two hundred thousand rubles they have withdrawn from the total merchant capital, as well as their own transformation. What merits! But what are the consequences of the benefactions received by them? The usual ones. In changing over from an active and industrious life to a condition that seems to them so much more brilliant, our merchant-noblemen become parasites, idlers, useless people. They live without performing any public duties and, ignorant of the obligations connected with their new status, evade them by all possible means; in so doing they give final demonstration of their own insignificance in this estate.

Ranks and noble status cannot be considered proper reward for the merchant class. These signs of distinction should belong only to those in the civil or military service. Each category of men should have advantages peculiarly its own. Thus, if the distinctions now available to the merchant status are not sufficient, the legislator can establish others suitable to it. The *rights* of citizens, without any doubt, should be equal, but their *privileges* cannot be the same. One of the legislator's most important objects is to make each member of society enjoy the estate in which he finds himself; so that the merchant, the artisan, the farmer, and so on, by putting all their pride into the zealous performance of their duties, may be certain that there are no degrees of distinction in good behavior, good name, and virtue, and that they compel equal respect from everyone.

Let us now consider the benefits derived from the following virtues assigned to the nobility: *justice* and *ever-present readiness to sacrifice oneself for the good of the country*. Most excellent obligations! How sacred you ought to be to a truly noble heart! Every step you take is a step toward virtue, every one of your traits is graven on the heart and remains there forever. Noblemen! How splendid is your station! What singular prerogatives you enjoy over other citizens! The monarchs have entrusted to you a most precious pledge—they have entrusted to you human beings like yourselves and, like you, members of society! This grace is from above, higher than humanity. Prove yourselves worthy of it! Greatness of soul should be your adornment. Array yourselves in it, be proud of it; it is the only pride you may be allowed, for it flows from a most noble source, from an elevation of the soul. Noblemen, love and respect justice; may this be your kindest feeling toward those in your power! Remember that the distance between you and them separates only two hearts, that Nature never loses her supremacy, and that yours must always bow to it. Remember that their contentment is your happiness, their happiness your glory, their love for you your immortality!

Justice is the salt of life, says Pythagoras. And in truth it safeguards everything, protects everything from injury; it renders the persons as well as the property of others inviolable and sacred. Man alone is master of himself; he lives in society for the sake of his security. In consequence, society must guarantee every member the possession of his own person, the exercise of his lawful rights, and the ownership of those things he has acquired by dint of his work and industry. From this it follows that no power on earth has the right to deprive man ⟨—the criminal excepted—⟩ either of his freedom, which is nothing but the possibility of laboring for his happiness in accordance with justice, or of his property, which includes everything he has or acquires by his efforts, talents, or dexterity. Man acquires just rights to all those objects which have required the application of his faculties to become what they are. His work, so to speak, fuses him with the object he has labored to shape, improve, make useful for either himself or others. Society becomes totally useless for us without security, without freedom, without property, and civil life is of advantage to us only because it protects these rights against injustice and infringement. *Justice* is the foundation of social and private welfare. Men are vicious and unhappy only because they are unjust; all moral virtues are based on justice.

Likewise, is there anyone from whom more services and more sacrifices should be demanded by the sovereign and the fatherland than the nobleman who enjoys extraordinary advantages in society and on whom the throne showers countless benefactions? Here then are the feelings, the sacred duties which the nobleman owes to his own title, to his monarch, and to his country: to be ready to sacrifice his life for the country at any moment; to have love of the common weal as his main goal; to repulse and destroy anything contrary to it; and to nourish in his breast that noble fire which is the source of all great deeds, which triumphs over time itself, which does not die down with the centuries, and which, being present in the magnanimous feats that adorn the world, instantly communicates its power, instantly flares up in sensitive and patriotic hearts.

But a nobleman who claims superiority because of his lineage and not because of the number of services rendered to his country, a nobleman who rests his fame on the merits of his ancestors and not on his own, a nobleman with a base soul who withdraws into himself, hates truth, and mocks virtue, believing that he has a claim to respect because of his wealth—such a nobleman belies his name completely, proves his contemptible ignorance, his vanity, and his brazen arrogance. Such a nobleman does not deserve to be called noble, he is unworthy of this distinction, he does not deserve to enjoy the rights connected with the status of nobility. Unfortunately, *with us as everywhere,*[25] noblemen in name only are scarcely fewer than those who are noblemen by virtue of their heart and qualities of soul. This circumstance alone would explain the need for the virtues I have assigned to this estate. The need is all the greater since the nobility, through the influence it has on the lives belonging to it, that is, on a large part of the population, can, if only it is oriented toward justice and readiness to sacrifice for the good of the country, more hopefully and surely promote the monarch's beneficent intentions.

Finally there remains to consider why *piety* and *exemplary conduct* ought to be the particular virtues of the clerical estate.

This much is surely not open to dispute: He who is entrusted with the sacred duty of preaching the word of God; who must be the teacher of the faith and impart the evangelical virtues without which there is no proper performance of civic duties; whose words should explain the wisdom, greatness, benevolence, and other divine attributes of the Almighty Creator that mold the Christian's heart and soul; who should lead the flock entrusted to his care in the path of righteousness, see to its piety, confirm it in the faith, reason with it in its perplexities, explain to it that religion brings true happiness to man; in short, he whose cloth and duties require that he impart so much knowledge and virtue to others—such a man must surely himself be filled with piety, must be himself of good conduct, so that he may influence others more by his example than by his teachings.

Thus we have defined the virtues of each of the four main estates of the realm, demonstrated the necessary benefits to be derived from the instilling of each one of these virtues, and in so doing have prepared a firm foundation on which the majestic edifice of public enlightenment should be erected. Anyone can then clearly see that, if these estates differ so much in their essence, in their virtues, they undoubtedly ought to differ also in the degree as well as in the pattern of their enlightenment.

A MANUAL FOR THE ENLIGHTENMENT
OF THE PRINCIPAL ESTATES
OF THE RUSSIAN REALM, NAMELY
THE AGRICULTURAL, BURGHER, NOBLE,
AND CLERICAL ESTATES [26]

The main goal of public education should be to give everyone the knowledge necessary for the proper performance of the duties to which he is called in society.

These obligations, however, cannot be the same for everyone, since society comprises various classes of citizens, and it follows that each member of

[25] Phrase struck out by the censor (note by copyist who copied Pnin's manuscript for resubmission to the censor in 1818).—I. K. Luppol, V. Orlov.

[26] Much of what follows is a paraphrase and adaptation of J. A. Chaptal's project for a system of national education for France.—V. Orlov.

society must receive an education corresponding to his estate, occupation, and way of life.

If we look at the composition of a populous nation whose members are united by a social contract, we note that all citizens occupy a place that is socially useful; we also note that the best-organized governments and the happiest nations are those in which every citizen is in his place, where no one is forgotten, where public offices are respected at every level, and where the government, taking care of everything, maintains order in all parts and protects the rights of every category of citizens.

If we take this as our premise and also feel convinced that education ought not to be the same for all citizens, it remains to determine what education should consist in with respect to the estates I have mentioned earlier. I shall proceed in order and, without going into all the details, indicate only the main principles on which we can base the books it will be necessary to prepare for uniform instruction in the schools and the moral education of the citizens.

The virtues I have defined for every estate must be carried as a motto on all the moral statutes which will be issued for them. Therefore:

1. Let *industry* and *temperance* be the motto for the statute intended for agricultural schools.

2. But inasmuch as this statute is issued solely to serve as the most convenient method for the farmer's true enlightenment, it follows that the farmer's primary knowledge must pertain to his calling and to his duties. For what can be dearer to him than himself? It is consequently necessary to begin by defining:

3. What is a farmer (*zemledelets*)?

4. How many types of farmers are there?

5. What is their significance in the state?

6. What is the state?

7. What is it called?

8. What kind of government does it have?

9. Having shown that it is a monarchy or an autocracy, one has to determine:

10. What is a monarch or a sovereign?

11. What does the sovereign power consist in?

12. What established powers or authorities are there in Russia?

13. What are their means of action?

14. Knowledge of these authorities is essential to farmers, as they are always in relations with them; the former give orders, the latter execute them.

15. Hence arise mutual obligations: the *obligations of authority* and the *obligations of subordination*.

16. What does each consist in?

17. Anyone who has public obligations must also have his own rights.

18. Consequently, the farmer must not be deprived of the rights belonging to him.

19. It must be determined what a right is and what it should consist in.

20. But as the very first and most sacred of civil rights is the right to property, it follows that the farmer must have property and that this property must be inviolable and protected by law.

21. Here it is necessary to indicate what law is and who has the power to issue laws.

22. What is property and how is it acquired?

23. The obligations, rights, and property of farmers having been defined in this manner, it is necessary to impress on them to the utmost the benefits and happiness that result from an industrious and sober life.

24. Lastly, as no morals can exist without religion, it is necessary to give the farmers a clear idea of God and of the faith and duties of a Christian.

These are the principal rules which I consider sufficient for drafting a statute for the moral education of citizens belonging to this estate.

Reading ought to be taught according to this statute (parish priests may be entrusted with the task); this will result in a double benefit, for in learning the pupil will not only acquire his letters but will also of necessity obtain knowledge of his obligations in society. He will learn who he is and what he is intended for. As a result, imperceptibly he will be educated morally.

Parish schools must be open to all, irrespective of age.

*Let us now consider what the farmer's training
should consist in*

As the farmers' lot is to labor and to work the land, whose fruits nourish men of all conditions, it follows that their only purpose ought to be agriculture; agriculture, however, will not flourish, will not reach perfection as long as the government's full attention, help, and encouragement are not given to it.

As agriculture is the sole purpose of the farmer, it is quite natural that his training should be focused on the subject most in keeping with this purpose. In short, the farmer should be taught farming.

Like all sciences, agriculture has its laws and may be enriched by the experience of all nations; it would be vain to expect from the [mere] passage of time what the [systematic] acquisition of knowledge may give us. For in the working of the fields, habit and methods transmitted from generation to generation eliminate even the very thought of improvement.

It is necessary, therefore, that knowledgeable men investigate without prejudice, test without passion, and propose without frenzy all that agriculture may offer in the line of discoveries and improvements. To convince the skeptical and prejudiced farmer, one must show him the results of experiments; it is necessary that he see clearly and be convinced that what you are proposing is incomparably better, more convenient, and more profitable than what he is accustomed to. Only in this way can we spread the useful methods whose success is beyond doubt.

The organization of these agricultural or parish schools should be as simple as their purpose.

For this reason I think it will be adequate if they comprise two grades. The subject of the *first grade* will be agricultural mechanics, that is, buildings and all mechanical equipment that may be to the advantage of agriculture and make it easier.

The *second grade* will have as its subject the nature and cultivation of soils, the nature and preservation of seeds and the storing of crops, work on natural and artificial meadows and swamps, the clearing of ground for plowing, and, lastly, the raising and improvement of cattle and the veterinary art.

If, in addition to these subjects reading, writing, and the basic operations of arithmetic, as prescribed in Chapter II, Paragraph 32, of the Preliminary Regulations for Public Education, are taught and if the entire curriculum is arranged in a systematic and pedagogically convenient order along the lines I have suggested earlier for the elaboration of a moral code, then the citizens of this estate will receive all the essentials for their enlightenment. In due course, the state will find its own true sons in these providers of our food, who possessing hearts formed by morality and minds shaped by learning, will perform their duties properly, serve their country with benefit, and harbor in their souls gratitude to the monarch who cares for them.

Guiding rules for the education of the burgher estate

Composing the middle estate in Russia and enjoying freedom, the burghers are not numbered among either the farmers or the nobility. The state may expect a great deal from citizens of this estate if only they receive the right guidance, that is, if the government gives them its attention and raises them to the level of social usefulness from which they are still so far removed at present.

The burghers need moral education as much as instruction in the subjects pertaining to their calling. Consequently, it is also necessary to draft a *moral statute* for them and engrave on it as a motto the virtues assigned to them. In many respects this statute should include the rules I suggested earlier for the agricultural statute, the only difference being that the burghers' statute be as closely relevant to their estate as possible. Its rules may, for example, include the following:

1. In the first place, burghers ought to know what a burgher is.
2. What place does he occupy in the state?
3. What are his obligations with respect to the state?
4. What rights and privileges is he accorded in the state?
5. What should he do to preserve them, and what must he avoid so as not to lose them?

6. It is the obligation of the burghers also to know all the laws of their country, for this constitutes a very important part of their duties.

7. Love of country and of the common weal should constitute their most treasured emotion. In this respect the immortal Minin can show the way leading to these most noble ends.[27]

8. An effort should be made to stimulate in the burghers a love for their estate, to bind them to it as closely as possible, so that in acquiring wealth they do not develop a disgust for their calling. For experience shows that almost all the merchants who have grown rich have an aversion to being merchants and endeavor, by all possible means, to turn their children at least, if not themselves, into nobles.

9. They should be impressed with the idea that true dignity does not consist in titles, but in honesty and lack of cupidity; without these no title will protect them from ignominy and contempt.

10. Their rights, privileges, and duties with respect to the state having been defined, the burghers ought to be shown their obligations with respect to their fellow-men, members of society like themselves.

11. To this end religious instruction must be part of the moral statute.

12. Finally, every possible effort should be made to inculcate in the burghers who follow the calling of merchants the virtues designated for them, that is, *punctiliousness* and *honesty;* by practicing them they will only consolidate their reputation and prosperity.

In my opinion, these rules are essential in drafting a moral statute for the merchants, a statute that can also serve for the burghers engaged in various trades, crafts, and arts. It is indeed indisputable that the lowliest artisan must know his rights and duties with respect to the state, and his obligations with respect to his fellow-man as well, and that without such virtues as good conduct and industry he will achieve neither prosperity nor happiness. In any case, the publication of this statute may be of general use, for parents who teach their children how to read at home will obviously prefer this book to all those of necessity in use at the present, and consequently half the task will have been completed even before their children have entered school.

Subjects of instruction for burghers who follow the merchant's calling.   It would be pointless to enumerate the benefits accruing to the state from trade. They are palpably clear to anyone who has dealt ever so little with this kind of subject. Trade may be considered a spontaneous development common to all nations, for there is no nation that does not more or less engage in it. By virtue of her extended possessions and the richness of her natural resources, Russia occupies a first place among the world's powers; and for this reason she requires that, for its part, the government give all possible attention to the improvement of such an important area. But advances in trade depend on the degree of enlightenment on the part of the citizens conducting it; in the absence of such enlightenment neither the

[27] History testifies that, fired by love for his country, Minin sacrificed all his possessions and his life to save it.

most useful institutions nor the best of legislative intentions can serve their purpose. This alone should explain the unavoidable necessity for the establishment of schools aiming primarily at the moral instruction of merchants in the knowledge requisite for their calling. In short, the establishment of commercial schools is as necessary for Russia as is commerce itself.

Chapter I, Paragraph 6, of the Preliminary Regulations for Public Education provides for the establishment of *at least one* district (*uezd*) school in every district town; consequently, no fixed number is set for such schools and there may be more than one in each town. For my part, I would consider it very useful if two schools were established in some towns, depending on their location and the nature of their population. In one school burghers would be taught various trades, crafts, and arts, while the other would be attended only by those preparing themselves for the merchant's calling. The latter, by its very nature, would be a merchants' or commercial school. The program of instruction in these schools might be as follows:

In the first type, that is the burghers' school, consisting of two grades, the lower and upper, the following should be taught in the lower grade:

1. Reading and writing in Russian.
2. Also reading and writing in the local language, such as Polish, German, Tatar, etc.
3. The grammar of all these languages.
4. The first part of arithmetic.
5. Pertinent information about the Russian Empire.
6. Summary survey and main periods of Russian history.
7. Introduction to world history and geography.

In the upper grade:

1. Second part of arithmetic.
2. Geometry and trigonometry.
3. Mathematical and physical knowledge about the world.
4. Physics.
5. Natural history and technology.
6. Practical information useful in local industry and for regional needs.

In the second school, that is, the commercial, in addition to the subjects listed above, there should also be taught:

1. Reading, writing, and grammar of the English language.
2. Algebra.
3. All types of commercial accounting.
4. Single- and double-entry bookkeeping.
5. History of trade and navigation, knowledge of commerce and wares, and finally, summary notions of anatomy, physiology, and dietetics.

If in some districts there is no need for two schools, all the subjects listed can be taught in one school, the instruction being split among the required number of grades, so that both artisans and merchants may have all the necessary facilities for their education.

At this point it may not be superfluous to mention that the freedom teachers are given in some schools to follow their own methods of teaching and a failure to provide special government-published books for the teachers' guidance to produce uniformity of instruction not only will prevent the successes expected of these schools from materializing but will even deprive us of the hope of seeing the schools in operation. While there are teachers on whose qualities and talents one may depend, the majority are such that they cannot be entrusted with a free choice in selecting the authors to guide them in their teaching. This is a task for the government, which has at its disposal all the necessary means; it should assume the responsibility of publishing classical books for compulsory use by teachers, who would also maintain as much uniformity of methods and rules as possible.

Let us now consider what the enlightenment
of the nobleman should consist in

The government has always paid most attention to this estate of the realm. Among the institutions benefiting the nobility, those that could serve its enlightenment have not been neglected. For the nobles, cadet schools (*korpusy*) and general schools were established, while all other estates were forgotten by the government and left in the darkness of their insignificance. At long last, Time, which holds sway over everything and transforms everything, saw the injustice so long inflicted on citizens of the lower order by keeping them in ignorance, and revolted against it. And wishing to ensure Russia's well-being, Time gave her Alexander, the gentle, philanthropic monarch who no sooner ascended his ancestors' throne than enlightenment flowed into all corners of the vast Russian Empire, passing from one estate to another and illuminating all of them with its beneficial light.

Undoubtedly, the nobles require a privileged education, for amidst their ranks the country must be able to find its brave defenders, skillful and virtuous heroes, as well as wise, honest, and just lords and magistrates. But how can such essential qualities be inculcated? Solely through education, I say.

If we examine the institutions existing at present for the education of noble youths, we shall see that most have departed from their true object. All education is limited to the teaching of subjects; consequently, the young men are being schooled but not educated. In some cadet schools the main effort consists in teaching the children the manual of arms and drill, and this excessively rigid instruction occupies them more than the basic sciences that should prepare them to fill with dignity and honor the posts they will have to occupy upon leaving the school. The military science taught in these schools consists entirely in this mechanical drill. Anyone can judge for himself, therefore, whether such training can produce skillful officers and generals.

The authorities in charge of the young noblemen's education must be selected by the government most strictly. For what can be more precious than this trust, which holds within it the individual and the social happiness? In his book *Opyt voennogo vospitaniia otnositel'no blagorodnogo iunoshestva* [Essay on the Military Education of the Young Nobility], Mr. Bestuzhev has drawn up a sound system of instruction for this category of citizens, and he has also pointed out those qualities that must distinguish the director and all those who are in charge of the pupils. The book is very useful, especially for a government that is concerned about public education, without which no state can be either strong or happy. It has facilitated my task very much, for it contains almost everything needed for drawing up a moral statute for the nobility as well as a curriculum of subjects necessary for its instruction. I need not, therefore, spell out fully the rules for the composition of such a statute and the methods to be used in instructing the young noblemen. In his book, Mr. Bestuzhev has already provided a splendid answer to the question of what the nobility's enlightenment should consist in. I shall note only the following:

As the nobles try to enroll their children only in the cadet schools, it is essential that these be set up in such a way as to prepare men fit not only for the military but also for the civil service. An officer should be both a skillful soldier and a learned magistrate. Everyday experience demonstrates how much harm stems from the fact that officers graduated from the cadet schools transfer to the civil service after a few years of [military] service without possessing the required knowledge of civil affairs, laws, or national institutions. It is saddening to enumerate the misfortunes resulting from this ignorance! Instead of protecting the innocent and saving a man unjustly oppressed, those occupying important state offices frequently do not know how to extend a helping hand and even become the instrument of his utter ruin. This happens because, being themselves ignorant, they have to resort to the knowledge of third persons, to turn over to them affairs they should have attended to themselves. These persons, called secretaries, on whose conscience one cannot always depend, do not fail to abuse the trust reposed in them; gradually, the more they find themselves needed, the more power they acquire over their superiors and sometimes, in so doing, crown the misfortune of a whole province.

This is sufficient to make one aware of the need to improve the education offered in the cadet schools. *Jurisprudence should certainly be part of their curriculum,* in particular the national laws, state institutions, and the conduct of civil affairs. An officer thus educated, if forced by circumstances to transfer to the civil service, will still be in the right place to fulfill his duty with honor; and at all times society will find him a most useful member. And must it not seem strange to everyone that there is no calling—scholarship, a craft, or trade—which a man may take up without going through all the stages leading to it and giving proof of his merits and skills, and yet in the civil service men are appointed indiscriminately, without any test. At times ranks are conferred on them that require them to fill most important posts without having any talents except that they can read and sign their name. Is it surprising that the civil service does not have the dignity it should have, that it is not respected, and that many avoid it solely out of fear that they may come under the authority of men who deserve no respect but only scorn? In purpose, the civil service is perhaps more important than any other, for its object is the internal ordering of the state, the foundation of the people's peace and happiness, and it therefore needs the most honest, virtuous, enlightened, and zealous individuals.

For this reason I think it would be most useful to establish, in addition to the existing school, *three* more *military (iunker) schools,* in order that—provided this is *considered desirable*—the nobility may continue to exist without loss of the rights granted to it by law. One of these military schools might be established in Moscow under the direction of the Senate, another in Kazan, and the third in Vilno, under the direction of the [school] overseers of the districts in which they will be located. These schools should be open exclusively to the nobility and on the same conditions as the existing school here,[28] except that the latter admit no children below the age of fourteen nor without elementary schooling, whereas the schools I propose would enroll children from seven to nine years of age, even if they had had no previous instruction whatsoever, and would start teaching them from the day of their admission.

Many right-thinking people have long felt the need for such institutions, particularly parents who want their children to have a career in the civil service. But not having the means, they are forced, against their will and against their children's inclinations and abilities, to send them to cadet schools whose purpose is to train officers for military service.

The curriculum of the schools I am proposing should correspond to their purpose.

This is all I have found necessary to suggest with respect to the enlightenment of the nobles; lastly, let us consider *what ought to be done with respect to the enlightenment of the clergy.*

Guides for educating the clergy

If we just think of the purpose for which clergymen are appointed, or of the duties they are obligated to perform, or of the respect they demand for their cloth, or of the influence they have on popular opinion, then we shall find that the government has not yet done everything for them. For many are the priests who, instead of possessing the requisite education, are in a state of most pernicious ignorance; who, instead of setting an example in spiritual and civic virtues, give themselves over to shameful passions and thus offer others a pretext for leading an indecent and debauched life. In short, is the flock to be entrusted to the care of this kind of shepherd? Must the Church have servants who conduct themselves in this way? Are these the priests who are to safeguard the holiness of religion and the stability of its altars? Of course not. For its part, the government must give all possible attention to the education of the clergy, which is, by its nature, such an important estate.

The necessity of a *moral statute* for the clerical calling, therefore, has

28 Presumably the St. Petersburg Corps of Cadets.—Editor.

been demonstrated. Piety and exemplary conduct (the virtues assigned to the clergy) will be the motto of the statute, which may be drafted along the lines of the statutes I have suggested earlier, the only difference being that its rules should be fully in keeping with the function of the priests.

With regard to the method of instruction in seminaries, the only places where men are prepared for the ecclesiastical estate, it requires some pruning and some improvements. Why teach the subjects in Latin and not in the native tongue? This time-honored custom hampers instruction a great deal, for a student who does not have a perfect command of Latin (and what need is there to know it to perfection?) will never adequately know what the instructor teaches in this language. Similarly, what is the use of teaching dead languages? Would it not be more useful to teach the languages that are most used, those which have obtained, so to speak, the rights of citizenship in all of Europe? Even more I would wish that, instead of the all too thick-strewn flowers of rhetoric, instead of the pompous style which in its extravagance hides the ideas and produces boredom or derision, our gentlemen instructors might see to it that in composing sermons their pupils endeavor to write in the simplest, clearest, and most readily intelligible language. The students should be reminded that they are to address themselves not to scholars but to the people; their eloquence should consist in the art of attracting their listeners' attention and producing in them the desired effect by the truths they propound. It is, therefore, necessary that the art of elocution be part of the seminary curriculum.

In this connection I cannot forbear mentioning that it is necessary for the government to take steps of its own to secure a decent maintenance for the priests. This would eradicate the shameful and debasing customs that are quite inappropriate for the priestly cloth; for example, on the great holidays of the year—Christmas, Easter Sunday, and others—priests would not have to go from house to house to collect offerings, a practice that makes them appear in such a disgusting aspect that one wonders how the government not only tolerates but even approves of such customs.

Now that I have proposed a system of general education for Russia, it remains for me to resolve a last, but rather important, question: What can best promote enlightenment? That is to say, what are the means that can stimulate and feed this spirit of enterprise so necessary to all estates of the realm in fulfilling their mutual obligations?

The principal means is *encouragement*. Wise governments, both past and present, demonstrate how far this all-conquering force can go. *Encouragement* pulls people out of irresponsibility and despondency, it gives birth to courage, it produces competition, and it moves the spirit to great and useful deeds. When talent and merit are encouraged, when virtues are duly respected, pygmies stride with giant steps, the impossible becomes possible, the sleeping genius awakes, and what would have required several years for completion if left to time is rapidly brought to successful completion. In short, wherever the government rewards labor, encourages talent, crowns patriotic feats with glory, patronizes the arts, crafts, and sciences, there patriots, artists, scholars, and philosophers will never fail to see the light of day.

But encouragement is needed most of all in a state that is, so to speak, still in its youth, in which one sees but the beginnings of everything. And the government which has chosen encouragement as the means for improvement has without doubt chosen the surest way to hasten the desired success.

Enlightened rulers alone can feel the people's need for enlightenment and consequently know the benefits which encouragement produces. Only wisdom can restore the rights of reason to the oppressed and the wronged, and free reason from the fetters imposed by malicious ignorance. Blessed are the rulers and the countries in which the citizens, free to think, can impart without fear the truths involving the common weal!

Of all the humanitarian and most benevolent prospects opened up by our most beloved monarch for the good of the fatherland, none is more splendid than the one manifested in the establishment of the Ministry of Public Education; indeed it may be called the trunk and all the other plans its branches.

Taking into account, therefore, the institutions existing at the present for the people's enlightenment, I maintain that encouragement alone can provide the means for making up the all too noticeable lack of books, classical and other, in our language. To this end the government must compile a list of the books it deems most useful for translation into Russian and announce to all practicing men of letters that the best translation will be accepted [for publication] and the translator duly rewarded by the government. In this way we shall soon have available in our language the most needed and the best works of foreign writers, and the government will also be able to revive the taste for everything beautiful and give this revival a desirable orientation.

If the establishment of ministries was aimed at facilitating the administration of the state by dividing it into eight major branches, thereby enabling each to function in the easiest, most convenient, surest, and steadiest way, we must assume that every department entrusted to the ministers ought to include everything pertaining to its domain. This being so, I cannot help mentioning here that all public theaters, because of their very nature and importance, definitely ought to be under the direction of the Minister of Public Education.

I shall not go into details concerning the good or harm done by theaters. This would distract me from my subject too much. Everybody knows that in either case it depends entirely on the nature of the government, on the direction it gives to the theaters, and on the authorities to whose care it entrusts them. I shall only say that, under wise direction, theaters will have no less influence on the success of universal education than the schools established to this end. This proves that the theaters are a branch of public education. I would like to see theaters established in some of the provinces and put under the direction of truly enlightened men, knowledgeable in this art and concerned for the good of the country. It is also necessary to provide for the upkeep of the actors, as the majority of those composing the local company lack even the basic necessities. They do not see themselves encouraged in any way, but, on the contrary, they are put far below foreign actors and enjoy little esteem in the public's opinion; for this reason they not only fail to be stimulated by competition but even lose the spirit that could develop their talents.

As a Russian who loves his country, I can say that it is impossible to look at the condition of our national theater without deepest sorrow. I shall not conceal the fact that I would like to see the Russian theater, with all its faults, preferred to all others; I would like to see the salary of our best actors and actresses at least equal to, if not double, that of the best French actors and actresses. The same goes, naturally, for our best dancers and ballerinas as compared with the French ones here. Anyway, even if one can find arguments against the idea, one can, of course, say even more in its favor. Such a policy will greatly encourage the Russian actors. A comfortable living will raise them from their despondency, stimulate their desire to excel, and thus, setting them on the path to glory, give them a new soul for their life in the theater.

One of the main defects of our theater is a shortage of plays worthy of performance and corresponding to the purpose of the theater as an institution. The public grumbles about it, and its grumbling is justified in this case. For if we look into the reason for this defect, we shall discover that there is no special curator who would, so to speak, supervise the moral condition of the theater. But as the theater is nothing else than a school of manners, it follows that everything touching on the economics of the theater can be left in its present state, under the control of existing authorities; but as to the selection of plays to be produced, the choice of plays to be translated into our language to make up for the lack of plays afflicting the Russian theater, assignment of subjects for plays to our authors, encouraging them with the promise that no play submitted by them and approved by the government would remain unrewarded—all these matters can hardly be disposed of more justly and more fittingly than by making them the responsibility of the Minister of Public Education. For who else could act better and in greater accord with the government's views?

I have only the following to say in conclusion: When all the major branches of government have been properly ordered, when they have acquired their due solidity and strength, then will the whole state be revivified, and the concord of its citizens will serve to revive the national spirit, which in the mirror of history will represent the character of past government and, consequently, also the epoch of Russia's happiness and the wise reign of Alexander.

8.

Petr Iakovlevich Chaadaev

ca. 1794-1856

The wars against Napoleon and particularly Russia's role in the liberation of Europe from French domination (1813–15), the gradual penetration of romantic ideas stressing the creative role of a nation's character, and finally the *crise de conscience* produced by the Decembrist revolt led the Russian intelligentsia to raise some basic questions concerning the nature of their country's past and its relationship to Western Europe. The public debate was opened by the publication in 1836 of the first of the so-called "Filosoficheskie Pis'ma" (Philosophical Letters) of Petr Iakovlevich Chaadaev. As Herzen put it, the publication of the letter had the "effect of a pistol shot in the dead of night." The furor it caused was immense. Nicholas I felt that Chaadaev had insulted Russia and the imperial regime itself. *Teleskop,* the journal in which the letter appeared, was banned, its editor, N. I. Nadezhdin, exiled, the censor reprimanded, and Chaadaev declared insane and put under house arrest.

The other letters, eight in all, which Chaadaev wrote were not printed in his lifetime. Taken together, these letters (ostensibly addressed to a woman friend of Chaadaev's) are a comprehensive historiosophical tract concerned in the main with religious questions. But the first letter sharply delineates the problem of Russia's relationship to the West (which Chaadaev equates with Roman Catholicism) and its role in the history of human culture and progress. The first letter alone, the only one to become known at the time, helped precipitate a lively debate on the character of Russia's past and of its mission in the future.

Letters on the Philosophy of History

First Letter

Adveniat regnum tuum

MADAM,

It is your candor and sincerity that I most cherish and respect in you. Imagine, therefore, how surprised I was by your letter! It was those delightful qualities of yours that charmed me when I made your acquaintance and caused me to speak to you of religion, although everything about you should have made me keep silent. Once again, imagine my astonishment on receiving your letter! That, Madam, is all I have to tell you concerning the opinion you think I have of your character. Let us say no more about it, but turn at once to the serious part of your letter.

To begin with, what causes this confusion in your mind, a confusion which so agitates you and, as you say, exhausts you to the point of affecting your health? Is this the sad result of our conversations? The new sentiment awakened in your heart should have brought you peace and tranquillity; instead, it has caused qualms, anguish, almost remorse. Yet is that so surprising? It is but the natural consequence of our present lamentable state of affairs, which affects all hearts and minds. You have merely allowed yourself to be swayed by the forces which move us all, from the most exalted members of our society to the slave who exists only for his master's pleasure.

How could you have resisted? The very qualities which set you apart from the crowd must make you the more vulnerable to the ill effects of the air you breathe. How could the little I was able to say to you have clarified your ideas, in the midst of all that surrounds you? Could I purify the

Translated by Valentine Snow from Petr Iakovlevich Chaadaev, "Lettres sur la philosophie de l'histoire: Lettre première," in *Sochineniia i pis'ma P. Ia. Chaadaeva*, ed. M. O. Gershenzon, Vol. I (Moscow, 1913-14), pp. 74-93. This letter, the only one to be published during Chaadaev's lifetime—probably against his will—first appeared in *Teleskop*, No. 15 (Moscow, 1836) although it was written several years before.

Gershenzon's volume also contains two more of the letters, all printed in the original French. Five others were discovered in the twentieth century and published in a Russian translation, "Neizdannye pis'ma P. Ia. Chaadaeva," ed. D. Shakhovskoi, in *Literaturnoe nasledstvo*, Vol. 22-24 (Moscow, 1935). A German translation of this Russian version may be found in Heinrich Falk, S.J., *Das Weltbilt Peter J. Tschaadajews nach seinen acht "Philosophischen Briefen"* (Munich, 1954).

atmosphere in which we live? I should have foreseen this consequence; I did, in fact, foresee it. Hence my frequent silences, which could hardly have inspired you with confidence and which must certainly have bewildered you. Had I not been persuaded that, whatever suffering an incompletely awakened religious feeling may cause, it is still better than total slumber, I would have had to repent of my zeal. But the clouds which now darken your sky will one day, I hope, dissolve into a life-giving dew which will germinate the seed fallen into your heart. The effect on you of a few valueless remarks is a sure sign that the work of your own intelligence will in future produce much greater results. Abandon yourself without fear, Madam, to the emotions aroused in you by religious ideas; only pure feelings can come from that pure source.

Insofar as external matters are concerned, let it be enough for you today to know that the doctrine which is founded on the supreme principle of *unity* and of the direct transmission of the truth through the unbroken succession of its ministers cannot but come closest to the true spirit of religion; for it is wholly contained in the idea of the fusion of all the moral forces in the world into a single thought, a single emotion, and in the progressive establishment of a social system, or *Church,* which is to make the truth reign among men. Any other doctrine, if only because it has split off from the original one, negates the sublime invocation of the Saviour, who prayed that "they may be one as we are" [1], and opposes the realization of the reign of God upon earth. But it does not follow that you must proclaim this truth to the world; that is certainly not your calling. On the contrary, the very principle from which that truth is derived imposes upon you the duty, seeing your position in the world, to maintain it as an inner torch of your faith, and nothing more. I deem myself happy to have helped to turn your thoughts toward religion; but I should have been most unhappy, Madam, if at the same time I caused you qualms of conscience which in the end would be bound to lessen your faith.

I believe I once said to you that the best way to preserve religious feeling is to observe all the rites prescribed by the Church. This exercise in submission, which encompasses more than is commonly thought and which the greatest minds have imposed upon themselves after due deliberation, is the true homage one pays to God. Nothing so fortifies the spirit in its faith as the strict practice of all the obligations of that faith. Besides, most of the rites of the Christian religion, dictated by the highest reason, are truly effective when practiced by those who have understood the truths they express. There is only one exception to this otherwise general rule: when one finds oneself holding beliefs of a higher order than those professed by the masses, beliefs which raise the soul to the very wellspring of all our certitude and which at the same time support, rather than contradict, the beliefs of the people, then, and then only, is it permissible to neglect external observances in order to engage all the better in more important tasks. But woe to him who mistakes the illusions of his vanity and the deceptions

[1] John 17:11.

of his reason for special grace which dispenses him from the general law! In your case, Madam, what better thing could you do than wrap yourself in the cloak of humility, so becoming to your sex? Believe me, that is the best way to calm your agitation and to bring sweet peace into your life.

Besides, is there—even in the eyes of the world—a more natural existence for a woman whose cultivated mind finds pleasure in study and in the grave emotions of meditation than a somewhat earnest life, much of which is spent in reflecting on and practicing religion? You say that nothing in your reading so captivates your imagination as descriptions of tranquil and thoughtful lives, the image of which, like the view of a fair countryside in the setting sun, brings repose to the spirit and for a moment takes us out of our painful or dull reality. Well, those are not mere fantasies; you can, if you wish, make one of these charming figments come true; you lack nothing for such an achievement. You see that I am not preaching an austere morality; it is in your own tastes, in the pleasantest fancies of your imagination, that I look for that which can bring peace to your soul.

There is a side in our life which relates not to the physical, but to the thinking, being. It should not be neglected; there is a regimen for the spirit as there is one for the body, and we must learn to submit to it. That is an old saying, I know; but I think that in our country it often has the merit of novelty. It is one of the most deplorable traits of our peculiar civilization that we are still discovering truths which other peoples, even some much less advanced than we, have taken for granted. The reason is that we have never marched with the other peoples. We do not belong to any of the great families of the human race; we are neither of the West nor of the East, and we have not the traditions of either. Placed, as it were, outside of time, we have not been touched by the universal education of the human race.

The admirable linking of human ideas over successive periods, the history of the human spirit which has brought it to its present state everywhere else in the world, have had no effect on us. That which elsewhere has long been absorbed into the life of society is to us still a matter of conjecture and speculation. You, for example, if I may say so, Madam, who are so well constituted to receive all that is good and true in the world, you who are capable of experiencing all the sweetest and purest joys of the soul, what have you achieved with these advantages? You are still seeking to fill not a life, but a day. You lack completely the very things which elsewhere form the framework of existence, where all the day's events find their appointed place—that being as essential for a healthy moral life as good air is for a healthy physical life. You will understand that I am now speaking not of moral principles or philosophical maxims, but merely of a well-ordered existence, of habits and routines which set the mind at ease and give a rhythm to the soul.

Look around you. Everyone seems to have one foot in the air. You would say we are all travelers on the move. No one has a fixed sphere of existence; there are no good habits, no rules that govern anything. We do not even have homes; we have nothing that binds, nothing that awakens our sympathies and affections, nothing that endures, nothing that remains. Everything passes, flows away, leaving no trace either outside or within us. We seem to camp in our houses, we behave like strangers in our families; and in our cities we appear to be nomads, more so than the real nomads who graze their flocks in our steppes, for they are more attached to their desert than we are to our towns. And do not imagine that this is a trifling matter. Poor wretches that we are, let us not add to our miseries by misunderstanding ourselves; let us not aspire to a life of pure intelligence; let us learn to live reasonably in our present reality. Let me discourse a little longer on our country; I shall not be departing from my subject. Without this preamble, you would not be able to understand what I have to say.

Every people passes through a period of violent agitation, frenzied unrest, and thoughtless activity, when men roam through the world, in mind and in body. This is a time of great emotions, great undertakings, great passions. It is a time of violent movement for the peoples, without apparent motive, but not without profit for posterity. All societies have passed through such a period. It endows them with their most vivid recollections, their legends, their poetry, all their most durable and fecund ideas; these are the very foundations of society. Otherwise they would have no memories to treasure; they would have nothing to love but the dust of their native soil. This fascinating epoch in the history of peoples is the adolescence of nations; it is the time when their faculties reach their peak, the memory of which is the joy and the lesson of their maturity. As for us, we have nothing of the kind. A brutal barbarism to begin with, followed by an age of gross superstition, then by a ferocious and humiliating foreign domination, the spirit of which has passed into the national state—that is the sad history of our youth. We have known nothing resembling that age of exuberant activity, that exultant play of a people's moral forces. The epoch in our society which corresponds to that period was one of a dreary and somber existence, without force or energy, enlivened only by crime, made sweeter only by servitude. There are no delightful recollections or charming images in our national memory, no powerful lessons in our national tradition. Let your eye roam over all the centuries we have traversed, all the land we have spread over, and you will not discover a single cherished memory, a single venerable monument which forcefully recalls the past and recreates it in a lively and picturesque manner. We live in a narrow present, without a past as without a future, in the midst of a dead calm. On the few occasions when we do rouse ourselves, we do so neither in the hope nor in the desire of achieving some common good, but with the thoughtlessness of a child who sits up and stretches its hand for the rattle held out by its nurse.

The true development of human beings in society does not begin for a people until life has become better regulated, easier, and pleasanter than in the midst of the uncertainties of its first period. How can the seeds of good germinate in a society which, without convictions and without rules, still vacillates even in daily matters, and in which life has not yet taken a definite shape? Ours is still the stage of chaotic fermentation in the moral sphere, resembling the physical upheavals of our planet which preceded its present period. We are still in that stage.

Our early years, spent in animal passivity, have left no trace on our minds, so that we have nothing of our own to serve as a basis for our thinking; but, having been isolated by a strange destiny from the universal progress of humanity, neither have we acquired any of the *traditional* ideas of the human race. Yet it is on such ideas that the life of nations is founded; it is such ideas that determine their future and shape their moral development. If we wished to evolve an attitude resembling that of other civilized peoples, we would, as it were, have to repeat for ourselves the entire process of the education of the human race. To this end, we would have before us the history of nations and the results of the strivings of centuries. This is, of course, a difficult task, and perhaps no one man can accomplish it; but first of all we must know what it is. What is this education of the human race, and what place do we occupy in the general scheme of things?

Nations live only through the strong impressions left by ages past and through relations with other peoples. In this way, every individual is conscious of being in contact with all mankind.

What is the life of man, says Cicero, if memory of earlier events does not relate the present to the past? But we [Russians], who have come into the world like illegitimate children, without a heritage, without any ties binding us to the men who came before us on this earth, carry in our hearts none of the lessons preceding our own existence. Each one of us must endeavor to restore the broken family bonds. We must deliberately hammer into our heads things which have become habit and instinct with other peoples. Our memories go back no further than yesterday; we are, so to say, strangers to ourselves. We move so oddly in time that, as we advance, the immediate past is irretrievably lost to us. That is but a natural consequence of a culture which is wholly imported and imitative. There is no internal development, no natural progress, in our society; new ideas sweep out the old, because they are not derived from the old but come from God knows where. Since all our ideas are ready-made, the indelible trace left in the mind by a progressive movement of ideas, which gives it strength, does not shape our intellect. We grow, but we do not mature; we move, but in a diagonal, that is, a line which does not lead to the desired goal. We are like children who have not been taught to think for themselves; when they become adults, they have nothing they can call their own—all their knowledge is on the surface, their soul is not within them. That is precisely our condition.

Peoples, like individuals, are moral beings. It takes centuries for their education, as it takes years for that of persons. We may be said to be an exception among peoples. We are one of those nations which do not appear to be an integral part of the human race, but exist only in order to teach some great lesson to the world. Surely the lesson we are destined to teach will not be wasted; but who knows when we shall rejoin the rest of mankind, and how much misery we must suffer before accomplishing our destiny?

The peoples of Europe have a common physiognomy, a family look. Despite their broad division into Latins and Teutons, into Southerners and Northerners, there is a tie which binds them together into one and which is readily apparent to anyone who has studied their general history. You know that not too long ago all Europe called itself Christendom, and the term was used in public law. In addition to this general character, each of these peoples has a character peculiar unto itself, shaped by its history and tradition. These, between them, furnish their patrimony of ideas. Each individual enjoys his share thereof, and in the course of his lifetime picks up without effort or difficulty these ideas that are prevalent in his society, and turns them to account. Draw the parallel for yourself and see how many fundamental ideas we are thus able to gather in ordinary social intercourse and to make some use of as guidance in life. Please note that I am speaking not of study or reading, of literary or scientific endeavor, but merely of contact with other minds—of those ideas which the child imbibes in his cradle, by which he is surrounded when at play, which his mother imparts to him in her caresses; which, in the form of various emotions, penetrate to the marrow of his bones with the air he breathes, and shape him into a moral being even before he goes out into the world as a member of society. Do you want to know what these ideas are? They are the ideas of duty, justice, right, and order. They derive from the events which have formed European society; they are part and parcel of the social fabric of these countries.

That is the atmosphere of the West; it is more than history, more than psychology—it is the very physiology of European man. What have we to put in its place? I do not know whether any absolute notion can be deduced from what I have said, and a definite principle drawn; but it will readily be seen that the strange situation of our people, which cannot link its thinking to any sequence of ideas progressively developed by society and slowly succeeding each other, which has taken part in the general movement of the human mind only by a blind, superficial, and often clumsy imitation of other nations, must have a profound influence on the thinking of each of its individual members.

You will therefore find that we all lack a certain assurance, a certain method in our thinking, a certain logic. The syllogism of the West is unknown to us. There is something more than frivolity in our best minds. The finest ideas, for lack of coherence or sequel, dazzle for a moment but are sterile and congeal in our brains. It is natural for man to feel lost when he is unable to establish a connection with what preceded him and with what follows. He loses all certainty, all feeling of consistency. Not being guided by a sense of unbroken continuity, he feels that he has gone astray in the world. There are such lost creatures in all countries; but with us this is a general characteristic. Ours is not the levity which used to be thrown up to the French and which in fact was merely a facility of understanding that did not preclude either depth or breadth of intellect and gave infinite grace and charm to social intercourse. We are scatterbrained; we live without gaining experience or providing for the future; our life is reduced to the ephemeral existence of the individual separated from his species, concerned neither with acquiring glory nor with promoting some cause, nor even with those inherited family interests and the many prospects and prescriptions which, in a society based on a memory of the past and an understanding of the future, are the essence of both public and private life. There are absolutely no general notions in our heads; everything is particular, and everything is unattached and incomplete. Even in our gaze, I find, there is something oddly vague, cold, and uncertain, resembling somewhat the look of people on the lowest rungs of the social ladder. Abroad, especially in the South, where faces are so animated and expressive, many a time when I have compared my compatriots with the local inhabitants, I have been struck by the mute appearance of our countenances.

Foreigners have commended us for a certain careless temerity, which is to be found mainly among our lower classes; but, having been able to observe only a few isolated traits of our national character, they could not evaluate it as a whole. They failed to see that the very thing which sometimes makes us so bold also renders us totally incapable of depth and perseverance; they failed to see that what makes us indifferent to the hazards of life makes us equally indifferent to all good, all evil, every truth and every lie, and that for this reason we lack the powerful motives which other men have for self-improvement; they fail to see that it is precisely because of this lazy audacity that—painful as this is to admit—in our country even the upper classes are prone to vices which elsewhere afflict only the lowest; finally, they failed to see that, while we have some of the virtues of young and not highly civilized peoples, we have none that characterize mature peoples with a high level of culture.

I do not, of course, mean to say that we have only vices and the nations of Europe only virtues—God forbid! But I do say that, in order to judge a people, one must study the general spirit which permeates their existence, for it is only that spirit, and not any one trait of their national character, which can lead them to greater moral perfection and promote unending progress.

The masses are guided by certain forces which are at the summit of society. They do not think for themselves; there are among them a few who think for them, who furnish the impetus for the collective intelligence of the nation and make it advance. While this small number cogitates, the rest feel, and a general movement results. With the exception of a few besotted races which are human only in appearance, this is true of all the peoples of the globe. The primitive peoples of Europe, the Celts, the Scandinavians, the Germans, had their druids, their skalds, their bards, who were powerful thinkers in their way. Look at those peoples of North America whom the materialistic civilization of the United States is so busily destroying; there are men of admirable profundity among them.

But where are our wise men, may I ask, where are our philosophers? Who has ever thought for us, who thinks for us today? And yet, placed between the two great divisions of the world, between the East and the West, resting one elbow on China and the other on Germany, we ought to combine in ourselves the two great principles of human intelligence, imagination and reason, and fuse in our civilization the history of all parts of the globe. But that is not the role Providence has assigned to us. On the contrary, It seems to have given no thought to our destiny. Excluding us from Its beneficent influence on the minds of men, It has left us entirely to ourselves; It would have none of us, and It has taught us nothing. The experience of the ages has passed us by; eras and generations succeed each other without leaving us anything of value. To look at us, one might come to believe that the general law of mankind has been revoked in our case. We are alone in the world, we have given nothing to the world, we have taught it nothing. We have not added a single idea to the sum total of human ideas; we have not contributed to the progress of the human spirit, and what we have borrowed of this progress we have distorted. From the outset of our existence as a society, we have produced nothing for the common benefit of all mankind; not one useful thought has sprung from the arid soil of our fatherland; not one great truth has emerged from our midst; we have not taken the trouble to invent anything ourselves and, of the inventions of others, we have borrowed only empty conceits and useless luxuries.

Strange to say, even in the realm of science, which is universal, our history is linked to nothing, explains nothing, proves nothing. If the barbarian hordes which turned the world topsy-turvy had not crossed the land we inhabit before invading the West, we would barely have furnished one chapter to world history. To be taken notice of at all, we have had to spread from the Bering Strait to the Oder. On one occasion a great man sought to civilize us; and, in order to give us a foretaste of enlightenment, he flung us the mantle of civilization; we picked up the mantle, but we did not touch civilization itself. Another time, another great prince, associating us with his glorious mission, led us victorious from one end of Europe to the other; returning home from that triumphant march across the most civilized countries of the world, we brought back only ideas and aspirations which resulted in an immense calamity, setting us back half a century. There is something in our blood that resists all real progress. In a word, we have lived, and we live now, merely in order to furnish some great lesson to a remote posterity that will come to know it; today, say what you will, we are a blank in the intellectual order. I never weary of marveling at this vacuum, at the astonishing isolation of our society. In part this is the fault of our unfathomable fate; but in part it is certainly the work of men, as is everything in the moral world. Let us take another look at history, for it is history that explains a people.

What were we doing while the struggle between the vigorous barbarism of the Northern peoples and the lofty concepts of religion was giving rise to modern civilization? Driven by a fatal destiny, we went to wretched Byzantium, which those peoples profoundly despised, for the moral code that was to educate us. Shortly before, an ambitious spirit [2] had removed that race from the brotherhood of man; thus what we received was an idea distorted by human passions. At that time the life-giving principle of unity permeated everything in Europe. Everything sprang from it, everything converged upon it. The intellectual trend of the time was toward unity of human

---

[2] Photius.

thought, and every impulse stemmed from that powerful need to evolve a universal idea which is the genius of modern times. Alienated from this remarkable principle, we became a prey to conquest. After we freed ourselves from the foreign yoke, we might, had we not been separated from the great family of man, have benefited by the ideas which during this time had emerged among our Western brethren; instead, we fell into a servitude that was harsher still, sanctified as it was by our deliverance.

How many bright rays had by that time pierced the darkness which had enveloped Europe! Most of the knowledge in which the human mind takes pride today was already being surmised; society had already taken shape; and, falling back on pagan antiquity, the Christian world had rediscovered the beauty it still lacked. But we were deep in our schism, and nothing of what happened in Europe reached us. We took no part in the world's great business. The remarkable qualities with which religion had endowed the modern peoples and which, in the eyes of reason, placed them as high above the peoples of antiquity as the latter were above the Hottentots and the Laplanders; the new powers with which it had enriched human intelligence; the customs and manners which submission to an unarmed authority had made as gentle as they had once been brutal—we had none of these in our country. While Christianity was majestically advancing along the path traced for it by its divine Founder and drawing whole generations after it, we did not move, for all that we called ourselves Christians. While the entire world was rebuilding itself, we constructed nothing, but went on squatting in our thatched huts. In brief, the new destinies of the human race were not for us. Christians though we were, the fruit of Christianity did not ripen for us.

I ask you, is it not absurd to suppose, as is usually done in our country, that we can in one fell swoop, without so much as taking the trouble to discover what brought it about, appropriate the results of a progress achieved in Europe gradually and under the direct and manifest influence of a unique moral force?

They misunderstand Christianity entirely who fail to see that it has a purely historical aspect, which is so integral a part of its dogma that it may be said to express the whole Christian philosophy, since it shows what Christianity has done for man and what it must do for him in the future. Thus the Christian religion is not merely a moral system conceived in mortal human minds but a divine, eternal power, ever at work in the world of the intellect, whose visible action should be a constant lesson to us. That is the true meaning of the dogma which is symbolized by faith in a universal Church. In the Christian world, everything must of necessity contribute to the establishment of a perfect order upon earth, and indeed everything does. Otherwise the Lord's words would be belied by actuality, and he would not be within his Church to the end of time. The new order, the reign of God, which is to be brought about by redemption, would be no different from the old order, the reign of evil, which it was to annihilate. We would be left with nothing save that imaginary perfectibility which is a philosopher's dream and which is denied by every page of human history—

that vain agitation of the mind which serves only our material needs and which has never raised man, be it ever so little, save in order to plunge him into a deeper abyss.

But, you will say, are we not Christians, and is there no way of being civilized other than the European? Of course we are Christians, but so are the Abyssinians. Certainly one can be civilized without being civilized in the European way. Is that not true of Japan, even more so than of Russia, if we are to believe one of our compatriots? But do you think that the Christianity of the Abyssinians and the civilization of the Japanese will bring about that order of things I have spoken about, which is the final destiny of the human species? Do you think that these absurd aberrations of divine and human truths are capable of bringing Heaven down to earth?

Christianity has two very distinct aspects. The first is its action on the individual; the second, its action on the universal intelligence. They are naturally merged in Supreme Reason and of necessity work toward the same end. But the time required for the accomplishment of the eternal designs of Divine Wisdom cannot be encompassed by our limited vision. We must distinguish between divine action manifesting itself in a finite period of human lives, and the action taking place in infinity. On the day when the work of redemption is completed, all hearts and minds will be fused into a single emotion, a single thought, and the walls separating peoples and faiths will tumble. But today it is important for each of us to know what his place is in the general order of the Christian vocation, that is to say, what resources he finds in himself and in his surroundings for working toward the predestined end of the entire society of man.

Hence in the society where this end is to be achieved, that is to say, where revealed thought must ripen and reach its fullness, minds of necessity move in a certain circle of ideas. That circle, that moral sphere, naturally produces a certain mode of life and a point of view which, without being exactly the same for everyone—this applies to us as well as to all European peoples—nevertheless create the same way of being for all, which is the result of the immense intellectual labor of eighteen centuries in which all the passions and interests, all suffering, all the imaginings and efforts of the intellect have had their part.

All the nations of Europe held each other by the hand in advancing through the centuries. Whatever they do today to strike out on their own, they always meet again on the same road. To visualize the development of this family of peoples, it is not necessary to study history. Just read Tasso, and you will find them all prostrating themselves before the walls of Jerusalem. Remember that for fifteen centuries they had but one language in which to address God, but one moral authority, but one faith. Consider that for fifteen centuries, every year on the same day, at the same hour, in the same words, they raised their voices in unison to the Supreme Being to celebrate His glory in His greatest benefaction. Wondrous concert, a thousand times more sublime than all the harmonies of the physical world! This sphere in which the Europeans have their being and which alone can enable the human species to reach its appointed end, is the result of the influence of religion upon them. Hence it is clear that since the weakness of our faith or the inadequacy of our dogma has kept us out of this universal movement in which the social concept of Christianity was formulated and developed, relegating us to the category of peoples who are to profit only indirectly and very late from the full effects of Christianity, we must seek by every means at our command to revive our faith and to give ourselves a truly Christian impetus; for everything in Europe was achieved through Christianity. This is what I meant when I said to you that we must repeat for ourselves the education of the human race.

The whole history of modern society takes place in the realm of opinion. Consequently, true education lies there. Initially organized on that basis, modern society has progressed solely through thought. Its interests have always followed, and never preceded, ideas. Opinions have always given rise to interests, and never interests to opinions. All its political revolutions were, in principle, moral revolutions. Men sought the truth, and found freedom and prosperity. This is the explanation of the phenomenon of modern society and its civilization; it would otherwise be incomprehensible.

Religious persecutions, martyrdoms, the spread of Christianity, heresies, Church councils—these events fill the first centuries. The entire trend of that epoch, not excluding the barbarian invasion, is comprised of these infant efforts of the modern spirit. The formation of a hierarchy, the centralization of spiritual power, and the continued spread of the Christian religion in the lands of the North make up the second epoch. Next comes a supreme exaltation of the religious feeling and the consolidation of religious authority. The development of philosophy and literature and the cultivation of customs and manners under the guidance of religion complete this history, which has as much right to be called sacred as that of the Chosen People of ancient times. Lastly, it was once again a religious reaction, a new impetus given to the human spirit by religion, which shaped present-day society. Thus opinion was always the greatest, one may say the only, consideration of modern peoples; all material, positive, and personal interests were absorbed in it.

I know that some, instead of admiring this powerful thrust of human nature toward possible perfection, have termed it fanaticism and superstition. But, whatever they say, judge for yourself how deep an impression must have been made on the character of these peoples by a social development stemming entirely from a single emotion, for good as for evil! Let superficial philosophy noisily voice its disapproval of religious wars and of pyres lighted by intolerance; as for us, we can but envy the fate of peoples who, in these clashes of opinion, these bloody conflicts in the cause of truth, have created for themselves a world of ideas which we cannot even imagine, far less transport ourselves to it body and soul, as we presume to do.

Once again, all is not reason, virtue, and religion in the countries of Europe—far from it. Yet everything there is mysteriously guided by a power which has ruled in sovereignty for many centuries; everything there is the result of that long sequence of events and ideas which has shaped modern society. Here is one proof out of many. The people whose traits are most clearly marked, whose institutions are the most representative of the modern spirit—the English—have, properly speaking, only a religious history. Their last revolution, to which they owe their freedom and prosperity, and the whole chain of events from the reign of Henry VIII onward which led to that revolution were but one long religious development. Throughout this period, purely political considerations appeared only as a secondary motive and sometimes vanished altogether or were sacrificed in favor of opinion. Even as I write these lines [1829], that privileged land is once again being agitated by religious ideas. But, generally speaking, what European people would not, if it troubled to look, find in its national conscience this special element which, in the shape of sacred thought, has been the life-giving principle, the soul of its society, throughout its entire existence?

The action of Christianity is not confined to its direct and immediate influence on the minds of men. The vast results it is destined to produce will be but the effect of a multitude of moral, intellectual, and social combinations in which the complete freedom of the human spirit will necessarily find the greatest possible scope. Everything that has occurred since the first day of our era—or rather from the moment the world's Saviour said to His disciples: "Go . . . preach the gospel to every creature"—including all the attacks on Christianity, is in complete accord with this concept of Christianity's general influence. It is sufficient to see Christ wielding sway over all hearts, whether they know it or not, whether they accept or resist His dominion, to recognize that His words have come true. Thus, despite all the imperfections, faults, and vices of European society as it is today, it is nonetheless true that the Kingdom of God finds itself in some sort realized there, because it contains the principle of continuous unlimited progress and harbors in embryo all the necessary elements for [God's Kingdom] one day to be finally established upon earth.

Before concluding these reflections on the influence of religion on society, Madam, I should like to transcribe here something about it that I once wrote in a piece with which you are not familiar.

It is certain, I said, that anyone who does not see the effect of Christianity whenever human thought comes in contact with it in any way, even if only to combat it, does not have a clear idea of it. Wherever the name of Christ is spoken, that name alone wins men over, whatever they may do. Nothing is more indicative of the divine origin of this religion than its absolute universality, which enables it to enter men's souls in all possible ways, to take possession of their minds without their knowledge, to dominate and subdue them even when they seem to resist it most, by imparting to the intelligence truths formerly unknown to it, awakening in the heart emotions never experienced before, and inspiring us with feelings which, we know not how, fit us into the general scheme of things. Thus this religion determines the use to be made of each personality and directs all actions toward a common goal. When we look at Christianity from this point of view, each prophecy of Christ becomes a palpable truth. We then see distinctly the operation of all the levers that His all-powerful hand sets in motion to lead man to his destination without infringing upon his freedom, without immobilizing any of the forces of his nature but, on the contrary, intensifying and raising to an infinite degree whatever powers of his own he has. We see that no moral element remains inactive in this new economy, that the vigor of thought, the generous flow of emotion, the heroism of a strong soul as well as the submission of a meek spirit, all alike find a place and an application in it. Accessible to every intelligent being, instinct in the very pulsing of our hearts, revealed thought carries everything with it, feeds and grows on the very obstacles it encounters. In a genius, it rises to a height to which other human beings cannot aspire; in a timid soul, it advances slowly, hugging the ground; in a meditative mind, it becomes absolute and profound; in a soul dominated by the imagination, it is ethereal and fanciful; in a tender and loving heart, it is dissolved into love and charity; in all cases, it moves forward with each intelligence that surrenders to it, filling it with warmth, strength, and clarity. See what a variety of natures, what a multiplicity of forces it sets in motion, how many different capacities it adds up to a single one, how many unlike hearts it causes to beat for the same idea! But the influence of Christianity on society as a whole is even more admirable. If you unroll the long scroll of the development of contemporary society, you will see that Christianity has transformed all human interests into its own, replacing material needs by moral, giving rise in the realm of thought to those great debates which are without parallel at any other period or in any other society, to those terrible struggles between opposing views in which the whole life of a people was reduced to one great idea, one boundless emotion. You will see that everything has turned into Christianity, and Christianity alone: private and public life, the family and the fatherland, science and poetry, reason and imagination, memories and hopes, joy and pain. Happy are those who, in this great impetus given to the world by God Himself, know in their innermost hearts what the results of their efforts are! But not all men are sentient instruments, not all act knowing what they do; of necessity, whole multitudes move blindly, like lifeless atoms, inert masses, without being aware of the forces which set them in motion or glimpsing the goal toward which they are propelled.

It is time I returned to you, Madam. I confess that I am loath to tear myself away from these general considerations. It is in the picture that I see from this height that I find all my consolation. It is in the sweet belief in man's future happiness that I take refuge when, obsessed by the wretched reality that surrounds me, I feel the need of a breath of purer air, of a look at a more serene sky. Yet I do not think I have wasted your time. I had to explain to you the viewpoint from which we should contemplate the Christian world and our role in it. I must have seemed bitter to you in speaking of our country; yet I spoke only the truth, and less than the whole truth. Besides, the spirit of Christianity will tolerate no blindness, and national prejudice least of all, since that is what divides men most.

This is a very long letter, Madam, and I feel we both need to catch our breath. As I began it, I thought that I could tell you what I had to say in a few words; on second thought, I find that I could fill a volume. Would you like that, Madam? Let me know. In any event, you cannot avoid a second letter, for we have merely broached our subject. In the meantime, I hope you will regard the prolixity of the first as compensation for the long time I have kept you waiting for it. I took up my pen the very day I received your own letter; but I was preoccupied by sad and wearisome concerns and had to finish with them before speaking to you of such serious matters, and then I had to recopy my scribbling, which was absolutely illegible. This time, you shall not have long to wait: I will take up pen again tomorrow.

Necropolis, December 1, 1829

9.
Ivan Vasil'evich Kireevski
1806-1856

Chaadaev had affirmed that a basic opposition existed between Western European culture and Russia's historical
experience. Like Chaadaev, the Slavophiles saw the essence of this opposition
in the domain of religious and spiritual
life. The Slavophiles drew their inspiration from Schelling's idea that a people
or a culture develops organically, manifesting distinctive spiritual traits in all
major aspects of its social and national
life. Interested primarily in the organic
totality of a social or cultural entity, the
Slavophiles recoiled from everything that
would lead to the dissection and destruction of its integrity—in particular,
logical analysis, individual particularism,
the atomization of society. In this respect
they foreshadowed some of the criticisms
that have been levied at Western culture
by twentieth-century romantic and ex-
istentialist writers.

Such were the basic notions on which
the leading spokesman for the early
generation of the Slavophiles, Ivan
Vasil'evich Kireevski, based his argument. Like all the members of the philosophic and literary circles of the 1830's,
Kireevski had a very careful and wholly
Western education. He grew up in the
most enlightened and sophisticated sa-

lons of Moscow and St. Petersburg and
then traveled and studied in Western Europe. At first he was an enthusiastic admirer of the West, especially of its
achievements in the realm of philosophy.
But in the late 1830's he underwent a
religious crisis, turned to the study of the
patristic writings, and emerged from this
experience a deeply devout son of the
Russian Orthodox Church. He saw the
history of Western civilization, as well
as that of old Russia, only through the
prism of a value system based on his
own understanding of Orthodox Christianity. Naturally, his assertions should
not be taken as statements of historical
fact.

Quite clearly Kireevski was less interested in historical truth than he was
in a critique of contemporary Russia,
since his goal was to bring about a
thoroughgoing transformation of his
country's social and spiritual condition.
For this reason the government of
Nicholas I—always concerned with preserving a status quo which it felt was
preeminently glorious for Russia—reacted almost as negatively to Kireevski's
praise of old Russia as it had to Chaadaev's condemnation. The censor felt,
not incorrectly, that Kireevski glorified

those elements of Russia's past which were least compatible with the modernization of Russia and the institutional framework inherited from Peter the Great. The periodical *Moskovskii sbor-* *nik* (Moscow Collection), in which the article appeared, was closed, and Kireevski was prevented from further publication of his views.

On the Nature of European Culture and Its Relation to the Culture of Russia

Letter to Count E. E. Komarovskii

At our last meeting, you and I had a long discussion about the nature of European culture and the characteristics that distinguish it from the culture which Russia called her own in ancient times, traces of which are to this day observable in the customs, manners, and ways of thinking of the common people; nay more, which permeate the soul, the turn of mind, the whole inner content, so to say, of any Russian who has not yet been transformed by Western education. You urged me to put down on paper my thoughts on this subject, but I was unable to comply with your request at that time. Now that I am to write an article on the same topic for the *Moskovskii sbornik,* I ask your permission to cast it in the form of a letter addressed to you. The idea that I am talking to you will lend life and warmth to my solitary meditations.

Certainly few questions nowadays are more important than the question of the relation of Russian to Western culture. How we pose and resolve it in our minds may determine not only the dominant trend of our literature but the entire orientation of our intellectual activity, the meaning of our private lives, and the nature of our social relationships. And yet only a short time ago this question could not have been posed or, what amounts to the

Translated by Valentine Snow from Ivan Vasil'evich Kireevski, "O kharaktere prosve shcheniia Evropy i o ego otnoshenii k prosveshcheniiu Rossii," in *Polnoe sobranie sochinenii,* Vol. I (Moscow, 1911), pp. 174–222. Ostensibly written as a letter to Count E. E. Komarovskii in 1852, this article first appeared in *Moskovskii sbornik,* an irregular periodical published by the Slavophiles of Moscow. During 1852 the periodical was published by A. Koshelev and edited by I. S. Aksakov; it had previously appeared in 1846–47 under the title *Moskovskii literaturnyi i uchenyi sbornik.*

same thing, could have been resolved so readily that there was no point in posing it. The consensus of opinion was that the difference between European and Russian culture was merely a difference in degree and not in kind, their spirit and basic principles being the same. We (it was then said) used to be barbarians; our civilization began only when we started to imitate Europe, which had immeasurably outdistanced us in intellectual development. In Europe, learning was in full flower before we had any, and it has come to fruition, while ours is still at the budding stage. Hence the Europeans are our teachers and we their students; still, it was usually added with complacency, we are clever students and learn so quickly that we shall probably soon outstrip our masters. In Riga in 1714 Peter said, draining his glass while on a newly launched ship:

> Who would have thought, lads, who would have thought thirty years ago that you, Russians, would be building ships with me here in the Baltic Sea and feasting in German dress? Historians [he added] assume that Greece was the ancient seat of learning; from Greece learning passed to Italy and spread through all the European lands. But the uncouthness of our forefathers stopped it from penetrating beyond Poland, although before that the Poles, and all other foreigners as well, had been plunged into the darkness in which we still live, and it was only owing to the unremitting efforts of their rulers that they were finally able to open their eyes and assimilate European knowledge, art, and style of life. I would liken this movement of learning upon the earth to the circulation of blood in the human body; and it seems to me that one day learning will leave its present seat in England, France, and Germany and pass to us for a few centuries, in order then to return to its birthplace, Greece.

These remarks explain the enthusiasm with which Peter addressed himself to his task and to a great extent justify the extremes to which he went. Love of enlightenment was his passion. He saw it as Russia's sole salvation, and Europe as its only source. This conviction survived him by a whole century among the educated class of Russian society—or, better, the class he had re-educated; and some thirty years ago you would hardly have found a thinking man who conceived the possibility of any culture other than that borrowed from Western Europe.

Since then, however, a change has taken place both in Western European culture and in European-Russian culture.

In this second half of the nineteenth century, European culture has attained such a fullness of development that its special significance has become consummately clear to any thoughtful observer. Yet this comprehensive development, this manifest achievement, has brought about an almost universal feeling of dissatisfaction and disappointment. Western culture has proved unsatisfying not because learning has lost its vitality in the West; on the contrary, it appears to flourish more richly than ever before. Again, the reason is not that there are some forms of public life which impede human relationships or prevent them from proceeding in the prevailing direction; on the contrary, a struggle against an external obstacle would only strengthen the dominant trend, and it would seem that never before have men found it easier to arrange their public lives to meet their intellectual requirements. No, men whose mental lives are not circumscribed by passing interests experience a feeling of dissatisfaction and disconsolate emptiness simply because the very triumph of the European mind has revealed the narrowness of its basic aspirations; because, despite the great abundance and magnitude of individual discoveries and advances in learning, what all that knowledge adds up to has been only of negative value for man's inner spirit; because, despite all the brilliance, the comforts and amenities of modern existence, life itself has been drained of its essential meaning; not being bolstered by a strong generally held conviction, it can neither be made fair by lofty ideals nor warmed by deep compassion. Cold analysis, practiced over many centuries, has destroyed the very foundations of European culture, so that the principles in which that culture was rooted, from which it has grown, have become irrelevant, even alien to it, and in contradiction to its end result. All that is left to it is this very analysis which has severed it from its roots, this self-propelling scalpel of reason, this abstract syllogism which recognizes only itself and individual experience, this autonomous intelligence, or—to put it more accurately—this logical faculty of the mind divorced from all man's other faculties of cognition save the coarsest and most primitive perceptions of the senses on which it erects its ethereal dialectical edifices.

It should be remembered, however, that the feeling of dissatisfaction and despondency now experienced by Western man did not set in at once when the triumph of his destructive rationality became manifest. Having abandoned his age-old convictions, he placed boundless trust in the omnipotence of his abstract reasoning precisely because the convictions it had destroyed had been so great, strong, and comprehensive. In the first moments of victory his joy was not only unmixed with regret; on the contrary, intoxicated with self-confidence, he reached a state of poetic exaltation. He believed that by using his own abstract reason he could forthwith build a new and rational life for himself and transform the earth into a veritable paradise. He was not deterred by his dreadful, bloody experiences; his gross failures did not dash his hopes; individual suffering only set a martyr's crown on his head, leaving him still bedazzled; an eternity of unsuccessful attempts might, it would seem, have tired him but not shattered his self-confidence had not that same abstract reason he had relied upon reached a point in its development at which it became aware of its own inadequacies and limitations.

This latest result of European civilization has not yet, it is true, become general, but it is beginning to preoccupy the leading thinkers of the West. It belongs to the newest, and probably the last, epoch of abstract philosophical thinking. Philosophical views do not, however, remain for long the monopoly of the schools. What is today the product of the meditation of a scholar closeted in his study will tomorrow be the credo of the masses; for men who have no faith save in rational science, who recognize no other source of truth save their own logic, find that the fate of their entire intellectual life is governed by the fate of philosophy. Philosophy is more than just a meeting place for all branches of learning and all human affairs—a node, as it were, of universal consciousness; for from this node, this common consciousness, guiding lines reach out again into all branches of learning and all human affairs, giving them meaning, establishing links between them, and shaping them according to their own bias.

Thus it has often been known to happen that in some remote corner of Europe an unnoticed idea will germinate in the brain of some scholar whose very face is barely noticed by the crowd around him, and that twenty years later this unknown man's unknown idea will rule the minds and desires of that selfsame crowd in the guise of some dramatic historical event. This happens not because some obscure thinker seated in his dark corner can order history about at will, but because history, through the mediation of his system, reaches the consciousness of itself. He merely notes and adds up the dominant trends, and any arbitrary element in his thought robs it of all power over reality; for only that philosophic system attains dominance which follows as an inevitable conclusion from the dominant convictions preceding it. Thus for peoples whose convictions are based solely on their own reasoning, the philosopher's brain is, as it were, a necessary natural organ through which their life-force circulates, rising from external events to inner consciousness and from that consciousness returning once more to the sphere of overt historical action.

Hence it may be said that it is not that Western thinkers have become convinced of the one-sidedness of logical reason, but that Europe's logical reason itself, having reached the highest possible level of its development, has become aware of its limitations and, having grasped the laws of its own operation, has discovered that the full scope of its self-propelling force does not extend beyond the negative aspect of human knowledge; that its theoretical linkage of derived concepts requires premises taken from other sources of knowledge; that the higher truths, the living insights, the basic convictions of the mind all lie outside the abstract circle of its dialectics and, although they do not contradict its laws, are nevertheless not derived from them and are in fact beyond its reach if its activity has been forcibly separated from that of the other faculties of the human spirit.

Thus Western man, having through the exclusive development of his abstract reason lost faith in all convictions not derived from it, has now, owing to that same development, lost his last faith—faith in the omnipotence of that reason. He has been compelled, therefore, either to content himself with a semi-animal indifference toward anything higher than sensual concerns and commercial calculations (which many do, but many are unable to do, being the product of earlier trends of European life) or to return to those rejected convictions which animated the West before abstract reason reached the acme of its development. Some have done so, but others have not been able to, because those convictions, as shaped by the historical development of Western Europe, have themselves been subject to the disintegrating action of abstract reason, and have lost their fullness and independence and been brought down to the level of a logical system, so that Western man sees them not as supreme life-giving principles, but as having all the one-sidedness of reason itself.

What then is intellectual Europe to do? Go back still further, to the pristine purity of those basic convictions before they had felt the effect of Western European rationality? Return to those principles as they had been before Western development began? This is a well-nigh impossible undertaking for minds surrounded and saturated by all the delusions and prejudices of Western civilization. It is perhaps for this reason that most European thinkers, unable to accept either a narrowly selfish life bounded by sensual goals and personal considerations or a one-sided mental life in direct contradiction with the fullness of their mental powers, and unwilling to be left without any convictions or to hold convictions they knew to be false, have sought their way out of the impasse by separately, each on his own, inventing new basic principles and verities for the world at large, finding them in the play of their individual dreamy ratiocinations, mixing the new with the old and the impossible with the possible, surrendering themselves wholly to the wildest hopes, each contradicting the others and each demanding general acceptance. Like so many Columbuses, they all embarked on voyages of discovery within their own minds, seeking new Americas in the vast oceans of impossible expectations, individual assumptions, and strict syllogisms.

This state of the European mentality had the opposite effect in Russia from that which it has more recently had in the West. Only a few, and then but passingly, were beguiled by the superficial glitter of these extravagant systems, deluded by that artificial comeliness which was rotten at the core; most of the men who had followed the developments of Western thought became aware of the inadequacies of Western civilization and turned their attention to those cultural principles, underestimated by the West, which were once peculiar to Russia and traces of which were still to be found in it despite the influence of Europe.

The result was active historical research, comparison, publications. In this we owe a great deal to our government, which discovered so many valuable historical documents gathering dust in forgotten archives and remote monasteries and published them for all to read. Perhaps for the first time in 150 years, Russian scholars took an objective, searching look at themselves and their own country and, in studying elements of intellectual life that were new to them, were struck by a strange phenomenon: they saw with amazement that they had been mistaken about nearly everything having to do with Russia, its history, its people, its faith, the roots of its culture, and the imprints—still visible, still warm—of that culture on the Russian past and on the mind and character of the Russian people; they had been mistaken not because anyone had sought to deceive them, but because their strong bias toward Western civilization and their boundless prejudice against Russian barbarism had made it impossible for them to understand Russia. In the past, being swayed by the same prejudices, they may themselves have helped to spread the delusion. The spell was so potent that it concealed from them the most obvious objects which were under their very noses; but to make up for this, the awakening is astonishingly rapid. Daily we see men who followed the Western orientation, many of them men with highly cultivated minds and firm characters, change all their convictions simply through having made an objective and profound study of themselves and their country. In the latter, they study the basic principles which went into the making of the particular Russian style of life, while in themselves they discover those vital faculties of the spirit for which Western intellectual development found no place and to which it offered no nourishment.

It must be said, however, that it is not as easy as some may think to understand and formulate the basic principles which underlie the Russian style of life. For the fundamental principles of Russian culture have not manifested themselves as clearly in Russia as have the principles of Western culture in the history of the West. One must look for them in order to discover them; they do not catch the eye, as does European civilization. Europe has had its full say. In the nineteenth century Europe may be said to have completed the process of development it began in the ninth. Although in the early centuries of its history Russia was no less civilized than the West, it was constantly hampered and set back in its cultural growth by external and presumably fortuitous events, so that it was able to bequeath not a complete and perfect culture to the present, but only such features of it as hint at its true meaning, only some of its first principles and their first impress on the minds and lives of Russians.

What are these principles of Russian culture? In what do they differ from the principles which are the basis of Western culture, and are they capable of further development? And if they are, what can they do for the intellectual life of Russia, what promise do they hold for the intellectual life of Europe? For, after the recent interpenetration of Russia and Europe, we can no longer conceive of any intellectual development in Russia that would not affect Europe, nor of any advance in European intellectual life that would not affect Russia.

The principles underlying Russian culture are totally different from the component elements of the culture of European peoples. True, the civilization of each of these peoples has features peculiar to it; but their individual ethnic, political, or historical peculiarities do not prevent them from forming a spiritual whole, into which they all fit as limbs do into a living body. Hence, despite all the accidents of history, they have always developed in close and sympathetic contact. Russia, having spiritually broken away from Europe, lived a life separate from Europe's. The Englishman, the Frenchman, the Italian, the German never stopped being Europeans, while always preserving their national characteristics. The Russian, on the other hand, had nearly to destroy his national personality in order to assimilate Western civilization; for both his appearance and his inner cast of mind, which explained and supported each other, were the result of an entirely different type of life, flowing from an entirely different fountainhead.

Apart from ethnic differences, three historical circumstances gave the entire development of culture in the West its specific character: the special form in which Christianity reached it; the special aspect of the civilization of the ancient world which it inherited; and, lastly, the special elements which entered into the formation of its political organization.

Christianity was the soul of the intellectual life of the peoples of the West, even as it was in Russia. But it was transmitted to Western Europe solely through the Roman Catholic Church.

Naturally, each patriarchate, each nationality, each country in the Christian world retained its individual personality, while being part of the great union represented by the Church. Each people, owing to local ethnic or historical factors, placed emphasis on some one phase of intellectual activity; naturally, in its spiritual life and in the writings of its theologians we find a reflection of its special character—the face it had been born with, so to speak, but illuminated from on high. Thus the theologians of the Syrian lands appear to have concentrated on man's inner life, the life of contemplation, attained by renouncing the world. The Roman theologians were most concerned with the practical application and the logical relationship of religious concepts. The theological writers of enlightened Byzantium seem to have paid more attention than others to the relationship between Christianity and the particular disciplines which flourished around it, at first warring against it, then later submitting. The theologians of Alexandria, waging a double war—against paganism and against Judaism—and surrounded by philosophical, theosophic, and gnostic schools, concentrated above all on the speculative side of the Christian doctrine. All these divergent paths led to a common goal, so long as those who followed them were mindful of that goal. Everywhere particular heresies sprang up, each closely related to the trend prevailing among the people who gave it birth; but they were all put down by the unanimity of the Universal Church, in which all the particular churches were united in holy concord. There were times when entire patriarchates stood in danger of deviation, on occasions when a doctrine which was contrary to that preached by the Universal Church was nevertheless in conformity with the prevailing trend and the turn of mind of the peoples belonging to that particular church; but in those times of trial, when the particular church faced the irrevocable choice between splitting away from the Universal Church and sacrificing its private views, the Lord saved His churches through the unanimity of the whole Orthodox world. The specific character of each particular church could have led it into a schism only if it had renounced its tradition and broken off communion with the other Churches; so long as it remained faithful to the common tradition and the common covenant of love, each particular church, through the special character of its spiritual activity, only added to the common wealth and fullness of the spiritual life of all Christendom. Thus the Roman Church, too, had what we might call its legitimate peculiarity before it broke away from the Universal Church. Once it split off, however, it was naturally forced to transform its distinguishing features into exclusive forms through which alone the Christian doctrine could penetrate among the peoples under its control.

The civilization of the ancient pre-Christian world—the second element which entered into the making of European culture—was until the mid-fifteenth century known to the West almost exclusively in that special form which it had assumed in pagan Rome; its other aspect, Greek and Asian civilization, virtually did not reach Europe in its pure form until after the fall of Constantinople. Yet, as we know, Rome could not lay claim to representing all pagan culture; it had merely held physical mastery over the world, whereas the intellectual supremacy had been exercised by Greek civilization and the Greek tongue. Hence to apprehend the entire experience of the human mind, the entire wealth it had amassed by dint of an effort continued over six thousand years, solely in the form given to it by the Roman civilization meant to apprehend but one aspect of it, with the certain risk of imparting the same one-sidedness to one's own civilization. That is precisely what happened in Europe. And when in the fifteenth century Greek exiles flocked to the West carrying their precious manuscripts with them, it was too late. True, European culture was reanimated, but its spirit remained the same: the mind and life of European man had been given their special cast. Greek learning broadened the scope of European knowledge and taste, stimulated thinking, set minds in motion; but it was no longer able to change the dominant trend of intellectual life.

Lastly, the third element of Western culture—its polity—was characterized by the fact that not one of the peoples of Europe attained their political organization through a peaceful development of national life and national consciousness, where dominant religious and social concepts, translated into daily life, grew naturally in strength and produced a unanimity of views reflected in the harmonious unity of the body politic. On the contrary, owing to some strange historical accident, political organization in nearly every country of Europe was brought about through violence arising out of a death struggle between two hostile races—out of the oppression exercised by the conquerors, out of the resistance of the conquered, and finally out of the fortuitous settlements reached at the end of the conflict between two antagonistic forces of unequal strength.

These three elements peculiar to the West—the Roman Catholic Church, the civilization of ancient Rome, and polity arising out of the violence of conquest—were entirely alien to old Russia. Having accepted the Christian religion from Greece, Russia was in constant contact with the Universal Church. The civilization of the pagan world reached it through the Christian religion, without driving it to single-minded infatuation, as the living legacy of one particular nation might have done. It was only later, after it had become firmly grounded in a Christian civilization, that Russia began to assimilate the last fruits of the learning and culture of the ancient world—at which point Providence, it would seem, saw fit to arrest its intellectual development, thus possibly saving it from the one-sidedness which must surely have been its fate if its mental education had begun before Europe had completed the process of its own intellectual development; for, not having yet made a final evaluation of the results, Europe would have drawn Russia surely and instinctively into its own limited and one-sided cultural pattern. When Christianity penetrated into Russia, it did not meet with the immense difficulties which it had to overcome in Rome, Greece, and the European countries steeped in Roman civilization. The Slavic world did not present those insurmountable obstacles to its pure influence on spiritual and social life which Christianity encountered in the self-contained civilization of the classical world and the one-sided civilization of the Western peoples. In many respects, even the ethnic characteristics of the Slavic customs favored the assimilation of Christian principles. Furthermore, the basic concepts of the rights and duties of man and of his personal, family, and social status did not evolve in violence through formal agreements between warring races and classes as, after a war, artificial boundaries are traced between neighboring states in obedience to the dead letter of a treaty obtained by compromise. Not having been conquered, the Russian people organized its polity in its own way. The enemies who afflicted it always remained alien to it, and did not interfere with its internal development. The Tatars, the Poles, the Hungarians, the Germans, and the other scourges sent to it by Providence could only stop its intellectual development—and did, in fact, stop it—but could not change the essential meaning of its spiritual and public life.

These three elements of early European civilization which were unknown to Russia—the Roman Catholic Church, the ancient Roman world, and the emergence of national states through conquest—were like three points in space, determining the circle which passed through them.

The influence of what had survived from the destruction of ancient Roman civilization on the emerging civilization of the West was all-embracing. Ancient Rome left its imprint on the basic structure of society, on the laws, the language, the ways and customs, the early arts and learning of Europe; it was, therefore, bound to impart to every aspect of Western life something of that specific character which had distinguished it from all other peoples; and that specific character was bound to affect the very substance of Western man's existence, shaping and transforming all other influences to conform to that main trend.

Consequently, the principal distinguishing feature of the Roman mentality had to be reflected in the mentality of the West. If we were to describe the dominant feature of the Roman civilization in one general formula, we could, I think, with justice say that it consisted in the preference for mere cerebration as against the inner essence of things. This is clearly to be seen in Roman public and family life, where natural and moral human relationships were ruthlessly distorted in the name of logic, according to the literal interpretation of a law cast in a certain form by pure chance. We find the same characteristic in Roman poetry, which was concerned with perfecting forms of foreign inspiration. The language of the Romans, too, bears the same stamp, for its grammatical constructions are so rigid and artificial that they stifle all natural freedom and spontaneity of emotion. We see the same thing when we look at the famous Roman laws, with their amazing logical perfection of form and an equally amazing absence of essential justice. Roman religion, which concentrated on the formal aspect of rites until their mystical significance was almost forgotten, presents the same picture of a formal sequence of ideas [arrived] at the expense of all living meaning. The Roman religion was a congeries of many heterogeneous, and frequently opposed, deities of the pagan world, concordant formally but discordant in essence, yet all made part of a logical system of symbolic worship, where philosophy was used to cloak an essential absence of faith. The same rationalistic tendency was manifest in the mores of ancient Rome, where external activity was so highly esteemed and so little attention was paid to its inner meaning; where pride was held to be a virtue; where each man was guided in his actions solely by his own logical convictions; where, consequently, each person regarded himself as being not merely distinct but different from his fellow-men and could conceive of no relationships with them save those which could be logically deduced from the external circumstances of life. For this reason, the Roman was hardly aware of any possible bond between people save the bond of mutual interest, or any unity save party unity. The very patriotism of the Roman—the most disinterested emotion of which he was capable—was not what it was in the case of the Greek. He did not love the smoke of his fatherland; even the smoke of a Greek hearth had greater attraction for him. What he loved in his country was his party's interests and, even more, the fact that it flattered his pride to be a Roman. But he was almost impervious to spontaneous human feelings. He regarded his compatriots much as great Rome regarded the cities which surrounded it: equally ready for alliance or war, he chose one or the other on the basis of self-interest, being ever sensible to the dictates of that passion which is generally uppermost in arid, logical, and self-seeking minds—the desire to dominate, which occupied the same place in the soul of the Roman that the blind love of glory held in the soul of the compassionate Greek. In brief, in all the characteristics of the Roman, in all the aspects of his intellectual and spiritual activity, we find the same common trait—that the formal harmony of his logical concepts was more essential to him than their essence, and that the internal equilibrium of his being, so to say, consisted for him solely in the balance of rational ideas and of external formal activities.

Christianity, when it sprang into being in the midst of the pagan world, was naturally in direct opposition to the Roman's bent toward self-seeking and arrogant cerebration. In turning the spirit toward the inner integrity of being, Christianity not only prevented it from being carried away by passion—even on the most plausible of pretexts—but, by turning the mind to meditation and self-knowledge, also prevented that state of spiritual disintegration in which the faculty of reasoning splits away from all the other faculties of the spirit and fancies itself able to find the truth in the formal relationships of concepts. Whereas to this external, rationalistic wisdom the Christian doctrine looked like utter madness, from the heights of Christianity this arrogant rationalism could itself be seen in all the poverty of its insentient blindness. Hence during the first centuries of the Church we find even Roman theologians frequently attacking the fallacies of pagan philosophizing. At the same time, their purely Christian orientation did not alter their specifically Roman cast of mind, which, as already noted, when kept within its proper limitations presented no obstacle to the true life of the spirit, but, quite to the contrary, even enriched its various manifestations, leading into error only whenever its excesses destroyed the inner equilibrium of the spirit. Thus Tertullian, perhaps the most eloquent of Rome's theological writers, astounds us by his brilliant logic and the formal coherence of his theses; many of his works will always remain an ornament of the Church, although the hypertrophy of his logical faculty or, more accurately, its separation from the other faculties of the mind led him to extremes where his doctrine cleft from the pure Christian doctrine. His famous disciple, St. Cyprian, was more fortunate, although no less remarkable for his powerful logic. But of all the Church Fathers both early and late, surely no one had so marked a predilection for the logical interconnection of truths as St. Augustine, often called the Teacher of the West. Some of his works are like an iron chain of syllogisms, link tightly fitting into link. He may occasionally have allowed himself to be carried away and, intent on formal harmony, failed to notice the one-sidedness of the inner meaning of his thought, for in the last years of his life he found himself obliged to refute some of his own earlier assertions.

If this special fondness of the Roman world for the formal coherence of ideas represented a pitfall for the Latin theologians even at a time when the Roman Catholic Church was a living part of the Universal Church and when the joint thinking of the entire Orthodox world maintained a reasonable balance between such special trends, it will readily be understood that after Rome's splitting away this peculiarity of the Roman mind was bound to become predominant in their teachings. It may even be that this Roman peculiarity, this abstract rationalism, this excessive liking for the formal coherence of ideas, had itself been one of the main reasons for Rome's defection. This is hardly the place to analyze either the causes or the circumstances of that defection, and to pose the question whether its architects were secretly moved by the Roman spirit of domination or by other reasons. Any such hypotheses are controversial; but what is not open to doubt is the pretext that was actually used—the addition of a dogma to the earlier symbol, an addition which was contrary to the ancient tradition and universal consciousness of the Church and was justified only by the logical deductions of the Western theologians.

We make special mention of this fact because—better than any other—it helps to explain the character of Western civilization, where, from the ninth century on, Roman abstract rationalism penetrated into the very teaching of the theologians, destroying with its one-sidedness the harmony and wholeness of their introspective speculation.

If we look at the matter from this angle, it becomes clear why Western theologians, for all their rational honesty, were incapable of visualizing the unity of the Church in any other form than that of a formal unity under one bishop; why they were able to ascribe essential merits to man's tangible good works; why, in the absence of such works, they could see no other means of salvation for a soul which was inwardly ready for it than through a specified period in Purgatory; why, finally, they were able to credit some persons with an actual excess of good works and use that excess to offset some other deficiency, again because of overt actions performed for the external benefit of the Church.

In this way, having subordinated faith to the logical conclusions of reason, the Western Church back in the ninth century sowed within itself the inescapable seeds of the Reformation, which later summoned it before the court of that very abstract reason which it had itself elevated above the common consciousness of the Universal Church; and at that time a thinking man could already have seen Luther looming behind Pope Nicholas I, even as, according to the Roman Catholics, a thinking man could, in the sixteenth century, have discerned Strauss behind Luther.

It is obvious that the same moral cause, the same bias toward logic, which gave rise to the doctrine of the necessary external unity of the Church was bound to produce also the doctrine of the infallibility of its visible head. This was a direct consequence of the special type of civilization which was beginning to predominate in the Western world. Because of this turn taken by the European mind, the Emperor of the Franks was able to offer, and the Bishop of Rome to accept, secular power in his bishopric. Later, for the same logical reason, the Pope's half-spiritual power was bound to extend over all the rulers of the West, giving birth to the so-called Holy Roman Empire and laying its stamp on the historical development of the Middle Ages, where secular power was constantly confused with the spiritual and constantly fought it, each preparing for the other's future downfall in the popular mind, while a similar struggle was taking place in the mind of Western man between faith and reason, tradition and personal presumption. Even as the Church sought to base its spiritual power on secular might, so Western man attempted to base his faith on syllogisms.

Having thus contrived to bring about external unity by giving itself a single head who wielded both spiritual and secular power, the Western Church caused a cleavage in its spiritual activities, its internal interests, and its external relations with the world at large. The twin towers which usually top a Catholic church may serve as a fitting symbol of this dichotomy.

In the meantime, the secular rulers, having accepted the supremacy of the tiara-crowned ruler of the Church, thereby sanctioned the feudal organization of the so-called Holy Roman Empire. It may well be that this was the only reasonable solution for peoples whose political organization had arisen out of conquest. The relentless struggle between two warring races, the oppressors and the oppressed, had resulted, throughout their historical development, in a lasting antagonism between opposing classes which continued to face each other, with their mutually exclusive rights, the exclusive privileges of the one and the profound discontent and endless complaints of the other, the steady envy on the part of the middle class which arose between them, and the continuous and always painful fluctuations in their relative strength; the latter determining the formal and forcible terms of their reconciliation, terms with which all parties were dissatisfied and which might have been somewhat acceptable only when based on a principle external to the state. Meanwhile, the fewer the rights that were granted to the class which descended from the conquered, the less did the class which descended from the conquerors respect the rule of law. Every nobleman strove to be a law unto himself in his relations with others. The notion of a unified state or nation could not enter into their independent hearts, which were shielded on all sides by steel and pride. The only limitation they would admit to their arbitrary actions was in the form of rules governing external relations, rules which they themselves formulated and voluntarily accepted. Although the codes of honor arose in response to the needs of the times as the only possible substitute for law in the face of utter lawlessness, yet their nature revealed such a one-sidedness of public life, such emphasis on the external and formal aspect of human relationships, and such disregard of their essence that, in themselves alone, they could serve as a faithful mirror of all of Western polity's development.

Each noble knight within his castle formed a separate state. For that reason, relations between nobles could be only external relations, entirely formal in character. That same external, formal character had to mark their relations with other estates. For that reason, civil law in Western states, as it developed, was marked by the same formality, the same disputatious emphasis on the letter of the law, which constituted the very basis of public relations. Roman law, which continued to survive and be applied in a few European cities, still more strengthened this formalistic tendency of European jurisprudence. For Roman law, too, displays this same formalism which concentrates on the wording at the expense of true justice—the reason possibly being that in Rome, too, national life developed as a result of the unremitting struggle of two hostile nationalities compelled by force to form one polity.

Incidentally, this is the explanation of why Roman law, which was foreign to the European peoples, was so readily accepted by them, with the exception of the few countries which were not formed through conquest and which, therefore, gave promise of a more harmonious future evolution.

Having been born of violence, the European states were forced to develop through upheavals, for the development of a state is simply the unfolding of the essential principles on which it is founded. Hence European societies, founded on violence, cemented by formal personal relationships, permeated with narrow rationalism, were forced to produce not a public spirit, but a spirit of individual separatism, and were held together only by private and party interests. Consequently, although the history of European states often presents external indications of a flourishing public life, in fact the semblance of a public life merely disguised the activity of separate private parties, which pursued their own purposes and individual policies at the expense of the state as a whole. Papal parties, imperial parties, city parties, church parties, court, private, governmental, religious, political, popular, interclass, and even metaphysical parties were ever contending in the European states, each trying to upset the existing system in order to attain its own particular aims. Consequently European states developed not through peaceful growth but always through cataclysms of varying degrees of intensity. Revolution was the precondition of all progress, until it became not a means to an end, but in itself the distinctive end of popular striving.

It is obvious that in these circumstances European civilization was bound in the end to destroy the whole social and intellectual edifice which it had itself erected.

However, this cleavage of the intellect into separate faculties, this predominance of reason over the other components of the human spirit, which was ultimately to destroy the entire edifice of European medieval civilization, had an opposite effect in the beginning, and its very imbalance resulted in an accelerated development. For such is the law of intellectual deviation: external brilliance is coupled with inner darkness.

The Arab civilization evolved even more rapidly, for while it too leaned toward abstract reasoning, as did medieval Europe, it was even more onesided. It was easier for the Mohammedan culture to shape its basic beliefs by formal logic than it was for the essentially living and integral Christian culture to do so. The systematization of abstract concepts was the highest goal the Mohammedan could set himself; indeed, it may be said to have been the very basis of his faith. It demanded of him only the abstract recognition of certain historical facts and the metaphysical recognition of the oneness of God; it did not require an integrated inner self-knowledge, but calmly allowed the disjointed nature of man in its unreconciled duality to persist; it did not indicate to him the supreme purpose of being but, on the contrary, held out to him gross sensual pleasures not only as the greatest reward of life on earth but as the highest aim of the afterlife. Consequently the Mohammedan's intellectual requirements were confined to abstract logical unity, a formal arrangement of ideas and their systematic correlation. The supreme metaphysical problem which the inquiring Mohammedan mind could set itself—the very poetry of the Mohammedan's philosophy—consisted in evolving tangible formulas for the intangible activities of the spiritual world by searching for talismanic links between the laws of the world beyond the stars and the laws of the sublunar world. Hence their passion for logic, hence their astrology, alchemy, chiromancy, and all their abstract-rational and sensual-spiritual disciplines. This also explains why, although the Arabs had borrowed their civilization from the Syrian Greeks and maintained close relations with Byzantium, they exerted almost no influence on the evolution of Greek culture. But their impact on Western Europe was particularly great because they brought it the brilliance of their sciences at the very time when Europe lived in almost total ignorance. There can be no doubt that the abstract-logical trend of their learning influenced European scholarship in the same direction; and, albeit only for a little while, the sparkling stream of their talismanic concepts mingled with the dominant current of European thought. They were the first to acquaint the Latin theologians with the works of Aristotle, which first reached Europe in translation from the Arabic, with Arabic commentaries—so little was Greek culture then known to these theologians.

Aristotle, whose work was never understood as a whole but was studied ad infinitum in fragments, was, as we all know, the heart and soul of scholasticism, which in its turn represented the entire intellectual development of Europe at that time and was its clearest expression.

Scholasticism was nothing but an attempt to evolve a sciencelike theology; for in those days theology was both the supreme goal and the wellspring of all knowledge. It was the task of scholasticism not only to combine theological concepts into a reasonable system, but also to give them a rational-metaphysical basis. The main tools used were the writings of St. Augustine and Aristotle's works on logic. The highest achievement of the schools consisted in dialectical debates on articles of faith. The most famous theologians attempted to deduce religious dogmas from their logical ratiocinations. From John Scotus Erigena to the sixteenth century, there was probably not a single theologian who did not attempt to balance his belief in God on the edge of a cunningly honed syllogism. Their voluminous works were filled with abstract subtleties, purely rational concepts woven together by logic. To them, the least substantial types of thinking were the subjects of science, the programs of parties, the purpose of life.

It is not the abstract arguments of the nominalists and realists, nor the strange debates about the Eucharist, grace, the conception of the Holy Virgin, and the like, which can best give us an understanding of the actual spirit of scholasticism and the mental attitudes of the time; no, these are most clearly revealed by what constituted the core of these debates and engaged the attention of the most learned philosophers of the day—the posing of nonexistent problems based on unlikely assumptions and the analyzing of all possible arguments for and against them.

This endless, tiresome juggling of concepts over seven hundred years, this useless kaleidoscope of abstract categories revolving constantly before the mind's eye, was bound in the end to blind it to those living beliefs which lie above the sphere of logic and reason—beliefs to which man does not attain through syllogisms, and whose truth, on the contrary, syllogisms can only mutilate, if not utterly destroy.

A spontaneous, integral approach to man's inner spiritual life and a spontaneous, unbiased observation of the world of nature were alike excluded from the charmed circle of Western thought, the first being disdained as "mysticism"—which by its very nature was an abomination to scholastic rationalism (and, incidentally, also embraced those parts of the doctrine of the Orthodox Church which were not in accord with the Western systems)—and the second persecuted as "godlessness" (and included those findings of the sciences which were in contradiction with the views of contemporary theologians). For scholasticism had indissolubly tied its faith to its narrow interpretation of science.

That is why when, after the fall of Constantinople, the fresh, uncontaminated air of Greek thought poured in from the East and thinking men in the West began to breathe more easily and freely, the entire edifice of scholasticism collapsed instantaneously. Nevertheless, minds brought up on scholasticism were stamped by its bias. The object and direction of thought were changed; but the emphasis on rationality and the blind neglect of living truths were hardly altered.

The great originator of modern philosophy affords an instructive example of this fact. He thought that he had completely thrown off the shackles of scholasticism; yet, all unbeknown to himself, he was still so much a captive that, despite his marvelous insight into the formal laws of reason, he was so strangely blind to manifest truths that he did not regard his inner direct conviction of his own existence as sufficient proof thereof until he had deduced such proof by abstract syllogistic reasoning! This example is all the more remarkable in that it reveals not an individual peculiarity of the philosopher but a general mode of thinking. Descartes' logical deduction did not remain his exclusive property, but was hailed with delight and became the basic principle of most modern philosophers until almost the middle of the eighteenth century. Even today, profound thinkers may perhaps be found who rest upon it their certainty that they exist, thereby satisfying their educated need for solid conviction. In any event, the writer still vividly remembers a time in his own life when such artificial thinking processes assuaged his thirst for intellectual peace.

I forbear to dwell upon another of Descartes' peculiarities, which was that, being carried away by the rigorous necessity of his conclusions, he was able good-naturedly to convince himself that all animals except man are mere machines skillfully constructed by the Creator and, having no consciousness, can feel neither pain nor pleasure.

It is hardly surprising, therefore, that his disciple and successor in dominating philosophy, the famous Spinoza, was able to knit together so skillfully and strongly a network of logical deductions concerning the First Cause, the supreme order, and the workings of the entire universe that through the close meshes of his theorems and syllogisms he was unable to see the Living Creator in all of creation, or notice the inner freedom of man. Owing to similar excesses of logical reasoning, the great Leibniz was unable to perceive, through the network of his abstract concepts, the obvious connection between cause and effect, and to explain it he had to invent his Preestablished Harmony, a theory which, however, makes up for some of its one-sidedness by the poetry of its basic conception.

I say the poetry of the conception makes up for some of the one-sidedness of the theory because it seems to me that when logical merit is reinforced by esthetic or moral merit, this very combination of qualities enables the mind itself to recapture some of its primal wholeness and thus brings it closer to the truth.

Is it necessary to continue this enumeration of the leading exponents of Western philosophy and to recall their systems in order to be convinced of the universal one-sidedness of the Western school? Is there any need to recall that Hume—that direct and inevitable result of another branch of Western philosophy, a follower of Bacon, Locke, and similar thinkers—the dispassionate Hume, using the faculty of impartial reason, proved that no truth of any kind exists in the world and that verities and lies are equally subject to doubt? Or that the illustrious Kant, trained in the German school and influenced by Hume, deduced from the laws of pure reason themselves incontestable proof that for pure reason the higher truths are not susceptible of proof?

This may have been but one step from the truth—but the Western world was not yet ripe for it.

One abstract aspect of Kant's system was further developed by Fichte, who proved, through a remarkable chain of syllogisms, that the whole external world is but a phantom of the imagination, and that the only thing that has a real existence is the self-developing *Ego*. Starting from the same premise, Schelling developed the reverse of this hypothesis, to the effect that, while the external world does in fact exist, its spirit is none other than this human *Ego*, which develops through the life of the universe only in order to achieve self-knowledge in man. Hegel still further strengthened and elaborated upon this system of the independent development of human self-awareness. At the same time, probing more deeply than anyone before him into the very laws of logical thinking by bringing his vast extraordinary genius to bear upon them, he carried these laws to their ultimate conclusion, thereby enabling Schelling to prove the limitations of all logical thought. Thus Western philosophy now finds itself in a situation where it can no longer continue along its path of abstract rationalism, having recognized its limitations; nor is it in a position to strike out along a new path, since all its strength has lain precisely in the development of the faculty of abstract reasoning.

In the meantime, while Roman theology developed along the line of scholasticism, the writers of the Eastern Church did not allow themselves to be lured into the narrow byways of syllogistic reasoning but retained that breadth and wholeness of vision which have ever been a distinguishing feature of Christian philosophy. For we must not forget that at that period all contemporary culture was concentrated in Byzantium. Educated Greeks were familiar with the ancient Christian and pagan writers, particularly the philosophers, and there are manifest traces of a thorough study of these predecessors in most religious writings until the middle of the fifteenth century; at the same time the West, uneducated and even ignorant in comparison with Byzantium, was restricted in its thinking, virtually until the fourteenth century, to the narrow circle of Latin writers, in addition to a very few Greeks. It is not until the middle of the fourteenth century that the first learned academy was founded in Italy by the famous monk Barlam, Petrarch's teacher—that same miserable betrayer of the Orthodox Church who, having become infected with Western reliance on logical reasoning, had rejected certain dogmas of the Christian doctrine he was unable to understand, and had in consequence been condemned by the Council of Constantinople and expelled from Greece in disgrace, a circumstance which led to his being welcomed in Italy with great honors.

There is no doubt that the work of Aristotle was far better known to the Greeks than to the Latin writers, although possibly without the additions by which Arab and Latin scholars had enriched it and which, until the collapse of scholastic education in Europe, were a required condition of all intellectual development in the West. Nevertheless, not only did the Greek thinkers show no particular predilection for Aristotle, but, on the contrary, the majority of them clearly preferred Plato: not that the Christian philosophers accepted the pagan concepts of the one or the other, but because they probably found that Plato's very mode of thought came closer to engaging the integral faculties of the mind and because his speculative thinking was distinguished for greater warmth and harmony. Hence very nearly the same relation in which the two philosophers of the ancient world stood to each other is to be found between the philosophy of the Latin theologians which developed into scholasticism and the spiritual philosophy expounded by the writers of the Eastern Church, particularly by the Holy Fathers who lived and wrote after the defection of Rome.

It is worthy of note that the spiritual philosophy of the Eastern Church Fathers who wrote after the tenth century was a wholly and purely Christian philosophy, profound, alive, elevating the mind from mechanical reasoning to the highest realms of morally free speculation, a philosophy which even a nonbeliever could well find instructive because of the remarkable wealth, depth, and subtlety of its psychological observations. Despite all its merits (I speak here of intellectual merits only, leaving aside its theological value), this philosophy was so little capable of being grasped by the West, with its rationalistic tendency, that it not only was never properly appreciated by Western thinkers but, what is even more astounding, has to this day remained almost totally unknown to them. It is, at any rate, not mentioned by a single philosopher or historian of philosophy, although in every history of philosophy there are lengthy disquisitions on the philosophy of India, China, and Persia. The treatises of the Eastern writers were for a long time utterly unknown in Europe; many still are; others, while known, have attracted no attention because they have not been understood; still others have been published only recently and their merit, too, has not been recognized. Although a few Western theologians did remark on certain distinguishing characteristics of the Eastern writers, they understood those characteristics so little that their comments frequently give an impression which is the direct opposite of the truth. Lastly, in practically none of the theologians of the West do we note living traces of the influence which the writings of the Eastern Church would certainly have left on them, had they known them even half as well as they knew the ancient pagan writers. Perhaps the only exception to this rule is Thomas à Kempis—or Gerson—if the book [1] ascribed to him was really written by him and is not, as some think, a translation from the Greek, slightly altered to fit Latin views.

Naturally, we cannot look for anything new as regards Christian doctrine in the writers of the Eastern Church who lived after the defection of Rome —anything that may not be found in the writers of the early centuries of Christianity. But that is precisely their merit; their distinguishing characteristic is that they preserved and maintained the basic Christian doctrine in all its purity and fullness and, being themselves situated at the heart, so to say, of true belief, they were able to discern more clearly both the laws of the human mind and the way it should follow to achieve true knowledge, as well as the external symptoms and internal causes of its various deviations.

[1] *De imitatione Christi.*—Editor.

In point of fact, even the early Church Fathers, who lived before Rome's defection and were consequently recognized by the East and the West alike, were not always understood in the same way in the West as in the East. This difference may have arisen because the East was at all times fully familiar with *all* the writers and teachers of the Universal Church; while Western scholars were acquainted mainly with the Latin writers and with only a few of the Greeks, whom they approached with minds already formed by their Roman teachers. Hence even in recent times, when they acquired some familiarity with Greek literature, they involuntarily went on looking at it through the same narrow window with its dark, if not colored, glass. There is no other explanation of how they could for so long have persisted in their biased rationalistic trend, which should have crumbled under the joint impact of all the early Church Fathers. Having maintained their narrow bias, they either took no notice of or simply did not know those ancient writers whose work presented the very opposite aspect, and complacently rejected it under the name of mysticism.

Hence, in addition to holding unlike concepts, the East and the West also differed in the very *method* of theological and philosophical thinking. For, in seeking to arrive at the truth through speculation, the Eastern thinkers were primarily concerned with the proper inner condition of the thinking spirit, while the Westerners were more interested in the external coherence of concepts. The Eastern thinkers, in their effort to attain the complete truth, sought to achieve an inner wholeness of the intellect—that concentration of intellectual powers which brings all the separate faculties of the mind together in a supreme and living unity. The Western philosophers, on the other hand, assumed that the complete truth could be discerned by separate faculties of the mind, acting independently and in isolation. They used one faculty to understand moral, and another to grasp esthetic, matters; for practical affairs they had yet a third; to ascertain the truth, they employed abstract reasoning; and none of these faculties knew what any of the others was doing until its action was completed. They assumed that each path led to a final goal, which had to be attained before the faculties could unite and make common progress. They deemed cold unemotional reasoning and the unrestrained sway of passions to be equally legitimate human attitudes; and when the Western scholars in the fourteenth century learned that the Eastern contemplative thinkers sought to preserve serenity and inner wholeness of spirit, they jeered at the idea and invented various mocking appellations for it.

True, at times they used the same expressons as the Eastern theologians, and spoke of the "internal còncentration of the spirit," the "turning of the mind on itself," and the like; but the meaning given to these expressions was generally quite different: not the concentration, the assembling, the integration of the powers of the spirit, but merely their being strained to the utmost. It may be said in general that they were not concerned with finding the center of spiritual being. Western man had no comprehension of that living union of the highest intellectual powers in which not one acts without a reaction on the part of the others, or that equilibrium of inner life which marks even the external actions of a man brought up in the traditions of the Orthodox world; for in his actions, even during the most acute crises of his life, there is a deep calm, a natural moderation, a dignity coupled with resignation, which bear testimony to the serenity, depth, and integrity of his spiritual being. The European, on the other hand, always ready to give way to passion, forever fidgeting—when he is not being theatrical—and eternally restless, can only by a conscious effort impose an artifical moderation on his internal and external reactions.

The teachings of the Fathers of the Orthodox Church reached Russia, so to say, with the first pealing of the Christian church bells. It is under their guidance that the authentic Russian mind, which is the foundation of the Russian style of life, was formed.

The vast land of Russia, even when it was divided into petty principalities, thought of itself as a single living organism, held together not so much by a common language as by the unity of convictions which resulted from a common faith in the dicta of the Church. Over its vast expanse, like an unbroken net, lay scattered a countless multitude of isolated monasteries which were linked together by sympathetic bonds of spiritual communion. They radiated a uniform and harmonious light of faith and learning to all the separate tribes and principalities. Not only did the people derive their spiritual notions from them; all their ethical, social, and legal concepts were subjected to their educative influence and came back to them bearing the stamp of uniformity. The clergy, whose members were drawn without distinction from all classes of society, from the highest to the lowest, in turn transmitted to all social classes that higher learning which it obtained directly from primary sources, from the very center of contemporary learning, which then meant Constantinople, Syria, and Mount Athos.

This learning spread in Russia so quickly and to such a degree that even today it amazes us to recall that some of the appanaged princes of the twelfth and thirteenth centuries had libraries which the library of Paris, then the largest in the West, could barely rival in number of volumes [2] ; that many of them spoke Greek and Latin as fluently as Russian, while some knew other European languages as well [3] ; that in some manuscripts preserved from the fifteenth century [4] we find extracts from Russian transla-

[2] See Schlözer's comments on Nestor, Vol. I. [Reference is to August Ludwig Schlözer, *Nestor. Russische Annalen in ihrer Slavonischen Grundsprache* (4 vols.; Göttingen, 1802–05). Russian translation by D. Iazykov, *Nestor, russkie letopisi na drevne-slavianskom iazyke* (3 parts; St. Petersburg, 1809–19).—Editor.]

[3] See *Istoriia russkoi slovesnosti* [History of Russian Letters] by Prof. Shevyrev, 2d fascicle. This book, one of the most remarkable recently published in our country, must without doubt produce a radical change in our general concept of our ancient state of learning. [Reference is to the nationalistic literary historian, Stepan P. Shevyrev (1806–64) and his course of lectures published under the title of *Istoriia russkoi slovesnosti, preimushchestvenno drevnei* (4 parts; Moscow, 1846–60).—Editor.]

[4] See the writings of Nil Sorskii. [Nikolai Feodorovich Maikov, as a monk under the name of Nil Sorskii (1433–1508), was a leading spokesman for the antiproperty movement in the Russian Church at the end of the fifteenth and the beginning of the sixteenth century, and a strong advocate of a "spiritualistic" (as opposed to institutional and ritualistic) orientation in Russian religious life.—Editor.]

tions of Greek works which not only were not known in Europe but which had been lost in Greece itself during its decline and have been only recently rediscovered with great effort in the unplundered treasure-trove of Athos; that in the silence and isolation of their cells, often in the depths of the forest, monks studied and copied (those ancient manuscripts having survived to this day) Slavonic translations of Church Fathers whose profound writings, representing theological and philosophical thinking in its highest form, may even today be beyond the grasp of many a German professor of philosophy (although none of them is likely to admit this fact); lastly, that this learning was so widespread, so strong, so highly developed, and so deeply rooted in Russian life that despite the fact that a century and a half has elasped since our monasteries ceased to be centers of culture, despite the fact that the entire thinking portion of the people, in its upbringing as in its views, has largely departed from, and in some cases completely abandoned, the former Russian style of life and erased the very memory of it from its mind—this Russian style of life, fashioned according to, and impregnated with, the ideas of our former learning, has survived almost without a change among the lower classes of the people. It has survived, although it is now practiced almost unconsciously, as a matter of tradition, no longer shaped and directed by a guiding thought, no longer revivified, as in the olden days, by the concerted influence of the upper classes, nor harmonizing, as once upon a time, with the main current of the country's intellectual life.

How great a force it must have been that has produced so lasting an effect! Too, this stability of custom inherited from our earlier culture has been manifested by the same people who had so readily shed their pagan culture when they embraced Christianity.

Hence these Russian customs and the early life of Russia which is reflected in them are precious to us, especially because they still show traces of the pure Christian principles which had been voluntarily accepted by the Slavic tribes. It is not because of any inborn merits of the Slavic race that we place such high hopes in its future; no! Racial characteristics are like the soil on which a seed is cast. The soil can only retard or accelerate the germination of the seed by giving it good or scanty food; it can let it grow in freedom in God's world or strangle it in weeds; but what the fruit will be depends on the seed itself.

Whatever we may think of the coming of the Varangians—whether we hold that Russia as a whole asked them to come, or that one party invited them in order to get the better of another party—in any event, their coming did not represent an invasion by a foreign tribe; neither can it have been a conquest, for if it was so easy to expel them, or a considerable part of them, from Russia 150 years later, could they have so easily conquered it before? And how could they have remained there undisturbed against Russia's will? [5] During their presence, the formation of Russian society and the

[5] Cf. the article of my brother Petr V. Kireevskii, "O drevnei russkoi istorii" in *Moskvitianin*, No. 3 (1845), which in my opinion gives the clearest picture of the original

Russian polity proceeded calmly and naturally, without any innovations being introduced by force, and purely as an outgrowth of Russian moral concepts. With the coming of Christianity, the moral concepts of the Russian changed, and with them his attitude toward society; hence all the social organization of Russia, as it developed, was also bound to change to conform to the Christian doctrine.

The best example of the readiness of the Russians, from the very outset, to put their newly accepted creed into practice in full was St. Vladimir's initial and unconsidered (but so beautifully unconsidered!) intention to forgive all criminals. The Church itself stopped him from carrying out his purpose, thereby drawing the line between personal spiritual obligations and those of secular government. At the same time, the Church established, once and for all, clear boundaries between itself and the state, between the absolute purity of its high principles and the worldly compromises of the social system, remaining always outside and high above the state and its material interests, like an unattainable, radiant ideal which men should strive toward and which did not mingle with their earthly motivations. In ruling the private convictions of men, the Orthodox Church never had any ambition to master their wills or to acquire any powers of secular government, still less to seek official dominion over government authorities. The state, it is true, depended on the Church: its foundations were the stronger, its structure the more harmonious, its internal life the more integrated, the more it was permeated by the Church's influence. But the Church never desired to be the state, even as the state, for its part, humbly recognizing its worldly purpose, never called itself "holy." If the Russian land was sometimes called "Holy Russia," that was solely because it abounded in sacred relics, monasteries, and churches, and not because its structure represented an interpenetration of the ecclesiastical and the secular like that of the "Holy Roman Empire."

Thus, in ruling society as the spirit rules the body, the Church did not endow worldly institutions with an ecclesiastical character, producing nothing similar to the monastic orders of knights, the trials of the Inquisition, and other half-secular, half-religious institutions of the West; but, by suffusing all the intellectual and moral convictions of men, it invisibly led the state toward a realization of the highest principles of Christianity, while never hindering its natural development. The Church was able to have so full and pure a spiritual influence on this natural growth of society because there was no historical obstacle to prevent men from allowing their inner beliefs to be expressed in their external relationships. Since Russia had not been crushed underfoot by conquest, its internal structure had not been twisted out of shape by the violence and oppression bound to arise from the struggle of two races which hate one another and which are compelled to live together in constant hostility. In Russia, there were neither conquerors

---

organization of old Russia. [Petr V. Kireevskii (1808–56) was a student of folklore and collector of Russian folk songs.—Editor.]

nor conquered. It knew neither a rigid separation of immobile social estates, nor privileges granted to one estate at the expense of the others, nor the resulting political and moral struggle, nor class contempt, class hatred, and class envy. Consequently, it was also spared the inevitable result of such a struggle: artificial formality in public life and a painful process of social development proceeding through the forcible alteration of the laws and the violent overthrow of institutions. The princes, the boyars, the clergy, the people, and the troops maintained respectively by the princes, the boyars, the towns, and the rural communities—all these classes and strata of the population were imbued with the same spirit, the same convictions and beliefs, and a like desire for the common weal. There might have been differences of opinion on details, but there was hardly ever any discord in essential matters.

Thus Russian society developed independently and naturally, under the influence of the same credo, nurtured by the Church and the popular tradition. Nevertheless—or perhaps we should say *for that very reason*—it was as free from utopian egalitarianism as it was from unfair privilege. It represented not a plane, but a ladder with a great many rungs; but these rungs were not meant to be fixed forever, for they were set up naturally, as the needs of society required, and not violently, owing to the contingencies of war, or deliberately, to correspond to logical categories.

Anyone who attempts to visualize Western society in feudal times is bound to see it as a profusion of fortified castles, each inhabited by a noble knight and his family and surrounded by the huts of the lowborn rabble. The knight was a person; the rabble were merely part of his domain. The warring of these individual castles with each other and their relations with the free cities, the king, and the Church form the entire history of the West.

If, on the contrary, we visualize the Russian society of ancient times, we see neither castles, nor lowborn rabble, nor noble knights, nor a king struggling against them. We see instead a countless multitude of small communities scattered over the face of the Russian land, each of them under a leader who operates within certain limitations, each of them representing its own consensus, its own small world; these microcosms, these tiny accords, merge together in other, larger accords, which in turn form territorial and then tribal accords; out of the latter is formed the one vast accord of the entire Russian land under the Grand Duke of All the Russias, serving as the foundation for the edifice of society, the groundwork for its political structure.

Given such a natural, simple, and concordant relationship, the laws by which Russia was governed could not have been marked by artificial formality; but, arising out of two sources—popular tradition and inner conviction —they were bound, in spirit, content, and application, to be concerned more with the essential truth than with the appearance of truth, preferring evident genuine justice to literal formal meaning, sacred tradition to logical deductions, and the demands of morality to those of expediency. I am not, naturally, speaking of any one law in particular, but of the general tendency of ancient Russian law, which gave preference to genuine equity over superficial formalism.

Whereas Roman and Western jurisprudence draw abstract logical conclusions from every legal form, saying: *"The form is the very law,"* and endeavor to link all forms into a coherent system, each part of which follows logically from the whole, with the whole itself constituting not merely a reasonable text but *reason itself expressed in writing,* customary law in Russia, springing as it did from daily life, knew nothing of abstract logic. In Russia laws were not formulated in advance by some learned jurists; they were not ponderously and eloquently discussed at some legislative assembly; and they did not subsequently fall like an avalanche in the midst of the astounded citizenry, wrecking some existing custom or institution of theirs. A law in Russia usually was not composed, but merely written down after the idea of it had been formed in people's minds and had gradually, through actual necessity, become part of their customs and way of life. Logical progress in the law is conceivable only where public life itself rests on artificial foundations, and where consequently the further development of the social order must be governed by *opinion,* whether of all or of some. Where, on the contrary, the life of society rests on a basic unanimity of views, any impairment of the stability of manners, the sanctity of tradition, or the continuity of customary relationships is bound to destroy the very fabric of social life. In such a society, every change introduced by force as a result of logical reasoning would be a stab to the heart of the social organism. For such a society is based on *convictions,* and for its development to be governed by *opinions,* even opinions generally held, would deal it a death blow.

Opinion and conviction are two wholly different mainsprings of two entirely different kinds of social order. Opinion differs from conviction not only in that the former is more temporary while the latter is more lasting and in that the former stems from logical reasoning while the latter is the result of a lifetime's experience. From the political viewpoint, we can see yet another distinction: conviction is a spontaneous awareness of the sum total of social relations; opinion is an undue preference for only those social interests which happen to coincide with the interest of some one party, whereby its narrow selfishness is given the deceptive appearance of a desire for the common good.

Hence in an artificial society, one founded on a formal concordance of interests, every improvement is introduced as a result of some deliberate plan; a new relationship is instituted because today's opinion gains ascendancy over yesterday's order of things; and each decision overthrows those preceding it. Development, as already noted, proceeds by means of upheavals, engineered either from above or from below, depending on where the victorious party has concentrated its forces and where the victorious opinion has directed them. On the other hand, in a society which has arisen naturally, through the independent development of its basic principles, every change in direction is an illness, and is fraught with some danger; to such a society, the law of upheavals is not a precondition for improvement but a threat of dissolution and death; for it can only develop harmoniously and imperceptibly, following the law of the natural growth of unified organisms.

One of the basic differences between the legal systems of Russia and the West lies in the fundamental conception of the right of land ownership. All Roman civil law may be said to be no more than an outgrowth of the unconditional character of this right. The social structure of Western European countries also arose out of various combinations of these original entitlements, which were initially absolute, and only in social relationships were subjected to some limitations by mutual agreement. The entire edifice of the Western social order may be said to rest on the development of the personal right of ownership, so that personality itself—in juridical terms—is no more than an expression of this right.

In the Russian social order, personality was the primary subject of the law, and the right of ownership was merely one of its *accidental* attributes. The land belonged to the community (*obshchina*) because the community was comprised of families which consisted of persons who were able to cultivate the land. As the number of persons in a family increased, the amount of land at its disposal increased also; as the number decreased, so did the amount of land. The community's rights over the land were limited by the rights of the landowner [6]; the landowner's rights were determined by his position vis-à-vis the state. The relationship of the landowner to the state did not derive from his estate, but the estate depended on the personal relationship of the owner to the state. His position depended in part on the services rendered by his father, in part on his own; it might be lost if the services could not be continued, or it might be enhanced if his personal qualities made him clearly superior to others in a like position. In a word, unconditional ownership of land in Russia could only be an exception. Society was made up not of private property to which persons were attached, but of persons to whom property was attached.

Any confusion which may subsequently have arisen in the upper strata of society when small principalities were abolished and merged into one administrative structure was accidental and appears to have been the effect of outside causes, so that it was not part of the inevitable evolution of the fundamental spirit of Russian polity, but a deviation. In any event, this very special position, altogether unlike that obtaining in the West—in which a person defined himself in terms of his landed property—was an intrinsic part of public, social, and moral relationships.

Consequently, the relationships of the Russians among themselves were also different from those of the West. I am not speaking of minor differentiations, which may be regarded as negligible national idiosyncracies. No, the very nature of popular custom, the very meaning of public relationships and

---

[6] Kireevskii here speaks of *pomeshchik ili votchinnik*, following the old distinction between one who possessed an estate (*pomest'e*) in return for service to the state, on a theoretically temporary basis, and one who owned land on the basis of a right of inheritance (*votchina*, or patrimony). In the subsequent discussion, however, only the term *pomeshchik* is used in its nineteenth-century sense of owner of land and serfs.—Editor.

private morals were quite different. Western man fragments his life into separate aspirations, and although he then unites them logically into a coherent plan, yet at every moment of his life he is like a different person. One corner of his heart shelters the religious feeling on which he calls on occasions of ritual observance; another, quite separate, harbors the faculties of reason and practical good sense; a third, his sensual desires; a fourth, his ethical concepts and love of family; a fifth, self-interest; a sixth, his esthetic sense; and each of these separate strivings and desires is subdivided further into drives, each of which is accompanied by a separate state of mind, each of which manifests itself separately, and all of which are bound together only by abstract reason. Western man is easily able to pray in the morning with fervent, intense, amazing zeal; then rest from that effort, forgetting prayer and exercising other faculties as he does his work; then rest from his work not only physically, but morally, forgetting its dull occupations in laughter and the sound of drinking songs; and then forget the rest of his day and indeed his whole life in the enjoyment of a make-believe world which captures his imagination. Next day he will be ready, with similar ease, to recommence turning the wheel of his outwardly rational life.

Not so the Russian. When he prays in church, he does not scream in exaltation, beat his breast, or swoon with emotion; on the contrary, during the act of prayer he makes a supreme effort to preserve sobriety of mind and integrity of spirit. Then, when the fullness of self-realization in prayer—rather than mere intensity of feeling—floods his soul and his heart is touched by emotion, his tears flow quietly and no passion troubles the deep serenity of his spiritual state. On the other hand, neither does he sing drinking songs; he partakes of his dinner with a prayer. It is with a prayer that he begins and finishes every task. It is with a prayer that he enters and leaves a house. The lowliest peasant appearing in the palace before the Grand Duke (to defend whose honor he may but yesterday have risked his life in some skirmish with the Poles) would not greet his host before bowing to the holy ikon, such as is also to be found in a place of honor in every hut, large or small. Thus the Russian has always linked all his doings, important or not, directly with the highest concepts of the mind and the deepest concentration of the heart.

It must, however, be admitted that this constant striving for the unity of all moral faculties may have its dangerous aspect. For it is only in a society in which all classes are imbued with the same spirit, where universally respected and numerous monasteries—those popular schools and institutions of higher learning of a religious state—govern all minds, where, consequently, men who have attained to spiritual wisdom may at all times direct others who are not yet so mature: it is only in such a society that such a disposition must lead man to the heights of perfection. But if he lacks the care and guidance of a superior mind before he has himself attained to the maturity of spiritual life, he may easily fall into the error of excessive effort resulting in undue exhaustion. Hence we sometimes see a Russian throw himself into his work and accomplish more in three days than the prudent German will in thirty; but then he will for a long time be unable to resume his task voluntarily. Because of the Russian's lack of maturity in the absence of a sympathetic guide, the German, for all the limitations of his mind, by tabulating and dividing into hours the extent and degree of the Russian's endeavors, can regulate and order the latter's work better than he can himself.

In ancient Russia, however, this spiritual integrity, which was fostered in the people by their very customs, was also reflected in their family life, where constant, recurring self-sacrifice was not a heroic exception but a general and ordinary obligation. Among our peasants, the family still maintains this character of unity. If we study the life that goes on in the peasant's hut, we shall see that no member of the family, while constantly at work and at pains to keep the whole household operating successfully, ever thinks of his own selfish interests. He has cut off at the root any thought of personal gain. The integrity of the family is the one common goal and motivating power. Any surplus in the household goes to the head of the family, who is accountable to no one; all private earnings are conscientiously handed over to him in full. The mode of living of the family as a whole usually improves little when the head of the family reaps additional benefits; but the various members do not seek to find out how these are used or even what they amount to: they continue their eternal labors with the same selflessness, as a moral duty, as a mainstay of family concord. In the old days this was even more striking; for families, composed not only of children and grandchildren, were larger and stayed together as the clan multiplied. Nevertheless, even today we can see on every hand how readily, when there is serious trouble, how willingly—I would even say how gladly—one member of a family will sacrifice himself for another when he feels that his sacrifice is for the good of the family as a whole.

In the West, family ties were weakened by the general trend of Western civilization: from the higher classes this tendency spread to the lower, both through the direct influence of the former on the latter and through the latter's irresistible urge to copy the manners of their betters. This passion for imitation is all the more natural the more homogeneous is the civilization of the different classes, and it bears its fruits the more readily the more artificial that civilization is and the more subject it is to the influence of private opinion.

In the higher strata of European society, generally speaking, family life very soon became a secondary matter even for the women. From their very birth, the children of noble families were brought up without the mother's care. Particularly in those countries where it was fashionable for upper-class [parents] to rear their daughters outside the family, behind the impenetrable walls of convents, the mother almost lost her family function. Leaving the convent only in order to go to the altar, she at once entered the charmed circle of worldly duties without having learned what her family duties were. For that very reason, she was more concerned with social than with family relationships. The ambitious and noisy delights of the drawing room replaced for her the alarms and joys of the quiet nursery. The social graces and knowledge of the fashionable life, developing freely at the expense of other virtues, became the most essential elements of feminine merit. The brilliant salon soon became for both sexes the main source of pleasure and happiness, of wit and culture, and of public influence, and the principal and engrossing goal of their artificial life. Hence, particularly in countries where women of quality were educated away from home, there was a marvelous and enchanting development of social refinement accompanied by the moral degeneration of the ruling class, which contained the first germ of what was later to become the notorious doctrine of the complete emancipation of women.

In Russia, in the meantime, the various forms of social life, being the reflection of a unified whole, never underwent any separate, independent development, were never sundered from the life of the entire people, and therefore could neither stifle family feeling nor prevent a balanced and unified moral growth. The striking peculiarity of the Russian character in this respect was that an individual, in his relationships with others, never stressed his personal characteristics as giving him special merit; individual ambition was confined to the desire to be a correct expression of the general spirit of society. Even as the salon does not rule a state all parts of which are in sympathy with the whole; even as individual opinion does not dominate a society which is founded on unshakable conviction; even so such a society is not governed by the whim of fashion, for fashion is thwarted in it by the stability of custom.

Such being the temper of the Russian people, the simplicity of their life and their needs was not the result of a lack of means or of inadequate education, but was in line with the fundamental nature of Russian culture. In the West, luxury was not a contradiction but the logical consequence of the fragmented aspirations of man and society; it may be said to have been inherent in the West's artificial civilization. The clergy, going against the general view, may have condemned it, but in the popular mind it was almost a virtue. People did not give in to it as to a weakness, but rather were proud of it, as of an enviable privilege. In the Middle Ages, the common folk gazed with respect at the outward glitter which surrounded a person of consequence, and in their minds this external glitter merged piously with the idea of a man's inner worth. The Russian, on the other hand, venerated the rags of the holy fool rather than the gold brocade of the courtier. Luxury did penetrate into Russia, but as a disease caught from the neighbors. Apologies were made for it; Russians succumbed to it as to a vice, being always aware that it was wrong, not only from the religious, but from the moral and social standpoints.

Western man sought to relieve the burden of his internal shortcomings by developing material wealth. The Russian endeavored to avoid the burden of material needs by raising his spirit above them. Had the science of political economy existed in those days, there can be no doubt that the Russian would have found it incomprehensible. He would have been unable to reconcile the existence of a separate science of wealth with his comprehensive view of life. He would not have understood that people could be deliberately aroused to greater awareness of their material needs merely in order that they might intensify their efforts to produce goods. He knew that the formation of wealth is a secondary factor in a country's life and should, therefore, not merely be closely connected with other, higher factors, but be entirely subordinate to them.

However, while luxury was able to penetrate into Russia as a sort of infection, artificial comfort with its exquisite effeminacy, any other deliberately artificial ways of life, any tendency toward debilitating reverie, could never have gained a foothold in it, being directly and clearly contrary to its dominant spirit.

For the same reason, if there had been time for the fine arts to develop in ancient Russia, they would certainly have taken a very different form from that which they took in the West. In the West their development followed the general trend of ideas; consequently, the same fragmentation of the spirit which in the intellectual sphere resulted in abstract logic produced fancifulness and dissociation of emotions in the fine arts. Hence the pagan veneration of abstract beauty. Instead of maintaining an eternal bond between beauty and truth—a bond which, it is true, may slow down the separate progress of each, but which safeguards the integrity of the human spirit and preserves the genuineness of its manifestation—the Western world founded its ideal of beauty on the lies of the imagination, on a dream it knew to be false, or on a supreme straining of an isolated emotion, born of a deliberate dissociation of the mind. For the Western world did not realize that a flight of fancy is a lie told by the heart, and that an inner wholeness of being is essential not only for cognition of the truth but also for full esthetic enjoyment.

This trend of the fine arts was not without effect on the life of the Western world. Free art is born of the sum total of human relationships and, having made its entrance into the world, it again reaches into the depths of the human spirit, strengthening or weakening it, uniting or scattering its forces, as the case may be. I believe, therefore, that the mistaken trend of the fine arts distorted European culture even more than did the trend of philosophy, which can be a mainspring of development only when it is also its fruit. But the voluntary, continuous, and, so to say, enthusiastic striving for a deliberate dichotomy of the human consciousness shatters the spirit's forces at the root. Intelligence is then transformed into cleverness, emotion into blind passion, beauty into illusion, truth into opinion, learning into a syllogism, reality into a springboard for the imagination, virtue into smugness; while theatricality becomes life's inseparable companion, serving as an external cover for falsehood even as idle fancy provides its internal mask.

In mentioning smugness I have touched upon yet another fairly general difference between the Westerner and the Russian. Western man, generally speaking, is nearly always satisfied with his moral state; almost every European is ready at any time, proudly placing his hand on his heart, to declare to himself and to others that his conscience is clear, that he is innocent before God and man, and that his only prayer is that all others should be like him. If his overt acts should happen to be at variance with the generally accepted notions of morality, he will invent a system of ethics of his own, and thus once more set his conscience at peace. The Russian, on the other hand, is always keenly aware of his shortcomings, and the higher he rises along the ladder of moral development, the more he demands of himself and consequently the less satisfied he is with himself. When he departs from the true path, he does not seek to deceive himself by some ingenious argument and to lend an appearance of rightness to his essential error; on the contrary, even when most carried away by passion, he is always ready to recognize the passion as immoral.

But let us stop here and summarize all that we have said on the difference between Western European and ancient Russian culture; for surely we have noted enough particulars to be able to add them up and arrive at a general definition of the two types of civilization.

Christianity was conveyed to the Western peoples solely through the teaching of the Roman Catholic Church, while in Russia it was kindled by the lights of the entire Orthodox Church; in the West theology became a matter of abstract logic, while in the Orthodox world it retained the integrity of its spirit; there the forces of the mind were split asunder, while here every effort was made to maintain them as a living whole; there the mind sought to find the truth by establishing a logical sequence of concepts, while here men aspired to it by endeavoring to elevate their consciousness and achieve unity of heart and concentration of spirit; there we see a search for an external, dead unity, while here we find a striving toward an inner, living essence; there the Church mingled with the state, uniting spiritual with temporal power and merging the ecclesiastical and the secular in a system of a mixed character, while in Russia the Church remained aloof from worldly institutions and purposes; there we see scholasticism and law in the universities, while in ancient Russia we find higher learning cultivated in the monasteries, in the midst of prayers; there we observe a scholastic and logical approach to the higher verities, while here we note an endeavor to grasp them spontaneously and completely; there pagan and Christian civilization grow into one another, while here a constant effort is made to keep the truth pure; there statehood is the result of violent conquest, while here it arose through the natural development of popular customs based on the unity of fundamental belief; there we find a hostile separation of estates, while in ancient Russia we see them united in purpose yet still maintaining their natural differences. There the formal relationship of the nobles' castles with their manors resulted in the formation of separate states, while here universal consent gives spiritual expression to indissoluble unity; there land ownership is the basis of civil relationships, while here property is merely an accidental expression of personal relationships; there the law is built on formal logic, while here it grows out of local custom; there the law leans toward the appearance of justice, while here preference is given to the essence of justice; there jurisprudence strives to codify the law along logical lines, while here, instead of looking for formal connections, it seeks the link between legal doctrine and the precepts of faith and custom; there laws are made to conform with prevailing opinion, while here they are born naturally out of the general way of life; there improvements are always effected by means of violent change, here [they occur] through natural harmonious growth. There we find the turbulence of the party spirit, here the steadfastness of basic conviction; there the whim of fashion, here the stability of a way of life; there the precariousness of individual willfulness, here the solidity of family and social ties; there ostentatious luxury and artificiality, here simplicity of needs and moral fortitude; there a tendency toward effeminacy and fancifulness, here a healthy integrity of the mental faculties; there an inner anxiety coupled with an intellectual conviction of virtue, here a profound peace and tranquillity of the inner self, coupled with constant self-mistrust and an incessant striving for moral improvement; in a word, there a dichotomy of the spirit, dichotomy of thought, dichotomy of learning, dichotomy of the state, dichotomy of estates, dichotomy of society, dichotomy of morals and emotions, dichotomy of the sum total and of all separate aspects of human life, both social and individual; and in Russia, on the other hand, an overwhelming reaching out for wholeness of being, both external and internal, social and individual, intellectual and worldly, artificial and moral. Thus, if what we have set forth is correct, *dichotomy* and *integrity, ratiocination* and *intelligence,* are the ultimate expressions of Western European and ancient Russian culture.

The question naturally arises: Why, then, did not Russian culture develop more richly than the European before Western learning was imported into Russia? Why did not Russia outstrip Europe? Why did it not head the intellectual advance of all mankind, having so many prerequisites for correct and comprehensive spiritual development?

If we were to say in reply that it was by the will of Providence that the development of the Russian mind was held back for several centuries from what would appear to be its appointed time, that would be true enough, but it would be begging the question. Holy Providence does not lengthen or shorten a man's appointed path unless he gives It moral cause. The people of Israel might have accomplished the journey across the Arabian desert from Egypt to the Promised Land in forty days; they took forty years to traverse it only because their souls failed to cleave to God, Who led them.

We have already mentioned, however, that each patriarchate of the Universal Church, each nation, each person, in placing his own individual characteristics at its service, finds that the very development of those characteristics presents a danger to his inner balance and his remaining in concord with the general spirit of Orthodoxy.

What, then, were the individual characteristics of Russia as compared with other nations of the Orthodox world, and what was the danger threatening it? Did these characteristics perchance develop to excess, so that its mind was deflected from the direct path it should have taken to reach its appointed goal?

We are, of course, in the realm of surmises. As for my personal opinion, I believe that Russia's distinguishing feature was the very fullness and purity of expression of the Christian doctrine throughout its social and family life. This was the great strength of its civilization; but it also held within it the main danger to its development. Being pure, the expression was so close to the spirit expressed that it was easy for a man to confuse the two and to respect the form as much as the inner meaning. He was, of course, protected against such confusion by the very nature of Orthodox doctrine, which was primarily concerned with preserving the integrity of the spirit. Yet the type of doctrine a man accepts does not liberate him from the weakness common to all mankind. Thus no teaching and no decrees will destroy the moral freedom of will in a man or in a nation. And so we see that in the sixteenth century esteem for the form becomes in many ways preponderant over respect for the spirit. Perhaps the origins of this imbalance should be looked for even earlier; but in the sixteenth century it becomes plainly visible. Certain distortions which had crept into the prayer books and certain peculiarities in the Church ritual persisted among the people, despite the fact that constant contact with the East should have shown them that the practice of the other churches was different. At the same time we see that particular legal decisions taken by Byzantium were not only studied, but were respected almost as much as the decisions of the whole Church, and that there was a tendency to apply them in Russia as if they were generally binding. At the same time the monasteries, while preserving their outward splendor, began to allow a certain laxity in the daily regimen of the monks. At the same time the relationship between the boyars and the gentry[7] deteriorated into the ugly and complicated formalism of the *mestnichestvo* system.[8] At the same time the proximity of the Uniate Church, inspiring fear of innovations from abroad, served to augment the general eagerness and anxiety to preserve every single bit of ancient Russian Orthodox culture, including even its external and literal aspects.

In this way respect for tradition, which was Russia's strength, was insensibly transformed into respect for its external manifestations rather than for its life-giving spirit. This gave rise to an imbalance in Russian civilization of which Ivan the Terrible was a striking consequence, and which, a century later, caused the schisms and, later still, by its one-sidedness, caused some thinking people to swing to the opposite extreme and eagerly to embrace foreign forms and a foreign spirit.

But the essence of Russian civilization still lives on among the people and, what is most important, in the Holy Orthodox Church. Hence it is on this foundation and on no other that we must erect the solid edifice of Russian enlightenment, built heretofore out of mixed and for the most part foreign materials and therefore needing to be rebuilt with pure native stone. The construction of this building can be carried out only when that class of our nation which is not wholly occupied with working to provide for its material needs and whose appointed role in society is therefore to shape

[7] Kireevskii here contrasts *boiar* and *pomeshchik,* implying that the former is the Muscovite service aristocracy, while the latter is a small landowning serviceman from the provinces. As his use of the terms is far from correct in the technical sense, the translation of *pomeshchik* as "gentry" seems to convey best the contrast he has in mind.—Editor.

[8] A system calculating seniority in service according to one's ancestors' service position (see note on p. 57).—Editor.

the public consciousness—when that class, I say, which is still saturated with Western ideas, becomes at last fully convinced of the one-sidedness of European culture; when it grows more keenly aware of the need for new intellectual principles; when, in a rational desire for the whole truth, it turns to the pure fountainhead of its people's ancient Orthodox faith and, with its responsive heart, will harken after the distinct echoes of this holy faith still clearly to be heard in Russia's former native life. Then, having thrown off the yoke of the logical systems of European philosophy, the educated Russian will find in the depths of the special, living, integral philosophy of the Holy Fathers of the Church—a philosophy incomprehensible to the Western mind—complete answers to those very questions of the mind and heart which most perturb a soul disillusioned by the latest results of Western thinking. [A study of] his country's former life will enable him to understand how a different culture may be evolved.

It will then be possible for learning to develop in Russia on native principles, different from those which European culture offers us. The arts can then flourish in Russia, growing from native roots.[9] And public life in Russia will then proceed in a direction different from that in which it would have been led by Western civilization.

In using the word "direction," however, I deem it necessary to add that it delimits sharply the extent of my desire. For, if ever I were to see in a dream that some external feature of our former life, long since outgrown, had suddenly been revived and, in its former shape, become part of our present existence, I would not rejoice at such a vision. On the contrary, I would be frightened. For such an intrusion of the past into the new, the dead into the living, would be tantamount to transferring a wheel from one machine into another, of a different type and size: in such a case, either the wheel or the machine must break. My only wish is that those principles of life which are preserved in the doctrine of the Holy Orthodox Church should become part and parcel of the beliefs of all estates and strata of our society; that these lofty principles, in dominating European culture, should not force it out but rather engulf it in their fullness, thus giving it a higher meaning and bringing it to its ultimate development; and that the *integrity* of being which we observe in the ancient should be preserved forever in our present and future Orthodox Russia. . . .

---

[9] A. S. Khomiakov expressed a number of profound ideas on the present state of the arts and their future development back in 1845, in his article, "Pis'mo v Peterburg" [Letter to St. Petersburg], published in *Moskvitianin*, No. 2 (1845). But his views seem to have been found premature by his public; for our literature did not respond to those living ideas in the way that might have been expected if a more reasonable frame of mind had prevailed.

10.
Aleksei Stepanovich Khomiakov

1804-1860

The foremost Slavophile polemicist and lay theologian, Aleksei Stepanovich Khomiakov, was more interested in practical affairs and contemporary issues than most of his Muscovite friends. But he also believed that the West was in the throes of a deepening crisis—that its institutional framework was cracking because its philosophical foundation was erroneous. Russia, he was convinced, not only could escape the decline of Europe but could even provide the principles and institutions for the West's salvation. Therein lay Russia's historical mission and claim to spiritual primacy —but only if its own elite returned to the hallowed spiritual traditions of the Russian people.

Better attuned than Kireevskii to practical and institutional questions, Khomiakov stressed the economic and social function of the village commune as the foundation for the regeneration of civilization. In addition, he recognized that Peter the Great had made an important contribution by moving Russia from the dead point of seventeenth-century cultural isolationism and xenophobia. Progress—both material and spiritual—was to be welcomed. Khomia-

kov was not even averse to technology and displayed a lively interest for modern science and engineering. But he felt that material progress had to be subordinated to social harmony and equity as well as to religious and spiritual values.

As a religious thinker Khomiakov did much to single out and develop the concept of conciliarity (sobornost'), which he saw as the distinctive trait and source of superiority of Russian Orthodoxy. For the true Russian believer, Khomiakov never tired of repeating, religious experience could have validity only within the church, amidst the congregation of the faithful assembled in prayer. The individual's voice had to fuse into the chorus of all believers; only then would he become fully himself; there could be no valid existence except as part of a community of faithful. For Khomiakov the village commune was clearly the secular counterpart of the spirit of conciliarity. That is why he laid the two at the basis of the truly Christian and genuinely national civilization of the future which it was Russia's mission to bring to the decrepit West.

On Humboldt

Recently, discoursing on the destinies of the human race, Humboldt attacked Hegel's doctrine that the course of history is ruled by necessity.[1] Humboldt speaks as a proponent of the theory of the accidental and the particular in history. He is right in attacking Hegel's system of history, for that system is fallacious from beginning to end; but he is not right either in the manner of his attack, which is too superficial, or in his conclusions, which, were they correct, would rob historical science of all its worth and even of the right to be called science.

Humboldt has apparently failed to see the full absurdity of the Hegelian school's notions of necessity.[2] Here is Hegel's reasoning: "Whatever exists is rational and necessary; consequently, past history is conditioned by what exists in the following epoch, and so on up to our time, by which, of course, the entire past is conditioned." There is no need to analyze the first premise, for it obviously cannot stand up to criticism. Even if it were correct, it would still be out of place in any treatise on the historical sciences. It would transform them into a kind of teleological mysticism, which would merit neither attention nor study on the part of a thinking being. Whatever concept may be held of necessity in general, every science must discover the necessity for its facts within itself, and not through universal propositions which will always remain outside it.

Hegel's entire historical system is nothing but an unconscious transposition of the categories of cause and effect. There can be no doubt that every effect conditions its cause—but is there a rational person in the world who would maintain that the cause derives from the effect? I gaze at the dome of

---

[1] Wilhelm von Humboldt (1767–1835), philologist and Prussian statesman. George Wilhelm Friedrich Hegel (1770–1831), German philosopher.—Editor.

[2] While fully recognizing Hegel's enormous achievements in the sphere of philosophy and human thought in general, I cannot refrain from passing a harsh judgment on a system which has misled many serious and gifted students of the science of history. Hegel's wholehearted admirers may regard it as a great impertinence on my part, but a great genius cannot be appreciated unless his mistakes are clearly understood, even as true respect for the works of a thinker is utterly impossible if one blindly and superstitiously admires every single link in his system.

Translated by Valentine Snow from Aleksei Stepanovich Khomiakov, "Po povodu Gumbol'-dta," in *Polnoe sobranie sochinenii*, Vol. I (3d ed.; Moscow, 1900–04), pp. 143–74. Probably written in 1849, this essay was not published until the first edition of Khomiakov's complete works came out in 1861–73.

St. Peter's, built by Michelangelo Buonarroti; from the fact that I see the dome it clearly follows that it exists and that it was built, let us say, by Michelangelo. In my mind the past is conditioned by this present impression. I would not be able to see the dome if it did not exist. I do see it; therefore it exists. The conclusion is correct. But what if I should say that it was built because I see it? Any man in his senses would call me mad. In order to avoid such an absurd yet inevitable conclusion, Hegel's disciples have had to invent a world spirit, a living and active personality distinct from all the individuals who compose the human race, developing in accordance with rigorous laws of logical necessity and reducing all individual human beings to ciphers, symbols, or puppets, by means of which it explains to itself the innermost mysteries of its own internal meaning. Having been transformed into puppets, individuals blindly obey external laws, and history is no longer concerned with the logic of their inner development, although that is the only thing that truly matters. This is a second absurdity, which, as I have said, has been introduced in order to avoid the first, without, naturally, being stated in so many words; instead, it is cleverly insinuated by means of half-positive, half-metaphorical assertions. Such is the whole process of Hegel's history.

Obviously, the great philosopher has confused two opposite processes: the process of synthetic evolution and that of analytical reasoning. The two are identical but opposite in direction, and to transpose the concept of necessity from one realm of thought to the other is to make a childish mistake, which there would be no need to refute did not experience teach us that there is no error so obvious but that it can, if only for a time, delude even the most intelligent. In general, confusing the analytical process with that of real synthesis is an error into which nearly all German thinkers constantly fall. Apparently they cannot distinguish a fact from the understanding of it. This error has been passed on from teacher to student, and it has led repeatedly to the most absurd and ludicrous conclusions. Humboldt, with his great mind, has nevertheless failed, like all his compatriots, to see this error; he senses obscurely that the historical system of Hegel and his school conceals a fallacy, but he has failed to understand the nature and essence of the fallacy.[3] The net result of Humboldt's discourse and his attack on Hegel is to bring history back to its former particularism. What a pitiful reward for so much mental labor!

Humboldt is aware of the poverty of his conclusions, and so he sadly and timidly hints at shadowy religious ideas. The reader too is saddened to see how difficult, how almost impossible it is for this entire old German school to turn to true religious ideas and, at the same time, how much it misses them. This can be sensed in the great Goethe, in the odd ending of his *Faust;* it is also to be seen in the last works of the aging Humboldt, a contemporary of Goethe's and his twin in the depth, harmony, and Grecian grace of his intellect.

[3] Let us note in passing that Hegel carried this error into his discussions of mathematics, astronomy, etc. Thus he explains the cause of the earth's rotation around the sun by the formula of that rotation.

Humboldt's conclusion, as I said, plunges historical science into the sense-lessness of its former particularism, and at what a time!

There are epochs in which the slow and almost imperceptible development of the spiritual principles, convictions, and ideas which form the basis of human society conceals from the observer the rationality of the historical laws themselves. There are epochs in which these spiritual principles, having already proved to be one-sided, impotent, or false, still, as it were, seek to deceive the stern logic of history by clever maneuvers, by attracting other and unlike principles, by forming an alliance with purely material interests, and even by making a truce with principles which are their very opposite. In such a case it is not easy for an observer to discern the truth. But there are other epochs in which the development of the spiritual principles which governed the course of history in the past is over; their wiles have been exhausted, and the incorruptible logic of history passes its sentence on them. In such epochs blindness is unforgivable.

Such is our epoch.

Never before have there been such vast, such general upheavals without external and, in the true sense of the word, inner storms; never has there been such destruction of all earlier spiritual principles without an emergence of new principles to which men could look with desire or hope; never has there been such popular turmoil, and such general unrest, without outstanding personalities to head or direct it. It is true that newspaper slander and public indignation have of late seized upon some men named Hecker, Caussidière, and Barbès; but the conscientious observer knows how much either the newspaper screams or the wrath of the salons intent on avenging their threatened comfort is really worth. It would be a shame to ascribe any significance to these Heckers, Caussidières, Blancs, and Proudhons.[4] They are weak and mediocre men who stand out only because those who surround them are even weaker; they are the foam which any turbulence brings to the top. It is true that occasionally some principles are propounded to which the restless throng adheres for a while. But what principles are these? They are preached without being honestly believed in, they are embraced without real hope; here and there they have served as a pretext, but they have never been the cause of any movement. Societies do not collapse because of some great cataclysm, or in consequence of some struggle—they fall even as old trees which have lost all their vital sap but still have just recently withstood a severe storm sometimes fall, thundering and booming, on a still night when there is not movement enough in the air to stir a leaf on the healthy trees; they die as old men die who, as the people say, are *tired of living*. Only a closed mind would fail to see in this a historical necessity.

And, indeed, all or nearly all have understood this necessity to some degree. The particularist historian would not know how to deal with our epoch. The historical necessity of the current phenomena is obvious. Princi-

[4] French radical political writers and leaders active primarily during the days of the Second Republic.—Editor.

ples on which the life of society was based are dead; humanity has lost faith in something—but in what? Not everyone knows. Explanations based on the public life of Western nations are inadequate; criticism of the form of government does not suffice—Switzerland has fared no better than France or Prussia. It is true that Western Europe seems to be making an effort to rid itself of irrational political structures, a bitter legacy left it by Germanic conquests and medieval feudalism; but this alone explains nothing. Society is revolting not against its own form but against its very essence, its inner laws. North America finds as few admirers as the Ottoman Porte or the Spain of Philip II. It is not the formal structure but the underlying spiritual principles that have withered, not social conditions but the faith by which societies, and the men who compose them, lived. This deadening of the human spirit manifests itself in the convulsions of the social institutions, for man is a noble being—he cannot, he must not, live without faith.

The phenomena which are currently attracting everyone's attention were preceded, some ten years ago, by a different phenomenon, which was noticed by many though not by all—a strong awakening of interest in religious matters. Roman Catholicism and Protestantism seemed ready to resume their fight; but neither the one nor the other was able to withstand the criticism to which every phenomenon is subjected in our century; neither was able to answer the questions put to it. Interest in religion appeared to die down; but the discord that had been stirred in men's souls and not quieted by any reasonable resolution was bound to bear fruit, and so it has done. The logic of history passes judgment not on the formal structure but on the spiritual life of Western Europe. Nothing else could have been expected. When the two spiritual principles, or rather the twin forms of the same principle, by which Europe had lived and been governed for so many centuries were seen to remain mute in the face of criticism, the very realm of the spirit was laid waste, the inner life of the soul ceased, faith in rational development perished, and the avid impatience for material gains (to some extent legitimate) could take no other way than the way of explosion and violence.

To the men of the West its present condition must seem to be a riddle without an answer. Only we, nurtured in a different spiritual tradition, can read this riddle.

Scholarship has recognized that the modern European world is the creation of Christianity. This is true in the following sense. Christianity, in the fullness of its divine doctrine, propounded the ideas of unity and freedom indissolubly joined together in *the moral law of mutual love*. The legalistic Roman world was incapable of grasping that law. It saw unity and freedom as two opposing and mutually antagonistic forces; of the two, it of necessity regarded unity as superior and sacrificed freedom to it. Such was the influence of the Roman genius. The Germanic genius, being contrary to the Roman, would have preferred to retain the other principle, but this it could not do—it was itself a conqueror and an invader in Western Europe. Because of its position it accepted the same principle which the Roman genius had chosen by inclination. Thus, Western Europe developed not under the influence of Christianity but under that of Roman Catholicism, which was a one-sided concept of Christianity as a law of external unity. Those who have an understanding of history will readily discern the gradual development of this principle in the idea of all Christendom (*tota Christianitas*) taken to mean a state, in the struggle between the emperors and the popes, in the Crusades, in the militant monastic orders, in the adoption of a single ecclesiastical and diplomatic language (Latin), and so forth. They will see—in the feudal hierarchy, the aristocracy, the conception of law, the conception of state power, and so forth—that all of Western life was imbued with this principle and developed in complete dependence on it. For those who have learned their history by rote from foreign writers, too much would have to be said. Consequently we shall not here examine the history of Western Europe from this viewpoint.

That was the first period of Western history; the second was a period of reaction. The one-sidedness of Roman Catholicism called forth resistance, and gradually, after many unsuccessful attempts and a prolonged struggle, there began the period of Protestantism, as one-sided as Roman Catholicism had been but leaning in the opposite direction—for Protestantism retained the idea of freedom and sacrificed to it the idea of unity. This could not have been otherwise, for a reconciliation of the two was impossible for the West, nurtured in the principles of Catholicism, under the conditions of Germanic conquest and Roman legalism. The entire modern history of Europe bears the stamp of Protestantism, even in supposedly Catholic countries. Just as the idea of Roman Catholic unity was external, so was the idea of Protestant freedom; for freedom that is stripped of rational meaning is a purely negative and consequently an external concept. Over a period of several centuries Protestantism avoided total self-annihilation only by means of arbitrary covenants; but it carried the seeds of its own destruction within it, and those seeds were bound to germinate. They did. Protestantism retreated from dogmatic religion and entered the vague reaches of philosophic thought, that is, philosophic skepticism; in the sphere of public life it produced the state of boundless ferment which now shakes the Western world. Arbitrary covenants could not withstand the probing either of rational criticism or of personal passions, for an arbitrary covenant cannot of itself be sacred; it can only be sanctified from without, and Protestantism had already done away with whatever could so sanctify it. In our day history is about to pronounce judgment on both Catholicism and Protestantism. That is the meaning of the present agitation.

Thus far no new spiritual principle capable of filling the void left in men's souls by the final collapse of the Catholic-Protestant principle has emerged, nor can it emerge. All attempts (and there have been many) to discover or create such a principle have failed. This is the explanation of the appearance and collapse of the several systems which have attracted more or less notice under the hallmark of Owen or Saint-Simon, under the names of communism or socialism. All these systems, ostensibly generated by the material diseases of society and having the ostensible purpose of healing these diseases, were in fact born of an internal malady of the spirit and were aimed at filling the void left in it by the collapse of former faith or its phantom. They have all met, or are meeting, with failure for one and the same reason, namely, their arbitrary subjective basis.

German philosophy as represented by Hegel, or, more precisely, by his disciples, arrived at the same point by another path. Rigorous (although incomplete) in its analysis, worthless in its synthesis, Hegelianism in its collapse revealed the depth of the spiritual abyss on the brink of which all German philosophy had long stood, unbeknownst to itself; it revealed a sore which it could not heal. Yet even that is beyond doubt a great service. All future attempts to proceed along the line of pure philosophy are impossible after Hegel; all future attempts along the line of dated Owenism or new socialism will be unsuccessful and negligible for the same reasons that their predecessors were unsuccessful and negligible. Their sentence is being imposed upon them by contemporary history; the verdict, however, was handed down some years ago in a book by Max Stirner, *Der Einzelne und sein Eigenthum* [The Single Individual and His Property],[5] a book ineptly put together and repellent from the ethical standpoint but mercilessly logical. This book, from which the school that gave it birth shrank back in horror, which no ethical (*sittlicher*) German can speak of without deep indignation, has a historical significance which was missed by the critics and of which the author himself is naturally even less aware—it is the most profound, the ultimate protest of the free spirit against all arbitrary attempts to shackle it. It is the voice of a soul, to be sure an amoral soul, but amoral only because it has been deprived of all ethical foundation; a soul which, albeit unconsciously, proclaims at every turn the possibility and wisdom of allowing itself to be governed by a principle which it can understand and in which it can believe; a soul which bitterly and indignantly rebels against the daily trickery of the Western systematizers, who do not themselves believe and yet demand to be taken on faith, who forge shackles for the spirit and expect others meekly to put them on. Contemporary history is a living commentary on Max Stirner, an actual protest of life itself in its simplicity against the bookish cerebrations which seek to inject into it phantom spiritual principles of their own invention at a time when the spiritual principles by which it was once truly governed no longer exist.

It was the will of Providence, or (if it is too presumptuous on my part to seek to divine the ways of the Almighty) it was the sense of world history, that mankind, having failed to understand Christianity or having taken a one-sided view of it, should through denial come to see its own error. Neither the useless efforts of thinkers holding antiquated views nor the useless wiles of princes of the church who debase faith by forming a shabby Jesuitical alliance with political passions and parties will resurrect or even prolong the Catholic-Protestant epoch. The former error cannot be repeated; man

[5] Max Stirner (1806–56), a German social philosopher, rejected all traditional and institutional ties of the individual. His main work (incorrectly cited by Khomiakov), *Der Einzige und sein Eigentum* (Leipzig, 1845), enjoyed great popularity for a short time after its appearance. It has been translated into English by S. T. Byington (New York, 1907). —Editor.

can no longer see the eternal truth of primitive Christianity except as a whole, which is to say, as the coincidence of unity and freedom, manifested in the law of spiritual love. That is Orthodoxy. Any other concept of Christianity is henceforth impossible. Orthodoxy is represented by the East, and mainly by the Slavic countries, headed by our Russia, which long ago, with God's blessing, embraced pure Christianity and became a strong vessel thereof, perhaps because of that communal principle which has ever been its mainstay and without which it cannot live. Russia has passed through great trials, defending its social and traditional principles in long and bloody struggles, especially the struggle which resulted in Michael's accession to the throne (as I mentioned in an earlier article [6]); and, having first secured these principles for itself, it must now be their exponent before the whole world. That is its mission, its future destiny. We may look ahead boldly and without fear.

Having discovered the meaning of the present disturbances and the mission of Russia in world history, we arrive at the deep conviction that Russia will fulfill its mission; but the question also arises how it can be fulfilled and what agencies for individual endeavor can be found in these times to express and make manifest Russia's inner principles.

To pose the question is to arouse involuntary and justifiable doubt.

Only he can expound his spiritual principles to others who has understood them himself; only a whole and harmonious spiritual organism can impart strength and harmony to other organisms which are weak and disunited. The thought and life of a people can be expressed and manifested only by those who fully share in that life and thought. Is that true of us, educated as we have been?

In my letter on England,[7] I said:

> The proper and successful evolution of a rational society is the result of two different but harmonious and concordant forces. One of these, the fundamental, the essential, force, inherent in the whole body and the entire past history of the society, is the force of life developing in its own way from its first principles, its organic origins. The other, the force of the individual intellect, based on the force of society and living only through it, is a force which never creates or means to create anything but which is ever-present in the work of general development and prevents it from blindly following deadening instinct or from becoming unreasonably one-sided. Both forces are indispensable, but the second, the conscious force of the mind, must be linked by living and loving faith to the force of life and creation. Where the bond of faith and love is broken, discord and conflict set in.

In England such discord was caused by the one-sidedness of Catholicism, which called forth Protestantism, and possibly by other social factors. In our country the same discord has resulted from another course of historical development.

[6] "Mnenie russkikh ob inostrantsakh" (Russian Opinion Concerning Foreigners); cf., *Polnoe sobranie sochinenii*, Vol. I, especially pp. 54–55.—Editor.

[7] "Pis'mo ob Anglii," *ibid.*, pp. 127–28.

In the early days in all of Russian society, despite its turmoils and the efforts within communities already formed to merge together in one great Russian community, there was a long time during which the life-force of society did not seek to suppress the rational development of the individual. The realm of thought was free, and all that is human was accessible to man (depending, naturally, on his knowledge and strength of intellect). Perhaps the first, that is, the social, principle was somewhat more preponderant than it should have been, because of the internecine strife which had preceded the consolidation of the state and because of external threats (the Tatars and the Poles), which required the concentration and exertion of all the forces of society for defense; but the realm of individual thought was nonetheless quite extensive. The genius of the people was not at war with the universal, even when the universal came to us bearing a foreign label. As evidence let me cite the knowledge of foreign languages and especially the fact that this knowledge was held in respect, the importation of artists from abroad, the readiness to associate with foreigners and even with foreign clergy, the influence of Western art on Novgorod ikon painting, the borrowing of many Western tales, the familiarity with the German sagas of the Nibelungenlied (as evidenced by the chronicler of Novgorod), and, lastly, the sympathy for happenings in the Western world in part deserving of such sympathy (for instance, the Crusades), and much else. It would seem that mistrust and hatred of Western thinking began to manifest themselves to a marked degree after the Council of Florence and the Catholic oppression in the Russian lands then subject to Poland. They developed to the full as a result of the deep and insane hatred of Russians shown by Sweden and by the Baltic merchants and barons, and most of all as a result of the hostility and treachery of the Polish magnates and the Catholic clergy. Little by little, the genius of the people became exclusive and hostile to everything alien.

The realm of the human spirit was constricted; but such constriction, being contrary to universal truth as well as to the requirements of the Russian genius and to the foundations of Russia's inner life, was bound to call forth a resistance which swung to the opposite extreme. The struggle of 1612 was not merely a civil and political struggle but also a spiritual one. Europeanism, with its good and evil, its seductions and its truths, came to Russia in the guise of the Polish party. The Saltykovs and their friends were exponents of Western thought. It is true that from the moral standpoint they were not deserving of respect. This could not have been otherwise—the baser souls more readily draw away from the sacred fount of the people's life. True, the men who wanted to change the old traditions were at the same time traitors to their country, but that was a historical accident; in point of fact their orientation, a reaction against the fortuitous distortion of the traditions of the people that had led to the suppression of freedom of thought, was not altogether wrong.

The strength of the Russian spirit triumphed; Moscow was set free, a Russian tsar was on the throne; but the demand made by reason itself, in rebellion against the constricting despotism of local customs and traditions, was not without its proponents. Its worst aspect was reflected in such men as the corrupt fugitive and slanderer Kotoshikhin, or in Khvorostinin, who said, "The Russian people are so stupid there's no living with them"; [8] but what was good in it struck a responsive chord in the best and noblest minds. There can be no doubt that in time this demand would have been satisfied, as it deserved to be; possibly it might have reached an extreme, having been brought forth by the opposite extreme. However that may be, it found a defender who gave it satisfaction and quick victory. That defender, one of the mightiest minds and perhaps the strongest will recorded in the annals of the nations, was Peter. No matter how harshly history may judge him in the future (and it is not to be denied that severe charges can be brought against his memory), it will recognize that the trend he represented was not altogether wrong; it became wrong only in its triumph, and that triumph was perfect and complete. It hardly needs to be said that all the Kotoshikhins, Khvorostinins, and Saltykovs rushed headlong in Peter's footsteps, overjoyed at having been delivered from the onerous demands and moral laws of the Russian spirit and at being able, so to speak, to feast on Russia's day of fast. Such truth as there was in Peter's victorious protest attracted many, including the best; in the end, worldly temptation seduced everyone.

Thus in Russia historical accident brought about the same cleavage that had occurred in England because of the deficiencies and fallacies of its spiritual laws.

One-sided development of the individual mind which has rejected the history and traditions of society—that is the meaning of Whiggism in England. That is the meaning of Whiggism in any country. Its general features, which I analyzed in my letter on England, are everywhere the same; nevertheless, the trend of Russian society (our home-grown Whiggism) is quite different from the English, and the differences, naturally, are not in our favor. Born of inherent deficiencies and fallacies of the spiritual laws which were England's historical foundation, the Whig movement in England was a natural and, one might say, legitimate, development of one aspect of its genius. It retained its bonds with the people and with the spiritual essence of the country even when it broke with its traditions and its historical past. An English Whig remains wholly an Englishman; his ways and habits, his spiritual life, even his outward appearance—all are English; he has not yet condemned himself to total social and moral impotence.

Whiggism in our society is quite another matter. Generated not by the inner law of the people's spiritual life but merely by the historical chance of Russia's foreign relations and the passing despotism of local custom,

[8] Grigorii Kotoshikhin or Koshikhin (ca. 1630–67), a clerk of the Bureau for Foreign Affairs in the reign of Tsar Aleksei Mikhailovich. He escaped to Sweden, where he wrote a comprehensive description of contemporary Muscovy (*O Rossii v tsarstvovovanie Alekseia Mikhailovicha,* 1666). Prince Ivan Andreevich Khvorostinin (d. 1625) became very much interested in Western culture (in its Polish form) and in Roman Catholicism during the Time of Troubles. His irreverent attitude toward Russian traditions and his criticism of religious practices and beliefs led to his imprisonment and eventual banishment to remote monasteries. He has often been considered the first example of Russia's "inner emigration" and a precursor of its intelligentsia.—Editor.

Whiggism started as a protest against that chance circumstance but then, possibly obeying an imperative law, turned into a protest against the very essence of the people's life: it abjured the entire Russian principle and broke away from it. Impotent, as all outcasts must be, devoid of any inner content (for it was purely negative), deprived of any spiritual nourishment (for it had uprooted itself from its native soil), it was compelled to cleave to another historical movement, the powerful intellectual movement of the West, whose disciple and slave it became. This spiritual enslavement to the Western world, this bitter antagonism toward Russia, manifested over an entire century, represents a most curious and instructive phenomenon. Rejection of everything Russian, from names to customs, from trifling details of dress to the basic principles of life, reached unimaginable extremes. There was a passion in it, a ludicrous exaltation, which betrayed both the greatest poverty of intellect and absolute complacency. Such excesses are, of course, more characteristic of the earlier period of our Europeanization than of the recent; and yet the recent, while more dispassionate, is marked by a greater contempt for, and a more complete rejection of, everything pertaining to the Russian people.

Such are the consequences of our social trend, our home-grown Whiggism.

I have demonstrated in earlier articles the influence of this trend on our learning, our art, and our manners or, rather, the inability of learning, art, and manners to develop under such a trend. Repetition would be useless; but at a time when, as I said, world history, having irrevocably condemned the one-sided spiritual principles which used to govern Western thought, calls to life the more perfect, the living principles of which our Holy Russia is the vessel, it may not be amiss for me to say a few more words on the subject, so that each of us—those of us who read, write, and live in our enlightened society—may, in all conscience, without bias, decide to what degree he or those around him are capable of acting as exponents of Russian life and Russian thought.

In my earlier articles I mentioned the mediocrity of learning in Russia and the reasons for that mediocrity. The fact itself is incontestable, and the reasons for it are clear. Learning cannot advance until the cause of its inanition—the inner cleavage I have described—has been removed; but it is interesting to see how stubbornly it defends its vested mediocrity and how passionately it resists any attempt to disturb its mental trance. Properly speaking, learning in our society falls into two categories. The majority is content with the by now traditional education in the French manner, and continues with quiet satisfaction to repeat the old lessons, now almost in their third generation, enlivening them with modern variations borrowed from the weightier French journals. There seems to be no unity of opinion among this majority, but the true bases of opinion are the same for all; the only difference is that one man will regard *La Presse* as his oracle, another *Le National*, a third the *Journal des Débats*, and so on. This majority may be described generically as the pupils of the French journals.

The minority has gone much further; it has plumbed the depths of German learning. Some twenty years ago, placing all its faith in Schelling, it subjectivized, objectivized, and subject-objectivized the whole world; later, together with Hegel, rejecting almost with contempt the poetic dreaminess of Schelling's day, it used the process of phenomenology to desiccate the same world down to its skeleton, or, rather, to the mere shade of a skelton, to a being identical with nonbeing, and then breathed new life and substance into it through a complex apparatus of logical steps. That era, too, passed away. Intellectual Germany joined hands with intellectual France, which it had disdained for nearly half a century, and the cream of our educated class followed suit. The erudite minority, those pupils of German philosophy, flocked with the German universities to the banners behind which the majority had been marching all along—the banners of French journalism.

Where are the fruits of the intellectual training which that minority received from Germany and which might have deceived a superficial observer? Where is the passionate interest which caused men who did not know German, but who wished to belong to the erudite minority, to misquote German authorities whom they did not understand or to weary the general public with dry and obscure formulas which defied comprehension? Where is the passionate belief which turned other, more conscientious and better-informed, men into veritable martyrs of learning who spent sleepless nights in endless disputes on philosophical abstractions, not only in the warm haven of friendly drawing rooms but in the bitter cold of St. Petersburg and Moscow streets? It is true that in some men this training awakened an intellectual activity which has resulted in new and original thinking, but they can be counted on the fingers of one hand, while most have played with ideas without being nurtured by them, have abandoned these ideas without thinking them through, and constantly take up the new trends from overseas and, one might say, the new beliefs of the moment—all with the same childlike trust with which they mouthed the formulas of German philosophy. To them, the pseudoscientific German manner was only a fashion, and sooner will a St. Petersburg *élégante* (or society woman) put on a dress made in the fashion of three years ago than will our erudite use or discuss the philosophic formulas which once they worshiped.

Naturally, in these circumstances true learning is impossible. And if somehow, by some chance, a thought is expressed that was born on Russian soil, the half-educated majority and the erudite minority greet it with the same lack of understanding (which is very natural, since it takes an effort for the human mind to leave its rut) and with the same hostility, caused by the equally natural desire to preserve their mental slumber. The new idea is unanimously proclaimed a paradox (as in the well-known scene in *Woe from Wit:* "This is somehow odd!" [9]; the majority declares that the new paradox is not quite seemly (for our political Whiggism has strong pretensions to conservatism and Toryism, being unaware of its own nature and failing to understand that Toryism is out of the question for those who have split away from the people and their life), while the minority hastily pro-

---

[9] Reference to the famous satirical comedy *Gore of Uma*, by A. S. Griboedov (1794–1829).—Editor.

duces some stupid objection and, to the general delight, passes it on to the penny-a-liners. That is the end of the matter.

I can cite a recent example. One of those rare men who have succeeded in thoroughly familiarizing themselves with Western learning, thinking it through, and going on to become original thinkers recently expressed the idea that *love alone* is the proper basis of society and social science. How was that idea received? A representative of the erudite minority, or of what might be termed the schoolboy school, promptly denied it, arguing that a society can just as readily be founded on mutual hostility as on mutual love. Any right-thinking person could have told him, of course, that hostility which is given free rein cannot serve as a foundation for anything and that it must be suppressed or restrained by conciliatory agreement. The conclusion of such an agreement is motivated either by mutual benefit or by mutual fear; but neither fear nor gain can ensure the observance of the agreement, since they depend merely on personal and haphazard considerations [on the part] of any member of society and cannot in themselves give the agreement the force of law. On the other hand, as I have said, no agreement can be sacred in itself; sanctity or justice can only be conferred on it from without. Consequently, the basis of society will be not hostility but the principle which sanctifies the agreement. Hence hostility can be an accidental component of a society, but it can in no case become its norm; the idea of mutual love, however, can be both part of the process of social development and society's final norm. The issue was clear and the nullity of the counterargument obvious, and yet the objection served a purpose.[10] That was the contribution of the minority.

The majority, for its part, declared that the principle thus advanced was what might be called a naive and idyllic dream and that it postulated a society of saints. There is no need to refute this. In my letter on England, speaking of the observance of Sunday quiet in England and of the observance of fasts in all Russian villages and truly Russian towns, I have already shown the difference between a social norm and individual will, but to many the distinction is not yet clear.

That is how the reading public received an idea which merited a different evaluation. They are looking for this idea in the West as the only possible solution to social questions, but they are unable to find it; for it cannot spring either from the West's social principles, which are based on conflict and conquest, or from its outworn spiritual principles, one-sided and mutually antagonistic; it cannot be the accidental outcome of individual thought; it must be rooted in spiritual and social values—in faith—in order to exist, and in the historical foundations of society in order to manifest itself. It was, at long last, a truly Russian idea, and that is why it had such a friendly reception! The example is instructive but not unique. The same

[10] My remarks about this ill-chosen objection in no way prevent me from having a sincere esteem for the highly gifted objector. If he and many of his colleagues, also highly gifted, sometimes seem inconsistent in the light of strict logic, this may be attributed to the deficiencies of the school itself, not to the individual shortcomings of any of its members.

reception awaited an attempt to show the difference between the lofty Christian concept of the individual and two Western views of the individual, first, as the sum total of chance circumstances constituting human personality and second, as a numerical unit. The same reception was given to the definition of unison as an expression of moral unity, in contradistinction to the majority as an expression of physical strength, or of unanimity as a majority carried to its extreme, and so forth. It would seem that learning, in its present state, cannot yet aspire to being an exponent of Russian life and thought.

The situation is clearer still where the arts are concerned. Neither the verbal nor the plastic arts nor the art of sound as yet begin to express the inner meaning of Russian life or to grasp the Russian ideals.

This could hardly be otherwise, for art, which is an involuntary and, as it were, unplanned translation of a people's moral and spiritual laws into visible and harmonious objects, is impossible when the executant (no matter how gifted artistically) has no contact with the people's life. Such isolation of the personality breeds impotence and an irreconcilable inner discord. The isolated personality is so utterly incapable of being an origin or a source of art that its intrusion mars and distorts the work of art; it must either obey the general law or suffer for having violated it. It is not to be denied that minor currents of Russian values ripple through the best works of our literature; but they are very sparse, although their play and sparkle should be a comforting promise of future development. Let me remark in passing that the general success of even inferior works in a branch of our letters which is close to the people's needs quite clearly points out those needs, and that in that very branch we can boast an eloquent practitioner who has no peer in the contemporary literature of the West and few rivals in its past. Pushkin admired him, Iazykov studied him.[11]

The art of sound presents a picture of even greater impotence, and with very few exceptions the formal music of one of the most musical peoples in the world is unworthy of attention; its rare attempts at capturing the spirit of the Russian people generally attest to a sad lack of inspiration and, in their pitiful weakness, fall as short of expressing the Russian soul in music as Del'vig's songs do of expressing it in words.

Lastly, the plastic arts not only do not exist but in their pathetic struggle to come into being serve as an object lesson demonstrating the reasons for the nonexistence of the other arts as well. A young man may feel the need to express in terms of visible beauty something which is hidden in his soul and of which he is only obscurely aware. Honorable schools founded through enlightened love of the arts hospitably open their doors to him, and he gladly accepts their invitation. There follow endless drawing and modeling of eyes, noses, faces, bodies, and groups of bodies, and endless study of every possible ideal, except, of course, the ideals of which the young man is himself the unconscious bearer. The course of training in the plastic arts continues for

---

[11] Khomiakov is probably referring to Ivan A. Krylov (1769–1844), author of fables and satirist.—Editor.

several years, and the student, having successfully, perhaps even brilliantly, completed it, emerges confused, having lost his bearings, having been seduced by the harmonious vision of other minds whose place is in the past, incapable henceforth of reading in his own soul, no longer loving what he used to love and having acquired no other loves—in a word, incapable forever after of being an artist.

Yet that eventuality was possible. But it was possible only with the proviso that the ties which bound the student to the people should not be broken. In every period of history, in every nation, the plastic arts fall into only two categories: the secular (genre) and the sacred (ikon). In an earlier article [12] I pointed out that schools of painting are dependent on the life of the people; that remark related mainly to genre painting, which includes various subdivisions (so-called historical, landscape, and so on)—everything, indeed, except ikons. The highest development of this highest form of art obeys some of the same laws, but it is also subject to other laws, which depend less on the accident of time or nationality. An ikon is not a religious picture, even as church music is not religious music; the ikon and the chant are immeasurably higher. Works of a single person, they are not expressions of his personality; they express all men who live by the same spiritual values—this is art at its highest. I am not, of course, speaking of any particular chant or any given ikon; I am speaking of general laws and their meaning. The picture which, when you approach it, seems an alien thing and the singing to which you listen as a stranger are not an ikon and a liturgic chant—they bear the mark of what is accidental in a person or a people. The Madonna di Foligno, despite its perfection, misses being an ikon. Not everyone would have so placed the Angel, hardly anyone would have so placed Christ; this is an Italian fancy of the great Raphael, and it disturbs you and prevents the picture from being an image of your inner world, your ikon. That is why, for a Christian, an ikon belongs only in a church, in the unity of the ecclesiastical consciousness; that is why (in its ideal form) it is so much higher than any other work of art, representing the furthest limit toward which art must strive if it hopes to grow. For the very reason that the ikon is an expression of communal, rather than personal, feelings, it demands on the part of the artist complete communion not with the dogmatics of the Church but with its entire social and artistic tradition as it has come down through the centuries to the Christian community.

Hence the plastic arts, in both their genre and their sacred modes, are accessible to the Russian artist only to the extent that he communes with the daily and spiritual life of the Russian people; and the artist's training and development should consist simply of clarifying the ideals which he already cherishes unconsciously. To this circumstance no heed is ever paid. That is the reason why we have no plastic arts, and that same reason prevents all other arts from flourishing. Obviously, art is even less fit than learning to be the expression of Russian life and thought.

---

[12] O vozmozhnosti Russkoi khudozhestvennoi shkoly" (On the Possibilities of a Russian Art School), in *Polnoe sobranie sochinenii*, Vol. I, pp. 73-104.—Editor.

The situation is still clearer where Russian manners are concerned. These are composed of trifles which, on the face of it, are insignificant; but giant cliffs have been formed of the microscopic remains of Ehrenberg's infusoria, and the trifling details of a people's manners make up the towering mass of custom—the only reliable mainstay of the national and social order. The importance of custom is still underestimated. Custom is law; but it differs from the law in that the latter is imposed from the outside as an accidental admixture, whereas custom is an internal force which permeates the entire life of the people and the conscience and thinking of all its members. Commenting on the struggle between law and custom, one of the greatest jurists of France said: "La désuétude est la plus amère critique d'une loi" [the harshest criticism of any law is its rejection by custom]. A witty Englishman remarked recently that England's sole salvation and its greatness lay in the conservative force of custom. Lastly, it may be said that the purpose, the final aim, of every law is to become customary, to enter the people's flesh and blood and to need no written confirmation. Such is the importance of custom; and anyone who has at all seriously studied current events will surely have realized that the lack of custom is one of the principal causes which accelerated the downfall of France and Germany.

Custom, as I have said, consists wholly of the accretion of manners; but who among us will not admit that for us custom does not exist, and that our constantly changing ways are incapable of being transformed into custom? The past does not exist for us; yesterday seems to us like olden times, while the recent era of powder, embroidered camisoles, and hoop skirts is practically Egyptian antiquity. It is a rare family that knows anything about its great-great-grandfather save that he was a sort of savage in the opinion of his enlightened great-grandchildren. Would the Sheremetevs be aware of the people's esteem for the Sheremetev who was a contemporary of Ivan the Terrible, or the Karamyshevs of their forebear's exploits, had not popular songs taken the trouble to preserve their memory, naturally embroidering fact with fancy? We have young men just out of school, and young men making their way in life by following the bent given them by their schooling or by modern ideas; then we have gray-haired young men, then decrepit young men—but old men we have none. Old age presupposes tradition, not the handing down of tales but the transmission of custom. We are always brand new; the old reposes in the people. That should inspire us with respect; but we lack not only custom, not only manners capable of engendering custom, we lack even respect for custom. Every personal whim of ours, every puerile notion of some improvement that stirs in our small minds gives us the right to disregard or violate any one of our people's customs, no matter how widespread or how ancient.

There is no need to look for proof—anyone who searches his conscience will admit that I am right—but I can think of a rather diverting recent instance. It occurred to someone to promote forest conservation in Russia—a useful and indeed a necessary measure. What was his solution? He proposed that the custom of cutting down young birches for Trinity Day—which he argued was ruinous for our forests—should be done away with![13] Let us suppose that the man who had this notion was an ignorant town dweller who had never been in the woods; but surely even a town dweller, if he had any respect for the people's customs, could have inquired whether this particular custom was really harmful. He would then have discovered that in a growth of healthy young birches (some five or six years old) there are often well over thirty thousand young trees to a *desiatina*,[14] barely a thousand of which survive to the age at which birches are cut down for firewood.[15] Hence, through entirely harmless thinning, every *desiatina* of young birches will yield up to thirty thousand trees for Trinity Day. Was there anything to make a fuss about? Was there any reason to propose the abolition of an old custom? In England such a notion would not have occurred even to the most hardened Whig. It is true that lately a good many people have been advocating the compilation and publication of popular customs. Such collections will present to the ages to come the curious spectacle of a paper graveyard of dead customs. This would seem to be a scholar's fancy, not in the least indicative of respect. Lack of respect may, of course, be justified by utter ignorance, but on the other hand such utter ignorance would not be possible but for utter disrespect. This vicious circle does great credit to our alleged Toryism.

When I speak of our ignorance of Russian manners and customs, I have in mind not merely the minor details but even those aspects which are its greatest enrichment and security. Not long ago, a very learned and gifted writer, commenting on the Russian mir,[16] called it a primitive attempt at communal life and said that it was not a civil order but only a step toward such an order. I hesitate to think that he meant to say that a village is not a state. That conclusion is so obvious that he would not have bothered either to draw it or to set it down. If he holds (and I fail to see any other possibility) that the organization of the mir is a childish or obsolete form of communal association on a small scale, then I can only regret that he failed to mention the form of association (naturally, also on a small scale) which is well known to him and which would be better than our mir, with its communal ownership of land and its public hearings of all civil cases, certain criminal cases, and even some family disputes—for the family, while part of the mir, is subject to its authority.

It is true that the same writer, speaking recently of ancient Russia and of the decisions of the town assembly (*veche*), said that those decisions were taken without any proper rules of procedure, in a random, haphazard way, just like the decisions made by the gathering of a village mir. This is the crux of the matter. The writer's error stems entirely from his lack of respect for the village gathering, and is thus excusable, being caused by ignorance—that is, if the ignorance itself can ever be excused. But which of his readers will

[13] Reference to the traditional custom of bringing birch branches to church to be blessed on Whitsunday and Trinity.—Editor.

[14] 2.7 acres.—Editor.

[15] I have counted over forty thousand saplings in a seven-year-old stand of oaks, which never grow as thickly as birches do.

[16] Communal village organization and assembly in the northern and central parts of European Russia.—Editor.

dare to censure him? Because of the utter disunity of our Whig society, have we not all left Russian life so far behind that we would be incapable even of taking part in a village gathering? I would go further and say that we have no concept of the legal grounds on which all its decisions are based. Not one of us would question that statement. That is but another proof of the gulf dividing us, a gulf so deep that an Englishman would never suspect it and would have difficulty believing it. In fact, the decisions of the village gathering are always based—or at least an effort is always made to base them—on legal principles which are peculiar to our people and which our lawyers do not entirely comprehend.

To illustrate what I mean, I should like to relate an incident I happened to witness. A few years ago, in the fall, I was driving from Elets along a country road, in my own carriage. While the horses were being fed I got out, saw a gathering about to begin, and followed the people in the hope of observing and (may the reader forgive me!) perhaps learning something of value. The gathering had been called to parcel out vegetable plots. The discussions lasted for perhaps two hours, whereupon the gathering reached some kind of decision, of no particular interest to anyone except the village itself. After the discussion, as the gathering was about to break up, a youth of eighteen or so came out of the crowd, bowed to the assembled mir, and voiced a complaint against an old man, a second cousin of his, for cheating him. He presented the case as follows. Three brothers (including the eldest brother, the head of the household, who was being complained against) and a cousin, the complainant's father, used to live together. The cousin left the family and set up his own household when his children were small; shortly thereafter he died. The youth was accusing the cousins of not having given his father his just share. The old man began to argue that the accusation was false, and that one-fourth of the household property had been given to the deceased, as was his due. The young man admitted this, but said that, as the family had been dealing in grain, seed, and hides, there had been about twenty-five hundred rubles outstanding in accounts payable; that one-fourth of that sum (about six hundred rubles) had been owed to his father, who would have received it had he lived; but that since the sum had not been paid to the widow (his mother), it was now owed to himself and his brothers. The old man argued, grew excited, and used abusive language; the gathering listened and remained silent; here and there timid voices were raised in favor of the complainant. The old man, as I learned later, was the richest peasant in the village. The young man now appeared confused and at a loss for words.

At this point a peasant of some forty years of age took the youth's part. He started proving to the old man that he had collected nearly all the outstanding debts and that one-fourth thereof, in cash or in kind, should be paid to his nephews; voices from the crowd clearly expressed approval. The old man was getting angrier and angrier and cursing more and more. The young man's defender replied courteously but firmly; finally, having stated the whole case, he began to repeat: "It's a sin to wrong orphans; pay them." The old man, losing his temper, shouted: "Who are you to keep telling me to pay? Are you my master?" "If I'm right, then I'm master," said the plaintiff's self-appointed counsel. The old man was staggered by this reply. There was no way of refuting it; he saw that in the eyes of all those present, he felt it in his own heart. He was silent for a bit, then, with a wave of his hand said, "Well, let the mir decide!" and left the gathering. I left it too, and I remembered that I left it with a high heart.

It would appear that ancient customs and the traditional community gatherings have their own legal principles. True, these differ from the legal norms accepted in other lands; but let us not forget that in the Middle Ages a Bologna jurist laughed at English common law, and that nowadays Europe imitates that law in many respects. But the process is not complete. Our conscience still examines a fact only in order to ascertain its existence. It would seem also to be its duty—and it will be its duty—to examine that fact with regard to its morality. When that is done, all further improvement of the law will stem from Slavic ways and customs. Part of the job has been finished, the rest remains to be done. I will no doubt be told that such principles are too vague and lack the requisite legal precision, etc., etc. I regard such objections as frivolous. The earliest legal rules are indeed rigidly formalistic, for example, "He who kills shall be killed"; but then the law attains a higher stage, and efforts are made to ascertain whether the killing was willful or accidental, whether the killer was in full possession of his faculties or out of his mind, whether he attacked or killed in self-defense, with premeditation or in a moment of rage, out of malice or because his patience had been exhausted by repeated injuries, etc., etc. Formalism tends to disappear. Let the Bologna jurist shrug all he will! The law is ceasing to be the property of the student and becoming that of man; but it can reach so high a stage of development only when the customary and spiritual principles on which society rests are in concert.

Be that as it may, it is obvious that, where manners are concerned, we are least fit to act as vehicles of Russian life and thought.

Such is the rich harvest of our widespread Whiggism! I believe I have described it impartially and without exaggeration. The picture is not encouraging. At the very time when the course of world history, having condemned the imperfect and one-sided principles which governed it hitherto, calls upon our Holy Russia to come forward with the more balanced and comprehensive principles which have nurtured it and on which it is founded, they cannot be communicated to others because there is no medium for their expression. In this respect it is clear that Russia is in an immeasurably more difficult position than England and that the Whiggism of our society is incomparably worse than, and far beneath, the Whiggism which constitutes one of England's political parties. That is the conclusion at which one would arrive at first glance.

But one should not stop there. A thorough study of the question leads to a diametrically opposite conclusion. English Whiggism, a natural Protestant reaction against the one-sidedness of Roman Catholic principles, was a necessity, an inevitable and legitimate development; its triumph is also inevitable, as is the triumph of any wholly logical idea. Hence, as I have already said, the future in England belongs to the Whigs—unless that country accepts other, more complete spiritual principles from elsewhere. Our situation is altogether different; our Whiggism is the consequence of a historical and, so to say, external chance, and is in no way derived from our communal or spiritual principles. The fruit of temporary circumstance, it can have only temporary significance and existence; not only can it not be said that the future belongs to it, but it may be confidently stated that it has no future. Legitimate in its fortuitous inception, senseless in its general development, it is approaching its end. Neither individual efforts, nor the half-meant paradoxes of outdated admiration for Western schools of thought, nor the stubbornness of society, nor even the immovable mass of public apathy and mental sloth can keep it alive. Logic has its inalienable rights, and the impartial observer, looking forward to the future, can already find some encouragement in signs which are apparent in the present. The return of Russians to the Russian principles has already begun.

By the word "return" I do not mean the return of our gentle compatriots who, like so many doves, having spread their little wings and fluttered for a while over the turbulent sea of Western society, return fatigued to the Russian rock and praise its solidity. No, they return to Holy Russia but not to Russian life; they praise the firmness of their landing place without realizing (like the rest of us) that all our activity amounts to a constant undermining of its very base. Luckily, our hands and crowbars are too weak, and our weakness saves us from our own blindness. Nor do I mean by "return" another, not too rare, phenomenon in our society which may well become a passing fashion: when men who have split away completely from Russian life—and, instead of grieving, complacently delight in their imagined superiority—give condescending praise to the Russian people, deigning, as it were, to say a kind word for them, make a show of their knowledge of Russian ways and manners, and in the process calmly endow the Russian people with feelings and ideas which the Russian people have never dreamed of. In order to give voice to the thought of the people, one must live with them and in them.

I am speaking of another kind of return. There are men, and fortunately their numbers are increasing, who return not to the Russian soil but to Holy Russia, their spiritual mother, and who greet their brethren with joy and loving repentance. This intellectual return is both important and reassuring. Despite the blind resistance of the erudite and the slothful inertia of the half-literate majority, learning is not only beginning to pay attention to the true requirements of Russian life but, gradually freeing itself from its former schoolboy shackles, is manifesting a trend toward awareness of our native values and the definition of truths latent in our own life and until now unrecognized. Such labors are not altogether unrewarded. There are many who sympathize with them throughout the land of Russia, possibly more in the outlying areas than in those supposed centers of our enlightenment which are in truth merely centers of Western schooling. Even cultivated Westerners, who are ready to respect our thinking as soon as it really becomes our own and not merely an imitation of alien thought, sympathize with this effort.

The progress of the arts is slower than that of learning, but that is only natural. The arts demand an inner world and an inner wholeness which we cannot have as yet; nevertheless, the stream of Russian thought is beginning to run through them ever more strongly. Never before has our spiritual world—the true requirement of the Russian soul—resounded with such marvelous music nor been enriched with such profound ideas as those which come from the greatest of contemporary practitioners; never has the art of letters, in that branch which is concerned with the life and customs of the people, had a Russian representative such as it has today. Even in the plastic arts the same return can be sensed. Our gifted young turn lovingly to the strait path once shown us by Byzantium and then concealed from us by the storms of our turbulent history. Enlightened lovers of the arts, having recognized the high worth of this path, are now ready to restore to the roster of Russian painters a name once shining in the annals for the founding of the school of ikon painting.[17] Finally, men faithful to conviction, seeing the connection between the little things of everyday life and general intellectual development, endeavor to adapt their mode of living, at least to some extent, to Russian ways and customs.

In addition to such positive signs, there are negative signs which are no less comforting. There is no other way to understand the fury with which the teachers and youngsters of the dying imitative school attack everything that pertains to ancient Russia. This is no mere delusion on the part of the critics, no error into which Kachenovskii [18] and his disciples have fallen—it is a passion, a veritable passion. One man denies, for all to hear, that the village commune (*obshchina*) [19] exists in Russia, whereas hardly a line of Russian history can be understood unless one has a clear idea of the commune and its internal life. Another, in the teeth of tradition and record, does away with trade in ancient Russia, not noticing that, according to his own testimony, Novgorod alone paid annually into the Grand Duke's treasury a sum (derived, naturally, from trade) equivalent to one-fourth of the tribute which the Normans exacted from all of England, and over one-eighth of the truly staggering tribute levied by those same victorious Normans on all of France—and surely everyone knows how harsh a thing a war tribute is! Lastly, a third authority takes it into his head to whitewash Ivan the Terrible and ascribes the unfortunate hardening of the Tsar's heart to the vile deeds of the people and the boyars. Neither in Ivan's own self-justificatory letters nor in the testimony of contemporaries, foreign and Russian, is there the shadow of a fact to support his thesis—but no matter! Ancient Russia must be found guilty, and the reader of periodicals must be

[17] Khomiakov probably has in mind A. Rublev (d. ca. 1430).—Editor.

[18] Mikhail Trofimovich Kachenovskii (1775–1842), the founder and leading exponent of the so-called skeptical school of Russian historiography. Subjecting the historical writings of the eighteenth century to search analysis and criticism, he laid the foundations for a modern scientific approach to the study of the earliest period of Russian history.—Editor.

[19] *Obshchina*, in the technical sense, refers to the village commune as an economic unit, whereas *mir* refers to it as a social and judiciary institution. In nontechnical literature the two terms tend to be used interchangeably.—Editor.

credulous.[20] Such attitudes might appear somewhat offensive and indicative of a desire to blacken unjustly the memory of our forefathers, but these scholastic passions are to some extent excusable. The fury with which ancient Russia is being attacked reveals the rage of impotence. The fault of ancient Russia is not that it was, but that it still is—and even lays claim to future existence and development. The same explanation applies to attacks in print on the personalities, the outward appearance, and indeed the domestic affairs of men who have been so bold as to express sympathy for, and faith in, the Russian principles. Raging impotence cannot be fastidious in choosing its means. This negative sign is as encouraging as the positive signs.

Without undue bedazzlement, as without the despondency which was bred in the partisans of the spiritual and communal Russian principles by the one-time triumph of imitative scholarship, I cannot but note that a change, although a slow one (which is as it should be), is taking place in our public thinking; but hope should not give rise either to excessive certainty or to indolent unconcern. Much time must elapse, much intellectual struggle awaits us. The slumber of the mind is not dispelled at once, convictions alter slowly, and habits acquired over a century and a half change more slowly still. The only task men can perform in our time is that of self-education. It is not our destiny to be the exponents of Russian thought; we will be doing well if we become vessels capable of containing it. A better fate awaits future generations; through them, the spiritual forces and principles which form the foundations of Holy Orthodox Russia will find their full expression. But in order that this may come to pass, the life of every individual must be in full accord with the life of all, so that there will be no disunity either within the individual or in society. Individual thought can be powerful and fruitful only when there has been a strong development of common thinking; and that can take place only when learned men are bound to the main body of society by ties of free and rational love and when the intellectual powers of every individual are revivified by the intellectual and spiritual lifeblood circulating in his people. History calls upon Russia to take the lead in universal enlightenment; it gives Russia this right because of the comprehensiveness and completeness of Russian principles; and a right which history confers upon a people is an obligation imposed upon each one of its members.

[20] On the other hand, how happy was the author later, when a zealous and gifted scholar explained the executions ordered by Ivan the Terrible as a struggle between the boyars and the Tsar over the right of departure. I cannot agree with Mr. Solov'ev entirely; but in any event, the idea he subsequently expressed has nothing in common with the attempt to justify Ivan the Terrible by invoking the immorality of the Russian people. [The "right of departure" refers to the right of noble servicemen of Russian princes to take up service with whatever ruler they wished without losing their estates. The custom flourished in the thirteenth and fourteenth centuries and was eventually brought to an end by the emergence of the Grand Duke of Moscow as the sole ruler of all Russian lands. The historian referred to, Sergei M. Solov'ev (1820–79), is the patriarch of modern Russian historiography.—Editor.]

11.

Konstantin Sergeevich Aksakov

1817-1860

Russia's defeat in the Crimean War and the collapse of the system of Nicholas I created a new atmosphere anticipating social and political reform. Taking advantage of this optimistic mood, Konstantin Sergeevich Aksakov submitted his analysis of Russia's political condition to the new Emperor, Alexander II. Any dispassionate reader of this memorandum will readily understand why it failed to make an impact on the Emperor's thinking. In effect, it suggested eliminating everything that had been accomplished in politics, economic development, and cultural life over the last century and a half for the sake of a return to Aksakov's own idealized (and mythical) vision of pre-Petrine Muscovy.

Aksakov's memorandum offered the clearest and fullest expression of Slavophile political ideology. We see how the basic religious, moral, and historical conceptions of the Slavophiles led to the advocacy of a primitive patriarchal monarchy hardly applicable to a modern nation. At the same time, by denying that Russia needed a comprehensive framework of political institutions, Aksakov came close to defending a peculiar form of anarchy as well. As his friends' and his own writings make clear, the Slavophiles were essentially apolitical; they were incapable of seeing and understanding the role that power and authority play in the preservation of the social bond. This doomed them to hopeless political daydreaming and impotence. Scorned by radicals and liberals alike, rejected by the very autocracy they claimed to uphold, their practical political role was negligible. But by focusing the attention of both government and society on the need for a national consensus and better channels of communication between the people and the authorities, they contributed—paradoxically—to the ideological storehouse of the constitutional movement in the latter half of the nineteenth century.

On the Internal State of Russia

In order to be able to discuss the internal state of a country, on which its external condition depends, one must first examine and determine the essential principles of its people in general, principles which are reflected in every particular thing and which are fragmented and reproduced in each individual who regards that country as his fatherland. It will then be easier to assess social defects and shortcomings, for these are caused for the most part by a lack of understanding of the essential principles of the people, or of their improper use or incorrect manifestation.

I

The Russian people is not a people concerned with government; that is to say, it has no aspiration toward self-government, no desire for political rights, and not so much as a trace of lust for power. The first proof of this is to be found in the beginnings of our history, when the Russians of their own free will invited foreigners to rule over them—the Varangians, Riurik and his brothers. An even more telling proof is to be seen in the Russia of 1612, when there was no tsar, when the whole administrative structure of the state lay in ruins, and when the victorious people, still under arms, rejoiced at their triumph over their enemies after having set Moscow free. What did this mighty people do, having been defeated under the Tsar and the boyars, and having been victorious without the Tsar and the boyars, under the leadership of Prince Pozharskii and the butcher Koz'ma Minin, whom they had themselves elected? What did they do? Even as they had done in 862, in 1612 the people called upon others to rule them; they chose a tsar and, having wholly entrusted their fate to him, they peaceably laid down their arms and turned to their separate homes.

These two pieces of evidence are so striking that it hardly seems necessary to add anything more. But if we cast a glance over the whole of Russian history, the truth of the above will become even more manifest. Russian

Translated by Valentine Snow from Konstantin Sergeevich Aksakov, "O vnutrennem sostoianii Rossii," in *Rannie Slavianofily: A. S. Khomiakov, I. V. Kireevskii, K. S. i I. S. Aksakovy*, ed. N. I. Brodskii (Moscow, 1910), pp. 69–96. Originally submitted as a memorandum to the Emperor Alexander II in 1855, this article was first published in *Rus'*, Nos. 26–27 (1881).

history does not record a single uprising against authority to obtain political rights for the people. Novgorod itself, once it had recognized the power of the Tsar of Muscovy, never attempted to restore its earlier form of government by rebellion. There are instances in Russian history of uprisings to defend the lawful authority against an unlawful one; the Russian people may at times have mistaken the lawful authority, yet nonetheless such uprisings testify to their law-abiding spirit. Never has there been a popular attempt to take any part in the government. There were pitiful attempts in that direction by the aristocracy under Ivan IV and Michael, but they were weak and of no import. A flagrant attempt was made later, in Anne's reign. But none of these found any sympathy among the people, and all disappeared quickly without leaving a trace.

Such is the evidence offered by history. Let us now turn from history to present conditions. Who ever heard of the common people in Russia rebelling or plotting against the tsar? No one, of course, for this has never happened and does not happen. In this connection, perhaps the best proof can be seen in the Schism [Raskol]; [1] it is well known that schismatics are found among the common people—among the peasants, the merchants, and the townspeople. The schism constitutes a tremendous power in Russia, for it commands many adherents and great wealth and is spread throughout the land. And yet the schism has never been of any political significance, although one would imagine that it very easily could be. In England, for example, it would have been. This would happen in Russia, too, if only it possessed the slightest political element. But the Russian people has no sense of politics, and Russian schismatics resist only passively, although they have no lack of strength. Russian schismatics flee, go into hiding, are ready to accept martyrdom, but they never acquire political significance. Order has never been maintained in Russia by governmental measures, nor is it now, but it is not in the spirit of the people to wish to disturb it. Were it not for this circumstance, no repressive measures would have helped; rather, they would have furnished a pretext for disturbances. The spirit of the people is the guarantee of tranquillity in Russia and security for the government. Were it at all otherwise, Russia would have had a constitution long ago, for her history and internal conditions have provided enough opportunities for such a development; but the Russian people do not want to govern.

That such is the spirit of the Russian people is not open to question. Some may grieve and call it a slave mentality, while others rejoice and call it a spirit of law and order, but both sides will be mistaken, for these are views of Russia taken in the light of Western concepts of liberalism and conservatism. It is hard to understand Russia unless we renounce Western concepts, on the basis of which we seek in each country—and hence in Russia as well—revolutionary or conservative elements; for both the one and the other are alien to us; they are the opposite extremes of the political spirit; and neither is to be found in the Russian people, for the Russian

---

[1] Reference to the seventeenth-century break from the official Church organization by those who refused to accept the reforms and innovations in the Church ritual.—Editor.

people lack the very spirit of politics. We shall leave aside for the time being the various explanations and interpretations that might be put forward of the absence of political spirit in Russia and the consequent absolute power of the government. Suffice it to say that this is how Russia views the situation, that this is what Russia requires.

For Russia to fulfill her destiny, she must follow her own ideas and requirements, and not theories which are alien to her, whether imported or homemade—theories which history so often explodes. It may be that Russia will put the theoreticians to shame and reveal an aspect of her greatness that no one has ever suspected.

The wisdom of a government consists in doing all it can to help the country it governs to fulfill its destiny and to do the good it was meant to do on earth; it consists in understanding the spirit of the people, by which the government should constantly be guided. Failure to understand the needs of that spirit and opposition to those needs result either in internal disturbances or in the slow exhaustion and disintegration of the forces both of the people and of the state.

Thus the first, and patently obvious, conclusion to be drawn from the history and characteristics of the Russian people is that the Russian people *has no concern for government,* that it does not seek to take part in the administration, that it has no desire to limit in any way the powers of the authorities, and that, in a word, it is apolitical and consequently does not contain so much as an embryo of revolution or a trace of desire for a constitutional order.

Is it not strange, therefore, that the Russian government is forever taking measures to prevent the possibility of revolution and fears a political uprising—events which would be contrary to the very essence of the Russian people? All such fears on the part of the government and also of society arise because those who harbor them do not know Russia and are more familiar with the history of Western Europe than with that of their own country; hence they see in Russia specters from the West which cannot exist here. Such preventive measures by our government—measures for which there is no need and no basis—must of necessity be harmful, as drugs are to a healthy man who does not require them. Even if they do not produce the very thing they are needlessly seeking to avert, they destroy confidence between the government and the people; that in itself is a great harm, and a gratuitous one, for the Russian people, because of their very nature, will never encroach on the power of the government.

II

But what do the Russian people want for themselves? What is the basis, the aim, the preoccupation of their national life, if they are totally bereft of the sense of politics, which is so active a factor in other peoples? What did our people want when, of their own accord, they called upon the Varangian princes to "reign and rule" over them? What did they want to retain for themselves?

They wanted to retain not their political but their internal communal life, their customs, their way of life—the peaceful life of the spirit.

Even before the coming of Christianity, being ready to accept it and having a foreknowledge of its great truths, our people developed a communal life, which Christianity later consecrated. Having renounced political government, the Russian people reserved for themselves the domain of communal life and entrusted the state with the task of enabling them to lead such a life. Without wishing to *rule,* our people wish to *live,* not in the animal sense alone, of course, but in the human sense. Without seeking political freedom, they seek moral freedom, the freedom of the spirit, communal freedom—life in society within the confines of the people. Being perhaps the only Christian people on earth (in the true sense of the word), they remember the saying of Christ: "Render unto Caesar the things that are Caesar's, and unto God the things that are God's"; and this other saying: "My kingdom is not of this world." Hence, leaving the kingdom which is of this world to the state, the Russians, being a Christian people, set their feet on another path—the path to inner freedom, to spiritual life, to the kingdom of Christ: "The Kingdom of God is within you." That is the reason for their unequaled submission to authority; that is the reason for the complete security of the Russian government; that is why there can be no revolution on the part of the Russian people; that is why there is tranquillity within Russia.

That does not mean that the Russian people is composed wholly of righteous men. Russians are sinners, because man is sinful. But the essential qualities of the Russian people are good, its beliefs are holy, its way is righteous. Every Christian, being human, is a sinner, but the path he follows as a Christian is the path of righteousness.

Neither does it mean that the very nature of government and worldly power precludes those who exercise them from also treading the path of Christianity. Every government official, being a man and a Christian, is capable of human and Christian heroism. The feat of heroism performed by the government in the public sphere is to secure for the people their moral life and to protect their spiritual freedom from violation. It is a heroic deed to stand guard outside a temple while the divine service goes on within and the community prays together—to stand guard and ward off any possible interference with the feat of prayer. But this analogy is not exact, for it is the *institutions* of government which stand apart from the nonpolitical life of society, whereas any government official, as *a human being,* may still take part in the life of the people as distinct from that of the state.

Thus, the Russian people, having renounced the political realm and given unlimited political powers to the government, reserved for themselves *life*—their moral and communal freedom, the high purpose of which is to achieve a Christian society.

Although this statement requires no proof—for a close look at Russian history and at the Russian people as they are today will suffice—attention may yet be drawn to a few particularly striking features. One such feature is the ancient division, in the Russian mind, of all Russia into the tsardom (*gosudarstvo*) and the land (*zemlia*), or the government and the people, which gave rise to the expressions, "tsar's business" (*gosudarego delo*) and "land business" (*zemskoe delo*). "Tsar's business" meant all matters of state *administration*, both external and internal, and primarily military matters, as the most obvious expression of state power. The "tsar's service" is still the common people's name for military service. In a word, "tsar's business" referred to the government and the state in all their aspects. "Land business" referred to the people's whole way of life, their entire existence, and comprised, in addition to matters of spiritual and communal life, economic activities—agriculture, industry, and trade. Hence "tsar's men," or "men of service," was the name given to all those who served the state, while "men of the land" were all those who were not in government service and who formed the core of the country: the peasants, the townspeople, and the merchants.

It is of interest to note that both the tsar's men of service and the men of the land also had official appellations; thus the former, in their petitions to the tsar, from the foremost boyar to the lowliest soldier, called themselves his "bondmen" (*kholopy*). The men of the land, in their petitions, called themselves the tsar's *siroty*. These appellations accurately reflected the status of each of the two classes. The word "bondman" now seems to us derogatory and almost insulting, but originally it simply meant "servant." The tsar's bondman signified a servant of the tsar. Hence it is not surprising that all men of service should have been called the tsar's servants, servants of the head of the state to whose sphere of activity they belonged. What then was the meaning of the word *sirota*? In Russian the word does not merely mean "orphan," for it is frequently applied to parents who have lost their children. Hence it refers to a state of helplessness; a *sirota* is a helpless person in need of support and protection. We can now understand why the men of the land should be so designated. The land needs the protection of the state; and by calling the state its protector and itself the *sirota* of the state it indicates this need. Thus in 1612, before Michael ascended the throne and prior to the restoration of the state, the country called itself orphaned—tsarless and grieved to be in that condition.

As further evidence of the essential qualities of the Russian people we may cite the opinions of the Poles in 1612. They reported with surprise that the Russian people talked only of religious matters, neglecting political conditions.

III

Thus the land of Russia entrusted its defense to the state, in the person of the tsar, that it might live under his shelter in peace and happiness. Having separated itself from the state, having made the distinction between the protected and the protector, the land, or the people, does not wish to cross the boundary that it has itself established; it does not wish to govern, but wishes instead to lead a rational life worthy of human beings. Can there be a juster or wiser relationship? How noble a task it is for the state to secure to the people a peaceful and untroubled existence based on moral freedom, the cultivation of Christian virtues, and the development of all their God-given talents! How noble is the people who, having renounced all ambition, all yearning for worldly power, desires not political freedom, but freedom to enjoy the life of the spirit and peaceful prosperity! Such an attitude is a guarantee of peace and tranquillity. It is the attitude of Russia, and of Russia alone. All other peoples aspire to popular sovereignty.

IV

Not only is such an order consonant with the spirit of Russia—and therefore essential for her, if only for that reason—but it may also be stated positively that it is the only proper order to be found on earth. The great question of the state versus the people cannot be better solved than it has been by the people of Russia. Man's vocation is to achieve a spiritual approach to God, to his Saviour; man's law is within him, and that law is unstinted love of God and of his neighbor. If men were like that, if they were saintly, there would be no need for the state, for we would have the Kingdom of God upon earth. But men fall short of this ideal and, what is more, fall short of it in different degrees; the law that is within them does not suffice and, once again, does not suffice in varying degrees. The cut-throat who has no law in his soul and who is not restrained by external law may kill an honest, virtuous man and commit all kinds of evil deeds. Therefore, because of the weakness and sinfulness of human nature, we need external law, we need a state as the embodiment of worldly power. But man's vocation still remains a moral, inner one; the state exists only to enable him to lead it. How then is the state conceived by a people which sets the highest value on moral development and aspires to freedom of the spirit, freedom in Christ—in brief, how does a truly Christian people regard the state? As a *protection*, and by no means as an object of the desire for power.

Whenever a people aspires to political power, it is thereby distracted from its inner, its moral, endeavors, and external political freedom serves only to undermine inner freedom, the freedom of the spirit. The exercise of government then becomes the people's goal, while the higher aim—inner truth, inner freedom, and spiritual striving—disappears. The people should not be the government. When the people is the sovereign, when the people is the government, the people as such ceases to exist.

On the other hand, if the people conceive the state to be a protection and not a target for ambition, the state too must act as the protector of the people, the custodian of its freedom, so that its spiritual powers may reach their full development under its guardianship.

v

On the premise that the people should not meddle in government, the power of the state must be absolute. What form should such absolute authority take? The answer is not difficult—it must be a monarchy. Any other form of government, such as a democracy or an aristocracy, allows the participation of the people to a greater or lesser extent, with a consequent limitation of state power, and consequently fails to meet either the requirement that the people should not meddle in government or the requirement that the government's authority should be absolute. Obviously a mixed constitution (sic), like the English, will not answer these demands. Even if we were to elect ten archons—as Athens did once—and give them full powers, inasmuch as they would constitute a council they could not truly wield absolute power. They would become a governing group and hence would form a kind of *national* life; as a result, that vast society, the nation, would be ruled by a miniature of itself. A society, however, is subject to its own laws of development which alone can freely achieve unity. But the governing group can have no such unity, for any unity would be disrupted, be made impossible, or become compulsory because of the needs of government. It is obvious that a group cannot govern.

Outside society, beyond the bounds of social life, there can only be the individual. Only an individual can possess unlimited authority, only he can free the nation from any participation in government. Hence we need a sovereign, a monarch. Only a monarch's power can be absolute. Only under an absolute monarchy can a people draw a line between itself and the state and, freeing itself from all participation in government, from all political significance, reserve unto itself a communal moral life and the pursuit of spiritual freedom. It is this very type of monarchy that was chosen by the Russian people.

This attitude on the part of the Russian shows him to be a *free man*. In recognizing the absolute power of the monarch, he retains complete independence of spirit, conscience, and thought. Since he is aware of his moral independence, the Russian, in all fairness, is not a slave but a free man. In his view, the absolute monarchy is not an enemy but a friend and protector of freedom—that true freedom of the spirit the test of which is the open expression of opinion. Only when it enjoys such freedom to the fullest extent can the people be of use to the government. Political freedom is not freedom. True liberty, the liberty bestowed upon us by our Saviour—"where the spirit of the Lord is, there is liberty"—can exist on earth only when a people refuses to take any part in the government and places itself under the protection of an absolute monarchy which affords it full possibility of moral development.

VI

Since the Russian people regard the government as a beneficent and necessary authority subject to no limitation, since they have recognized it not under duress, but freely and consciously, they consider it to be, in the Saviour's words, "the power of this world": only the Kingdom of God is not of this world. The Russian people render unto Caesar that which is Caesar's, and unto God that which is God's. Since the government is a worldly, man-made institution, they do not deem it to be perfect. Hence the Russian people do not pay divine homage to the tsar, do not make him into an idol, and are guiltless of that idolatry of authority which is shown by the excessive adulation that has come to Russia along with Western influences. The adulation invokes the most sacred notions—the attributes of God—to celebrate and glorify the monarchy and present them to the people, who, on the other hand, have a proper understanding of what is sacred. Thus, Lomonosov in one of his odes says of Peter the Great:

> O Russian land, he was your God!
> He clothed himself in human flesh
> As he descended from on high . . .

The dissenters [Old Believers], however, cite those very lines of Lomonosov's as an argument against the Orthodox faith. Despite such adulation, which is greatly on the increase, the Russian people (in the mass) have not changed their proper concept of the government. This concept, on the one hand, secures the people's unfailing and unalterable submission to the government and, on the other, eliminates the egregious, impious radiance with which the government allows its adulators to surround it. Indeed, even in the Christian community the monarchy has acquired an aura of sanctity, so that although the phrase "God on earth" has not become one of the tsar's official titles, it is allowed as an interpretation of the tsar's power. The Christian faith bids its adherents to obey the authorities, and thereby supports them; but it does not give to the authorities that aura of excessive sanctity which followed later. The Russian people understand this and take the same view of the authorities, no matter how hard the flatterers may try to convince both the tsar and his subjects that the latter hold him to be a god on earth. The Russian people know that *there is no power but of God.* Being Christians, they pray for the tsar, obey him, and honor him, but they do not worship him. That is the very reason why submission and respect are solidly ingrained in them, and why they are incapable of revolution.

VII

Such is the sober view the Russian people take of government. But look at the West. The Western nations, having abandoned the spiritual path, the path of religion, have been lured by vanity into striving for power. Believing as they do in the possibility of a perfect government, they have formed republics, composed constitutions of every imaginable kind, embraced the vanity of worldly power, and become spiritually the poorer; they have lost their faith and, despite the ostensible perfection of their political order, are ready at any moment to totter and suffer dreadful upheavals, if not a final collapse.

VIII

It is now clear to us what the government and the people stand for in Russia. In other words, we see that Russia has two facets—the tsardom and the land. Although the tsardom and the land—or the government and the people—are clearly demarcated in Russia, and although they do not mingle, they nevertheless impinge on each other. What is their mutual relationship? First of all, the people do not meddle in governmental or administrative matters; the state, for its part, does not meddle in the life and ways of the people, does not force them to live according to its rules. It would be strange indeed if the state required the people to rise at seven o'clock, eat dinner at two o'clock, and the like; and no less strange if it forced the people to comb their hair in a certain way or to wear a given kind of dress. Thus the first relationship between the government and the people is that of mutual *noninterference*. But this relationship (being negative) is incomplete; it must be supplemented by a positive relationship. The positive duty of the state to the people is to safeguard and protect their life, to give them material security, and to provide them with all the requisite means and ways to enable them to prosper, attain their full development, and fulfill their moral destiny on earth. Administration, justice, the making of laws—all these, within their purely political limitations, are the inherent attributes of the government. It is an undisputed fact that the government exists for the people, rather than the people for the government. Having honestly accepted this principle, the government will never seek to violate the independence of the people's life and conscience.

The positive duty which the people owe to the state is to carry out its demands, give it the strength it needs to put its plans into execution, and supply men and money when these are required. This relationship of the people to the state is merely the direct consequence of their recognition of the state. It is one of submission and not of independence, and it does not allow the state *to see the people as such.* What, then, is the *independent* relationship between an apolitical people and the state? When does a state see, so to say, the *people as such?* An independent relationship between a powerless people and an all-powerful state can take only one form—that of *public opinion.* There is no political element in public or popular opinion; it has no force other than moral force, and therefore has no compelling, as contrasted to moral, power. Public opinion (which, naturally, must be openly expressed) shows the state what the country wants, how it conceives its purpose, what its moral needs are, and, consequently, by what principles the state must be guided, for we must not forget that the purpose of the state is to enable the country to fulfill its vocation. It is thus one of the state's duties to protect freedom of public opinion, as an expression of the country's moral activity. At important junctures in the life of the state and the land, the government itself must ask for the country's opinion, but for its *opinion* only, which (it goes without saying) the government is free to accept or to reject. *Public opinion* constitutes the independent service which the people can and must render to their government; it is the living, moral, and in no way political link which can and must exist between them.

Our wise tsars understood this, and for this we owe them eternal gratitude. They knew that those who sincerely and consciously want the country's weal and prosperity must know, and on some occasions ask for, its opinion. For this reason, our tsars often convoked Assemblies of the Land (*Zemskie sobory*),[2] consisting of representatives of all the social classes, and invited them to discuss some particular question relating to the state and the land. Our tsars, who understood Russia well, never hesitated to convene such assemblies. The government knew that it would not forfeit or curtail any of its rights thereby, while the people knew that they would neither acquire nor confer any rights. The bond between the government and the people was not shaken, but only strengthened. This was a friendly relationship between the government and the people, based on mutual confidence.

The Assemblies of the Land were attended not only by men of the land but also by men of service or tsar's men—boyars, court dignitaries, and plain nobles;[3] but these were summoned in their capacity as constituent members of the people, to give counsel. The clergy, too, was present, as an essential component of the whole Russian society. Thus it might be said that Russia herself foregathered in full at these assemblies and on these occasions, fulfilled its true meaning of *land*—that is why these gatherings were called Assemblies of the Land.

When we consider these famous assemblies and the statements of the representatives who attended them, it becomes evident that their only purpose was to elicit expression of *opinion*. All statements began in this way: "O Tsar, what should be done in this case is for you to decide. *Do* as it pleases you; but this is what we *think*." Thus to take action was a right of the state, and to hold an opinion was the country's. In the best interests of the country, each side must be able to exercise its right—the land must not hinder the *action* of the state, while the state must impose no restrictions on the opinion of the land.

[2] Assemblies of representatives of the service nobility, the major towns, and—to a small extent—the free peasantry. The first assemblies met in the middle of the sixteenth century and the last in the 1680's. The extent of their role and representative character is still subject to scholarly dispute. The most famous (and most "democratic" in membership) was the *sobor* which elected Michael Romanov Tsar in 1613.—Editor.

[3] *Boiarin, okol'nichii, stol'nik, dvorianin.* An *okol'nichii* was a high courtier of rank below *boiarin;* a *stol'nik* was a steward of court rank below that of *okol'nichii;* a *dvorianin* was a service nobleman.—Editor.

Since the people of Russia gathered at these assemblies at the summons of their tsar, and not out of a vainglorious desire to orate, as they do in Parliament, or to seek power—in a word, since they did not come of their own accord—they often regarded attendance at the assemblies as an onerous duty and were in no hurry to come; thus in the archives we find missives to outlying cities, such as Perm and Viatka, asking for representatives to be sent as soon as possible, as "on their account the tsar's business and the land's are at a standstill."

In addition to [convoking] these assemblies, our forever-remembered tsars, the founders of Russian might, would ask for the people's opinion wherever and whenever they could. The price of bread went up in Moscow, and Tsar Alexis summoned the merchants to the Red Square to ask their advice on what was to be done. The government consulted public opinion on every suitable occasion; when it was necessary to prepare regulations for military service in village garrisons (*stanichnyi*) or in the field (*polevoi*), a boyar was ordered to consult the entire garrison force; when the government issued a decree, a boyar was instructed to find out what the people said about it. Our tsars gave free rein to public opinion among the peasantry as well, by asking them to elect judges, to order general perquisitions, which were of extreme importance in their day; by allowing, in addition to the elected judges, elected representatives of the people to be present in court; and, lastly, by giving full latitude to peasant meetings to decide all matters pertaining to their own administration.

In so doing, our tsars were able to leave to our emperors a Russia which had been freed from the Tatar yoke, had acquired three kingdoms,[4] had emerged with glory from the year 1612, had reconquered the Ukraine, had produced a code of laws, and had done away with the nobles' disputes about the *mestnichestvo* system,[5] which had so hindered governmental action: a renovated and reinvigorated Russia that was free from all elements of internal disintegration; a Russia strong and stalwart. Surely no one will question either that our tsars wielded absolute power or that the spirit of revolution was completely absent in ancient Russia. There was also much that our tsars did not have time to do; after the dreadful upheavals she had undergone, Russia needed strengthening for a long period. Unhurriedly, gradually, and solidly did our wise sovereigns perform their heroic task, without abandoning Russian principles, without changing Russia's course. They did not shun foreigners—whom the Russian people have never shunned—and they did their best to catch up with Europe in the matter of enlightenment, in which Russia had been left behind as a result of two centuries of the Mongol yoke. They knew that to achieve this, Russians need not cease to be Russians or renounce their customs, language, and dress, still less their essence. They knew that enlightenment is really useful only when a man acquires it not in a spirit of imitation but in one of independence. Tsar Alexis increased diplomatic contacts with European

[4] Reference to the conquests of Kazan, Astrakhan, and Siberia in the reign of Ivan IV. —Editor.

[5] A system of calculating seniority in government service. Cf p. 57.—Editor.

powers and read foreign journals; the first Russian ship, the *Eagle* (*Orel*) was built in his reign; his boyars were already men of culture; enlightenment was beginning to spread quietly and peacefully. Tsar Theodore founded in Moscow an institution of higher learning, a university, albeit under another name: the Slavic-Greco-Latin Academy, whose statute was written by the famous Simeon of Polotsk.

IX

We must now speak of a period when the government—not the people—violated the principles of Russia's civil order and swerved Russia from her course. The last of the tsars, Theodore, convoked two assemblies during his brief reign: an assembly of the men of service of the state, on matters of precedence which were of interest to the men of service only, and an Assembly of the Land, for the purpose of equalizing taxes and service obligations throughout Russia. While this second assembly was meeting, the Tsar died. It will be remembered that in obedience to the Tsar's will his youngest brother, Peter, was chosen to reign. It is probable that this same Assembly of the Land, which was then meeting in Moscow, confirmed Peter as Tsar, following the wishes of Theodore. However that may be, this Assembly of the Land was dissolved in the name of Peter, then still a minor; but a few years later Peter began to act on his own.

I have no intention of relating in detail the story of Peter's revolution; no intention of disputing the greatness of that greatest of all great men. But the revolution wrought by Peter, despite all its outward brilliance, shows what immense spiritual evil can be done by the greatest genius as soon as he acts alone, draws away from the people, and regards them as an architect does bricks. Under Peter began that evil which is still the evil of our day. Like every evil that is not remedied, it grew worse with the passage of time, and is now a dangerous deep-lying cancer for Russia. I must define this evil.

If the people do not encroach upon the state, the state must not encroach upon the people. Then, and only then, is their union strong and beneficent. In the West there is constant conflict and contention between the state and the people, for they do not understand their proper relationship. Russia knew nothing of such conflict and contention. The people and the government, without mingling, lived in a happy union. Calamities either came from outside or were caused by the imperfections of human nature, and not by a mistaken choice of course or a confusion of concepts. The Russian people remained true to their views and did not encroach on the state; but the state, in the person of Peter, encroached upon the people, invaded their life and customs, and forcibly changed their manners and traditions and even their dress. Attendance at social gatherings was enforced by the police. Even tailors who made clothes in the old Russian style were exiled to Siberia. The men of service who previously, in their private capacity rather than as servants of the state, had identified themselves with the people by sharing their ideas, their way of life, their customs, and their manner of dress, suffered more than anyone from Peter's encroachments upon the moral principles which governed their daily life, and bore the brunt of Peter's revolution. Although the government made the same demands upon all classes of society, including even the peasants, it made them less in-sistently, and the declared intention not to allow a single peasant to come to the city wearing a beard was later abandoned; instead, beards were taxed. In the end, men of the land were permitted to live and dress as they had done before; but their position in Russia was completely changed. A cleavage had taken place in Russian society. The men of service, or the upper class, had been torn loose from Russian principles, concepts, and customs, as well as from the Russian people; they began to live, dress, and speak like foreigners. The sovereign was displeased with Moscow, and trans-ferred his capital to the edge of Russia, to a new city he had built himself and called by the German name of Sankt-Peterburg. In that city, Peter was surrounded by a whole immigrant population of newly transformed Russians —officials deprived even of their native ground, for the indigenous popula-tion of St. Petersburg is foreign.

That is how the breach between the Tsar and the people occurred; that is how the ancient union of the land and the state was torn asunder and replaced by a *domination* of the state over the land, so that the land of Russia became, as it were, conquered territory and the state its conqueror. That is how the Russian monarch was transformed into a despot, and his willing subjects into slaves held captive in their own country!

The newly transformed Russians, in part driven by force, in part tempted, into adopting foreign ways, soon reconciled themselves to their condition, for the license of their borrowed manners, the ostentation and brilliance of their new society and, lastly, the new rights accorded to the nobles strongly appealed to human passions and weaknesses. Contempt for Russia and for the Russian people soon became an attribute of every edu-cated Russian intent upon aping Western Europe. At the same time the newly transformed Russians, now that their manners and morals were sub-ject to state control and they themselves were in a new position—that of slaves—vis-à-vis the authorities, felt a stirring of political ambition. Among the social classes which had been sundered from the people, particularly among the nobility, a desire for power now manifested itself. Several revolu-tionary attempts were made and—a thing hitherto unknown—the Russian throne became the illicit plaything of rival factions. Catherine I ascended to the throne unlawfully; unlawful, too, was the ascent of Anne, and on that occasion the aristocracy even planned a constitution, but the attempt fortu-nately miscarried. Elizabeth came to the throne with the aid of soldiers. Is there any need to speak of the deposition of Peter III? At last, the un-Russian principles imported by Peter the Great found their fruition in the revolt of December 14,[6] a revolt by the upper class, which had been severed from the people, for the soldiers, as we know, were tricked into it.

[6] In 1825—the abortive effort of officers of the St. Petersburg garrison to prevent the accession of Nicholas I and to establish a constitutional monarchy.—Editor.

Such was the conduct of the upper class, which had renounced its Russian principles. And how did the people, who had remained faithful to the Russian principles—the merchants, the townspeople, and particularly the peasants, who more than anyone remained loyal to the Russian ways and spirit—conduct themselves?

During all this time, the people, as should have been expected, remained calm. Is not this calm of theirs the best proof that revolution in any form is contrary to the Russian spirit? The nobles rebelled, but when did the peasants ever rebel against their sovereign? The clean-shaven face and German dress rebelled, but when did the Russian beard and the peasant coat (*kaftan*) rebel?

The mutiny of the *strel'tsy* [7] under Peter is a special case; but it was an outbreak of lawlessness rather than a mutiny and, what is more, the *strel'tsy* found no support among the people. On the contrary, the army recruited from the people zealously fought the *strel'tsy* and defeated them. In order to win over the bondmen, the *strel'tsy* tore up the deeds of bondage and scattered them in the streets, but the bondmen declared that they would have none of this freedom, and fought the mutineers. Thus, the people were the first to be outraged by the willful violence of the *strel'tsy*, and, far from supporting, opposed them. There was, it is true, one terrible uprising in more recent times, but whose name served as its deceptive banner? [8] The name of Peter III, the lawful sovereign. Is not this the final proof that the Russian people—the real mainstay of the throne—are wholly antirevolutionary?

Indeed, so long as the Russian people remain Russian, internal tranquillity and the security of the government are assured. But the system introduced by Peter the Great and the foreign influence which is inseparable from it continue to operate, and we have seen what effect they have had on those many Russians whom they have lured away from the fold. We have seen that the slave mentality—which is generated when the government encroaches upon men's very lives—is accompanied by a spirit of revolt, for a slave is not aware of that dividing line between himself and the government, a line which is perceived by the free man with an independent spiritual life. The slave sees only one difference between himself and the government: he is oppressed, and the government is the oppressor. His base servility can at a moment's notice change to insolent audacity; the slave of today is the rebel of tomorrow, and out of his chains are forged the merciless knives of revolt. The Russian people—that is to say, the common people—adhere to their ancient principles and still resist both the slave mentality and the foreign influence of the upper class. But Peter's system has been in effect for 150 years; it is at last beginning to penetrate to the people, and what reaches the people is its frivolous but harmful aspect. Already in some villages Russian

[7] "Musketeers"—corps of professional soldiers (see note on p. 36).—Editor.

[8] Peasant rebellion (1773–75) led by Emel'ian Pugachev, who claimed to be the deposed Peter III, who was murdered.—Editor.

dress is being discarded and even peasants start to talk of fashion, and along with such frivolous matters an alien way of life and alien notions creep in, and Russian principles begin to totter.

As soon as the government takes away the people's *inner, communal* freedom, it forces them to seek external, political freedom. The longer Peter's system of government continues (although on the face of it, it is not as harsh as it was in his time)—a system so alien to the Russian people, infringing on the freedom of life of the community, restricting the freedom of conscience, thought, and opinion and turning the subject into a slave—the more will foreign ideas infiltrate into Russia, the greater will be the number of people who lose touch with their native Russian soil, the more will the foundations of the Russian land be shaken, and the more terrible will be the revolutionary attempts which in the end will destroy Russia when she has ceased to be Russia. The only danger which threatens Russia is *that she may cease to be Russia,* and that is where Peter's system of government is leading her. God grant that this may not come to pass!

It will be said that Peter exalted Russia. It is true that he brought her much outward glory, but within her essential integrity he implanted corruption; he sowed the seeds of conflict and destruction in Russian life. Besides, he and his successors were able to perform their glorious exploits by mobilizing the strength of a Russia which had grown and matured in an ancient tradition in another spirit. Our soldiers are still recruited from among the common people, and even the transformed Russians, subjected as they are to a foreign influence, have still not wholly forgotten Russian principles. Thus Peter's state is able to be victorious by drawing on the strength of pre-Petrine Russia; but strength is waning, for Peter's influence is increasingly felt among the people, despite the fact that the government has begun to talk of Russian nationality,[9] even to demand it. But for its good intention to be transformed into a good action, the government must understand the spirit of Russia and embrace Russian principles, which have been rejected since Peter's day. Russia's outward glory, under the emperors, has been truly brilliant, but outward glory is durable only when it stems from inner greatness. The source must not be muddied, nor must it be allowed to dry up. Besides, how can any external brilliance compensate for the loss of inner well-being and inner harmony? What unstable outward glory and unreliable outward strength can compare with stable inner greatness and reliable inner strength? Outward strength can continue to exist only while the inner, albeit undermined, persists in being. If a tree is rotten at the core, it does not matter how strong and thick its bark; one gust of wind and, to the general astonishment, the tree will fall. Russia has stood because her inner strength, which is the heritage of many centuries, has not yet disappeared despite constant abuse and attack, because pre-Petrine Russia still survives in her. Thus the first and highest aim of the people and, naturally, of the government, must be to maintain inner greatness.

[9] Reference to the so-called doctrine of "official nationality" (*narodnost'*) promoted by the government of Nicholas I.—Editor.

X

Russia's present condition is one of internal dissension, glossed over by unscrupulous lies. The government—and with it the upper classes—has drawn away from the people and has become a stranger to them. The people and the government follow divergent paths and are guided by different principles. Not only is the people's opinion not sought; every private person is afraid to express an opinion. The people have no trust in the government; the government has no confidence in the people. The people are ready to see a new measure of oppression in each governmental act; the government is constantly afraid of revolution and senses mutiny in every independent expression of opinion; petitions signed by many or even several persons are no longer permitted, whereas in ancient Russia it is they that would have received every consideration. The government and the people do not understand each other, and their relationship is not friendly. This inner dissension is the soil from which, like a weed, has sprung up a rich growth of unscrupulous adulation which assures us that all is well and turns the respect due to the Emperor into idolatry by treating him as if he were a god. A writer in *Vedomosti* [10] produced the following passage: "The children's hospital was consecrated according to the ritual of the Orthodox Church; it was consecrated a second time by the visit of His Majesty the Emperor." It is now customary to say that "His Majesty *deigned* to receive the Sacrament," whereas any Christian would say that he was *permitted* or *privileged* to receive it.

It may be said that these are isolated instances; no, this is the general attitude toward the government. I have chosen but insignificant examples of divine worship of earthly authorities, but examples thereof abound, both in words and in deeds; to list them all would fill a book. Frankness and mutual confidence having vanished, the lie has taken over and deception is everywhere. The government, for all its absolute power, cannot command honesty and truthfulness, for where there is no freedom of opinion these are not to be had. Everyone lies to everyone else; everyone knows it; yet everyone continues to lie, and who knows where this will end? The general corruption and the weakening of moral principles in society have reached vast proportions. Bribery and organized robbery by officials are terrifying. They are now, so to speak, part of the air we breathe, so that not only dishonest men are thieves in Russia; nay, very often kind, excellent, even in a sense honest, men are thieves also—the exceptions are few. Stealing is no longer a personal, but a social sin; it is a symptom of the immorality of our entire society, of our internal social order.

[10] Record or Gazette (see note on p. 71).—Editor.

XI

The main root of the evil is our repressive system of government—repression of freedom of opinion and of moral freedom, since the Russian people do not even aspire to political freedom. The suppression of all opinion, of all expression of thought, has reached a point where some officials prohibit the expression even of opinion favorable to the government, because they prohibit the expression of any opinion. They will not even permit praise of steps taken by the authorities, holding that higher officials are not concerned with the approval of their underlings, and that these should not presume to exercise their own judgment and pronounce themselves in favor of something done by their superiors or by the government. What does such a system lead to? To total indifference, to the complete destruction of all human feeling; a man is not even expected to think right, he is expected not to think at all. If this system were to be successful, it would turn man into a beast which obeys without reasoning and without conviction! But even if men could be reduced to that state, what government would set itself such a goal? All that is human in man would perish; and why does man live upon the earth if not in order to be human, in the fullest, the highest sense? Furthermore, men who have lost their human dignity will not come to the rescue of their government. In times of great trials, human beings in the true sense will be needed; where will the government find them then, where will it find the compassion it has taught them not to feel, human talents, human inspiration, the human spirit?

But to reduce men to the level of beasts cannot be the conscious goal of any government. Besides, men cannot really sink to that level; but their human dignity can be destroyed, their minds dulled, and their feelings deadened, so that they come close to the level of the beasts. At any rate, that is what the system of stifling the originality of communal life, of thought, of expression, leads to. This system, with its injurious effects on man's mind, talents, all his moral powers and moral dignity, engenders inner discontent and despondency. That same repressive system of government makes the emperor an idol, to whom all moral convictions and aspirations are sacrificed. "My conscience," says the man. "You have no conscience," he is told; "how dare you have a conscience of your own? The emperor is your conscience, and you may not question him." "My country," says the man. "It is no business of yours," he is told. "What concerns Russia does not—without special authorization—concern you. The emperor is your country, and you may not even love him freely but must be slavishly devoted to him." "My religion," says the man. "The emperor is the head of the Church," he is told (in contradiction to Orthodox doctrine, which holds that Christ is the head of the Church). "The emperor is your religion." "My God," the man says at last. "The emperor is your God, for he is God on earth!"

Thus the emperor has become a mysterious force which may not be discussed or analyzed and which saps men of all their moral strength. As a result, men become dehumanized and, with instinctive cunning, they cheat, rob, and steal wherever they can.

This system is not always brought out clearly and frankly; but such, without exaggeration, is the inner meaning, the very spirit, of our present system.

Great is the rot at Russia's core, a rot which flattery attempts to conceal from the emperor's eyes; deep is the gulf between the government and the people, which loud professions of slavish adulation seek to mask. The intrusion of the authorities into the life of society continues; the people are becoming more contaminated daily, and public corruption thrives in all its many forms, among which bribery and defrauding the government have become nearly universal and virtually accepted. Secret discontent among all classes of society is on the increase.

XII

And why all this? For no good reason! Simply because the government does not understand the people and has violated that necessary frontier between the people and itself which alone makes a strong and mutually beneficial union possible. All this could easily be remedied at least in its essentials.

The specific remedy for the ills of modern Russia is *to understand Russia* and to revert to the essential principles which are consonant with her spirit. The specific remedy for the disease caused by a course of action which is against Russia's nature is to abandon that unnatural course of action and to return to one which is in conformity with Russian concepts and the essence of Russia.

As soon as the government learns to understand Russia, it will realize that desire for political power is contrary to the spirit of the Russian people; that fear of revolution in Russia is utterly groundless; that multitudes of spies serve only to corrupt those with whom they come in contact; and that the government is absolute and secure because the Russian people wish it so. The people want these things only: freedom to lead their own life, spiritual freedom, freedom of speech. As they themselves do not meddle in matters of state, they do not want the state to interfere in their spiritual life and their ways, which the state has meddled with and has been repressing for 150 years—even to the point of telling them what to wear. The government must once again grasp the basic relationship between itself and the people —the ancient relationship between the state and the land—and restore it. Nothing more is required. Since it was the government itself that violated this relationship when it encroached upon the people's rights, it can eliminate the violation. This is not difficult and calls for no forcible action. As soon as the oppression of the land by the state is done away with, it will be simple for the government to establish the true Russian relationship between itself and the people. A sincere union between the sovereign and the people, a union based on mutual trust, will then be brought about. Lastly, to crown this union, the government must not be content to know that popular opinion exists, but it must want to learn what that opinion is and on certain occasions must seek and demand that opinion, as used to be done under the tsars in the old days.

I say that the government itself should on occasion seek the country's opinion. Does that mean that it should call an Assembly of the Land?

The answer is no. To convene an Assembly of the Land nowadays would be futile. Of whom would it be composed? Of nobles, merchants, townspeople, and peasants. But it is enough to name these classes of society to realize how far apart they have drawn, how little unity there is between them today. The nobility severed the bonds uniting them with the people 150 years ago, and now for the most part look down on the peasantry with haughty disdain or regard it as a source of their income. The merchants, on the one hand, imitate the nobles and, like them, look to the West; on the other, they cling to a kind of ancient tradition they seem themselves to have invented, wearing a waistcoat over a Russian blouse, a tie and a long-skirted coat with Russian boots. This costume is a symbol of their notions, which are a similar mixture. The townpeople are a pale imitation of the merchants; they are the most pitiful social class in Russia, and also the most heterogeneous. The peasants, long removed from any contact with history in the making, take part in it only by paying taxes and furnishing recruits for the army. They alone have largely preserved the essence of the Russian tradition in all its purity; but what could they say, who have so long been silent? The voice of the entire Russian land should make itself heard at an Assembly of the Land, but the different social classes cannot now speak with that voice.

Thus, at the present time an Assembly of the Land would serve no useful purpose and should not be convened. At present it might be possible, and would be truly useful, if the government were to convene separate gatherings of the social classes on certain occasions, to discuss some question of concern to some one class, as, for example, a meeting of elected representatives of the merchants on matters of trade. It is essential that the government convene such gatherings for a special purpose, setting forth one or another subject for discussion. During the past century and a half, the regular meetings of the nobility, the merchants, and the townspeople have acquired a particular character of their own, and it is not the habit of those who attend them to express their opinion frankly and truthfully; that attitude might well persist if the government should suddenly decide to put forward some topic for discussion at those meetings. Hence in my view it would be better to call extraordinary gatherings of some one social class whenever a question arises about which the government deems it necessary to ask for the opinion of that class. It should not be obligatory for the government to call such meetings, as well as Assemblies of the Land (when these become feasible), nor should they be called at regular intervals. The government should convene an assembly and elicit opinion whenever it sees fit.

At the present time, public opinion can to some extent serve as a substitute for an Assembly of the Land. At the present time, public opinion can give the government the requisite information and indication—something which an Assembly of the Land, when it becomes possible to hold one, can supply in a clearer form.

By giving the country social and spiritual freedom, the government also gives it freedom of public opinion. How can public opinion express itself? In speech and in writing. Consequently the repression of the spoken and the written word must cease. Let the state return to the land what belongs to the land—freedom of thought and speech—and the land will give back what belongs to the government—its own confidence and strength.

God created man as a being endowed with reason and the gift of speech. The exercise of reason and spiritual freedom are man's vocation. Spiritual freedom finds its fullest and worthiest expression in freedom of speech. Hence freedom of speech is an inalienable human right.

At the present time the word—the land's one means of expression—is subject to severe repression. The greatest tyranny is exercised over the written word (by which I mean the printed word as well). It is natural that under such a system censorship should have reached the heights of absurdity. Many instances of incredible absurdities are, indeed, known to all. This dread repression of the word must cease.

Does that mean the abolition of censorship? It does not. Censorship must continue, to protect the individual person. But censorship must be liberal as possible in regard to every expression of thought and opinion so long as they do not concern personalities. I will not define the limits of this freedom beyond saying that the wider they are, the better. If there should be ill-intentioned people who desire to disseminate harmful ideas, there will also be well-intentioned people who will unmask the former, undo the harm, and, by making truth triumph, give it greater strength. The truth, when it has freedom of action, is always strong enough to defend itself and to refute any lie. If truth cannot defend itself, nothing can defend it. But not to believe in truth's power to triumph is not to believe in truth itself. That is a sort of godlessness, for God is truth.

In time, there must be complete freedom of the spoken and written word, once it has been realized that freedom of expression is indissolubly linked with the absolute monarchy—that it is its mainstay, a pledge of peace and tranquillity, and an inherent part of moral improvement and human dignity.

There are some sores in the body of Russia which cry out for special treatment—such as religious dissent, serfdom, and bribery. I do not offer any views on them, for they are outside the scope of this memorandum. I have sought to analyze the basic causes of Russia's internal condition, which constitute the main problem and which profoundly influence Russia as a whole. Let me say only that the proper relationship between the state and the land, once it has been restored, and public opinion, once it is given free rein, will, by breathing new life into the body of Russia, have a healing effect on these sores as well—and most particularly on bribery, which shrinks before publicity. In addition, public opinion can indicate remedies for the ills which beset the people and the state, as for all other ills.

May the ancient union between the government and the people, between the state and the land, be restored on the firm foundation of true traditional Russian principles.

Let there be reserved for the government unlimited freedom *to rule,* which is its prerogative, and for the people full freedom of social and spiritual *life* under the government's protection. Let the *government have the right to action* and consequently the power of the law; let the *people have the right of opinion* and consequently freedom of speech.

That is the Russian civil order! That is the only true civil order!

12.
Vissarion Grigor'evich Belinskii

1811-1848

After the publication in 1836 of *The Inspector General* N. V. Gogol (1809–52) was acclaimed not only as a great writer and a truthful painter of Russian life but also as a forceful critic of the evils of serfdom and bureaucratic corruption. This reputation was reinforced in 1842 by the publication of the first part of *Dead Souls.* Great, therefore, were the shock and indignation of the progressive intelligentsia when they read in 1847 his *Selected Passages from a Correspondence with Friends (Vybrannye mesta iz perepiski s druz'iami).* Indeed, in this book Gogol proclaimed that Russia's ills were due solely to the moral failings of individuals, not to her social, economic, or political system. He further argued that the way to the much-needed national regeneration was through complete submission to the teachings of the Church and the paternal guidance of the autocratic Tsar. To the intellectuals of the 1840's such a viewpoint could have but one meaning: apology for the brutal tyranny of Nicholas I that held all of Russia in thrall. They felt betrayed by the man they had acclaimed as one of their leaders because he had earlier pointed his finger at Russia's sores.

The most outraged and famous reaction came from the pen of Vissarion Grigor'evich Belinskii. This was to be expected. Belinskii was a passionate man who took ideas and literature very seriously; in particular, he saw literature as the educator of Russians, the defender of right, and the denouncer of all the social and spiritual ills that afflicted his country. And it was Belinskii who had hailed the powerful effect of Gogol's earlier writings in fighting the status quo. That he may have misinterpreted Gogol's intentions is beside the point.

Belinskii's letter to Gogol is a landmark in Russian intellectual history. Not only did it forcefully denounce the consequences Gogol's point of view might have for the future development of Russian society, but it explicitly stated the Westernizing intelligentsia's belief in the interconnection of material, political, and spiritual progress in the tradition of the eighteenth-century Enlightenment. Belinskii also dramatically restated his conviction that under prevailing conditions of Russian life, literature had to be *engagée* (on the side of right, of course) since an author had a special responsibility as leader and spokesman for his nation's better hopes. Belinskii's viewpoint on the primacy of social over esthetic criticism in literature was to remain predominant among the Russian intelligentsia until after the end of the nineteenth century.

Letter to N. V. Gogol

You are only partly right in saying that in my article you detect an "angry" [1] man: the adjective is too mild to describe the state I was in after reading your book. But you are not right at all when you ascribe my reaction to your admittedly not altogether flattering references to those who admire your talent. No, the reason was a more important one. An injury to one's pride is, after all, bearable, and I would have had the wit to pass the matter over in silence if that had been all there was to it; but an injury to one's sense of truth, one's sense of human dignity, is not to be borne, and one cannot remain silent when, under the cloak of religion and the protection of the knout, falsehood and immorality are being preached as truth and virtue.

Yes, I have loved you with all the passion with which a man who has a deep sense of kinship with his country can love its hope, its honor, and its glory, can love one of its great leaders on the road of self-awareness, growth, and progress. And you had reason enough to lose your equanimity, if only for a minute, when you lost the right to such a love. I say this not because I regard my love as a fitting reward of your great talent, but because in this I represent not myself alone, but a multitude of people, the great majority of whom neither you nor I have ever seen and who, in their turn, have never set eyes on you. I am incapable of giving you the slightest idea of the indignation which your book aroused in all noble minds, or of the howl of wild joy with which its appearance was greeted by all your enemies—both

---

[1] Belinskii refers to Gogol's remark: "I read your article about me in No. 2 of *Sovremennik* [The Contemporary] with sorrow—not because I was saddened by the public humiliation you wanted to inflict upon me, but because I could hear in it the voice of a man who was angry at me."

Translated by Valentine Snow from Vissarion Grigor'evich Belinskii, "Pis'mo k N. V. Gogoliu," in *Polnoe sobranie sochinenii*, Vol. X (Moscow, 1956), pp. 212–21. Belinskii's letter to Gogol, written on July 15, 1847, was first published by A. I. Herzen in the review *Poliarnaia zvezda* in 1855, in a faulty version (hundreds of handwritten copies of the letter had been circulated prior to publication). The notes have been adapted from those by K. P. Bogaevskaia in the Soviet edition.

those not concerned with literature (the Chichikovs, the Nozdrevs, the town mayors, and their sort[2]) and the men of letters, whose names you know well. You yourself must be well aware that even men who, one would have thought, are imbued with the same spirit as your book[3] have repudiated it. Even had it been written out of a deep and sincere conviction, it would still have made the same impression on the public. And if everyone (with the exception of a handful of people whom it is enough to see and know not to rejoice at their approval) saw in your book a clever but overdone trick for attaining purely earthly ends by divine means, the fault is yours alone.

This is not surprising in the least; what is surprising is that you should find it so. I believe the reason must be that you know Russia well only as an artist and not as a thinking man, a part which you so unsuccessfully assumed in your fantastic book. This is not to say that you are not a thinking man; but you have been accustomed for many years now to gaze at Russia from your "fair faraway retreat,"[4] and, as we all know, nothing is easier than to see objects from far away as we would like them to be. Living in that "fair faraway retreat" of yours, you remain a total stranger to Russia and live by and in yourself, or in a single-minded little coterie which shares your views and is unable to resist your influence.[5] Hence you have failed to notice that Russia sees her salvation not in mysticism, not in asceticism, not in pietism, but in the achievements of civilization, enlightenment, and humanitarianism. What she needs is neither sermons (of which she has heard enough!) nor prayers (she has mumbled enough of those!), but an awakening in her people of the sense of human dignity, which has been trampled down in mud and manure for so many centuries; she needs rights and laws conforming not to Church doctrine but to common sense and justice, and she needs to have them rigorously enforced. Instead, she offers the dreadful spectacle of a country in which men trade in men, without so much as the excuse invented by the wily American plantation owners who claim that a negro is not a human being; a country where people refer to themselves not by their proper names but by degrading nicknames such as Van'ka, Steshka, Vas'ka, Palashka; a country, finally, which not only affords no guarantees for personal safety, honor, and property but which cannot even maintain internal order and has nothing to show but vast corporations of office-holding thieves and robbers.

The most topical, the most vital national questions in Russia today are the abolition of serfdom, the repeal of corporal punishment, and the introduction, as far as possible, of the strictest possible application of at least those laws which are already on the books. Even the government itself is becoming aware of these things for it knows full well what the landowners

[2] Characters in Gogol's *Dead Souls* and *The Inspector General.*

[3] The reference is to the Slavophiles, particularly the Aksakov family.

[4] Quoted from *Dead Souls*, Chapter 9: "Russia, Russia, I see you, from my enchanting fair faraway retreat I see you"; an allusion to Gogol's lengthy stay abroad.

[5] In the late 1840's Gogol lived in Rome, where he associated largely with Russian mystics—A. O. Smirnova, the V'el'gorskii family, and others.

do to their peasants, and how many of the former have their throats cut by the latter every year), as is shown by its timid and futile half-measures in favor of our white "negroes" and the ludicrous replacement of the knout by a three-thonged whip.[6] These are the questions by which Russia is stirred in her apathetic half-sleep! And at such a time a great writer, one who has so powerfully stimulated Russia's self-awareness by his marvelously artistic, deeply true works, enabling her, as it were, to see herself in a looking glass, comes forward with a book in which he teaches the cruel landowner in the name of Christ and of the Church to squeeze more money out of his peasants, whom he curses as "unwashed brutes"! And you are surprised that I should be indignant? Why, if you had made a direct attempt on my life I could not hate you more than I do for those shameful lines!

And after this you expect people to believe in the sincerity of your book? No, if you were truly full of the wisdom of Christ and not of the devil's doctrine, it is not thus that you would have written to your landowning disciple. You would have written to him that since his peasants are his brothers in Christ, and since a brother cannot be his brother's slave, he must give them their freedom or, at the very least, make use of their labors in the way most advantageous to them, being aware in the depths of his own conscience of the falseness of his position vis-à-vis them. As for the expression: "Why, you unwashed mug!"[7]—what Nozdrev, what Sobakevich have you overheard using it, that you communicate it to the world as a great discovery with which to admonish and edify the Russian muzhiks, who do not wash for the very reason that, believing their masters, they do not regard themselves as human beings? And what about your concept of the national Russian court and the punishments it should mete out, the ideal of which you picked up from the stupid woman in Pushkin's tale,[8] in whose judgment the innocent and the guilty alike should be whipped? That is precisely what often is done in our country, although in most cases the innocent man alone is whipped if he is too poor to buy himself off—and is held guilty although he has committed no crime! And such a book is supposed to be the fruit of a difficult mental process, indicating a high degree of spiritual illumination! Never! Either you are sick, and must see a doctor at once, or—I dare not complete my thought.

Advocate of the knout, apostle of ignorance, champion of obscurantism and reactionary mysticism, eulogist of Tatar customs—what are you doing? Look at what is beneath your feet: you are standing on the brink of an abyss. That you should tie in your ideas with the Orthodox Church I can understand—it has ever been the support of the knout and the toady of

---

[6] Act on Criminal and Corrective Punishment (1845).

[7] Quoted from the article "The Russian Landowner," in which Gogol advises landowners to address "worthless" and "hard-drinking" peasants in some such fashion as: "Why, you unwashed brute! You're so covered with soot that your eyes barely show, yet you won't give honor where honor is due!"

[8] In Pushkin's novel *The Captain's Daughter,* the captain's wife orders an underling to look into a quarrel between two of her serfs: "See which of them is right and which is wrong. And punish them both."

despotism; but why do you bring in Christ? What do you think He has in common with any Church, and particularly the Orthodox Church? He was the first to teach men the ideals of liberty, equality, and fraternity, and He illustrated and proved the truth of His teaching by His martyrdom. And it was men's salvation only until a Church was organized around it, based on the principle of orthodoxy. The Church was a hierarchy, and hence a champion of inequality, a toady to power, an enemy and persecutor of brotherhood among men, and so it continues to be to this day. The true meaning of Christ's teaching was revealed by the philosophical movement of the last century. That is why a Voltaire, who used the weapon of mockery to put out the bonfires of fanaticism and ignorance in Europe, is certainly far more a son of Christ, flesh of His flesh and bone of His bone, than all your priests, bishops, metropolitans, and patriarchs, in the East as in the West. Can it be that you do not know this? It is no longer news to any high-school student.

Hence can it be that you, the author of *The Inspector General* and *Dead Souls,* have sincerely and from the heart eulogized the abominable Russian clergy, placing it far above the Catholic clergy? Let us suppose you do not know that the latter at least was something once, whereas the former has never been anything more than the servant and slave of worldly power; but can you really and truly not know that our clergy is held in general contempt by Russian society and the Russian people? About whom do the Russian people tell dirty stories? About the priest, his wife, his daughter, and his hired man. Whom do the Russian people call "the idiot breed," "cheats," "stud horses"? Their priests. Is not the Russian priest regarded by everyone as a symbol of gluttony, avarice, sycophancy, bawdiness? And still you are unaware of all this? Strange! According to you, the Russian people are the most religious people in the world; that is a lie! The basis of religious feeling is piety, awe, the fear of God. But the Russian speaks the name of God while scratching his posterior. He says of an ikon: "If it does some good, pray to it; if it doesn't, use it as a pot cover." Take a closer look, and you will see that the Russian people are deeply atheistic by nature. They still have many superstitions, but not a trace of religious feeling. Superstition dies away with the advances of civilization, but the religious feeling frequently persists; we have a living example in France, where there are still many fanatically devout Catholics among educated and cultured people, and where many others, having abandoned Christianity, nevertheless stubbornly believe in some sort of deity. The Russian people are different; mystical exaltation is foreign to them; they have too much common sense, lucidity, and firmness of mind: therein may be the pledge of their future historical greatness. Religious feeling has not taken root even among the Russian clergy, for a few isolated, extraordinary individuals given to a quiet, cold, ascetic kind of meditation prove nothing. The great majority of our priests have always been remarkable for their big bellies, their theological pedantry, and their incredible ignorance. It would be wrong to accuse them of religious intolerance and fanaticism; rather, they might be praised for exemplary indifferentism in matters of faith. True religious feeling in Russia has manifested itself only among the schismatics, who are so different in spirit from the great mass of the people and so insignificant numerically.

I shall not dwell on your panegyric of the love affair between the Russian people and their rulers. Let me say straight out that this panegyric pleased no one, and it lowered you in the esteem even of persons whose views in other respects are very close to yours. As for myself, I leave it to your conscience to enjoy the contemplation of the divine beauty of autocracy (it is a safe pursuit and, it is said, a profitable one for you); but please continue wisely to contemplate it from your "fair faraway retreat"; at close range it is neither so beautiful nor so harmless. I will only say this: When a European, especially a Catholic, becomes possessed by the religious spirit, he turns to denouncing unjust authority, like the Hebrew prophets, who denounced the great of the earth for flouting the law. In Russia, on the other hand, if a man (even a decent man) develops the illness known to the psychiatrists by the name of *religiosa mania,* he at once proceeds to burn more incense to the earthly god than to God in Heaven; what is more, he overdoes it to such an extent that much as the recipient would like to reward him for his slavelike devotion, he knows that by so doing he would compromise himself in the eyes of society. What scoundrels we Russians are!

It also occurs to me that in your book you affirm—as if it were a great and undeniable verity—that literacy is not only not good for common folk, but positively harmful. What can I say to this? May your Byzantine God forgive you for this Byzantine thought, provided that when you put it down in black and white you knew not what you did.

You may say to me: "Let us assume that I have erred and that all my ideas are false; but why am I denied the right to err, and why will no one believe in the sincerity of my errors?" Because, I would say in reply, such views are far from a novelty in Russia. Only a short time ago they were fully expounded by Burachok [9] and others of his ilk. Naturally, more intelligence and even talent is to be found in your book (although it does not abound in either) than in their writings; but on the other hand they developed the doctrine you hold in common more forcefully and more consistently, pursuing it boldly to its ultimate conclusion; they gave all to the Byzantine God, leaving nothing for Satan; whereas you, desirous of burning a candle to each, fell into a contradiction. Thus you defended Pushkin, literature, and the theater, which from your own point of view—had you had the integrity to be consistent—can do nothing to further the salvation of the soul, but may do much for its damnation. Now who could stomach the idea that Gogol and Burachok stand for the same thing? You have won too high a place for yourself in the esteem of the Russian public for it to be able to believe that you can be sincere in holding such convictions. What seems natural in fools cannot appear natural in a man of genius. Some people reached the conclusion that your book was the fruit of a mental derangement approaching actual insanity. But they soon gave up their notion, for it is obvious that your book took not a day, a week, or a month to write, but a year or possibly two or three years; it is coherent; a planned

[9] S. A. Burachok was the publisher of the progovernment review *Maiak* (The Beacon).

design shows through the careless writing; and the hosannas to the powers that be are meant to better the worldly situation of the pious author. That is why it was rumored in St. Petersburg that you wrote this book with the aim of being appointed tutor to the son of the heir to the throne. Even earlier, the contents of your letter to Uvarov became known in St. Petersburg—the letter in which you say with sorrow that your writings are being misconstrued in Russia, in which you next express dissatisfaction with your earlier works, and in which you declare that you will be satisfied with your books only when he who, etc.[10] Judge for yourself, now—is it surprising that your book should have lowered you in the public esteem as a writer and, still more, as a man?

As far as I can see, you do not rightly understand the Russian public. Its mood results from the condition of Russian society, in which fresh forces are on the rise and trying to break through, but, being brutally repressed and unable to find an outlet, cause only despondency, apathy, and gloom. Only in literature, despite our Tatar censorship, is there any life and progress left. That is why the calling of writer is held in such respect in our society, and why it is so easy to achieve literary success, given even a modicum of talent. The title of poet, the calling of man of letters have long ago acquired a greater luster in our society than the tinsel glitter of epaulettes and motley uniforms. That is why any so-called liberal tendency is so richly rewarded by general attention in Russia even in the absence of any marked talent, and why great poets so quickly lose their popularity once they decide, sincerely or insincerely, to serve Orthodoxy, Autocracy, and Nationalism. A striking example is afforded by Pushkin, who had only to write two or three loyal poems and don the livery of a Gentleman of the Bedchamber in order suddenly to forfeit the people's love. You are greatly mistaken if you seriously think that your book failed not because of its pernicious thesis but because of the unpleasant truths which you presumably told us all. I am willing to assume that you could have had this idea about professional scribblers, but how could the cap fit the general public? Do you think that you told it less bitter, less unpalatable truths, and with less realism and talent, in *The Inspector General* and *Dead Souls?* It really was furiously angry at you then, but just the same *The Inspector General* and *Dead Souls* did not fail, whereas your latest book was a most dismal failure. And the public is right: it holds the Russian writers to be its only leaders, its only defenders and saviours from the black night of Autocracy, Orthodoxy, and Nationalism, and hence it is always ready to forgive a writer for a bad book, but never for a pernicious one. This shows how much fresh and healthy feeling, even though it is still embryonic, there is in our society; it also shows that our society has a future. If you love Russia, rejoice with me at the failure of your book!

Allow me to tell you, not without a touch of smugness, that I believe I

---

[10] "You will be satisfied with your books only when he who, etc." refers not to a passage in Gogol's letter to Uvarov but to a draft of an official letter which Gogol intended to send to Nicholas I.

know the Russian public a little. Your book frightened me because I thought it might have a bad effect on the government and on the censors, but not on the public. When the rumor swept through St. Petersburg that the government wanted to print many thousands of copies of your book and sell them for next to nothing, my friends were despondent; but I told them even then that, no matter what, the book would not be successful and would soon be forgotten. And indeed, it is now remembered for all the articles that were written about it rather than for itself. The Russian has a deep, even if undeveloped, instinct for truth.

Your conversion may, I suppose, have been sincere, but to bring it to public notice was a most unfortunate idea. The days of naive piety have long since passed even in our society. We have come to realize that it makes no difference where one prays, and that only those seek Christ in Jerusalem who never had Him in their hearts, or lost Him.[11] He who can suffer at the sight of the suffering of others, who is pained at the spectacle of utter strangers being oppressed, has Christ in his heart and need not go to Jerusalem on foot. The humility you preach is not new to begin with; besides, it smacks of overweening pride on the one hand, and, on the other, of a most shameful surrender of human dignity. The idea of attaining a sort of abstract perfection, of rising through humility above everyone else, can only be dictated by pride or imbecility, and in either case it must inevitably lead to hypocrisy, sanctimoniousness, and empty ritualism. In addition, you have descended to using cynically low language not only about others (that would have been merely uncivil), but about yourself, and that is disgusting: for whereas a man who slaps another in the face arouses indignation, a man who slaps himself in the face provokes contempt. No! You have been plunged into darkness rather than enlightened; you have understood neither the spirit nor the form of contemporary Christianity. What is to be found in your book is not a revelation of the Christian doctrine, but a morbid fear of death, hell, and the devil. And what language, what expressions! "What limp rags and rubbish ye are all become!" Can you really think that by saying "ye are" instead of "you have" you achieve a biblical style? It is a great truth that when a man gives himself over to falsehood, his intelligence and talent forsake him! If your book did not bear your name, and if the passages in which you speak of yourself as a writer were omitted, who would think that this pompous and untidy jumble of words and phrases had come from the pen of the author of *The Inspector General* and *Dead Souls?*

As for me personally, I repeat: You are wrong in thinking that my article reflected my irritation with you because of your comments about me as one of your critics. Had that been all that had angered me, I would have reacted to that point alone with irritation, and dealt with everything else calmly and impartially. But it is true that your remarks about your admirers are doubly reprehensible. I can understand the need to discourage a fool who

[11] In the preface to his book Gogol announced that he intended to make a pilgrimage to Jerusalem.

by his ecstatic praise of me only makes me ridiculous; but that need is painful, because it is somehow humanly embarrassing to repay even a mistaken love with hostility. But you had in mind men who, even if they were not of the highest intelligence, were yet no fools. These men, in their amazed delight, may have done more ecstatic exclaiming about your works than solid analysis of them; and yet the enthusiasm you aroused in them came from so pure and noble a source that you surely should not have delivered them to their and your common enemies, accusing them into the bargain of deliberately misconstruing your writings. I understand, of course, that you did this because you were carried away by the thesis of your book and through lack of foresight; but Viazemskii, that prince among the aristocracy and lackey in literature, developed your thought and published a veritable denunciation of your admirers (myself foremost among them). He probably did it out of gratitude to you for having promoted him, a pitiful versifier, to a great poet—apparently, if I remember rightly, for his "flabby verse that drags along the ground." [12] All this is not good! That you were merely biding your time until you were in a position to pay their just due to the admirers of your talent (having with proud humility paid it to your enemies) I did not know, could not have known, and, truth to tell, would not have cared to know. What I had before me was your book, not your intentions. I read and reread it a hundred times, and I could still see nothing but what was in it; and what was in it I found repellent and deeply offensive.

If I were to give free rein to my feelings, this letter would fill a thick notebook. I never meant to write to you on this subject, although I ached to do it and although you have publicly invited each and every one to write to you without hesitation, being concerned only with the truth. Living in Russia, I would have been unable to do it, for the local Shpekins [13] open other people's letters not merely for their private pleasure but in the line of duty, to be able to inform on the writers. But a case of consumption, which developed this summer, drove me abroad, and N. forwarded your letter to me in Salzbrunn, whence I am going this very day with An[nenkov] to Paris via Frankfurt-am-Main. [14] The unexpected receipt of your letter allowed me to tell you all I have been holding against you because of your book. I cannot say things by halves, nor can I dissemble—that is not my nature. If you or time itself should prove to me that I was mistaken in my conclusions concerning you, I would be the first to rejoice, but I would not regret having told you what I have. What is at stake is not my person or yours, but something immeasurably higher than myself, and even than you; what is at stake is truth, Russian society, and Russia herself. Here is the very

[12] This is a reference to an article by P. A. Viazemskii, "Iazykov i Gogol," which appeared in 1847 and in which Viazemskii, an old enemy of Belinskii's, accused the critic of spreading revolutionary ideas. Belinskii misquotes Gogol slightly; the actual line is: ". . . that heavy verse of Viazemskii's, which seems to drag along the ground and which is fraught at times with a bitter, stinging Russian sadness."

[13] Shpekin, a character from *The Inspector General*, is a postmaster who enjoys opening other people's letters.

[14] N. probably refers to the poet N. A. Nekrasov.

last thing I have to say: having had the misfortune with haughty humility to repudiate your truly great works, you must now with true humility disown your latest book, and redeem the heinous sin of having published it by producing new writings which will remind us of your earlier ones.

Salzbrunn, July 15, 1847

13.

Nikolai Aleksandrovich Dobroliubov

1836-1861

While the Slavophiles had based their ideas on the primacy of the Christian spirit, the generation that came to maturity in the middle of the nineteenth century turned to the natural sciences, especially biology, for the formulation of their views. Tired of what they considered the lofty and essentially idle discussions of their predecessors, the young members of the intelligentsia in the 1850's hoped to find in the discoveries of science the inspiration and guidelines for useful action in a Russia that was finally beginning to change after the long freeze of Nicholas I's reign. Using critical essays and book reviews as their vehicle, they felt that their first task was to acquaint the Russian reading public with Western scientific knowledge. The books that served as pretext for their critical essays (such as those mentioned in Dobroliubov's review) have been justly forgotten. It was not the contents of second-rate scientific popularizations that influenced the history of Russian thought but rather the use the Russian intellegentsia made of them to provide the sanction of scientific evidence for their own moral and social ideals and their critique of contemporary Russian society.

For a brief time Nikolai Aleksandrovich Dobroliubov was perhaps the most energetic and influential of the young social critics. Continuing the line of approach developed by Belinskii toward the end of his life but not shying away from its logical conclusion, Dobroliubov questioned the traditions, aspirations, and educational practices which had helped to shape the idealistic attitudes of the intelligentsia of the previous generation. As he could not state his most extreme ideas explicitly because of Russian censorship, he had to express them in allusions ("Aesopian language"). The present article should therefore be read as more than merely an exposition of simple physiological facts and pedagogical views; Dobroliubov was concerned not so much with the education of children according to the most modern principles of bodily and mental hygiene as with the transformation of Russian society itself.

Those who had come from the lower classes—many, like Dobroliubov, were sons of priests—held in contempt the intelligentsia of an earlier generation who had not made more of their privileged position in society. Man and society were the products of purposeful struggle, of the triumph of will and mind over inert matter and slothful traditions. Education, properly understood and based on "scientific" evidence, was but another form of this struggle and helped the individual in developing his will and his physical and mental energy. This was the essential message of Nihilism, of which Dobroliubov was a leading exponent during his short life.

The Organic Development of Man in Connection with His Mental and Spiritual Activities

Both the works mentioned [1] appeared in Russian rather long ago but, we think, did not attract particular attention on the part of the Russian public. And yet these two books are really remarkable, especially for us, who have been misled by the high-flown theories of learned pedagogues who say such things about the spiritual development of man as to make one's hair stand on end. Thus Schnell, without resorting to any subtle theorizing, says bluntly that "the supreme object of education should be the cultivation of sound health." He commences his book with this definition and ends with it, and it runs consistently through all sections of his work. Dr. Bock also affirms that the most important thing in education is concern for health, the constant exercise of all the senses, and their adjustment to diverse impressions.

There can be no doubt that Schnell's definition, being extremely simple, will at once be understood by every reader. But there can be no doubt also

---

[1] The two German books reviewed, which had recently been translated into Russian, were K. F. Schnell, *Organicheskoe vospitanie v primenenii k samoobrazovaniiu i k razvitiiu zdorov'ia pitomtsev* (Organic Education Applied to Self-Education and to the Cultivation of Health), trans. F. Böhmer (St. Petersburg, 1857) and Dr. K. E. Bock, *Kniga o zdorovom i bol'nom cheloveke* (A Book on the Healthy and Sick Man), trans. J. Paulsen and F. Böhmer (St. Petersburg, 1857).—Editor.

Translated by J. Fineberg from N. A. Dobroliubov, *Selected Philosophical Essays* (Moscow, Foreign Languages Publishing House, 1948), pp. 72–103. Reprinted with minor changes. Originally titled "Organicheskoe razvitie cheloveka v sviazi s ego umstvennoi i nravstvennoi deiatel'nost'iv," the essay was first published in *Sovremennik* (The Contemporary), No. 5 (1858). Words and phrases unfinished in the manuscript have been supplied in angular brackets (⟨ ⟩).

that many will hasten to interpret it in a very limited sense and, as a consequence, will hurl well-intentioned ridicule at Bock and Schnell, as well at us, who regard this as a very sensible principle. "Your idea is not new," we shall be told with biting irony. "You have the honor of sharing it with Madame Prostakova, with Mr. Skotinin,[2] and with the parents of Pan Khalyavsky,[3] whom Osnovyanenko describes—and, in general, with all the mamas and papas who regard the word *education* as being synonymous with *fattening*. Unfortunately, your theory that the *object of education should be sound health* still has many advocates among the dying generation of provincial grandmothers, aunties, and nurses, who welcome their wards on returning home from the university with the words: 'Good Lord, how they have tortured you there! It was a pleasure to look at you when you went away. But you are as thin as a matchstick now! That's the result of your accursed education!' Your idea will gladden the hearts of all the numbskulls who learn nothing until they are fifteen, but whose faces are as ruddy as apples because they do nothing from morning till night," and so on and so forth.

In answer to all these arguments raised by our enlightened opponents we can say that not every ailment emaciates a man, and not all stoutness is a sign of good health. We ask them to remember the poetic complaint of the corpulent old fellow who asserts that people

> From the immensity of my girth
> Get a wrong impression of my worth—

not knowing that

> Though so robust in appearance,
> With rosy cheeks and belly round,
> Against cruel fate I have a grievance,
> For my health is far from sound.

Yes, the mistake Madame Prostakova and her ilk made was not that they were concerned about the health of their children, but that they did not know what good health was. Mother stuffs her Mitrofanushka [4] with food. For example, she gives him ten slices of pork and five or six griddlecakes for supper. He goes to bed and tosses about all night and in the morning goes around in a daze. Is this sound health? If sound health means that the functions of vegetable life can proceed in a man unhindered, and that his body does not know the constant feeling of acute pain, then, perhaps, one may agree that all fat idiots are absolutely healthy. But in that case a man afflicted with paralysis and also one who is suffering from delirium tremens must also be regarded as healthy. We, however, regard both as sick men, and

---

[2] Prostakova and Skotinin are characters in Fonvizin's comedy *The Hobbledehoy*.—Translator.

[3] Hero of the historical novel of the same title by the Ukrainian author Kvitko-Osnovyanenko.—Translator.

[4] Mitrofanushka, a pampered little boy, is the principal character in *The Hobbledehoy*.—Translator.

very sick men at that. More than that, we also regard as sick, or at all events not quite healthy, a man who constantly suffers from hysteria, spasms, migraine, all sorts of nervous disorders, etc. Afflictions of all kinds such as deafness, blindness, etc., must also be included in the category of sicknesses. And this applies also to the special, abnormal conditions in which some people find themselves, such as, for example, insomnia, or apathy toward everything, complete loss of memory, all sorts of monomanias, general debility, incapacity for any effort of will, etc. In short, sound health must not be regarded merely as the external soundness of the body, but as the natural harmonious development of the entire organism in general, and the correct performance of all its functions.

This too may be challenged, and on fairly good grounds. Reference may be made to the lower class of the people, who are usually of better physical health than the upper classes; reference may be made to savages who enjoy perfect health and possess enormous physical strength; on the other hand, reference may be made to numerous great scholars, poets, and statesmen who are emaciated, sick, and feeble. From this comparison a conclusion may be drawn which at first sight may seem to have some grounds: if the entire development of a man is directed toward the sole purpose of making him healthy, then we should take as ideal the Iroquois, who, it is said, have no knowledge of sickness in any form, and deny all importance to great men who are famous for their mental and spiritual activities.

If this objection is closely examined, however, it will be rejected as absolutely unsound, and for many reasons. First of all we must repeat that by a healthy organism we do not mean only the physical fitness of the body. We regard as ridiculous and pitiful the ignorant claims of crude materialism, which degrades the lofty mission of the spiritual side of man by arguing that a man's soul consists of some kind of very fine matter. The absurdity of these arguments has been proved so long ago and so irrefutably—they so thoroughly contradict the findings of the natural sciences—that at the present time only the most backward and ignorant can still withhold their contempt for them. We do not wish to say that bodily activity is more important than spiritual, nor do we wish to present physical pleasure as our sole object in life. On the contrary, we want to say that our bodies, as an instrument that serves spiritual activity, are often spoiled by various weaknesses and ailments and are unable to fulfill their functions. We protest against the fact that often we only pay lip service to spiritual improvement, but in practice we do not try to subjugate the body to the spirit; abandoning ourselves to sensuousness, we derange our bodies and do not allow our spiritual faculties to manifest themselves properly; for the deranged organs of the body become unfit to serve lofty spiritual activity. This is proved by constant experience, it is proved by our inner consciousness, by our faith; and it is confirmed by the results of modern research in natural history. It is this truth, which has even become threadbare from frequent repetition, the truth that *mens sana,* a sound mind, must be *in corpore sano,* in a sound body, that we intend to prove by pointing to the indisputable facts of natural history. And it is in this sense that all our observations on the inseverable connection between spiritual and bodily activity must be understood.

But let us return to the objection mentioned above. In addition to its one-sided and narrow conception of health, it is fallacious also because it compares objects under not altogether equal conditions. Difference of race and difference in occupation exercise considerable influence on a man's potential degree of development in all respects. If we could take health in the abstract, there would be no need for us to refer to human beings; we could quote the example of animals. Where will you find a stronger and healthier organism than in the elephant, or the lion, or even in the ox? It is not for nothing that the saying goes: "He's as strong as an ox." But the very structure of the organism of these animals differs from ours, and we shall therefore leave them alone. There are worms which can be cut in half, and the two halves will crawl in different directions as if nothing had happened; but we cannot take these as examples. Nor can the Iroquois serve as an example for European scientists. Moreover, it must be observed that sickness did not, of course, facilitate the useful discoveries and researches of these scientists. In the majority of cases sickness did not affect the organs needed for their specialties (we may quote Beethoven as an exception, but his hearing was not so badly affected at the time he composed his finest works); in this case local afflictions must be left out of account.[5] Byron, of course, was lame, but that did not prevent him from being a great poet; similarly, weak sight was not a hindrance to many great scientists, philosophers, and so forth. But everybody will agree, of course, that external injury can least of all be called a sickness of the organism. On the other hand, everybody will agree that every morbid sensation in the body will, for a moment at least, disturb our spiritual activity, and that consequently if great scientists were absolutely sound in health they would do even more than they do when they suffer from various ailments.

It is said that the contrary is the case, that sometimes bodily sickness stimulates greater spiritual activity. Many examples are quoted. Several poets are mentioned who became conscious of their talents and revealed it to the world after they had become blind. Here, of course, Homer and Milton are brought up, and Pushkin's lines to the blind Russian poet are quoted:

> Bard, when the mundane world
> Vanished before thee in gloom
> Thy genius awakened in a flash,[6] etc.

Reference is also made to Ignatius Loyola, who, when he was sick, heard the call to form his order; to Mohammed, who heard the call of Allah during fits of epilepsy; to the ascetics whose visions occurred as a result of

---

[5] Actually, Beethoven produced his finest works in the last years of his life, when he was stone deaf.—Translator.

[6] From Pushkin's poem "To Kozlov," the blind poet.—Translator.

the torments to which they subjected the flesh, etc. Thousands of examples could be quoted on this subject; and cases in which the antagonism between the spiritual and physical nature of man is revealed are also numerous. But in all this perplexity reigns. At first the crude materialists were to blame for this, but later, the dreamy idealists, in refuting the former, committed the same error. We intend to dwell on this in greater detail because we think that an explanation of precisely this point is most essential to convince one of the importance of a healthy organism not only for the bodily but also for the spiritual activities of man.

We shall begin by saying that it is quite natural and inevitable that a man should note the antagonism between objects as soon as his consciousness is awakened. As long as we fail to note the difference between objects, we exist unconsciously. The first act of consciousness is that we distinguish ourselves from the other objects in the world. This very distinction that we draw contains a contrast, and the more we recognize our own independent existence the stronger this contrast becomes. Regarding himself as something separate from everything else, man must necessarily arrive at the conclusion that he has a right to live and act by himself, to live a separate and independent life. Actually, however, he constantly meets with insurmountable obstacles in the pursuit of his own strivings, and, realizing his impotence, but not yet clearly realizing his connection with the universal laws of nature, he places himself in opposition to the latter. It seems to him that there are certain forces in nature hostile to man and constantly fighting him. Gradually, this gives rise to the conception of dark forces which are constantly doing man harm. And yet once man has already distinguished himself from nature he cannot help observing also her beneficial forces, and thus, simultaneously with the conception of dark forces, there arises the conception of light and benign forces which protect man. This marks the beginning of that dualism which we find at the basis of all natural religions; Vishnu and Siva, Ormuzd and Ariman, Belbog and Chernobog [White God and Black God], etc., etc., are the personifications of man's original conceptions of the forces of nature. Later on in man's development, as he acquired more experience, the general idea split up into numerous separate ideas, which were applied to every single phenomenon. Thus arose the conception of the conflict between light and darkness, warmth and cold, sea and land, ⟨the earth and the pagan heaven⟩, etc. Finally, man turned from the external world to himself, and he gradually became conscious of a conflict between certain antagonistic impulses within his own nature. Unable as yet to grasp the idea of universal unity and harmony, he also assumed the existence within himself, as well as in nature, of different, mutually hostile principles. In his search for their origin, still almost completely under the influence of the impressions of the external world, he did not hesitate to ascribe their origin to the hostile forces that he has already noted in nature. Discovering within himself certain vague strivings, a certain discontent with the external, he naturally concluded that within him there exists a special being, superior to that which revealed itself in his external activities. Hence the conclusion that there are two hostile beings in man—one springing from the element of good, the inner and higher element, and the other created by the evil, the external, coarse, and dark force.

Thus arose that gloomy conception of the body as the prison of the soul which existed among the peoples before they adopted Christianity. Under Christianity the ancient dualism gradually began to disappear and, to some extent, to lose its potency in the public mind. But the scholastics of the Middle Ages were reluctant to abandon the old concepts, and so they clutched at dualism as an inexhaustible source of dialectical controversy. Indeed—what would there be to argue about if everything were so simple, natural, and harmonious? Far better that there should be two principles, two forces, two opposite propositions, with which, armed cap-à-pie with sophistries, one could enter the arena of idle dialectics. It was these very wise scholastics who retarded the progress of general common sense, which, of course, should have understood long ago that the final object of knowledge is not struggle but conciliation, not antagonism but unity. The scholastics of the Middle Ages tried to separate the soul from the body, and, looking upon it as a being that was totally alien to the body, they began to speculate on the question as to how the soul combined with the body. In ancient times Aristotle also pondered over this question, but he, of course, could be pardoned for this. He imagined that the body was crude matter and that the soul was also matter, but of a very fine texture, and, consequently, the question he raised might be to some extent understood in the chemical sense. This explains the origin of his excellent theory of *influxus physicus,* with which he explained the connection between the soul and the body. The scholastics of the Middle Ages could not subscribe to Aristotle's assumption concerning the material nature of the soul. They were all Christians; most of them belonged to the clergy, and all believed in the spirituality and immortality of the soul, and yet they discussed a question which could have arisen only on the basis of Aristotle's assumption. How did the soul combine with the body? they asked. What place does it occupy in the body? By what means is pain inflicted on the body conveyed to the soul? Through what channels are thoughts and the desires of the will conveyed to the body? In asking these questions the scholastics failed to understand that in regarding the soul as an ideal being mechanically introduced into the body they were themselves dropping into the crudest materialism. If the soul occupies a definite place in the body, then, of course, it is material; if it combines with the body through certain external connections, we arrive at the same inevitable conclusion. To this error was added another, also pagan, that the body was under the influence of an evil force, through which all impurities enter the soul. On the basis of this contention the ascetics of the Middle Ages even excelled the Indians in the cruel and bloody torments they inflicted upon themselves in their religious frenzy. The degree of madness reached by them in the endeavor to subdue the flesh is known. And we also know how many witches and how many unfortunate people who were said to be "possessed" were burned to death at that time owing to the conviction that the devil had entered their bodies. . . .

In our days the successes achieved by the natural sciences, which have already rid us of many prejudices, have enabled us to form a sounder and simpler idea of the relation between man's spiritual and corporeal activities. Anthropology has clearly proved to us, first of all, that all our efforts to picture to ourselves an abstract spirit bereft of all material qualities, or positively to determine its nature, have always been, and always will be, absolutely fruitless. Science has also explained that all man's activities can be noted only to the extent that they are revealed in corporeal, external manifestations, and consequently that we can judge of the activities of the soul only by their manifestations in the body. At the same time we have learned that the simple substances that enter into the composition of our bodies have no separate existence of their own; consequently, the vitality we reveal depends not on this or that substance, but on a certain combination of all of them. With this precise knowledge it was now impossible to adhere to crude, blind materialism, which regarded the soul as a minute piece of the finest ethereal matter; it now became impossible to raise questions concerning the organic life of man in the way they were raised by the ancient pagan philosophers and by the scholastics of the Middle Ages. A broader and clearer view was needed; it was necessary to bring about unity in what hitherto had been deliberately separated; it became necessary to generalize what had hitherto been pictured as separate ⟨disconnected⟩ parts. This elevation of apparent contradictions to natural unity is the great service rendered by modern science. Modern science alone refuted the scholastic dualist conception of man and began to study him as a complete, undivided whole, corporeal and spiritual, without attempting to separate the two. It discerned in the soul the force which permeates and inspires the whole of man's body. Guided by this conception, science today no longer regards corporeal activities separately from spiritual, and vice versa. On the contrary, in all, even the most minute, corporeal phenomena science discerns the action of the same force, which unconsciously takes part in the formation of blood, the assimilation of food, etc., and reaches the heights of consciousness in the functions of the nervous system, and mainly of the brain. Distinguished for its simplicity and for the truthful explanation it gives of the facts of life, in harmony with the highest Christian conception of man's personality as an independent individual, the view of true science is superior in still another respect. It establishes beyond doubt the truth that the soul unites with the body not by means of external connections, that it has not been accidentally introduced into the body and does not occupy a certain corner in it, but necessarily, firmly, and inseparably merges with it, completely permeates it; that without it, without this inspiring force, it is impossible to conceive of the living human organism ⟨and vice versa⟩.

Once one understands this view, it is not difficult to understand in what sense sound health may be accepted as the supreme object of a man's development. If all spiritual activity inevitably manifests itself in external symbols, and if the organs of our body necessarily serve as the instruments of its manifestations, it is clear that the proper manifestation of spiritual activity needs properly developed and healthy organs. Much as he would like to heed good advice and see good examples, a blind and deaf man can no more fulfill his wish than a legless man can walk, a dumb man speak, and so forth. Similarly, if our nerves are deranged we cannot be calm and patient; if our brain is affected we cannot reason well, and so forth. In all these cases we are unhealthy, although we do not feel any acute physical pain. Nor can we call an organism a healthy one in which one side is developed too much at the expense of the other. Thus, an organism in which the development of the cerebral functions absorbs everything else develops abnormally, morbidly. Also abnormal is the development of the organism in which the development of the nervous system, and of the brain in particular, is restricted and stunted by intense muscular activity. In this respect, therefore, pale, emaciated, overeducated children, as well as savages who possess enormous physical strength but are coarse and uneducated, are both one-sidedly developed, and this one-sidedness may be called the organism's lack of complete sound health.

This, of course, does not in the least prevent the proper functioning of those organs which are properly developed, although it prevents the development of complete harmony in the organism. That is why we always see so much feverishness and convulsiveness in the activities of enthusiasts whose feelings and imaginations predominate over their reason. That is why the intelligence of people who spend all their lives in physical labor is so limited and dull; animal health is not enough for man; he needs human health, health in which the development of the body will not hinder but will facilitate the development of the soul. When that is not the case we get one-sided, unhealthy development, in the course of which—quite naturally—the morbid state of some organs stimulates others to intensified activity. Strictly speaking, every ailment may be defined as a disturbance of the proper relation between the parts that make up our organism. Consequently the fact, for example, that the imagination is heightened when the body is exhausted by disease does not contradict but rather confirms the general harmony of the organism. It has long been noted that nature tries to compensate man for defects in some organs by greater perfection in others. Thus, the blind are gifted with good hearing and touch, the deaf frequently enjoy very good sight, and so forth. The same thing must occur in the activities performed through the medium of the brain. The less other activities are developed, the more the brain activities will be developed. Thus, loss of sight necessarily compels the blind man to drop certain public occupations and, in addition, deprives him of the opportunity of obtaining new impressions through his eyes. It is quite natural that, finding himself in such a state, a blind man will turn to his subjective world and begin to analyze the impressions he received in the past. Similarly, a Loyola might mentally draw up the grandest of plans in spite of his physical weakness during convalescence. This is very natural: it is well known that the enfeeblement of the body as a consequence of prolonged starvation ends in delirium, and, in general, delirium most often appears in sicknesses which exhaust the organism. In such phenomena we should discern harmony rather than antagonism.

By treating man as a single whole, as an indivisible being, as a true individual, we eliminate the innumerable contradictions that the scholastics found between corporeal and spiritual activity. It goes without saying that if a man were dissected we would find a host of irreconcilable contradictions, as we would find in everything else under such circumstances. What would happen if, for example, we set out to find what part of a violin contains the sounds that it emits—the strings, the bridge, the sound holes, or the top? What amusing arguments the attempt to settle this question, which by its very nature cannot be settled, would lead to! Something of the same kind happened to the scholastics who tried to contrast the body to the spirit. How can the soul rejoice when the body feels pain? they asked. How can the soul fail to note an object when the eyes are looking at it? How can the soul fail to feel cold when the hand touches a warm object directly after a hot one? etc. The contradictions were endless, and from them the scholastics— without any grounds, incidentally—drew a rather curious conclusion, viz., that the soul in man was quite separate from the body; one functioned in accordance with its own laws and the other in accordance with its own quite different laws. Absurd as this conclusion was, it was accepted on faith for a long time until the results achieved by the natural sciences helped to determine more precisely the organic nature of man. Now nobody has any doubts that all efforts to draw a line of demarcation between the spiritual and corporeal functions of man are useless, and human knowledge can never achieve this. We cannot learn of the existence of internal activity without material manifestation, and the material manifestation takes place in the body. Is it possible to separate an object from its characteristics? And what remains of an object if we destroy our conception of all its properties and characteristics? We get an absolutely simple and logical explanation of the apparent antagonism within human nature when we treat man simply as a united, indivisible organism. Then the fact, for example, that we sometimes look and do not see is very simply explained. Vision is not merely the reflection of the visible object in our eyes; the main thing here is that the visual nerve should be irritated and convey the impression of the object to the brain. The seat of vision, as of all our senses, is in the brain; if, for example, the eye nerve is severed, objects will be reflected in the eye as before, but we shall not see them. Hence, there is nothing strange in the fact that when our mind is occupied with important thoughts, i.e., when intense activity is going on in the brain, the feeble irritation of the visual nerve, sensitive enough in other cases, now becomes inadequate and fails to make the brain conscious of it. But as soon as the irritation of the nerve becomes too strong our attention is at once diverted from the subject of our thoughts and turns to the object which caused the irritation. In the same natural way physiology explains all the contradictions invented by the scholastics, who, unbeknown to themselves, dropped into extremely crude materialism.

After these preliminary explanations we believe the reader is no longer left in perplexity as to what we mean by the healthy development of the organism, and why we attach so much importance to it. Generally speaking, it has become the custom in our days to echo the high-flown utterances of the poets, to complain about the materialism and the practical trend of the age. But we think that physicians and physiologists have far more grounds for complaining about the one-sided and shortsighted idealism of our times. Indeed, look at the contempt with which we regard physical labor, and what little attention we devote to the exercise of physical strength. True, we love beauty, litheness, and grace, but here too our contempt for the simple and healthy development of the organism often finds expression. Often we like to see the dreamy, transcendental expression in faces, and the pallor that is "the sign of melancholy"; in bodily structure we like the waist that can be embraced with one arm, and as for small hands and feet, that goes without saying. There is nothing positively bad in all this; it cannot be asserted that a large foot is nicer than a small one; but still our preference, which is based not on the conception of the symmetrical development of all organs of the human body but on some unaccountable caprice, is proof of a one-sided, false idealism. Muscular, strongly developed arms and legs awaken in us thoughts of physical labor, which, as is well known, develops these members, and this is what we do not like. On the other hand, small, dainty hands show that the lady or gentleman who possesses them is not engaged in coarse toil but in some gentler activity. And this is exactly what we want. We are constantly betraying a distorted idealism. For example, we are very stern in our strictures of the conduct of other people and are very much inclined to demand that everybody should be the incarnation of virtue. Only very rarely do we pay any attention to a man's condition, to the circumstances of his life, to various mitigating circumstances (but very often we say with amazing heroism: "He told a lie; that's enough: I think he is a dishonest man"). Well, is this not an idealistic line of thought? What about our pleasures? We organize charity balls, charity lotteries, noble theatrical performances, also for charitable objects: can one fail to discern in this lofty strivings alien to material calculation? We admire all the arts and say that the strains of Verdi's operas and Kalam's landscapes attune us to something lofty, pure, and ideal. As a matter of fact, all this perhaps merely conceals the pleasant satisfaction felt by the organs of hearing and vision and perhaps even a desire to drive off ennui; but we do not confess this, and so our striving after some ideal finds expression. We are ashamed to see things as they really are; we always try to beautify, ennoble them, and often take up a burden too heavy for us to carry. Who of us has not sometimes tried to give a shade of heroism, magnanimity, or subtle wit to our simplest action, sometimes performed quite casually? Who has not adorned in the rosy colors of idealism the ordinary and very intelligible desire for a woman? And finally, how many educated people—we have our readers in mind—have spoken confidently and sometimes even with rapture about Homer and Shakespeare, perhaps about Beethoven, and Raphael and his Madonna, and yet, in their heart of hearts, have not understood what they were talking about? No, say what you like, the desire to play the idealist is very strong in us. The physicians and naturalists have "good reason" for their reproaches.

But in no sphere is this false and sterile idealism so clearly expressed and does it do so much harm as in the sphere of education. In what circles do we see any concern for adjusting education to the individual organism of a child? In what circles is education by demonstration commenced with children at an early age? Who seeks for his children a healthy development of their organism instead of the inculcation of all sorts of abstractions, often of a freakish kind? In the old days people loved to fatten their children; today they starve them so that they shall not become fat and stupid. In the old days education was not commenced until the child had reached the age of fifteen, as much as to say: let the children romp a little longer, school will not run away. Today, however, children are not allowed to romp; they are compelled to sit still and learn their lessons. There was a time when children were sent to bed early so as not to weary themselves, and they slept nearly twelve hours a day. Today, however, children are compelled to pore over their lessons until their heavy heads sink on their desks. Even a two-year-old boy has the prospect of going to school dinned into his head, and at five, and sometimes even earlier, attempts are made to knock into his head lofty ideas about his mission in life—to be an architect, an engineer, a general, a lawyer, and so forth. Perhaps this conceals within itself the crudest form of materialism, but its results are by no means beneficial for the child's physical health and development. Today it is by no means rare to find a mother who with pride and secret self-satisfaction relates how her son did not sleep at night, lost his appetite, and became as thin and dry as a matchstick during the period of his examinations. Needless to say, to take pride in one's children's diligence and love of knowledge is extremely praiseworthy—but we are sorry for the children.

One cannot fail to note a pseudoidealistic trend combined with neglect of the organic development of children in their subsequent education. For example, parents would like their son to become a famous general. They realize, of course, that this object cannot be attained if their child should die, and so they try to guard him from death, that is to say, they do not permit him to romp and play, they safeguard him against colds and draughts, muffle him up, keep him on a medical diet, and so forth. The child is, of course, feeble and sick, but he is safeguarded against accidental illnesses, although not always. The time to go to school arrives, and at once tales of heroic deeds and great historical examples are dinned into the child's head. Weakness and cowardice are shameful, he is told; he must always be brave and cool-headed. Such were Leonidas of Sparta, Alexander of Macedon, Julius Caesar, and so forth. Look at the hardships Suvorov went through; look what dangers Napoleon faced; this is what Mucius Scaevola, Horatius Cocles, etc., etc., performed. The praiseworthy qualities and feats of these gentlemen and the eloquent admonitions of the parents create a strong impression on the child. He is ready to go to war and perform miracles of valor right now. But *right now*, unfortunately, he cannot even go into the garden because it rained yesterday and the ground is still damp. The boy would also be delighted to emulate Mucius Scaevola, but he is checked by the recollection of the hubbub that was raised all over the house a day or two before when the future hero dropped some hot wax on his finger when sealing a letter. He himself roared so loudly that he was heard all down the street, his mother swooned, a doctor was hastily sent for, his finger was bandaged, and the hero was kept in bed for two days. And so the boy realizes that it is rather difficult to become a Mucius Scaevola, and all the lofty admonitions to which he is treated are almost wasted, since they are intended to affect *only* the spirit, while utterly neglecting the body.

And this is what we do in everything that concerns the development of children. The children whose mission it is to study in general, to become *educated,* are the ones who suffer particularly from this. First of all they are compelled to pore over books and learn from them what they should really learn from actual experience. Thus a boy who lives in St. Petersburg receives information about many things that surround him only when he begins to learn various subjects. From geography he learns that St. Petersburg is situated on the Neva, which flows into the Gulf of Finland, forming several islands in the process; from history he learns about the St. Petersburg Side, Peter the Great's cottage, and so forth; from natural history he learns of the existence of granite, etc. But think how long it takes before he comes to all these subjects if he follows our textbooks. It is not surprising that we hear anecdotes like the one we heard recently, which we will relate here for the sake of curiosity. A very *educated* boy was taken to high school. He passed the examination for the second form and went to live with his uncle. Next day, when his parents had gone, he complained at dinner that he could not eat anything because the uncle's Triphon was bad ⟨Triphon ought to be flogged, he said⟩. There was nobody named Triphon in the uncle's house and so nobody could understand what the boy was complaining about, nor could he explain. All he did was to repeat his abuse of and complaints about Triphon. And so the problem remained unsolved. But the same thing was repeated the following day, and only then was it learned that the cook at the boy's parents' country house was named Triphon, and this *educated* boy, who had been prepared for the second form at high school, had never asked himself what Triphon meant, and did not know the meaning of the word *cook!*

All this clearly shows how little the necessity of connecting organic functions with the action of the internal spiritual faculties is understood among us. We din into children's heads an enormous amount of abstract concepts of different kinds that are totally alien to the children ⟨God knows by whom and how invented, and often totally unnecessary⟩, and yet we will not take the trouble properly and rationally to train those organs which are necessary to ensure that mental and spiritual activity properly proceeds. In our unpractical—and perhaps all too practical—dreams we forget that the human organism has appropriate physical conditions for every kind of spiritual action, that it is impossible to speak without a tongue, hear without ears, or feel and think without a brain. The latter is forgotten most often, and consequently no care at all is taken among us properly to develop the activity of the brain during the child's education. And yet this is the most important obstacle to the achievement of successful results in our education, which is undoubtedly extremely wise and moral, but one-sided as regards methods. The following is what Dr. Bock, a scholar very well known in Germany, has to say about this:

Weak mental faculties and diseases of the brain [he says] may be due not only to natural deficiencies, but also to insufficient nutrition of the brain and excessive mental strain. The latter, with its deplorable consequences, is particularly fatal to children whose brains are too soft and insufficiently developed to perform hard work. And yet how often they are tortured with abstractions which are totally unintelligible to them at their age and their power of perception, how often feeble, anemic children are expected to achieve success in their studies equal with healthy children! Add to this irrational rest and food unsuitable to the child's age, and you will understand that nothing can be more harmful than this kind of mental drilling!

We find the same opinion expressed by Schnell, the author of the other book, the title of which is given at the beginning of this essay. He gives vent to the following tirade on this subject:

Knowledge is acquired far more easily by natural than by artificial means, i.e., the reading of books. Books burden the spirit with alien material and, therefore, often bring no benefit and upset the health of the spirit. Sicknesses of the brain that we meet with among children of an early age are rather often due not so much to premature education as to bad, unnatural methods of education; they are due to the fact that education is not commenced by practical demonstration, as it should be, but by stuffing the child's head with forms, abstractions, and ideas which subsequently begin to decay, so to speak, and infect the entire structure of the brain. In later years, too, the superficial assimilation of abstract forms may completely dull receptiveness to healthy, sensual impressions, i.e., to nature and to life. We already know that the incomplete, or imperfect, reception of impressions by the organs of external senses give rise to fantasies, i.e., subjective impressions, or delusions. Similarly, fantastic images created by the imagination and the mind are due to the imperfect assimilation by the spirit of abstract forms, or to inadequate, unclear, and insipid spiritual sustenance. Under such circumstances, the mind pictures to itself not objects that really exist in the external world, not actual things, but its own (subjective) products of fantasy, delirium, which gradually completely overpower the mental forces. If the number of insane and semi-insane people whose mental derangement manifests itself either in lack of restraint and unruliness or in slavish, apathetic, and unthinking obedience is actually increasing day after day, as psychologists tell us, it is not a historically necessary phenomenon arising from the present order of things, but the result of a parasitic spiritual life.

One may disagree with the last remark in the above passage, because the defects in education are, of course, a historical phenomenon which springs from the present order of things. But the author's protest against the abstract education that predominates in our times is fully justified. All the requirements and methods of modern education reveal utter contempt for the organic life of man as a man and not as a calculating machine, a machine for performing feats of valor, constructive work, heroism, honesty, universal learning, and so forth. By stuffing the heads of children with all sorts of abstractions we of course stimulate their brains to activity, but to one-sided and morbid activity, because we persist in ignoring the connection between the functioning of the brain and the condition of the entire organism. This unfavorably affects the mental and spiritual activities of man. Physiology has lately proved by a continuous series of researches and discoveries the undoubted connection that exists between man's spiritual life and the structure and development of his brain, and it is a great pity that to this day our educated public shows so little interest in the results obtained with the aid of the natural sciences. Having this in mind, we take the liberty of presenting here several commonly known facts related to our subject.

Moleschott, one of the most celebrated naturalists of modern times, was driven by his researches to the conclusion that thinking influences the material composition of the brain and, vice versa, the composition of the brain influences thinking. This conclusion is elaborated in one of his works in some detail, which we think it superfluous to quote here. We shall only remind the reader of the proposition, long known in comparative anatomy, that in the uninterrupted gradation of animals, commencing with the lowest organisms and ending with man, the size of the brain is in direct proportion to the mental faculties. The lowest animals have no real brain but only nerve nets, which represent rudiments of the brain. The smallest brains are found among amphibians and fish, the largest among dogs, elephants, and apes, i.e., among the animals who are distinguished for their intelligence. Man has a larger brain than all the other animals. The size of the brain considered here is, of course, relative to the size of the body—those parts of the brain which form the central organs of locomotion and perception are not taken into account here. The mental faculties also stand in the same relation to the composition and structure of the brain. Thus, the researches of Bibra have shown that the development of the thinking faculties of animals is determined by the amount of fat and phosphorus in the brain. The more fat and phosphorus the brain contains, the more perfect are those faculties. According to the researches of another naturalist, intelligence and ease in thinking are in direct proportion to the weight of the brain. Cushke's [7] observations have shown that the higher an animal stands in the scale of mental development, the more winding and deeper are the convolutions of the surface of the brain, and the more they lack visible regularity and symmetry. All this applies perfectly to man. His brain fat contains a larger quantity of phosphorus than that of any other animal, his brain is heavier, and the convolutions are deeper and more peculiar. Differences in all these respects are observed not only as between humans and the lower animals, but also between humans of different tribes, of different modes of life, of different ages, and of different sexes. The amount of fat in the brains of newborn children is relatively smaller than in the brains of adults; in general, the infant brain is thinner, softer, and contains more white matter

[7] E. G. Cusco.—Editor.

than gray matter, which increases only later with the development of the mental faculties. Vogt asserts that the development of a child's mental faculties proceeds strictly parallel with the development of the cerebral hemispheres. In general, brain matter continues to develop and grow in man up to the age of forty or fifty; in old age, however, it begins to grow smaller; it shrinks and becomes viscous and more watery. Accordingly, in old age we observe failing memory, loss of quick and firm comprehension, etc.

The same relation is observed in the weight of the brain. The weight of the ordinary human brain ranges from three to three and one-half pounds.[8] Numerous observations have shown that a woman's brain generally weighs from one-fourth to one-sixth of a pound less than the brain of a man. This is in complete conformity with their mental development: it is well known that (probably as a result of the conditions of our civilization) women's reasoning faculties are less developed than those of men. This difference exists also in the weights of the brains of people of varying abilities. Thus, Cuvier's brain weighed over four pounds, and the brains of several imbeciles weighed by Tiedeman weighed only from one to two pounds.

We do not think it necessary to deal with the differences between the skulls of negroes and other lower races of man and the skulls of people of civilized nations. Who is not aware of the strange development of the upper part of the skull among these races, so much so, in fact, that some of them, the New Hollanders, for example, have no upper part of the brain at all? And who, at the same time, is not aware that as regards development of the mental faculties, these tribes are at an incomparably lower level than the people of the Caucasian race?

We shall also point to remarkable facts which prove the inseverable connection that exists between the brain and the mind, and the spiritual life of men in general. A man's occupation influences the condition of his brain. Mental activity increases its volume and strengthens it in the same way as gymnastics strengthen our muscles. The observations of certain naturalists have shown that the brains of scientists, thinkers, etc. are firmer, contain more gray matter, and have more convolutions. In general, the front part of the skull of people belonging to the educated class is more developed than among the common people. Every mental derangement affects the condition of the brain. The evidence of medical men who have studied the corpses of the insane shows that injury to the brain is inevitably found in every case of mental derangement. Moreover, many undoubted cases have been met with of loss of memory accompanying local injuries to the brain, and what is particularly remarkable, often there was no complete loss of memory, but only loss of memory of certain objects. Some, for example, forgot events in certain years of their lives, others forgot one of the languages they had known very well before, others again ceased to recognize their friends, etc. Each of the above cases was due to local injury to the brain.

In general, the connection between spiritual activity and the functioning of the brain is recognized beyond a doubt in the works of all the best and most conscientious naturalists. Valentine says that if we slice the brain of

[8] I.e., Russian pounds: 1 pound = 14.5 ounces.—Translator.

any one of the mammals, the manifestations of its internal activity diminish in proportion to the diminution in size of the brain; and when the so-called brain cavities are reached, the animal becomes dead to all sensibility. This proposition becomes absolutely obvious from the experiments of Flourens, who cut horizontal slices from the top of the brain of certain animals which can bear injury to the brain. He made such experiments on chickens, and by gradually slicing off the brain he brought them to a state in which they ceased to display any signs of higher vital activity. They even lost the ability of locomotion and all perceptiveness to external impressions. But life in them did not cease; it was sustained by artificial feeding, and the chickens vegetated like this for several months and even gained in weight.

In face of all these facts, one cannot help admitting the importance of the proper development of the brain to ensure proper spiritual activity. And as man excels the lower animals most in that he possesses a more perfectly constructed brain, this organ of spiritual activity must be of exceptional importance for him. In this connection we may repeat the words of Dr. Bock:

⟨Only⟩ the higher and more perfect development of the brain distinguishes man from the lower animals; defects in the brain, imperfect development, or morbid changes in it more or less weaken the mind, weaken the spiritual faculties, the ability to feel and the ability to move at will. The most important defects in the brain sometimes place men much below the animals. Consequently, a man's soul is conditioned primarily by a healthy brain.

But in order that the brain may be healthy and develop properly, certain special conditions are needed. Not a single part of the human organism exists independently without connection with the other parts; but no part of our body is so closely connected with its other parts as is the brain. Without going into details, it is sufficient to say that in it are concentrated the nerves of locomotion and sensation. The close connection that exists between the action of the brain and the general condition of the body will therefore be understood. Obviously, every change in the organism must also affect the brain, if not the thinking, then the sensitive part. Physiological research has not yet fully explained the microscopic structure of the particles and the chemical composition of the brain; it is therefore impossible as yet to say what material changes in the organism are due to this or that aspect of the brain's activity. Nevertheless, it has now been reliably ascertained that in addition to protecting the brain from injury, two main conditions are essential for its development: *wholesome nutrition and proper exercise.* Nutrition for the brain is produced in the blood. Consequently, its proper nutrition requires proper blood formation, blood circulation, and blood purification in the body. Examples of how deterioration of the blood harmfully affects the functioning of the brain are not rare. Such cases occur during overflow of the bile, delirium, rabies, etc. In addition to nutrition, the development of the brain needs exercise in the shape of the absorption of external impressions. Dr. Bock says:

A healthy brain must develop its mental faculties gradually with the aid of the five senses and external impressions. The whole process of education is based on this. A man who is completely removed from the society of men immediately after birth will not have even a trace of human reason; surrounded, under the same circumstances, exclusively by animals, he will inevitably acquire all their habits, insofar, of course, as his human organism permits this.

The study of the history of the spiritual development of man undoubtedly confirms Bock's opinion, for it shows that the fewer external impressions a man obtains, the narrower is the circle of his conceptions and consequently the more restricted is his power of judgment. Many oppose this thesis on the grounds that man is born with conceptions and judgment, for if he were not he would be no different from the animals, whose outward senses are as perfect as and in some cases even more perfect than man's. Furthermore, they say, if all conceptions were acquired from the outside world, children brought up under the same influences should be equally intelligent. This argument is utterly groundless; it disregards the fact that outward impressions are felt not by the sense organs, but by the brain. The brain of man differs from the brain of animals, and there is even some difference in the brains of different men. That certain specific features in body structure, temperament, and disposition are inherited by children from their parents is a fact which, though not yet explained by natural science, is nevertheless fully proved. Hence, the same impressions often affect different people in different ways. For the purpose of comparison we can recall the remarkable fact presented by medicine. Medicine that is administered to the sick does not affect all the organs of the body in the same way; it mainly affects the particular organs for which it is intended. But the process by which the organism absorbs the medicine is the same in all cases; it enters the blood and with it spreads over the whole body. In its circulation, however, as the result of the operation of sometimes known and sometimes unknown chemical laws, it is attracted to one or another part of the body. Thus it may be assumed that when the brain functions, certain impressions affect it more strongly than others, and the impressions which, so to speak, pass unobserved through the sense organs of one man may have a powerful effect upon another.

That a man does not develop conceptions within himself but obtains them from the outside world is proved beyond doubt by numerous studies that have been made of people who live under exceptional conditions. For example, those who are born blind have no conception of light or color; those who are born deaf can have no conception of music. People who are born in forests, in the society of animals, and have no association with human beings are distinguished for their wildness and undeveloped conceptions. Sometimes this lack of development reaches the stage of almost complete absence of all signs of intellect, as was the case, for example, with the celebrated Kaspar Hauser, that "unsuccessful attempt at rational existence," as a German writer expressed it.

The same is confirmed by observations of children living even under normal conditions. In the first period of its life the infant displays no conscious activity. In the opinion of physiologists, it does not even feel pain or hunger; it takes its mother's breast, but it does so quite unconsciously, mechanically, simply as a consequence of a certain physiological process in its nerves. It cries and wriggles because its sensory nerves, on being irritated, pass the irritation on to the nerves of locomotion. Examples of such involuntary movement are not infrequently observed in corpses and in bodies in the vegetable kingdom. As regards consciousness, a newborn infant does not and cannot possess one. Bock says:

> External impressions produce no sensations or pain in an infant because its organ of sensation and consciousness, i.e., its brain, is not yet able to function. An infant cries quite unconsciously because its irritated sensory nerves affect the nerves of the vocal organs. Consciousness and sensation appear later, only with the development of the brain.

How conscious life gradually develops in man is described in rather great detail in Dr. Bock's book. We think it will not be superfluous to present here his main ideas.

In Dr. Bock's opinion consciousness appears in the child rather early. "Unfortunately," he says, "most parents think that reason, i.e., the ability of the brain to feel, think, and desire, appears not in infancy but much later, and therefore it never occurs to them that a child at the breast already needs a proper education."

The education that Dr. Bock proposes, however, is not the abstract education that so much fuss is made about in our midst, but dietetic education. At first the senses of the newborn infant are extremely dull, so that it cannot distinguish even its mother's milk from the bitterest substances, and only the fact that it becomes accustomed to sweet things gradually teaches it to distinguish between sweet and bitter. In the same gradual way, as a consequence of its becoming accustomed to impressions of a certain kind, it develops all its other senses. Consequently, at this stage it is easy to imbue the infant with many habits and requirements that may later become deeprooted. The first sense that the infant develops is the sense of touch of its lips, with which it seeks its mother's breast; later, sight, hearing, etc. develop. During the first months of life the infant's eyes are totally inactive; that is why its gaze is quite senseless and indefinite. In the fifth or sixth week the infant already begins to look at surrounding objects, and, as a consequence, the first sensory impressions, that is to say, mental pictures, are made on the brain and gradually become more and more distinct. Gradually they become so distinct that the infant can conceive of them even when the objects themselves are not before its eyes. This marks the beginning of the functioning of the faculty of imagination. Hearing develops parallel with sight, and both organs help each other in their development, so that impressions created on the hearing, for example, induce the child to open its eyes and look in the direction from which the sound came. In the third month of its life the infant already manifests a desire to take hold of visible objects, but a complete absence is observed of any conception of distance and size, as well as of ability to exercise the muscles. The child reaches out for an object but usually *misses* it, and if the object is put into its hand, it is unable to hold it. But gradually the sense of touch develops in the infant. At three months the infant already begins to babble or "gurgle," as it is called. If the infant often hears the same word combined with the presence of any particular object, the two concepts—the name of the object and the object itself—are combined in its mind, so that when it hears the object named, it can picture its shape and understand what is meant. Only the connection between objects and the order in which actions are performed still remain strange to the infant; coherent speech is altogether unintelligible to it.

At the same time (i.e., in the fifth or sixth month) the infant begins to distinguish between gentle and angry speech. Two months later it acquires a vague understanding of the order in which certain things are done, and why they are done. Having reached this stage of mental development, the child already attempts to talk, but this ability is acquired sooner or later, according to the degree in which its organs of locomotion are developed. The will develops last of all, only in the second year, when the child is able to walk without assistance, and when it already has a sufficient stock of impressions to enable it to form its own judgment and draw its own conclusions. All this shows how important are the first impressions that are made on the child's brain for molding its character and future conduct. It has been observed that children whose mothers or wet nurses chatted merrily and played with them in the first months of their lives later developed kind and cheerful dispositions. Many children who had long been kept in leading strings and had not been allowed to walk without assistance grew up to be irresolute in character and always lack confidence in their own strength. Children who, in the first year of their lives, were accustomed only to pleasant sensations and were relieved of everything unpleasant the moment they cried, subsequently found it very difficult to bear anything displeasing and lost their temper at the slightest mishap. Most of the children who are taught to speak, that is to say, have words repeated to them without showing them the objects referred to, subsequently reveal extreme superficiality.

External impressions are still more important for children entering their third or fourth year. Up to that time, in Bock's opinion, reward and punishment, even corporal punishment, may still be inflicted, not as a rational pedagogical measure, however, but only out of consideration for the fact that the child's organs of rational activity are not yet developed and animal spontaneity still predominates. Thus a lazy horse will steadily cover the entire journey if a loaded hay cart is proceeding in front of it; thus a horseman will put spurs to his horse to make it run faster. It is precisely in this sense that reward and punishment may be resorted to in the early, almost unconscious, life of the child. Beginning with the fourth year, however, they become superfluous and must be replaced by persuasion. In Dr. Bock's opinion, "the expectation of the usual reward for good conduct may imbue the child with the elements of covetousness, venality, and egoism."

Punishment, of course, frightens children, and, according to Bock, "fear is the beginning of cowardice, hypocrisy, and baseness." Beginning with the fifth and particularly with the sixth year, the child must be taught to reason and to understand everything it does. Hence, a child should never be forced to do anything that is beyond its understanding, and of the reasonableness of which it cannot convince itself with the aid of the small stock of knowledge it has obtained from its observations of the outside world. The child's external senses must be exercised as much and as correctly as possible in order to enlarge the stock of impressions in its brain. If that is done, intelligent views and judgments of the various relations between objects will inevitably arise in its mind of their own accord. Stuffing the child's head with various conceptions beyond its understanding, however, will only make it impossible for the child to analyze its sensations, subordinate them to its will, or free itself from them. Dr. Bock says:

> Many teachers think, of course, that such an education cultivates noble and lofty sentiments in children, but in this they are mistaken. The result is entirely different; that is to say, it cultivates not men and women with noble sentiments, but sentimental dreamers who are totally unfit for practical life and useless to themselves and others.

The few data we have quoted can, we think, give us some idea of the connection that exists between the functions of the nerves and brain and the mental activities of man. Incontrovertible facts clearly show that for correct thinking and expression of thoughts we must have a healthy and properly developed brain. Consequently, if we want the *mental* side of our beings to develop, we must not ignore the physical development of the brain.

But the question may arise in the mind of the reader: "What must be done for *moral* development, upon which the brain must exercise not direct but indirect influence?" On this point we have already quoted in passing several observations made by Dr. Bock, but here we can add a few more reflections. They are very simple and, therefore, will not be lengthy.

If we accept the ancient (and still generally accepted) division of man's spiritual faculties, we must consider not only the mind, but also the emotions and will. The emotions are usually attributed to the heart and are completely divorced from the brain. It cannot be said that this opinion is well grounded. Properly speaking, the heart is not in the least responsible for our emotions and passions. All that we have been accustomed to ascribe to the heart is engendered in the brain. But there are special *heart nerves* which run from the brain to the heart and are connected with all the other nerves of the body; hence every irritation, however slight, and no matter where it may occur or why, is immediately communicated by the brain, or spinal cord, to the heart nerves and causes the heart to beat faster. As it is easier for us to note the beating of the heart than the activity of the brain nerves, we ascribe all emotions to the heart. But the fact that the primary cause of all emotion is the brain can easily be proved by the following:

emotion arises in us as a result of impressions produced upon us by objects in the outside world. But we can become conscious of these impressions only when they affect the brain. Otherwise, we would look at things and not see them; a severed nerve could be irritated by every possible means, but we would feel no pain, because the nerve is disconnected from the brain. Hence, it is obvious that, before it is reflected in the heart, every emotion must appear in the brain as a thought, as the consciousness of an impression, and then affect the organism and manifest itself in the beating of the heart. Consequently, emotion must be influenced by means of thought. Some feelings are more developed in us than others, some people feel one way, some another—all this is true. But the cause of this difference does not lie in the development of the heart, of that hollow muscle which pumps up the blood. This cause lies mostly in the difference in the original impressions obtained by our brain. If, for example, a man has been accustomed from early childhood constantly to hear melodious sounds, naturally his musical sense will be developed; if a man has not been accustomed since childhood to experience unpleasant sensations, then, of course, the slightest unpleasantness will upset his temper; if successful efforts are made to retard the free activity of a child's mind, the child will inevitably develop a feeling of repugnance for mental activity, etc. In general, it must be said that our bad feelings are invariably the consequence of an incomplete, incorrect, or utterly distorted perception of impressions by the brain. Just as we fail to hear a moderate but fairly audible sound after hearing a loud sound, or see nothing when suddenly passing from a brightly lit to a dimly but sufficiently lit place, so we sometimes receive wrong impressions and, consequently, feelings with regard to objects directly affecting our spiritual activity. A man who has been accustomed to hear constant praise is displeased, and even angry, when he is praised less than usual; he who is accustomed to a life of idleness and has experienced few strong impressions is frightened at the prospect of having to make the slightest effort and imagines that he is incapable of performing it; a man who has been accustomed from childhood to witness sordid and ugly scenes finds pleasure in the company of a vulgar circle if it is just slightly more decent than the company he was used to. Thus all our good and bad feelings and passions are entirely dependent upon the degree of development and on the health or ill health of the brain. Both the development of sympathetic feelings simultaneously with education and the predominance of egoistic feelings when education is lacking are phenomena known to all.

On the basis of these data we may positively say that the efforts of many teachers to *influence the heart* of a child without imbuing it with sound conceptions are absolutely wasted. The result of such "influencing the heart" is usually a man habitually amiable, but totally lacking firm and potent convictions. It can be emphatically asserted that only that kindness and that nobility of feeling are absolutely reliable, and may be truly useful, which are based on firm convictions, on well-developed thinking faculties. Without this, the morality of a *kindhearted* man, and particularly his usefulness to others, cannot be guaranteed. Let us remember that "an obliging bear is more dangerous than an enemy."

In the process of education, therefore, feeling develops of its own accord if mental perceptions are correct, consistent, and clear. We often see how pleased children are when some new object, or some new idea, becomes clear to them. They seem to be bathed in light, their eyes shine, their faces beam, they begin to chatter in this ebullience, express opinions, devise plans, etc. This shows that they have grasped the idea with sufficient fullness and clarity to rouse an inner feeling in them—and happy is the teacher who is often able to rouse his pupils to such a state. In this connection Mr. Schnell quite rightly observes:

> During lessons there is no need to deliver fervid speeches, to declaim, etc., to cause ideas to affect also the feelings of the pupil. All true teaching in itself supplies rich material for feeling, for knowledge enlightens not only the mind but also the heart, it animates and rejoices it. Knowledge and joy are closely akin.

As regards will, it more than feeling depends upon the impressions created upon our brain by the outside world. Everybody in our days understands that there is no such thing as absolute free will for man, that he, like all phenomena of Nature, is dependent upon her eternal laws. Except for Mr. Bervi, the author of "Fiziologichesko-psikhologicheskii sravnitel'nyi vzgliad na nachalo i konets zhizni" [A Physiologico-psychological View on the Beginning and End of Life], nobody today can say that man exists outside of the conditions of space and time, and can change the universal laws of nature at will. Everybody understands that man cannot do everything he pleases; consequently, his freedom is relative, restricted freedom. Moreover, the briefest reflection will convince anyone that there can be no absolutely free actions, actions dependent upon nothing but our will. In our decisions we are constantly guided by certain feelings or considerations. To assume the opposite means assuming the possibility of action without cause.

Strictly speaking, it is impossible to assume the existence of will as an innate faculty separate from and independent of other faculties. All its actions are determined, and are even inevitably produced, by that stock of knowledge which we have accumulated in our brain, and by the degree to which our nerves can be irritated. The instrument for the fulfillment of our wishes is the nerves of locomotion which run from the brain to all the muscles. Consequently, the degree to which the muscles are developed also determines our activity. The nerves of the muscles must also be connected with the brain, otherwise they will not obey us, and we shall not be able to move.

That desire appears first in the brain is proved by the fact that desire is always centered upon some object, or some goal. This shows that desire must have an object which must first create an impression on our brain, for it is impossible to desire anything of which we have no conception. Furthermore, the object must produce a pleasant impression, i.e., one that will soothe and not irritate our natures: like everything else in the world, man strives only for what conforms to his nature in some respect or other, and turns away from what is repugnant to it. Thus so-called freedom of choice really means the possibility, which exists in our minds, of comparing several objects and determining which of them is the best. Here it is very appropriate to recall the well-known aphorism that "every criminal is primarily a poor calculator." Indeed, most crimes and immoral acts are committed as a result of ignorance, of a lack of sound conceptions of things, an inability to understand the existing state of affairs and the consequences of the given act. Only a few immoral acts are committed as the result of firm but false conviction. This enables us to distinguish frivolous conduct from grave error. Some immoral people justify themselves on the ground that their line of reasoning is correct and act accordingly. But the number of such people is not very large. Most people commit offenses of various kinds because they have no definite conception of anything in particular and just waver between good and evil. When a man is in a good mood it seems to him that a certain act would be immoral. When that mood passes, the same act may appear to him to be moral. A man may feel he would like to take a glass of something for the sake of his stomach, but he knows perfectly well that he must not drink much. When in company, however, he will not refuse another glass, and another, and here his conceptions turn right the other way. As long as a man has money and is not in need he will think it dishonest to accept gratuities; but the same man may even solicit gratuities if hard pressed by want.

In this way all bribetakers, frauds, and blackmailers gradually acquire the habit and achieve a certain amount of skill in this art. Sometimes practice engenders theoretical convictions which harmonize with that practice. Most often, however, moral convictions remain in the head as abstractions, while practice proceeds on its own way. All this is because the conception of morality is not worked out in the minds of many people independently, but enters their minds in passing, from what they hear from others at a time when they are not yet capable of understanding such things. The conception of morality held by many people can be compared to our conception of the evil, for example, of smoking tobacco, drinking tea or coffee, etc. We have all heard something about these evils, but we have heard so much about other things too. It is rather difficult to acquire a clear and correct judgment about the harmfulness of tobacco and tea, and in what cases they are harmful, and we therefore content ourselves with rumors, and even these we often forget. One cannot recall the exhortations of medical men every time one smokes a cigarette or drinks a cup of tea; and besides, these admonitions may be wrong. Similarly, many people forget about morality in their everyday conduct. In general, caprice, which so many confuse with true freedom, means the very opposite, means slavish subordination to the first impression one receives. That is why children whose every caprice is indulged, no matter how absurd, grow up to be as little free morally as the children in whom every manifestation of will, that is to say, every attempt to discuss things independently, is suppressed at the very beginning of their lives.

Mr. Schnell rightly says concerning this:

> Mainly, we must safeguard ourselves and others from caprice. Whoever blindly obeys a passing mood, whoever is guided in his conduct only by caprice and fails to subordinate his will to the higher power of reason and justice, will be either weak and spineless or a tyrant and oppressor of himself and others. This happens even with children. . . . Cruel men, the tormentors of mankind, have all been educated in this way. They are the most unhappy and most dangerous of men. They are not to be trusted, even though they themselves preach fraternity and lawful civil liberty; for caprice, which serves as the lever of all their actions, is also the source of injustice, cruelty, and villainy.

The influence which organic development undoubtedly exercises on the mental and spiritual activities of man has long been the object of study by naturalists. The way this influence is exercised, and its very nature, is explained more and more clearly every day by the latest physiological researches. Basing ourselves on these researches, we may now boldly assert that the natural, correct, and healthy development of all the forces of the organism means much more for mental activity than all sorts of artificial admonitions. The healthy state and normal development of the brain, however, affect our feelings and desires far more strongly and more often than all the moralizing platitudes and fervid exhortations that we have learned by heart, in most cases without any useful result.

In pointing, in this essay, to some of the results of physiological research, we have not gone into any detail to explain the structure of the organism in general, the composition and structure of the brain, the nervous system, etc. We refrained from introducing these details into our essay because they would have made it far too long and would not in any case have given the reader who is unfamiliar with anatomy and physiology a perfectly clear conception of the structure of our organism. Such a conception can be obtained only from books that deal especially with this subject. In fact, we wrote this essay only for people who are totally unfamiliar with physiology; those who have studied this subject to any extent will probably not find a single new fact or idea in it. But even those who are unfamiliar with the present state of physiology may find this essay unsatisfactory precisely because of the absence of details. Stern critics will observe that, consequently, our entire essay is useless, and was written in vain! Anticipating such a conclusion, we hasten to say that we do not attach any special significance to our observations. Our only object has been to rouse in readers to whom the natural sciences are utterly strange at least some interest in them, and at the same time to draw the attention of the public to two books which may very well serve as an introduction to physiology and to the process of human development. The readers may find all the details concerning anatomy and physiology that are lacking in this essay in Dr. Bock's book, *A Book on the Healthy and Sick Man,* which is written in an exceedingly simple and popular style. The application of the principles of physiology to education may be found in Schnell's book, in which many useful and correct ideas are expounded, although sometimes the author is carried away by dreams which, strictly speaking, are totally unnecessary for the proper organic development of man.

14.
Feodor M. Dostoevsky

1821-1881

The Emancipation of the serfs in 1861 ushered in administrative and economic changes which transformed the social fabric of Russia as well. None of the views and ideals the Russian elite had previously held seemed suitable to the new conditions: the Slavophiles' retrospective utopia was but a hopeless dream; the Nihilists' reliance on natural sciences for social progress proved to be naive and unrealistic; the eighteenth-century faith in reason, education, and enlightenment was hardly relevant to the masses of illiterate peasants and the gradually emerging urban proletariat. The old questions of the nature of Russia's national identity and her relationship to the outside world, mainly Western Europe, had acquired a new form without losing any of their acute topicality. And what about the role of the intelligentsia, who in the past had suggested the answers? Had it not failed? And was its failure to provide effective leadership perhaps due more to its members' intellectual and moral makeup than to the repressive controls of Nicholas I? In his *Selected Passages from a Correspondence with Friends* Gogol had hinted at this aspect of the question—an aspect that Belinskii chose

to disregard in his passionately outraged reply. The young generation of Nihilists—who found a spokesman in Dobroliubov—emphatically rejected the leadership claims of the idealistic and esthetically minded intellectuals.

As the old groupings and classes of pre-reform Russia disintegrated, the nature and makeup of the isolated individual became the crucial concern of all perceptive observers of the Russian scene. No one probed more deeply and gave a more searching, truthful, and disturbing portrayal of the existential condition of man in modern society than Feodor M. Dostoevsky. In the final analysis, Dostoevsky concluded, man's happiness and salvation depended entirely on his spiritual resources. But these resources could be fully brought into play only if the person had meaningful relationships with his fellow men; he could preserve his individual identity only if he had respect and sympathy for the spiritual truths of others and shared his own moral truth with them.

What was true of an individual was also true of a nation; for Dostoevsky, a child of Romanticism, believed that every nation had its own spiritual and moral truth but that this truth was to be shared with others. The really great and genuinely national poet who expressed his people's moral and spiritual values also guided them in fulfilling their highest universal mission. In Russia this was the role played by Aleksandr S. Pushkin. By becoming aware of what he tried to express through his poetry we discover the real nature of the Russian people and their contribution to the progress of mankind.

Pushkin

A Sketch

"Pushkin is an extraordinary, and perhaps a unique, phenomenon of the Russian spirit," said Gogol. For my own part, I will add: and a prophetic one. Yes, in his appearance, to all us Russians, there is something indisputably prophetic. Pushkin appeared precisely at the very inception of our true self-consciousness, which was then just coming into being and which originated in our society after a whole century following Peter's reform; and his appearance greatly helped to illuminate our obscure path with a new guiding light. It is in this sense that Pushkin is a prophecy and a revelation.

I divide the activity of our great poet into three periods. I am not speaking now as a literary critic: when referring to Pushkin's creative work, I merely wish to explain my conception of his prophetic significance to us, and my understanding of this word. In passing, I may remark, however, that it seems to me that between the periods of Pushkin's activity there are no clearly defined lines of demarcation. To my mind the inception of *Eugene Onegin*, for instance, belongs to the first period, while its concluding part should be placed in the second period, when Pushkin had already found his ideals in his own country, and had fully and affectionately absorbed them in his loving and perspicacious soul. It is said that, in his first period, Pushkin imitated the European poets—Parny, André Chénier, and others —but particularly—Byron. Yes, no doubt, the poets of Europe did exercise a strong influence upon the development of his genius; and maintained it

Reprinted with the permission of Charles Scribner's Sons from *The Diary of a Writer*, F. M. Dostoievsky, Volume II, pp. 967–80, translated by Boris Brasol. Copyright 1949 Charles Scribner's Sons. Originally delivered before Obshchestvo Liubitelei Rossiiskoi Slovesnosti (the Society of Lovers of Russian Literature) on June 8, 1880, this essay was first published under the title "Pushkin: Ocherk" (Pushkin: A Sketch) in Dostoevsky's own irregularly published periodical, *Dnevnik pisatelia*, for 1880.

throughout his life. Nevertheless, not even his earliest poems were mere imitations, so that even in them the extraordinary independence of his genius was revealed. In imitations one never finds such personal suffering and such depth of self-consciousness as Pushkin revealed, for instance in his *Gypsies,* a poem which I ascribe entirely to the first period of his creative life. I do not speak of the creative potency and impetuosity which could not have been expressed so strongly had it been merely imitative.

In the character of Aleko, the hero of the poem *Gypsies,* there is already revealed a strong, deep, and purely Russian concept, which was subsequently expressed in such harmonious perfection in *Eugene Onegin,* where virtually the same Aleko is shown not in a fantastic light but in a palpably real and intelligible guise. In Aleko, Pushkin had already discerned and ingeniously noted that unhappy wanderer in his native land, that traditional Russian sufferer detached from the people who appeared in our society as a historical necessity. And, of course, Pushkin found him not only in Byron. Aleko's is a true and unmistakably conceived character, a lasting character long since native to our Russian land. These homeless Russian ramblers are wandering still, and it seems it will be long before they disappear. If, in our day, they no longer visit gypsy camps with their wild and odd mode of living in a quest for their universal ideals and in order to seek refuge in the bosom of nature from the confused and incongruous life of our Russian educated society—all the same they embrace socialism, which did not exist in Aleko's times, and with their new creed they journey to another field, eagerly tilling it, believing, even as Aleko, that through this fantastic labor they will attain their goal and happiness not for themselves alone but for all men. A Russian sufferer in order to find peace needs precisely universal happiness: with nothing less than that is he content—of course, as long as the proposition is confined to theory. Essentially, it is the same Russian who appeared in a different epoch.

This character, I repeat, came into being among our educated society detached from the people's might in the beginning of the second century after the great reform of Peter. Oh, an overwhelming majority of Russian intellectuals served peacefully in the days of Pushkin—just as now—as civil servants, in the government or on railroads and in banks, or otherwise earned their livelihood, or were even engaged in scientific work, in lecturing—in a regular, leisured and peaceful fashion, receiving salaries, playing preference,[1] with no inclination to take refuge whether in gypsy camps or in other places more suited to our time. At the utmost they play at liberalism "with a tinge of European socialism" to which a certain benign Russian flavor is conveyed, but, after all, this is merely a matter of time. What of the fact that one man has not even begun to worry while another, encountering a locked door, has already smashed his head against it?—In due time all men will meet the same destiny, unless they choose the salutary road of humble communion with the people. And even if not all men meet this destiny: it suffices if "the chosen," one tenth, start worrying; the great majority will lose peace through them.

[1] A game of cards popular in Pushkin's time.—Translator.

Of course, Aleko as yet does not know how to express correctly his anguish: in him all this is still an abstract mood: yearning for nature; complaints against fashionable society; universal aspirations; laments over truth, somewhere and somehow lost, which he can nowhere find. In this there is something akin to Jean-Jacques Rousseau. Wherein that truth is, in what form and where it can appear, and precisely when it was lost, of course, he does not know himself, but his is sincere suffering. A fantastic and impatient creature, he still awaits salvation preeminently from external things, as needs he must: "Truth," it is implied, "is somewhere without him, somewhere in other lands—European, perhaps—with their solid historical order, with its settled social and civic mode of life." Nor will he ever comprehend that first of all truth is within himself. How can he understand this?—He is an alien in his own country; for a whole century he has been unaccustomed to work; he is devoid of culture; he has grown up as a damsel in a convent within closed walls; he has fulfilled strange and unaccountable obligations associated with this or that of the fourteen ranks into which Russian educated society is divided. He is still nothing but a blade of grass torn from its root and blown about by the wind. This he feels; this makes him suffer—not seldom quite acutely! What if, perhaps belonging to hereditary nobility and possibly owning serfs, taking advantage of his noble birth, he, for once, allowed himself to indulge in a little whim of taking a fancy to people living "without laws" in a gypsy camp, leading a bear which performs? Naturally a woman, "a wild woman," as the poet calls her, more than anyone could inspire him with the hope of deliverance from his anguish, and so, with light-minded but passionate credulity he throws himself into the arms of Zemphira: "Here"—says he—"is my escape; here, perhaps, is my happiness—here, in the bosom of nature, far from fashionable society; here—among men without civilization and without laws!"

And what is the outcome?—At his first encounter with the conditions of wild nature he fails to restrain himself, and he stains his hands with blood. The poor dreamer proves unequal not only to universal harmony but even to those gypsies who cast him away without vengeance, without malice, in naive dignity:

> Depart from us, thou haughty man:
> We're wild, we have no binding laws,
> We neither punish nor torment.

Of course, all this is fantastic, but "the haughty man" is genuine and is cleverly conceived. First he has been conceived in Russia by Pushkin;—and this should be remembered. Quite so: the moment something goes against his grain, he is ready to devour his adversary to avenge his offense, or—which is still handier—recalling his appurtenance to one of the fourteen ranks, he may appeal (this did happen) to the chastising and torturing law, provided his personal wrong be thus avenged.

Nay, this is an ingenious poem—not an imitation! Here, indeed, we have the Russian answer to the "accursed question" in terms of the people's faith and truth: "Humble thyself, proud man; above all, break thy haughtiness!

Humble thyself, idle man, and, first of all, labor on thy native land!"—Such is the solution according to the people's truth and wisdom. "Truth is within—not without thee. Find thyself within thyself. Not others shouldst thou subdue; subdue thyself; be master of thyself—and thou shalt perceive truth. Not in things, not outside thee nor overseas is this truth, but above all in thine own labor for self-betterment. If thou conquerest thyself, if thou humblest thyself, then wilt thou be free beyond dreams; thou wilt labor upon a great task; thou wilt make others free and thou wilt find happiness, since thy life will be full, and thou wilt, finally, understand thine own people and their sacred truth. Neither with the gypsies nor elsewhere is universal harmony provided if thou thyself art unworthy of it—if thou art given to malice and pride, if thou demandest life as a gift without even comprehending that it has to be paid for."

This solution of the question is clearly indicated in Pushkin's poem. It is expressed still more clearly in *Eugene Onegin,* a poem which is no longer fantastic but tangibly realistic, in which genuine Russian life is incarnated with such creative potency and completeness as have never been witnessed either before or, perhaps, also since Pushkin.

Onegin arrives from Petersburg—necessarily from Petersburg: it is imperative for the poem, and Pushkin could not miss such an important realistic trait in the biography of his hero. Onegin—I repeat—is the same Aleko, particularly where he later exclaims in anguish:

> Oh, why, like Tula's poor assessor,
> Am I not lying paralyzed?

However, in the beginning of the poem, he is still half a dandy and half a man of the world; as yet, he has not lived long enough to be completely disillusioned in life. Even so, "the noble fiend of secret boredom" begins to visit and annoy him.

It stands to reason that in the remote heart of his motherland he is in exile, not at home. He knows not what to undertake, and feels as if he were a guest in his own home. Later, when he roams, seized with anguish for his own land, in foreign countries and among strangers, as an unquestionably clever and sincere man he feels even more a stranger to himself. True, he, too, loves his country, but he does not trust it. Of course, he has heard about its ideals but he has no faith in them. He merely believes in an utter impossibility of any kind of work in his native land, and he looks upon the few—now as heretofore—who believe in this possibility with a sad smile. He killed Lensky out of mere spleen—which may have been an outgrowth of a longing for some universal ideal: this is so typical of us, so plausible.

Quite different is Tatiana: hers is a strong character, firmly standing on her own soil. She is deeper than Onegin, and of course wiser than he. With her noble instinct she foresees where and in what truth resides, and this is revealed in the finale of the poem. Perhaps Pushkin might have done better had he called his poem by the name Tatiana, and not Onegin, since she is undeniably its protagonist. She is a positive, not a negative, character; she is a type of real beauty and an apotheosis of Russian womanhood, and it is to her that the poet assigned the task of expressing the idea of the poem in the famous scene of her last meeting with Onegin. It may even be said that so beautiful and genuine a type of Russian woman has virtually never reappeared in our literature—save, perhaps, for the image of Liza in Turgenev's *A Gentlefolk's Nest.*

However, the habit of looking down upon people accounts for the fact that Onegin altogether failed to understand Tatiana when, in a remote place, he met her first, in the humble guise of a pure and chaste girl, so abashed by his presence. He was unable to discern perfection in that poor girl, and perhaps he even took her for a "moral embryo." She—an embryo! And this—after her letter to Onegin! If there is a moral embryo in the poem it is, of course, Onegin himself—this is undeniable. Nor was he capable in the least of comprehending her, for did he know the human soul?—All his life he was an abstract man, a restless dreamer. And again he failed to appraise her later in Petersburg as a *grande dame* when, according to his own words in his letter to Tatiana, he began "to comprehend her full perfection." But these were only words: unrecognized and unappreciated she passed through his life, and therein lay the tragedy of their love. Oh, had only Childe Harold, at the time, in that country place, at their first meeting, or by some chance Lord Byron himself, arriving from England and taking notice of her timid, modest charm, pointed it out to him—oh, then Onegin would have been at once astonished and struck with admiration; for there is, at times, in these universal sufferers a good deal of spiritual servility! But this did not happen, and this seeker of universal harmony, having read to her his sermon and, after all, having honestly dealt with her, started off with his *Weltschmerz,* and with his hands stained with blood spilt in senseless anger, to roam in his native land forgetful of Tatiana, full to the brim with health and strength, exclaiming with a curse:

> Oh, I am young, and full of vigor!
> On naught but anguish can I figure!

This Tatiana understood. In immortal strophes of his romance the poet shows her visiting the dwelling of that man who was then still fascinating and mysterious to her. I need not speak here about the artistic perfection and inimitable beauty of these lines. Here she is shown in his study. She examines his books, his various possessions. She seeks, through them, to divine his soul—her riddle—and finally "that moral embryo," after a wistful pause, with a strange smile, foreseeing the solution of the enigma, gently whispers: "Isn't he a parody perchance?"

Yes, this she had to whisper—she did divine him. Long afterwards in Petersburg, when they had met once more, she had completely comprehended his quality. By the way, who was it that said that life in the *beau monde* and at court had a pernicious effect upon her soul and that the position of a lady of fashion and the newly engendered ideas of fashionable society were partly the cause of her refusal of Onegin? No, this is not so. No, it is the same, the former rustic Tanya! She is not spoiled; on the contrary, half-broken, she suffers and feels oppressed by the pomp of Petersburg life.

She hates her position as a lady of fashion, and he who judges her differently utterly fails to understand what Pushkin sought to express. With firmness she tells Onegin:

> Pledged to another husband, I
> To him stay loyal, till I die.

She says this precisely as a Russian woman; therein is her apotheosis. She expresses the truth of the poem. Oh, I shall not say a word about her religious convictions, about her attitude toward the sacrament of marriage —upon this I shall not touch. Well, did she refuse to follow him, despite having said to him: "I love you," because "as a Russian woman"—and not a Southern or some French woman—she is incapable of so bold a step, or has no strength to break her chains, to sacrifice the lure of honors, riches, and her social position, the conventions of virtue?—Nay, brave is the Russian woman. She will boldly follow that in which she believes—and this she has proved. But "having been pledged to another man," she will be "loyal to him unto death." To whom, to what is she faithful? To what obligations?— To that old general whom she cannot love, since she loves Onegin, and whom she married because "her mother wept, adjured, besought her," while in her offended and wounded soul there was then only despair, and no hope, no ray of light?—Yes, she is loyal to that general, her husband, an honest man, who loves and respects her and takes pride in her. Even though her mother did "beseech" her, it was she, Tatiana, and no one but her, who gave her consent, and it was she who swore to be his faithful wife. Even though she married him in despair, now he is her husband, and perfidy on her part would disgrace and shame him and this would be his death. But can one's happiness be founded upon another's unhappiness?—Happiness is not confined to the mere delights of love; it also involves the supreme harmony of the spirit. What will assuage the spirit if there is in the past a dishonest, merciless, inhuman act? Dare she run away for the only reason that here might be her happiness?—But what kind of happiness would it be if it were based upon somebody's unhappiness?—Please suppose that you yourself are erecting an edifice of human destiny in order to bestow upon men at last tranquillity and peace. And imagine, further, that for this end it is necessary and inevitable to torture to death only one human creature, moreover—not even so worthy a creature, which to some people may even seem ridiculous—not some Shakespeare, but simply an honest old man, the husband of a young wife whose love he blindly trusts, without, however, knowing her heart at all; whom he respects; of whom he is proud—a husband who is happy with her and who has found his peace. And now it is he who must be dishonored, disgraced and tortured to death in order to erect upon the suffering of this disgraced old man your edifice! In these circumstances would you agree to be the architect of such an edifice?—That's the question. And can you conceive, though for an instant, that men, for whom this edifice was erected, would agree to accept from you happiness if it were founded upon the suffering, let us say, of some negligible creature but one mercilessly and unjustly tortured to death; or, if they accepted it, that they would forever stay happy?—Tell me, could Tatiana with her lofty soul, with her heart so ennobled by suffering, have answered otherwise?—Nay, a pure Russian heart gives this reply: "Let me alone be deprived of happiness; let my unhappiness be immeasurably greater than that of this old man; finally, let no one ever, including the old man, learn about and appreciate my sacrifice, but I refuse to be happy by ruining another man!" —This is tragedy: it does transpire, and Tatiana sends away Onegin.

It may be argued that Onegin is also unhappy; that by saving one man she ruined the other!—Well, perhaps this is the cardinal point in the poem. By the way—the question why Tatiana refused to follow Onegin has, at least in our literature, a rather peculiar history. That is why I deemed it possible to elaborate on it. What is most characteristic is that the moral solution of this question has for a long time been in doubt. I reason this way: even if Tatiana had become free; even if her old husband had died and she had become a widow—even then she would not have gone away with Onegin. One has to comprehend the essence of her character: she knows who he is: he, the eternal wanderer; he meets by chance the woman whom he had formerly neglected, in a new, brilliant, unattainable setting. Why, perhaps the essence of the matter is in that setting: the young girl whom he virtually used to despise is now worshiped by the *beau monde*— that terrible authority to Onegin, who, despite his universal aspirations, throws himself, dazzled, at her feet! "This"—he exclaims—"is my ideal! Here is my salvation! This is my escape from my anguish, I failed to notice it and yet . . . 'So possible was happiness, so near!' "

And even as Aleko in the past turned to Zemphira, Onegin is now drawn to Tatiana, seeking all solutions in his new whimsical fantasy. And doesn't Tatiana perceive this in him? Hasn't she appraised him long ago? She is firmly convinced that, strictly speaking, he merely loves his new fancy, and not her, the hitherto humble Tatiana! She knows that he takes her for something different—not for what she actually is; that it is not she whom he loves; that he is even incapable of loving anyone, despite the fact that he suffers so acutely!—He loves his fantasy. But he himself is but a fantasy! Were she to follow him, the very next day he would be disillusioned and would regard his infatuation scoffingly. He is devoid of any soil; he is a blade of grass caught in a gust.

Tatiana is very different!—Even in despair, in the agony of her lucid recognition of the fact that her life is ruined—she is herself solid, unshakable, something upon which her soul relies. These are the reminiscences of her childhood, of her birthplace, in a rural wilderness, where her humble and pure life began,

> Ay, of that burial-ground so quiet,
> Where my poor nurse reposes now
> Beneath her cross and shadowing bough.[2]

[2] Aleksandr S. Pushkin, *Evgeny Onegin*, trans. Oliver Elton (London, Pushkin Press, 1939).

Oh, these reminiscences, these pictures of the past, to her are now more precious than anything else; these images—nothing else is left to save her soul from ultimate despair. Nor is this a bagatelle; nay, there is much in this, because this is a whole foundation, something indestructible and solid. Here is the link with the motherland, with her own people, with their sanctity.

And what, by contrast, has he to offer? Who is he?—Certainly she would not follow him from mere compassion, to gratify him, to give him out of boundless loving pity, for a while at least, illusive happiness, knowing certainly in advance that tomorrow he would deride it. Nay, there are deep and firm souls which, even though from infinite compassion, will not surrender their sanctity by dooming it to dishonor. Nay, Tatiana never could have followed Onegin.

Thus, in *Onegin,* in that immortal and inimitable poem, Pushkin, as no one ever before him, revealed himself as a great national writer. With one stroke, in a most precise and perspicacious manner, he indicated the innermost essence of the upper stratum of our society standing above the level of the people. Having traced the type of the Russian wanderer of all time; having been the first—by reason of his ingenious instinct, his historical fate, his immense significance to our future destinies—to place side by side with this type a character of positive and unquestioned beauty in the person of a Russian woman, Pushkin—also first among the Russian writers in his other creations of the same period—showed us a whole gallery of genuinely beautiful Russian characters which he discovered in the Russian people. Their principal beauty lies in their incontestable and tangible truth, so that it is impossible to deny them, and they stand there as though sculptured.

Once more, I reiterate: I am not speaking as a literary critic, and for this reason I shall not dwell in any literary detail upon these ingenious creations of our poet. For instance, it would be possible to write a whole book about the character of the annalist-monk, revealing the great importance and significance to us of this stately Russian figure unearthed by Pushkin in the Russian soil. He revealed and molded it, forever placing it before us in its indisputable, humble, and spiritually noble beauty as evidence of that potent spirit of Russian national life which is capable of producing characters of such incontestable truth. This character has been established; it is here; it cannot be denied by the assertion that it is mere fiction or a fantasy and idealization of the poet. You contemplate it, and you admit: yes, this exists. Therefore, the spirit of the people that conceived it must exist, and it is great and boundless.

Everywhere in Pushkin there sounds a faith in the Russian character, in its spiritual might, and where there is faith there is hope, great hope for the Russian:

> With hope for all the good and glory,
> I look ahead, devoid of fear,

said the poet himself, referring to another subject; yet these words are directly applicable to his entire national creative work. And never was any

Russian writer, either prior to Pushkin or since, so wholeheartedly and germanely at one with his people as he. It stands to reason that we have many writers who are connoisseurs of the people; they write about the people with much talent, pointedly and lovingly; and yet, compared with Pushkin, they are verily, with one or at most two exceptions, among his latest followers, merely "gentlemen" writing about the people. In the most talented among them, even in these two exceptions just mentioned, now and then, suddenly there appears something haughty, something belonging to a different world and mode of living, something of an effort to lift the people to these writers' level and thereby to bestow happiness on them. In Pushkin, however, there is precisely something *genuinely* akin to the people which reaches in him the point of almost naive emotionalism. Take his story about *The Bear* and the peasant who killed his "lady bear's mate"; or recall the verses "Kinsman John, when we start drinking," and you will understand what I mean.

All these artistic treasures and gems of creative insight were left by our great poet as mere landmarks for future artists and workers in the same realm. It may be positively asserted that had there been no Pushkin the men of talent following him would be nonexistent. At least they would not have revealed themselves so potently and so clearly, despite their great gifts, as they did reveal themselves later, in our day.

Still, the point is not confined to poesy alone, to mere artistic creation: had there been no Pushkin, perhaps our faith in our Russian individuality, in our national strength, and our belief in our future independent mission in the family of the European nations, would not have manifested itself with so unyielding a force as it did later (although not in everybody but only in very few). This exploit of Pushkin becomes particularly clear when what I call the third period of his creative work is examined.

As stated, there are no clear-cut divisions between these periods. For instance, certain works of the third period could even have appeared at the very beginning of the creative work of our poet, since Pushkin was always, so to speak, a complete and homogeneous organism bearing within it at once all the beginnings, and not acquiring them from without. External stimuli merely called forth in him what lay hidden in the depth of his soul. Even so, that organism developed, and the stages of its development may actually be traced; in each one of them its intrinsic character may be indicated and the gradual transformation from one period to another may be discerned.

Thus, that group of his works may be placed in the third class which preeminently reflects universal ideas, poetic images of other nations in which their genius is incarnated. Some of these works appeared only after Pushkin's death. It is in this period that our poet reveals something almost miraculous and unheard-of, something never before recorded in any nation. In fact, in European belles-lettres there were geniuses of immense creative magnitude—Shakespeare, Cervantes, Schiller. But please point to even one of these geniuses who possessed such a universal susceptibility as Pushkin. And this faculty, the major faculty of our nationality, Pushkin shares with our people, and by virtue of this he is preeminently a national poet. Even the greatest of the European poets were never able to embody in themselves with such potency as Pushkin the genius of an alien, perhaps neighboring people—their spirit, its hidden depth, its longing for its predestination. In dealing with foreign nations it may be said, on the contrary, that the European poets reincarnated in them their own nationality, interpreting them from their own national point of view. Even in Shakespeare, his Italians, for instance, are almost invariably Englishmen. Pushkin alone—among all world poets—possesses the faculty of completely reincarnating in himself an alien nationality. Take his *Scene from Faust, The Covetous Knight,* or his ballade *Once There Lived a Poor Young Knight.* Read again his *Don Juan,* and had it not been signed by Pushkin you would never have guessed that it was not written by a Spaniard. What deep, fantastic images in the poem *A Feast During the Plague!* But in these fantastic images one discerns the genius of England: this admirable song about the plague sung by the hero of the poem; and *Mary's Song,* with those verses

> Our children's cheerful voices
> In the noisy school were heard,—

these English songs, this anguish of British genius, its lamentations, its suffering presentiment of its future. Recall the strange poem:

> When wandering once amidst a valley wild . . .

This is almost a literal rendition of the first three pages of a strange mystical book, written in prose by an ancient English sectarian—but is it a mere rendition?—In the sad and ecstatic music of these verses there sounds the soul of northern Protestantism, of an English sectarian leader, a boundless mystic with his dull, gloomy and irresistible aspirations and unrestraint of mystical reverie. When reading these queer verses, one feels the spirit of the age of the Reformation; one begins to understand the militant fury of early Protestantism, history itself; and one grasps it not only rationally, but as if one were physically present there, as if one had walked through an armed camp of sectarians, had sung their hymns with them, wept with them in their religious ecstasies and shared their creed with them.

Apropos: compare this religious mysticism with the religious strophes from the Koran, or *Imitations of the Koran:* isn't this a Mohammedan? Isn't this the very spirit of the Koran, its sword, the naive stateliness of its creed and its threatening power?

And again—here is the ancient world, here are *The Egyptian Nights;* here are the earthly gods who seated themselves as such on the people's backs, gods already despising the genius of the people and their aspirations, no longer believing in that genius—gods who in fact became segregated gods, who grew mad in their isolation, who in their weariness foresaw death, and who in their agony sought diversion in fantastic brutalities, in the voluptuousness of creeping things, of a female spider devouring its male.

Nay, I assert emphatically that never has there been a poet with such a universal responsiveness as Pushkin. But it is not only a matter of susceptibility but also of its amazing depth—that reincarnation in his spirit of the spirit of foreign nations, an almost complete, and therefore miraculous, reincarnation. This phenomenon has been revealed in no other poet in the world. This we find in Pushkin alone, and in this sense he is a unique and unheard-of phenomenon, and to my mind a prophetic one . . . since it is exactly in this that his national, Russian strength revealed itself most—the national character of his poetry, the national spirit in its future development and in our future, which is concealed in that which is already present —and this has been prophetically revealed by Pushkin. For what else is the strength of the Russian national spirit than the aspiration, in its ultimate goal, for universality and all-embracing humanitarianism? Having become fully a national poet, having come in contact with the people and their vigor, Pushkin at once began to foresee their future destiny. In this he was a diviner and a prophet.

In fact, what has Peter's reform meant to us, not only from the standpoint of its effect upon the future but even in that which has already come to pass and stands in full view? What was the meaning of this reform?—Surely, it was not a mere adoption by us of European dress, habits, inventions, and science. Let us scrutinize the matter, let us examine it attentively. Yes, it is very possible that at first Peter conceived the reform in this narrow utilitarian sense. Later, however, in the subsequent elaboration of his idea, he certainly must have obeyed a certain concealed instinct which impelled him in his work to aspire unquestionably for future, greater aims than mere utilitarianism. Likewise, the Russian people accepted the reform not from mere utilitarian motives, but, no doubt, because they at once felt an infinitely loftier goal than mere utilitarianism. I repeat: they felt it unconsciously, and yet in a direct and vital manner. Indeed, at once we began to strive impetuously for the most vital universal all-humanitarian fellowship. Not inimically (as it would seem it should have happened) but in a friendly manner, with full love, we admitted into our soul the genius of foreign nations, without any racial discrimination, instinctively managing—almost from the first step—to eliminate contradictions, to excuse and reconcile differences, thereby manifesting our readiness and proclivity to enter into an all-embracing, universal communion with all the nationalities of the great Aryan races.

Yes, the Russian's destiny is incontestably all-European and universal. To become a genuine and all-around Russian means, perhaps (and this you should remember), to become brother of all men, *a universal man,* if you please. Oh, all this Slavophilism and this Westernism is a great, although historically inevitable, misunderstanding. To a genuine Russian, Europe and the destiny of the great Aryan race are as dear as Russia herself, as the fate of his native land, because our destiny is universality acquired not by the sword but by the force of brotherhood and our brotherly longing for fellowship of men. If you analyze our history after Peter's reform, you will find traces and indications of this idea, of this fantasy of mine, in the character of our intercourse with European nations, even in our state policies. For what else has Russia been doing in her policies, during these

two centuries, than serving Europe much more than herself? I do not believe that this took place because of the mere want of aptitude on the part
of our statesmen.

Oh, the peoples of Europe have no idea how dear they are to us! And
later—in this I believe—we, well, not we but the future Russians, to the last
man, will comprehend that to become a genuine Russian means to seek
finally to reconcile all European controversies, to show the solution of European anguish in our all-humanitarian and all-unifying Russian soul, to
embrace in it with brotherly love all our brethren, and finally, perhaps, to
utter the ultimate word of great, universal harmony, of the brotherly accord
of all nations abiding by the law of Christ's Gospel!

I know, I know too well, that my words may sound ecstatic, exaggerated,
and fantastic. Be it so: I do not feel sorry for having uttered them. This had
to be said, especially now, at the moment of our triumph, of the celebration
of the memory of our great genius, who, in his creative work, incarnated
precisely this idea. Besides, it has been expressed before: I am saying nothing new. What is most important—all this may sound conceited: "Is such a
destiny"—it might be said—"to be bestowed upon our crude land! Are we
destined to utter the new word to mankind?" Well, do I speak of economic
renown, of the glory of sword or science?—I am speaking merely of the
brotherhood of men and of the fact that the Russian heart is more adapted
to universal, all-humanitarian brotherly fellowship than any other nation. I
perceive this in our history, in our gifted men, in the creative genius of
Pushkin. Let our land be poor, but this destitute land "Christ, in a serf's
garb, has traversed, to and fro, with blessing." Why shouldn't we embrace
His ultimate word? Wasn't He Himself born in a manger?

I repeat: at least we are already in a position to point to Pushkin, to the
universality and all-humanitarianism of his genius. For wasn't he capable of
embracing in his soul foreign genius as his own? In art, at least, in creative
achievement, he has indubitably revealed this universality of the Russian
spirit, and this in itself is a great indication. If my idea is a fantasy—at least
it has its support in Pushkin. Had he lived longer, perhaps he might have
revealed great and immortal images of the Russian soul which would be
intelligible to our European brethren; he might have attracted them to us
much more than they are attracted at present; perhaps he might have explained to them the whole truth of our aspirations, and thus they would
comprehend us better than at present and might foresee our destiny; they
would cease to look upon us as suspiciously and haughtily as they still do.
Had Pushkin lived longer, perhaps there would have been among us, too,
less strife and misunderstanding. But God willed differently: Pushkin died
in the full bloom of his creative power, and no doubt he carried with him
into his grave some great secret. And now we, with him no longer among us,
are endeavoring to solve it.

15.

Konstantin Dmitrievich Kavelin

1818-1885

Dostoevsky's "Pushkin speech" gave rise to a lively polemic that revived some of the themes debated by the men of the 1830's and 1840's. But it did not produce a similar intellectual ferment, for conditions had changed. Russian society was engrossed in the newly opened opportunities for constructive action. Science and scholarship, economic development (especially industrialization), urbanization, democratization of society —these were the main concerns, not metaphysical, theological, and historical speculations. The prevailing atmosphere was conducive to empirical investigation and practical compromise.

The leading figures on Russia's intellectual stage were no longer drawing-room philosophers, amateur theologians, and litterateurs but men of science, scholars, professional men with a set role in society, a commitment to active participation in the modernization of their country.

Such a man was Konstantin Dmitrievich Kavelin, a leading historian of the so-called juridical school of Russian historiography. A prominent Westerner and a moderate liberal, he had taken an active part in implementing the Emancipation of the serfs. Strongly influenced by the theories of social development rooted in positivism and Darwinism, he believed that Russia's special condition was but a reflection of an earlier stage of social development, a stage that was rapidly being overcome by the transformation ushered in by the reforms of the 1860's.

He was mainly concerned with the practical implications of the debate opened by Dostoevsky. This allowed him to bring the scholar's detachment to his analysis of the implications of Dostoevsky's highly personal, passionately moralistic approach. He was able, therefore, to summarize the old positions, to criticize their weak spots and to point to the direction in which a practical, empirical solution might be sought. Putting his faith in the evolution of social and political institutions, Kavelin—unlike Dostoevsky—was primarily interested in the means of bringing about conditions that would lead to a moral as well as material regeneration of Russian society.

A Letter to F. M. Dostoevsky

DEAR SIR:

Your ecstatic speech in Moscow on the occasion of the unveiling of the monument to Pushkin made a tremendous impression on listeners belonging to the very different camps into which Russian thought is at present divided. The ensuing polemic between you and Professor Gradovskii has aroused great interest among the general public, and the issue of *Dnevnik pisatelia* [Diary of a Writer] devoted to the debate has already appeared in a second printing.[1] All this proves that the questions you touched upon with your exceptional talent, unfailing sincerity, and deep conviction are indeed ripe in the minds and hearts of thoughtful people in Russia and are of great moment for them. This can only be welcomed as a sign of revival after many years of unhealthy, lethargic indifference toward the higher concerns of man. What are we? Where are we going? Where should we be going? These national Russian questions, close to all of us as such, become universal human questions when they are posed as in your debate with Professor Gradovskii—and as they are by almost all thoughtful people in our country. Which is more important, which is more of the essence, which should be put in the forefront—personal moral improvement or the elaboration and perfection of the conditions under which man lives in society? Some say: Strive for inner, spiritual, moral truth, come to love it with all your soul, and the perfect social life will take shape of itself. Others retort: Make social life, the social conditions, as nearly perfect as possible; then individuals will quite naturally and automatically be steered onto the path of virtue, of moral growth and perfection.

Ultimately the doctrines of the Slavophiles and the Westerners, and all that is being thought, said, and written at present, boil down to this basic question. The Slavophiles put forward as their banner the first of the two solutions to this problem, identifying it with the essence of Greco-Eastern

---

[1] The one issue of Dostoevsky's *Dnevnik pisatelia* published in 1880 contained the text of his Pushkin speech as well as an answer to Aleksandr D. Gradovskii's criticism of it. Gradovskii (1841–89) was a leading historian of Russian public law and an active propagandist for Western-style moderate liberalism.—Editor.

Translated by Gertrude Vakar from Konstantin Dmitrievich Kavelin, "Pis'mo F. M. Dostoevskomu," in *Sobranie sochinenii*, Vol. II (St. Petersburg, 1897–1900), cols. 1021–52. The letter, written in 1880, was first published in *Vestnik Evropy*, No. 11 (1889).

Christianity and the Slavic national genius; as clearly and firmly, the so-called Westerners set forth the second solution, linking it inseparably with the spirit of Peter's reforms and of Western European culture. Despite all the ramifications and changes in the Slavophile and Western views, and no matter how close some of their branches at times came to each other, the basic tenor of their difference, mentioned above, has persisted to this day. Now as before, the best men in both camps admit that their opponents are right to a certain extent; but neither side has ever conceded that the other might be right in the principle on which its philosophy is built. Any mutual concessions are made very cautiously, with important reservations, and are instantly revoked if they can give rise to the slightest doubts as to the fundamental disagreement.

This, it seems to me, is what makes the controversy between you and Professor Gradovskii extremely important and why it is particularly desirable that it should be brought sooner or later to a conclusion. It concerns principles deeply rooted in life and consciousness. Their struggle began before our time and is not likely to end in our lifetime. For thousands of years, the most profound and most enlightened minds have been actively engaged in it.

I have been very interested in the subject during the last few years and have given it a great deal of thought; everything led me back to it almost despite myself. I hope, therefore, that you will find it only natural if I join in your discussion from the sidelines, so to speak, unbidden and uninvited. I certainly do not consider myself called upon to resolve it but only to help in clarifying it and in putting it on the right footing. This is always the main thing, but especially with us—because of the incredible chaos in our ideas, which prevents even two individuals from reaching any kind of agreement.

You have uttered the words "reconciliation of the parties." Yes, it is time, high time, to close private accounts, to stop the literary jousts turning on witticisms, to discard the trite and vulgar mutual accusations! It is time to forget personalities and mutual irritation and to explain ourselves calmly and frankly on all points. But reconciliation in the sense of agreement—that is a different matter! You, a man of undoubted sincerity, certainly cannot mean a diplomatic compromise, an armed truce, when you speak of reconciliation. A bad peace is good, better than a good war, in practical affairs, because daily life is a continuous series of compromises, half-sincere, half-cunning, with reservations in the back of one's mind; but in problems of science, faith, principles, a good war—until genuine, honest peace—is much better! But such a peace is still very far away. God knows when it will come! Our Russian arguments are poisoned from the very beginning because we seldom argue against what a man says but nearly always against what he may be thinking at the time—against his supposed intentions and secret thoughts. That is how we face one another, and how we enter upon various transactions: ever on guard, with a stone hidden in the bosom. Therefore our arguments nearly always turn to personalities, and our business relations are so vague and indefinite that they constantly lead to lawsuits and litigation. The objective meaning of words and things has little importance in our eyes; we must always rummage around in a person's soul. You, too, did not prove quite free of this common weakness of ours when you put in the Westerner's mouth thoughts that would never occur to a responsible person but only to some harebrain at best.

Let us, you and me at least, rid our differences of this worthless appendage. We ourselves shall gain a great deal, and our readers are sure to be grateful.

I

To begin, I shall discuss your view of the relations between our common people and the educated strata of society, because it epitomizes a character-istic feature of the Slavophile doctrine. Like the Slavophiles of the forties, you believe that the loftiest moral ideas are embodied in the spiritual virtues and perfections of the Russian people, more precisely the peasantry, which has had no part in the apostasy from the Russian national spirit that is supposed to taint the upper, educated classes.

The heated, sometimes bitter polemics that the Slavophiles and Western-ers used to conduct are, it seems to me, already a thing of the past. To understand now their real meaning we must turn to the history of our culture and shuffle archives. Today, if you tell someone unacquainted with our party battles that the Russian people is a model of moral perfection, he will stare at you in amazement or begin to enumerate aspects of Russian life that will make your flesh crawl. Tell an educated person who has merely heard of the Slavophiles but does not know their doctrines that he is a traitor to the Russian popular traditions and a renegade to his country, and he will either feel insulted or decide that you have gone out of your mind. Everybody knows by now that the Russian peasantry is far from being the summit of perfection, and that educated people are as devoted to their country as the popular masses—there are no longer any arguments on the subject, and there cannot be. If in the past people thought, spoke, and wrote differently about it, there were reasons for this, now forgotten, but which we must recall in order to grasp the full meaning of your views.

All men and all nations on earth learn from other men and other nations and always have, not only in childhood and youth, but also in their mature years. The difference is that in childhood and youth both men and nations tend mainly to imitate, whereas, having reached maturity, they utilize the experience and knowledge of others consciously, critically, with discrimina-tion. In childhood and youth, they strive to become exact copies of those who serve them as models; having reached maturity, they already have a sense of individuality and assimilate what they borrow, without trying to become the very image of those whose experience and knowledge they use.

Such was also our case. We learned from the whole world, from whomever we came in contact with—from practically all the Oriental nations, from the Byzantine Greeks, from our western and northern neighbors; but somehow we forgot about it and remembered again much later, not long ago. With particular zeal and haste we began to learn from the nations of Western Europe. Necessity forced us to; and Peter's impassioned nature lent an extraordinary headlong quality to our learning. The Tsar genius wanted to achieve in a quarter of a century what normally takes centuries! We remember the time of our schooling very well, because by then we had already begun to be conscious of ourselves. It has been said that Peter and his collaborators were transforming us into Europeans indiscriminately, but that is wholly untrue: both he and they were Russians to the core, loved their motherland fervently, saw and sought in the European borrowings nothing but the good of their country, without a thought of putting her into any kind of material or moral bondage to the European nations.

But Peter's work suffered the fate that almost inevitably overtakes great ideas and great enterprises: the basic thought becomes diffused in the details of its practical application and is little by little forgotten, while the details move into the foreground and become the important thing. When the methods thus replace the central idea, dead schemata, stereotypes, routine replace the former live, intelligent approach to the task. Few reforms and turnings in the life of an individual or a nation escape such setbacks. Once Peter's work had passed from the hands of his genius into the unskilled, untalented hands of his successors, it soon became stereotype and routine. The borrowings from Europe, meant to be assimilated on Russian soil, fossilized instead; Europeanism, which according to Peter's plan was to serve merely as a subsidiary to Russian life, grew into an independent factor and began to live a life of its own, albeit artificial, on Russian soil. The classes which since ancient times have dominated our popular mass were the first, because of their social position, to absorb European elements—in whose educational role they presently found a justification, a consecration as it were, of their own political and social role and of their domination of the uneducated. In this way the Europeanism which Peter and the statesmen of his school intended to be an instrument of enlightenment turned into an instrument of oppression, and also opened wide the doors into Russia to all sorts of European adventurers and rogues who, under the cloak of European enlightenment, tended their own affairs or served interests that were alien or hostile to the interests of the country.

As Russia grew and took form, the unnatural, antinational role in it of the kind of Europeanism that emerged in the post-Petrine period began to be felt more and more. The best minds, examining the situation and trying to find the causes of the torpor and gloom that blighted Russian life, came to two conclusions: some explained the malady by the fact that the educational process initiated by Peter with the aid of European influences had become arrested and had degenerated into depressing, crusty formalism retaining only a deceptive appearance of Europeanism, while the invigorating European spirit, the great, universally valid European ideas had evaporated. Therefore, they thought, one must let these ideas flow freely into Russia and thus redeem Russian life withering away under the heavy load of deadening, fossilized forms long since outdated and already abandoned by Europe herself. Others saw the cause of the stagnation and lethargy in the fact that the Russian mind had been stunned, confused, by Peter's forcible reform; hence everything European, the bad as well as the good, had become an object of servile, slavish, almost superstitious veneration. What was needed, these people thought, was to restore buoyancy, independence, enterprise to the Russian mind; then it would become what it naturally is; it would reveal the riches of the Russian national genius, now lying hidden because of false humility vis-à-vis Europe.

These were the two currents of Russian thought that later developed into the two so-called parties—which are not really parties—of Westerners and Slavophiles. As has been noted long ago, and quite rightly, both trends, which became more clearly defined in the forties, grew from one soil. That is why at first they existed peacefully side by side. Both were expressions of dissatisfaction with the conditions under which the sad life of Russia wended its colorless way, in an outward halo of unprecedented political and international glory and might. The reproach that Westerners were renegades to their country is quite unjust; they were, on the contrary, Russian people profoundly devoted to their motherland, loving it ardently, and dreaming of a great and bright future for it no less than the Slavophiles. It was not Europe they put their hopes in but the European ideas, which they regarded as valid for all mankind. Like you, they highly prized the exceptional responsiveness of the Russian people and saw in it a pledge of its great historical destinies; they were enthralled with its ability to encompass all that is human—the very quality that enthralls you. At first, the Westerners did not have the slightest animosity toward the Slavophiles, nor was there any reason for it: the attitude of the two trends toward our pseudo-Europeanism was equally negative, and their demands were essentially the same but formulated differently. The Westerners wished to see the great ideals of mankind realized in Russia; the Slavophiles did not want these ideals foisted upon Russia but rather realized through the free initiative, the independent efforts of the Russian people themselves. The two trends complemented each other. But before they understood this, before the rapprochement—which did become a fact twenty years ago—had time to take place, enmity divided them into two opposite camps.

The history of this schism in Russian thought is very interesting because it shows the level of our development at the time it began, and also the development of Russian thought and Russian self-awareness.

If the inertia, the moribund state of Russian life, came from our being depressed by pseudo-Europeanism and by the obsolete, fossilized European patterns, this meant that our earlier life had lacked the resiliency and firmness to resist their entrenchment, or, once having admitted them, to modify them according to our own national genius—in other words, that we had not yet reached adulthood; but our having begun to feel oppressed by pseudo-Europeanism and by our own passivity and inertia was a sure sign of awakening national genius and enterprise. That is, Russian life itself was putting the problem as follows: The period of school learning and mimicry was over; it was time to begin thinking for ourselves, to look critically at ourselves and others, to think and act only after a thorough appraisal of our own and others' ideas and deeds. Such a view implied that we had not yet worked out, in the past, well-defined forms of thinking and living that could serve as base and support for future work; but it also excluded the possibility of realizing the great human ideals in our country otherwise than in national forms peculiar to us and evolved by us out of our own resources; to put it differently, mankind's ideals can only be the products of the autonomous activity of a nation's genius; they result from a nation's life and cannot be transferred and transplanted from one country into another.

When thought and life in Russia began to stir, our understanding of all this was dim and jumbled; therefore our development proceeded unevenly and took roundabout paths.

For a long time we confused the human with the European, mistaking the latter for the former, as we still often do. This was unquestionably the weak side of the Westerners. The Slavophiles fell into another error. Having demanded independent national development—which was their chief merit—they set out to determine what were the basic traits of the national character that should serve as starting points for the future activity, social and moral, of the Russian people. But discovering them was like squaring the circle. Pseudo-Europeanism had become established in our midst and acquired citizenship rights precisely because our national character had not yet formed, had not taken on clear-cut traits. Only life and spontaneous activity forge the character and the distinctive traits of a man or a people; we had been apprentices of one nation after another until recently, had not lived by our own intelligence, and therefore had had no chance of developing a distinct national personality. How then could one detect the fundamental characteristics of the Russian genius? Past history was merely a chronicle of schoolboy days; it showed clear traces of our mentors' and teachers' influences and barely outlined still fluid, and hence elusive, traits of national character and genius. Since it was impossible to know, one had to invent. This was as great a mistake on the part of the Slavophiles as confusing the human with the European was on the part of the Westerners.

The logic of facts, which plays the role of the ancients' Fate in the history of modern peoples, confuted both of these trends. We no longer have pure Slavophiles nor pure Westerners—both have left the stage. In continuing to contrast their opinions, it seems to me, you are reviving an old quarrel that has already been settled by the development of Russian life and thought. Are you, for instance, an authentic Slavophile? Or those with whom you polemize real Westerners? You yourself exonerate the best among them. But who else is left? The conciliation of the two trends you are wishing for was tacitly accomplished twenty years ago, when Slavophiles and Westerners shook hands over the abolition of serfdom.

We have since entered a new period of development. Today the problems are posed differently; the labels of Slavophile and Westerner no longer fit the new trends in Russian thought. Leave it to mediocrities and phrase-makers to mouth over the old lessons! You will not make them see reason, and of course it is not for them that you write.

You will not find a single thoughtful and sensible Russian today who looks down on our popular masses because of some theoretical preconceptions, or who thinks Russia is a blank sheet of paper on which anything at all can be written. Everyone realizes that peoples, like individuals, have their own character, their own peculiarities, their own physical and spiritual physiognomy, which cannot be changed and must be taken into account when one discusses their future destiny or what is good for them in the present. Likewise, every thinking and sensible Russian understands that the new conditions introduced from the beginning of the seventeenth century cannot be deleted from our history, and that however lovingly we may regard the popular masses, it is impossible, in their present state, to consider them the acme of perfection. One has but to listen to what is being thought and discussed at present to distinguish the two trends in Russian theoretical thought that I outlined at the very beginning. One of them, basing its thesis on the formative nature of public institutions, expects all good to come solely from their reorganization, fully convinced that good institutions re-educate people and foster in them the qualities needed for orderly community life—qualities that we, unfortunately, still lack to a considerable degree. The other school of thought, also starting from our want of organization, does not believe in the omnipotence of institutions and, seeing the root of all evil in our moral condition—very unenviable, to be sure—proposes various other means of raising our morality, apart from improving our institutions. Many consider the two trends a continuation of the two older ones. Evidently you share this view. But it is hardly correct. The fresh approach to the problem is obviously a step forward in Russian thought, which could not be taken until many of the misunderstandings that had in the past led the Westerners and Slavophiles to violent disputes, oral and sometimes in the press, had been clarified. Still, one cannot deny a certain kinship and some degree of continuity between the old and the new conceptions of Russian life and the tasks it faces. The belief in the potency of institutions does recall the point of view of Peter and the champions of his cause on Russian soil, which the Westerners certainly were; while the idea of moral regeneration as the sole means of renewal brings its proponents close to the Slavophiles. The parallels stand out even more clearly when we remember that most of our social ideals still follow European prototypes, and that our moral ideals are almost entirely taken from the Slavophiles' program. But these similarities should not blind us to the substantial differences between the old and the new trends in Russian thought. The Slavophile and Western theories were the first, still immature, attempts at independent criticism; the new trends shift the Russian problems to a purely theoretical plane and thus make them apply to mankind in general.

It would seem that the two currents now forming in Russian thought also should complement rather than exclude each other. In fact, what they offer is not two differing solutions of one problem but two means of eliminating two aspects of one and the same evil. Yet, judging by certain signs, we shall not be spared a new rift and a new struggle similar to the one the Westerners and the Slavophiles used to wage. There are reasons for it on both sides, and weighty ones.

It began to be clear to me long ago that the basic trouble with European societies, not excluding our own, was the insufficiently formed and developed inner—moral and psychic—side of human nature. The effects of this flaw are all the greater since it is not especially noticeable and hardly any efforts are made to remedy it. In practical life, the firm conviction prevails that any lack of personal moral discipline can very well be balanced by good legislation, good courts of law, good administration; in scholarship, ethics is ignored: today ethics lacks a proper scientific foundation and clings to old, rusty, routine theories in which no one believes any more and which are devoid of any authority in the eyes of our contemporaries; in education, moral training plays the sorriest role: it has been supplanted by mechanical drilling to fit people for life within a society, and this is deemed to be all there is to morality.

I confess that one of the features which most attracts me in the Slavophile theories has always been their emphasis on inner, psychic, moral truth, on generally neglected and forgotten moral beauty. Perhaps I am letting myself be carried away by a golden dream, but I have a notion that the new word awaited by many will concern a new, correct presentation of the problem of morality, in science, education, and practical life, and that it is we who shall say this vivifying word. The obscure hopes of young Russian minds and hearts are circling around this problem, eagerly attentive to anything that may hold an answer to it. This problem is bound up, in all sorts of vague combinations, with hazy ideas about the future role of the Russian and Slavic race in the world's destinies. The immense success of your speech about Pushkin is due mainly to your having struck this strongly resounding chord and having identified moral beauty and truth with the Russian national psyche.

Why it is precisely this question that stands first in line and knocks on all doors at once, where the hopes come from that it may be our lot and not some other nation's, if not to solve the problem, at least to work at solving it—this I shall not stop to consider here. I should have to talk for a long time, and I would rather not digress from what I want to say to you.

At the moment, the main task facing all of us volunteers in the field of Russian thought is to pose the problem of moral truth squarely, boldly, tellingly, in such a way that the problem itself and its urgency shall become obvious and unmistakable to all, in such a way that no one can keep silent or elude it with commonplaces and pompous words. Sermons will be useful, even necessary, later; their time has not yet come. First we must work out the problem in the laboratory of strict and exact science; we must, by dint of proof, by the arguments of up-to-date knowledge, confront people with moral truth, demonstrate that all roads inevitably lead to it, that there is no escape, that to pass it by or detour it is entirely impossible.

I jumped at your polemics with Professor Gradovskii in the avid hope of finding in it at least a hint of this necessary foreword to the new word; but I found nothing of the kind. The same old Slavophile argumentation, which cannot satisfy anyone today. Were the old Slavophile leaders alive in our time, after all the things we have experienced, they would, I am sure, bring out new arguments in defense of their thesis. The formula in which they cast it has turned out to be wrong and poorly supported, and you have added nothing to it; you do not even try to correct it.

Like the Slavophiles of the forties, you refer to the exalted, matchless moral qualities of the Russian people. When the Slavophiles first spoke of this, it was indeed new and stimulating. The Russian intelligentsia groveled before Europe and everything European; national consciousness was half asleep; we were aware only of our physical strength and proud of it, hardly suspecting how little it means when it is not buttressed by intellectual and moral strength. Since then an immense change has come over Russian society and the Russian intelligentsia. Where are the so-called kvass patriotism [2] and the reliance on the bear's strength? Hasn't the servile adulation of Europe given way in our time to an unexampled upsurge of national feeling, which even spills over into hypersensitivity, arrogance, and pugnacity? One does not have to be a Westerner to blush at the behavior in which these feelings sometimes find expression. The Moscow Slavophiles, pure idealists that they were, would of course have condemned them severely. Theirs was a vision of quite different ideals of nationalistic feeling.

In your enthusiasm over the spiritual treasures of the Russian national genius, you say: "All of our destitute, disordered land, with the exception of its upper stratum, is like one man. All the eighty million of its population exhibit such a spiritual unity as, of course, does not and cannot exist anywhere in Europe."

I leave it to ethnographers and statisticians to reduce that figure by twenty or twenty-five million; among the remaining fifty-five or sixty there is indeed a striking unity, but of what kind? Racial, religious, political, linguistic—yes; as to spiritual, in the sense of moral, conscious, unity—that is debatable! So far, we have before us only a fact of tremendous import, whose inner, spiritual meaning we cannot define—it is all in the future; we should look for it vainly in the present or the past.

II

Equally perplexing is your opinion of the common Russian people's moral qualities, their significance and their origin.

Like the Slavophiles of the forties, you consider our national virtues an established, indubitable fact and ascribe them to our people's being imbued with the Orthodox faith and carrying it deep in their heart.

Let me observe, in the first place, that one can hardly ascribe moral virtues to an entire people, especially when one belongs to it by birth, education, one's whole life, and all one's sympathies. What people does not consider itself the best, the most moral in the world? On the other hand, once having adopted such a viewpoint, one might, despite reason and com-

[2] A kind of homespun, uncritical nationalism that admires everything that seems to be rooted in popular custom.—Editor.

mon sense, regard entire peoples as immoral, or even as particularly prone to immoral acts of a specific kind—such opinions have been expressed.

You will extol the artlessness, meekness, humility, candor, kindness of the Russian people; someone else, with no less justification, will point out its bent for thieving, deceit, cheating, drink; the savage, revolting treatment of women. You will be given a multitude of examples of inhuman, ferocious cruelty. Who is right? Those who extol to the skies the moral qualities of the Russian people or those who trample it in the mud? Every one of us has repeatedly pondered this problem. And it is insoluble! When we discuss morality and immorality, we concentrate not on the *how* of the people's attitude to the object of its faith and convictions, but on *what* that object is; and the *what* is entirely a result of the school the people went through, of foreign influences—in short, of its history, development, and culture. Therefore, to evaluate a people correctly, one must speak not of its good or bad moral qualities, which may change, but of the characteristics inherent in its spiritual nature, those that give it a physiognomy unlike any other and which it retains throughout its history, whatever the freaks of fate.

Does the Russian people possess such characteristic traits? No doubt it does—like any other people, even the most insignificant tribe doomed by history to be swallowed up by another nation. But should you ask me what I think they are, I could not, to my shame and the great temptation of many, give you a clear-cut, categorical answer. I am unable to distinguish a single trait in the spiritual physiognomy of the Russian people of which I could say with absolute certainty that it is basic, typical of its character and not due to its historical age, its surroundings, or the circumstances of its past or present life.

That the Russian people is richly endowed by nature can hardly be questioned—this is conceded even by our ill-wishers and enemies. But exactly what its natural talents are eludes definition, it seems to me. I shall be told: great mental alertness, daring, and agility, the level-headed approach to all things, the broad sweep? But those are attributes common to all gifted peoples in their youth. Weren't the ancient Greeks the same in their time? We are supposed to be terrific realists. Many single out this trait as basic to the Russian national character, but let them show me a people who is more inclined than the Russians to pursue abstract ideas, castles in the air, mirages and utopias of all kinds! How are we realists then? We are just lively adolescents as yet. Others cite our astonishing ingenuity in the most varied circumstances, our skill in adapting ourselves to them, our skill in adapting ourselves to other people and nations. But are these properties basic national traits? We have only to remember the territory we are sitting on, the peoples and tribes that surround us, the past great sufferings of the Russian people, to see instantly how we came by these traits. If they had not been cultivated for centuries, you and I would not be discussing the Russian people today: there would be none to discuss. And in youth everything is borne and endured more buoyantly, cheerfully, easily, than in middle age or old age. You note, quite correctly, the Russian people's exceptional empathy, its exceptional ability to "identify itself with the genius of foreign nations, an almost complete identification." But this undoubted and very valuable faculty of the Russian people also is, alas! no more than a trait of a very gifted and intelligent people, but a people not even in its youth but in its infancy; a young man, even an adolescent, as soon as he has in the least matured and has something of his own to say, gradually loses this ability. In a word, whichever salient trait of the Russian people one takes, each bespeaks remarkable aptitudes and at the same time extreme youth—an age when it is still impossible to guess what kind of spiritual physiognomy that talented adolescent will develop when he becomes a man.

Since the character of our spiritual nature is still so indistinct and unclear, I am obliged to regard with some mistrust your basic idea that we are imbued with the Christian spirit. That many of our high moral qualities are the fruit of Christianity cannot be doubted. Throughout our history, all over the Russian land, there stretch long lines of Christian ascetics, of saints who renounced the world, retired into the wilderness, and dedicated themselves to fasting, prayer, and contemplation; among laymen, still recently one could find in families, cities, and peasant huts not a few types of striking moral beauty, whose genuine piety, purity, simplicity, and meekness recalled apostolic times. All who knew them remember them and will never forget them. But observe that all of them—laymen as well as monks—shunned the world, retired from the turbulence of workaday life into prayer and meditation. The daily, humdrum, material life went its way, hardly in accord with the teaching of Christ, while saintly people avoided it and wanted no part in it. It has to be either one or the other: either the confession of Christianity is incompatible with living and working in the world—and if so, how could the Russian people be imbued with Christian principles?—or, on the contrary, peoples cannot find salvation unless they are imbued with Christian truths in their public and private life; but if so, then our daily life was not thus imbued, since holy men left it to go into forests and deserts and found salvation only in estrangement from the world.

My queries suggest an explanation of many phenomena of Russian life and history that differs from yours. The most pious people, the most fervid patriots complain that ritual predominates over faith in the minds and lives of our common people, as if religion were one thing and life another, separate, thing. It has been pointed out more than once that we need internal missionaries to enlighten the people still steeped in crude pagan prejudices and superstitions. Even illiterate peasants complain of their womenfolk's utter ignorance of the most common prayers. All this shows that the enlightenment of the popular masses in the spirit of Christianity still awaits its workers. It has not been accomplished so far because the truly zealous Christians thirsting for spiritual perfection retired from the world and served only as models of the saintly life and as objects of veneration to the laymen who yearned for spiritual enlightenment and perfection; the enormous majority, immersed in the worries and vanities of daily life, imagined the Christian faith to consist in church services and ritual; frequent attendance at church and strict observance of the holy ritual—that was what the majority imagined to be the whole meaning of Christianity. This predominantly formalistic attitude of our forebears amazed foreigners so much that Fletcher,[3] for instance, simply called us pagans. Is it any wonder that daily life, left to itself, went badly and looked outside the fatherland, to foreign parts and foreign people, for examples to follow and a way out toward a better order of things? If moral improvement in the spirit of Christ required renouncing the world, then the improvement of the secular order obviously had to be achieved apart from the Church and its influences; one was the natural and inevitable outcome of the other. Unprepared by a gradual betterment of the mores, it was made in leaps and starts, through legislative measures after foreign patterns. The harshness and suddenness of Peter's reforms, the sharp opposition of the temporal to the spiritual, of the Slavophiles' moral ideals to the Westerners' social ideals, were but consequences of the belief, which had come to permeate our flesh and blood, that perfection in the Christian sense is possible only away from the world and its temptations.

This conception of Christianity has its basis in the philosophy of the ancient East. Separation from the world, mortification of the flesh, spiritual contemplation as the greatest good and the highest perfection had traditionally appeared to the inhabitants of the East as the sole escape from the ills, adversities, and troubles of earthly life. The principle of fighting and eliminating them, of controlling external phenomena with the aid of science and art, had no place in Eastern philosophy; and since men and nations accept truth insofar as they can encompass it, the inhabitants of the East adopted the form of Christianity that was most congenial to them. Scholars and philosophers, mostly Greek, applied themselves to the study and exegesis of creed and dogma; those who sought moral perfection retired into the wilderness, purified themselves through fast and prayer, and gave themselves over to spiritual contemplation.

But Christianity has innumerable facets and can be looked at from innumerable points of view. The Western European peoples entered upon its adoption with different dispositions and premises and therefore assimilated it mainly in one of its other aspects. In their lands, Nature is generous only to those who know how to make her serve them. This fact alone early challenged the European to work hard and to fight his environment, and fostered in him the certitude that with knowledge, labor, and perseverance he could eliminate the harmful, utilize the propitious, and create for himself surroundings that suited his needs and tastes. This point of view was also implicit in the rich heritage left by the Greco-Roman world, which the Western peoples at first absorbed unconsciously, from the mere fact of living on classic soil, and later deliberately made their own through long study. Acquaintance with this world was bound to confirm and strengthen the

---

[3] Giles Fletcher, who wrote *Of the Russe-Common-Wealth* (1591), one of the best-known descriptions of Russia in the reign of Ivan the Terrible.—Editor.

Western European in his belief that not only nature but social conditions, too, could be adapted to the needs of man, just as man can and must adapt and accustom himself to the conditions of properly organized community life. Therefore a Western European would not think of meekly suffering unfavorable conditions or leaving his environment when it does not satisfy him; he tries, on the contrary, to master them, subject them to his will, transform them to suit his requirements and tastes. A man of such outlook and habits, on adopting Christianity, naturally used it as a powerful means of expanding his knowledge, improving the conditions of social and private life, and educating people. To the Western European, Christianity opened new horizons, unsuspected till then—new ways of developing and perfecting reality and man's whole surroundings. You will say that such an application of Christianity to material needs and to the conditions of everyday life has blurred and dulled in Western European consciousness the divine image of the Saviour, who said that His kingdom was not of this world? I can agree with this, though not without serious qualifications. Since no spiritual doctrine can be compressed into a formula, any attempt to capture the spirit of Christianity and frame it in a set of rules is bound to distort it; I am willing to go even further and add that in focusing exclusively on Christianity's application to science, knowledge, and society, the Western European has lost sight of man's inner, moral, spiritual world, which is just the one to which the Gospel addresses itself. This, it seems to me, is the Achilles' heel of European civilization; here lies the root of the sickness that undermines it and saps its strength. The Western European has entirely devoted himself to ameliorating the objective conditions of life, persuaded that they alone hold the key to human welfare and perfection; the subjective side is ignored. But I go along with you only so far; from here on, we diverge radically. The Slavophiles of the forties, and now you, in condemning the Western Christians, overlook the fact that they represent—even if imperfectly, incompletely—the active, reformatory side of Christianity in the world. According to the Western European conception, Christianity is meant to improve, perfect, renew not only the individual but also mankind's whole way of life, to nurture not hermits alone but also people living in the world, amid all its petty annoyances and daily temptations. According to the European ideal, a Christian should not retire from the world in order to preserve his purity and saintliness—he should live in the world, fight evil, and overcome it. In Catholicism, the creation of the Romance peoples' genius, you see only the ugly organization of the Church after the pattern of a secular state, with a spiritual emperor at its head; and in Protestantism, the conception of Christianity according to the spirit of the Germanic peoples, you see only the one-sided limitless freedom of individual thought, leading in the end to atheism; but Western Europe has produced much more than the pope and atheism under the unquestionable influence of Christianity. You contradict yourself when you admire European science, art, literature, in which the same spirit breathes that also produced both Catholicism and Protestantism. To be consistent, you should reject all if you reject these—there is no middle ground.

III

I am coming at last to the theoretical basis of your whole argument—your conception of morality and of its meaning and role in human society.

Disagreeing with Professor Gradovskii, you deny the distinction between social ideals and personal and moral ideals. You ask: "How are you going to unite people for the attainment of your civic goals if you don't have the great primary idea of morality for a basis?" And you continue: "And moral ideas are of one kind only: they are all based on the idea of absolute personal self-perfection as an ideal ahead, because it comprises everything, all the aspirations, all the thirsts; and consequently your civic ideals also derive from it." This thought, one of the major points of controversy, seems wrong to me.

In the first place, there are no moral *ideas,* just as there is no *social* morality, Professor Gradovskii notwithstanding. Morality is above all personal, a cast of the soul, a lay of feelings, which set the tone and direction of our thoughts, intentions, and acts. That is the reason it is impossible to seize hold of morality and put it into any kind of thought or formula. Morality is primarily what we call Spirit. Deep down in his heart every man knows whether what he is planning or doing is good or bad. He carries the feeling of good and evil within himself. But if you ask what evil is, or what good is, no one will be able to answer you. Ask the same question about a specific thought, deed, undertaking, and the densest illiterate will have no trouble answering it. You may find his answer wrong, or consider that he calls good evil, or vice versa; but in terms of his own feeling and consciousness he will be a moral man if he refrains from plans and actions that he perceives as bad. How this elusive, so to speak shapeless, feeling of good and evil develops in man and illumines every thought and act for each in a way peculiar to him—that is another question. The point is that everyone has such a private tuning fork. Who is faithful to it in thought and deed is a moral person, and who is unfaithful, who disobeys it, is immoral.

Our concepts, or ideas, of what is good and what is evil are something else altogether. Every idea is a formulated, definite thought about an object, that is to say, about something we conceive of as existing outside ourselves, something objective. A *concept* of what is good or evil (here I speak only of our social concepts) is a judgment based on considerations stemming not from a vague and shapeless feeling but from the conditions and facts of organized common life with other people.

You will say that, after all, the inner awareness of good and evil, that is, the voice of conscience, also develops under the influence of the social milieu? Certainly—and that is why the conscience of the ancient pagan Greeks spoke otherwise than the Christian conscience. The inner awareness of good and evil and the concepts of good and evil are identical in content; but there is the essential difference that the first, conscience, expresses man's unmediated personal attitude toward his own thoughts and acts; it is a feeling that cannot be fitted into any formula. A concept, on the other hand, is no longer something personal but something objective, concrete, accessible to all, and subject to discussion and verification. Moreover, a concept of what is good and what is evil recedes from the individual even further, becomes to him even more objective and external, when it is made into a compulsory law that all must obey whether they want to or not, to which all must conform in their outward conduct.

For these reasons I cannot agree with you when you speak of moral *ideas*, or with Professor Gradovskii when he speaks of *social* morality. Morality, as a purely personal fact particular to each human being, cannot be an idea, a formulated concept of a number of people. By the same token, there cannot be any social morality; for if we mean by this expression that the majority of people in a given society are moral, it is inaccurate, since it transfers to an aggregate of people something that is a characteristic attribute of each separate individual; and if we relate the expression to some idea that they all accept, it is entirely wrong, because ideas cannot be moral or immoral—they are correct or incorrect. A moral man is a man who in thought and deed is always true to the voice of his conscience, which tells him whether his thoughts and deeds are good or bad; morality consists solely in man's attitude toward himself, and moral truth consists solely in the accord of thought and deed with conscience. *What* conscience prompts, *why* it approves of some thoughts and deeds and condemns others—that is beyond the scope of morality and is determined by concepts, or ideas, which form under the influence of society and therefore vary greatly at different times and in differing circumstances.

Concepts or ideas must on no account be confused with *ideals*. The latter are pluperfect intellectual models, facts or ideas elevated in our consciousness to a higher plane through a process of generalization. In this sense, one can speak of both a moral ideal (not idea) and social ideals. The moral ideal would be the constant, total, instantaneous, unhesitating subordination of every thought and act to the voice of inner consciousness, or conscience; a sensitivity to that voice developed to the highest degree; an extremely refined sensitivity, refined to a high degree through exercise, of conscience itself, and so on. Of social ideals there may be a great many, as many as there are social ideas and formulas, and every one of the ideals will be an image of the full and most perfect realization of these formulas in actual life.

Until we sort out these conceptions, our arguments will go on endlessly and lead nowhere. We confuse concepts, ideas, ideals, with morality. The result is an unbelievable muddle.

In the second place, the ideas you call moral define the mutual relations of people in an organized society, presenting them in formulas. These formulas are general and abstract because they deal not with this or that person but with people in general, or, if you wish, with the average man, considering only his general, not his individual, traits; and as soon as you define the relations of the average man with other, also average, people in an organized community, you create social ideas for really existing individuals.

You say that social or civic ideals (that is, ideas) derive from the idea of absolute personal self-perfection as an ideal ahead. Apart from the inaccuracy of expression I pointed out earlier, I maintain that morality and social ideas, personal ideals and social ideals, have nothing in common and that confusing them can result only in chaos.

Orsini and Charlotte Corday were patriots, people of superior morality, while Dumollard, who raped, killed, and robbed a number of women and terrorized a whole neighborhood, was a villain, a brute; yet all three had transgressed the social law and ended under the blade of the guillotine.

The social idea, in formulating the requisites for orderly human coexistence, ignores the inner man and his relationship to himself; it deals only with the outward behavior of people and their relations with other people and with the community. In the formulation of social ideas, inner life and hidden thoughts are taken into account only insofar as they affect behavior.

Dealing as it does with the outward, not the inward, life of man, the social formula sets a rule or a law compulsory for that external side and enforces conformity and obedience by equally external means and methods. What inner motives make people conform to the social law is of no interest whatever from the standpoint of society. The social law does not look into a man's soul—and woe to the society in which it does.

You believe that morality itself contains everything that the social laws or formulas require? That is a big mistake! What you would call a moral idea—loving one's neighbor more than oneself, self-abnegation in favor of others—is a social idea or formula, since it defines our relationship to others within a society: it expresses the ideal of that relationship. The only moral aspect of these virtues is their sincerity and completeness, the strength of conviction. Otherwise you would have to describe as immoral the fanatic who thought he served God when he burned heretics at the stake—and whom the Catholic Church has canonized.

You may ask where the ideal nature of the social virtues comes from if not from moral ideas? I have already answered this: social or civic ideas do not deal with individuals but with abstract average man; they reproduce not single facts but a general abstract formula for facts, which for this very reason, when applied to really existing people, becomes a compulsory law, the ideal norm to which they aspire or at least conform in their outward behavior for fear of punishment.

You say that "the ideal of civic order in human society . . . is wholly a product of the moral self-perfection of individuals and begins with it, and this has been so forever and will remain so forevermore." Such a view contradicts the facts of history. It is by no means the moral self-perfection of people that engenders civic ideas but the practical concrete necessity of ordering their coexistence within society in such a way that each and every one will be as safe, free, and generally comfortable as possible and able to look after his affairs in peace. I should say, rather, that social ideas form and are formulated because some of the people in a society break the requirements of well-ordered coexistence and thereby compel the others to formulate them, to enact them into laws, and by various means, including threat of punishment, to ensure their strict observance by all. Not personal self-improvement but, on the contrary, the lack of discipline, the willfulness of some of the people, their disregard of the rights and needs of others, cause the standards of proper community life to be summed up in social ideas and formulas. In maintaining the opposite, you forget that individuals grow up and develop within society, not outside it; that as far back as man remembers himself in history he has been a member of a society, if at first only of a family; and that apart from community life with others he is unable to perfect himself. What you call the moral idea is the fruit of human coexistence, the result of its long development and elaboration. Before the requisites for ordered social life had crystallized in the human conscience and become what you call the moral ideal, they already existed in embryo, in a crude, raw form, in the fact itself of community life and the customs and laws that evolved from it. Overlooking this, you speak only of voluntary societies freely created by people drawn together by their religious beliefs. Many communities did begin in this way, and not only for religious reasons; but observe that such associations presuppose already mature people, and they could become mature only in contact with others of their kind, that is, within some human society. Moreover, only the tiniest fraction of human societies were formed by voluntary agreement. The immense majority came into being independently of human volition, through accidents of birth, conquest, the mere fact of living in the same place, and so on. In those at any rate, moral self-perfection could not possibly have been at the root of social ideas; on the contrary, it is the latter, developed in response to the community's practical needs and made into laws applying to all, that have become a powerful means of educating people in proper community life; it is they that have implanted and fostered in people what you call moral ideals. In my opinion this is another and most weighty argument against your contention that moral ideas have engendered the civic and social ideas. Just the opposite: the imperative practical need of regulating community life has engendered the social ideas, and these in turn have educated individual men into moral personalities, have developed and strengthened in them the feeling of good and evil. I shall go even further and assert that only in rare, exceptional cases can human societies—and then only voluntary ones—consist entirely of moral people following only the dictates of their conscience; the immense majority of human societies contain only a few people living by the promptings of their inner awareness of truth and untruth; the mass everywhere and always conforms to the laws of society out of habit or for reasons of expediency and personal advantage. Finally, there always will be a certain number of people who refrain from gross infraction of the social laws merely out of fear of punishment—people ready to break the law as soon as they see a chance of doing so with impunity. The proportion of these categories of people may vary, inclining now to one side, now to the other, and their relative sizes indicate whether the condition of a given society at a given time is sound or not; but none of these categories can disappear completely because their existence is determined by human nature and by the extreme diversity of individuals in societies that were not created by choice but came into being independently of the human mind and will.

But if so, you will say, where does morality come in? What would be its use? Having admitted that social ideas are indispensable, that we cannot do without them, and that they are imposed on people and prevail, if not willingly accepted, through force of circumstance and fear of punishment, we shall have to agree, if we reason consistently, that morality is superfluous, of no use at all. But such a conclusion, too, would be utterly erroneous. Social, civic ideas and formulas do not hang in the air or fall from the sky—they are born from community life and serve people. Without people they would have no meaning, they would be pure abstractions. They exist only in people, not apart from them; and since they cannot exist otherwise than in people, they appear either as formulated conscious concepts or as a formless feeling, the voice of conscience. That is why morality is indispensable. As to its practical usefulness, this comes from the fact that moral people are the only immediate, living carriers of the social ideas and formulas. As soon as these formulas and ideas cease to be reflected in conscience, this is our clue that they have outlived their time and must be replaced. Moral people are the only disinterested guardians of social ideas and formulas in the country. Habit is an unreliable bulwark; personal advantage chooses the path of profit, unmindful of ideas and formulas, which serve it merely as means to achieving its own ends; and immoral people always watch for the instant when they can throw off the distasteful bridle of social ideas and formulas. The role of morality in society stands out vividly if we reverse the question and ask: Can a society exist that is entirely composed of people who do not believe in social ideas and formulas, comply with them grudgingly, and are ready at the first opportunity to flout them? Obviously such a society cannot exist, because there is no one to support the social order and to apply the social ideas and formulas in practice. But morality, I repeat, does not create them—it only realizes and guards them in actual life. A man may be very moral and yet favor outdated ideas and formulas no longer consonant with the society's needs or actually hampering progress— for they must change, evolve, with changing conditions, while the moral ideal is always the same: man's ardent, complete, unselfish devotion to good and truth as his conscience sees them.

What is the conclusion to be drawn from all this? That you are in error when you contend that "social civic ideals as such, not organically related to moral ideals but having their own being, as a separate half cut off from the whole . . . do not exist, never have existed, and never can exist." When you said this, you did not pursue your analysis to the end. It seems to me that a correct, exhaustive analysis leads to the conclusion that the ideal social life is built on good social institutions and morally mature people. Both solutions to the problem that I mentioned at the very beginning of this letter are right and wrong at the same time if we oppose them to each other. Good social conditions educate people in virtue and truth; bad ones confuse and corrupt them. Professor Gradovskii stresses this, without denying the role of personal morality, and, of course, he is right. It would indeed be very one-sided to worry only about good institutions: civic ideals cannot materialize and become established in life if the people do not have a well-developed sense of morality and have not learned good moral habits; in this sense, I have repeatedly spoken up for personal morality and the need for it. But your opinion that moral self-perfection can replace civic ideals is equally one-sided.

The spirit of Christ wholeheartedly embraced by people, engrossing their thoughts and lives, becoming to them the highest, inmost moral truth and through them the vital principle of a social order and a daily life organized on the basis of precise, positive, empirical knowledge—this is what humanity will achieve sooner or later, judging by the whole course of history. So far, those who have confessed Christianity in spirit, not only in words and ritual, have either fled the world or exhausted themselves in vain efforts to install truth among people by putting it into laws, science, and art. Christ's teaching can reside only in the hearts of human beings. When it engrosses them so completely that they act in the Christian spirit without fleeing into a desert but right in the midst of our fallen, sinful, tormented world—then it will have become reality and life. This is the only possible meaning of the new word you are expecting.

Now you will fully understand why your view of our common people as the depository of Christian truth, and of our educated classes as apostates from that truth, as Alekos, Bel'tovs, Tentetnikovs, and their like [4]—as representative of apostasy and the sufferings it causes—why all this does not stand up under scrutiny in my opinion and is no more than a beautiful, talented, poetically expressed paradox. I simply cannot see our common people as custodians of the Christian truth, though I am filled with compassion for their cruel lot; for as soon as one of them makes a little money and climbs out of his poverty he immediately turns into a "kulak," [5] not a whit better than the "yid" you dislike so much. Take a closer look at the types of common Russians which we find so endearing and which really are beautiful: theirs is the moral beauty of a people in its infancy! The greatest virtue to them is avoiding evil and temptation in a purely Oriental fashion, not getting involved in anything if they can possibly help it, taking no part in any civic affairs. The "quiet fellow," the "simple soul," is the man everybody respects for clean living, probity, candor, piety, but who for these very reasons always effaces himself, attending only to his personal business; in community affairs or in public office he is no good at all because he always keeps silent and yields in everything. Therefore the doers are only the bold, the adroit, the resourceful, nearly always of dubious morality or

[4] Characters in Russian poetry and fiction personifying the "superfluous man" and his purely negative attitudes, criticized by Dostoevsky in his Pushkin speech.—Editor.

[5] A rich, grasping peasant—in Kavelin's time, the Russian equivalent of the pushy, self-reliant, tight-fisted farmer of the American frontier.—Editor.

downright dishonest. You consider that the Alekos break with the people out of pride? Oh, come, now! They are merely the same Orientals again who out of "great sadness of heart" over various disorders in society or in their private life, or out of liking for the European social and domestic patterns, abandoned everything and went away, some to live abroad, some on their estates. They are the hermits and anchorites over again, the "quiet fellows" of our villages, only with different ideals. A European in their place would try to realize his ideals as far as possible within his allotted big or small sphere of action, would combat his environment for all he was worth, and sooner or later transform it to suit him; but we Orientals, we run from life and its troubles, preferring to keep faith with the moral ideal in all its purity, and feeling no urge, or not knowing how, to realize it at least partly in our own surroundings—little by little, through long, sustained, obstinate work.

Then you, too, dream of our becoming Europeans? you will say. I dream, I shall reply, of one thing only: that we stop talking about moral, spiritual, Christian truth and begin to act, behave, live according to that truth! This will not turn us into Europeans, but we shall cease being Orientals and shall become in fact what we are by nature—Russians.

16.

Lev Nikolaevich Tolstoy

1828-1910

Revolution became the overarching fact of Russian life in the first years of the twentieth century. The changes introduced by the reforms of the 1860's had undermined the old social, economic, and administrative patterns. Forces had been unleashed which neither the rigid autocracy nor the moderate enlightened intelligentsia were able to direct or contain. Violence and chaos threatened everywhere, at home and abroad; the old world order seemed to shake and crumble.

The progressive members of the Russian Establishment hoped that rapid industrialization and economic modernization would stave off and eventually cure the country's ills. The Marxist or proto-Marxist revolutionaries saw in the turmoil, suffering, and dislocation the inevitable but transitory birthpangs of a new order. But many thinkers, imbued with the values of traditional Russian individualism, humanism, and Christianity, could not view with equanimity the evil and violence around them. Some—the symbolists—escaped into the ivory towers of rarefied estheticism; others turned to metaphysical speculation and the expectation of an imminent apocalyptic end of the world. Still

others felt they could no longer accept anything of the established order, least of all its optimistic intellectualism and materialism, which they held responsible for all that was happening. The modern world *en bloc* was bad—it was engaged on a path bound to lead to perdition. There could be only one escape: to reject the corruption of urban civilization and return to the simplicity of primitive agricultural life guided only by the words of the Saviour.

Count Lev Nikolaevich Tolstoy was the most eloquent spokesman for Christian anarchism and an advocate of a return to pastoral simplicity. His appeals and pronouncements on the burning questions of the day had a wide circle of readers and quite a few converts (even abroad, as the translation below proves). His popularity, however, was due perhaps not so much to the soundness of his logic as to the earnestness of his moral conviction and to his fame as a writer. The reader will judge for himself whether Tolstoy's solution —genuine political anarchism and passive resistance—was not merely a denial of reality and a consolation only to those who were too weak or too disoriented to live in man's world.

The Meaning of the Russian Revolution

We live in glorious times. . . . Was there ever so much to do? Our age is a revolutionary one in the best sense of the word—not of physical but moral revolution. Higher ideas of the social state, and of human perfection, are at work. I shall not live to see the harvest, but to sow in faith is no mean privilege or happiness.—W. E. CHANNING

For the worshipers of utility there is no morality except the morality of profit, and no religion but the religion of material welfare. They found the body of man crippled and exhausted by want, and in their ill-considered zeal they said: "Let us cure this body; and when it is strong, plump, and well nourished, its soul will return to it." But I say that that body can only be cured when its soul has been cured. In it lies the root of the disease, and the bodily ailments are but the outward signs of that disease. Humanity today is dying for lack of a common faith: a common idea uniting earth to heaven, the universe to God.

From the absence of this spiritual religion, of which but empty forms and lifeless formularies remain, and from a total lack of a sense of duty and a capacity for self-sacrifice, man, like a savage, has fallen prostrate in the dust, and has set up on an empty altar the idol "utility." Despots and the Princes of this world have become his High Priests; and from them has come the revolting formulary: "Each for his own alone; each for himself alone."—MAZZINI

When He saw the multitude, He was moved with compassion for them, because they were distressed and scattered, as sheep not having a shepherd.—MATT. 9:36

A revolution is taking place in Russia, and all the world is following it with eager attention, guessing and trying to foresee whither it is tending and to what it will bring the Russian people.

To guess at and to foresee this may be interesting and important to outside spectators watching the Russian Revolution, but for us Russians, who are living in this revolution and making it, the chief interest lies not in guessing what is going to happen, but in defining as clearly and firmly as

Translated by Louise and Aylmer Maude from Leo Tolstoy, *The Russian Revolution* (Christchurch, Hants, Eng., Free Age Press, 1906), pp. 1–52. Reprinted with minor changes. The essay was originally published under the title "Znachenie russkoi revoliutsii" in 1906.

possible what we must do in these immensely important, terrible, and dangerous times in which we live.

Every revolution is a change of a people's relation toward power.[1]

Such a change is now taking place in Russia, and we, the whole Russian people, are accomplishing it.

Therefore to know how we can and should change our relation toward power, we must understand the nature of power: what it consists of, how it arose, and how best to treat it.

I

Always and among all nations the same thing has occurred. Among people occupied with the necessary work natural to all men, of providing food for themselves and their families, by the chase (hunting animals), or as herdsmen (nomads), or by agriculture, there have appeared men, of their own or another nation, who forcibly seized the fruit of the workers' toil: first robbing, then enslaving them, and exacting from them either labor or tribute. This used to happen in old times, and still happens in Africa and Asia. And always and everywhere the workers (occupied with their accustomed, unavoidably necessary, and unremitting task—their struggle with nature to feed themselves and rear their children), though by far more numerous and always more moral than their conquerors, submitted to them and fulfilled their demands.

They submitted because it is natural to all men (and especially to those engaged in a serious struggle with nature to support themselves and their families) to dislike strife with other men; and feeling this aversion, they preferred to endure the consequences of the violence put upon them, rather than to give up their necessary, customary, and beloved labor.

There were, certainly, none of those contracts whereby Hugo Grotius and Rousseau explain the relations between the subdued and their subduers. Neither was there, nor could there be, any agreement as to the best way of arranging social life, such as Herbert Spencer imagines in his *Principles of Sociology;* but it happened in the most natural way that when one set of men did violence to another set, the latter preferred to endure not merely many hardships, but often even great distress, rather than face the cares and efforts necessary to withstand their oppressors; more especially as the conquerors took on themselves the duty of protecting the conquered people against internal and external disturbers of the peace. And so the majority of men, occupied with the business necessary to all men and to all animals (that of feeding themselves and their families), not only endured the unavoidable inconveniences and hardships, and even the cruelty, of their op-

[1] The word "power" occurs very frequently in this article, and is, as it were, a pivot on which it turns. We have been tempted in different places to translate it (the Russian word is *vlast'*) by "government," "authorities," "force," or "violence" according to the context. But the unity of the article is better maintained by letting a single English word represent the one Russian word, and we have followed this principle as far as possible. —Translators.

pressors without fighting, but submitted to them and accepted it as a duty to fulfill all their demands.

When speaking about the formation of primitive communities the fact is always forgotten that not only the most numerous and most needed but also the most moral members of society were always those who by their labor kept all the rest alive; and that to such people it is always more natural to submit to violence and to bear all the hardships it involves than to give up the necessary work of supporting themselves and their families in order to fight against oppression. It is so now, when we see the people of Burma, the Fellahs of Egypt, and the Boers surrendering to the English, and the Bedouins to the French; and in olden times it was even more so.

Latterly, in the curious and widely diffused teaching called the science of sociology, it has been asserted that the relations between the members of human society have been, and are, dependent on economic conditions. But to assert this is merely to substitute for the clear and evident cause of a phenomenon one of its effects. The cause of this or that economic condition always was (and could not but be) the oppression of some men by others. Economic conditions are a *result* of violence, and cannot therefore be the *cause* of human relations. Evil men—the Cains—who loved idleness and were covetous, always attacked good men—the Abels—the tillers of the soil, and by killing them or threatening to kill them, profited by their toil. The good, gentle, and industrious people, instead of fighting their oppressors, considered it best to submit: partly because they did not wish to fight, and partly because they could not do so without interrupting their work of feeding themselves and their neighbors. On this oppression of the good by the evil, and not on any economic conditions, all existing human societies have been, and still are, based and built.

II

From the most ancient times, and among all the nations of the earth, the relations of the rulers to the ruled have been based on violence. But this relation, like everything else in the world, was and is continually changing. It changes from two causes. Firstly, because the more secure their power becomes and the longer it lasts, the more do those in power (the leisured classes) grow depraved, unreasonable, and cruel, and the more injurious to their subjects do their demands become. Secondly, because as those in power grow more depraved, their subjects see more and more clearly the harm and folly of submitting to such depraved power.

And those in power always become depraved: firstly, because such people, immoral by nature, and preferring idleness and violence to work, having grasped power and used it to satisfy their lusts and passions, give themselves up more and more to these passions and vices; and secondly, because lusts and passions, which in the case of ordinary men cannot be gratified without meeting with obstacles, not only do not meet such obstacles and do not arouse any condemnation in the case of those who rule, but on the contrary are applauded by all who surround them. The latter generally benefit by the madness of their masters; and besides, it pleases them to imagine that the virtues and wisdom to which alone it is natural for reasonable men to submit are to be found in the men to whom they submit; and therefore the vices of those in power are lauded as if they were virtues, and grow to terrible proportions.

Consequently the folly and vice of the crowned and uncrowned rulers of the nations have reached such appalling dimensions as were reached by [such despots as] Nero, Charles, Henry, Louis, John, Peter, Catherine, and Marat.

Nor is this all. If the rulers were satisfied with their personal debauchery and vices they would not do so much harm; but idle, satiated, and depraved men, such as rulers were and are, must have something to live for—must have some aims and try to attain them. And such men can have no aim except to get more and more fame. All other passions soon reach the limits of satiety. Only ambition has no limits, and therefore almost all potentates always strove and still strive after fame, especially military fame, the only kind attainable by depraved men unacquainted with, and incapable of, real work. For the wars devised by the potentates, money, armies and, above all, the slaughter of men are necessary; and in consequence of this the condition of the ruled becomes harder and harder, and at last the oppression reaches a point at which the ruled can no longer continue to submit to the ruling power, but must try to alter their relation toward it.

III

Such is one reason for alteration in the relations between the rulers and the ruled. Another still more important reason for this change is that the ruled—believing in the rights of the power above them and accustomed to submit to it—as knowledge spreads and their moral consciousness becomes enlightened, begin to see and feel not only the ever-increasing material harmfulness of this rule, but also that to submit to such power is immoral.

It was possible five hundred or a thousand years ago for people, in obedience to their rulers, to slaughter whole nations for the sake of conquest, or for dynastic or religio-fanatic aims to behead, torture, quarter, encage, destroy, and enslave whole nations. But in the nineteenth and twentieth centuries subjugated people, enlightened by Christianity or by the humanitarian teachings which have grown up out of it, can no longer without pangs of conscience submit to the powers which demand that they should participate in the slaughter of men defending their freedom (as was done in the Chinese, Boer, and Philippine wars) and can no longer with quiet consciences, as formerly, know themselves to be participators in the deeds of violence and the executions which are being committed by the governments of their countries.

As a result force-using power destroys itself in two ways.

It destroys itself through the ever-growing depravity of those in authority, and the consequent continually increasing burden borne by the ruled, and through its ever-increasing deviation from the ever-developing moral perception of the ruled. Therefore, where force-using power exists, a moment must inevitably come when the relation of the people toward that power must change. This moment may come sooner or later according to the degree and the rapidity of the corruption of the rulers, the amount of their cunning, the quieter or more restless temperament of the people, and even the way their geographical position helps or hinders the intercourse of the people among themselves; but sooner or later that moment must inevitably come to all nations.

To the Western nations, which arose on the ruins of the Roman Empire, that moment came long ago. The struggle of people against government began even in Rome, continued in all the states that succeeded Rome, and still goes on. To the Eastern nations—Turkey, Persia, India, China—that moment has not yet arrived. For the Russian people, it has now come.

The Russian people are today confronted by the dreadful choice of either, like the Eastern nations, continuing to submit to their unreasonable and depraved government in spite of all the misery it has inflicted upon them or, as all the Western nations have done, realizing the evil of the existing government, upsetting it by force, and establishing a new one.

Such a choice seems quite natural to the nonlaboring classes of Russia, who are in touch with the upper and prosperous classes of the Western nations and consider the military might, the industrial, commercial, and technical improvements, and that external glitter to which the Western nations have attained under their altered governments to be a great good.

IV

The majority of the Russian nonlaboring classes are quite convinced that the Russian people at this crisis can do nothing better than follow the path the Western nations have trodden and are still treading: that is to say, fight the power, limit it, and place it more and more in the hands of the whole people.

Is this opinion right, and is such action good?

Have the Western nations, traveling for centuries along that path, attained what they strove for? Have they freed themselves from the evils they wished to be rid of?

The Western nations, like all others, began by submitting to the power which demanded their submission: choosing to submit rather than to fight. But that power, in the persons of Charles the Great, Charles V, Philip, Louis, and Henry VIII, becoming more and more depraved, reached such a condition that the Western nations could no longer endure it. The Western nations, at different times, revolted against their rulers and fought them. This struggle took place in different forms, at different periods, but always found expression in the same ways: in civil wars, robberies, murders, and executions, finishing with the fall of the old power and the accession of a new one. And when the new power became as oppressive to the people as that which had been overthrown, it too was upset, and another new one was put in its place, which by the same unalterable nature of power became in due course as harmful as its predecessors. Thus, for instance, in France there were eleven changes of power within eighty years: the Bourbons, the Convention, the Directory, Bonaparte, the Empire, again the Bourbons, a republic, Louis Philippe, again a republic, again a Bonaparte, and again a republic. The substitution of new powers for old ones took place among other nations too, though not so rapidly as in France. These changes in most cases did not improve the condition of the people, and therefore those who made these changes could not help coming to the conclusion that the misery they suffered did not so much depend on the nature of the persons in power as on the fact that a few persons exercised power over many. And therefore the people tried to render the power harmless by limiting it. Such limitation was introduced in several countries in the form of elected Chambers of Representatives.

But the men who limited the arbitrariness of the rulers and founded the assemblies, becoming themselves possessors of power, naturally succumbed to the depraving influence which accompanies power, and to which the autocratic rulers had succumbed. These men, becoming sharers in power even though not singly, perpetrated, jointly or separately, the same kind of evil, and became as great a burden on the people as the autocratic rulers had been. Then, to limit the arbitrariness of power still more, monarchical power was abolished altogether in some countries, and a government chosen by the whole people was established. In this way republics were instituted in France, America, and Switzerland; and the referendum and the initiative were introduced, giving every member of the community the possibility of interfering with and participating in legislation.

But the only effect of all these measures was that the citizens of these states, participating more and more in power, and being more and more diverted from serious occupations, grew more and more depraved. The calamities from which the people suffered remained however, exactly the same under constitutional, monarchical, or republican governments, with or without referendums.

Nor could it be otherwise, for the idea of limiting power by the participation in power of all who are subject to it is unsound at its very core, and self-contradictory.

If one man with the aid of his helpers rules over all, it is unjust, and in all likelihood such rule will be harmful to the people.

The same will be the case when the minority rules over the majority. But the power of the majority over the minority also fails to secure a just rule; for we have no reason to believe that the majority participating in government is wiser than the minority that avoids participation.

To extend the participation in government to all, as might be done by still greater extension of the referendum and the initiative, would only mean that everybody would be fighting everybody else.

That man should have over his fellows a power founded on violence is [fundamentally] evil; and no kind of arrangement that maintains the right of man to do violence to man can cause evil to cease to be evil.

Therefore among all nations, however they are ruled, whether by the most despotic or the most democratic government, the chief and fundamental calamities from which the people suffer remain the same: the same ever-increasing, enormous budgets; the same animosity toward their neighbors, necessitating military preparations and armies; the same taxes; the same state and private monopolies; the same deprivation of the right to use the land (which is given to private owners); the same enslaving of subject races; the same constant threatenings of war, and the same wars, destroying the lives of men and undermining their morality.

V

It is true that the representative governments of Western Europe and America—constitutional monarchies as well as republics—have uprooted some of the external abuses practiced by the representatives of power, and have made it impossible that the holders of power should be such monsters as were the different Louis, Charleses, Henrys, and Johns. (Although in representative government not only is it possible that power will be seized by cunning, immoral, and artful mediocrities, such as various prime ministers and presidents have been, but the construction of those governments is such that only that kind of people can obtain power.) It is true that representative governments have abolished such abuses as the *lettres de cachet,* have removed restrictions on the press, have stopped religious persecutions and oppressions, have submitted the taxation of the people to discussion by their representatives, have made the actions of the government public and subject to criticism, and have facilitated the rapid development in those countries of all sorts of technical improvements giving great comfort to the life of rich citizens and great military power to the state. As a result the nations which have representative government have doubtless become more powerful industrially, commercially, and militarily than have despotically governed nations, and the lives of their leisured classes have certainly become more secure, comfortable, agreeable, and esthetic than they used to be. But is the life of the majority of the people in those countries more secure, freer, or, above all, more reasonable and moral?

I think not.

Under the despotic power of one man, the number of persons who come under the corrupting influence of power and live on the labor of others is limited, and consists of the despot's close friends, assistants, servants, and flatterers, and their helpers. The infection of depravity is focused in the court of the despot, whence it radiates in all directions.

Where power is limited, i.e., where many persons take part in it, the number of centers of infection is augmented, for everyone who shares power has his friends, helpers, servants, flatterers, and relations.

Where there is universal suffrage, these centers of infection are still more diffused. Every voter becomes the object of flattery and bribery. The character of the power itself is also changed. Instead of power founded on direct violence, we get a monetary power, also founded on violence—not directly, but through a complicated transmission.

As a result under representative governments, instead of one or a few centers of depravity, we get a large number of such centers—that is to say, there springs up a large class of people living idly on others' labor, the class called the "bourgeois," i.e., people who, being protected by violence, arrange for themselves easy and comfortable lives, free from hard work.

But as, when arranging an easy and pleasant life not only for a monarch and his court but for thousands of little kinglets, many things are needed to embellish and to amuse this idle life, it results that whenever power passes from a despotic to a representative government, inventions appear, facilitating the supply of objects that add to the pleasure and safety of the lives of the wealthy classes.

To produce all these objects, an ever-increasing number of working men are drawn away from agriculture and have their capacities directed to the production of pleasing trifles used by the rich, or even to some extent by the workers themselves. So there springs up a class of town workers so situated as to be in complete dependence on the wealthy classes. The number of these people grows and grows the longer the power of representative government endures, and their condition becomes worse and worse. In the United States, out of a population of seventy million, ten million are proletarians, and the relation between the well-to-do and the proletariat classes is the same in England, Belgium, and France. The number of men exchanging the labor of producing objects of primary necessity for the labor of producing objects of luxury is steadily increasing in those countries. It clearly follows that the result of such a trend of affairs must be the ever-greater overburdening of that diminishing number which has to support the luxurious lives of the increasing number of idle people. Evidently such a way of life cannot continue.

What is happening is [like what would happen if a man's] body went on increasing in weight while the legs that supported it grew continually thinner and weaker. When the support had vanished the body would have to fall.

VI

The Western nations, like all others, submitted to the power of their conquerors only to avoid the worry and sin of fighting. But when that power bore too heavily upon them, they began to fight it, though still continuing to submit to power, which they regarded as a necessity. At first only a small part of the nation shared in the fight; then, when the struggle of that small part proved ineffectual, a greater and greater number entered into the conflict, and it ended by the majority of the people of those nations (instead of freeing themselves from the worry and sin of fighting) sharing in the wielding of power: the very thing they wished to avoid when they first submitted to power. The inevitable result of this was the increase of the depraving influence that comes of power, an increase not affecting a small number of persons only, as had been the case under a single ruler, but affecting all the members of the community. (Steps are now being taken to subject women also to it.)

Representative government and universal suffrage resulted in every possessor of a fraction of power being exposed to all the evil attached to power: bribery, flattery, vanity, self-conceit, idleness, and, above all, immoral participation in deeds of violence. Every member of Parliament is exposed to all these temptations in a yet greater degree. Every deputy begins his career of power by befooling people, making promises he knows he will not keep; and when sitting in the House he takes part in making laws that are enforced by violence. It is the same with all senators and presidents. Similar corruption prevails in the election of a president. In the United States the election of a president costs millions to those financiers who know that when elected he will maintain certain monopolies or import duties advantageous to them, on various articles, which will enable them to recoup the cost of the election a hundredfold.

And this corruption, with all its accompanying phenomena—the desire to avoid hard work and to benefit by comforts and pleasures provided by others; interests and cares, inaccessible to a man engaged in work, concerning the general business of the state; the spread of a lying and inflammatory press; and, above all, animosity between nation and nation, class and class, man and man—has grown and grown, till it has reached such dimensions that the struggle of all men against their fellows has become so habitual a state of things that science (the science that is engaged in condoning all the nastiness done by men) has decided that the struggle and enmity of all against all is a necessary, unavoidable, and beneficent condition of human life.

That peace, which to the ancients who saluted each other with the words "Peace be unto you!" seemed the greatest of blessings, has now quite disappeared from among the Western peoples; and not only has it disappeared, but by the aid of science, men try to assure themselves that not in peace but in the strife of all against all lies man's highest destiny.

And really, among the Western nations, an unceasing industrial, commercial, and military strife is continually waged; a strife of state against state, class against class, labor against capital, party against party, man against man.

Nor is this all. The chief result of this participation of all men in power is that men, being more and more drawn away from direct work on the land, and more and more involved in diverse ways of exploiting the labor of others, have lost their independence and are forced by the position they live in to lead immoral lives. Having neither the desire nor the habit of living by tilling their own land, the Western nations were forced to obtain their means of subsistence from other countries. They could do this only in two ways: by fraud, that is, by exchanging things for the most part unnecessary or depraving, such as alcohol, opium, weapons, for the foodstuffs indispensable to them; or by violence, that is, robbing the people of Asia and Africa whenever they saw an opportunity of doing this with impunity.

Such is the position of Germany, Austria, Italy, France, the United States, and especially Great Britain, which is held up as an example for the imitation and envy of other nations. Almost all the people of these nations, having become conscious participators in deeds of violence, devote their strength and attention to the activities of government, and to industry and to commerce, which aim chiefly at satisfying the demands of the rich for luxuries; and they subjugate (partly by direct force, partly by money) the agricultural people both of their own and of foreign countries, who have to provide them with the necessaries of life.

Such people form a majority in some nations; in others they are as yet only a minority; but the percentage of men living on the labor of others grows uncontrollably and very rapidly, to the detriment of those who still do reasonable, agricultural work. As a result a majority of the people of Western Europe are already in the condition (the United States is not so yet, but is being irresistibly drawn toward it) of not being able to subsist by their own labor on their own land. They are obliged in one way or another, by force or fraud, to take the necessaries of life from other people who still do their own labor. And they get these necessaries either by defrauding foreign nations or by gross violence.

From this it necessarily results that trade, aiming chiefly at satisfying the demands of the rich, and of the richest of the rich (that is, the government), directs its chief powers not to improving the means of tilling the soil, but to making it possible by the aid of machines to somehow till large tracts of land (of which the people have been deprived), to manufacturing finery for women, building luxurious palaces, producing sweetmeats, toys, motorcars, tobacco, wines, delicacies, medicines, enormous quantities of printed matter, guns, rifles, powder, unnecessary railways, and so forth.

And as there is no end to the caprices of men when they are met not by their own labor but by that of others, industry is more and more diverted to the production of the most unnecessary, stupid, depraving products, and draws people more and more from reasonable work; and no end can be foreseen to these inventions and preparations for the amusement of idle people, especially as the stupider and more depraving an invention is—such as the use of motors in place of animals or one's own legs, railways to go up mountains, or armored automobiles armed with quick-firing guns—the more pleased and proud of them are both their inventors and their possessors.

VII

The longer representative government lasted and the more it extended, the more did the Western nations abandon agriculture and devote their mental and physical powers to manufacturing and trading in order to supply luxuries to the wealthy classes, to enable the nations to fight one another, and to deprave the undepraved. Thus, in England, which has had representative government longest, less than one-seventh of the adult male population is now employed in agriculture, in Germany 0.45 of the population, in France one-half, and a similar number in other states. At the present time the position of these states is such that even if they could free themselves from the calamity of proletarianism, they could not support themselves independently of other countries. All these nations are unable to subsist by their own toil; and just as the proletariat are dependent on the well-to-do classes, so are they completely dependent on countries that support themselves and are able to sell them their surplus: such as India, Russia, and Australia. England supports from its own land less than a fifth of its population; and Germany less than half, as is the case with France and with other countries; and the condition of these nations becomes year by year more dependent on the food supplied from abroad.

In order to exist, these nations must have recourse to the deceptions and violence called in their language "acquiring markets" and "colonial policy"; and they act accordingly, striving to throw their nets of enslavement farther and farther to all ends of the earth, to catch those who are still leading rational lives. Vying with one another, they increase their armaments more and more, and more and more cunningly, under various pretexts, seize the land of those who still live rational lives, and force these people to feed them.

Till now they have been able to do this. But the limit to the acquirement of markets, to the deception of buyers, to the sale of unnecessary and injurious articles, and to the enslavement of distant nations is already apparent. The peoples of distant lands are themselves becoming depraved, are learning to make for themselves all those articles which the Western nations supplied them with, and are, above all, learning the not very cunning science of arming themselves and of being as cruel as their teachers.

As a result the end of such immoral existence is already in sight. The people of the Western nations see this coming, and feeling unable to stop in their career, comfort themselves (as people half aware that they are ruining their lives always do) by self-deception and blind faith; and such blind faith is spreading more and more widely among the majority of Western nations. This faith is a belief that those inventions and improvements for increasing the comforts of the wealthy classes and for fighting (that is, slaughtering men), which the enslaved masses for several generations have been forced to produce, are something very important and almost holy, called in the language of those who uphold such a mode of life "culture," or even more grandly, "civilization."

As every creed has a science of its own, so this faith in "civilization" has a science—sociology, the one aim of which is to justify the false and desperate position in which the people of the Western world now find themselves. The object of this science is to prove that all these inventions—ironclads, telegraphs, nitroglycerine bombs, photographs, electric railways, and all sorts of similar foolish and nasty inventions that stupefy the people and are designed to increase the comforts of the idle classes and to protect them by force—represent not only something good, but even something sacred, predetermined by supreme unalterable laws; and that, therefore, the depravity they call "civilization" is a necessary condition of human life, and must inevitably be adopted by all mankind.

And this faith is just as blind as any other faith, and just as unshakable and self-assured.

Any other position may be disputed and argued about; but "civilization" —meaning those inventions and those forms of life among which we are living, and all the follies and nastiness which we produce—is an indubitable blessing, beyond all discussion. Everything that disturbs faith in civilization is a lie; everything that supports this faith is sacred truth.

This faith and its attendant science cause the Western nations not to wish to see or to acknowledge that the ruinous path they are following leads to inevitable destruction. The so-called "most advanced" among them cheer themselves with the thought that without abandoning this path they can reach not destruction, but the highest bliss. They assure themselves that, by again employing violence such as brought them to their present ruinous condition, somehow or other, from among people now striving to obtain the greatest material, animal welfare for themselves, men (influenced by socialist doctrines) will suddenly appear, who will wield power without being depraved by it, and will establish an order of things in which people accustomed to a greedy, selfish struggle for their own profit will suddenly grow self-sacrificing, and all work together for the common good, and share alike.

But this creed, having no reasonable foundation, has lately more and more lost credibility among thinking people and is held only by the laboring masses, whose eyes it diverts from the miseries of the present, giving them some sort of hope of a blissful future.

Such is the common faith of the majority of the Western nations, drawing them toward destruction. And this tendency is so strong that the voices of the wise among them, such as Rousseau, Lamennais, Carlyle, Ruskin, Channing, W. L. Garrison, Emerson, Herzen, and Edward Carpenter, leave no trace in the consciousness of those who, though rushing toward destruction, do not wish to see and admit it.

And it is to travel this path of destruction that the Russian people are now invited by European politicians, who are delighted that one more nation should join them in their desperate plight. And frivolous Russians urge us to follow this path, considering it much easier and simpler, instead of thinking with their own heads, slavishly to imitate what the Western nations did centuries ago, before they knew whither it would lead.

VIII

Submission to violence brought both the Eastern nations (who continue to submit to their depraved oppressors) and the Western nations (who have spread power and its accompanying depravity among the masses of the people) not only to great misfortunes, but also to an unavoidable collision between the Western and the Eastern nations, which now threatens them both with still greater calamities.

The Western nations, besides their distress at home and the corruption of the greater part of their population by participation in power, have been led to the necessity of seizing by force or fraud the fruits of the labor of the Eastern nations for their own consumption; and this by certain methods they have devised called "civilization," they succeeded in doing until the Eastern nations learnt the same methods. The Eastern nations, or the majority of them, still continue to obey their rulers, and, lagging behind the Western nations in devising things needed for war, were forced to submit to them.

But some of them are already beginning to acquire the depravity or "civilization" which the Europeans are teaching them, and, as the Japanese have shown, they can easily assimilate all the shallow, cunning methods of an immoral and cruel civilization, and are preparing to withstand their oppressors by the same means that these employ against them.

And now the Russian nation, standing between the two—having partially acquired Western methods, yet till now continuing to submit to its government—is placed, by fate itself, in a position in which it must stop and think: seeing on one side the miseries to which, like the Eastern nations, it has been brought by submission to a despotic power; and on the other hand, seeing that among the Western nations the limitation of power and its diffusion among the people has not remedied the miseries of the people, but has only depraved them and put them in a position in which they have to live by deceiving and robbing other nations. And so the Russian nation must naturally alter its attitude toward power, but not as the Western nations have done.

The Russian nation now stands, like the hero of the fairy tale, at the parting of two roads, both leading to destruction.

It is impossible for the Russian nation to continue to submit to its government. It is impossible, because having freed themselves from the prestige which has hitherto enveloped the Russian government, and having once understood that most of the miseries suffered by the people are caused by the government, the Russian people cannot cease to be aware of the cause of the calamities they suffer, or cease to desire to free themselves from it.

Besides, the Russian people cannot continue to submit to the government, because now a government—such a government as gives security and tranquillity to a nation—no longer exists in reality. There are two envenomed and contending parties, but no government to which it is possible quietly to submit.

For Russians to continue to submit to their government would mean to continue not only to bear the ever-increasing calamities which they have suffered and are suffering: land-hunger, famine, heavy taxes, cruel, useless, and devastating wars; but also and chiefly it would mean taking part in the crimes this government, in its evidently useless attempts at self-defense, is now perpetrating.

336 LEV NIKOLAEVICH TOLSTOY

Still less reasonable would it be for the Russian people to enter on the path of the Western nations, since the deadliness of that path is already plainly demonstrated. It would be evidently irrational for the Russian nation to act so; for though it was possible for the Western nations, before they knew where it would lead them, to choose a path now seen to be false, the Russian people cannot help seeing and knowing its danger.

Moreover, when they entered on that path, most of the Western people were already living by trade, exchange, and commerce, or by direct (negro) or indirect slaveowning (as is now the case in Europe's colonies), while the Russian nation is chiefly agricultural. For the Russian people to enter on the path along which the Westerners went would mean consciously to commit the same acts of violence that the government demands of them (only not for the government, but against it): to rob, burn, blow up, murder, and carry on civil war, and to commit all these crimes knowing that they do so no longer in obedience to another's will, but at their own. And they would at last attain only what has been attained by the Western nations after centuries of struggle; they would go on suffering the same chief ills that they now suffer from: land-hunger, heavy and ever-increasing taxes, national debts, growing armaments, and cruel, stupid wars. More than that, they would be deprived, like the Western nations, of their chief blessing—their accustomed, beloved, agricultural life—and would drift into hopeless dependence on foreign labor, and this under the most disadvantageous conditions, carrying on an industrial and commercial struggle with the Western nations, with the certainty of being vanquished. Destruction awaits them on this path and on that.

IX

What, then, is the Russian nation to do?

The natural and simple answer, the direct outcome of the facts of the case, is to follow neither this path nor that.

To submit neither to the government which has brought it to its present wretched state; nor, imitating the West, to set up a representative, force-using government such as those which have led those nations to a still worse condition.

This simplest and most natural answer is peculiarly suited to the Russian people at all times, and especially at the present crisis.

For indeed, it is wonderful that a peasant husbandman of Tula, Saratov, Vologda, or Khar'kov Province, without any profit to himself, and suffering all sorts of misery, such as taxation, law-courts, deprivation of land, conscription, etc., as a result of his submission to government, should till now, contrary to the demands of his own conscience, have submitted, and should even have aided his own enslavement: paying taxes, without knowing or asking how they would be spent, giving his sons to be soldiers, knowing still less for what the sufferings and death of these [children,] so painfully reared and to him such necessary workers, were wanted.

It would be just as strange, or even stranger, if such agricultural peasants, living their peaceful, independent life without any need of a government, and wishing to be rid of the burdens they endure at the hands of a violent and to them unnecessary power, instead of simply ceasing to submit to it, were, by employing violence similar to that from which they suffer, to replace the old force-using power by a new force-using power, as the French and English peasants did in their time.

Why! the Russian agricultural population need only cease to obey any kind of force-using government and refuse to participate in it, and immediately taxes, military service, and all official oppressions, as well as private property in land and the misery of the working classes that results from it, would cease of themselves. All these misfortunes would cease, because there would be no one to inflict them.

The historic, economic, and religious conditions of the Russian nation place it in exceptionally favorable circumstances for acting in this manner.

In the first place, it has reached the point at which a change of its old relations towards the existing power has become inevitable after the wrongfulness of the path traveled by the Western nations (with whom it has long had the closest connections) has become fully apparent.

Power in the West has completed its circle. The Western peoples, like all others, accepted a force-using power at first in order themselves to escape from the struggles, cares, and sins of power. When that power became corrupt and burdensome, they tried to lighten its weight by limiting (that is, by participating in) it. This participation, spreading out more and more widely, caused more and more people to share in power; and finally the majority of the people (who at first submitted to power to avoid strife and to escape from participation in power) have had to take part both in strife and in power, and have suffered the inevitable accompaniment of power—corruption.

It has become quite clear that the pretended limitation of power only means changing those in power, increasing their number, and thereby increasing the amount of depravity, irritation, and anger among men. (The power remains as it was: the power of a minority of the worse men over a majority of the better.) It has also become plain that an increase in number of those in power has drawn people from the labor on the land natural to all men, to factory labor for the production (and overproduction) of unnecessary and harmful things, and has obliged the majority of Western nations to base their lives on the deception and enslavement of other nations.

The fact that in our days all this has become quite obvious in the lives of the Western nations, is the first condition favorable to the Russian people, who have now reached the moment when they must change their relation toward power.

For the Russian people to follow the path the Western nations have trodden would be as though a traveler followed a path on which those who went before him had lost their way, and from which the most farseeing of them were already returning.

[In the second place], while all the Western nations have more or less abandoned agriculture and are living chiefly by manufacture and commerce, the Russian people have arrived at the necessity of changing their relation toward power while the immense majority of them are still living an agricultural life, which they love and prize so much that most Russians, when torn from it, are always ready to return to it at the first opportunity.

This condition is of special value for Russians when freeing themselves from the evils of power; for while leading an agricultural life men have the least need of government; or rather, an agricultural life less than any other gives a government opportunities of interfering with the life of the people. I know some village communes which emigrated to the Far East and settled in places where the frontier between China and Russia was not clearly defined and lived there in prosperity, disregarding all governments, until they were discovered by Russian officials.

Townsmen generally regard agriculture as one of the lowest occupations to which man can devote himself. Yet the enormous majority of the population of the whole world are engaged in agriculture, and on it the possibility of existence for all the rest of the human race depends. As a result in reality, the human race [is a race of] husbandmen. All the rest—ministers, locksmiths, professors, carpenters, artists, tailors, scientists, physicians, generals, soldiers—are but the servants or parasites of the agriculturist. As a result agriculture, besides being the most moral, healthy, joyful, and necessary occupation, is also the highest of human activities, and alone gives men true independence.

The enormous majority of Russians are still living this most natural, moral, and independent agricultural life; and this is the second, most important, circumstance which makes it possible and natural for the Russian people, now that they are faced by the necessity of changing their relations toward power, to change them in no other way than by freeing themselves from the evil of all power, and simply ceasing to submit to any kind of government.

These are the first two conditions, both of which are external.

The third condition, an inner one, is the religious feeling which according to the evidence of history, the observation of foreigners who have studied the Russian people, and especially the inner consciousness of every Russian, was and is a special characteristic of the Russian people.

In Western Europe—either because the Gospels printed in Latin were inaccessible to the people till the time of the Reformation, and have remained till now inaccessible to the whole Roman Catholic world, or because of the refined methods which the Papacy employs to hide true Christianity from the people, or in consequence of the especially practical character of those nations—there is no doubt that the essence of Christianity, not only among Roman Catholics but also among Lutherans, and even more in the Anglican Church, has long ceased to be a faith directing people's lives, and has been replaced by external forms, or among the higher classes by indifference and the rejection of all religion. For the vast majority of Russians, however—perhaps because the Gospels became accessible to them as early as the tenth century, or because of the coarse stupidity of the Russo-Greek Church, which tried clumsily and therefore vainly to hide the true meaning of the Christian teaching, or because of some peculiar trait in the Russian character, or because of their agricultural life—Christian teaching in its practical application has never ceased to be, and still continues to be, the chief guide of life.

From the earliest times till now, the Christian understanding of life has manifested, and still manifests, itself among the Russian people in various traits peculiar to them alone. It shows itself in their acknowledgment of the brotherhood and equality of all men, of whatever race or nationality; in their complete religious toleration; in their not condemning criminals, but regarding them as unfortunate; in the custom of begging one another's forgiveness on certain days; and even in the habitual use of a form of the word "forgive" when taking leave of anybody; in the habit not merely of charity toward, but even of respect for, beggars, which is common among the people; in the perfect readiness (sometimes coarsely shown) for self-sacrifice for anything believed to be religious truth, which was shown and still is shown by those who burn themselves to death or castrate themselves and even (as in a recent case) by those who bury themselves alive.

The same Christian outlook always appeared in the relation of the Russian people toward those in power. The people always preferred to submit to power, rather than to share in it. They considered, and consider, the position of rulers to be sinful and not at all desirable. This Christian relation of the Russian people toward life generally, and especially toward those in power, is the third and most important condition which makes it most simple and natural for them at the present juncture to go on living their customary, agricultural, Christian life, without taking any part either in the old power or in the struggle between the old and the new.

Such are the three conditions, different from those of the Western nations, in which the Russian people find themselves placed at the present important time. These conditions, it would seem, ought to induce them to choose the simplest way out of the difficulty, by not accepting and not submitting to any kind of force-using power. Yet the Russian people, at this difficult and important crisis, do not choose the natural way, but, wavering between governmental and revolutionary violence, begin (in the persons of their worst representatives) to take part in the violence, and seem to be preparing to follow the road to destruction along which the Western nations have traveled.

Why is this so?

X

What has caused, and still causes, this surprising phenomenon—that people suffering from the abuse of power which they themselves tolerate and support do not free themselves in the most simple and easy way from all the disasters brought about by power, that is to say, do not simply cease obeying it? And not only do not act thus, but go on doing the very things that deprive them of physical and mental well-being: that is to say, either continue to obey the existing power, or establish another similar force-using power and obey that?

Why is this so? People feel that their unhappy position is the result of violence, and are dimly aware that to get rid of their misery they need freedom; but, strange to say, to get rid of violence and gain freedom, they seek, invent, and use all sorts of measures: mutiny, change of rulers, alterations of government, all kinds of constitutions, new arrangements between different states, colonial policies, enrollment of the unemployed, trusts, social organizations—everything but the one thing that would most simply, easily, and surely free them from all their distresses: the refusal to submit to power.

One might think that it must be quite clear to people not deprived of reason that violence breeds violence; that the only means of deliverance from violence lies in not taking part in it. This method, one would think, is quite obvious. It is evident that a great majority of men can be enslaved by a small minority only if the enslaved themselves take part in their own enslavement.

If people are enslaved, it is only because they either fight violence with violence or participate in violence for their own personal profit.

Those who neither struggle against violence nor take part in it can no more be enslaved than water can be cut.

They can be robbed, prevented from moving about, wounded, or killed, but they cannot be enslaved: that is, made to act against their own reasonable will.

This is true both of individuals and of nations. If the two hundred million Hindus did not submit to the power which demands their participation in deeds of violence, always connected with the taking of human life: if they did not enlist, paid no taxes to be used for violence, were not tempted by rewards offered by the conquerors (rewards originally taken from themselves), and did not submit to the English laws introduced among them, then neither fifty thousand Englishmen, nor all the English in the world, could enslave India, even if instead of two hundred million there were but a thousand Hindus. So it is in the cases of Poles, Czechs, Irish, Bedouins, and all the conquered races. And it is the same in the case of the workmen enslaved by the capitalists. Not all the capitalists in the world could enslave the workers if the workmen themselves did not help, and did not take part in their own enslavement.

All this is so evident that one is ashamed to mention it. And yet people who discuss all other conditions of life reasonably not only do not see and do not act as reason dictates in this matter, but act quite contrary to reason and to their own advantage. Each one says, "I can't be the first to do what nobody else does. Let others begin, and then I too will cease to submit to power." And so says a second, a third, and everybody.

All, under the pretense that no one can begin, instead of acting in a manner unquestionably advantageous to all, continue to do what is disadvantageous to everybody, and is also irrational and contrary to human nature.

No one likes to cease submitting to power, lest he should be persecuted by power; yet he well knows that obeying power means being subject to all sorts of the gravest calamities in wars foreign or civil.

What is the cause of this?

The cause of it is that people when yielding to power do not reason, but act under the influence of something that has always been one of the most widespread motives of human action, and has lately been most carefully studied and explained; it is called "suggestion" or hypnotism. This hypnotism, preventing people from acting in accordance with their reasonable nature and their own interest, and forcing them to do what is unreasonable and disadvantageous, causes them to believe that the violence perpetrated by people calling themselves "the government" is not simply the immoral conduct of immoral men, but is the action of some mysterious, sacred being, called the state, without which men never have existed (which is quite untrue) and never can exist.

But how can reasonable beings, men, submit to such a surprising suggestion, contrary to reason, feeling, and their own interest?

The answer to this question is that not only do children, the mentally diseased, and idiots succumb to hypnotic influence and suggestion, but all persons do, to the extent to which their religious consciousness is weakened: their consciousness of their relation to the Supreme Cause on which their existence depends. And the majority of the people of our times more and more lack this consciousness.

The reason that most people of our time lack this consciousness is that having once committed the sin of submitting to human power, and not acknowledging this sin to be a sin, but trying to hide it from themselves, or to justify it, they have exalted the power to which they submit to such an extent that it has replaced God's law for them. When human law replaced divine law, men lost religious consciousness and fell under the governmental hypnotism, which suggests to them the illusion that those who enslave them are not simply lost, vicious men, but are representatives of that mystic being, the state, without which it is supposed that men are unable to exist.

The vicious circle has been completed; submission to power has weakened, and partly destroyed, the religious feeling in men; and the weakening and cessation of religious consciousness has subjected them to human power.

The sin of power began like this: The oppressors said to the oppressed, "Fulfill what we demand of you; if you disobey, we will kill you. But if you submit to us, we will introduce order and will protect you from other oppressors."

And the oppressed, in order to live their accustomed lives, and not to have to fight these and other oppressors, seem to have answered: "Very well, we will submit to you; introduce whatever order you choose, we will uphold it; only let us live quietly, supporting ourselves and our families."

The oppressors did not recognize their sin, being carried away by the attractions and advantages of power. The oppressed thought it no sin to submit to the oppressors, for it seemed better to submit than to fight. But there was sin in this submission—and as great a sin as that of those who used violence. Had the oppressed endured all the hardships, taxations, and cruelties without acknowledging the authority of the oppressors to be lawful, and without promising to obey it, they would not have sinned. But in the promise to submit to power lay a sin (ἁμαρτία, error) equal to that of the wielders of power.

In promising to submit to a force-using power, and in recognizing it as lawful, there lay a double sin. First, that in trying to free themselves from the sin of fighting, those who submitted condoned that sin in those to whom they submitted; and secondly, that they renounced their true freedom (i.e., submission to the will of God) by promising always to obey the power. Such a promise (including as it does the admission of the possibility of disobedience to God in case the demands of established power should clash with the laws of God), a promise to obey the power of man, was a rejection of the will of God; for the force-using power of the state, demanding from those who submit to it participation in killing men, in wars, executions, and laws sanctioning preparations for wars and executions, is based on a direct contradiction to God's will. Therefore those who submit to power thereby renounce their submission to the law of God.

One cannot yield a little on one point, and on another maintain the law of God. It is evident that if in one thing God's law can be replaced by human law, then God's law is no longer the highest law incumbent at all times on men; and if it is not that, it is nothing.

Deprived of the guidance given by divine law (that is, the highest capacity of human nature) men inevitably sink to that lowest grade of human existence where the only motives of their actions are their personal passions and the hypnotism to which they are subject. Under such an hypnotic suggestion of the necessity of obedience to government lie all the nations that live in the unions called states; and the Russian people are in the same condition.

This is the cause of that apparently strange phenomenon, that a hundred million Russian cultivators of the soil, needing no kind of government, and constituting so large a majority that they may be called the whole Russian nation, do not choose the most natural and best way out of their present condition (by simply ceasing to submit to any force-using power) but continue to take part in the old government and enslave themselves more and more; or, fighting against the old government, prepare for themselves a new one which, like the old one, will employ violence.

XI

We often read and hear discussions as to the causes of the present excited, restless condition of all the Christian nations, threatened by all sorts of dangers; and of the terrible position in which the demented, and in part brutalized, Russian people find themselves at present. The most varied explanations are brought forward; yet all the reasons can be reduced to one. Men have *forgotten God*, that is to say, they have forgotten their relations to the infinite Source of Life, forgotten the meaning of life which is the outcome of those relations, and which consists, first of all, in fulfilling, for one's own soul's sake, the law given by this Divine Source. They have forgotten this, because some of them have assumed a right to rule over men by means of threats of murder; and others have consented to submit to these people and to participate in their rule. By the very act of submitting, these men have denied God and exchanged His law for human law.

Forgetting their relation to the Infinite, the majority of men have descended, in spite of all the subtlety of their mental achievements, to the lowest grade of consciousness, where they are guided only by animal passions and by the hypnotism of the herd.

That is the cause of all their calamities.

Therefore there is but one escape from the miseries with which people torment themselves: it lies in re-establishing in themselves a consciousness of their dependence on God, and thereby regaining a reasonable and free relation toward themselves and toward their fellows.

And so it is just this conscious submission to God and the consequent abandonment of the sins of power and of submission to [power] that now stand before all nations that suffer from the consequence of this sin.

The possibility and necessity of ceasing to submit to human power and of returning to the laws of God are dimly felt by all men, and especially vividly by the Russian people just now. And in this dim consciousness of the possibility and necessity of re-establishing their obedience to the law of God and ceasing to obey human power lies the essence of the movement now taking place in Russia.

What is happening in Russia is not, as many people suppose, a rebellion of the people against their government in order to replace one government by another, but a much greater and more important event. What now moves the Russian people is a dim recognition of the wrongness and unreasonableness of all violence, and of the possibility and necessity of basing one's life not on coercive power, as has been the case hitherto among all nations, but on reasonable and free agreement.

Whether the Russian nation will accomplish the great task now before it (the task of liberating men from human power substituted for the will of God) or whether, following the path of the Western nations, it will lose its opportunity and leave to some other happier Eastern race the leadership in the great work that lies before humanity, there is no doubt that at the present day all nations are becoming more and more conscious of the possibility of changing this violent, insane, and wicked life for one that shall be free, rational, and good. And what already exists in men's consciousness will inevitably accomplish itself in real life. For the will of God must be, and cannot fail to be, realized.

XII

"But is social life possible without power? Without power men would be continually robbing and killing one another," say those who believe only in human law. People of this sort are sincerely convinced that men refrain from crime and live orderly lives only because of laws, courts of justice, police, officials, and armies, and that without governmental power social life would become impossible. Men depraved by power fancy that as some of the crimes committed in the state are punished by the government, it is this punishment that prevents men from committing other possible crimes. But the fact that government punishes some crimes does not at all prove that the existence of law-courts, police, armies, prisons, and death penalties holds men back from all the crimes they might commit. That the amount of crime committed in a society does not at all depend on the punitive action of governments is quite clearly proved by the fact that when society is in a certain mood, no increase of punitive measures by government is able to prevent the perpetration of most daring and cruel crimes that imperil the safety of the community, as has been the case in every revolution, and as is now the case in Russia to a most striking degree.

The cause of this is that men, the majority of men (all the laboring folk), abstain from crimes and live good lives not because there are police, armies, and executions, but because there is a moral perception common to the bulk of mankind, established by their common religious understanding and by the education, customs, and public opinion founded on that understanding.

This moral consciousness alone, expressed in public opinion, keeps men from crimes, both in town centers and more especially in villages, where the majority of the population dwell.

I repeat that I know many examples of Russian agricultural communities emigrating to the Far East and prospering there for several decades. These communes governed themselves, being unknown to the government and outside its control, and when they were discovered by government agents, the only results were that they experienced calamities unknown to them before and received a new tendency toward the commission of crime.

Not only does the action of governments not deter men from crimes; on the contrary, it increases crime by always disturbing and lowering the moral standard of society. Nor can this be otherwise, since always and everywhere a government, by its very nature, must put in the place of the highest, eternal, religious law (not written in books but in the hearts of men, and binding on every one) its own unjust, man-made laws, the object of which is neither justice nor the common good of all, but various considerations of home and foreign expediency.

Such are all the existing, evidently unjust, fundamental laws of every government: laws maintaining the exclusive right of a minority to the land—[which should be] the common possession of all; laws giving some men a right over the labor of others; laws compelling men to pay money for purposes of murder, or to become soldiers themselves and go to war; laws establishing monopolies in the sale of stupefying intoxicants, or forbidding the free exchange of produce across a certain line called a frontier; and laws regarding the execution of men for actions which are not so much immoral as simply disadvantageous to those in power.

All these laws, and the exaction of their fulfillment by threats of violence, the public executions inflicted for the nonfulfillment of these laws, and above all the forcing of men to take part in wars, the habitual exaltation of military murders, and the preparation for them—all this inevitably lowers the moral social consciousness and its expression, public opinion.

As a result not only does governmental activity not support morality, but, on the contrary, it would be hard to devise a more depraving action than that which governments have had, and still have, on the nations.

It could never enter the head of any ordinary scoundrel to commit all those horrors: the stake, the inquisition, torture, raids, quarterings, hangings, solitary confinements, murders in war, the plundering of nations, etc., which have been and still are being committed, and committed ostentatiously, by all governments. All the horrors of Stenka Razin, Pugachev,[2] and other rebels were but results, and feeble imitations, of the horrors perpetrated by [such rulers as] John,[3] Peter,[4] and Biron,[5] and that have been and are being perpetrated by all governments. If (which is very doubtful) the action of government does deter some dozens of men from crime, hundreds of thousands of other crimes are committed only because men are educated in crime by governmental injustice and cruelty.

If men taking part in legislation, in commerce, in industries, living in towns, and in one way or other sharing the advantages of power can still believe in the beneficence of that power, people living on the land cannot help knowing that government only causes them all kinds of suffering and deprivation, that it was never needed by them and only corrupts those of them who come under its influence.

As a result to try to prove to men that they cannot live without a government, and that the injury the thieves and robbers among them may do is greater than the injury both material and spiritual which government continually does by oppressing and corrupting them, is as strange as it would have been to try to prove to slaves that it was more profitable for them to be slaves than to be free. But just as, in the days of slavery, in spite of the obviously wretched condition the slaves were in, the slaveowners declared and created a belief that it was good for slaves to be slaves, and that they would be worse off if they were free (sometimes the slaves themselves became hypnotized and believed this), so now the government and the people who profit by it argue that governments which rob and deprave men are necessary for their well-being, and men yield to this suggestion.

[2] Stenka Razin and Pugachev were famous Russian rebels of the seventeenth and eighteenth centuries.—Translators.

[3] Ivan the Terrible.—Editor.

[4] Peter the Great.—Editor.

[5] Biron, the favorite of the Empress Anne, who ruled Russia for ten years (1730–41). —Translators.

Men believe in it all, and must continue to do so; for not believing in the law of God, they must put their faith in human law. Absence of human law for them means the absence of all law; and life for men who recognize no law is terrible. Therefore, for those who do not acknowledge the law of God, the absence of human law must seem terrible, and they do not wish to be deprived of it.

This lack of belief in the law of God is the cause of the apparently curious phenomenon that all the theoretical anarchists, clever and learned men—from Bakunin and Proudhon to Reclus, Max Stirner, and Kropotkin—who prove with indisputable correctness and justice the unreasonableness and harmfulness of power, as soon as they begin to speak of the possibility of establishing a society without that human law which they reject, fall at once into indefiniteness, verbosity, rhetoric, and quite unfounded and fantastic hypotheses.

This arises from the fact that none of these theoretical anarchists accepts that law of God common to all men, which it is natural for all to obey; and without the obedience of men to one and the same law—human or divine—human society cannot exist.

Deliverance from human law is only possible on condition that one acknowledges a divine law common to all men.

XIII

"But if a primitive agricultural society like the Russian can live without government," will be said in reply, "what are those millions to do who have given up agriculture and are living an industrial life in towns? We cannot all cultivate the land."

"The only thing every man can be is an agriculturist," is the correct reply given by Henry George to this question.

"But if everybody now returned to an agricultural life," it will again be said, "the civilization mankind has attained would be destroyed, and that would be a terrible misfortune; and therefore a return to agriculture would be an evil and not a benefit for mankind."

A certain method exists whereby men justify their fallacies, and it is this: People, accepting the fallacy into which they have fallen as an unquestionable axiom, unite this fallacy and all its effects into one conception, and call it by one word, and then ascribe to this conception and word a special, indefinite, and mystical meaning. Such conceptions and words are *the Church, Science, Justice, the State,* and *Civilization.* Thus, *the Church* becomes not what it really is, a number of men who have all fallen into the same error, but a "communion of those who believe rightly." *Justice* becomes not a collection of unjust laws framed by certain men, but the designation of those rightful conditions under which alone it is possible for men to live. *Science* becomes not what it really is, the chance dissertations which at a given time occupy the minds of idle men, but the only true knowledge. In the same way *Civilization* becomes not what it really is, the outcome of the activity (falsely and harmfully misdirected by force-using governments) of the Western nations, who have succumbed to the false idea of freeing themselves from violence by violence, but the unquestionably true way towards the future welfare of humanity. "Even if it be true," say the supporters of civilization, "that all these inventions, technical appliances, and products of industry are now only used by the rich and are inaccessible to working men, and cannot therefore as yet be considered a benefit to all mankind, this is so only because these mechanical appliances have not yet attained their full perfection and are not yet distributed as they should be. When mechanism is still further perfected, and the workmen are freed from the power of the capitalists and all the works and factories are in their hands, the machines will produce so much of everything, and it will all be so well distributed, that everybody will have the use of everything. No one will lack anything, and all will be happy."

Not to mention the fact that we have no reason to believe that the working men who now struggle so fiercely with one another for existence, or even for more of the comforts, pleasures, and luxuries of existence, will suddenly become so just and self-denying that they will be content to share equally the benefits the machines are going to give them—leaving that aside—the very supposition that all these works with their machines, which could not have been started or continued except under the power of government and capital, will remain as they are when the power of government and capital have been destroyed is a quite arbitrary supposition.

To expect it is the same as it would have been to expect that after the emancipation of the serfs on one of the large, luxurious Russian estates, which had a park, conservatories, arbors, a private theatrical troupe, an orchestra, a picture gallery, stables, kennels, and storehouses filled with different kinds of garments—[to expect that] all these things would be in part distributed among the liberated peasants and in part kept for common use.

One would think it was evident that on an estate of that kind neither the houses, clothes, nor conservatories of the rich proprietor would be suitable for the liberated peasants, and they would not continue to keep them up. In the same way, when the working people are emancipated from the power of government and capital, they will not continue to maintain the arrangements that have arisen under these powers, and will not go to work in factories and works which could only have come into existence owing to their enslavement, even if such factories could be profitable and pleasant for them.

It is true that when the workers are emancipated from slavery one will regret all this cunning machinery which weaves so much beautiful stuff so quickly and makes such nice sweets, looking glasses, etc., but, in the same way, after the emancipation of the serfs one regretted the beautiful racehorses, pictures, magnolias, musical instruments, and private theaters that disappeared. But just as the liberated serfs bred animals suited to their way of life and raised the plants they required, while the racehorses and magnolias disappeared of themselves, so the workmen, freed from the power of government and capital, will direct their labor to quite other work than at present.

"But it is much more profitable to bake all the bread in one oven than for everybody [to bake] his own, and to weave twenty times as quickly at a factory as on a handloom at home," say the supporters of civilization, speaking as if men were dumb cattle for whom food, clothing, dwellings, and more or less labor were the only questions to solve.

An Australian savage knows very well that it would be more profitable to build one hut for himself and his wife, yet he erects two, so that both he and his wife may enjoy privacy. The Russian peasant knows very decidedly that it is more profitable for him to live in one house with his father and brothers; yet he separates from them, builds his own cottage, and prefers to bear privations rather than obey his elders, or quarrel and have disagreements. "Better but a pot of broth, and one's own master be!" I think the majority of reasonable people would prefer to clean their own clothes and boots, carry water, and trim their own lamps rather than go to a factory and do obligatory labor for one hour a day to produce machines that would do all these things.

If coercion is no longer used, probably nothing of all these fine machines that polish boots and clean plates, nor even of those that bore tunnels and impress steel, etc., would remain. The liberated workmen would inevitably let everything that was founded on their enslavement perish, and begin to construct quite other machines and appliances, with other aims, of other dimensions, and very differently distributed.

This is so plain and obvious that men could not help seeing it if they were not under the influence of the superstition of civilization.

It is this widespread and firmly fixed superstition that causes all indications of the falseness of the path the Western nations are traveling and all attempts to bring the erring peoples back to a free and reasonable life to be rejected, and even to be regarded as a kind of blasphemy or madness. This blind belief that the life we have arranged for ourselves is the best possible life also causes all the chief agents of civilization—its government officials, scientists, artists, merchants, manufacturers, and authors—while making the workers support their idle lives, to overlook their own sins and to feel perfectly sure that their activity is not an immoral and harmful activity (as it really is), but a very useful and important one, and that they are, therefore, very important people and of great use to humanity; and that all the stupid, trifling, and nasty things produced under their direction, such as cannons, fortresses, cinematographs, cathedrals, motors, explosive bombs, phonographs, telegraphs, and steam printing-machines that turn out mountains of paper printed with nastiness, lies, and absurdities, will remain just the same when the workers are free, and will always be a great boon to humanity.

Yet to people free from the superstition of civilization, it cannot but be perfectly obvious that all those conditions of life which among the Western nations are now called "civilization" are nothing but monstrous results of the vanity of the upper, governing classes, such as were the productions of the Egyptian, Babylonian, and Roman despots: the pyramids, temples, and seraglios; or such as were the productions of the Russian serf-owners: palaces, serf-orchestras, private theatrical troupes, artificial lakes, lace, hunting packs, and parks, which the slaves arranged for their lords.

It is said that if men cease to obey government and return to an agricultural life, all the industrial progress they have attained will be lost, and that, therefore, to give up obeying government and to return to an agricultural life would be a bad thing. But there is no reason to suppose that a return to agricultural life, free from government, would destroy such industries and achievements as are really useful to mankind and do not require the enslavement of men. And if it stopped the production of that endless number of unnecessary, stupid, and harmful things, on which a considerable portion of humanity is now employed, and rendered impossible the existence of the idle people who invent all the unnecessary and harmful things by which they justify their immoral lives, that does not mean that all that mankind has worked out for its welfare would be destroyed. On the contrary, the destruction of everything that is kept up by coercion would evoke and promote an intensified production of all those useful and necessary technical improvements which, without turning men into machines and spoiling their lives, may ease the labor of the agriculturists and render their lives more pleasant.

The only difference will be that when men are liberated from power and return to agricultural labor the objects produced by art and industry will no longer aim at amusing the rich, satisfying idle curiosity, preparing for human slaughter, preserving useless and harmful lives at the cost of useful ones, or producing machines by which a small number of workmen can somehow produce a great number of things or cultivate a large tract of land; but they will aim at increasing the productiveness of the work of those laborers who cultivate their own allotments with their own hands, and help to better their lives without taking them away from the land or interfering with their freedom.

XIV

But will people be able to live without obeying some human power? How will they conduct their common business? What will become of the different states? What will happen to Ireland, Poland, Finland, Algeria, India, and to all the colonies? How will the nations group themselves?

Such questions are put by men who are accustomed to think that the conditions of life of all human societies are decided by the will and direction of a few individuals, and who therefore imagine that the knowledge of how future life will shape itself is accessible to man. Such knowledge, however, never was, nor can be, accessible.

If the most learned and best-educated Roman citizen, accustomed to think that the life of the world was guided by the decrees of the Roman Senate and emperors, had been asked what would become of the Roman

Empire in a few centuries, or if he had himself thought of writing such a book as Bellamy's, you may be sure that he never could have foretold, even approximately, the barbarians, or feudalism, or the Papacy, or the disintegration of the peoples and their reunion into large states. The same is true of those twenty-first-century Utopias, with flying machines, X-rays, electric motors, and Socialist organizations of life, which are so daringly drawn by Bellamy, Morris, Anatole France, and others.

Men cannot know what form social life will take in the future—and more than that, harm results from their thinking they can know it. For nothing so interferes with the straight current of their lives as this fancied knowledge of what the future life of humanity ought to be. The life of individuals as well as of communities consists only in this—that men and communities continually move toward the unknown, changing not because certain men have formed brain-spun plans as to what these changes should be, but in consequence of a tendency inherent in all men to strive toward moral perfection, attainable by the infinitely varied activity of millions and millions of human lives. Therefore the relation in which men will stand toward one another and the forms into which they shape society depend entirely on the inner characters of men, and not at all on forecasting this or that form of life which they desire to adopt. Yet those who do not believe in God's law always imagine that they can know what the future state of society should be, and not only define this future state, but do all sorts of things they themselves admit to be evil, in order to mold human society to the shape they think it ought to take.

That others do not agree with them, and think that social life should be quite differently arranged, does not disturb them; and having assured themselves that they can know what the future of society ought to be, they not only decide this theoretically, but act: fight, seize property, imprison and kill men, to establish the form in which, according to their ideas, mankind will be happy.

The old argument of Caiaphas, "It is expedient that one man should die, and that the whole nation perish not," seems irrefutable to such people. Of course they must kill, not one man only, but hundreds and thousands of men, if they are fully assured that the death of these thousands will give welfare to millions. People who do not believe in God and His law cannot but argue thus. Such people live in obedience only to their passions, to their reasonings, and to social hypnotism, and have never considered their destiny of life, nor wherein the real happiness of humanity consists—or, if they have thought about it, they have decided that this cannot be known. And these people, who do not know wherein the welfare of a single man lies, imagine that they know, and know beyond all doubt, what is needed for the welfare of society as a whole: know it so certainly, that to attain that welfare, as they understand it, they commit deeds of violence, murders and executions, which they themselves admit to be evil.

At first it seems strange that men who do not know what they themselves need can imagine that they know clearly and indubitably what the whole community needs; and yet it is just because they do not know what they need that they imagine they know what the whole community needs.

The dissatisfaction they (lacking all guidance for their lives) dimly feel, they attribute not to themselves, but to the badness of the existing forms of social life, which differ from the one they have invented. And in cares for the rearrangement of society they find a possibility of escaping from consciousness of the wrongness of their own lives. That is why those who do not know what to do with themselves are always particularly sure what ought to be done with society as a whole. The less they know about themselves, the surer they are about society. Such men for the most part are either very thoughtless youths or the most depraved of social leaders, such as Marat, Napoleon, and Bismarck; and that is why the history of the nations is full of most terrible evil doings.

The worst effect of this imaginary foreknowledge of what society should be, and of this activity directed to the alteration of society, is that it is just this supposed knowledge and this activity which more than anything else hinder the movement of the community along the path natural to it for its true welfare.

Therefore, to the question "What will the lives of the nations be like which cease to obey power?" we reply that not only do we not know, but we ought not to suppose that anyone can know. We do not know in what circumstances these nations will be placed when they cease to obey power; but we know indubitably what each one of us must do, that those conditions of national life should be the very best. We know, without the least doubt, that in order to make those conditions the very best, we must first of all abstain from the acts of violence which the existing power demands of us, as well as from those to which men fighting against the existing power to establish a new one invite us; and we must therefore not obey any power. We must refuse to submit, not because we know how our life will shape itself in consequence of our ceasing to obey power, but because submission to a power that demands that we should break the law of God is a sin. This we know beyond doubt, and we also know that as a consequence of not transgressing God's will and not sinning, nothing but good can come to us or to the whole world.

XV

People are prone to believe in the realization of the most improbable events under the sun. They believe in the possibility of flying and communicating with the planets, in the possibility of arranging socialistic communes, in spiritualistic communications, and in many other palpably impossible things; but they do not wish to believe that the conception of life in which they and all who surround them live can be altered.

And yet such changes, even the most extraordinary, are continually taking place in ourselves, and among those around us, and among whole communities and nations; and it is these changes that constitute the essence of human life.

It is not necessary to mention changes that have happened in historic times in the social consciousness of nations. At present in Russia, before our very eyes, an apparently astonishing change is taking place with incredible rapidity in the consciousness of the whole Russian nation, a change of which we had no external indication two or three years ago.

The change only seems to us to have taken place suddenly because the preparation for it, which went on in the spiritual region, was not visible. A similar change is still going on in the spiritual region inaccessible to our observations. If the Russian people, who two years ago thought it impossible to disobey or even to criticize the existing power, now not only criticize but are even preparing to disobey it and to replace it by a new one, why should we not suppose that in the consciousness of the Russian people another change in their relation toward power—more natural to them—is now preparing, a change which will consist in their moral and religious emancipation from power?

Why may not such a change be possible among any people, and why not at present among the Russians? Why, instead of that irritated, egotistical mood of mutual strife, fear, and hatred which has now seized all nations, instead of all this preaching of lies, immorality, and violence now so strenuously circulated among all nations by newspapers, books, speeches, and actions—why should not a religious, humane, reasonable, loving mood seize the minds of all nations, and of the Russian nation in particular, after all the sins, sufferings, and terrors they have lived through: a state of mind which would make them see all the horror of submitting to the power under which they live, and feel the joyful possibility of a reasonable, loving life without violence and without power?

Why should not the consciousness of the possibility and necessity of emancipating themselves from the sin of power, and of establishing unity among men based on mutual agreement and on respect and love between man and man, be now ripening, just as the movement now manifesting itself in the revolution was prepared for by decades of influence tending in one particular direction?

Some ten or fifteen years ago the French writer Dumas *fils,* a talented and intelligent man chiefly occupied with esthetic and social questions, wrote a letter to Zola in which he, when already old, uttered some strikingly prophetic words. Truly the spirit of God "bloweth where it listeth"! This is what he wrote:

> The soul, too, is incessantly at work, ever evolving toward light and truth. And so long as it has not reached full light and conquered the whole truth, it will continue to torment man.
>
> Well! The soul never so harassed man, never so dominated him, as it does today. It is as though it were in the air we all breathe. The few isolated souls that had separately desired the regeneration of society have, little by little,

sought one another out, beckoned one another, drawn nearer, united, comprehended one another, and formed a group, a center of attraction, toward which others now fly from the four quarters of the globe like larks toward a mirror. They have, as it were, formed one collective soul, so that men in future may realize together, consciously and irresistibly, the approaching union and steady progress of nations that were but recently hostile one to another. This new soul I find and recognize in events seemingly most calculated to deny it.

These armaments of all nations, these threats their representatives address to one another, this recrudescence of race persecutions, these hostilities among compatriots, are all things of evil aspect, but not of evil augury. They are the last convulsions of that which is about to disappear. The social body is like the human body. Disease, in this case, is but a violent effort of the organism to throw off a morbid and harmful element.

Those who have profited, and expect for long or forever to continue to profit, by the mistakes of the past are uniting to prevent any modification of existing conditions. Hence these armaments and threats and persecutions; but look carefully and you will see that all this is quite superficial. It is colossal, but hollow. There is no longer any soul in it—the soul has gone elsewhere; these millions of armed men who are daily drilled to prepare for a general war of extermination no longer hate the men they are expected to fight, and none of their leaders dares to proclaim this war. As for the appeals, and even the threatening claims, that rise from the suffering and the oppressed—a great and sincere pity, recognizing their justice, begins at last to respond from above.

Agreement is inevitable, and will come at an appointed time, nearer than is expected.

I know not if it be because I shall soon leave this earth, and the rays that are already reaching me from below the horizon have disturbed my sight, but I believe our world is about to begin to realize the words, "Love one another"—without, however, being concerned whether a man or a God uttered them.

The spiritual movement which one recognizes on all sides and so many naive and ambitious men expect to be able to direct, will be absolutely humanitarian. Mankind, which does nothing moderately, is about to be seized with a frenzy, a madness, of love. This will not, of course, happen smoothly or all at once; it will involve misunderstandings—even sanguinary ones perchance—so trained and so accustomed have we been to hatred, even by those, sometimes, whose mission it was to teach us to love one another. But it is evident that this great law of brotherhood must be accomplished some day, and I am convinced that the time is commencing when our desire for its accomplishment will become irresistible.

I believe that this thought, however strange the expression "seized with a frenzy of love" may seem, is perfectly true, and is felt more or less dimly by all men of our day. A time must come when love, which forms the fundamental essence of the soul, will take the place natural to it in the life of mankind and will become the chief basis of the relations between man and man.

That time is coming; it is at hand. Lamennais wrote:

We are living in the times predicted by Christ. From one end of the earth to the other, everything is tottering. In all institutions, whatever they may be, in all the different systems on which the social life of men is founded, nothing stands firm. Everyone feels that soon it must all fall to ruins, and that in this temple too, not one stone will be left on another. But as the destruction of Jerusalem and its temple, from whence the living God had departed, foreboded and prepared for the erection of a new city and a new temple, whither the people of all races and of all nations would come together at their own free will—so on the ruins of the temples and towns of today, a new city and a new temple will be erected, predestined to become the universal temple and the common fatherland of the human race, disunited till now by teachings hostile to one another, that make brothers into strangers and sow godless hatred and revolting warfare among them. When that hour, known to God alone, arrives—the hour of union of the nations into one temple and one city—then indeed will the kingdom of Christ come—the complete fulfillment of his divine mission. Did he not come with the one object of teaching men that they must be united by the law of love?

Channing said the same:

Mighty powers are at work in the world. Who can stay them? God's word has gone forth, and "it cannot return to him void." A new comprehension of the Christian spirit—a new reverence for humanity, a new feeling of brotherhood, and of all men's relation to the common Father—this is among the signs of our times. We see it; do we not feel it? Before this, all oppressions are to fall. Society, silently pervaded by this, is to change its aspect of universal warfare for peace. The power of selfishness, all-grasping and seemingly invincible, is to yield to this diviner energy. . . . "On earth peace" will not always sound as fiction.

XVI

Why should we suppose that people, who are entirely in the power of God, will always remain under the strange delusion that only human laws —changeable, accidental, unjust, and local as they are—are important and binding, and not the one, eternal, just law of God, common to all men? Why should we think that the teachers of mankind will always preach, as they now do, that there is and can be no such law, but that the only laws that exist are special laws of religious ritual for every nation and every sect; or the so-called scientific laws of matter and the imaginary laws of sociology (which do not bind men to anything) or, finally, civil laws, which men themselves can institute and change? Such an error is possible for a time, but why should we suppose that people to whom one and the same divine law written in their hearts has been revealed in the teaching of the Brahmins, Buddha, Lao-tse, Confucius, and Christ will not at last follow this one basis of all laws, affording as it does moral satisfaction and a joyful social life—but that they will always follow that wicked and pitiful tangle of Church, scientific, and governmental teaching which diverts their attention from the one thing needful and directs it toward what can be of no use to them, as it does not show them how each separate man should live?

Why should we think that men will continue unceasingly and deliberately to torment themselves, some trying to rule over others, others with hatred and envy submitting to the rulers and seeking means themselves to become rulers? Why should we think that the progress men pride themselves on will always lie in the increase of population and the preservation of life, and never in the moral elevation of life? That it will lie in miserable mechanical inventions by which men will produce ever more and more harmful, injurious, and demoralizing objects, and not in greater and greater unity one with another, and in that subjugation of their lusts which is necessary to make such unity possible? Why should we not suppose that men will rejoice and vie with one another, not in riches and luxuries, but in simplicity and frugality and in kindness one toward another? Why should we not suppose that men will see progress, not in seizing more and more for themselves, but in taking less and less from others, and in giving more and more to others; not in increasing their power, not in fighting more and more successfully, but in growing more and more humble, and in coming into closer and closer union, man with man and nation with nation?

Instead of imagining men unrestrainedly yielding to their lusts, breeding like rabbits, establishing factories in towns for the production of chemical foods to feed their increasing generation, and living in these towns without plants or animals—why should we not imagine chaste people, struggling against their lusts, living in loving communion with their neighbors amid fruitful fields, gardens, and woods, with tame, well-fed animal friends; only with this difference from their present condition, that they do not consider the land to be anyone's private property, do not themselves belong to any particular nation, do not pay taxes or duties, prepare for war, or fight anybody; but on the contrary, have more and more of peaceful intercourse with every race?

To imagine the life of men like that, nothing need be invented or altered or added in one's imagination to the lives of the agricultural races we know in China, Russia, India, Canada, Algeria, Egypt, and Australia.

To picture such life to ourselves, one need not imagine any kind of cunning or out-of-the-way arrangement, but need only imagine to oneself men acknowledging no other supreme law but the universal law expressed alike in the Brahmin, Buddhist, Confucian, Taoist, and Christian religions —the law of love to God and to one's neighbor.

To imagine such a life we need not imagine men as some new kind of beings—virtuous angels. They will be just as they now are, with all weaknesses and passions natural to them; they will sin, will perhaps quarrel, and commit adultery, and take away other people's property, and even slay;

but all this will be the exception and not, as now, the rule. Their life will be quite different owing to the one fact that they will not consider organized violence a good thing and a necessary condition of life, and will not be trained amiss by hearing the evil deeds of governments represented as good actions.

Their life will be quite different because there will no longer be that impediment to preaching and teaching the spirit of goodness, love, and submission to the will of God that exists as long as we admit, as necessary and lawful, governmental violence demanding what is contrary to God's law, and involving the acceptance of what is criminal and bad in place of what is lawful and good.

Why should we not imagine that, through suffering, men may be aroused from the suggestion, the hypnotism, under which they have suffered so long, and remember that they are all sons and servants of God, and therefore can and must submit only to Him and to their own consciences? All this is not difficult to imagine; it is even difficult to imagine that it should not be accomplished.

XVII

"Except ye become as little children, ye shall in no wise enter the Kingdom of Heaven" does not refer to individuals only, but also to human societies. As a man, having experienced all the miseries caused by the passions and temptations of life, consciously returns to a state of simplicity, kindness toward all, and readiness to accept what is good (the state in which children unconsciously live) and returns to it with the wealth of experience and the reason of a grown-up man, so human society also, having experienced all the miserable consequences of abandoning the law of God to obey human power, and of attempting to arrange life apart from agricultural labor, must now consciously return, with all the wealth of experience gained during the time of its aberration, from the snares of human power, and from the attempt to organize life on a basis of industrial activity, and must submit to the highest, divine law, and to the primary work of cultivating the soil, which it had temporarily abandoned.

Consciously to return from the snares of human power, and to obey the supreme law of God alone, is to admit as always and everywhere binding upon us the eternal law of God, which is alike in all the teachings— Brahminist, Buddhist, Confucian, Taoian, Christian, and to some extent in Mohammedan (Babist)—and is incompatible with subjection to human power.

Consciously to live an agricultural life is to acknowledge it to be not an accidental and temporary condition, but the life which makes it easiest for man to fulfill the will of God, and which should therefore be preferred to any other.

For such a return to an agricultural life and to conscious disobedience to power, the Eastern nations (and among them the Russian nation) are most favorably situated.

The Western nations have already wandered so far on the false path of changing the organization of power, and exchanging agricultural for industrial work, that such a return is difficult and requires great efforts. But, sooner or later, the ever-increasing annoyance and instability of their position will force them to return to a reasonable and truly free life, supported by their own labor and not by the exploitation of other nations. However alluring the external success of manufacturing industry and the showy side of such a life may be, the most penetrating thinkers among the Western nations have long pointed out how disastrous is the path they are following, and how necessary it is to reconsider and change their way, and to return to that agricultural life which was the original form of life for all nations, and which is the ordained path making it possible for all men to live a reasonable and joyful life.

The majority of the Eastern peoples, including the Russian nation, will not have to alter their lives at all. They need only stop their advance along the false path they have just entered, and become clearly conscious of the negative attitude toward power and the affectionate attitude toward husbandry which was always natural to them.

We of the Eastern nations should be thankful to fate for placing us in a position in which we can benefit by the example of the Western nations: benefit by it not in the sense of imitating it, but in the sense of avoiding their mistakes, not doing what they have done, not traveling the disastrous path from which nations that have gone so far are already returning, or are preparing to return.

Just in this halt in the march along a false path, and in showing the possibility and inevitableness of indicating and making a different path, one easier, more joyful, and more natural than the one the Western nations have traveled, lies the chief and mighty meaning of the revolution now taking place in Russia.

17.
Aleksandr Aleksandrovich Blok

1880-1921

For over a century the dominant pre-occupation of the Russian intelligentsia had been their alienation from the people. Both Slavophiles and Westerners had looked for ways to bridge the gap that separated the educated classes from the peasant masses. The problem became even more critical when, after the Emancipation, vast numbers of peasants crowded into urban centers and formed a rapidly growing, miserable, and disoriented proletariat. In the nineteenth century, because of their ties to the landed estates, the majority of the intelligentsia had believed that they retained some understanding of the peasants and could therefore expect to be able to re-establish contact with them. But the intelligentsia at the dawn of the twentieth century discovered that nothing could bridge their distance from the "people" in the cities. In addition, the intelligentsia grew frightened of the cultural and spiritual implications of industrialization and urbanization. Little wonder that industrial civilization gave rise to anxiety and gloomy forebodings.

The leading poet of Russia's Silver Age, Aleksandr Aleksandrovich Blok, was particularly sensitive to the gulf separating him (or rather his esthetic and moral sensibilities) from the masses. His passionate appeals to the intelligentsia to understand the people and re-establish ties with them expressed his deep sense of guilt for the misery of the Russian nation. His feelings of guilt led him not only to forgive but to justify the people's hostility to the cultural values of the intelligentsia. Blok's sensitive ear was also attuned to the ominous rumblings of the impending catastrophe.

It is not surprising that Blok welcomed the hurricane of the Revolution as an inevitable and deserved retribution. In his apocalyptic mood and his fervent belief that the elemental forces of moral passion and spiritual energy sweeping the world must be understood and accepted, Blok echoed Nietzsche's message. Blok was thinking in the terms posed by the "cursed questions" (discussed on p. 8 of this volume) of the Russian intelligentsia; but his intuitions and answers were relevant to the broader crisis of Western civilization as well.

The People and the Intelligentsia

. . .

The love for the common people that awoke in the Russian intelligentsia during Catherine's reign has never diminished. They keep collecting materials for the study of "folklore"; cram their bookcases with anthologies of Russian songs, epics, legends, incantations, dirges; investigate Russian mythology, wedding and funeral rites; grieve for the people; go to the people; [1] are filled with high hopes; fall into despair; even give up their lives, face execution or starve to death for the people's cause. Possibly they have even come to *understand the people's soul*. But how do they understand it? Isn't understanding *everything* and loving *everything*—even the inimical, even that which requires abjuring what one values most—isn't that the same as understanding *nothing, loving nothing?*

All this on the part of the "intelligentsia." It certainly cannot be said that they have always been sitting by idly. They did put their will, heart, and mind into studying the people.

But from the other side—ever the same faintly ironical smile, the knowing silence, the gratitude for "instruction" and apologies for "ignorance," with an undertone of "for the present, till our time comes." A dreadful laziness and dreadful torpor, it always seemed to us; or else the slow awakening of a giant, as it seems to us more and more. A giant waking with a singular smile on his lips. No *intelligent* smiles like that; one would think we knew all the ways of laughing there are, but in face of the muzhik's [2] smile—which has nothing in common with the irony that Heine and the Jews have taught us, or with Gogol's laughter through tears, or with [Vladimir] Solov'ev's loud laughter—all our laughing instantly dies; we are troubled and afraid.

Is all this really as I say, or is it all invented—does the terrible gulf exist

[1] A reference to the "going to the people" movement of the 1870's.—Editor.

[2] Plain peasant.—Editor.

Translated by Gertrude Vakar from Aleksandr Aleksandrovich Blok, "Narod i intelligentsiia," in *Sochineniia v dvukh tomakh*, Vol. II (Moscow, 1958), pp. 85–91. This article, originally an address given before two literary societies in November 1908, was first published under the title "Rossiia i intelligentsiia" (Russia and the Intelligentsia) in *Zolotoe runo*, No. 1 (1909). The opening section, in which Blok criticized G. Baronov's address "On Demotheism," which attacked Gorky's deification of the people, has been omitted here.

only in our imagination? Sometimes one doubts that it can be true, but apparently it is—in other words, there actually exist not merely the two concepts but two realities: the people and the intelligentsia; a hundred and fifty million on the one hand, and a few hundred thousand on the other, unable to understand each other in the most fundamental things.

The thousands are in a state of hasty ferment, constantly changing direction, temper, banners. From the cities rises a din whose separate elements even a trained ear cannot distinguish, a din like the din which, according to legend, rose from the Tatar camp the night before the battle of Kulikovo.[3] Countless cartwheels screeching beyond the Nepriadva, a clamor of voices, and on the misty river the alarmed cries and splashing of geese and swans.

Among the millions, a stillness of sleep seems to reign. But so was Dmitrii Donskoi's camp wrapped in silence; yet the *voevoda* [4] Bobrok wept when he put his ear to the ground—he could hear the widow's disconsolate weeping, the mother trembling as she clung to her son's stirrup. Distant and ominous heat lightning flared above the Russian camp.

Between the two camps—the people and the intelligentsia—there is a line at which they can meet and agree. No such uniting line existed between the Russians and the Tatars in their frankly hostile camps. But how tenuous this line is today between the secretly hostile camps! How strange and rare are the meetings! How disparate the "tribes, tongues, conditions" that come together here! Workmen, sectarians, tramps, peasants meet with writers and public figures, officials and revolutionaries. But the line is tenuous. As before, the two camps do not see and do not want to know each other; as before, most of the people and most of the intelligentsia tend to regard all who desire peace and accord as traitors and defectors.

Is not the line as thin as the misty streamlet Nepriadva? The night before the battle it meandered limpid between the two camps; the night after the battle, and for seven more nights after that, it ran red with Russian and Tatar blood.

Once in a while, on the narrow line where the people and the intelligentsia communicate, great men and important events arise. These men and events always demonstrate, as it were, that the antagonism is deep and of long standing, that the problem of reconciliation is not an abstract but a practical problem, and that it must be solved in some special way, which we have not found as yet. The men who emerge from the masses and reveal the depths of the people's soul are immediately antipathetic to us, antipathetic because somehow incomprehensible in their innermost being.

It is known that Lomonosov was hated and hounded by the fraternity of scholars of his day; to us, the folk-story-tellers are amusing freaks; the Slavophile principles, deeply grounded in the people, have always been a

---

[3] The first Russian victory over the Tatar overloads won by the Grand Duke Dimitrii (Donskoi) in 1380. Blok is alluding to the account of the battle found in the medieval epic *Zadonshchina*.—Editor.

[4] Medieval Russian title for a military commander.—Editor.

fatal obstacle to the "intelligentist" [5] principles. Samarin was right when he wrote Aksakov about the "impassable line" between the "Slavophiles" and the "Westerners." Under our own eyes, the intelligentsia, who let Dostoevsky die in penury, treated Mendeleev with overt or secret hatred.

In their way the intelligentsia were right. Between them and these men there was that "impassable line" (Pushkin's expression) which constitutes Russia's tragedy. In recent times the tragedy has found its sharpest expression in the irreconcilability of the Mendeleevan and the Tolstoyan principles; their antithesis is even more acute and alarming than the antithesis between Tolstoy and Dostoevsky which Merezhkovskii has pointed out.[6]

The latest notable case on the line uniting the people and the intelligentsia is the phenomenon of Maxim Gorky. He, too, proved that the intelligentsia are terrified and baffled by what he loves and how he loves. He loves Russia, which we also love, but with a different, incomprehensible love. His heroes, who embody his love, are alien to us; they are taciturn, cunning men, with a half-smile auguring no one knows what. Gorky is not an *intelligent* by nature; "we" love the same thing but with a different love; for the corrosive poisons of "our" love he has an antidote—"healthy blood."

Baronov, in his predominantly "literary" paper, warns us not to deify the people. I think very few of us do that; we are not savages, to create gods of the unknown and the frightening. But if we have long since stopped worshiping the people we still cannot let it alone, dismiss it with a shrug; our love and our thoughts have tended in that direction for too long.

What is to be done, then?

Baronov says: "We must not deify the people but quite simply work with it, pull it out of the putrid Russian swamp (first, of course, we must pull ourselves out)."

This is the only nonliterary part of his address. No ways and means are indicated. But then no one person can indicate the means for which the whole of Russian literature is searching.

What we must do is love Russia, "travel around in Russia," as Gogol wrote just before he died. How does one begin to love one's brothers? To love people? The soul wants to love only the beautiful, and poor humanity is so imperfect, there is so little in it that is beautiful! How does one go about it? Begin by thanking God that you are a Russian. For Russians, the way is opening now, and the way is Russia herself. If a Russian comes to love Russia, he will also come to love everything there is in Russia. God himself is now leading us toward this love. Without the diseases and sufferings that have accumulated in the body of Russia in such abundance, and which are

---

[5] Blok's derogatory reference also implies that the more radical and narrow-minded members of the intelligentsia were uncritical worshipers of Western ideas that had no affinity with Russia's cultural tradition.—Editor.

[6] A reference to the pioneering study of Dimitrii Merezhkovskii, *Tolstoi i Dostoevskii* (St. Petersburg, 1901–2), which contrasts the "revealer of the flesh" with the "revealer of the spirit."—Editor.

our fault, none of us would be feeling compassion for her. And compassion is already "the beginning of love."

> Our monastery is Russia! Clothe yourself mentally in a monk's black cassock and, having completely mortified self as far as you, but not Russia, are concerned, go forth to work in her. She is now calling her sons more urgently than ever before. Already her soul is in pain, and the cry of her soul-sickness is heard. My friend! either your heart is unfeeling, or you do not know what Russia means to a Russian! [7]

Can an *intelligent* understand these words? Alas, even now they will sound to him like a dying man's delirium and provoke the same hysterical abuse as Belinskii, "the father of the Russian intelligentsia," heaped on Gogol.

Indeed, the words are incomprehensible to us which say that compassion is the beginning of love, that God is leading us toward love, that Russia is a monastery for which one must "mortify self as far as oneself is concerned." They are incomprehensible because we no longer know the love that is born of compassion, and because the problem of God is perhaps "the least interesting problem in our day," as Merezhkovskii has noted, and because in order to "mortify oneself," to renounce what is dearest and most personal, one must know why this must be done. The first, the second, and the third are alike incomprehensible to the "nineteenth-century man" of whom Gogol wrote, and a fortiori to twentieth-century man, before whom there looms "only the gigantic form of boredom, day by day growing more immeasurable in size." "Life is getting more and more arid. . . . All is smothered, all is a tomb" (Gogol).

Is the line dividing the intelligentsia from Russia indeed impassable? While such a barrier exists, the intelligentsia are condemned to ferment, move, and degenerate within a vicious circle; they have no incentive for denying the self as long as they do not believe that life itself demands such a renunciation. Not only can there be no abnegation, but one can even assert one's frailties—up to the frailty of suicide. What can I reply to a man driven to suicide by the imperatives of individualism, demonism, estheticism, or finally, by the least abstract, most ordinary imperative of *despair and depression,* when I myself am in love with estheticism, individualism, and despair—briefly, when I myself am an *intelligent?* When in myself there is nothing that I love more than my own individualistic love and my melancholy, which, like a shadow, always inseparably follows this kind of love?

Fewer and fewer educated people find salvation in the positive values of scholarship, public service, or art; we observe this, and hear about it, daily. This is natural, nothing can be done about it. Some different, higher principle is needed. Since there is none, rebellion and violence of all sorts take its place, from the vulgar "theomachy" of the decadents to unspectacular open self-destruction—debauch, drinking, all the forms of suicide.

---

[7] Quoted from Gogol's *Selected Passages from a Correspondence with Friends* (*Vybrannye mesta iz perepiski s druziami*).—Editor.

Nothing like this exists among the people. A man who embarks upon one of these fatal courses automatically exiles himself from the people's world, becomes an *intelligent* in spirit. The people's very soul loathes such things. If the intelligentsia are increasingly imbued with the "will to die," the people has always harbored a "will to live." This explains why even the unbeliever runs to the people to seek in it the life-force: he is led simply by the instinct of self-preservation. He runs to the people, and is brought up short by the smile and the silence, by disdain, condescending pity, the "impassable line," and perhaps by something even more dreadful and unexpected.

Gogol and many other Russian writers liked to imagine Russia as sleep and quiet incarnate; but the sleep is coming to an end, and the quiet is broken by a far-off, gathering rumble, unlike the mixed din of the cities.

It was Gogol, too, who pictured Russia as a flying troika. "Russia, whither are you speeding? Answer me." But there is no answer, only "the magic ringing cascade of the bell."

The rumble, growing so fast that with every passing year we can hear it more distinctly, is nothing else than the "magic ringing" of the troika's bell. What if the troika, around which "the rent air thunders and becomes wind," is *racing straight at us?* When we rush to the people, we are rushing to certain death under the mad troika's hoofs.

Why is it that two feelings visit us ever more often: the self-oblivion of rapture and the self-oblivion of anguish, despair, indifference? Soon there will be no room for any other feelings. Perhaps it is because darkness already reigns all around us? In that darkness no one is conscious of others, only of himself. Already, as in a nightmare or a frightening dream, we can imagine that the darkness overhanging us is the shaggy chest of the shaft-horse, and that in another moment the heavy hoofs will descend.

The Intelligentsia and the Revolution

"Russia is going under," "Russia is no more," "Memory eternal to Russia"—this is what I hear on all sides.

But before me is Russia—the Russia our great writers saw in terrifying, prophetic visions, the Petersburg that Dostoevsky saw, the Russia that Gogol compared to a racing troika.

Russia is in storm. Carlyle has said that democracy arrives "storm-girt."

Russia is destined to suffer torments, abasement, divisions, but she will come out of these humiliations renewed—and great in a new way.

In the torrent of thoughts and forebodings that caught me up ten years ago there was a mixed feeling about Russia: anguish, terror, guilt, hope.

Those were the years when autocracy for the last time achieved what it wanted: Witte and Durnovo [1] had tied the revolution with a rope; Stolypin wound the rope firmly around his tense, aristocratic hand. Stolypin's hand weakened. When this last nobleman was gone, the power passed to "journeymen," to use the expression of a certain high-ranking personage; then the rope slackened and slid off easily, by itself.

All this took only a few years, but the few years settled on our shoulders like a long, sleepless, ghost-filled night.

Rasputin was all, Rasputin was everywhere; Azefs, unmasked and not; [2] and finally the years of the European carnage. For a moment it seemed that it would clear the air, or so it seemed to us who were too impressionable; in reality it proved a fitting culmination to the sham, filth, and turpitude in which our motherland wallowed.

What is the war like?

Bogs, bogs, and bogs, overgrown with grass or covered with snowdrifts; in the west, a dreary German searchlight—groping—night after night. On a sunny day a German Fokker appears; it doggedly flies along one and the same path, as if a path could be worn and befouled even in the sky. Little puffs of smoke spread out around it, white, gray, reddish (that's us

---

[1] P. N. Durnovo was the rigidly conservative, even reactionary, Minister of the Interior after the Revolution of 1905.—Editor.

[2] Evno F. Azef was the head of the terrorist Executive Committee of the Socialist Revolutionary party who was unmasked as having also been a police agent.—Editor.

Translated by Gertrude Vakar from Aleksandr Aleksandrovich Blok, "Intelligentsiia i revoliutsiia," in *Sochineniia v dvukh tomakh*, Vol. II (Moscow, 1958), pp. 218–28. This article was first published in *Znamia truda*, No. 122 (January 19, 1918).

shooting at it, hardly ever hitting; like the Germans—at us). The Fokker is flustered, falters, but tries to stay on its foul little path; sometimes it methodically drops a bomb. This means that the spot it aims at has been punctured on the map by dozens of German staff officers. The bomb falls, now on a graveyard, now on a herd of cattle, now on a herd of people, but more often, of course, into a bog; that's thousands of the people's rubles in a bog.

Men gape at all this, perishing of tedium, devoured by idleness; they have already managed to drag over here all the filth of their prewar apartments: adultery, cards, drinking, squabbles, scandal.

Europe has gone insane. The flower of manhood, the flower of the intelligentsia, sits for years in a bog, sits with conscious determination (isn't that symbolic?) on a narrow strip a thousand versts long, which is called "the front."

People are tiny, the earth is huge. It is nonsense that the world war is so noticeable—on a small patch of land, the edge of a wood, one clearing, there is room for hundreds of dead bodies of men and horses. And how many of them can be dumped into one not very large hole, which will soon be covered with grass or powdered over with snow! Here is one tangible reason the "great European war" is so pathetic.

It is difficult to say which is more nauseating—the bloodshed or the *idleness*, the *boredom*, the *triviality*. They are called "the great war," "the war for the fatherland," "the war for the liberation of oppressed nationalities," and I forget what else. No, by *this* sign no one will be liberated.

By and by, overcome by the filth, the abomination of desolation, crushed by mad boredom and senseless idleness, people somehow dispersed, fell silent, and withdrew into themselves, as if they were sitting under glass domes from which the air was gradually being pumped out. This was when humanity really turned brutish, and the Russo-patriots in particular.

The torrent of premonitions that rushed over some of us between the two revolutions lost its force too, became muted, disappeared somewhere into the ground. I think I was not the only one to experience a sense of disease and anguish in the years from 1909 to 1916. Now, when the whole air of Europe has been changed by the Russian Revolution, begun as the "bloodless idyll" of February and irrepressibly, angrily growing, it seems at times that those recent years, so ancient and so remote, never were; and the torrent that had gone underground, flowing silent in the deep and the dark—it is sounding again, and there is a new music in its noise.

We used to love these dissonances, the roaring and ringing, the unexpected transitions—in an orchestra. But if we *truly loved* these sounds and were not merely titillating our nerves in a full concert hall after dinner, we must listen to them and love them now, when they pour from the world's orchestra, and, listening, understand that the theme is the same, still the same.

For music is not a plaything; and the cur who thought music was a plaything—let him now behave like a cur: tremble, crawl, hold on to what's his!

We Russians are living through an epoch that has few equals in grandeur. Tiutchev's words come to mind:

> Blessed is he who visited this world
> At its most fateful moments.
> He was invited by the gods
> As a companion to their feast,
> He's cospectator of their noble drama.[3]

It is not the artist's job to watch how intents are fulfilled, to worry whether they are fulfilled or not. In his art the prosaic, the workaday, the transient will find expression later, when it will have burned out in life. Those of us who survive, who are not "crushed by the onslaught of the noisy whirlwind," shall become masters over countless spiritual treasures. Probably only a new genius, like Pushkin's Arion, will be able to master them fully; "tossed ashore by a wave," he will sing "the old songs" and dry "his wet garment in the sun, at the foot of a cliff." [4]

The artist's job, the artist's *obligation,* is to see *what* is intended, to listen to the music thundering in the "wind-torn air." [5]

Well, then, what is intended?

To make everything over. Find a way to make everything different, to change our false, filthy, boring, hideous life into a just, clean, gay, and beautiful life.

When *such* an intent, concealed since the dawn of time in the heart of man, the heart of the people, breaks its confining bonds and rushes forth in a stormy torrent, tearing down the last dams, carrying off chunks of riverbank, this is called revolution. Lesser, tamer, lowlier things are called insurrection, riot, coup d'état. But *this* is called *revolution.*

It is akin to Nature. Woe to those who expect a revolution to fulfill merely their own dreams, however high-minded and noble. A revolution, like a hurricane, like a blizzard, always brings something new and unexpected. It cruelly deceives many, it easily maims the deserving in its vortex, it often carries the undeserving unharmed to dry land; but these are details, they change neither the main direction of the torrent nor its awesome, deafening roar. The roar is still about something *grand*—always.

The sweep of the Russian Revolution, which wants to engulf the whole world (no genuine revolution can desire less; whether the wish will come true isn't ours to forecast), is such that it hopes to raise a world-wide cyclone, which will carry warm winds and the sweet scent of orange groves to snow-covered lands, moisten the sun-scorched steppes of the South with cool northern rain.

"Peace and the brotherhood of nations" is the sign under which the

[3] The second stanza of F. I. Tiutchev's poem "Cicero."—Editor.
[4] A somewhat inaccurate quotation from Pushkin's poem "Arion."—Editor.
[5] An allusion to the last sentence of Part One of Gogol's *Dead Souls*, in which Russia is compared to an onrushing troika. The same line is more accurately quoted on p. 363. —Editor.

Russian Revolution runs its course. This is what its torrent roars. This is the music that all who have ears must hear.

Russian artists have had enough "premonitions and portents" to expect just such assignments from Russia. They never doubted that Russia was a big ship destined to journey far. Like the soul of the people that nurtured them, they were never noted for practical sense, moderation, tidiness; "all, all that threatens ruin" held for them "ineffable delights" (Pushkin).[6] A sense of trouble, of uncertainty about the morrow, was their constant companion. To them, as to the people in its innermost dreams, it had to be *all* or *nothing*. They knew that only the best is worth thinking about, even though "hard is the good," as Plato has said.

The great Russian artists—Pushkin, Gogol, Dostoevsky, Tolstoy—went down into darkness, but they also had the strength to dwell and lie low in the dark, because they believed in light. They knew the light. Each of them, like the whole people that had carried them in its womb, gnashed his teeth in the dark, in despair, often in hate. But they knew that sooner or later *everything would be different*, because *life is good*.

Life is good. What has a people or a man to live for who has inwardly lost faith in everything? Or a man who is disappointed with life, exists on its "handouts," "out of charity"? Or thinks that being alive "isn't too bad but not very pleasant either," because "everything goes its ordained way" —the way of evolution—and that people, generally speaking, are so shoddy and imperfect that the best they can expect, God willing, is to blunder through their life-span somehow, knocking together societies and states, blocking themselves off from one another with little walls of rights and obligations, conventional laws, conventional relationships.

This kind of thinking is wasteful; people who think like that might as well not live. Dying is easy. One can die quite painlessly—right now in Russia, as never before. It can even be done without a priest; no priest will humiliate you with the bribe of a funeral service.

Life is worth living only if we make boundless demands of it—all or nothing—if we expect the unexpected, if we believe not in things that "do not exist on this earth," but in those that ought to exist, no matter if they have not yet come and may not come for a long time. Life will *render* them to us—because it is *good*.

Mortal weariness is replaced by animal high spirits. After a sound sleep come fresh thoughts, washed by sleep; in the light of day they may seem *foolish*, these thoughts. But the light of day is lying.

We must understand where such thoughts flow from. Right away, now, we must realize that the Russian people is like Ivan the Simpleton, who has just tumbled out of bed, and in whose thoughts, which may seem foolish if not hostile to his older brothers, there is a tremendous creative power.

Why "*uchredilka*"?[7] (By the way, this isn't as disparaging as it sounds:

6 Quotation from "Feast at the Time of the Plague."—Editor.
7 The derogatory nickname of the Constituent Assembly (*Uchreditel'noe Sobranie*),

the peasants are used to *"potrebilka."* [8]) Because we ourselves pontificated about "electoral agitation," criticized officials for "abusing" it; because the most civilized countries (America, France) are just now choking on electoral rigging, electoral corruption.

Because (let me speak for the simpleton) I want to "check and control" everything myself, to do everything myself, not to be "represented" (there is a great elemental strength in this—Doubting Thomas' strength); and also because sooner or later in a colonnaded hall an important official will trumpet: "Upon the thirty-ninth reading, such-and such a bill has been rejected." In that trumpet voice there will be such a dull and dreadful somnolence, such a thunderous yawn of "organized public opinion," such nameless horror, that the more sensitive, more musical among us (Russians, French, Germans—all alike) will again and again rush into "individualism," into "flight from society," into the deep and lonely night. And finally, because God alone knows whom, and how, and to what today's illiterate Russia has elected—the Russia that cannot get it through her head that the Constituent Assembly is not a tsar.

Why "Down with courts of law"? Because there are tomes of "statutes" and tomes of "interpretation"; because the judge and the lawyer,[9] upper-class people both, talk between themselves about the "delict"; because the "arguments to the court" go on, over the head of a miserable little crook. The crook—well, he's a crook; he has already committed his sin, lost his soul; nothing is left but hatred or tears of repentance, escape or forced labor—anything to get out of sight. Why, on top of it all, make sport of the wretch?

A liberal lawyer has been depicted by Dostoevsky. While Dostoevsky lived he was hounded, but after his death he was called "the bard of the insulted and injured." Tolstoy, too, described the things I am talking about. And who erected a fence around that eccentric's grave? Who now vociferates that the grave might be "desecrated"? How do you know, perhaps Lev Nikolaevich [Tolstoy] would be pleased to have people sit by his graveside, throw cigarette butts, and spit? Spittle is God's, but a fence—hardly.

Why gouge holes in an ancient cathedral? Because for a hundred years a fat, belching priest took bribes and sold vodka here.

Why defile the gentry's beloved estates? Because peasant girls were raped and flogged there; if not at this squire's, then at his neighbor's.

Why the felling of century-old parks? Because for a hundred years, under the leafy lindens and maples, their owners paraded their power, taunting the beggar with their purse, the dunce with their education.

And that's how it is for everything.

I know what I'm saying. You can't get around these things. It is impossible to hush them up; yet everybody keeps silent about them.

elected in the fall of 1917, which met only once, in January 1918, and was prevented from reassembling on Lenin's orders.—Editor.

[8] A popular term for a consumers' union (*obshchestvo potrebitelei*) store.—Editor.

[9] Blok uses the illiterate form *ablakat*, which has the derogatory implication of the American "Philadelphia lawyer."—Editor.

I do not doubt anyone's personal integrity, anyone's personal sorrow; but we are responsible for the past—or aren't we? We are links of a single chain. Don't we answer for the sins of our fathers? If this is not felt by all, it must be felt by "the best."

Do not worry. Could even a grain of the truly precious be lost? We have loved too little if we fear for the things we love. "Perfect love casteth out fear." [10] Do not be alarmed when citadels, palaces, pictures, books are destroyed. They should be preserved for the people, but the people will not have lost all if it loses them. A palace that is being destroyed is no palace. A citadel that is being wiped off the face of the earth is no citadel. A tsar who has toppled off his throne by himself is no tsar. The citadels are in our hearts, the tsars in our heads. The eternal forms that have been revealed to us can be taken away only together with the heart and the head.

What did you think? That a revolution was an idyll? That creativity did not destroy anything in its path? That the people is a good little boy? That crooks, agents provocateurs, reactionaries, profiteers by the hundreds would not try to grab what can be grabbed? Finally, that the age-old discord between "black" and "white" bone, between the "educated" and the "un-educated," the intelligentsia and the people, would really be so "blood-lessly" and "painlessly" resolved?

Perhaps it is you who must now be woken from "age-long sleep"? You who need to be told, "Noli tangere circulos meos"? [11] For you loved too little, and much is demanded of you, more than of anyone. You lacked the inner, crystalline ringing, the music of love; you insulted the artist—all right, the artist—but in him you insulted the very soul of the people. Love works wonders, music charms beasts. But you (all of us) lived without music and without love. We had better be quiet now if there is no music, if we do not hear the music. For at this time everything except music, anything devoid of music, any "dry matter," can only arouse and enrage the beast. At this stage, the human being cannot be reached without music.

Yet even the best among us say, "We are disillusioned in our people"; the best sneer and snicker, are filled with spite, see nothing around them but coarseness and beastliness (while the human being is right there). The best people even say, "There hasn't been any revolution." The ones who were obsessed with hatred of "tsarism" are ready to fling themselves back into its arms, just to be able to forget what is going on now. Yesterday's "defeatists" wring their hands over the "German tyranny." Yesterday's "international-ists" weep for "Holy Russia." Born atheists are ready to light votive candles and pray for victory over the external and the internal foe.

I don't know which is more frightening, the arson and lynchings in one camp, or this oppressive lack of musicality in the other?

Remember that I am addressing the "intelligentsia," not the "bour-geoisie." The latter never dreamt of any music except the piano. To them

[10] I John 4:18.—Editor.
[11] "Do not touch my designs" (Archimedes).—Editor.

everything is quite simple: "Very soon our side is going to win," "order" will be restored, everything will be as before; civic duty consists in protecting one's assets and hide; the proletarians are "ruffians"; the word "comrade" is a dirty word; we've hung on to our property—and another day is gone: we might as well laugh at the fools who mean to stir up all Europe, yes, a good belly laugh, seeing that somehow we've managed a bit of profit.

One cannot argue with them, because their cause is indisputable—the interests of the belly. But these are "half-enlightened" or quite "unenlightened" people; all they have ever heard is what was grunted at them at home and in school. The same grunts are expected of them:

Family: "Obey papa and mama." "Save money for your old age." "Learn to play the piano, daughter, you'll get married sooner." "Don't play with street urchins, sonny, or you'll shame your parents and tear your overcoat."

Elementary school: "Obey the teachers and revere the principal." "Tell on bad boys." "Get better marks." "Be the first in your class." "Be willing and obliging." "Religion is the most important subject."

Secondary school: "Pushkin is our national pride." "Pushkin adored the Tsar." "Love the Tsar and the fatherland." "If you don't go to confession and communion, your parents will be called and you'll get a lower conduct mark." "Notice whether any of the boys read prohibited books." "Pretty chambermaid, mm."

University: "You are the salt of the earth." "The existence of God cannot be demonstrated." "Humanity advances on the path of progress, and Pushkin celebrated women's legs." "You are too young to take part in politics." "Give the Tsar a fig in your pocket." [12] "Note who spoke at the meeting."

Government service: "The internal enemy is the university student." "Not a bad-looking skirt." "You're not here to argue." "His Excellency is coming today, everybody be at your posts." "Observe Ivanov and report to me."

What can one expect of a man who conscientiously listened to all this and believed it all? But the intelligentsia are supposed to have "re-evaluated" these values? They have heard other words as well, haven't they? They have been enlightened by science, art, literature? They have drunk not only from these polluted springs but also from clear and vertiginously deep springs, into which it is perilous to look, and where the water sings songs that would amaze the uninitiated?

The ground under the bourgeois' feet is as concrete as the muck under the hog's: family, money, position, medal, rank, God on his ikon, the Tsar on his throne. Pull this out from under him, and everything flies topsy-turvy.

The *intelligent* has always boasted that he never had that kind of ground to stand on. His tsar can be taken away only together with his head. Skill, knowledge, methods, habits, talents are nomadic, winged possessions. We are homeless, family-less, rankless, poor—what have we to lose?

We should be ashamed to be haughty, to scoff, weep, wring our hands, moan over Russia now, when she is swept by the revolutionary cyclone.

[12] A coarse way of expressing one's scorn for someone.—Editor.

So we had been hacking away at the branch we were sitting on? A lamentable situation. With voluptuous malice we stuck firewood, shavings, dry logs into a heap of timber damp from the snows and the rains; but when the sudden flame flares up to the sky (like a banner), we run around, crying: "Oh, ah, we're on fire!"

I am not speaking of political figures whom "tactics" and "the demands of the moment" may forbid to bare their souls. I think that right now in Russia there are not a few people who rejoice in their hearts but frown out of duty.

I am speaking of those who are not engaged in politics, of writers, for instance. (If they engage in politics, they sin against themselves. "Chase two hares and you won't catch either"—they will not make policy, but they will lose their voice.) I think it is not only their right but their duty to be untactful, "tactless," [13] to listen to the grandiose music of the future that fills the air, without watching for single strident false notes in the august roar and ringing of the world's orchestra.

One would think a bear had stepped on the ears of the Russian intelligentsia: petty fears, pettier words. We should be ashamed to scoff at illiterate announcements or letters, written by well-meaning but unskilled hands, ashamed to meet "stupid" questions with haughty silence, ashamed of pronouncing the beautiful word "comrade" in quotation marks.

Any shopkeeper can do as much. This can only embitter the human being and arouse the beast in him.

We reap what we sow. If you think everybody is a sharper, only sharpers will come to you. There are a few hundred crooks in plain sight—and just out of sight there are millions of human beings, as yet "unenlightened," as yet "benighted." But it is not from you that their enlightenment will come.

Among them are some who are going insane from the lynchings, cannot stomach the blood that in their ignorance they have shed; some who pound their ill-starred heads with their fists: we are stupid, we cannot understand. And there are some in whom the creative drives are still dormant; these may yet speak such words as our tired, shopworn, bookish literature has not spoken in a long time.

Proud politicking is a great sin. The longer the intelligentsia remain aloof and sarcastic, the more terror and bloodshed there may be. Dreadful and dangerous is that elastic, dry, unsavory "adogmatic dogmatics" seasoned with patronizing soulfulness. Behind the soulfulness is blood. The soul attracts blood. Only the spirit can combat horror. Why bar with soulfulness the way to spirituality? The good is hard as it is.

And the spirit is music. Socrates' daemon once ordered him to obey the spirit of music.

With your whole body, your whole heart, your whole consciousness—listen to the Revolution.

---

[13] A play on the word *takt*, which means "beat" in the musical sense. Blok is implying that it is better not to have too keen an ear for music.—Editor.

18.

Viacheslav Ivanovich Ivanov

1866-1949

Mikhail Osipovich Gershenzon

1869-1925

Throughout the eighteenth and nineteenth centuries Russian thought had been concerned with the nature of culture, its relationship to both past and future, and its meaning for the individual. Peter the Great and those who sang his praises in the eighteenth century believed that culture resulted from the man-made creation of conditions of greater happiness and well-being; they saw the people primarily as the object of the elite's actions. However, for others—the Slavophiles, for instance—culture was the product of past history, the expression of spiritual values, and the fulfillment of Christ's purpose in the social bond of a people. If for the former group of thinkers culture was mainly a thing of utility, the matrix of man's worldly happiness, for the latter it was an esthetic and spiritual principle destined to further moral progress.

The outcome of the Russian Revolution naturally put into question with dramatic force the meaning of both culture and the Russian discussions concerning it. During the years of turmoil and deprivation the attention of the intelligentsia was too much absorbed by the difficult task of physical survival for them to carry on the discussion. But in

1920 two sophisticated representatives of the Silver Age of Russian culture were granted a brief spell of physical comfort and peace of mind in a rest home, which enabled them to take up the debate.

Viacheslav Ivanovich Ivanov was one of the most original and erudite poets of Russia's Silver Age. In his letters he echoed Chaadaev in his conviction that culture is the result of history and that it is essentially esthetic. During and after the Revolution he focused on the fate of the esthetic cultural values that he held dear and believed were essential if man was to fulfill his higher spiritual purpose. But he also very well knew that esthetic creation is the work of the individual, not necessarily dependent on any specific social, political, or economic conditions. The creative individual may therefore withdraw from worldly concerns, for the creative urge never dies and will assert itself under any circumstances. This outlook gave Ivanov a sense of belonging to history. He thus could also view the Revolution of 1917 and the conditions that had brought it about as part of history and as the seedbed of new esthetic and cultural forms. As with Chaadaev, this belief was bolstered by his faith in the fulfillment of Christian Providence as the overarching transcendental meaning of history.

Mikhail Osipovich Gershenzon, historian of ideas and essayist, had done more than anyone to explore and explain the character and history of the Russian intelligentsia of the first half of the nineteenth century. In spite of his sympathy for the Slavophiles, his basic orientation—unconsciously, perhaps—was that of the progressive Westerners. But the Russian Revolution—largely a result of the intelligentsia's actions for over a hundred years—had ended in the triumph of those forces most inimical to the intelligentsia's ideals, hopes, and traditions. Gershenzon found himself completely disoriented by this turn of events and fell into gloomy despondency. The Revolution led him to realize the futility of the intelligentsia's attempts to shape the tomorrow in which he still wanted to believe.

Realizing that what was worth discussing was too complex for verbal improvization, Ivanov and Gershenzon took to the pen. Although they lived in the same room, they exchanged ideas in writing. Their "correspondence" gave expression to the essence of the historical argument that had agitated the Russian elite for about a century and a half. But even their discussion did not culminate in a final conclusion.

A Corner-to-Corner Correspondence

I

TO M. O. GERSHENZON

I know, my dear friend and neighbor in another corner of the room we share, that you have come to doubt personal immortality and a personal God. And it may seem that it is hardly my place to defend to you the personality's right to metaphysical recognition and eminence. For, to tell the truth, I feel nothing in myself that could pretend to eternal life. Nothing save that presence which is certainly not I but the general and universal in me, and which, like some radiant guest, unifies and fills with spiritual meaning my bounded and inescapably temporary existence, with all its complex, odd, and fortuitous content. Yet it seems to me that this guest has

Translated by Gertrude Vakar from Viacheslav Ivanovich Ivanov and Mikhail Osipovich Gershenzon, *Perepiska iz dvukh uglov* (Petrograd, 1921). The verse passages have been translated literally, without any attempt at poetic rendering.

a definite purpose in visiting me and "making his abode" in me. His purpose, I think, is to bestow upon his host the immortality which my reason
cannot grasp. My personality is immortal not because it already exists but
because it is destined to come into existence. And like any coming into
existence, like my birth into this world, this is to me a pure miracle. I know
that I could not find in my supposed personality and its manifold manifestations a single atom in the least like even the merest germ of autonomous
true (that is, eternal) existence. I am a seed that has died in the soil; but a
seed's death is a precondition of its quickening. God will raise me from the
dead because He is with me. I know Him in myself as a dark, life-giving
matrix, as that forever higher Something that overmasters even the best and
most sacrosanct in me; as the vital principle of all being, richer in content
than I am, and therefore containing, along with my other powers and
attributes, also the attribute of personal consciousness that is mine. I am
born of Him and He abides in me. And if He does not forsake me He will
also create the form of His further abiding in me, that is, my personality.
God not only has created me but is continually creating me and will create
me further. For, of course, He wishes that I too should go on creating Him
in myself as I have been creating Him until now. There can be no descent
unless it is willingly received; in a way, the two achievements are equivalent, and the receiver becomes equal in worth to the One who descends. God
cannot abandon me as long as I do not abandon Him. Briefly, the inner
law of love engraved in us (for we easily read its invisible table) assures us
that the Old Testament psalmist is right when he says to God: "Thou wilt
not leave my soul in hell; neither wilt thou suffer thine Holy One to see
corruption." This is what I think about in my corner, my good neighbor,
since you wanted to know. And what will you tell me in reply, from
another corner of the square?

V. I.
June 17

II

TO V. I. IVANOV

No, V. I., it isn't that I have come to doubt personal immortality; like
you, I feel sure that the human person is the repository of true reality. But
it seems to me it is better not to talk or think of these things. You and I,
dear friend, are diagonal not only in this room but in spirit, too. I do not
like to let my thoughts roam the metaphyical peaks, although I delight in
watching you smoothly soaring above them. These other-worldly speculations which inevitably fall into systems obeying the laws of logic, this celestial
architecture in which so many among us so assiduously engage—I confess
that they seem to me idle and hopeless pursuits. Moreover, all these abstractions depress me, and not only they—the whole intellectual heritage of man,
all the discoveries, knowledge, values amassed and established through the
centuries, have begun to oppress me of late, like an annoying load or too

heavy, too stifling clothes. This feeling has long since troubled me off and on, but now it has become constant. I am thinking what bliss it would be to plunge into Lethe, wash off without trace the mind's memory of all religions and philosophical systems, of all science, art, poetry, and come out naked like the first man, naked, joyous, and light, and freely stretch out to the sky my bare arms, remembering nothing of the past except how heavy and stifling those clothes were, and how easy it is without them. Why this feeling has grown in me I do not know. Perhaps our opulent garments were no burden as long as they were whole, and looked good on us, and comfortably fitted our bodies; but now that they are ripped and hang in tatters, as in the last few years, one wants to tear them off altogether and fling them away.

M. G.

III

TO M. O. GERSHENZON

I am no architect of systems, my dear M. O., but neither do I belong to the frightened ones to whom everything that has been put into words is an untruth. I am used to ambling in the "forest of symbols," and I understand the symbolism of words as clearly as the symbolism in a kiss of love. The inner experience has its verbal tokens, and seeks them, and pines without them, for out of the abundance of the heart the mouth speaketh. There is no greater gift that men can bestow on one another than the affirmative revelation of their highest, most spiritual perceptions, if only foreshadowed and budding. One thing one must guard against—imparting an element of coercion to these communications, these confidences, that is, turning them over to the intellect. The latter is by its very nature coercive, while the spirit bloweth where it listeth. The word-symbols of the individual's inner experience must be of the spirit, and truly children of freedom. As a poet's song does not coerce but moves, so they too must move the listener's spirit rather than compel his reason like a demonstrated theorem. Metaphysics is guilty of arrogance and lust for power—a tragic guilt, for, having left the cradle of global spiritual cognition, the paternal house of primal religion, it was bound to aspire to a scientific form and to reach for the scepter of that great coercer, science. And the state of mind that bedevils you at present—this acute awareness of the excessive weight of the cultural heritage we drag along—stems essentially from understanding culture not as a treasure-trove of gifts but as a system of subtle coercions. And no wonder—for a system of coercions is just what culture has been striving to become. To me, however, it is a ladder of Eros and a hierarchy of reverences. And so many things and people in my surroundings fill me with reverence—from man and his tools and his great labor and his debased dignity down to the mineral—that I find it sweet to drown in that sea (*naufragar mi è dolce in questo mare*) —to drown in God. For my reverences are free; none is mandatory, all are open, unhampered, and each one rejoices my spirit. It is true that every reverence, as it changes into love, also perceives with the sharp eye of love the inner tragedy and the tragic guilt in everything that has withdrawn from the wellsprings of life and closed in upon itself—under every rose of life can be seen the outline of the cross from which it grew. But this is already a yearning for God, the attraction of the moth-soul to death in the flame. As Goethe has said so truly, he who does not know this elemental attraction suffers from another, hateful yearning, even if he never takes off his mask of cheer; he is "a dull guest on the dark earth." Our true freedom, our noblest happiness and noblest suffering, are always with us, and no culture can take them away. Bodily sickness is more to be feared, for the spirit is willing but the flesh is weak; man is more defenseless against poverty and disease than against dead idols. He will never cast off the hated yoke of his deadening heritage by abolishing it forcibly, because it is sure to grow back again, just as the hump stays with the camel even when the pack-load has been shed; the spirit can free itself of this yoke only by taking on another, "easy yoke." You are right when you say to man enslaved by his own riches, "Become" (werde), but you seem to forget Goethe's condition: "Die first" (stirb und werde). And death, that is, the personality's rebirth, is the liberation desired by man. Cleanse yourself with cold spring water—and be consumed. This is always possible—on any morning of the daily reawakening spirit.

V. I.
June 19

IV

TO V. I. IVANOV

Our casually begun correspondence from corner to corner is beginning to interest me. You remember—you wrote your first letter in my absence and put it on my desk before going out, and I replied to it when you were not at home. Now I am writing in your presence, while you, in quiet reflection, try to smooth out in thought the age-old folds of Dante's tercets, so that later, looking at the original, you may fashion their likeness in Russian verse. I answer in writing because my thought will thus be more fully expressed, and more distinctly perceived, like a sound amid silence. After lunch we shall both lie down on our beds, you with a sheet of paper and I with a small leather-bound volume; you will read to me your translation of *Purgatory*, the fruit of the morning's labor, and I shall compare and disagree. And again today, as in the past days, I shall savor the rich mead of your verses, but also experience again the familiar constriction of the heart.

O my friend, O swan of Apollo! Why were feelings so vivid, thought so fresh, words so meaningful then, in the fourteenth century, and why are our thoughts and feelings so dull, our language as if interspun with cobwebs? What you said about metaphysics as a system of barely perceptible coercions is good; but I was talking of something else—of our culture as a whole and the subtle emanations with which it has suffused the entire fabric of life;

not of coercions but of the seductions that have corrupted, debilitated, warped our spirit. And not even of this exactly, not of the consequences and the harm of culture, because assessing the good and the harm is the business of reason, and any argument that takes the sword perishes by the sword. Can we rely on our intellect in this matter, when we know full well that it has itself been reared by culture and naturally worships it as a witless slave the master who has elevated him?

Another, an incorruptible judge has raised his voice in me. Whether I am weary of carrying too heavy a load or whether, from under the mass of knowledge and habits, my primordial spirit suddenly shone through—a simple feeling, as undeniable as hunger or pain, has fastened in me. I am not judging culture, I am merely testifying that it stifles me. Like Rousseau, I imagine some blissful state of completely unencumbered freedom of the spirit, of heavenly insouciance. I know too much, and this baggage weighs me down. I did not acquire this knowledge myself, from live experience; it is common to all and not mine, it comes from our fathers and forebears; through the seduction of proof, it has gained access into my mind and has filled it. And because it is common, objectively proven, its incontestability chills my soul. The countless things that I know bind me like millions of unbreakable threads, all of them horribly immutable, neutral, inescapable. What do I need them for? The immense majority are of no use to me at all. In love and suffering I do not need them; it is not with their help that through fatal mistakes and chance achievements I slowly discern my life's purpose; and of course at the hour of my death I shall not give them a thought. Yet they clutter my brain like trash, they are there every minute of my life, they hang like a dusty veil between me and my joy, my pain, my every thought. From this immeasurable impersonal knowledge, the innumerable theories, truths, hypotheses, rules of logic, and moral laws stored in our memory, from this hoard of intellectual riches everyone of us has to carry, comes the exhaustion that is gnawing away at us. Take just one thing, the doctrine of noumenon and phenomenon. The great Kant discovered that we know nothing of the thing-in-itself, that all the attributes we perceive in it are our own representations. Schopenhauer confirmed this truth by demonstrating that we are completely enclosed in ourselves and have no means of stepping outside the bounds of our consciousness and coming in contact with the world. The thing-in-itself is not knowable; in apprehending the world, we actually apprehend only the phenomena and laws of our own spirit; we merely imagine or dream the external world—it does not exist, our perceptual apparatus is the sole reality. This discovery was logically irresistible. Like a light in darkness, the truth shone forth, and reason had to submit to it without demur. A tremendous revolution took place in the human mind: objects, people, I myself as a creature, briefly, all reality, formerly so solid and palpable, suddenly as if levitated, a foot above the ground, took on a spectral sheerness. Nothing had any substance; what seemed to be reality was no more than systematically constructed mirages with which our spirit peopled the void, God knows what for. This doctrine reigned for a hundred years and wrought profound changes in human consciousness. And now its end has come. Imperceptibly, it has lost its suasion and its luster; philosophers have found the courage to speak up for good old naive experience, the outer world has been handed back its indisputable reality, and nothing remains of the dazzling discovery but its modest germ: the truth, disclosed by Kant, that the formal categories of cognition, the categories of time, space, and causality, are not real but ideal, not of the world but of the mind, which superimposes them on experience like a grid on a map. The hundred-year phantasmagoria is over—but what dreadful traces it has left! The nightmare of illusoriness still envelops our minds in a web of madness. Man returns to the perception of reality like a convalescent after a serious illness, with the sick fear that everything he sees may be a dream. Thus abstract intellect in the workshops of science evolves knowledge and systems unimpeachable from its own point of view but uncongenial to the spirit; and when such a truth in time bursts at the seams and collapses, as inevitably it must, we ask ourselves sadly why it had to smother our thinking for so many years, impeding its free movement. As things sold in shops tempt us because they are pretty or handy, so theories and knowledge tempt us with idle seductiveness, and our spirit has become as cluttered with them as our houses with things. Ideas and knowledge are fruitful for me when they are born in myself in a natural way, out of my own experience or because I felt an imperative need of them; but when they are acquired from outside without real need they are like the stiff collars, umbrellas, overshoes, and watches traded from Europeans that naked savages sport in African jungles. Therefore I say, I am depressed by the multitude of manufactured things in my home, but I am infinitely more depressed by the acquired clutter in my spirit. I would gladly exchange all the knowledge and ideas I have gleaned from books, and in addition all those I may have been able to construct on top of them, for the joy of discovering for myself, from my own experience, just one bit of basic knowledge of the simplest kind but fresh as a summer morn.

I repeat, what matters is not the coercion you wrote about, but seduction; it is more coercive than coercion. Through the allurement of objective truth, abstract reason foists its discoveries upon the individual. You say that having cast off the load we shall inevitably gather another and saddle ourselves with it. No doubt this is so—we cannot get rid of our intellect or change its nature. But I believe, I know, that another kind of creativity is possible, a different kind of culture, that need not imprison every insight in a dogma, desiccate every good until it is mummified and every value until it becomes a fetish. For not I alone but many of us suffocate within these stone walls. Could you, a poet, live behind them without rebelling if you did not possess the happy gift of inspiration, to carry you occasionally beyond these walls, into the open air, the sphere of the spirit? I enviously watch your flights—yours and the other poets' of our time—for they prove that there are open spaces and that humanity does have wings! But my eyes—perhaps they are at fault?—see something else, too: the wings have become heavy and the swans of Apollo do not fly very high. And, come to think of it, how could a poet retain the strength and freshness of innate inspiration in our enlightened age? By the time he is thirty he has read so many books, taken part in so many philosophical discussions, is so steeped in the abstract intellectuality of his milieu!

Here it seems apropos to reply to your last exhortation. The rebirth of the personality, its true liberation, Goethe's *Flammentod* of which you speak at the end of your letter, also is a transport and flight of the spirit, akin to the poet's inspiration but incomparably more daring and decisive. That is why such events are so rare in our time, much rarer even than art works of genius. The "cultural heritage" presses on the personality with a pressure of 60 atmospheres and more, and its yoke, because of its seductiveness, is indeed an easy yoke. Most people do not feel it at all; and if someone does become aware of it and swings upward, how can he break through that solid mass? For it is not above him but in him; he himself is heavy, and nothing except perhaps the wings of genius can lift his spirit above his overloaded mind.

M. G.

V

TO M. O. GERSHENZON

My dear friend, we dwell in the same cultural environment as we do here in the same room, where each of us has his own corner but there is only one wide window and one door. Each of us has, besides, a permanent home, which you, like myself, would gladly exchange for another, under different skies. Life in the same environment is not the same for all its inhabitants and visitors. In one and the same element, both oil and soluble matter can float; algae, coral, and pearls grow; fish, whales, flying fish, dolphins, amphibians, and pearl divers move about. It seems to me—unless, let me say in my turn, "my eyes are at fault"—that you do not conceive of dwelling within a culture without essentially fusing with it. I should say, rather, that while consciousness can be entirely immanent in culture it can also be only partly immanent and partly transcendent—a point easy to illustrate by an example that has a particular bearing on our discussion. A man who believes in God will never admit that his faith is part of culture; on the other hand, a man in thralldom to culture will inevitably regard faith as a cultural phenomenon, no matter how else he may define its nature—as an inherited conception and a historically determined psychologism, or as metaphysics and poetry, or as a sociomorphic force and a moral value. He may see faith as all kinds of things, but he will be sure to place it within the sphere of cultural phenomena, which to him encompasses all spiritual life, and he will never agree with the believer that his faith is extraneous to culture, an independent, simple, primary phenomenon connecting the personality *directly* to the absolute. To the believer, his faith is by definition separate from culture, as nature is separate, or love. . . . And so?

So it depends on our faith in the absolute, which transcends culture, whether we shall have inner freedom—that is, life itself—or grovel inwardly before culture, long essentially godless since it imprisons man within himself (as Kant, too, has definitively stated). Only through faith, that is, the repudiation in principle of the original sin of culture, can its "seductions," which you feel so keenly, be overcome. But it is not by summarily destroying its outer marks and manifestations that original sin will be eradicated. Unlearning to read and write and banishing the Muses (to use Plato's words) would be only a palliative: written characters would appear again, and the new scrolls would once more reflect the same unchanging figurations as those of the prisoners chained to the rock in Plato's cave. Rousseau's dream originated in his lack of faith. By contrast, to live in God means that one is already not living wholly in man's relative culture but that a part of one's being is growing out of it, out into liberty. Life in God is truly life, that is, motion; it is spiritual growth, heaven's ladder, the journey to the mountain top. It suffices to start out, to find the trail; the rest will come of itself. Objects in our environment will reshuffle themselves, voices will recede, and new vistas open. The door to freedom is the same for all the inmates of the prison and is never locked. If one man leaves, another will follow. Perhaps all will file out one by one. Without faith in God, man cannot recover his lost innocence. It is useless to throw off the old worn-out clothes, one must shake off the old Adam. Only living water can rejuvenate. The new society "without the Muses and letters" that you envision, enticing as the idea may be, is a delusion and *décadence,* like all Rousseauism, unless it is a community of prayer and not a new crop of beings as corrupt as we are.

Should you reply to this that, even so, the very process of building a new culture, of writing new symbols on the *tabula rasa* of the human mind, would ensure to mankind a long era of renewed creativity, a fresh perception of the world, a return to youth, I could only shrug my shoulders, marveling at the bottomless optimism of your suggestion, obviously stemming from the failure—characteristic of Rousseau's time—to see the fatal truth that the very fountainhead of our spiritual-psychic life is poisoned, that the orphic and biblical assertions of some "original sin" are, alas, no lie. Our conversation in that case would recall another, ancient conversation, related by Plato in the *Timaeus.* Solon and an Egyptian priest were the conversants. "You Hellenes are children; there is not an old man among you," said the second to the first. Floods and fires periodically devastated the earth, but in the lands inhabited by Hellenes people rose to life again "without the Muses and letters," ἄμουσοι χαὶ ἀγράμματοι, after these destructive spasms of the earth, to begin once more their ephemeral building; meanwhile, the sacred Nile saved static Egypt, which preserved on its sempiternal tables the ancient memory of the forebears that the Hellenes themselves had forgotten—the great and glorious race that had thrown off the yoke of immemorial Atlantis. My dear fellow-questioner! Like that Egyptian and his Greek disciple, and Plato himself, I devoutly burn my incense on the altar of Memory, the mother of the Muses, and glorify her as "the pledge of immorality, the crown of consciousness," sure that no upward step on the ladder of spiritual ascent is possible without a step down on the ladder leading to her subterranean treasures: the taller the tree, the deeper the roots.

But should you reply that you would not venture, and even felt that you had no right, to predetermine the future thought patterns of the culturally renewed people but simply felt an imperative need, for yourself and for the coming generations, to leave the stifling vaults for an airy expanse, neither knowing nor wanting to know what you and they might find beyond the prison walls—this reply would mean a fatalistic indifference to the task of preparing the way to freedom, and complete despair as to your own liberation. May it not be so!

V. I.
June 30

VI

TO V. I. IVANOV

Dear neighbor, it is of no avail to tempt me with kindly persuasion to leave my corner and join you in yours. Your corner is also a corner limited by walls—there is no freedom in it. You say that if civilized man would only give himself up to faith he would be essentially free. I reply: Partly, burdened as he is with his cultural heritage, he is incapable of soaring toward the absolute; and if he does have faith, it shares the condition of all his other psychic states—it is tainted with reflection, distorted, and powerless. I repeat what I wrote in my last letter: Our consciousness cannot transcend culture, except in rare, unusual cases. Look how our friend Shestov [1] thrashes about in the net. How often you and I have discussed him with loving concern! Who if not he has seen through the vanity of intellectual speculations, the lethal dogmatism of theories and systems? Who hungers more than he for freedom? His yearning spirit helplessly seeks escape; now he tries to undo the knots of the dogmatic thinking that trammels humanity, now he excitedly relates some momentary breakthrough achieved by this or that individual, be it Nietzsche or Dostoevsky, Ibsen or Tolstoy, and their sad relapses into the prison. One cannot gain freedom with poisoned blood and exhaustion in the bones. Faith, love, inspiration, everything that could liberate the spirit, everything is contaminated in us and sickly, and hence does not liberate. How can you expect a soil cluttered with the rocks of centuries-old concepts and systems, with numberless shards of ancient, old, and new ideas, dotted haphazard with mausoleums of "spiritual values"—the unassailable values of faith, thought, art—how can you expect such a soil to produce mighty oaks and delicate violets? At best, a few poor tough bushes can grow on it, or the ivy that covers ruins.

---

[1] Lev Isakovich Shestov (1866–1938), philosopher and essayist. His philosophy may be characterized as a theocentric existentialism; in the 1920's and 1930's he did much to revive interest in Kierkegaard's thought in Germany. One of his earlier important philosophical works, referred to later on in the Correspondence, was *Apofeoz bespochvennosti* (The Apotheosis of Rootlessness), 1905.—Editor.

But this isn't what I wanted to speak about. You are right, I do not know and do not want to know what humanity will find "beyond the prison walls," and I frankly admit my complete indifference to "the task of preparing the way to freedom." All these are speculations, my friend, speculations again. I have more than enough of those that pervade the air around me and my own brain. I cannot bother with speculations. I "simply," as you say, feel an urgent need of freedom for my spirit, or consciousness—in the same way, probably, as a sixth-century Greek felt intolerably bound by the numerous gods on his Olympus with all their established attributes and claims, by the plethora of sacred myths and religious rites, or as, perhaps, some Australian aborigine chokes in the stifling, threatening atmosphere of his animism, his totemism, yet lacks the inner strength to free himself of them. Beyond the prison walls that Greek may have visualized himself willingly standing before the single, universal, unpersonalized God prefigured by his soul, and that Australian may have dreamt of the lighthearted freedom of a spirit not crushed by fear, and of the free choice of a mate, unrestricted by totemic taboo. Neither of them could have worded his desire or his hope. A man aspiring to freedom sees only the barrier and proclaims only his repudiation, but he always struggles and repudiates "in the name of" something—some positive ideal is already ripe in him and alone gives him the passion and the strength to fight. This ideal is dim and unspoken, the only kind that actuates the will. A conscious and formulable ideal is a system of barely alive, weakly impelling, precise ideas—a product of decay. What do I want? I want freedom of reason and of quest, I want a primeval freshness of spirit, that I may go wherever my fancy takes me, follow untrodden paths and uncharted trails, firstly because it will be fun, and secondly because—who knows—perhaps on the new roads we shall find more. But no, mainly because I am bored here, as bored as in our sanatorium. I have an urge to be off to the woods and meadows. I not only want to, I firmly believe that I shall. How else could this feeling have come to me? The strength and genuineness of my feeling are my guarantee that this will happen. You know, birds are descended from reptiles; my feeling is like the burning and itching in an amphibian's shoulders when the wings first began to sprout. The dim dreams of that Greek and that Australian were prefigurations and heralds of the liberty that arrived centuries later. Perhaps it was necessary for man to pass from his initial freedom through a long period of discipline, of dogmata and laws, in order to emerge, transformed, into freedom again. Perhaps. But' this is hard on the generations whose lot is the middle stage, the road of culture. Culture is disintegrating from within—we can see this clearly; it hangs in tatters from our exhausted spirit. Whether this is how liberation will come about, or whether it will explode in a catastrophe, as it did twenty centuries ago, I do not know, and of course I myself shall never reach the promised land, but my feeling is like Mount Nebo, from which Moses saw it. And I am not alone in discerning it through the curtain of fog.

M. G.

VII

TO M. O. GERSHENZON

" 'There is no motion,' said the bearded sage." In reply, his interlocutor gave him the symbolic advice to test his opinion empirically—"and he walked in front of him." The first one, of course, was no paralytic either; he, too, could move his legs; but he attached no importance to the movements of his body because he did not trust his own experience. I ascribe a large part of your reply to autosuggestion—to the hold of a preconceived abstract idea; the rest, to unsatisfied hunger for life. There is much despair in your words, but between the lines, in the inner tone and rhythm of the words, as also in your characteristic liveliness, there is so much youthful verve, such a thirst for novel experiences, for exploring untrodden paths, for nestling close to living nature, such a yearning for play and derring-do and the yet untasted gifts of the bountiful earth—*tant de désir, enfin, de faire un peu l'école buissonnière* [such a desire, finally, to play truant a little]—that it seems to me, my dear Doctor Faust in a new incarnation but not yet entirely free of the old fussy worries, it seems to me that Mephistopheles, after glancing at you, would not abandon all hope of success if he wanted to find for you, too, the appropriate temptation, the one that would draw the overtired member of four faculties out of his zealously guarded "corner" into the free, wide world. To be sure, he would have to devise a more subtle technique and on no account show you a seductive female form in the magical distance; it would be more expedient, after reminding you once again that theories are grey with age while the golden tree of life is eternally green, to begin by showing you a virginal grove and pretty flowers in an open meadow. Of course, after a series of new adventures, the new freedom too would turn out to be a hopeless prison. Or perhaps the last of Faust's temptations should come first for you: canals, the New World, and the illusion of a free land for a liberated people. Any number of planimetric designs and patterns can be drawn on a horizontal plane. The important fact is that the plane is horizontal. But I am no Mephistopheles and have no intention of enticing or luring you anywhere. In essence, what I am saying to you is that a vertical line can start at any point, in any "corner" on the surface of any culture, young or decrepit. To me, however, culture itself, in its proper sense, is not at all a flat horizontal surface, not a plain of ruins or a field littered with bones. It holds, besides, something truly sacred: the memory, not only of the earthly, external visage of our fathers, but of the high initiations they achieved. A live, permanent memory that never dies in those who partake in these initiations! For they were granted through the fathers to the remotest descendants, and not an iota of the signs once revealed and graven on the tables of the human spirit shall ever perish. In this sense, culture is not only monuments but spiritual initiation. For Memory, its supreme sovereign, makes her true votaries participate in the "initiations" of the fathers and, re-enacting them, gives them the vigor of new begettings and beginnings. Memory is a dynamic principle, while oblivion means weariness, interrupted motion, decadence, and a return to a state of relative stagnation. Let us, like Nietzsche, closely watch ourselves, lest we harbor the poisons of decay, the infection of *décadence*.

What is *décadence*? It is the feeling of a refined organic bond with the material legacy of a past high culture, coupled with a painful pride in being the last in its line. In other words, the numbness of a memory no longer creative, no longer a living link with our fathers' initiations and a spur to our own initiative; the knowledge that the oracles are silent, as, in fact, the decadent Plutarch entitled one of his essays ("On the Cessation of Oracles"). The whole work of our poor friend Lev Shestov is one long and complicated treatise on this subject. The spirit no longer speaks to the decadent through its former oracles, only the psyche of the times speaks to him. His spiritual barrenness makes him turn exclusively to the things of the mind, his interests become purely psychological and psychologistic. Would he understand Goethe's belief: "The truth has been found long ago; it unites the august company of spiritual minds. Seek to learn this old truth"? To the psychologist, truth is nothing but the old psychology. At any rate, the psychologist suspects everything spiritual and objective of being psychological and subjective. I am again reminded of Goethe's words— Faust's words about Wagner: "He digs for treasure and rejoices when he finds a worm." Isn't this like our friend, thirsting for the water of life but conducting psychological investigations which merely prove the vanity of theories? He had best be left to his daemon—let the dead bury their dead. To trust him would mean admitting to dry-rot in one's own spirit. Which, of course, does not diminish our love for him, or our tender compassion for this tragic and tenaciously alive gravedigger and his heroic labor. Let us have faith in the life of the spirit, in holiness, in revelations, in the unknown saints around us, among the numberless united throng of striving souls, and continue hopefully on our way, looking neither aside nor behind, measuring not the road, ignoring the voices of weariness and sloth that speak to us of "poisoned blood" and "tired bones." One can be a cheery traveler on this earth without leaving one's home town, and become poor in spirit without quite forgetting one's learning. We have long since decided that reason is a tool and a servant of the will; it is useful, just as the baser organs of the body are. The theories that pervade it, as you say, can be given away as we give away the books we no longer need, unless we let them repose in peace on the shelves of our libraries at home; but the vital sap of these theories and religions, their spirit and logos, their revelatory power—let us quaff them in deep drafts, for the sake of Goethe's "old truth," and thus, carefree and curious like strangers, pass by the countless altars and idols of historical culture, some neglected, some renovated and refurbished, stopping where we please, and sacrificing in abandoned places if we come upon imperishable flowers that, unseen by man, have grown from an ancient tomb.

V. I.

July 4

VIII

TO V. I. IVANOV

You are a siren, my friend—your letter of yesterday is bewitching. It seemed to me that culture herself was tempting me with her riches and affectionately warning me of the dangers of breaking with her. Yes, her voice is irresistible to me, for am I not her son? Not a prodigal son, as you think, but—which is harder to take—the son of a profligate mother. Your diagnosis, my dear physician, is decidedly wrong; I see it is time for me to express my thoughts more clearly. I have no desire to turn humanity back to the world-view and the way of life of Fiji Islanders, I do not want to unlearn writing and banish the Muses, my dreams are not of pretty flowers in a meadow. I think that Rousseau's dream, which stirred up all Europe, was not of a *tabula rasa* either; that would have been a vain, silly dream that could not have inspired anyone. This time, you have formulated the basic problem of our argument. Up to now you were under the impression that, bored with the external achievements of culture, I was ready, in vexation, to throw out the baby with the bath water. No, no! I have been talking all along of corruption of the spirit, of the poison in our very lifeblood; of, precisely, the highest achievements gained from millennial valid experience, of what you call the true initiations of our fathers, of objective, immutable truth. I say that this very wellhead of our spiritual life is poisoned and no longer vivifies but deadens the soul. The dynamism of an acquired truth, its stimulating effect on the spirit, is just the point. You say that Memory "makes her true votaries participate in the 'initiations' of the fathers and, re-enacting them, gives them the vigor of new begettings and beginnings." Oh, if only this were so! This was true long ago—and has ceased to be true. Somehow the revelations received by our fathers have become mummies or fetishes. They no longer pierce the soul like a beneficially destructive, galvanizing charge but bury it under the stones and rubble of disintegrating ideas. Objective truth both does and does not exist; it has reality only as a way, a point of orientation, but it does not exist as an ultimate datum that man can and should learn, as Goethe said and you quote. If "the truth has been found long ago," then, of course, life would not be worth living. What is valuable in the "initiations" of our fathers is not their content—for the content of any truth discovered by man is relative, and hence provisional and false—but their method, if the term is applicable here. You should know better than anyone that every expression of truth is symbolical—only a sign, a sound that wakes the inert mind from its slumber and makes it look in the direction from which the sound comes. When you speak of truth as invariably initiative, you depict life not as it is but precisely as I should like it to be. I say that our fathers' initiations have petrified, have become tyrannical values which, through allurement and fear, reduce the individual spirit to unprotesting, and even willing, submissiveness, or wrap it in a fog that obscures vision. But I have written of this before. To avoid repeating myself, let me quote those pages.

Everyone knew that Napoleon wasn't born an emperor. Some woman of the people, watching him from the crowd in a resplendent parade, might have thought: "Now he is the Emperor who has almost lost his own name, the ruler of nations—but when he was in swaddling clothes, he was nothing to the world, only his mother's child." This is how I think of a famous painting when I stand before it in a museum. The artist painted it for himself, and during the creative process he and his picture were one—he was in it, and it in him; and now it is enthroned before the whole world as a value in itself.

Every objective value originates in one human personality and at first belongs to it alone. No matter what the value is, its story invariably falls into three phases, the same as Napoleon passed through: first nothing to the world, then a soldier and leader on the battlefield, and finally the ruler. And like Napoleon at Ajaccio, a value is free and genuine only in its infancy, when, obscurely born, it plays, grows, and ails naturally, without attracting anyone's calculating eye. *Hamlet* bloomed only once in the fullness of its truth—in Shakespeare; the Sistine Madonna—in Raphael. Later the world draws the flowering value into its humdrum battles. In the world, no one needs it in all its fullness. People sense in the value the original force injected into it by its creator and want to utilize that force for their own ends; their attitude is one of self-interest, and self-interest is always practical. Therefore a value in common use always becomes differentiated, breaks up into special forces and particular meanings, lacking the fullness, and hence the essence, of the whole. As people need an oak tree not in its natural state but sawed up, so a value looks good to them only when its substance has been fragmented and it can be turned into a versatile commodity. Eventually the commodity becomes a generally recognized value and is crowned queen. A reigning value is cold and cruel; in time, it petrifies completely and becomes a fetish. Not a trace remains in its features of the frank, overt strength that illumined its countenance in the past. It has served so many passions, noble and vile! One wanted sunshine, another wanted rain, and it tried to please them all, to confirm to each his fictitious, subjective truth. Now it dictates to the world its own autocratic laws, deaf to individual appeals. What had been alive and personal, throbbing with the ardent blood of one man, has become an idol demanding the immolation of other values as alive and personal as it itself was when it first saw the light of day. Napoleon the Emperor and a picture enthroned in a museum are alike despots.

Besides the concrete and tangible fetish-values there are the vampire-values, the so-called abstract values, which in the realm of values are something like juristic persons. They are disembodied and invisible; they are formed of abstractions from concrete values, since the law of cohesion operates in the spiritual sphere exactly as it does in the physical world, where the vapors from the earth's waters aggregate into clouds. Out of many *Hamlets* and Sistine Madonnas there emerges, through abstraction, the generalized value Art; this is how all of them were born, Property and Morality, the Church and Religion, Nationality, Culture, and how many, many more—all from the emanations of the best blood of the most fervent human hearts. And every one of them has its cult, its priests, and its devotees. The priests authoritatively tell the populace of the "interests" and "needs" of the deified value and demand sacrifices so that it may continue to prosper. The State hungers for power, Nationality for unity, Industry for development, and so on; in this way, phantoms rule the world, and the more abstract a value, the greedier and more ruthless it is. Perhaps the late war was only an unexampled hecatomb that a few abstract values, having formed an alliance, jointly demanded from Europe through their priests.

Yet in every abstract value, no matter how inflated its insatiable belly, there glimmers, touchingly, a divine spark. The individual unconsciously reveres in it the sanctity of some personal, ineradicable longing that he has in common with all men; this feeling explains the value's power. When I eat, assuaging my hunger, or cover my nakedness, or pray to God, my actions are mine alone, simple and personal. And suddenly a private concern of mine is elevated into something social, impersonal, and from there even higher, into the empyrean of suprapersonal principles—and lo, a solitary feeling has been made into a hierarchical centralized system of the utmost complexity; around a simple prayer has grown the immense world of Theology, Religion, the Church. What was a cry of my heart has been declared my sacred duty; what was dear to me has been taken away and set up over me as an anointed ruler.

The poor heart, like a mother, still loves its child in the tyrant, yet weeps in submitting to his impersonal will. Sooner or later, love triumphs over submission: the mother dethrones the tyrant to embrace again the child. There comes a Luther with a fiery heart and demolishes ritual, doctrine, the papal Church, in order to rescue simple personal faith from a complex system: the French Revolution dispels the mystique of the throne and establishes a more direct, closer relation between the individual and his government. Today a new rebellion is shaking the earth: the personal truth of labor and ownership is breaking out of the centuries-old, intricate, monstrous web of social and abstract ideas.

Mankind still has a long way to go. Luther's Christianity, the republic, socialism, are but half the task; eventually the personal must again become purely personal, as it was at birth. But the past has not been in vain either. Man will return to his beginnings transformed, because during these long years his subjectivity has become a universal objective value which, up there in the heights, has blossomed forth in its eternal truth. We have here a kind of phylogeny in reverse. Having reached its peak, a movement descends transformed by the same road, stage by stage, as it had gone up. This is why every revolution is a revival of the past; monarchy is replaced by the single *veche,* or parliament; parliamentarianism by a still earlier form, federalism; and so on, ever farther back to the starting point. But a new spirit now animates the old forms. During its ascendancy, the community was weak, chaotic, and closed; descending, it is well organized and full of national meaning. The point of departure to which everything must return is the individual. He will encompass all the accrued fullness. In time, faith will again be simple and personal, work a joyous, personal, creative activity, ownership an intimate communion with things; for the individual, faith and work and ownership will be abiding and sacred, and for the world at large these concepts will be immeasurably richer in content, like an ear of corn grown from a grain. The goal is for the personal to become entirely personal again and yet to be apprehended as universal; for man to recognize in his every manifestation, like Mary, at once his own child and God.

Values, however, are not the whole problem; and, after all, they can be fought. But how do you fight those poisons of culture that have penetrated into our blood and polluted the very sources of our spiritual life? There are the cobwebs of theories, cobwebs of steel, woven by centuries of human experience. They shackle the spirit unnoticeably but surely. There are the habitual paths of consciousness, which our laziness is only too ready to follow. There are the routines of thought and of conscience, the routines of perception, the stereotyped emotions, and the innumerable clichés of speech. They ambush the spiritual embryos at their very inception, instantly envelop them as if in a loving embrace, and carry them along the beaten paths. Finally, there are the incalculable legions of known facts, frighteningly numerous and implacable. They flood the mind and install themselves in it as objective truths, never waiting for hunger to call forth those of their number that are needed; and the burdened spirit wilts in the crush, unable either to absorb them or to cast them out. Consequently, what I am talking about is not freedom from, but freedom of, intellectual speculation, or, rather, the freedom, spontaneity, and freshness of reflection, so that the ancestral wisdom will not frighten off the timid, or cater to laziness, or cloud vision, but so that a new perceptiveness and new thoughts may come into being, which will not instantly congeal in their every attainment but will always remain flexible, free to move on into infinity. Only then shall we have the cheerful pilgrim and the poor in spirit, carefree and curious, that you talk about. At present there are none, or only spurious ones; at present, no one *passes by* altars and idols like a stranger—even you, my friend, unbeknownst to yourself, sacrifice on many altars and unconsciously honor idols, because the poison, as I say, is in our blood. And it is not I who would keep mankind on a horizontal plane—it is you who write, "Let us continue on our way without looking around us and measuring not the road." What I say is that the vertical line along which the new culture must ascend is the human personality.

M. G.

IX

TO M. O. GERSHENZON

Our dialogue is getting difficult in that it is turning into a verbalism, which it was never meant to become. You are a monologist by nature, my dear friend. There is no luring you onto the highway of dialectic—logic is no law unto you. What do you care if you contradict yourself? I could present to you a list of your verbal inconsistencies as one presents a bill for payment, if good taste did not counsel me to refrain from such an attempt

upon the inner, the *soulfelt,* meaning of your confessions. Besides, we have
agreed that the truth should not be coercive. But what shall I do, then? Play
to you on my reed pipe and sing? "We piped unto you, and ye did not
dance; we wailed, and ye did not weep." So children reproach one another
in the Gospel, but we like to think that we are children no longer. "Well
sung," you will remark to the singer in passing, with a kindly smile, and go
your own way. I feel like calling after you, "A good journey to the promised
land!" since you have mentioned it, and of course it is what you dream
about—its vines and its fig trees ("They shall sit every man under his fig
tree," as the Bible says), its unexhausted pastures and cold springs. But
where exactly it is and what it is really like, or whether it isn't even beyond
the phenomenal world, you apparently feel no need to know; all that matters is reaching it (and of course one is bound to reach it, since it is the
"promised" land) or at least getting a glimpse of it from Mount Nebo, for in
it shines "the triad of perfection." And you will never exchange your nomadic restlessness and your burning thirst after cold water—the ancient
thirst of a forty-year journey through the desert—for the fleshpots of Egypt,
its temples, pyramids, and mummies, and all the Egyptian wisdom and secret
initiations. Like Moses, you have tasted of this wisdom and these mysteries,
and would rather forget it all; Egypt repels you—you loathe the mummy
culture and the wisdom that does not slake *your* thirst.

What a difference there is between you and Nietzsche—whose burden, as
uncongenial to you as all Egypt, you naturally did not attempt to lift onto
your shoulders, already overloaded with spiritual values and memorabilia.
Why indeed should you undertake together with him the hazardous pilgrimage to the valley of the Sphinx, whose melodious riddle ("Who and
what art thou, stranger?" . . . Oedipus answered, "A man.") sings a
different, unique song to each comer. Of course, your problem is the same as
Nietzsche's: culture and man, values, decadence and health, especially
health. And it is doubtful whether in today's cultural climate any personal
initiation can take place without the "initiate's" (as the theosophists say)
meeting him as the "guardian of the threshold." Nietzsche has said, "Man is
something that must be overcome"—whereby he declares once more that the
way of personal emancipation is a way up to the heights and down into the
depths, a vertical movement. Again the obelisk and the pyramid! "Could
be, could be," you hastily wave this aside, for your loins are girded and your
feverish eyes scan the desert's horizon: "First of all, out of here, out of
Egypt!" If at any time you had been to any degree a Nietzschean, you would
feel in yourself how it is when lion-claws cut through on man, on that camel-
like pack animal of culture (the metaphor is a find of Nietzsche's, its pathos
is yours); you would sense how the furious desert hunger of a beast of prey
rises in him, compelling him to tear to pieces some living creature he used to
fear, and to taste its blood. In the abstract language of the new Egypt, in its
sacred texts, these living, blood-filled creatures are called "values." They are
so prodigiously viable and alive because, as you say, humanity has filled
them with its own lifeblood, breathed into them its fiery soul, even if they
do now sit motionless on their thrones as "graven images and likenesses of

things that are in heaven above, and in the earth beneath, and in the waters underneath the earth." But Nietzsche is not only a tearer-to-pieces, a drinker of blood, and a psychophage—he is a lawgiver as well. Not yet having become the "child" into which, as he predicts, the lion must change, he smashes the tables of the old values, to engrave on new ones, *ungue leonis* [with the lion's claw], other signs. He wants to give a new covenant to the same ancient Egypt, to "transvalue" the same ancestral pagan heritage. He is one of the great creators of ideals; from an iconoclast, he turns into an ikon painter. Whereas you thirst for cold water, not for steaming blood; you are only a wayfarer in the desert, by no means a beast of prey; in Egypt itself, you are no destroyer but at most—before the priestly court of inquisition—a sower of doubt, of suspicion, of disintegration; you have no heart for lawmaking, and there isn't really anything to re-evaluate, because your own evaluations would, I daresay, coincide in their essence and core with the accepted values; but for some reason you have to start with a quasidethronement and a demonstrative abolition of the latter. Perhaps you feel that they may not revive unless they die, that they cannot be immortal deities if they do not pass the test of death. You are motivated, it seems to me, by a deep and secret impulse, the direct opposite of the impulses that have throughout the ages determined the world's successive image-making, which the Holy Scriptures call pagan. The pagan genius projected what was best and loftiest in it either into a transcendent image or into an invisible but transcendent idea—a suprasensory image—and objectified it in a symbol, a likeness, an ikon, an idol; and even "in the shallows of time," as you like to say, during the age of Kant, when reflection had completely immured the spirit in the solitary cell of the individual personality, it tried to save the "idea," in the guise of the "regulative idea" in the rational consciousness of man. Though you do not realize it, you are a typical representative of another equally ancient and inherently iconoclastic desire to let the idea drown in the twilight of the subconscious. The "regulative idea"—whether transcendent or immanent, still an idea—is of no use to you and is despotically restrictive; what you want is in fact a regulative instinct. God for you is not in the sky nor in man's invisible heaven but in the fiery soul of the living being, in his life-breath, in the pulse of his veins, and that is where you want Him to be. This thought, I repeat, harks back to hoary antiquity, no less ancient than the hieroglyphics of Egypt. I remember some verses of mine about primeval man, who did not fear death as we fear it:

> Man of old, you are stronger than we—
> You did not lower your childlike eyes
> Before inevitable fate.

Did he believe in the immortality of the soul? If he did, his faith surely gave him neither comfort nor hope; on the contrary, it must have filled him with inconsolable dejection.

> Yet, while hopelessness in secret crushed his spirit,
> And the darkness of the welcoming temple

Filled his imagination with fear,
In his sinews there ripened the strength that comes from the sun,
And, pouring heedless life through his veins,
"I am immortal," sang his very blood.

This is the real faith in immortality, isn't it? It follows from all your premises that instinct, with its immanent teleology, is the one perfect and true ideal (because it is consistent with nature). And that is why you do not really want to make use of the "freedom of intellectual speculation" which you nevertheless demand—and, true to yourself, you begin our correspondence with the statement that "it is better not to talk or think of such things as God and immortality."

Forgive this typological analysis of your psychic and intellectual makeup. *Amico licet.* But how else could one reply to a man who refuses the usual methods of persuasion (except one, and perhaps the most effective, the beauty of vocables) and simply declares, *"Hoc volo"*—this is my will, this is my thirst; *"ut sentio sitioque, ita sapio"* [as I feel and thirst, thus do I know]. It remains to examine the sources of the will and the nature of the thirst. But such an inquiry would be incomplete if we did not first determine the place of the will under study in our present general upheaval, in which it is an important factor. Well, then, what is going on these days? A wholesale abolition of cultural values? Their decay, which would mean that they are completely or partly dead? Or a reappraisal of the old system of values? Whatever it is, yesterday's values have been profoundly shaken, and you seem to be one of those who welcome the earthquake, for, according to you, unless the old Egypt is destroyed, the image of perfection that originally shone over the cradle of its every creation will remain buried forever in the inner sepulchers, under the weatherbeaten stones of the pyramids. But apparently history is not proceeding under your sign but stubbornly wants to remain *history*, that is, a new page in the annals of Egypt's culture. Let us disregard what is random, unpredictable, irrational in the course of events, and look at the prevailing trends. The anarchic tendencies are not dominant; essentially, they seem to be correlates and shadows of the bourgeois social structure. The so-called conscious proletariat stands entirely on the ground of cultural continuity. The struggle is not for abolishing the values of the old culture but rather—and this is seen as a task of prime importance—for the revival of everything in them that has objective and timeless significance; just at present, however, for their re-evaluation. The lion, who is not a transformed camel but who has come out of deep inner recesses and has pounced on the established values, is no common beast of prey but, as Nietzsche visualized him, a man-lion, to whom "nothing human is alien." And breaking the old tables, he tries, like his prototype given by Nietzsche, to scratch on new tables, *ungue leonis*, new laws. I think he will spoil much marble and durable bronze in the process, but I also think that some unique, deep trace of the lion-claw will show forever on the memorials of our ancient Egypt. Our topic, however, is the attitude toward cultural values, not the content of the new "twelve tables." The method of the

Revolution—which has relegated the two of us, tired and worn out, to a public sanatorium, where we discuss health—is primarily a historical and social, indeed a political, method, not utopian or anarchic (that is, individualistic); it is the method of settled people, of people who are going to stay, not of runners and nomads—inasmuch, let me add, as we are not at the moment discussing spiritual advance, the vertical growth in which the personal principle, each unique and irreplaceable human personality, claims all its rights and duties.

Here we are, back at its hallowed circle. I contend that Mount Nebo and the promised land itself lie within the human personality—in the spirit that animates it. You place personality and values in opposition when you speak of the mother who swaddled Napoleon and of the same mother as a stranger watching him on the throne of deadening glory, which must have looked to her like the cold and sumptuous sarcophagus of the former life and love. My friend, those Pharaohs who saw their main task in erecting suitable mausoleums for themselves exemplify very well the deepest urge of the human will. Every living thing wants not only self-preservation but self-revelation, aware in its every fiber that the latter means self-exhaustion, self-destruction, death—and perhaps eternal remembrance. The desire to leave a trace, to make one's life into the monument of a value, to disappear and be preserved in the cult of an inspiring principle—this is the source of mankind's inborn *arete,* as the Hellenes, the Dorians, called their categorical imperative of active valor. Man's initiation into the supreme mysteries has disclosed to him another, human-divine, aspect of this striving for death in order to live. Truth, love, and beauty want to be eucharistic: "Eat my flesh and drink my blood; my flesh is meat indeed, and my blood is drink indeed." Not the mother of Bonaparte before her son's throne but Mary at the foot of the cross symbolizes the human heart before the great truth of a universal value. A value must needs be crucified, and entombed, and covered with a stone slab, and sealed with seals; the heart will see it resurrected on the third day.

But here your voice unexpectedly joins mine, and both of us, in love and in common hope, prophesy in unison, no longer in my words but in your own, that the heart's thirst and the spirit's freedom will find fulfillment, that "the personal will be entirely personal again and yet apprehended as universal; and man will recognize in his every manifestation, like Mary, at once his own child and God."

V. I.
July 12

X

TO V. I. IVANOV

It amuses me that you treat me as a doctor his patient; my sickness grieves you as a friend, frightens you from a social point of view, and even irritates

you. From the first, you made a wrong diagnosis, and now you are astonished that your cures do not work. To put it more precisely, you make great
efforts to dispel my feeling with the arguments of historical reason, and you
blame your lack of success on my stubbornness. But it would do as much
good for a father to tell his son that the girl he loves will not make him
happy, or to tell a person suffering from thirst, "Drink no water, what you
have is an imaginary thirst, put up with it, it will soon pass." And I do not
completely refuse rational discussion: I do counter your numerous arguments with at least one argument, which methodologically meets all of
yours. Heraclitus said: *"Chalepòn thumò máchestai, psychés gar oneìtaí"* [It
is difficult to fight with one's heart, for the price is one's being]; following
his example, I say: The historically oriented intellect, in discussing culture,
is naturally predisposed to glorify it. If you think it is necessary to examine
the nature of my thirst, I have as much right to investigate the causes of
your satiety.

This brings me to your remarks about Nietzsche. You are again in error,
my good physician. I have read little of Nietzsche—he never appealed to
me; and today I see my "pathos," as you call it, not as identical with but as
antipodal to his pathos. A sick man himself, he nevertheless saw fit to
prognosticate about the disease of culture and to make laws for the future
on the basis of that prognosis. A lion must come out of cultural man, and
then a child out of the lion; therefore hurry and become lions, be daring,
claw to bits. But it seems to me that after the dreadful war of 1914–18 one
can hardly speak of the birth of lions any more. The war has shown, it is
true, that within cultured, educated modern man a bloodthirsty predator
has matured—but by no means a lion, and therefore I have little hope that
he will ever turn into a child. No, it does not behoove us to legislate to the
future. It is enough to realize that we are sick, and to desire healing; this
may already be the beginning of recovery. Nietzsche is forceful only in his
outcries of pain and in his descriptions of the cultural disease that saps
humanity's strength.

I seem to distinguish throughout your arguments one dominant note:
filial respect for history. You shrink from blaming it, you reverently accept
everything it has produced, and my impudent rebellion appalls you. Yet in
one of your previous letters you spoke with conviction of man's original sin,
by which you apparently meant the sin of falling away, of separating into
closed, self-assertive individualities. Then you do admit that man's will is
more or less free to determine the way he lives. Why then are you shocked
when I say that modern culture has resulted from a mistake, that man as we
know him has taken a wrong turning and lost his way in the woods? Of
course history is rational from beginning to end, in the sense that there has
always been sufficient cause for everything that has happened. But explanation does not mean evaluation. A deer develops antlers for a good reason, as
a means of intimidation and defense; but in some species, for the same good
reason, they grow so big that they interfere with running in the woods, and
the species dies out. Isn't the same happening to culture? Aren't our "val-

ues" like those antlers—first an individual adaptation, then a common possession of the species, and finally a weight, a hindrance, overdeveloped in the species and tormenting, fatal, to the individual?

You are right, your logic is no law unto me. The truth of history does not become a sacred truth at any one point; it is always in the making, being tested and verified by every individual person. My person, having weighed it against all that I feel, says that it is a lie and that I cannot worship it. I say to Perun [2] that he is a wooden idol, not God; God, to me, is invisible and omnipresent; and you try to persuade me that this idol is the symbol of my Godhead, and that if I only grasped its symbolism it would replace God to me. But although you expound its symbolic nature very interestingly and very profoundly—I could listen to you for hours, you almost convince me—it looks so frightening and so repulsive that I cannot control myself. I remember all the sacrifices we have made to it, and I think of all the others I shall still have to make, day after day, at the command of its priests— painful, bloody sacrifices! No, no! This is not God! *My* God, my invisible God, does not exact, or threaten, or crucify. He is my life, my motion, my freedom, my true will. This is what I meant when I told you that my thirst rejects the warm, spicy beverages of contemporary philosophy, art, poetry, and that only cold spring water could slake it. And in our way of life there is no fresh water any more; all our springs are enclosed in reservoirs, their water is channeled along miles of pipes, filtered, and sterilized, and finally this half-dead liquid undergoes additional treatment in our cities—we drink either boiled water or complex mixtures of the most varied tastes, colors, and smells. One can die of thirst amid these gorgeous containers of syrupy, tepid philosophy, of hot and aromatic poetry, for the lack of one swallow of cold water. Forgive this protracted metaphor. The heat is so trying these days; no coolness to be found anywhere; I keep drinking warm boiled water, have emptied our whole decanter, and am still thirsty. This is probably why I began talking about thirst. I had remembered how, on an equally hot day many years ago, I drank spring water from a dipper, in the shade of a wood near Kuntsevo. *There* was coolness, and the clear cold drink was delicious. Although, by a caprice of fate, by the decree of culture, I live in a city now, confined to a rest home, in an airless room with windows facing a wall, where I sip horrid boiled water and chase off swarms of flies—how can I forget that there are forests and coolness, and not feel homesick for them? And then there is this, no less valid:

> Would that our children be spared
> The difficult fate that is ours!

The logic of abstract thought has no power over my feeling; and the logic of history—in its superstitious respect for it—is equally powerless. You array against me not only the rationality of the past but its sequel, the events of the present day—they are your final and decisive argument. You urge me to look with open eyes at the Revolution going on around us. Its motto, you

---

[2] A pagan Slavic god of thunder and lightning.—Editor.

say, is not the abolition of the old cultural values: on the contrary, it wants to make them available to all. It is not a rebellion against culture but a struggle for culture, and "the proletariat stands entirely on the ground of cultural continuity." Very well, but what of it? All we can observe is that the proletariat is taking over the accumulated values from the hands of the few. But we have no idea what the proletariat sees in these values and why it is taking them over. Perhaps it sees them only as the tools of its long enslavement, and wants them only in order to take them away from the enslavers? Or possibly, after all these years of systematic enlightenment, it has come to believe the self-vaunting of culture and feels that its values will enrich it. But who knows? Having gained possession of them and looked at them more closely, the proletariat may find that there isn't anything in them except chains and trash, and throw them away in frustration and disappointment, and set out to create new, different values. Something else is possible too—the proletariat may lift them onto its shoulders and carry them onward, dutifully accepting the "cultural succession"; but in using the old values it may unconsciously infuse them with a new spirit, and before long their molecular structure may change so much that they will become unrecognizable. Perhaps (I really believe this) the proletariat fighting for the possession of the cultural values is honestly mistaken in thinking that it needs them for their own sake, when it actually needs them only as means toward other attainments. This is a common self-deception. Man invents the airplane, thinking only of its practical usefulness—I shall be able to fly back and forth at great speed and transmit stock-exchange news from New York to Chicago. He is unaware that his spirit drives him to construct wings not because of any earthly aims but in order to break free of the earth and rise above it; he is unaware that the dream of, and belief in, being able to fly to other worlds has reached its secret fruition, and that the airplane is no more than the merest beginning of the realization of this dream, which is strong and confident already—give me time, and some day I shall soar up never to return, I shall vanish without trace into the ether! In the same way, prehistoric man drew the first spark from flint and realized that darkness was unnecessary and that he had the power to overcome it—and we merely flip a switch to change night into day. Conscious intent does not reveal the real aim; the spirit sets its own hidden goals and tells consciousness only the direction of the first step, then of the second, and so on. The general direction of the road is known only to the spirit, and consciousness feels cheated after each step. Wundt called this phenomenon the heterogeny of goals. In the process of realization, the conscious goal is displaced or superseded by another, totally different from the first, and so on, link after link; the planned short line turns out to be a curve—unnoticeably but firmly the spirit steers the movement in the direction of its own vision, unknown to reason. Whatever we may observe in the Revolution today tells us nothing of the long-range designs for which the spirit has called it forth.

M. G.

XI

TO M. O. GERSHENZON

Perhaps, my dear friend, we have compromised ourselves long enough, each in his own way, I with my mysticism and you with your anarchic utopianism and cultural nihilism—as they would be branded by the "compact majority" (Ibsen's words) of today's gatherings and public forums. Hadn't we better retire to our respective corners and stay quietly on our cots?

> How can a heart expression find?
> How should another know your mind?
> Will he discern what quickens you?
> A thought once uttered is untrue.[3]

I do not like to abuse this sad admission of Tiutchev's; I prefer to think that it reflects not a permanent truth but the intrinsic untruth of our disjointed and scattered epoch, unable to produce a united mind, the epoch which sees the penultimate consequences of the original sin of "individuation" that has poisoned the whole historical existence of man—all of culture. We try daily, hourly, to surmount this deadly principle by ceaselessly creating major and minor cults—for any cult, as long as it lasts, represents collectivity, even if it unites only three or two votaries—and the collective principle flares up for a moment and flickers out again, and the many-headed Hydra of our culture, torn by internecine wars, proves unable to become one harmonious cult. But the craving for unity must not seduce us into concessions and compromises, that is, into establishing outward, apparent bonds where the very roots of consciousness, the blood vessels, as it were, of our spiritual selves, are not interwoven into a single web. In the ultimate depths, where we cannot reach, we all form a single universal circulatory system feeding the single heart of humanity. Nor must we, in advance of our feeling, which is granted us only as a distant, uncertain hint, substitute contrived imitations for the mystic, sacred reality. You and I have no common cult. You feel that oblivion brings freedom and life, while cultural memory means enslavement and death. I maintain that memory liberates, and forgetting enslaves and kills. I speak of ascent, and you tell me that the wings of the spirit are overloaded and have unlearned how to fly. "Let us go away," you invite, and I reply: "There is no place to go. Moving around on the same plane will not alter anything in the nature of the plane or in the nature of the moving body." Once I sang:

> For you—the ancestral trees
> And cramped graveyards;
> For us—by Beauty's decree—

[3] A quotation from F. I. Tiutchev's poem "Silentium" (as translated by V. Nabokov). —Editor.

> The nomad's freedom.
> Each day a new love,
> A new encampment daily.[4]

But right away the truthful muse forced the rebel against the cultural heritage to add:

> The Fata Morgana
> Of hopeless servitude.

Oh, for worship one does have to leave the old familiar places, the ancestral trees:

> Brothers, let us depart for the twilight of sacred forests . . .
> To a child of the gods the staff of exile is light,
> The flowering thyrsus of a new love.

Wide is the flowering earth, and many light-filled meadows on it

> Await our clinging lips
> And the dithyramb rhythm of our feet.

This is how it *will* be, my dear friend, even if there are as yet no signs of such a change. Culture will become a cult of God and of the Earth. But it is Memory, the Primeval Memory of man, that will bring this miracle about. Culture is not unitary at core, just as eternity is not, and as the human personality consists of diverse components.

> Seas within the deep sea move to dawns or to sunsets,
> The upper waves toward noon, and the waves blow—toward midnight;
> Many conflicting streams flow in the dark abysses,
> In the purple ocean there are underwater rivers.

In culture, too, there are unseen currents that draw us to the prime sources of life. An era of great, joyous, all-comprehending return will come. Cool springs will bubble among the old gravestones, and rosebushes grow from grey sepulchers. But to speed the advent of this day we must forge ahead, not turn back; retreat can only retard the closing of eternity's circle.

But we Russians, or very many of us, have always been great at running away. Something impels us to run, without as much as a backward glance. Personally, I have an invincible distaste for solving problems by flight. In a previous letter I said that the culture of "Egypt," as well as Nietzsche's ideas,

---

[4] An alternative rendition is that of C. M. Bowra in *A Book of Russian Verse* (London, Macmillan, 1947), p. 86:

> Wide acres you inherit,
> And graveyards populous;
> A tameless nomad spirit
> Is Beauty's fate for us.
>
> For us a daily Treason
> New camp-grounds every day.
> —Editor.

was alien to your nature. Egypt is uncongenial, and its culture an Egyptian captivity, to practically all of our intelligentsia—if we use this term in its narrow, special, socio-historical sense. And you are, of course, flesh of the flesh and bone of the bone of our intelligentsia, for all your rebellion against them. Of myself, this is hardly true; I should say that in one half of my being I am a son of the Russian land, although an exiled son; and in my other half I am a stranger, a disciple from Saïs, where they forget their kith and kin. The magic formula, to our intelligentsia, is *oproshchenie;* [5] this shows to what extent they are severed from the roots. They think that by "becoming simple" they will put down roots, be able to feel that they have roots. Lev Tolstoy was such a man, and he naturally attracts you. Dostoevsky was a man of a different stamp, and he just as naturally repels you. He did not want *oproshchenie;* what he wrote of the garden as the panacea of communal life, and of bringing up children in the great garden of the future, and even of factories in a garden, was not a dream but a spiritually right and historically justified program of social action. *Oproshchenie* is betrayal, oblivion, defection—a cowardly, listless reaction. The idea makes as little sense in relation to culture as it would in mathematics, which recognizes only *uproshchenie,* that is, the reduction of a complexity to a simpler, perfected, unified form. Simplicity is the supreme, crowning achievement, the victory of completion over the incomplete, of perfection over imperfection. The way to this longed-for and lovely simplicity leads through complexity. It is reached not by defecting from a given society or country but by moving upward. Everywhere—I repeat this again and again —there is a Bethel and a Jacob's ladder—in the center of anyone's world. This is the way of genuine, active, creative freedom; the freedom of oblivion is a stolen, hollow freedom. Those who forget their ancestry are runaways or manumitted slaves, not freeborn men. Culture is the cult of ancestors and, of course, their resurrection—as culture vaguely knows even now. The way man must follow is an ever-clearer consciousness of himself as a "God forgotten, and by himself forgot." He has trouble remembering his primogeniture, and no wonder—even the savage has already forgotten it. The philosophy of culture I put in the mouth of my Prometheus is *my* philosophy:

> They will invent and practice commerce,
> Art, mathematics, war,
> And governing, and being slaves—
> So that their days may pass in noise and fretting,
> And sensuality, to help them to forget
> In dreams the straight and solid purpose of existence.
> While in his desert
> The savage roams despondent . . .

The savage finds no joy in his pointless freedom, nor does the man who succumbs to the lure of oblivion and "simplifies" himself into the likeness of a savage; he is dejected and sad.

[5] "Going primitive," or "Back to the simple life!"—Editor.

The only way to avoid becoming "a dull guest on the dark earth" is to die in the fire of the spirit. *Dixi.*

V. I.
July 15

XII

TO V. I. IVANOV

You are angry—a bad sign. Annoyed at my lack of response, you put me in the ranks of those who practice *oproshchenie* and "forget their ancestry," of cowardly quitters, and so on, and even brand me an *intelligent* (while describing yourself very prettily, humbug that you are: a son of the Russian land, and a disciple from Saïs to boot!). What annoys you most of all is that I obstinately repeat my *Sic volo* and refuse rational discussion. But that is not true—I am quite keeping up with you in our debate. For example, in this letter you allege two things: one, that culture itself, in evolving, will lead us to the prime sources of life. We have only to forge ahead, and at the end of the road, according to you, the desired light will shine, "cool springs will bubble among the old gravestones, and rosebushes grow from grey sepulchers"—that is, our profligate culture, by persisting in being profligate, will recover its original chastity. To this I reply: I do not believe it, and see no reason for thinking so; only a miracle can change a whore into a St. Mary Magdalene. This, in your opinion, is one way—the spontaneous evolution of culture. It does not agree very well with your second thesis, that every individual must overcome culture through death in the fire of the spirit. Surely it has to be either one or the other? If culture itself, in evolving, leads us straight to God, then I, the individual, need not fuss; I can in all tranquillity go on with my daily tasks, lecture on the economic development of England in the Middle Ages, build a railroad from Tashkent to the Crimea, perfect long-range cannon and poison gases. I am even duty-bound to do this, in order to make culture move ahead faster in its own way, to speed up its hoped-for culmination. But in that case the individual *Flammentod* is not only unnecessary but bad, because a consumed and reborn personality is thereby removed from the ranks of cultural workers. I want to remind you of your own lines:

> He who has known the anguish of all that is earthly
> Also knows its beauty . . .

and further:

> He who knows its beauty
> Knows the Hyperborean's dream:
> Cherishing the stillness and fullness of his heart,
> He longs for the azure and the void.

Now *this* is true: *"He longs for the azure and the void."* He will at once stop lecturing, and he will never again address the learned society of which he was a member, or even visit it again. I hardly need to add that "death in the fire of the spirit" is as much of a rarity as the transformation of wantons into saints. Why do you say that I refuse logical discussion? As you can see, I reason and argue.

But these verses of yours do appeal to me, very much. Evidently there was a time when you, too, suffered from my depression and my thirst, but later you calmed down, lulled your unhappiness with sophistries about the ultimate transfiguration of culture and the ever-present possibility of personal redemption through fiery death. Such as you are at present, piously accepting all of history, we indeed lack a common cult. No, we do have certain things in common, as witness our friendship over so many years. I lead a strange, double life. Brought up in the tradition of European culture, I am steeped in its spirit and am not only completely at home in it but sincerely like or love much in it—its cleanliness and comfort; science, art, poetry; Pushkin. I feel at home in the cultural family, engage in lively discussions of cultural topics with friends and strangers, and am genuinely interested in these subjects and in the methods of treating them. In all this, you and I are at one; we share the cult of spiritual service in the market place of culture, we have the same habits of mind and a common language. This is the life I lead by day. But on a deeper level of consciousness I lead a different life. There, an insistent, persistent, hidden voice has been saying to me for years: No, no, this is not it! Some other kind of will in me turns away in misery and distaste from all of culture, from all that is being said and done around me. It finds all this tedious and vain, like a struggle of phantoms flailing about in a void; it seems to know another world, to foresee a different life, not yet to be found on earth but which will come and cannot fail to come, for only then will true reality be achieved. To me this voice is the voice of my real self. I live like a foreigner acclimatized in an alien land; the natives like me and I like them, I diligently work for their good, share their sorrows and rejoice in their joys, but at the same time I know that I am a stranger, I secretly long for the fields of my homeland, for its different spring, the smell of its flowers, and the way its women speak. Where is my homeland? I shall never see it, I shall die in foreign parts. At times I so passionately yearn for it! At such moments I take no interest in railroads and international politics, I see no point in the war of philosophical systems or in my friends' arguments about transcendent and immanent God—it all seems futile to me, and obfuscating like a cloud of dust on a road. But just as that stranger sometimes, in the tints of a sunset or the scent of a flower, recognizes with tenderness his native land, so I, too, here and now, sense the beauty and coolness of the promised world. I sense it in the fields and the woods, in the song of birds and in the peasant guiding his plow, in the eyes of children and sometimes in their words and their divinely kind smiles, in human affection, in true, disinterested simplicity, in an occasional fiery word or an arresting line of verse that cuts through the gloom like lightning, and in any number of other things—especially in suffering. All these will exist there, too; they are the flowers of my homeland, choked here by a proliferating harsh, scentless vegetation.

You, dear friend, live in your own country; your heart is here, where your home is, and your sky is above this land. Your spirit is not divided, and this wholeness charms me, because—whatever its provenance—it is itself a flower of that land which is our future common home. And therefore I think that in our Father's mansion the same quarters are readied for you and me, even if here on earth we stubbornly sit in opposite corners and disagree about culture.

M. G.

July 19

Selected Bibliography

For each author represented in this anthology there is a Russian bibliography too large to be cited here. For those able to read Russian the most convenient place to begin the study of particular authors is the *Russkii Biograficheskii Slovar'* (25 vols.; St. Petersburg, 1896–1918). For names not found in this biographical dictionary, consult the major Russian encyclopedias, such as *Entsiklopedicheskii Slovar'* (43 vols.; St. Petersburg, 1890–1907) or *Bol'shaia Sovetskaia Entsiklopediia* (51 vols.; Moscow, 1950–58). The books and journals listed below also contain, in most cases, references to the major Russian monographs and general studies on the subject.

But since this volume was designed for those unable to read Russian, the suggestions given here for further readings and biographical information have been limited to the most important general studies and most useful monographs in the major Western languages.

I. GENERAL BACKGROUND

1. *General histories of Russia*

ALEXANDER KORNILOV, *Modern Russian History* (New York, 1943).

ANATOLE LEROY-BEAULIEU, *L'Empire des tsars et les russes* (4th ed.; 3 vols.; Paris, 1897–98).

PAUL MILIOUKOFF, CHARLES SEIGNOBOS, and LOUIS EISENMAN, *Histoire de Russie* (3 vols.; Paris, 1935).

GÜNTHER STÖKL, *Russische Geschichte* (Stuttgart, 1962).

2. *Monographs on Russian intellectual history*

WOLF GIUSTI, *Due secoli de pensiero politico russo* (Florence, 1943).

RICHARD HARE, *Pioneers of Russian Social Thought* (London, 1951); *Portraits of Russian Personalities between Reform and Revolution* (London, 1959).

ALEXANDRE KOYRÉ, *La Philosophie et le problème national en Russie au début du XIX siècle* (Paris, 1929); *Études sur l'histoire de la pensée philosophique en Russie* (Paris, 1950).

MARTIN E. MALIA, *Alexander Herzen and the Birth of Russian Socialism, 1812–1855* (Cambridge, Mass., 1961).

THOMAS G. MASARYK, *The Spirit of Russia: Studies in History, Literature and Philosophy* (2 vols.; New York, 1955).

RUFUS W. MATHEWSON, JR., *The Positive Hero in Russian Literature* (New York, 1958).

PAUL MILIUKOV, *Outlines of Russian Culture* (3 vols.; Philadelphia, 1942); *Le Mouvement intellectuel russe* (Paris, 1918).

RICHARD PIPES, ed., *The Russian Intellgentsia* (New York, 1961).

HANS ROGGER, *National Consciousness in Eighteenth Century Russia* (Cambridge, Mass., 1960).

PETER SCHEIBERT, *Von Bakunin zu Lenin*, Vol. I (Leiden, 1956).

ALEXANDER VON SCHELTING, *Russland und Europa im russischen Geschichtsdenken* (Bern, 1948).

VASILII ZENKOVSKII, *A History of Russian Philosophy* (2 vols.; New York, 1953); *Russian Thinkers and Europe* (Washington, 1953).

3. *General histories of Russian literature*

DMITRIJ ČIŽEVSKIJ, *History of Russian Literature from the Eleventh Century to the End of the Baroque* (The Hague, 1960).

MODEST HOFMANN, G. LOZINSKI, CONSTANTINE MOTCHOULSKI, *Histoire de la littérature russe* (Paris, 1934).

DMITRI S. MIRSKY, *A History of Russian Literature* (New York, 1955).

II. PARTICULAR AUTHORS

BELINSKII: H. E. Bowman, *Vissarion Belinskii 1811–1848* (Cambridge, Mass., 1954); E. Lampert, *Studies in Rebellion* (New York, 1957).

BLOK: S. Bonneau, *L'Univers poétique d'Alexandre Blok* (Paris, 1946); R. Poggioli, *The Poets of Russia, 1890–1930* (Cambridge, Mass., 1960).

CHAADAEV: H. Falk, S. J., *Das Weltbild Peter J. Tschaadajews nach seinen acht "Philosophischen Briefen"* (Munich, 1954); Ch. Quénet, *Tchaadaev et les lettres philosophiques: Contribution à l'étude du mouvement des idées en Russie* (Paris, 1931).

DOSTOEVSKY: C. Motschoulsky, *Dostoevsky: Vie et oeuvre* (Paris, 1963). An English edition is forthcoming.

IVANOV: R. Poggioli, *The Phoenix and the Spider* (Cambridge, Mass., 1957); O. Deschartes, "Vyacheslav Ivanov," *Oxford Slavonic Papers*, V (1954), pp. 41–55.

KARAMZIN: R. Pipes, *Karamzin's Memoir on Ancient and Modern Russia* Cambridge, Mass., 1959).

KAVELIN (as an historian primarily): K. A. Grothusen, *Die historische Rechts-schule Russlands* (Giessen, 1962).

KHOMIAKOV: P. K. Christoff, *An Introduction to Nineteenth-Century Russian Slavophilism*, Vol. I, *A. S. Xomjakov* (The Hague, 1961); A. Gratieux, *A. S. Khomiakov et le mouvement slavophile* (2 vols.; Paris, 1939).

LOMONOSOV: B. N. Menshutkin, *Russia's Lomonosov: Chemist, Courtier, Physicist, Poet* (Princeton, N.J., 1952).

SHCHERBATOV: "State and Nobility in the Ideology of M. M. Shcherbatov," *American Slavic and East European Review*, XIX, 3 (October 1960), pp. 363–79.

TOLSTOY: Janko Lavrin, *Tolstoy: An Approach* (London, 1944).